KITĀB AL-IRSHĀD

THE BOOK OF GUIDANCE INTO THE LIVES OF THE TWELVE IMAMS

By:

SHAYKH AL-MUFĪD

Translated by:

I. K. A. HOWARD B.a., M.a., PH.D.

(Lecturer in Arabic and Islamic Studies at the University of Edinburgh)

With a perface by Seyyed Hossein Nasr

TRANSLITERATION

Arabic Letter	Transliteration
ء	’
ا	ā
ب	b
ت	t
ث	th
ج	j
ح	ḥ
خ	kh
د	d
ذ	dh
ر	r
ز	z
س	s
ش	sh
ص	ṣ
ض	ḍ
ط	ṭ
ظ	ẓ
ع	‘
غ	gh
ف	f
ق	q
ك	k
ل	l
م	m
ن	n
ه	h
و	w
ي	y
ة	t

Short Vowels

ـَ	a
ـُ	u
ـِ	i

Long Vowels

ـَا	ā
ـُو	ū
ـِي	ī

Diphthongs

ـَوْ	aw
ـَيْ	ay
ـِيّ	iyy
ـُوّ	uww

Persian / Urdu Letters

پ	p
چ	ch
ژ	zh
گ	g

بسم الله الرحمن الرحيم

IN THE NAME OF ALLĀH,
THE MERCIFUL, THE COMPASSIONATE

اللهم صلى على محمد وعلى آل محمد كما صليت على
إبراهيم وعلى آل إبراهيم وبارك على محمد وعلى آل
محمد كما باركت على إبراهيم وعلى آل إبراهيم إنك
حميد مجيد

O ALLĀH, SEND PEACE UNTO MUHAMMAD AND THE PROGENY OF MUHAMMAD AS YOU WERE SENDING PEACE UNTO IBRAHIM AND THE PROGENY OF IBRAHIM. AND SEND BLESSINGS UNTO MUHAMMAD AND THE PROGENY OF MUHAMMAD AS YOU WERE SENDING BLESSINGS UNTO IBRAHIM AND THE PROGENY OF IBRAHIM. SURELY YOU ARE THE MOST PRAISEWORTHY, THE MOST GLORIOUS

TABLE OF CONTENTS

PREFACE BY SEYYED HOSSEIN NASR i
INTRODUCTION iv
PREFACE - SHAYKH AL-MUFĪD xix

PART I
THE LIFE OF THE
COMMANDER OF THE FAITHFUL
'ALĪ B. ABĪ ṬĀLIB

CHAPTER I
BACKGROUND TO THE LIFE
OF THE COMMANDER OF THE FAITHFUL

Introduction 2
Reports of him, Peace be on him, Mentioning and Knowing about the Event (of his Death) before its Occurrence 7
Reports which have come down of the Motive for his Murder and of how the Event occurred 11
Reports about the Place of the Grave of the Commander of the Faithful, Peace be on him, and an Explanation of the Circumstances of his Burial 16

CHAPTER II
VIRTUES, QUALITIES AND ACHIEVEMENTS
OF THE COMMANDER OF THE FAITHFUL

Reports of his Priority in Belief in Allāh and His Apostle, of his Being the First of all responsible Men in (Faith) 19
Reports of his Outstanding Merit, Peace be on him, over Everybody in Religious Knowledge (*'Ilm*) 21
Reports of his Outstanding Merit, the Blessing of Allāh be on him 23

Reports of Love for him, Peace be on him, Being a Sign of Faith (in a Person) and Hatred of him Being a Sign of Hypocrisy (in a Person) 25
Reports of him, Peace be on him, and his Shī'a Being the Successful Ones 25
Reports of Friendship to him, Peace be on him, Being a Sign of Good Birth and Enmity to him Being a Sign of Disgraceful (Birth) 26
Reports of the Apostle of Allāh, may Allāh bless Him and His Family, Naming him, Peace be on him, Commander of the Faithful, during (the Prophet's) Lifetime 27
His Qualities
1. The Meeting of the Banū 'Abd al-Muṭṭalib 29
2. Circumstances of the Prophet's Emigration from Mecca 31
3. The Commander of the Faithful fulfils the Prophet's Obligations in Mecca 32
4. The Commander of the Faithful puts right the Crimes committed by Khālid b. Walīd 33
5. Keeping the Conquest of Mecca Secret 35
6. The Carrying of the Standard at the Conquest of Mecca 37
7. The Conversion of Yemen 38
8. Taking up the Standard at Khaybar 40
9. Delivery of the Verses of Renunciation in Mecca 41

CHAPTER III

THE MILITARY EXPLOITS

OF THE COMMANDER OF THE FAITHFUL

The Battle of Badr 43
The Battle of Uḥud 50
The Campaign against the Banū al-Naḍīr. 60
The Campaign against the Allies (Aḥzāb) 61
The Campaign against the Banū Qurayẓa 71
The Campaign of Dhāt al-Salāsil 74
The Campaign against the Banū al-Muṣṭaliq 77
The Expedition to al-Ḥudaybiyya 78
The Campaign against Khaybar 82

The Conquest of Mecca 86
The Campaign against Ḥunayn 93
Expeditions to Awṭās and al-Ṭā'if 101
The Expedition to Tabūk and the Commander of the Faithful's Deputising for the Prophet at Medina 103
The Campaign against 'Amr b. Ma'dīkarib 106
The Campaign of (Dhāt) al-Salāsil 110

CHAPTER IV

The Role of The Commander of The Faithful In The Last Year of The Prophet's Life

The Deputation of Christians from Najrān and the Contest of Prayer. 113
The Prophet's Farewell Pilgrimage and the Declaration at Ghadīr Khumm 116
The Circumstances of the Last Illness and Death of the Prophet. 123

CHAPTER V

Legal Decisions of The Commander of The Faithful

A. (Judgements of the Commander of the Faithful during the Lifetime of the Prophet) 134
   1. His Judgements in Yemen 135
   2. A Case outside Yemen during the Life of the Prophet 137
B. Judgements of the Commander of the Faithful during the Rule of Abū Bakr. 139
C. Reports of the Judgements of (the Commander of the Faithful) during the Rule of 'Umar b. al-Khaṭṭāb 141
D. Reports of the Judgements of the Commander of the Faithful during the Rule of 'Uthmān b. 'Affān 148
E. Reports of the Judgements of (the Commander of the Faithful), peace be on him, after the Pledge of Allegiance of the General Populace to him and the Death of 'Uthmān 150

CHAPTER VI

Memorable Words And Speeches of The Commander of The Faithful

His Words about Allāh 160
His Words about Knowledge (*'Ilm*) 163
His Words concerning Heresy 166
His Words about this World and the Next 167
His Words about Companions, Ascetics and his Shī'a 169
His Words concerning Death 170
Speeches Urging Men to Himself and his Family 171
Speeches about those who refrained from Pledging Allegiance to him and those who broke their Pledge 174
His Words before and after the Battle of the Camel 180
His Words about the Campaign against Mu'āwiya and the Battle of Ṣiffīn 185
His Words about the Truce and the Revolt of the Khārijites 190
His Words concerning the Syrian Raids after the Truce 192
His Words about the Succession and Men's Desertion of him 200
Some of his Words of Wisdom and Warning, Peace be on him 206

CHAPTER VII

Some of The Miracles of The Commander of The Faithful

The Miracle of his Wisdom while still a Boy 214
The Miracle of his Military Prowess 215
The Miracle of the Survival of his Reputation and his Family despite Suppression and Oppression 216
The Prophecies and Inner Knowledge of the Commander of the Faithful 219
His Miraculous Strength at Khaybar 235
The Miracle of Moving the Rock and the Water under it 236
His Miraculous Victory over the Jinn 240
His Sending back the Sun 244

The Miracle of Speaking to the Fish 246
The Commander of the Faithful and the Jinn 247
Some other miracles of The Commander of the Faithful 248

CHAPTER VIII
THE CHILDREN OF THE
COMMANDER OF THE FAITHFUL 251

PART II
THE LIVES OF THE OTHER IMAMS

CHAPTER I
IMAM AL-ḤASAN B. ʻALĪ 254
Al-Ḥasan's Succession to the Caliphate and his Abdication 255
Reports of the Cause of the Death of al-Ḥasan, Peace be on him, and of Muʻāwiya Poisoning him, the Story of his burial and the Actions and Statements concerning that 261
An Account of the Number and Names of the Children of al-Ḥasan b. ʻAlī, Peace be on them, and an Extract from the Reports about them 264

CHAPTER II
IMAM AL-ḤUSAYN B. ʻALĪ 270
The account of the martyrdom of al-Ḥusayn 273
The names of the members of the house who were killed with al-Ḥusayn at Karbalā 346
A sample of the outstanding virtues of Al-Ḥusayn b. ʻAlī, peace be upon him, the Merit in visiting (his Grave) and the Mention of his Tragedy 347
An account of the Children of al-Ḥusayn, peace be upon them 352

CHAPTER III
IMAM 'ALĪ B. AL-ḤUSAYN 353

A brief survey of the Reports about 'Alī b. Al-Ḥusayn, peace be upon him 355

An account of the Children of 'Alī b. Al-Ḥusayn, peace be upon them 364

CHAPTER IV
IMAM MUḤAMMAD B. 'ALĪ AL-BĀQIR 366

An Account of his Brothers and an Extract of the Reports about them 374

An Account of the Children of Abū Ja'far (Muḥammad b. 'Alī), Peace be on them, their Number and their Names 378

CHAPTER V
IMAM JA'FAR B. MUḤAMMAD AL-ṢĀDIQ 380

An Extract from the Accounts of Abū 'Abd Allāh Ja'far b. Muḥammad al-Ṣādiq, Peace be on them and from his Words. 388

The Number of Abū 'Abd Allāh's (Ja'far's) Children, their Names and an Extract of the Reports about them 401

CHAPTER VI
IMAM MŪSĀ AL-KĀẒIM 407

The Designation (*Naṣṣ*) of (Imam Mūsā) for the Imamate by his Father, Peace be on them. 407

An Extract of the Proofs, Signs, Indications and Miracles which Abū al-Ḥasan Mūsā (presented) 411

A Sample of his Virtues, Outstanding Qualities and Merits by which he was distinguished from others 418

Reports about the Reason for him Being Killed and a Sample of the Accounts about that 422

An Account of the number of his Sons and an Extract from the Reports about them 428

CHAPTER VII
IMAM ‘ALĪ B. MŪSĀ AL-RIḌĀ 431

Reports of his Nomination 431

A Sample of the Proofs concerning him and the Reports about him 435

An Extract from the Reports about the Death of al-Riḍā, ‘Alī b. Mūsā, Peace be on them and about its Cause 447

CHAPTER VIII
IMAM MUḤAMMAD B. ‘ALĪ AL-JAWĀD 450

An Outline of the Nomination and Indication of Abu Ja‘far Muḥammad b. ‘Alī (al-Jawād) for the Imamate by his Father 450

An Extract from the Reports, Proofs and Miracles of Abū Ja‘far (al-Jawād), Peace be on him 454

The Death of Abū Ja‘far (al-Jawād), Peace be on him, its Cause, the Place of his Grave and the Account of his Children 464

CHAPTER IX
IMAM ‘ALĪ B. MUḤAMMAD AL-HĀDI 465

An Extract from the Reports of his Nomination for the Imamate and of his Being Indicated for the Succession 465

A Survey of the Evidence for Abū al-Ḥasan, ‘Alī b. Muḥammad (al-Hādi), Peace be on him, his Proof and his Explanations 467

The Account of the Coming of Abū al-Ḥasan, (al-Hādi), Peace be on him, from Medina to al-‘Askar, his Death there and the Cause of it, the Number of his Children and a Survey of Reports about him 473

CHAPTER X
IMAM AL-ḤASAN B. ‘ALĪ AL-‘ASKARĪ 476

A Survey of the Reports put forward concerning his Nomination by his Father, Peace be on them, and the Indication of him for the Imamate after him 476

A Survey of the Reports about Abu Muḥammad (al-‘Askarī), Peace be on him, his Virtues, Sign and Miracles 480

The Account of the Death of Abū Muḥammad al-Ḥasan b. ‘Alī (al-‘Askarī), Peace be on him, the Place of his Grave and the Report about his Son. 491

CHAPTER XI
THE TWELFTH IMAM 493

Extract from the Evidence for the Imamate of the one who will undertake to (bring about) Truth (*al-Qā’im bi-al-Haqq*), the Son of al-Ḥasan, Peace be on them 494

Reports of the Nomination of the Imamate of the Leader of the Rest of time (*Ṣāḥib al-Zamān*), the Twelfth of the Imams, the Blessings of God on them all, and an Explanation of the Evidence 495

An Account of those who saw the Twelfth Imam, Peace be on him, an Extract from the Evidence and Proof for him 499

Extract from the Evidence, Proof and Signs for the Leader for the (Rest of) Time 501

The Signs of the Reappearance (*Qiyām*) of the (Imam) who undertakes the Office (*al-Qā’im*), Peace be on him, the Period of Time of his Appearance, an Explanation of his Life and an Extract of what is revealed about his State 510

The Year in which the *Qā’im* will arise 517

The Direction from which the *Qā’im* will come 517

The Dominion of the *Qā’im* 518

The Description of the *Qā’im* and his Appearance 519

The Actions and Manner of the Laws of the *Qā’im* at his Coming 519

CONCLUSION 524

BIOGRAPHICAL INDEX 525

PREFACE

The whole field of Islamic studies, and especially as it concerns the Twelve-Imam Shī'ism, has suffered until now from the paucity of reliable translations of primary sources in English. Analyses and descriptions have abounded while the arduous task of translating basic writing from Arabic, Persian and other Islamic languages has attracted relatively few scholars. It is therefore with particular joy that one is confronted in the pages that follow with a rendering into English of one of the most famous works of Shī'ism by one of the pillars of Shī'ite learning, the Shaykh al-Mufīd.

Abū Abdullāh Muḥammad al-Ḥārithī al-Baghdādī, known as al-Shaykh al-Mufīd and also Ibn al-Mu'allim (the Son of the Teacher), who was born in 336/948 or 338/950 and who died in 413/1022, is one of the foremost figures of Shī'ite history. A student of the Ibn Bābūyah al-Qummī, the great teacher of jurisprudence, the science of traditions (*ḥadīth*) and theology in the 4th/10th century, Shaykh al-Mufīd was in turn the teacher of such celebrated Shī'ite theologians as al-Shaykh al-Murtaḍā. The author of some 170 treatises concerned almost completely with theology, jurisprudence, *ḥadīth* and sacred history, Shaykh al-Mufīd soon became one of the main figures of Shī'ism and his works came to occupy a priviledged position in the traditional schools of Shī'ite learning. Over the centuries his writings have continued to enjoy great prominence in scholarly circles and also popularity as far as certain of his less obstruse treatises are concerned. To this day his writings remain, along with those of his teacher Ibn Bābūyah, al-Kulaynī and Shaykh Muḥammad al-Ṭūsī the core of the theological and juridicial curricula of Shī'ite *madrasahs*.

The particular significance of Shaykh al-Mufīd in the history of Shī'ism is that he constitutes a bridge between the school of earlier Shī'ism adhering strictly to the *ḥadīth* and usually referred to as "traditional" and the more rational interpretation of theology to be seen in the later period. Moreover, Shaykh al-Mufīd lived at a time of intense intellectual activity that permitted the composition of the imposing edifice which constitutes his writings. His life coincided with the Buyid domination of Persia and Iraq. Being Shī'ite and yet ruling over a pre-dominantly Sunni population, the Buyids sought to deal even-handedly with the two major denominations over whom they ruled and gave much greater freedom to intellectual activity among Shī'ites than had been hitherto possible. The city of Baghdād from which they ruled their empire, was a notable center of both Sunni and Shī'ite learning. Their court was witness to the presence of both Abu Bakr al-Bāqillānī, who was the most outstanding propagator of Ash'arite theology of the late 4th/10th and early 5th/11th centuries and Shaykh al-Mufīd who stood as foremost among the scholars of the Shī'ite community. History has in fact recorded some of the interactions, debates and controversies between these two leading authorities of Sunni and Shī'ite theology.

Shaykh al-Mufīd resided in Baghdād and occasionally even suffered political persecution as in 409/1018 when he was banished from the city following a violent riot caused by clashes between certain segments of the Sunni and Shī'ite community. But he was intellectually more an heir to the centers of Shī'ite learning in Qum and Khurasan whose "traditional" perspective he combined with the more "rational" approach of the Nawbakhtī family which has often been compared with the perspective of the Mu'tazilites. Shaykh al-Mufīd introduced into Shī'ite *kalām* the element of "intellectual introspection" or *naẓar*, usually translated as reason, which was to mark the work of his immediate student Shaykh al-Murtaḍā and which was to lead finally to the first systematic exposition of Shī'ite *kalām* by Naṣīr al-Dīn al-Ṭūsī in the 7th/13th century in his *Kitāb al-tajrīd*.

The concept of *naẓar* itself in its full meaning as used in Shī'ite *kalām* on the one hand and in Islamic philosophy on the other, is of great importance for an understanding of the incessant debates between the *mutakallimūn* and the philosophers and also the Shī'ite scholars and the Mu'tazilites. As far as Shaykh al-Mufīd himself was concerned, he did not display much interest in philosophy and was in fact opposed to it to the extent that he dealt with its teachings in contrast to later Shī'ite theologians such as al-Ṭūsī, 'Allāmah al-Ḥillī, Sayyid Ḥaydar Āmulī and 'Abd ar-Razzāq Lāhījī, who were at once *mutakallim* and *faylasūf*, or in certain cases at least sympathetic to *falsafah*.

Shaykh al-Mufīd was, however, much more interested in the relation between Shī'ite *kalām* and Mu'tazilite teachings which constitutes the subject matter of several of his works, the most important being *Awā'il al-maqālāt fi'l-madhāhib al-mukhtārāt* which deals with the difference between Shī'ites and Mu'tazilites concerning the doctrine of Divine Justice (*al-'adl*). Shaykh al-Mufīd was also anxious to delineate and accentuate the points of difference between himself and the strictly "traditional" Shī'ites of the earlier generations who were even further removed from the Mu'tazilite position. His famous *Sharh 'aqā'id al-Ṣadūq*, which is a commentary upon the *i'tiqādāt* of his teacher Ibn Bābūyah and which has remained a popular theological text to this day, is concerned more than anything else with those theological interpretations that distinguish him from the earlier "traditional" authorities.

While being a master jurisprudent (*faqīh*) and theologian (*mutakallim*), Shaykh al-Mufīd was also concerned with *ḥadīth* and sacred history to which he devoted many works. Among this category of his writings, the *Irshād* remains the most famous and perhaps the most important. Devoted to the life and sayings of the twelve Imams, it has been used as a definitive traditional reference by numerous later hagiographers and scholars of *ḥadīth* as well as being a standard source by preachers and religious orators. The treatment of the Imams is in chronological order with the greatest space devoted to the first Imam. Each section moreover deals not only with the life of an Imam but also his sayings which in Shī'ism form a part of *ḥadīth* literature and serve as one of the foundations for not only jurisprudence and theology but all the traditional sciences. The translation of this work into English therefore makes available a work concerned not only with Shī'ite history, but also with nearly the whole of Shī'ite studies.

The world of scholarship should be grateful to Doctor Howard for understanding the difficult task of translating this major opus into a very readable and at the same time scholarly English, combining exactitude in the translation from the original Arabic with faithfulness to the particular nature and genius of the English language, a feature that is unfortunately lacking in many present day translations. Dr. Howard has made available to the English speaking public a major work of Shī'ite learning which is important for all students of early Islamic history, and thought as well as those concerned with the later development of Islamic theology and philosophy in the Shī'ite world. The work is also of great value in that it provides an authentic account of how Shī'ism has always seen its Imams who play such a central role in not only Shī'ite theology but also in the everyday religious life of the Shī'ite community.

We must also be thankful to the Muḥammadi Trust which has undertaken the laudable task of making available the authentic sources of Shī'ism in English and is making possible the appearance of Shaykh al-Mufīd's *Kitāb al-Irshād* following its publication of the anthology of the sayings of the Imams. Such publications are necessary not only for a better understanding of a basic aspect of Islam by the outside world, but also for a more fruitful dialogue between Sunnism and Shī'ism which is being carried out in certain quarters with the hope of bringing about that harmony and unity which is the earnest desire of all Muslims seriously concerned with their own tradition and the future of the Islamic world in the family of nations. It is our hope and prayer that this important translation receives the wide attention that it deserves and that the Muḥammadi Trust will continue to enrich the field of Islamic studies with works of authentic traditional character and high scholarly quality.

Seyyed Hossein Nasr

INTRODUCTION

The Life and Times of al-Shaykh al-Mufīd

Al-Shaykh al-Mufīd's real name is Muḥammad b. Muḥammad b. Nu'man al-Baghdādī al-Karkhī. His *kunya* (i.e. the name by which an Arab is usually referred to and which refers to him as the father of someone, usually his eldest son) was Abū 'Abd Allāh. During his lifetime he was given the nick-name (*laqab*) of Ibn al-Mu'allim, the son of the teacher. The teacher (*mu'allim*) par excellence to the Arabs was Aristotle and this nick-name may refer to al-Shaykh al-Mufīd's great learning as being such that he could be regarded intellectually as if he were the son of Aristotle. The actual nick-name by which he was later known, al-Shaykh al-Mufīd, also refers to his great learning. *Shaykh* at this time meant "scholar" and *Mufīd* means "one who brings benefit".

He was born in the year 336/ 948 or 338/950 in 'Ukbarā in Iraq.[1] He was brought to Baghdād at a very early age. It was in Baghdād that he did most of his studying and teaching, hence he is called al-Baghdādī. The district of Karkh in Baghdād was inhabitated by a largely Shī'ite population and it is there that al-Mufīd probably resided and did much of his teaching. Hence he is called al-Karkhī.[2]

Al-Mufīd was a Shī'ite of the Imāmī persuasion. The period during which he lived in Baghdād was a period in which Shī'ite scholars enjoyed particular freedom and hence we see a blossoming of Shī'ite scholarship in Baghdād, and in particular of Imāmī-Shī'ite scholarship. The reason for this was that the dynasty which governed Baghdād, the Buwayhids, were very much inclined towards Shī'ism. Originally from Daylam in Iran they had conquered Baghdād in 334/945. They were probably of the Zaydī Shī'ite persuasion but the doctrines of the Imāmī-Shī'ites suited them politically.[3] Thus Imāmī-Shī'ites were given opportunities to proclaim their doctrine in a way that had rarely occurred to them before.

The fact that al-Mufīd became the exponent of the Imāmī-Shī'ite doctrine during his life and that his work *al-Irshād* (The Guidance) is concerned with the history of the twelve Imams of the Imāmī-Shī'ites and their relationship with the other Shī'ite sects, in addition to the good relationship which the Imāmī-Shī'ites enjoyed with the Zaydī Buwayhids would seem to necessitate some description

1 Al-Ṭūsī, *Fihrist*, (ed. Sprenger, reprint Mashhad, 1351 A.H.S) 314-5.

2 Ibn al-Jawzī, *al-Muntaẓam fī ta'rīkh al-mulūk wa-al-umam* (Haiderabad, 1358 A.H.) VIII, II cited by M. McDermott, *The Theology of al-Shaykh al-Mufīd* (Beirut, 1978), 8.

3 On the Buwayhids, cf. C. Cahen "Būyids", EI-2

of the stage Shī'ism had reached at this period.

There were at this time three main groupings of Shī'ites: Imāmīs, Ismā'īlīs and Zaydīs. The fundamental difference between the three groups lay in their conception of the Imamate. There were, also, differences in their legal doctrines. However, these differences were rather like the differences between the various schools of law outside Shī'ism.

The Ismā'īlīs and Zaydīs were much closer and both much nearer to the kind of law practised in Iraq.[4] The Imāmīs had a much more distinctive kind of law but some Zaydīs held legal views very similar to the Imāmīs.[5]

The Imāmīs and Ismā'īlīs had similar beliefs about the nature of the Imamate. They believed that men could not function properly without leadership, and that in order for man to fulfill his religious duties and worship God it was necessary for him to have this leadership. At first God had provided this leadership through prophets who presented His revealed guidance to the world. These prophets, in order that the truth of God's message be substantiated were protected from error. Whether a prophet was actually the ruler or not, he should, in fact, have been the ruler. The prophet was in a sense an Imam. The last of the prophets was Muḥammad and after Muḥammad God provided a series of Imams, who were protected from sin, to act as the custodians of faith for the world. The Imams were God's testimony to the world which guaranteed the world's continued existence. Without the Imams the world would cease to exist. The Imams were designated by God and this designation was made public by their predecessor. Thus the first Imam, 'Alī b. Abī Ṭālib, the son-in-law and cousin of the Prophet Muḥammad, was designated by Muḥammad and the Qur'ān. The second two Imams, al-Ḥasan and al-Ḥusayn, the sons of 'Alī, were each designated in turn. After al-Ḥusayn, they maintained that the Imamate went in the line of al-Ḥusayn. 'Alī b. al-Ḥusayn designated his son, Muḥammad al-Bāqir, and the latter designated his son, Ja'far al-Ṣādiq.

It is after the Imamate of Ja'far al-Ṣādiq, the sixth Imam, that the major difference between Imāmīs and Ismā'īlīs occurs. A group of Ja'far's followers maintained that he had designated his son, Ismā'īl, to succeed him. This man was believed to have died but these supporters of the Imamate of Ismā'īl divided into two groups: one maintaining that Ismā'īl had not died and that he was the last Imam who was in hiding and would return at the end of time and a

4 cf. I.K.A. Howard, "Mut'a Marriage Reconsidered", *Journal of Semitic Studies* (Spring, 1975), 90
5 *Ibid.*, 88-9

second group that maintained that the Imamate had been passed on to Muḥammad, Ismā'īl's son. This latter group became the nucleus around which the Ismā'īlīs formed. They traced the succession through Ismā'īl.[6] This group had now gained political power in Egypt and posed a serious threat to the central Islamic world dominated by the Buwayhids.

The Imāmīs favoured the view that Ja'far had designated his son Mūsā to be the seventh Imam. With the death of Mūsā there was another serious split. There were several traditions in circulation that there would only be seven Imams and the seventh Imam would be the Imam who would return. A group, then, maintained that Mūsā had not died and he would return at the end of time. This group was known as *al-Wāqifa*, "those who stop", and it still had a number of followers at the time of al-Mufīd. However, the main group of the Imāmīs maintained that there were in fact twelve Imams, son succeeding father after Mūsā: 'Alī al-Riḍā, Muḥammad al-Jawād, 'Alī al-Hādī, al-Ḥasan al-'Askarī and his son, the twelfth Imam. The traditions that the twelfth Imam was the last Imam who would go into occultation and return at the end of time are numerous. The Imāmīs hold that al-Ḥasan al-'Askarī kept the birth of his son secret and after al-Ḥasan's death, in 260/873, the twelfth Imam remained in hiding, keeping in contact with his followers through four especially appointed emissaries. On the death of the fourth of these emissaries, in 329/940, the Imam sent an announcement that he was going into permanent hiding and would only return at the end of time. These two periods are called the Lesser Occultation and the Greater Occultation. The Imam, although absent from his community, was still present in the world and thus would ensure that his community would persevere their true faith.

The Zaydīs were a much more amorphous grouping than the other two groups. Initially their two principal doctrines appear to have been that the true Imam is only Imam when he declares himself to be so and comes out in open revolt against the authorities and secondly that this Imamate belongs to the Husaynid branch of the 'Alid family. They seemed to have claimed these doctrines on the authority of Zayd b. 'Alī, the brother of Muḥammad al-Baqīr, who led such a revolt after the death of his brother.

Many of the Zaydīs seem to have accepted that Abū Bakr and 'Umar, the first two caliphs, were genuinely Imams and some also accepted the early part of the Caliphate of 'Uthmān. This attitude was formulated in the theological doctrine of the Imamate of the *mafḍūl* (the less excellent). It was agreed that 'Alī b. Abī Ṭālib was *al-afḍal* (the most excellent) and therefore the most appropriate for the

6 cf. Part II, 427

Imamate but it was conceded that the Imamate of the *mafḍūl* (the less excellent) could occur when the most excellent (*al-afḍal*) did not publically assert his right to the Imamate by armed revolt.[7] This doctrine involved a reassessment of 'Alī's nomination by the Prophet. If 'Alī's nomination had been public and clear to all, then the legitimacy of the Imamates of Abū Bakr, 'Umar and 'Uthmān could be gravely compromised. Thus, groups of the Zaydiyya maintained thal 'Alī's nomination by the Prophet had been a secret nomination (*al-naṣṣ al-khafī*) which had not been made public to all the faithful, as opposed to the doctrine of a public nomination (*al-naṣṣ al-jafī*).

The revolutionary tendencies of the early Zaydī movement soon led many of them to abandon the doctrine that the Imamate only belonged to a man from the line of al-Ḥusayn, who came out in armed revolt. Many Zaydī revolts in the second century of the Islamic era were in support of claimants who came from the line of al-Ḥasan, and some even who were much less directly connected by family to 'Alī b. Abī Ṭālib.

Included within the Zaydī movement was a group who had previously been supporters of Muḥammad al-Bāqir. After his death, they had become supporters of Zayd b. 'Alī. This group, under the leadership of Abū al-Jārūd, was known as the Jārūdiyya. They have a much closer relationship with the Imāmī-Shī'ites than the others. Their attitude to the Imamate was much closer to the Imāmī-Shī'ites, as was their legal doctrine. What seems to have attracted them to the Zaydī movment was its emphasis on armed rebellion in favour of an 'Alid claimant to the Imamate.[8] Nonetheless their close relationship to Imāmī-Shī'ite thought can be seen in the belief that some of them held that there would be an Imam who would go into occultation and return at the end of time.[9] It is also claimed that some members of the Jārūdiyya were prepared to accept the twelve Imams of the Imāmī-Shī'ites, but wanted some place to be found for Zayd within the Imamate.

However, such doctrines as the Imamate of the *mafḍūl* (less excellent) soon led to a quietist tendency among some elements in the Zaydī movement. They found that this doctrine allowed them to have a close working relationship with the 'Abbāsid caliphate.

The Buwayhids, as noted earlier, were probably of Zaydī inclinations, at

7 cf. 'Abd al-Jabbār al-Asadābādī, *al-Mughnī* (Cairo, 1965), XX, (ii) 184

8 W. Madelung, *Der Imam al-Qāsim ibn Ibrāhīm* (Berlin, 1965), 47

9 cf. J. Hussain, "The Historical Background to the Occultation of the Twelfth Imam" (unpublished Ph.D. Thesis. University of Edinburgh. 1979), 36-38, citing traditions from 'Abbad b. al-Ya'qūb al-'Aṣfarī, *'Asl Abū Sa'īd al-'Aṣfarī, Uṣūl al-Arba'mi'a*, MS. Teheran University no. 262.

least at the time of their conquest of Baghdād. At one time early on they even considered deposing the ʻAbbāsid Caliph and setting up an ʻAlid Imam. However, this would have led to an extremely difficult situation with regard to the majority of their subjects who were non-Shīʻite and accepted the ʻAbbāsid caliphate. The doctrine of the Imamate of the *mafḍūl* allowed them to work with the less excellent ʻAbbāsids. By encouraging Imāmī-Shīʻism, whose Imam was in occultation and would not return until the end of time, they could encourage Shīʻite aspirations without endangering their own political sovereignty. By the appointment of an ʻAlid Imam, they would have relegated themselves to much more subservient political status than they had by maintaining an ʻAbbāsid Caliph, whom they regarded, at best, as *mafḍūl* (less excellent.)

The Buwayhids provided an atmosphere in Iraq and Iran, which enabled groups previously under some pressure from the authorities to flourish. This was particularly true for the various strands of Shīʻism, with the exception of the Ismāʻīlīs with their dangerous threat to Iraq from their power base in Egypt. Another group which seems to have done well during this period was the Muʻtazila, a theological school which laid great emphasis on the use of reason. They had been moving steadily towards a view of ʻAlī as the most excellent (*al-afḍal*) of the Companions of the Prophet and therefore a more favourable attitude towards Shīʻism.

It was in this atmosphere that al-Mufīd was born, was educated and lived his life. He was educated in Baghdād by leading Imāmī-Shīʻite scholars and by leading members of the Muʻtazila.[10] Earlier Imāmī scholarship had not been able to present such a public voice. While there had been several Imāmī-Shīʻite theologians before al-Mufīd who had used reason in theological speculation, al-Mufīd became the leader of a theological trend within Imāmī-Shīʻism that firmly established reason in Imāmī-Shīʻite theological speculation.[11]

In fact, the vast bulk of earlier Imāmī-Shīʻite scholarship had concerned the collection of traditions from the Imams. The first collections of traditions, collected either directly from the Imams or at second-hand, were known as *uṣūl* or sources. There were said to be four hundred such *uṣūl*.[12] The next stage was to bring these collections into more systematic form according to subject matter. The most important of these systematic collections of traditions from the Imams was *al-Kāfī*. This vast collection of traditions was compiled by Muḥammad b. Yaʻqūb al-Kulaynī, who died in 329/940. Al-Mufīd studied this work under

10 M. McDermott, op. cit. (9-13).

11 *Ibid.*, 2-4.

12 Agha Buzurg al-Teheranī, *al-Dhāriʻa ilā taṣānīf al-Shīʻa* (Najaf, 1963-8,) II, 125-9

another great traditionist, Ibn Qūlawayh, (died 368/978-79).[13] Al-Mufīd also studied traditions under the second great collector of traditions, Ibn Bābawayh, also known as al-Shaykh al-Ṣadūq, who died in 381/991-92.[14]

With the occultation of the twelfth Imam, leadership of the Imāmī-Shī'ite community rested very much in the hands of the traditionists, who propagated the teaching of the Imams. Perhaps their greatest exponent during this period was Ibn Bābawayh. Al-Mufīd, with his great knowledge of traditions and his training in theoretical speculation, was able to cross the division between the two elements, the speculative theologians and the traditionists, and provide Imāmī-Shī'ism with a synthesis which combined speculative theology with an intelligent use of traditions.

Such was the breadth of his learning that he became recognised as the leading scholar of the Imāmī-Shī'ites.

Although the period was a much more favourable time for Imāmī-Shī'ite scholars, it was not without friction between the Shī'ites and their opponents. Two Shī'ite festivals had been established. The commemoration of Ghadīr Khumm on 18th of the month of Dhū al-Ḥijja, and 'Ashūrā' on the 10th of the month of Muḥarram. These festivals were instituted by the Buwayhid Mu'izz al-Dawla in 351/962. The Ghadīr Khumm festival commemorated the occasion on which the Prophet, when returning from the farewell Pligrimage, declared 'Alī, to be the *mawlā* (master) of the people and commended him to them. This was taken by Shī'ites to be an explicit designation of 'Alī for the Imamate. 'Ashūrā' commemorated the martyrdom of al-Ḥusayn in Iraq. In retaliation of these two festivals, the Sunnīs instituted two rival festivals in 389/999 on the 26th of Dhū al-Ḥijja and 18th of Muḥarram, on which they celebrated respectively Abū Bakr's stay in the cave with the Prophet during his emigration from Medina to Mecca, and the death of Muṣ'ab b. al-Zubayr, who had defeated the rebel al-Mukhtār, who had risen in vengeance for the death of al-Ḥusayn. These festivals became a frequent source of violence between Shī'ite and Sunnī partisans. There were several occasions on which serious violence occurred between the rival factions. On these occasions al-Mufīd was banished from the city of Baghdād because of disturbances but it does not appear that al-Mufīd was in any way responsible for instigating these disturbances. Rather it appears that the Buwayhids, in order to preserve order and give an appearance of even-handed justice, felt it necessary to find a scape-goat among the Shī'ites. Al-Mufīd was sufficiently important for them to pacify Sunnī sentiments.

13 Al-Ṭūsī, *Fihrist*, 328.
14 Al-Ṭūsī, *Fihrist*, 305.

However, these banishments were short-lived.[15]

Al-Mufīd was a great Imāmī-Shī'ite scholar in an era of great Imāmī-Shī'ite scholars. His older contemporaries and teachers, Ibn Qūlawayh and Ibn Bābawayh have already been mentioned. He was, however, himself the teacher of two very great Imāmī-Shī'ite scholars, the brothers, al-Sharīf al-Raḍī, (d.406/1015) and al-Sharīf al-Murtaḍā (d.436/1044). Al-Raḍī, who in fact died before al-Mufīd, was a great writer and poet and the compiler of *Nahj al-Balāgha*, a collection of the speeches of 'Alī b. Abī Ṭālib.[16] Al-Murtaḍā followed and developed al-Mufīd's work in speculative theology and must be regarded as one of the greatest Imāmī-Shī'ite theologians.[17] Another student of al-Mufīd who belongs to the ranks of the great Imāmī-Shī'ite scholars was the traditionist, jurist and theologian and later leader of the Imāmī-Shī'ite scholars, al-Shaykh al-Ṭūsī.[18]

Al-Mufīd's own literary output was enormous. He is credited with over two hundred works: many of these were short treatises of a polemical nature but he also wrote much lengthier works on the whole range of religious topics.

Al-Mufīd died in the year 413/1022. A vast crowd attended his funeral and the funeral prayer for him was led by his former pupil al-Sharīf al-Murtaḍā. He was at first buried in his own house but later moved to Kāẓimayn and buried alongside his former teacher, Ibn Qūlawayh.[19]

Kitāb al-Irshād

Kitāb al-Irshād was written by al-Mufīd before he was forty, as it is mentioned by Ibn al-Nadīm.[20] It is written in answer to a request for guidance about the lives of the Imams "so that you may distinguish obscure errors and proved facts and you may rely on the truth in it with the sureness of one who has justice and true beliefs of religion."

The book is really in two halves. The first deals with the first Imam, 'Alī b. Abī Ṭālib and the second half deals with the other eleven Imams. The first half of the book is mainly concerned with the inter-Islamic polemic. Al-Mufīd attempts

15 cf. M. McDermott, op. cit., 16-21.
16 Ibn Dāwud, *al-Rijāl* (Tehran.1342 A.H.S.) 307.
17 Al-Ṭūsī, *Fihrist*, 218-220.
18 Al-Ṭūsī, *Fihrist*, 285-288.
19 Al-Ṭūsī, *Fihrist*, 316.
20 Bayard Dodge (ed. And trans.), *The Fihrist of ibn Nadīm* (New York, 1970), I, 491.
Ibn Nadim died in 380/990. Therefore, *Kitāb al-Irshād* must have been wntten before that date.

to show that 'Alī was the most excellent of the followers of the Prophet and was designated by the Prophet to be his successor. The main concentration of it, therefore, concerns 'Alī's great exploits during the Prophet's life, the Prophet's trust in and reliance upon 'Alī and his designation of 'Alī. In this part al-Mufīd uses several accounts from historians of the life of the Prophet, in particular versions of the work of Ibn Isḥāq (d.151/768) and al-Wāqidī (d. 208/823), which are not always acknowledged. After giving the accounts, al-Mufīd attempts to draw the appropriate conclusions from them. Thus, most of these accounts are followed by an analysis which attempts to demonstrate that 'Alī must be the most excellent and therefore was the logical Imam after the Prophet. Many of these accounts concern 'Alī's bravery and heroism during the life of the Prophet when Islam was beset by so many dangers.

Another area, in addition to the military, where the leadership of an Imam was necessary, was in giving judgements in legal disputes. Al-Mufīd produces a collection of 'Alī's legal decisions which cover the time of the Prophet and the first three Caliphs. In some of these accounts there are Biblical reminiscences but al-Mufīd himself stresses the role of the legal knowledge of David. 'Alī, he claims, has a similar knowledge.

He does not give a detailed account of the period in which 'Alī ruled the Islamic Community. Rather at this point he relies on the speeches of 'Alī. He includes a fairly wide selection of the speeches of 'Alī and thus in *Kitāb al-Irshād* we have an earlier collection of the speeches of 'Alī than that of al-Mufīd's pupil, al-Raḍī's *Nahj al-Balāgha*. There are many speeches similar to those included by al-Raḍī and some that al-Raḍī has not used. Al-Mufīd's collection of speeches is more systematic than al-Raḍī's. He begins with speeches of a more theological nature and then lets 'Alī's words comment on the events of his caliphate as they happen, in more or less chronological order. Al-Mufīd goes on to deal with the miracles attributed to 'Alī. During the course of his presentation of the miracles, he takes great pains to argue against the rationalist tendency present in society, which denied miracles.

In the second half of the book al-Mufīd presents the other eleven Imams. These accounts are not full lives of the Imams but rather collections of traditions concerned with critical aspects of their Imamates. As such, this half of the book is much more concerned with the inter-Shī'ite polemic of al-Mufīd's own time. He is anxious to show his readers the Imāmī-Shī'ite position on matters which were subjects of dispute to Shī'ites of his own time.

The Imamates of al-Ḥasan and his brother al-Ḥusayn were generally accepted by the Shī'ites of his time so that there was no real argument within Shī'ism concerning them. With regard to al-Ḥasan, al-Mufīd is mainly concerned to show the circumstances surrounding his abdication, which made that abdication inevitable, and that al-Ḥasan's death was murder at the instigation of Mu'āwiya. In the case of al-Ḥusayn his main interest is to give an account of the martyrdom. In choosing to use the account of Ibn al-Kalbī and not that of his teacher Ibn Bābawayh, al-Mufīd seems to be opposing tendencies within and outside the Imāmī-Shī'ite community to exaggerate the historical circumstances of that martyrdom. In choosing the version of al-Kalbī he has opted for the one with the best historical pedigree, being derived, as it is in the main, from the tradition of Abū Mikhnaf.

The Imamate 'Alī b. al-Ḥusayn was a period in which there was a contestant for that Imamate. Al-Mufīd omits the story, which is common in Imāmī-Shī'ism, about the dispute between Muḥammad b. al-Ḥanafiyya and 'Alī b. al-Ḥusayn over the Imamate and how that dispute was settled by the Black Stone of the Ka'ba. Al-Mufīd dealt with it elsewhere in his works. He also refutes the doctrines of the Kaysāniyya, the group which upheld the Imamate of Muḥammad b. al-Ḥanafiyya, in another of his works. The reason for the absence of any detailed discussion of the Kaysāniyya and the Imamate of Muḥammad b. al-Ḥanafiyya from this work would appear that, although these matters were of great significance in early Shī'ism, they no longer had any relevance to Shī'ism in the time of al-Mufīd. The main thrust of al-Mufīd's arguments in favour of 'Alī b. al-Ḥusayn is the Imāmī-Shī'ite doctrine that there must always be an Imam and since, apart from Muḥammad b. al-Ḥanafiyya, there are no other claims made on behalf of any one else, it belongs to 'Alī b. al-Ḥusayn. He maintained that this was also confirmed by the designation on his Imamate by his grandfather, and his position as the only surviving son of al-Ḥusayn. For the rest al-Mufīd is concerned to demonstrate his piety and merit.

In his account of the Imamate of Muḥammad al-Bāqir, al-Mufīd emphasises the latter's great contribution to traditional knowledge. He particularly refers to the tradition reported by Jābir b. 'Abd Allāh al-Anṣārī that he (Jābir) would live until he met a descendant of the Prophet who would split knowledge open. Al-Mufīd also draws attention to certain documents which Muḥammad al-Bāqir inherited from the Prophet and Fāṭima. While the possession of such documents might well be regarded as one of the insignia of office, certainly of inherited wisdom, it is also maintained that these documents contained the actual names of the twelve Imams. In the course of this account al-Mufīd refers to the rebellion led by Muḥammad al-Bāqir's brother Zayd b. 'Alī. He is at pains to point out that Zayd's revolution was carried out to secure the Imamate for Muḥammad's appointed successor, his son Ja'far, and that the revolution was a spontaneous reaction by Zayd to humiliation which he received from the authorities. Al-Mufīd's version clearly belongs to the polemic between the Zaydīs and the Imāmī-Shī'ite of his own time.

During the Imamate of Ja'far al-Ṣādiq, the Ḥasanid line began to emerge as contestants for the Imamate. Al-Mufīd recounts a report from Abū al-Faraj al-Isfahānī's *Maqātil al-Ṭālibiyyīn* in which, at a meeting of the various branches of the Hāshimites, the claims of Muḥammad b. 'Abd Allāh to the title of the *Mahdī* were put forward. This claim Ja'far rejected with the assertion that the time was not appropriate for the Imamate. The doctrine of the *Mahdī*, the rightly guided Imam who would bring justice to the Shī'a and the world, was first attributed to Muḥammad b. al-Ḥanafiyya. The Kaysāniyya had claimed that he had not died but had gone into concealment and would bring justice to the world. The poet al-Sayyid al-Ḥimyarī had been a supporter of this belief. Al-Mufīd quotes a poem of his to show that he was converted to Ja'far's interpretation of this doctrine, namely that the *Mahdī* belonged to the line of Imams from 'Alī through al-Ḥusayn and his descendants. One of their number would eventually go into concealment and return as the *Mahdī* to bring justice to the world.

This belief served to emphasise the quiescent policy of the Imāmī-Shī'ites. Ja'far's reign was a particularly turbulent time for Shī'ite rebellions against the 'Umayyad authorities. The enthusiasm of some Shī'ite elements and popular reaction against the 'Umayyads was exhibited during Ja'far's own lifetime, in the rebellions of Zayd b. 'Alī and 'Abd Allāh b. Mu'āwiya. In addition the 'Abbāsid branch of the Hāshimites, using claims of succession through Muḥammad b. al-Ḥanafiyya, brought about the overthrow of the 'Umayyads. Even some of Ja'far's own sons, who were not to succeed him, seem to have dabbled in revolutionary Shī'ism. Thus there is some evidence that Ismā'īl, Ja'far's eldest son, was engaged in revolutionary activities.[21] Al-Mufīd, himself, gives an account of some of the revolutionary activities undertaken by his son, Muḥammad. There are also reports of his second son, 'Abd Allāh, who was not nominated by Ja'far as his successor, taking part in Muḥammad b. 'Abd Allāh's rebellion.[22]

Amid such turbulent conditions, Ja'far's own nomination to the Imamate by his father, Muḥammad al-Bāqir, takes on a new significance. Al-Mufīd pays particular attention to Ja'far's nomination by his father in a way that he had not done for the earlier Imams. For the latter, he had been content with general

21 cf. B. Lewis. *The Origins of Ismā'īlism* (Cambridge, 1940), 39.

22 *Maqātil al-Ṭālibiyyin*, (Cairo. 1949) 278. There is also a report that Mūsā took part with 'Abd Allāh (227) but this seems unlikely.

statements of their nomination. In the case of Ja'far and all the later Imams, he gives much more evidence from traditions by eye-witnesses of their nomination. Al-Mufīd also shows Ja'far asserting that the weapons of the Prophet, the symbols of authority, which would be used in the ultimate revolution, were in the safe-keeping of true Imams, that is, himself and his successors. Ja'far seems to have been compelled to make this assertion in response to claims that Muḥammad b. 'Abd Allāh had the Prophet's sword.

Al-Mufīd also reports Ja'far as maintaining that he had documents dictated by the Prophet to 'Alī. Again possession of these documents served to strengthen his claims to the Imamate. The nature of such documents served to underline the doctrine of the Imam as teacher, interpreter and ultimate guide in religion.

There were current in Shī'ite circles traditions that there would be only seven Imams. These traditions were later to lead to serious divisions within the Shī'ite movement. Some of Ja'far's supporters maintained that he nominated his eldest son Ismā'īl and that Ismā'īl was the seventh and last Imam. Al-Mufīd takes great trouble to demonstrate that Ja'far did not nominate Ismā'īl and that Ismā'īl died during Ja'far's own lifetime. Despite this, the Ismā'īlī branch of Shī'ism developed, claiming that the Imamate belonged to the successors of Ismā'īl.

The Imamate of Ja'far's successor Mūsā was a critical period for Imāmī-Shī'ism. Such was the influence of the rumours about the seventh Imam being the Imam who would be the *Mahdī* that the 'Abbāsid authorities kept a very close watch to see who would be designated as Ja'far's successor. As a result and in order to protect his successor, Ja'far appears, at least publicly, not to have made it clear who his successor would be. Although al-Mufīd quotes a considerable number of traditions about Mūsā's designation by Ja'far, this designation seems to have been made secretly and the majority of the Shī'a seem to have been uncertain who Ja'far's successor was. Al-Mufīd himself indicates that most of them, at first, followed Ja'far's second son 'Abd Allāh. However, they found his knowledge inadequate and eventually came to uphold the Imamate of Mūsā.

Once the Imamate of Mūsā was clearly established among the majority of the Imāmī-Shī'ites, the authorities paid increasing attention to his activities and eventually imprisoned him. The death of Mūsā is important to establish within the context of the inter-Shī'ite polemic, for the tradition of the seventh Imam being the "awaited" Imam was fairly widespread. Al-Mufīd uses the account reported by Abū al-Faraj al-Iṣfahānī for this purpose. The account reveals that Mūsā's body was publicly displayed so that people should have no doubt about his death. In the same context, Mūsā's designation of his son 'Alī al-Riḍā is of importance.

The Imamate of ʻAlī al-Riḍā was a time of great Shīʻite activity against the ʻAbbāsid caliph al-Ma'mūn. During this time al-Mufīd shows ʻAlī al-Riḍā as the reluctant instrument of al-Ma'mūn's attempt to reconcile the Shīʻite community. Al-Ma'mūn, professing great respect for the family of ʻAlī b. Abī Ṭālib, makes ʻAlī al-Riḍā his heir apparent. Then, later, he has ʻAlī al-Riḍā poisoned. The ordering of the court to wear green, another aspect of al-Ma'mūn's policy, has absolutely nothing to do with Shīʻism. ʻAlī al-Riḍā, when asked to lead the prayer by al-Ma'mūn, wears white, the colour traditionally associated with the family of the Prophet.

The succession of ʻAlī al-Riḍā was another moment of critical importance to Imāmī-Shīʻism. ʻAlī al-Riḍā left behind him only one son, Muḥammad al-Jawād, who was seven years old at the time of his death. As a result of this, several of his former supporters, now reverted to the idea that Mūsā was the awaited Imam who was in occultation and would return. To combat this, al-Mufīd quotes traditions of his nomination by his father. These traditions refer to Jesus having begun his mission while still a child. Al-Mufīd demonstrates that he was competent to be Imam although still a child by reporting his confrontation with one of the leading jurists of the time, Yaḥyā b. Aktham. In their discussion, Muḥammad al-Jawād shows himself to be not only conversant with jurisprudence but a much greater jurist then Yaḥyā b. Aktham. When reporting the death of Muḥammad al-Jawād, al-Mufīd refuses to accept reports of his murder. He, thus, shows himself to be in disagreement with his teacher, Ibn Bābawayh, who maintains that all the Imams were murdered. In fact al-Mufīd only seems to accept the murders of ʻAlī, al-Ḥasan, al-Ḥusayn, Mūsā and ʻAlī al-Riḍā.

With the death of Muḥammad al-Jawād, the Imamate passes to his son, ʻAlī al-Hādī. From the time of ʻAlī al-Riḍā onwards, the Imams had been kept under very close observation by the ʻAbbāsids. This is particularly true of Imams ʻAlī al-Hādī and al-Ḥasan al-ʻAskarī, his son. The traditions reported by al-Mufīd give us some insight into the secret organisation built up by the Imāmī-Shīʻites to escape ʻAbbāsid surveillance. The succession of al-Ḥasan al-ʻAskarī also presented the Imāmī-Shīʻites community with some problems. For ʻAlī al-Hādī had had another son, Muḥammad, whom observers thought that he intended to appoint as his successor. However Muḥammad died before ʻAlī al-Hādī. The situation is actually compared to that which existed when it was thought that Jaʻfar al-Ṣādiq would appoint Ismāʻīl as his successor.

The existence of the twelfth Imam is of crucial importance to Imāmī-Shīʻism.

Al-Mufīd maintains that he was born in 255/869. His birth was kept secret from the authorities and the child was sent to the Ḥijāz for safe-keeping. Al-Mufīd quotes traditions from men who claimed to have seen him there. The claims of Ja'far, the brother of al-Ḥasan al-'Askarī, to be the Imam are rejected. It is suggested that Ja'far was himself aware of the existence of the son of al-Ḥasan al-'Askarī. Al-Mufīd also quotes some of the traditions in favour of there being twelve Imams. The 'Abbāsid authorities were also aware of these traditions and took great care to try to detect the birth of the twelfth Imam. Al-Mufīd's main concern, then, is to show the contact that the Imam maintained with the Imāmī-Shī'ite organisation. He finishes his account of this Imamate by enumerating the signs which will precede the return of the twelfth Imam.

He presents the background to these matters by selective use of historical material. As already mentioned, al-Mufīd used versions of the historians, Ibn Isḥāq and al-Wāqidī, for the life of 'Alī.[23] He also relies on material from Imāmī-Shī'ite traditional sources. He had a copy of Abū al-Faraj al-Iṣfahānī's *Maqātil al-Ṭālibiyyīn*, written in the latter's own hand. He seems to have material from this in his account of 'Alī's death and al-Ḥasan's accession and abdication as well as of his death.

In these two cases, he quotes one of Abū al-Faraj's sources, Abū Mikhnaf, rather than the book itself, but a comparison of the two texts seems to indicate that he took it directly from Abū al-Faraj. Other places where he seems to have used Abū al-Faraj, are at Ja'far al-Ṣādiq's meeting with the Hāshimites at al-Abwā' near Medina (here he acknowledges the source), and also for the death of Mūsā al-Kāẓim as well as for some of the account about 'Alī al-Riḍā.

His historical account of the martyrdom of al-Ḥusayn, he attributes in the main to Ibn al-Kalbī and al-Madā'inī. However, his principal source seems to have been al-Ṭabarī's version of al-Kalbī,[24] which he has given in a somewhat abbreviated form.

The other major source used by al-Mufīd is al-Kulaynī's *al-Kāfi*. He had studied this under Ibn Qūlawayh and frequently he gives the full *isnād* (chain of authorities) from Ibn Qūlawayh and gives al-Kulaynī's *isnād*. However,

23 In fact on two occasions al-Mufīd cites Ibn Hishām's Recension of Ibn Isḥāq's *Sīra*. On both occasions the citation is not the same as the version we have of Ibn Hishām. In the main it seems likely that he used the version presented by al-Ṭabarī, though with additional material from Shī'ite sources.

24 However, he does include some details not described in al-Ṭabarī's version. He also Incorporates the arrival of 'Ubayd Allāh into the account, which al-Ṭabarī gives as an alternative to Ibn al-Kalbī on the authority of 'Umar b. Shabba.

sometimes he cuts his own reference and the *isnād* to the last two authorities and sometimes he omits the *isnād* altogether.

Another work which al-Mufīd mentions and commends to his readers is *Kitāb al-Ghayba* of al-Nu'mānī. This work is particularly concerned with the existence, occultation and signs for the return of the twelfth Imam and al-Mufīd probably made particular use of it in his chapter about that Imam.

Al-Mufīd also seems to have used a work by Yaḥyā b. al-Ḥasan al-'Alawī a follower of 'Alī al-Rīḍā.[25] This work he received from al-Sharīf Abū Muḥammad al-Ḥasan b. Muḥammad. Although the latter was regarded as generally weak, he seems to have had an interest in genealogy[26] and al-Mufīd uses him for reports on this subject from the work of Yaḥyā b. al-Ḥasan. Yaḥyā b. al-Ḥasan is also used extensively by Abū al-Faraj al-Iṣfahānī in *Maqātil al-Ṭālibiyyīn*. Al-Mufīd reports traditions from several other teachers, about whom we know very little. Other authorities whom we know something of are Ibn al-Ji'ābī, who was an expert in tradition, and the theologian Ṭāhir, the pupil of the Imāmī-Shī'ite theologian Abū al-Jaysh, as well as Abū al-Jaysh himself.

The Translation

The text used for this translation is the reprint (Tehran 1377 A.H.) of the lithographed version edited by Kāẓim al-Mūsawī al-Miyāmiwī.

In the translation, texts of letters and verses have been indented. Square brackets, [], have been used to separate the *isnād*, i.e. the chain of authorities, from the actual report. Ordinary brackets, (), have been used to identify persons who might otherwise be obscure, to give the meaning of words or phrases which may be a little unclear and sometimes to give the Arabic word in order to make clear what the translation refers to. Qur'ānic quotations have been referred to by giving the number of the *sūra* in Roman numerals and the number of the verse in ordinary numerals.

The chapter divisions have been given titles and some of the sections within the chapters have been joined together, or separated according to the logic of their contents. Sometimes a section has been given a title that is not given by al-Mufīd.

---

25 Al-Ṭūsī, *Fihrist*, 360. Where It is mentioned that he has a work on the genealogy of the family of Abū Ṭālib. The link in the chain of authorities for this book back to Al-Ṭūsī is his grandson, Abū Muḥammad al-Ḥasan b. Muḥammad whose name is given as Abū Muḥammad b. Akhī Ṭāhir (son of the brother of Ṭāhir).

26 Ibn Dāwud, *al-Rijāl* 443.

Mawlā, which is a rather difficult word to translate, depending very much on the context, has been usually translated "retainer". This is a rather loose translation, but gives the general idea of the status of the people generally referred to by this designation in the text. Where the meaning is entirely different, it has been translated differently, but the word is given in brackets.

The system of transliteration of Arabic used is that in general use in Britain. I have chosen to ignore the *ḥamzat al-waṣl* and have transliterated words as written and not as pronounced.

Following the translation is a biographical index which is designed to help identify the people referred to in the text.

I would like to thank the Muḥammadi Trust for financing the publication of this work. In this connection, I would particularly like to thank Mr. Abbās Gokal and Wing-Commander Husain Qasim, the secretary of the Muḥammadi Trust. The latter has been a constant source of encouragement and help and I would like to thank him for his kindness and understanding. I am also extremely grateful to colleagues and friends, Dr. Jāsim Hussain and Dr. 'Abd al-Raḥīm 'Alī, who helped me check the translation. In this connection I would also like to thank Dr. Dona Straley, whose help has been of great value. Finally I must acknowledge the debt I owe to my wife, Louise, without whom I do not think this work would ever have been finished.

I. K. A. Howard
University of Edinburgh.

AUTHOR'S PREFACE

In the name of ALLĀH, the Merciful the Compassionate

Praise be to Allāh for His inspiration of knowledge of Himself and of guidance towards Himself through obedience to Him. Blessings and salvation be upon the best of His creatures, Muḥammad, Lord of the Prophets and His sincere friend, and upon the rightly-guided Imams from his progeny. I am recording - Allāh grant me help and success - what you have asked for, of the names of the Imams of guidance and the dates of their lives; as well as mentioning the places of their tombs and the names of their children and some of their stories which will be useful for knowledge of their circumstances, so that you may become as thoroughly acquainted (with them) as one who knows them and so that the difference between (various) claims and beliefs about them is clear. Thus through considering (this account) you may distinguish between obscure errors and proved facts and you may rely on the truth in it with the sureness of one who has justice and the true beliefs of religion. I am answering what you have asked for, while taking care to be concise and brief in my answer as you have urged and requested that to be. I put my trust in Allāh and seek His guidance along the path of righteousness.

PART I

THE LIFE OF
THE COMMANDER OF THE FAITHFUL
‘ALĪ B. ABĪ ṬĀLIB

CHAPTER I

BACKGROUND TO THE LIFE OF THE COMMANDER OF THE FAITHFUL

Introduction

(This part gives) an account of the Commander of the Faithful, peace be on him, the first of the Imams of the believers, of the rulers (*wulāt*) of the Muslims and of Allāh's (appointed) successors in religion after the Apostle of Allāh, the truthful one and the trusted one, Muhammad b. 'Abd Allāh, the seal of the Prophets, blessings be on Him and His Pure Family. (He was) the brother of the Apostle of Allāh and his paternal cousin, and his helper (*wazīr*) in his affair, his son-in-law (being married) to his daughter, Fāṭima the chaste, mistress of the women of the universe. (The full name of) the Commander of the Faithful is 'Alī b. Abī Ṭālib b. 'Abd al-Muṭṭalib b. Hāshim b. 'Abd Manāf. (He was) the Lord of the testamentary trustees of authority (*waṣiyyīn*), the best of blessing and peace be on him. His *kunya* was Abū al-Ḥasan.

He was born in the Sacred House (i.e. the Ka'ba) in Mecca on Friday, the thirteenth day of the month of Rajab, thirty years after the Year of the Elephant (c.570). Nobody before or after him has ever been born in the House of Allāh, the Most High. (It was a mark) of him being honoured by Allāh, the Most High, may His name be exalted, and of his position being dignified in its greatness.

His mother was Fāṭima, daughter of Asad b. Hāshim b. 'Abd Manāf, may Allāh be pleased with her. She was like a mother to the Apostle of Allāh, may Allāh bless Him and His Family, and he (the Apostle) was brought up under her care.

He was grateful for her kindness and she was among the first to believe in him and she emigrated with him in the group of the emigrants. When she died, the Prophet shrouded her with his own shirt in order to protect her from the insects of the earth, and he laid her to rest in her grave in order that, through that, she might be protected from (the crushing pressure of) the narrow space within the grave. He dictated to her her last words (which were) the statement of the authority (*wilāya*) of her son, the Commander of the Faithful, peace be on him, so that at the examination after burial, she would be able to reply with those words. He singled her out with this great favour because of her position with Allāh, may He be magnified and exalted, and with him, peace be on him. The report of that is well known.

The Commander of the Faithful, 'Alī b. Abī Ṭālib, peace be on him, and his brothers were among the leading members of the second generation of descendants of Hāshim. In this way he gained two marks of nobility, through his growing up under the care and education of the Apostle of Allāh, may Allāh bless Him and His Family. He was the first of the family of the House and of the Companions to believe in Allāh and His Apostle. He was the first male whom the Prophet, may Allāh bless Him and His Family, summoned to Islam and who answered. He never ceased to support the religion and to strive against the polytheists. He constantly defended the faith and fought against those who supported deviation (from the truth) and despotism. He spread the teachings of the sunna (the practice of the Prophet) and the Qur'ān, judged with justice and enjoined (people) to do good.

He was with the Apostle of Allāh, may Allāh bless Him and His Family, twenty-three years after the (coming) of the (prophetic) mission. Of these, thirteen years were in Mecca before the emigration when he shared with him all the persecutions and bore most of his hardships. Then there were ten years in Medina after the emigration when he defended him against the polytheists and strove with him against the unbelievers. He protected him with his own life from the enemies of religion until the time Allāh, the Exalted, took (the Prophet) to His heaven, raised him to the highest place in heaven and bestowed His blessings and peace on Him and His Family. On that day the Commander of the Faithful, peace be on him, was thirty-three years of age.

On the day of the death of the Prophet, may Allāh bless Him and His Pure Family, the community differed over his Imamate. His Shī'a who were all the Banū Hāshim, Salmān, 'Ammār, Abū Dharr, al-Miqdād, Khuzayma b. Thābit - the man who is known as the possessor of two testimonies - Abū Ayyūb al-Anṣārī, Jabīr b. 'Abd Allāh al- Anṣārī, Abū Sa'īd al-Khudrī and people like them among the important emigrants and Anṣār, (all these) maintained that he was the successor (*khalīfa*) after the Apostle of Allāh, may Allāh bless Him and His Family, and the Imam. (They did this) because of his outstanding merit (*faḍl*) above all mankind, through the fact that there were gathered in him the qualities of outstanding merit, judgement and perfection, such as him being the first of the community to enter the faith, his superiority over them in knowledge of the laws, his precedence over them in fighting (*jihād*) and the distinction which set him apart from them in the extent of his piety, asceticism and righteousness.

Furthermore he had been specially singled out by the Prophet from among (all) his relations because of (the qualities) which no other relation, apart from him, shared with the Prophet and because of the nomination (*naṣṣ*) of his authority (*wilāya*) by Allāh, may Allāh be magnified and exalted, in the Qur'ān where He, may His name be exalted, says: *Your authority (walī) is Allāh and His Apostle and those believers who perform the prayer and pay alms (zakāt) while they are bowing (in prayer)*. (V 55) It is known that no one except him paid alms while bowing (in prayer).

It has been established in language that *walī* means "the most appropriate for authority" (*awlā*), without there being any opposition (to this definition). If the Commander of the Faithful, peace be on him, was, by the stipulation of the Qur'ān, more appropriate for authority among the people than themselves because of his being their *walī* according to the textual nomination (*naṣṣ*) in the Clear Explanation (i.e. the Qur'ān, *tibyān*), it was obviously necessary for all of them to obey him, just as obedience to Allāh, the Most High, and obedience to His Apostle, peace be on Him and His Family, was required because of the information about their authority (*wilāya*) over creatures which is given in this verse with clear proof.

(Another reason for their support for the Commander of the Faithful was) because of what the Prophet, may Allāh bless Him and His Family, said on the day (of the assembly) at his house. He had especially gathered the Banū 'Abd al-Muṭṭalib there in order to make the (following) solemn pledge: "Whoever helps me in this matter will be my brother, my testamentary trustee (*waṣī*), my helper (*wazīr*), my heir and my successor after me." Then the Commander of the Faithful, peace be on him, stood up before him among all the gathering of them, and on that day he was the youngest of them, and he said: "O Apostle of Allāh, I will help you."

Then the Prophet, may Allāh bless Him and His Family, said: "Sit down, you are my brother, my trustee, my helper, my inheritor and successor after me."

This is a clear statement about the succession (after the Prophet).

In addition, there is also what (the Prophet), peace be on Him and His Family, said on the day of Ghadīr Khumm. The community had gathered to listen to the sermon (in which he asked): "Am I not more appropriate for authority (*awlā*) over you than yourselves?"

"Yes," they answered.

Then he spoke to them in an ordered manner without any interruption in his speech: "Whomsoever I am the authority over (*mawlā*), 'Alī is also the authority over."

Thus he (the Prophet) required for him ('Alī), through laying down obedience to him and his authority (over them), the same authority as he had over them, and which he made them acknowledge and which they did not deny. This is clear (evidence) of the nomination (*naṣṣ*) of him for the Imamate and for succession to his position.

Furthermore there is (the Prophet's), peace be on Him and His Family, statement to him at the time of setting out to Tabūk: "You are in the same position with respect to me as Aaron (Hārūn) was to Moses (Mūsā) except that there is no prophet after me." Thus he required him (to have) the office of helping (i.e. administering) and to be characterised by love and outstanding merit over everyone. (He also required) his deputising for him both during his life and after his death. The Qur'ān gives evidence for all that coming to Aaron (Hārūn) from Moses (Mūsā), peace be on them, when Allāh, may He be magnified and exalted, said in giving a report of what Moses, peace be on him, said: "*Make Aaron, my brother, a helper for me from my family. Give me support through him and make him participate in my affair so that we may glorify You much and we may remember You frequently in that You have been a watcher over us.*" (XX 29-35). Allāh, the Most Exalted said: "*Your request is granted, Moses.*" (XX 36). This (verse) confirmed that Aaron had a share with Moses in prophecy, and in helping in delivering the message and his support was strengthened through him by his aid. (Moses) also told him of deputising for him (when he said): "....*Deputise for me among my people. Act for (their) benefit and do not follow the path of the corrupters.*" (VII 142) This confirms his succession by the precise statement of revelation. Therefore when the Apostle of Allāh, may Allāh bless Him and His Family, gave all the ranks which Aaron had from Moses to the Commander of the Faithful, peace be on him, in the same extent, except for prophecy, (all such things) were required of him as helping the Apostle, giving him support, outstanding merit and love, because these qualities were definitelyrequired by that. Then by the clear statement there is his deputising for him during his life and "after the prophethood" which (gives evidence of his succession) by specification of the exception, (of Prophethood) when he excludes him from it by mentioning "after".

Proofs similar to these are so numerous that it would make the book unduly long to mention them all, (especially) as we have examined thoroughly the statement of the evidence for them in other places in our books. Praise be to Allāh.

The Imamate of the Commander of the Faithful, peace be on him, was for thirty years after the Prophet, may Allāh bless Him and His Family. For twenty-four years and six months of these he was prevented from administering the laws (of the office) (and had to) exercise precautionary dissimulation (*taqiyya*) and withdrawal. For five years and six months of these, he was troubled by wars against the hypocrites, those who broke their pledges, the unjust and those who deviated (from the religion) and he was plagued by the seditions of those who had gone astray. In the same way the Apostle of Allāh, may Allāh bless Him and His Family, had been prevented from (administering) the laws (of his office) through fear and through being spied upon, and through being a fugitive and through being exiled, so that he had no power to fight the unbelievers and no means of defending the believers. Then he emigrated and for ten years after the emigration he remained making war on the unbelievers and being troubled by the hypocrites until the time that Allāh, may His name be exalted, took him unto Himself and made him dwell in the gardens of Paradise.

The death of the Commander of the Faithful, peace be on him occurred before dawn of Friday, the twenty-first of the month of Ramaḍān, in the year 40 A.H. He was a victim of the sword. Ibn Muljam al-Murādī, may Allāh curse him, killed him at the mosque of Kūfā, which he had come out to in order to wake the people for the dawn prayer on the night of the nineteenth of the month of Ramaḍān. He had been lying in wait for him from the beginning of the night. When he (the Commander of the Faithful) passed by him while the latter was hiding his design by feigning sleep amid a group of people who were asleep, he (Ibn Muljam) sprang out and struck him on the top of his head with his sword which was poisoned. He lingered through the day of the nineteenth and the night and day of the twentieth and the first third of the night of the twenty-first. Then he, peace be on him, died a martyr and met his Lord, Most High, as one who has been wronged. He, peace be on him, knew of that before its time and he told the people of it before its time. His two sons, al-Ḥasan and al-Ḥusayn, peace be on them, performed (the tasks) of washing him and shrouding him according to his bequest. Then they carried him to al-Gharī at Najaf in Kūfa and they buried him there. They removed the traces of the place of his burial according to his bequest which was made about that to both of them by him, because of what he, peace be on him, knew about the regime of the 'Umayyads (which would come) after him, and their hostile attitude towards him. (For he knew) the evil action and abuse to which they would be led by their wicked intentions if they had been able to know that (place). His grave, peace be on him, remained hidden until al-Ṣāḍiq Ja'far b. Muḥammad, peace be on them, pointed it out during the 'Abbāsid regime. For he visited it when he came to visit Abū Ja'far (al-Manṣūr) while the latter was in al-Ḥīra. Then the Shī'a knew of it and they began from that time to make visitation to his (grave), peace be on him and on his pure offspring.

On the day of his death he was 63 years of age.

Reports of him, Peace be on him, Mentioning and Knowing about the Event (of his Death) before its Occurrence

[It is reported on the authority of ʻAlī b. al-Mundhir al-Ṭarīqī, on the authority of Abū al-Faḍl al-ʻAbdī, on the authority of Fiṭr, on the authority of Abū Tufayl ʻĀmir b. Wāthila, may Allāh be pleased with him, who said:][1]
The Commander of the Faithful, peace be on him, gathered the people for the pledge of allegiance. ʻAbd al-Raḥmān b. Muljam al-Murādī, may Allāh curse him, came but he (i.e. ʻAlī) refused to accept his (pledge of allegiance) twice or three times. Then he (let him) make his pledge of allegiance to him. When he did so, he (i.e. ʻAlī) said to him: "What prevents the most wretched person of the community (from doing his wicked deed now)? For I swear by Him in Whose hand is my life, you will colour this (with blood) from this." And he put his hand on his beard and his head.

When Ibn Muljam withdrew and left him, he, peace be on him, recited the following:

> Stiffen your breast for death. Indeed death will meet you.
> Do not show grief at death, when it arrives in your valley.

[It is related from al-Ḥasan b. Maḥbūb, on the authority of Abū Ḥamza al-Thumālī, on the authority of Abū Isḥāq al-Sabīʼī, on the authority of al-Aṣbagh b. Nubāta, who said:]
Ibn Muljam came to the Commander of the Faithful, peace be on him, and pledged allegiance to him with the (others) who pledged their allegiance, and withdrew from him. Then the Commander of the Faithful, peace be on him, called him back and warned him to be trustworthy and to be sure that he was not treacherous and did not break his oath. He did that (i.e. promised to keep his word). Then he withdrew. A second time the Commander of the Faithful called him (back) and warned him to be trustworthy and to be sure that he was not treacherous and did not break his oath. Ibn Muljam, may Allāh curse him, said: "By Allāh, O Commander of the Faithful, I have not seen you do this with anyone else except me."

1 cf. *Maqātil al-Ṭālibiyyīn*, 31. The tradition is cited by Ibn Saʻd on the authority of al-Faḍl b. Dukayn, *al-Ṭabaqāt al-Kubrā* (Beirut, 1978), III, 33; al-Balādhurī has the same tradition on the authority of Ibn Saʻd, *Ansāb al-Ashrāf* (Beirut, 1974), II, 500. The text of *al-Irshād* had Abū Faḍl al-ʻAbdī. This has been corrected.

Then the Commander of the Faithful said:

> I want his friendship and he wants my death. The one who makes excuses to you is one of your bosom friends from (the tribe of) Murād.[2]

(Then the Commander of the Faithful continued): "Go, Ibn Muljam, I do not think that you will keep your word."

[It is related from Ja'far b. Sulaymān al-Dab'ī, on the authority of al-Mu'āllā b. Ziyād, who said:]
'Abd al-Raḥmāan b. Muljam, may Allāh curse him, came to the Commander of the Faithful, peace be on him, to ask to be provided with a horse.
"O Commander of the Faithful," he said, "provide me with a horse."
The Commander of the Faithful, peace be on him, turned toward him and then said to him, "You are 'Abd al-Raḥmān b. Muljam al-Murādī?"
"Yes," he replied.
"Ghazwan," called (the Commander of the Faithful), "provide him with the roan."

That man came with a roan horse and Ibn Muljam, may Allāh curse him, mounted it and took its reins. When he had gone away, the Commander of the Faithful, peace be on him said:

> I want his friendship and he wants my death. The one who makes excuses to you is one of your bosom friends from (the tribe of) Murād.

When he did what he did and struck the Commander of the Faithful, peace be on him, he was captured after he came out of the mosque and then brought to the Commander of the Faithful. The latter said to him: "I have treated you as I have done, even though I knew that you would be my murderer. Yet, I treated you that way in order to seek Allāh's support against you."

There are other reports in which he, peace be on him, announces his own death to his family and companions before his murder.

[Abū Zayd al-Aḥwal reported on the authority of al-Ajlaḥ, on the authority of the shaykhs of Kinda whom al-Ajlaḥ said he heard say more than twenty times:]
'Alī said on the pulpit: "What prevents the most wretched person of the community dyeing this red with blood from above it?" And he, peace be on him, put his hand on his beard.

---

2 This verse is also reported by *Maqātil al-Ṭālibiyyīn*, 31, Ibn Sa'd, op. cit., 34, with a different *isnād*. It is given in a slightly different story in the next report. The verse is also cited by Ibn Ziyād in his confrontation with Hani' b. 'Urwa, cf.

['Alī b. al-Ḥazawwar on the authority of al-Aṣbagh b. Nubāta, who said:]
'Alī preached in the month in which he was killed and he said: "The month of Ramaḍān has come to you. It is the lord of the months, and foremost of the year. In it the mill of authority makes a (new) turn and you will make the pilgrimage of the (new) year in one rank (i.e. without an Imam to lead you). The sign of that will be that I will no longer be among you."

[Al-Aṣbagh added:] He was announcing his own death but we did not understand.

[It is related from al-Faḍl b. Dukayn, on the authority of Ḥayyān b. al-'Abbās, on the authority of 'Uthmān b. al-Mughīra who said:]
When the month of Ramaḍān began, the Commander of the Faithful, peace be on him, had supper one evening with al-Ḥasan, one evening with al-Ḥusayn, peace be on them, and one evening with 'Abd Allāh b. al-'Abbās. He never had more than three mouthfuls (of food). One of those nights he was asked about that, he replied: "(I would rather) the decision of Allāh come to me while I was hungry." It was only a night of two nights later when he, peace be on him, was struck towards the end of the night.

[Ismā'īl b. Ziyād reported, on the authority of Umm Mūsā, a woman servant of 'Alī, peace be on him, and the wet-nurse of his daughter, peace be on her, who told me:]
'Alī, peace be on him, said to his daughter, Umm Kulthūm,: "O my little daughter, little time is left for me to be with you."
"Why is that, father?" she asked.
"I have seen the Apostle of Allāh, may Allāh bless Him and His Family, in my sleep," he replied. "He was rubbing the dust from my face and saying: 'O 'Alī, do not be concerned, you have accomplished what you had to.'"

Only three days later he was struck by that blow. Umm Kulthūm cried aloud (with sorrow).
"Don't do that, my daughter," he said. "For I see the Apostle of Allāh, may Allāh bless Him and His Family, pointing to me with his hand and saying: 'O 'Alī, come to us, for what we have is better for you.'"

['Ammār al-Duhnī reported on the authority of Abū Sāliḥ al-Ḥanafī, who said:]
I heard 'Alī, peace be on him, saying: "I saw the Prophet, may Allāh bless Him and His Family, in my sleep and I complained to him about the trouble and quarrelling which I had met from his community. Then I wept. He said: 'Don't weep, 'Alī, but turn around.' I turned around. Behold, there were two fettered

men, and then their heads were crushed by stones."[3]

[Abū Sāliḥ added:] I went to him in the morning as I had done every morning, and when I got to the (area of) the butchers I met the people who were saying: "The Commander of the Faithful, peace be on him, has been killed."

['Abd Allāh b. Mūsā related, on the authority of al-Ḥasan b. Dīnār, on the authority of al-Ḥasan al-Baṣrī, who said:]
The Commander of the Faithful, peace be on him, stayed up awake during the night on the morning of which he was killed and he did not go out to the mosque for the night prayer as was his custom. His daughter, Umm Kulthūm, the mercy of Allāh be on her, asked him: "What has kept you awake?"
"I will be killed, if I go out in the morning," he replied.

Then Ibn al-Nabbāḥ came to him and summoned him to the prayer. He walked out a little way then returned. Umm Kulthūm said to him: "Tell Ja'da to pray with the people."
"Yes, tell Ja'da to perform the prayer with the people," he answered. But then he said: "There is no escape from the appointed time."

He went out to the mosque and there was the man who had spent the whole night lying in wait for him. However, when it had become cold in the early morning before dawn, he had fallen asleep. Now, the Commander of the Faithful, peace be on him, moved him with his foot and said to him: "The prayer."
The man got up and struck him.

[In another account:]
The Commander of the Faithful, peace be on him, spent that night awake and he frequently went out and looked up to the sky, saying: "By Allāh, I have not lied nor have I been lied to. It is the night which I was promised."

Then he went back to his bed. When dawn rose, he put on his waist-cloth (*izār*) and went out saying:

> Stiffen your breast for death. Indeed death will meet you.
> Do not show grief at death, when it arrives in your valley.

When he reached the courtyard of his house, the geese met him and hooted in his face. (The people) began to drive them away but he said: "Leave them, they are those who wail (for my death)."

---

3 Reference to the punishment Ibn Muljam and Shabīb b. Bajura will receive from Allāh.

He, peace be on him, went out and was struck down.

Reports which have come down of the Motive for his Murder and how the Event occurred

[What is reported by a group of historians (*ahl al-siyar*), including Abū Mikhnaf, Ismāʿīl b. Rashīd, Abū Hāshim al-Rifāʿī, Abū ʿAmr al-Thaqafī and others who relate:][4]

A group of the Khārijites gathered at Mecca and they mentioned the leaders (of the people) and blamed them and their actions. They mentioned the people of al-Nahrawān and they asked Allāh's mercy for them. Then they said to each other: "If (only) we devoted ourselves to Allāh, and went to the leaders (Imams) of error (*ḍalāl*) and sought a moment when they were inattentive and then rid the country and men of them for the sake of Allāh, and also avenged our brothers, the martyrs of al-Nahrawān."

They made a compact to do that after performing the pilgrimage. ʿAbd al-Raḥmān b. Muljam, may Allāh curse him, said: "I'll take care of (killing) ʿAlī for you."
Al-Burak b. ʿAbd Allāh al-Tamīmī said: "I will take care of (killing) Mu'āwiya for you."
ʿAmr b. Bakr al-Tamīmī said: "I will take care of (killing) ʿAmr b. al-ʿAṣ for you."

They made a compact to do that and bound themselves to its fulfilment. They agreed (to carry it out) on the night of the nineteenth of the month of Ramaḍān. On that they separated.

Ibn Muljam, may Allāh curse him, set out - he was numbered among Kinda - until he came to Kūfa. There he met his colleagues. But he kept his task secret from them out of fear that something of it might get spread around. The situation was like this when one day he visited one of his colleagues from Taym al-Rabāb. At this man's house he met by chance Qaṭām, daughter of al-Akhḍar of Taym. The Commander of the Faithful, peace be on him, had killed her father and brother at al-Nahrawān. She was (also) one of the most beautiful of the women of her time. When Ibn Muljam, may Allāh curse him, saw her, he fell in love with her and his admiration of her became very intense. He asked to marry her and became engaged to her. Then she said to him: "What dowry do you suggest for me?"

4 The following account agrees with *Maqātil al-Ṭālibiyyīn*, 31-33. It is slightly rearranged and there are occasional small differences in words. Al-Mufīd even accepts Abū al-Faraj's collected *isnād* and cites his three principal authorities.

"Make your decision on that," he answered.

"I have decided," she said, "that you should give me three thousand dirhams, a young serving boy, a servant and the murder of 'Alī b. Abī Ṭālib."
"You can have all you asked for," he replied. "But as for the murder of 'Alī b. Abī Ṭālib, how can I do that?"

"You should look (for a time) when he is careless," she said. "If you kill him, I will cure myself (of my obsession against him) and life with me will be a pleasure for you. If you are killed, Allāh has nothing in this world which is better for you (than such a death)."
"The only thing which has brought me to this town (*miṣr*)," he said, "when I was a fugitive from it and could find no protection with its inhabitants, was to kill 'Alī b. Abī Ṭālib, which you have asked me for. So you will have what you have asked for."

"I have been looking for someone to help you and strengthen you in that (undertaking)," she said. Then she went to Wardān b. Mujālid (another) from Taym al-Rabāb. She gave him the information and asked help for Ibn Muljam, may Allāh curse him. He undertook to share responsibility for that for her.

Then Ibn Muljam, may Allāh curse him, went out and came to a man from Ashja' called Shabīb b. Bajura and said to him: "Shabīb, would you like nobility (*sharaf*) in this world and the next life?"
"What is that?" he asked.
"Will you help me to kill 'Alī b. Abī Ṭālib?"

Shabīb was one who held the view of the Khārijites, so he said to Ibn Muljam: "May a wailing woman wail for you (at your death), Ibn Muljam. For you have come to something which is horrific. How will you be able to do it?"

"We will lie in wait for him in the great mosque," Ibn Muljam, may Allāh curse him, replied. "Then when he comes to the dawn prayer, we will attack him. If we kill him, we will satisfy ourselves and attain our vengeance."

He insisted until he agreed and went with him into the great mosque to Qaṭām, while she was performing the rite of *i'tikāf*[5] there and put up a tent. They both said to her: "We have reached agreement on killing this man."
"When you want (to do) that," she said, "come to me in this place."

5 *i'tikāf* a ritual usually performed in Ramaḍān where a person cuts himself off from ordinary life by staying in a tent in a mosque.

Then they left her and waited for several days. They came to her finally on the night of Wednesday, the nineteenth of the month of Ramaḍān in the year 40 A.H. She ordered some silk which she tied around their chests. They put on their swords, and went out and sat opposite at the door from which the Commander of the Faithful, peace be on him, would come out to the prayer. However before that, they had told al-Ash'ath b. Qays of the resolution in their spirits to kill the Commander of the Faithful, peace be on him. Al-Ash'ath b. Qays, may Allāh curse him, agreed with them in what they had agreed upon.

Ḥujr b. 'Adī, may Allāh have mercy on him, was (also) spending that night in the mosque. He overheard al-Ash'ath saying to Ibn Muljam:
"Hurry, hurry to your task, for dawn is beginning to appear."

Ḥujr perceived the intention of al-Ash'ath and said to him: "You are going to kill him, you one-eyed man."

He left directly to go to the Commander of the Faithful, peace be on him, and tell him the news to warn him about the group. However, the Commander of the Faithful, peace be on him, missed him on the way and went into the mosque. Ibn Muljam came to him first and struck him. Ḥujr approached as the people were crying: "The Commander of the Faithful has been killed!"

['Abd Allāh b. Muḥammad al-Azdī has reported:][6]
On that night I was praying in the great mosque with men who were inhabitants of the town. During that month they used to pray from the beginning of the night to the end of it. I looked towards the men who were praying near the door and 'Alī b. Abī Ṭālib, peace be on him, came out for the dawn prayer. He began to call out: "The prayer, the prayer."

I was hardly aware of the call before I saw the flashing of swords and I heard someone saying: "Judgement belongs to Allāh, 'Alī, not to you and your companions."

Then I heard 'Alī, peace be on him, saying: "Don't let the man escape from you."

Then 'Alī, peace be on him, was struck and Shabīb b. Bajura came to strike him but he missed him, and his blow fell on air. The group fled towards the gates of the mosque and the people rushed to seize them.

---

6 The following account is almost identical with *Maqātil al-Ṭālibiyyīn*, 34-37. But the *isnāds* have been omitted and the order slightly rearranged. There is one brief addition concerning the people going to 'Alī and details about al-Ash'ath are omitted.

A man caught Shabīb b. Bajura, knocked him down and sat on his chest and took his sword to kill him with it. When he saw the people rushing towards him, he was afraid that they would act precipitately against him without listening to him. Therefore he jumped off him and let him go and threw the sword from his hand. Shabīb made his escape to his house.Then his paternal cousin came to him. He saw him untying the silk cloth from his breast and said: "What is that? Perhaps (it was) you (who) killed the Commander of the Faithful, peace be on him." (Shabīb) meant to say 'no' but he said "yes". His cousin went away and put on his sword. Then he went to (Shabīb) (again) and struck him with it until he killed him.

One of the men from Hamdān followed Ibn Muljam, may Allāh curse him. He flung his cloak over what was in Ibn Muljam's hand and took his sword from him. Then he took him to the Commander of the Faithful, peace be on him. In the meantime the third had escaped and dodged among the people.

When Ibn Muljam, may Allāh curse him, was brought before the Commander of the Faithful, peace be on him, the latter looked at him and said: "A life for a life. If I die, kill him as he killed me. If I live, I will consider my judgement on him."

"By Allāh", said Ibn Muljam, may Allāh curse him, "I have bought his life for a thousand lives. I have plotted against him for a thousand lives. If he has betrayed me, then may Allāh destroy him."
"Enemy of Allāh," cried out Umm Kulthūm, "you have killed the Commander of the Faithful, peace be on him."
"I have killed only your father," he retorted.
"Enemy of Allāh," she cried, "I hope that there is no danger for him."
"I think you are only crying for 'Alī," he replied. "Indeed, by Allāh, I struck him. If I had been divided among the people of the land, I should have destroyed them."

Then he was taken from his presence, peace be on him, while the people (wanted) to tear his flesh with their teeth as if they were wild beasts. They were crying out: "O enemy of Allāh, what have you done? You have destroyed the community of Muḥammad, may Allāh bless Him and His Family. You have killed the best of people."

He was silent and did not speak. He was taken to the prison.[7] Then the people went to the Commander of the Faithful, peace be on him, and said: "Commander

7 See above. The account, which follows, of the people visiting the dying 'Ali is not in *Maqātil al-Ṭālibiyyīn.*

of the Faithful, give us your order about the enemy of Allāh. For he has destroyed the community, and corrupted the faith."

"If I live," answered the Commander of the Faithful, peace be on him, "then I will consider my judgement on him. But if I die then do to him what the Prophet did with a murderer. Kill him and after that burn him in a fire."

When the Commander of the Faithful, peace be on him, died (the people) wept for him. (After) his family had finished his burial, al-Ḥasan, peace be on him, sat in council and ordered Ibn Muljam to be brought to him. He was brought to him and when he stood before him (al-Ḥasan) said: "O enemy of Allāh, you have killed the Commander of the Faithful and you have increased corruption in religion."
Then he ordered him to be beheaded. Umm al-Haytham, daughter of al-Aswad of al-Nakha'a asked to be given his corpse so that she could be in charge of burning it. He gave it to her and he made her burn it in a fire.[8]

The poet said about the affair of Qaṭām and the killing of the Commander of the Faithful peace be upon him:

> I have never seen a dowry, given by a generous man, like the dowry of Qaṭām (whether the man was) rich or needy.
> (It was) three thousand (dirhams), a slave and a young servant, and the striking of 'Alī with a sharp piercing sword.
> (There has been) no dowry more precious - and no violence except that it was less than the violence of Ibn Muljam.[9]

As for the two men who were in agreement with Ibn Muljam to kill Mu'āwiya and 'Amr b. Al. 'Āṣ, the one struck Mu'āwiya while he was bending (in prayer). However his blow was delivered weakly and he was saved from its consequences. The man was seized and killed immediately. As for the other he went (to carry out) his mission that night. However 'Amr had felt sick and had put a man in his place to pray with the people; the man was called Khārija b. Abī Ḥabība al-'Āmirī. He struck with his sword when he thought that it was 'Amr. He was seized and taken to 'Amr who had him killed. Khārija died on the second day.[10]

---

8 cf. *ibid.*, 41.
9 cf. *ibid.*, 37.
10 Summary of *ibid.*, 30.

Reports about the Place of the Grave of the Commander of the Faithful, Peace be on him, and an Explanation of the Circumstances of his Burial

[‘Abbād b. Ya‘qūb al-Rawājinī related: Hayyān b. ‘Alī al-‘Anazī told us: A retainer of ‘Alī b. Abī Ṭālib told me:]
When death was close to the Commander of the Faithful he said to al-Ḥasan and al-Ḥusayn, peace be on them: “When I die, you two put me on my bier. Then take me out and carry (me) in the back of the bier. You two will protect the front of it. Then bring me to al-Ghariyyayn. You will see a white rock shining with light. Dig there and you will find a shield and bury me at it.”

When he died, we took him out and began to carry him on the back of the bier while we guarded the front of it. We began to hear a rustling and whistling of the wind until we came to al-Ghariyyayn. Behold! There was a white rock whose light was shining. We dug there and behold, there was a shield on which was written: “This is one of the things which Noah has stored for ‘Alī b. Abī Ṭālib.” We buried him there and went away. We were happy at Allāh’s mark of honour to the Commander of the Faithful. A group of the Shī‘a followed us but they had not witnessed the prayer performed for him. We told them about what had happened and about Allāh’s mark of honour to the Commander of the Faithful.

Then they said: “We would like to see what you have seen of his affair.”
“Traces of the place have been removed according to his bequest,” we told them. They kept coming back and forth to us and they told us that they had dug but could not find anything.

[Muḥammad b. ‘Umāra related: Jābir b. Yazīd al-Ju’fī told me:]
I asked Abū Ja‘far Muḥammad b. ‘Alī al-Bāqir where the Commander of the Faithful was buried.

“He is buried,” he answered, “in the region of al-Ghariyyayn. He was buried before the dawn rose and al-Ḥasan, al-Ḥusayn, peace be on them, and Muḥammad, the sons of’ ‘Alī, and ‘Abd Allāh b. Ja‘far, may Allāh be pleased with him, went into his grave.”

[Ya‘qūb b. Yazīd reported on the authority of Ibn Abī ‘Umayr, on the authority of his men:][11]
Al-Ḥusayn b. ‘Alī, peace be on them, was asked: “Where did you bury the

11 *Ibid.*, 42.

Commander of the Faithful?" He answered: "We went out with him at night past the Mosque of al-Ash'ath until we brought him out on the upper ground beside al-Ghariyyayn. We buried him there."

[Muḥammad b. Zakariyyā reported: 'Abd Allāh b. Muḥammad told us on the authority of Ibn 'Ā'isha, who said: 'Abd Allāh b. Ḥāzim told me:]
We went out from Kūfa one day with (Hārūn) al-Rashīd to hunt. We came to the region of al-Ghariyyayn and al-Thawiyya. Then we saw some gazelle. We sent the falcons and dogs after them. They raced after them for an hour but then the gazelle took refuge in a hill. They stopped chasing them; the falcons flew down to the ground and the dogs came back. Al-Rashīd was amazed at that. Then the gazelles came down from the hill, and the falcons and dogs descended towards them. The gazelle returned to the hill, and the falcons and dogs came away from them. That happened three times.

Then (Hārūn) al-Rashīd said: "Hurry and bring me whoever you meet."
We brought him an old man (shaykh) of the Banū Asad. Hārūn asked him: "Tell me what this hill is."
"I will tell you, if you grant me a pledge of security," he replied.
"You may have the compact of Allāh and His guarantee that I will not be roused against you and harm you," said Hārūn.
"My father reported to me from his father," said the old man, "that they used to say that in this hill was the grave of 'Alī b. Abī Ṭālib, and that Allāh has made it a sanctuary (*ḥaram*) so that whatever seeks refuge there will be safe."

Hārūn got down and called for water. Then he made ritual ablutions and performed the prayer at the hill. He rolled in the ground there and began to weep. Then we left.

My mind could not accept that. Some days later I made the pilgrimage to Mecca. I saw there Yāsir, one of al-Rashīd's men. He used to sit with us. When we had made the *tawwāf* (circumambulation of the Ka'ba), the conversation went on until he said:
Al-Rashīd said to me one night when we had come from Mecca and stopped at Kūfa: "Tell 'Īsā b. Ja'far to come riding with me."

I rode with them both until we came to al-Ghariyyayn. 'Īsā threw himself down and slept. But al-Rashīd went to the hill and prayed there. Whenever he performed two *rak'as* he called out, wept and rolled in the ground of the hill. Then he said: "O cousin, I know your outstanding merit (*faḍl*), and your precedence (in Islam). By Allāh, you have sat in my *majlis* (council) while I was there and you were what you were: but your descendants are harming me and revolting against me."

After this he stood and prayed two *rak'as*, then he began speaking again, calling out and weeping until it was daybreak. Then he said: "Yāsir, wake 'Īsā." I woke him and he said to him: "'Īsā, wake up and pray at the grave of your cousin."
"What cousin of mine is this?" asked 'Īsā.
"This is the grave of 'Alī b. 'Abī Ṭālib," he replied.

Then 'Īsā made his ritual ablutions and stood up to pray. He did not stop doing that until the dawn arose. Then I said: "O Commander of the Faithful, morning has come." So we rode off and returned to Kūfa.

CHAPTER II

VIRTUES, QUALITIES AND ACIEVEMENTS OF THE COMMANDER OF THE FAITHFUL

(This Chapter includes) a sample of the reports about the Commander of the Faithful, peace be on him, (including) his virtues and his eminent qualities, together with (some of) what has been preserved of his wise sayings and sermons, and (some of) what is told of his miracles, legal judgements and explanations.[1]

Reports of his Priority in Belief in Allāh and His Apostle and of his Being the First of all Responsible Men in (Faith)

[Abū al-Jaysh al-Muẓaffar b. Muḥammad al-Balkhī informed me: Abū Bakr Muḥammad b. Aḥmad b. Abī Thalj informed us: Abū al-Ḥasan Aḥmad b. (Muḥammad b.) al-Qāsim al-Barqī told us: 'Abd al-Rahmān b. Ṣāliḥ al-Azdī told me: Asad b. 'Ubayda told us on the authority of Yaḥyā b. 'Afīf b. Qays, on the authority of his father ('Afīf b. Qays),[2] who said:)
I was sitting with al-'Abbās b.'Abd al-Muṭṭalib, may Allāh be pleased with him, in Mecca, before the affairs of the Prophet became known to the public. A man came and looked up towards the sky where the sun hovered above. He turned in the direction of the Ka'ba and stood to pray. Then a youth came and stood at his right and a woman came and stood behind them both. The man bowed, and the youth and the woman bowed. The man raised his hands and the youth and the woman raised their hands. Then he prostrated and they both prostrated.

"'Abbās!" I exclaimed, "it is a fantastic affair!"
"Indeed, it is a fantastic affair," replied al-'Abbās. "Do you know who that man is? He is Muḥammad b. 'Abd Allāh b.'Abd al-Muṭṭalib, my cousin. Do you know who that youth is? He is 'Alī b. Abī Ṭālib, my cousin. Do you know who that woman is? She is Khadīja, daughter of Khuwaylid. This cousin of mine (i.e. Muḥammad) has told me that his Lord is the Lord of the heavens and the earth, Who has ordered him to carry out this religion (*dīn*) which he is practising. No, by Allāh, there are not any on the face of the earth, who practise this religion

1 Although mentioned here by al-Mufīd, the arrangement of the chapters in the translations means that the sayings and sermons and miracles and legal judgments will be dealt with in separate chapters.

2 Al-Ṭabarī, *Ta'rikh* (Leiden 1879-1901) I, 1160-1. The *isnād* has the same three first authorities, but it seems from the full *isnād* that it was not taken from al-Ṭabarī.

except these three."

[Abū Ḥafṣ 'Umar b. Muḥammad al-Ṣayrafī informed me: Muḥammad b. Aḥmad b. Abī Thalj told me on the authority of Aḥmad b. Muḥammad b. al-Qāsim al-Barqī, on the authority of Abū Ṣāliḥ Sahl b. Ṣāliḥ - it was about the year 100 (A. H.) - who said I heard Abū al-Mu'ammar 'Abbād b.'Abd al-Ṣamad who said: I heard Anas b. Mālik say:]
The Apostle of Allāh, may Allāh bless Him and His Family, said: "The angels bless me and 'Alī for seventy years, because (for a time) only 'Alī and I raised the testimony to heaven that there is no God but Allāh and Muḥammad is the Apostle of Allāh."

[By the same chain of transmitters on the authority of Aḥmad b. (Muḥammad b.) al-Qāsim al-Barqī: Isḥāq told us: Nūḥ b. Qays told us: Sulaymān b. 'Alī al-Hāshimi Abū Fāṭima told us: I heard Mu'ādha al-'Adawiyya say:]
I heard 'Alī b. Abī Ṭālib say on the pulpit at Baṣra: "I am the greater testifier of truth (*ṣiddīq*) for I believed before Abū Bakr believed; I became a Muslim before he became a Muslim."

[Abū Naṣr Muḥammad b. al-Ḥusayn al-Muqrī al-Baṣrī al-Sayrawānī informed: Abū Bakr Muḥammad b. (Aḥmad b.) Abī Thalj told us: Abū Muḥammad al-Nawfalī told us on the authority of Muḥammad b.'Abd al-Ḥamīd, on the authority of 'Umar b.'Abd al-Ghiffār al-Faqīmī who said: Ibrāhīm b. Ḥayyān reported to me on the authority of Abū 'Abd Allāh, retainer of Banū Hāshim, on the authority of Abū Sukhayla, who said:]
I and 'Ammar went on the pilgrimage. We stopped at the house of Abū Dharr, may Allāh be pleased with him, and stayed with him for three days. When the time of our departure was at hand, I said to him: "Abū Dharr, we consider that nothing except confusion has come over the people. What is your view?"

"Cleave to the Book and 'Alī b. Abī Ṭālib," he replied, "then bear witness to the Apostle of Allāh, may Allāh bless Him and His Family, who said: "'Alī was the first to believe in me and will be the first to shake my hand in greetings on the Day of Resurrection. He is the greatest testifier of the truth (*ṣiddīq*) and discerner of truth and falsehood. He is the chief of the believers and money is the chief cause of wrong-doing.'"

Al-Shaykh al-Mufīd, may Allāh be pleased with him, comments: The reports with this meaning are numerous as testimonies (of it) are bulky.

[Among such are the words of Khuzayma b. Thābit al-Anṣārī, the man who gave two testimonies, in what was reported to me by Abū 'Abd Allāh Muḥammad b. 'Imrān al-Marzubānī on the authority of Muḥammad b. al-'Abbās who said:] Muḥammad b. Yazīd al-Nahwī recited to us on the authority of Ibn 'Ā'isha (the words) of Khuzayma b. Thābit al-Anṣārī, may Allāh be pleased with him:

> I never thought that this affair would leave the clan of Hāshim, and then within it (that) it would leave Abū Ḥasan (i.e. 'Ali).
>
> Was he not the first to pray with their (i.e. the Muslims') *qibla* (direction of prayer), and the most knowledgeable man in traditions and practice?
>
> (Was he not) the last of men with whom the Prophet made a covenant ('*ahd*), and the one whose helper was Gabriel in washing and shrouding (the body of the Prophet)?
>
> He it is in whom there is what others are not distinguished by. There is not among the people the good which is in him.
>
> What is it which makes you reject him, for we know him? Yet your pledge of allegiance is made through the greatest cheating.

Reports of his Outstanding Merit, Peace be on him, over Everybody in Religious Knowledge ('*Ilm*)

[Abū al-Ḥasan Muḥammad b. Ja'far al-Tamīmī al-Naḥwī informed me: Muḥammad b. al-Qāsim al-Muḥāribī al-Bazzāz told me: Hishām b. Yūnis al-Nahshalī told us: 'Ā'idh b. Ḥabīb told us on the authority of Abū al-Sabbāḥ al-Kinanī, on the authority of Muḥammad b. 'Abd al-Rahmān al-Sulamī, on the authority of his father, on the authority of 'Ikrima, on the authority of Ibn 'Abbās, who said:]
The Apostle of Allāh, may Allāh bless Him and His Family, said: "'Alī b. Abī Ṭālib is the most learned of my community and the most capable of giving legal decisions after me in (matters upon) which (men) differ."

[Abū Bakr Muḥammad b. 'Umar al-Ji'ābī informed me: Aḥmad b. 'Īsā Abū Ja'far al-'Ijlī told us: Ismā'īl b.'Abd Allāh b. Khālid told us: 'Ubayd Allāh b. 'Umar told us: 'Abd Allāh b. Muḥammad b.'Aqīl told us on the authority of Ḥamza b. Abī Sa'īd al-Khudrī, on the authority of his father (Abū Sa'īd al-Khudrī), who said:]
I heard the Apostle of Allāh, may Allāh bless Him and His Family, say: "I am the city of knowledge and 'Alī is its gate. Therefore whoever wants knowledge should learn it from 'Alī, peace be on him."

[Abū Bakr Muḥammad b. ʻUmar al-Jiʻābī informed me: Yūsuf b. al-Ḥakam al-Ḥannāt told us: Dāwud b. Rashīd told us: Salama b. Ṣāliḥ al-Aḥmar told us on the authority of ʻAbd al-Malik b. ʻAbd al Raḥmān, on the authority of al-Ashʻath b. Ṭalīq who said: I heard al-Ḥasan al-ʻAranī relating on the authority of Murra, on the authority of ʻAbd Allāh b. Masʻūd, who said:]
The Apostle of Allāh, may Allāh bless Him and His Family, summoned ʻAlī and went apart with him. When he returned to us, we asked him: "What covenant (*ʻAhd*) did he make with you?" He replied: "He taught me a thousand doors of knowledge and he opened from each (of these) doors a thousand (more) doors."

[Abū al-Ḥasan Muḥammad b. al-Muẓaffar al-Bazzāz informed me: Abū Mālik Kuthayyir b. Yaḥyā told us: Abū Jaʻfar Muḥammad b. Abī al-Sirrī told us: Aḥmad b. ʻAbd Allāh b. Yūnis told us on the authority of Saʻd al-Kinānī, on the authority of al-Aṣbagh b. Nubāta who said:]
When the pledge of allegiance was made to the Commander of the Faithful, peace be on him, for the caliphate, he went out to the mosque wearing the turban and cloak of the Apostle of Allāh, peace be on Him and His Family. He went up on the pulpit. After praising and glorifying Allāh, and giving admonition and warning, he sat down confidently, knitted his fingers together and placed them on his stomach. Then he said: "Question me before you lose me. Question me, for I have the knowledge of those who came earlier and those who will come later. If the cushion (on which a judge sits) was folded for me (to sit on), I could give judgements to the people of the Torah by their Torah, to the people of the Gospels by their Gospels, to the people of Psalms by their Psalms and to the people of the Furqān (i.e. Qur'ān) by their Furqān, so that each one of these books will be fulfilled and will declare, 'O Lord, indeed ʻAlī has given judgement according to Your decree.' By Allāh, I know the Qur'ān and its interpretation (better) than anyone who claims knowledge of it. If it were not for one verse in the Book of Allāh, most High, I would be able to inform you of what will be until the Day of Resurrection." Then he said: "Question me before you lose me, for by Him Who split the seed and brought the soul into being, if you questioned me about (it) verse by verse, I would tell you of the time of its revelation and why it was revealed, I would inform of the abrogating (verse) and the abrogated, of the specific and general, the clearly defined and the ambiguous, of the Meccan and the Medinan. By Allāh, there is not a party who can lead astray or guide until the Day of Resurrection, without me knowing its leader, the one who drives it forward and the one who urges it on."

Examples of such reports are (so many) that the book would become (unduly) long in (reporting) them.

Reports of his Outstanding Merit, the Blessing of Allāh be on him

[Abū al-Ḥasan Muḥammad b. al-Muẓaffar al-Bazzāz informed me: 'Umar b. 'Abd Allāh b. 'Imrān told us: Aḥmad b. Bashīr told us: 'Abd Allāh b. Mūsā told us on the authority of Qays b. Abī Hārūn who said: I went to Abū Sa'īd al-Khudrī and asked him whether he had witnessed (the battle of) Badr. He said:]
On that day (the Battle of Badr), I heard the Apostle of Allāh, may Allāh bless Him and His Family, speak to Fāṭima, peace be on her, when she came to him weeping and saying: "O Apostle of Allāh, the women of Quraysh are reviling me because of the poverty of 'Alī peace be on him."
"Aren't you satisfied that I have married you to the first Muslim and the most knowledgeable of them?" the Prophet, may Allāh bless Him and His Family, asked her. "Indeed, Allāh, the Most High, looked thoroughly over the people of the earth and chose your father from them and made him a Prophet. Then He looked over them a second time and chose your (present) husband (*ba'l*) and made him a trustee of authority (*waṣī*). Allāh inspired me to marry you to him. Didn't you know, Fāṭima, that through Allāh's kindness to you, your husband is the greatest of men in clemency, the most knowledgeable of men and the first of them in Islam."

Fāṭima laughed and rejoiced. Then the Prophet, may Allāh bless Him and His Family, continued: "Fāṭima, 'Alī has eight molar teeth. No one before and after him will have the like. He is my brother in the world and the hereafter. No one else of the people has that (rank). Fāṭima, the mistress of the women of heaven, is his wife. The grandsons of mercy, my grandsons, will be his sons. His brother, who will be adorned by two wings in heaven, will fly with the angels wherever he wishes. He has the knowledge of those who came before and those who will come after. He is the first who believed in me and he will be the last of the people to see me. He is my trustee of authority (*waṣī*) and the inheritor (*wārith*) of (all) the trustees of authority (*waṣiyyīn*)."

[Al-Shaykh al-Mufīd, may Allāh be pleased with him, said: I have found (the following report) in the book of Abū Ja'far Muḥammad b. al-'Abbās al-Rāzī who said: Muḥammad b. Khālid told us: Ibrāhīm b. 'Abd Allāh told us: Muḥammad b. Sulaymān al-Daylamī told us on the authority of Jābir b. Yazīd al-Ju'fī, on the authority of 'Adī b. Ḥakīm, on the authority of 'Abd Allāh b. al-'Abbās, who said:]
We, (the members) of the house (*Ahl al-bayt*) have seven qualities none of which the (rest of the) people have:

From us (came) the Prophet may Allāh bless Him and His Family;
From us came the trustee of authority (*waṣī*), the best of this community after him (i.e. Prophet), 'Alī b. Abī Ṭālib, peace be on him
From us came Ḥamza, the lion of Allāh and of His Apostle, and the lord of martyrs;
From us came Ja'far b. Abī Ṭālib who is adorned by two wings with which he flies in heaven wherever he wishes;
From us (came) the two grandsons of this community, the two lords of the youth of paradise, al-Ḥasan and al-Ḥusayn;
From us (came) the (one who will undertake the Imamate for the rest of time) *Qā'im* of the family of Muḥammad, by which Allāh graced His Prophet;
From us (came) the one who was given (final) victory (*al-manṣūr*).

[Muḥammad b. Ayman related on the authority of Abū Ḥāzim, retainer of Ibn 'Abbās, who said:]
The Apostle of Allāh, may Allāh bless Him and His Family, spoke to 'Alī b. Abī Ṭālib, peace be on him:
"'Ali, you will be engaged in disputes but you will overcome any dispute by seven qualities, the like of which no one else has: you are the first of those who believed with me, the greatest of them in war, the most knowledgeable of them in the battles (*ayyām*) on behalf of Allāh, the one of them who is most loyal in keeping the covenant (*'Ahd*) of Allāh, the most compassionate of them towards subjects, the most capable of giving equal treatment and the greatest of them in distinction before Allāh."

Reports like this and in the same sense as this, which are better known by both the general populace and the Shī'a (*khāṣṣa*) are (so clear) that there is no need to lengthen (matters) with an explanation. Yet if there was only the tradition whose story is well known, whose narration has been spread abroad, of the bird and the words of the Prophet, may Allāh bless Him and His Family: "O Allāh, bring the creature most lovable to you to eat (some) of this bird with me," and then the Commander of the Faithful, peace be on him, came, it would be sufficient (to show that) he was the most lovable creature to Allāh, the greatest in reward from Him, the nearest to Him, and the most outstanding in his action. (Similar) is the case of the words of Jābir b. 'Abd Allāh al-Anṣārī when he was asked about the Commander of the Faithful, peace be on him, and he said, "He is the best of men. Only an unbeliever could doubt clear proof." Jābir had supported that in a narrative which has come through an uninterrupted chain of transmitters, and is well known to the traditionists (*ahl al-naql*). The evidences for the fact that the Commander of the Faithful, peace be on him, is the most outstanding person after the Apostle of Allāh, may Allāh bless Him and His Family, are mutually verifiable. If our purpose was to establish it (by reporting and analysing all the reports) we would have to set aside a book for it. The reports of what we have outlined are sufficient in so far as our intention is to give a summary, and put that in its (appropriate) place in this book.

Reports of Love for him, Peace be on him, Being a Sign of Faith (in a Person) and Hatred of him Being a Sign of Hypocrisy (in a Person)

[Abū Bakr Muḥammad b. 'Umar - known as Ibn al-Ji'ābī al-Ḥāfiẓ - told us: Muḥammad b. Sahl b. al-Ḥasan told us: Aḥmad b. 'Umar al-Dihqān told us: Muḥammad b. Kathīr told us: Ismā'īl b. Muslim told us: al-A'mash told us on the authority of 'Adī b. Thābit, on the authority of Zirr b. Ḥubaysh, who said:]
I saw the Commander of the Faithful, 'Alī b. Abī Ṭālib, on the pulpit and I heard him say: "By Him Who split the seed and brought the soul into being, the Prophet made a promise (*'ahd*) to me: 'Only believers will love you and only hypocrites will hate you!'"

[Abū 'Abd Allāh Muḥammad b. 'Imrān al-Marzubānī informed me: 'Abd Allāh b. Muḥammad b. 'Abd al-'Azīz al-Baghawī told us: 'Ubayd Allāh b. 'Umar al-Qawārīrī told us: Ja'far b. Sulaymān told us: al-Naḍr b. Hamīd told us on the authority of Abū al-Jārūd, on the authority of al-Ḥārith al-Hamdānī who said:]
I saw 'Alī, peace be on him. One day he came and went up on the pulpit. He praised and glorified Allāh. Then he said: "A decree which Allāh, the Most High, decreed by the tongue of the Prophet, may Allāh bless Him and His Family, was that only believers will love me and only hypocrites will hate me. Whoever forges a lie is lost."

[Abū al-Ḥasan Muḥammad b. al-Muẓaffar al-Bazzāz informed me: Muḥammad b. Yaḥyā told us: Muḥammad b. Mūsā al-Barbarī told us: Khalaf b. Sālim told us: Wakī' told us: al-A'mash told us on the authority of 'Adī b. Thābit, on the authority of Zirr b. Ḥubaysh, on the authority of the Commander of the Faithful, peace be on him, who said:]
The Prophet, may Allāh bless Him and His Family, made a promise (*'ahd*) to me: "Only believers will love you and only hypocrites will hate you."

Reports of him, Peace be on him, and his Shī'a Being the Successful Ones

[Abū 'Abd Allāh Muḥammad b. 'Imrān al-Marzubānī informed me: 'Alī b. Muḥammad b. 'Abd Allāh al-Ḥāfiẓ told me: 'Alī b. al-Ḥusayn b. 'Ubayd al-Kūfī

told us: Ismā'īl b. Abān told us on the authority of Sa'd b. Ṭālib, on the authority of Jābir b. Yazīd, on the authority of Muḥammad b. 'Alī al-Bāqir, peace be on them both, who said:]
Umm Salama, the wife of the Prophet, may Allāh bless Him and His Family, was asked about 'Alī b. Abī Ṭālib, peace be on him, she said: "I heard the Apostle of Allāh say: "'Alī and his Shī'a are the successful ones'"

[Abū 'Abd Allāh Muḥammad b. 'Imrān informed me: Aḥmad b. Muḥammad al-Jawharī told me: Muḥammad b. Hārūn b. 'Īsā al-Hāshimī told me: Tamīm b. Muḥammad b. al-'Alā told us: 'Abd al-Razzāq told us: Yaḥyā b. al-'Alā told us on the authority of Sa'd b. Tarīf, on the authority of al-Aṣbagh b. Nubāta, on the authority of 'Alī, peace be on him, who said:]
The Apostle of Allāh, may Allāh bless Him and His Family said: "Allāh, the Most High, has a cane of ruby which none will obtain except us and our Shī'a. The rest of the people are excluded from it."

[Abū 'Abd Allāh informed me: 'Alī b. Muḥammad b. 'Abd Allāh al-Ḥāfiz told me: 'Alī b. al-Ḥusayn b. 'Ubayd al-Kūfī told us: Ismā'īl b. Abān told us on the authority of 'Amr b. Ḥurayth, on the authority of Dāwūd b. al-Salīl, on the authority of Anas b. Mālik, who said:]
The Apostle of Allāh, may Allāh bless Him and His Family said: "Seventy thousand of my community will enter Heaven without any reckoning and punishment against them." Then he turned to 'Alī, peace be on him and said: "They are your Shī'a and you are their Imam."

[Abū 'Abd Allāh informed me: Aḥmad b. 'Īsā al- Karkhī told me Abū al-'Aynā Muḥammad b. al-Qāsim told us: Muḥammad b. 'Ā'isha told us on the authority of Ismā'īl b. 'Amr al-Bajalī, who told us: 'Umar b. Mūsā told me on the authority of Zayd b. 'Alī b. al-Ḥusayn, on the authority of his father, on the authority of his (Zayd's) grandfather, on the authority of 'Alī, peace be on them, who said:]
I complained to the Apostle of Allāh, may Allāh bless Him and His Family, about the people's envy of me. He said: "'Alī, the first four to enter heaven are myself, you, al-Ḥasan and al-Ḥusayn. Our progeny (will come) behind us and our loved ones will be behind our progeny. To our right and left will be our Shī'a."

Reports of Friendship to him, Peace be on him, Being a Sign of Good Birth and Enmity to him, Being a Sign of Disgraceful Birth

[Abū al-Jaysh al-Muẓaffar b. Muḥammad al-Balkhī informed me: Abū Bakr Muḥammad b. Aḥmad b. Abī al-Thalj told us: Ja'far b. Muḥammad al-'Alawī

told us: Aḥmad b. ‘Abd al-Mun‘im told us: ‘Abd Allāh b. Muḥammad al-Fazārī told us on the authority of Ja‘far b. Muḥammad, on the authority of his father, peace be on them, on the authority of Jābir, b. ‘Abd Allāh al-Anṣārī, who said:]
I heard the Apostle of Allāh, may Allāh bless Him and His Family, say to ‘Alī b. Abī Ṭālib, peace be on him: “Shall I not make you happy, give you a gift, tell you good news?”
“Please do, Apostle of Allāh,” he replied.

“Both I, myself, and you have been created from one (piece of) clay. Part of it was left over and from that Allāh created our Shī‘a. On the Day of Resurrection (all) the people will be summoned by the names of their mothers except our Shī‘a. They will be summoned by the names of their fathers because of their good birth.”

[Abū al-Jaysh al-Muẓaffar b. Muḥammad informed me on the authority of Muḥammad b. Aḥmad b. Abī al-Thalj who said: Muḥammad b. Muslim al-Kūfī told us: ‘Ubayd Allāh b. Kathīr told us: Ja‘far b. Muḥammad b. al-Ḥusayn al-Zuhrī told us: ‘Ubayd Allāh b. Mūsā told us on the authority of Isrā’īl, on the authority of Abū Ḥusayn, on the authority of ‘Ikrima, on the authority of Ibn ‘Abbās:]
The Apostle of Allāh, may Allāh bless Him and His Family, said: “On the Day of Resurrection all the people will be summoned by the names of their mothers except our Shī‘a. They will be summoned by the names of their fathers because of their good birth.”

[Abū al-Qāsim Ja‘far b. Muḥammad al-Qummī told us: Abū ‘Alī Muḥammad b. Hammām b. Suhayl al-Iskāfī told us: Ja‘far b. Muḥammad b. Mālik told me: Muḥammad b. Ni‘ma al-Salūlī told us: ‘Abd Allāh b. al-Qāsim, told us on the authority of ‘Abd Allāh b. Jabala, on the authority of his father, who said: I heard Jābir b. ‘Abd Allāh b. Ḥizān al-Anṣārī say:]
One day a group of us Anṣār were with the Apostle of Allāh, may Allāh bless Him and His Family. He said to us: “O people of the Anṣār, instill in your children a love for ‘Alī b. Abī Ṭālib, peace be on him. Whoever loves him should know that he is rightly guided and whoever hates him should know that he is in error.”

Reports of the Apostle of Allāh, may Allāh bless Him and His Family Naming him, Peace be on him, Commander of the Faithful during (the Prophet’s) Lifetime.

[Abū al-Jaysh al-Muẓaffar b. Muḥammad al-Balkhī informed me: Abū Bakr

Muḥammad b. Aḥmad b. Abī al-Thalj informed me: al-Ḥusayn b. Ayyūb informed me on the authority of Muḥammad b. Ghālib, on the authority of 'Alī b. al-Ḥusayn, on the authority of al-Ḥasan b. Maḥbūb, on the authority of Abū Ḥamza al-Thumālī, on the authority of Abū Isḥāq al-Sabī'ī, on the authority of Bashīr al-Ghiffārī, on the authority of Anas b. Mālik, who said:]
I was a servant of the Apostle of Allāh, may Allāh bless Him and His Family. One night Umm Ḥabība, daughter of Abū Sufyān, brought water for ablutions to the Apostle of Allāh, may Allāh bless Him and His Family. He said to me: "Anas, at this moment there will come to you through this door the Commander of the Faithful, the best of testamentary trustees of authority (*waṣiyyīn*), the foremost of the people in Islam, and the most knowledgeable and most mindful of them."
"O Allāh, make him one of my tribe," I said.

However, almost immediately 'Alī b. Abī Ṭālib, peace be on him, came through the door. The Apostle of Allāh, may Allāh bless Him and His Family, performed his ablutions. Then the Apostle of Allāh threw the water into, the face of the Commander of the Faithful, peace be on them both, so that both his eyes were filled with water.

"Apostle of Allāh, has any impurity occurred in me?" asked 'Alī.
"Only good has been occasioned in you," replied the Prophet, may Allāh bless Him and His Family. "You belong to me and I belong to you. You will act on my behalf, fulfill my duties, wash my (corpse) and bury me in my grave. You will listen to the people's (questions) about me and you will explain to them after me."

"Apostle of Allāh," 'Alī said, "haven't you told them?"
"Yes, but you will explain the things they differ on after me."

[Abū al-Jaysh al-Muẓaffar b. Muḥammad informed me on the authority of Muḥammad b. Aḥmad b. Abī al-Thalj who said: My grandfather told me: 'Abd Allāh b. Dāhir told us: My father, Dāhir b. Yaḥyā al-Aḥmarī al-Muqrī told me on the authority of al-A'mash, on the authority of 'Abāya al-Asadī, on the authority of Ibn 'Abbās:]
The Prophet, may Allāh bless Him and His Family, said to Umm Salama, may Allāh be pleased with her: "Listen and bear witness that this 'Alī is the Commander of the Faithful and the master of the testamentary trustees."

[With the same *isnād* on the authority of Muḥammad (b. Aḥmad) b. Abī al-Thalj who said: my grandfather told me: 'Abd al-Salām b. Ṣāliḥ told us: Yaḥyā b. al-Yamān told us: Sufyān al-Thawrī told us on the authority of Abū al-Jaḥḥāf, on

the authority of Mu'āwiya b. Tha'laba who said:]
Abu Dharr, may Allāh be pleased with him, was told: "Make a will."
"I have made my will," he answered.
"To whom?" he was asked.
"To the Commander of the Faithful," he replied.
"To 'Uthmān?"
"No," he said. "To the Commander of the Faithful, 'Alī b. Abī Ṭālib, peace be on him. Indeed he is the pivot of the earth and the master of this community. If you lost him, you would not know the earth and those who were on it."

The report of Burayda b. Ḥuṣayb al-Aslamī is famous and well known among the religious scholars with (so many) *isnāds* that their full elucidation would be very long. He reported:
The Apostle of Allāh, may Allāh bless Him and His Family, ordered me while I was the seventh of a group of seven which included Abū Bakr, 'Umar, Ṭalḥa and al-Zubayr: "Greet 'Alī with the title of Commander of the Faithful."
We greeted him with that title while the Apostle of Allāh, may Allāh bless Him and His Family, lived among us.

There are many reports like these which would make the book too long (to report them all). Allāh is the bringer of truth.

HIS QUALITIES

As for his many qualities, the fact that they are so famous, so well authenticated and reported by tradition and by the consensus of the religious scholars (means) that they do not need their chains of authority to be put forward; for since they are (also) so numerous their full explanation would make the book too long. In our outline, an extract from them will do instead of reporting them all, in accordance with the purpose which we set down for this book, Allāh willing.

1. The Meeting of the Banu 'Abd al-Muṭṭalib

Among these is the account that the Prophet, may Allāh bless Him and His Family, gathered his own family and tribal kin together at the beginning of his mission for Islam. He showed them the faith and sought their help against the people of unbelief and enmity, and guaranteed for them, if they did that, favour and honour in this world and a reward in heaven. None of them answered him except the Commander of the Faithful, 'Alī b. Abī Ṭālib, peace be on him. Because of that he granted him the achievement of brotherhood (with himself), the office of helping him, of being his nominated trustee, his inheritor and his successor, and announced that his going to heaven was inevitable.

This is reported in the account of the (meeting in the) house, whose authenticity the reporters of tradition are agreed upon:
When the Apostle of Allāh, may Allāh bless Him and His Family, gathered members of the clan of ‘Abd al-Muṭṭalib in the house of Abū Ṭālib, they were more or less forty men on that day as the reporters mention. He ordered food to be set for them, a leg of a ewe with a measure of wheat. He measured a *ṣā‘a* of milk. Each man of them was known to be able to eat a lamb in one sitting and to drink a *farq*[3] of drink in the same sitting. He, peace be on Him and His Family, intended by preparing little food and drink for their gathering, to reveal a clear sign to them through satisfying them and quenching their thirst with what would not normally satisfy and quench the thirst of one of them. He ordered the food and drink to be offered to them. From that little amount the whole group ate (and drank) until they were full and what they had eaten and drunk was not clear. He dazzled them by that and showed them the clear sign of his prophetic mission and the evidence for his truthfulness, through the proof of Allāh, the Exalted, with regard to it. After they had eaten and drunk their fill, he said to them: “Banū ‘Abd al-Muṭṭalib, Allāh has sent me to all creation and He has especially sent me to you. He has said: *Warn your clan (who are your) kin* (XXVI 214). I call you to make two statements light to the tongue but heavy in the scales (of Allāh). By them you will be master of Arab and foreigner, by them nations shall submit to you, by them you will enter heaven and by them you will escape from hell. They are the (two fold) testimony that there is no God but Allāh and that I am the Apostle of Allāh. Whoever answers me in this matter, helps me in it and in carrying it out, will be my brother, my trustee, my helper, my inheritor and my successor after me.”

None of them answered.

The Commander of the Faithful reported: I stood up before him amid them. At that time I was the youngest of them, still with very thin legs and with dirt still in the corners of my eyes. I said: “Apostle of Allāh, I will help you.”
“Sit down,” he told me. Then he repeated his words to the people again. They were silent and I arose and said the same as I had said the first time. Again he told me to sit down and he repeated his words to the people a third time. None of them spoke a word. I arose and said:
“I will help you, Apostle of Allāh, in this matter.”
“Sit down,” he said and then he went on, “You are my brother, my trustee, my helper, my inheritor, and my successor after me.”

3 A *ṣā‘a* and *farq* are measures of cubic capacity.

The people got up and they were saying to Abū Ṭālib: "Abū Ṭālib, you should be congratulated today that you have entered the religion of your nephew and he has made your son a commander over you."

This outstanding quality is exclusive to the Commander of the Faithful, peace be on him. None of the first emigrants or the Anṣār share in it, nor does anyone else of the people of Islam. No one else has the equal of it in merit, nor even an approximate in (the) circumstance (of it). What is shown by the report of it is that through him, peace be on him, the Prophet, may Allāh bless Him and His Family, was able to communicate his message, to make public his mission and declare the truth of Islam. If it had not been for him, the religion would not have been established, the law of Islam (*sharī'a*) would not have been set down and the mission would not have been made public. He, peace be on him, is the support of Islam, the helper of the one who undertook its mission on behalf of Allāh, the Mighty and High. Through his guaranteeing support to the Prophet of guidance, peace be on Him and His Family, he brought about for (the Prophet) what he wanted with regard to the prophetic mission. In that there is such merit that not even the weight of mountains could outweigh it, nor do all other virtues go beyond it in position and rank.

2. The Circumstances of the Prophet's Emigration from Mecca

Another example of his qualities occurs when the Prophet, may Allāh bless Him and His Family, ordered the emigration after the council of Quraysh had decided to kill him and he, peace be on him, would not have been able to defeat their plans by leaving Mecca. For He, peace be on him, wanted to keep his departure secret and keep the reports about him hidden from them so that he could carry out his departure in safety from them. He told his news to the Commander of the Faithful and made him keep it secret. He gave him the responsibility of protecting him by spending the night on his (i.e. the Prophet's) bed so that they would not know that it was 'Alī who was sleeping on the bed and they would think that the Prophet, may Allāh bless Him and His Family, was sleeping there as he had normally done on previous nights.[4] The Commander of the Faithful, peace be on him dedicated his life to Allāh, the Exalted, devoted it to Allāh, the Exalted, in obedience and exchanged it for His Prophet, the blessings and peace of Allāh be on Him and His Family, in order that he might save him from the plots of his enemies and thus make sure of his safety and survival and also arrange properly his purpose in summoning (the people) to the faith, establishing the religion and making public Allāh's law (*sharī'a*). He, peace be on him, spent the night on the bed of the Apostle of Allāh, may Allāh bless

4 cf. al-Ṭabarī, I, 1232-3, citing Ibn Isḥāq; Ibn Hishām, *Sīra* (Gottingen, 1858-60), 325-6.

Him and His Family, hidden by his waist-cover (*izār*). The people who had plotted to kill the Prophet, may Allāh bless Him and His Family, came to him and surrounded him. They were carrying weapons. They waited until the dawn rose so that they could kill him openly and thus his blood would be shed in such a way that Banū Hāshim would see that his murderers were from all the clans (of Quraysh). Then it would not be possible for them to take vengeance (on them) for him because everyone had shared in taking his blood and every tribe would be spared from fighting his group and being separate from his family.

That (i.e. 'Alī's action) was the reason for the Prophet, may Allāh bless Him and His Family, being saved, his blood being kept safe and his survival until he died at (the time of) his Lord's command. If it had not been for the Commander of the Faithful, peace be on him, and his action, it would not have been possible for the Apostle of Allāh, may Allāh bless Him and His Family, to propagate and carry out (his mission), nor would he have remained alive and continued to survive. Thus through him he overcame the envy (of the people) and his enemies. In the morning when the people were intending to rush upon him, he, peace be on him, rushed towards them. They scattered from him when they recognized him and departed. Their plot against the Prophet, peace be on Him and His Family, had gone wrong. The preparations they had made to kill him had been destroyed. Their plans had been betrayed and their hopes brought to nought. In this way was the faith properly set up, Satan humiliated and the people of unbelief and enmity betrayed. None of the people of Islam share this achievement with the Commander of the Faithful, peace be on him, nor is any equal to it in any circumstance known, nor is there anything approaching it in merit according to any correct consideration. Concerning the Commander of the Faithful, peace be on him, and the night he spent on the (Prophet's) bed, Allāh, glory be to Him, revealed: *Whoever among the people sells his life out of a desire to please Allāh, Allāh is kind to (such) servants* (II 207).

3. The Commander of the Faithful fulfils the Prophet's Obligations in Mecca

(Another example) of that is that the Prophet, may Allāh bless Him and His Family, was the one trusted by the Quraysh with the things which they wished to deposit. When the situation occurred which required his sudden flight from Mecca, he could not find anyone among his people and his family to entrust (the things) which he had been entrusted with except the Commander of the Faithful, peace be on him. He appointed him (i.e. the Commander of the Faithful) as his deputy to return the things deposited with him to their owners and to pay the debts which he owed.[5] Then he gathered his daughters, the womenfolk of his family and his wives and their emigration was entrusted to him for he did not consider that anyone could take his (i.e. the Commander of the Faithful's) place among all the people. Thus he set his trust on his faithfulness, depended upon his courage and bravery, and in the defence of his family and his close associates he relied upon his fearlessness and his ability. He rested upon his reliability to look after his family and his womenfolk. He recognized in his piety and protection from error that by which the soul could feel sure of his reliability in those matters.

'Alī, peace be on him, carried out (these tasks) very well: he returned every deposit to its owner; he paid every debt to the person to whom it was owed; he looked after the daughters and womenfolk of the Prophet, may Allāh bless Him and His Family; and he emigrated with them, he himself going on foot to protect them from the enemies and guard them against adversaries; he took them gently on the journey until he brought them to him at Medina, (having provided them) with complete protection and guarding, good companionship and excellent organization. The Prophet gave him accommodation in his house when he arrived in Medina[6] and allowed him to stay with him and mix with his womenfolk and children. He did not exclude him from anything which was special to himself, nor did he withhold from him the inner meaning and the secrets of his affair. This is a quality which is uniquely held by (the Commander of the Faithful) peace be on him, from among all his house and Companions. None of his followers or supporters shared in it and there occurred in no other creature any merit like it, which equalled it in appearance and came near to it in its testing quality. It was in addition to his outstanding achievements which we have mentioned and their overwhelming merit and their nobility in the hearts of those who think.

4. The Commander of the Faithful puts right Crimes committed by Khālid b. al-Walīd[7]

(Another example) of that is that Allāh, the Exalted specified him for the task of putting right what had been done wrong by those who opposed the orders of His Prophet, may Allāh bless Him and His Family, and of reforming what had been corrupted so that through him the causes of righteousness were established. It (i.e. righteousness) was brought about by his hand, by the happiness of his

5 cf. al-Ṭabarī, I, 1244, citing Ibn Isḥāq; Ibn Hishām, *Sīra*, 334-5.

6 cf.*ibid.*

7 The full accounts of Khālid's mission and 'Alī's rectification of it are in al-Ṭabarī, I, 1649, citing Ibn Isḥāq; Ibn Hishām, *Sīra*. 833-40, al-Wāqidī, *al-Maghīzī*, (Oxford, 1966), II, 875-84.

endeavour, his good organization, and the necessary success (he brought) to the affairs of the Muslims. Through him, the pillars of religion were held firm.

The Prophet, may Allāh bless Him and His Family, sent Khālid b. Walīd to the Banū Jadhīma to summon them to Islam and he did not send him to make war (on them). He disobeyed his order, renounced his treaty, rebelled against his religion and killed people who had embraced Islam. He betrayed their protected status when they were people who had accepted the faith. In that he had been acting according to the wild ways of the Jāhiliyya and the methods of people of unbelief and enmity.

The result of his evil action (would have affected) Islam and through it those whom its Prophet, peace be on Him and His Family, had called to the faith, would have broken away and it is likely that the system of organization in religion would have been brought to nothing as a result of his action. Therefore the Apostle of Allāh, may Allāh bless Him and His Family, sought to repair the wrong that had been done and to reform what had been corrupted. He gave the blood-wit according to the law from Allāh for that to the Commander of the Faithful, peace be on him, and sent him to conciliate the people, to draw out their hatred and to show gentleness to them in making firm their faith. He told him to pay the blood-wit for the dead and in that way satisfy the next of kin responsible for keeping their blood alive (by vengeance).

The Commander of the Faithful, peace be on him, achieved complete satisfaction in that, for he gave more than was necessary by making a personal contribution to them from money which he had. He said to them: "I have paid the blood-wit for your dead and in addition to that I have given you money which you can hand down to your successors so that Allāh may be pleased with His Apostle and you may be pleased with his kindness to you." The Apostle of Allāh, may Allāh bless Him and His Family, made a public renunciation in Medina of Khālid's action against them, which he, then, had communicated to them. By the Apostle of Allāh's, may Allāh bless Him and His Family, renunciation of Khālid's crime, and by the conciliation of the Commander of the Faithful, peace be on him, the people agreed (to be reconciled) despite what had been done to them. In that way righteousness was achieved and those who carried out corrupt acts were foiled. No one was entrusted with that task except the Commander of the Faithful, peace be on him, nor did anyone else from the community (*jamā'a*) except him undertake such actions, nor was the Apostle of Allāh, may Allāh bless Him and His Family, satisfied to entrust anyone else with such a task. This is an achievement which is greater in merit than any claimed by men other than the Commander of the Faithful, peace be on him. No one else among them shared in it, nor was an action equal to it carried out by anyone else.

5. Keeping the Conquest of Mecca Secret[8]

Another example of that is that when the Prophet, may Allāh bless Him and His Family, wanted to conquer Mecca, he asked Allāh, may His name be exalted, to keep the reports of it hidden from Quraysh so that he could enter it unexpectedly. He, peace be on him, had based the plan for his going there on the secrecy of that. However, Ḥāṭib b. Abī Balta'a wrote to the Meccans to inform them of the decision of the Apostle of Allāh, may Allāh bless Him and His Family, to conquer it. He gave the letter to a black woman who had come to Medina to seek intercession there for the people and to ask for them to be forgiven. He instructed her to take it to some Meccans whose names he gave her and he ordered her not to take the (main) road. Revelation about that came down on the Apostle of Allāh, may Allāh bless Him and His Family. He summoned the Commander of the Faithful, peace be on him, and told him: "One of my companions has written to the Meccans to inform them about us. I had asked Allāh, the Mighty and High, to keep the reports about us hidden from them. The letter is with a black woman who has not taken the (main) road. Take your sword, follow her and take the letter from her. Let her go and bring it to me."

Then he summoned al-Zubayr b. al-'Awwām and told him: "Go with 'Alī b. Abī Ṭālib on this mission."

The two departed and did not take the (main) road. They caught up with the woman. Al-Zubayr got to her first and he asked her about the letter which was with her. She denied it and swore that she had nothing with her and wept.

"I can't see a letter with her, Abū al-Ḥasan," said al-Zubayr. "Let us go to the Apostle of Allāh, may Allāh bless Him and His Family, and tell him that her journey is innocent."
"The Apostle of Allāh, may Allāh bless Him and His Family, told me that she had a letter," replied the Commander of the Faithful, peace be on him, "and he ordered me to take it from her. You say that she has no letter."

Then he drew his sword and advanced towards her and said to her: "By Allāh, if you don't produce the letter, I will compel you to show it. Then I'll cut off your head."
"Since there is no escape from doing that," she answered, "turn your face away

8 cf. al-Ṭabarī, 1626-7, citing Ibn Isḥāq; Ibn Hishām, *Sīra*. 810-11, al-Wāqidī, *al-Maghīzī*, II, 797-9. In the first two accounts it is 'Alī who makes the women give up the letter. In al-Wāqidī's account both men are equally responsible for making her give it up.

from me, Ibn Abī Ṭālib."

He, peace be on him, turned his face away from her. She took off her veil and took the letter from her hair. The Commander of the Faithful, peace be on him, caught hold of it and took it to the Prophet, may Allāh bless Him and His Family. He ordered that the call should be given: "The prayer is general" (*al-ṣalāt jāmi'a*) (i.e. everybody should attend). The call was made among the people and they gathered at the mosque until it was crowded with them. Then the Prophet, may Allāh bless Him and His Family, went up on the pulpit and he took the letter in his hand. He said: "People, I had asked Allāh, the Mighty and High, to keep reports about us hidden from Quraysh. However, one of you wrote to the Meccans to inform them about us. Let the writer of the letter stand up. If he does not, then revelation will make him known."

No one stood up. The Prophet repeated his words a second time. He said: "Let the writer of the letter stand up. If he does not, then revelation will make him known:"

(At this) Ḥāṭib b. Abī Balta'a stood up. He was shaking like a palm-bough on the day of a violent storm. He said: "Apostle of Allāh, I am the writer of the letter. I have committed no (other) act of hypocrisy after becoming a Muslim, nor have I had any (other) doubt after my firm conviction (in Islam)."
"What made you write this letter?" the Prophet, may Allāh bless Him and His Family, asked him.
"Apostle of Allāh, I have a family in Mecca," he said, "and I have no other tribal connections (*'ashīra*) there. I was afraid that they would be overcome on account of us. So this letter of mine was (an attempt) to offer a helping hand to my family, (to give) support to them. I did not do it because of any doubt on my part in the religion."

"Apostle of Allāh," said 'Umar b. al-Khaṭṭāb, "command me to kill him. He has committed an act of hypocrisy."
"He is one of the men (who fought) at Badr," said the Apostle of Allāh, may Allāh bless Him and His Family. "Perhaps Allāh will look down on them and forgive them. Take him out of the mosque."

[He reported:]
Then people began to push him in the back until they had taken him out, while he had been turning towards the Prophet, may Allāh bless Him and His Family, begging him for mercy. The Apostle of Allāh ordered him to be brought back and he said to him: "I have forgiven you and your crime, so seek the forgiveness of

your Lord and never do such a crime as you committed again."

The achievement belongs with his other achievements, peace be on him, which have been mentioned earlier. As a result of it, it was possible for the Apostle of Allāh, may Allāh bless Him and His Family, to organise the entry into Mecca, to protect against trouble from the people and to avoid their knowledge of his intention towards them until he had come upon them unawares. In the matter of extracting the letter from the woman, he could only trust the Commander of the Faithful, peace be on him. In that he did not regard anyone else as a faithful adviser except him, nor did he rely on anyone else. Through him, peace be on him, the task was carried out and his purpose attained; his organization was properly established as was the advantage of the Muslims in the matter, and the religion was able to be spread. No merit can be attributed to al-Zubayr in terms of him being sent with the Commander of the Faithful, peace be on him, because he did not fulfil his task and he was useless in carrying it out. The Apostle of Allāh, may Allāh bless Him and His Family, only sent him because he was included in the number of Banū Hāshim through his mother, Ṣafiyya, daughter of 'Abd al-Muṭṭalib, and he wanted to entrust the task, in the execution of which there was need for secrecy, to those specially belonging to his family. Al-Zubayr had courage and boldness in addition to the relationship which there was between him and the Commander of the Faithful, peace be on him. He (the Prophet) knew that he (al-Zubayr) would help him (the Commander of the Faithful) in his mission since they both had (an interest) in the fulfilment of the task and since it referred to them both it so far as what was general to Banū Hāshim was specific to them both. Al-Zubayr was a follower of the Commander of the Faithful, peace be on him. There occurred from him during his mission (actions) which did not conform to correct reasoning and the Commander of the Faithful, peace be on him, prevented him (from following these actions).

In what we have explained in this story, there is clear evidence for the special achievement and virtue of the Commander of the Faithful, peace be on him, which is shared by no one else. No one else approached him with any merit without him having more than it. Allāh be He Who is praised.

6. The Carrying of the Standard at the Conquest of Mecca.[9]

(Yet another example) is the fact that the Prophet, may Allāh bless Him and His Family, gave the standard to Sa'd b. 'Ubada on the day of the conquest of Mecca and ordered him to carry it in front of him into Mecca. Sa'd took it and began

9 This account is based on al-Ṭabarī, I, 1632, citing Ibn Isḥāq, Ibn Hishām, *Sīra*, 816; for a fuller version cf. al-Wāqidī, al-Maghāzī, II, 821-2.

to declare: "Today is the day of slaughter, the day of capturing (any) daughter."

"Haven't you heard what Sa'd b. 'Ubada is saying?" some of the people asked the Prophet, may Allāh bless Him and His Family. "We are afraid that today will (simply mean) to him, attacking Quraysh."

"'Alī, go to Sa'd," he, peace be on him, told the Commander of the Faithful, peace be on him, "and take the standard from him. You be the one to enter with it."

Thus the Apostle of Allāh, may Allāh bless Him and His Family, set right through the Commander of the Faithful, peace be on him, what was about to go astray in the organization through Sa'd rushing forward and attacking the Meccans. He knew that the Anṣār would not be pleased if any (other) person had taken the standard from their leader Sa'd and taken that position from him except one who was similar in circumstance to the Prophet, may Allāh bless Him and His Family, through the exaltedness of his rank, his high position, and the duty of obeying him, and someone who would not make Sa'd delay in giving up that command to him. If there had been with the Prophet, may Allāh bless Him and His Family, someone suitable for that other than the Commander of the Faithful, peace be on him, he would have set the affair right through him, or he would have mentioned there his suitability for what the Commander of the Faithful, peace be on him, undertook. Since decisions are only required by virtue of the actions which actually happened and what the Prophet, may Allāh bless Him and His Family, did to the Commander of the Faithful was to magnify and exalt him, to consider him worthy of what he did consider him worthy in terms of putting right affairs and attaining what would not have been possible through the action of any one else as we have mentioned, it is necessary to judge him in this achievement as someone set apart from others who were not equal to him, and (someone) preferred through the honour of it over all others.

7. The Conversion of Yemen[10]

(Another example) of that which is agreed upon by all the historians (biographers *ahl al-sīra*) is that the Prophet, may Allāh bless Him and His Family, sent, Khālid b. Walīd to the people of Yemen to call them to Islam. With him, he sent a group of Muslims, among whom was al-Barā' b. 'Āzib, may Allāh have mercy on him. Khālid stayed with the people for six months calling them (to Islam) but no one of them responded. That depressed the Apostle of Allāh, may Allāh bless Him and His Family. He summoned the Commander of the

10 This report is the same as reported by al-Ṭabarī, 1, 1731-2.

Faithful, peace be on him, and ordered him to send back Khālid and those who were with him. However, he told him that if anyone of those who had been with Khālid wanted to stay, he should let him.

[al-Barā' reported:]
I was one of those who followed him. When we came to the first people among the Yemenīs and the news reached the people (generally), they gathered before him. 'Alī b. Abī Ṭālib, peace be on him, prayed the dawn prayer with us, then he advanced in front of us. He praised and glorified Allāh. Then he read the letter of the Apostle of Allāh. The whole of Hamdān became Muslim in one day. The Commander of the Faithful, peace be on him, wrote about that to the Apostle of Allāh, may Allāh bless Him and His Family. When he read his letter, he was pleased and delighted. He prostrated in thanks to Allāh, the Exalted. He raised his head and sat. He said: "Greetings to Hamdān. After the submission to Islam of Hamdān, (the rest of) the people of Yemen will follow (them) into Islam."

This is another achievement of the Commander of the Faithful, peace be on him, which no other of the Companions had done anything like or similar to. For (the Prophet), when he wanted to stop Khālid from carrying on with the mission on which he had sent him and he was afraid that corruption would be caused by him, could not find anyone to succeed him except the Commander of the Faithful, peace be on him. So he asked him (i.e. 'Alī) and the latter undertook it in the best possible manner. And as was Allāh's custom with him, he performed it with success since it conformed to the preference of the Prophet, may Allāh bless him and grant him peace. He was a man of righteousness, gentleness, good administrative ability and sincere intentions in obedience to Allāh, the Mighty and High, (a man) with the ability to guide those of the people who would be guided, and to respond to those of them who responded to (the call of) Islam. He was (an important element) in the building of the religion, the strength of the faith in (explaining) the message of the Prophet, may Allāh bless Him and His Family, according to the meaning he (the Prophet) had traced for him. (Indeed he was capable) of organising matters in a way which delighted him (i.e. the Prophet). The promise of heaven was revealed about him (as was) his delight in his perfection among all the people of Islam. It has been confirmed that obedience is of great importance by virtue of the great importance of the benefit gained by it, just as sin is of great consequence by virtue of the great harm which comes through it. Thus prophets, peace be on them, are the creatures with the greatest rewards by virtue of the greatness of their benefit through their call to the rest of the beneficial things (which can be gained) by acts (performed) by the rest of the people.

8. Taking up the Standard at Khaybar[11]

Similar to that was the putting to flight of those who were put to flight at Khaybar. The exalted rank of carrying the standard is considered highly. By the (standard-bearer's) being put to flight, there occurred such disarray as could not be hidden from those with discernment. Then the standard was given to another man after that. However, he was put to flight in the same way as the first man had been before. In that there was fear for Islam and its position after two men (carrying its standard) had been put to flight. That troubled the Apostle of Allāh, may Allāh bless Him and His Family, and made public the disobedience to him and the bad attitude towards him. So he said in a (public) announcement: "Tomorrow, I will give the standard to one whom Allāh and His Apostle love. Allāh and His Apostle love him as one who returns to the battle without fleeing: he will not come back until Allāh has brought victory at his hands."

Then he gave (the standard) to the Commander of the Faithful, peace be on him, and victory came at his hands. His words, peace be on him, guided and prevented those who wanted to flee from leaving the rank which had been assigned to the Commander of the Faithful, peace be on him. Thus by the Commander of the Faithful, peace be on him, coming out to attack, giving support to the battle and restoring the situation at Khaybar, which had been beyond everyone else, there is evidence of his unequalled merit which no one else shared. Concerning that al-Ḥassān b. Thābit al-Anṣāri said:

> 'Alī was ashen-eyed needing medicine, even then he did not find (the help of anyone) to nurse him.
>
> The Apostle of Allāh healed him with saliva. He blessed the healer (*raqī*) and He blessed the healed.
>
> He said: I will give the standard today to a dauntless man, brave, one who loves Allāh as a follower.
>
> He loves my Allāh and Allāh loves him. Through him Allāh will overcome the fortress returning it to Allāh.
>
> He distinguished 'Alī by that apart from all other creatures and he named him his helper (wazīr) and brother.

---

11 cf. al-Ṭabarī, I, 1579, Ibn Hishām, *Sīra*, 761-2. The two defeated men are identified as Abū Bakr and 'Umar. The verses are not reported by either authority.

9. Delivery of the Verses of Renunciation in Mecca[12]

Similar to that is the story of (the document of renunciation (*barā'a*)) which the Prophet, may Allāh bless Him and His Family, gave to Abū Bakr so that he could abrogate the alliance with the polytheists through it. When he had travelled far away, Gabriel, peace be on him, descended to the Prophet, may Allāh bless Him and His Family. He told him: "Allāh recites His greeting to you and says to you that the act of renunciation should not be performed for you except by yourself or a man (related) to you."

The Apostle of Allāh, may Allāh bless Him and His Family, summoned 'Alī, peace be on him, and told him: "Ride my camel, al-'Aḍbā', and go after Abū Bakr. Take (the document of) renunciation from him and go with it to Mecca. You abrogate the alliance with the polytheists through it. Give Abū Bakr the choice of continuing to ride with you or of returning to me."

The Commander of the Faithful, peace be on him, rode al-'Aḍbā', the camel of the Apostle of Allāh, may Allāh bless Him and His Family and caught up with Abū Bakr. The latter was disturbed at being caught up with by him.
"Why have you come, Abū al-Ḥasan?" he asked as he greeted him. "Are you going to travel with me? Or is it for some other reason?"
"The Apostle of Allāh, may Allāh bless Him and His Family, ordered me to come after you," the Commander of the Faithful, peace be on him, said, "to take the verses of renunciation (*barā'a*) from you and to abrogate the treaty with the polytheists through them. He ordered me to let you choose between going with me or returning to him."
"Indeed, I will return to him," he said.

He went back to the Prophet, may Allāh bless Him and His Family. When he came to him, he said: "Apostle of Allāh, you regarded me as worthy to undertake a mission on account of which men craned their necks towards me. When I had set out on it, you dismissed me from it. What has come down in revealed message (Qur'ān) concerning me?"

"The trusty one, Gabriel, peace be on him, came down to me from Allāh, the Mighty and Exalted," the Prophet, may Allāh bless Him and His Family, answered, "with (the command) that: 'The act of renunciation should not be performed for you except by yourself or a man (related) to you.' 'Alī is related to

12 This account follows most closely the account given in al-Ṭabarī, 1720-1, however it makes Gabriel responsible for the change. The name of the Prophet's camel is given by Ibn Hishām, *Sīra*, 922.

me and it should only be performed for me by ‘Alī.”

(This account occurs) in a famous tradition. The abrogation of a treaty was limited to the one who made it or to one who could take his place in terms of the necessary obedience, dignified regard, high rank, noble position, and one who was above suspicion in his actions and whose words could not be (legitimately) opposed - one who was the same as the maker of the treaty and whose affair was his affair. Since it was judged by what he had done in the past it was established and was secure from opposition and (since) the strength of Islam, the completion (of the laws) of religion, the well-being of the Muslims, the conquest of Mecca, and the good organization of well-being was involved in the abrogation of the treaty, Allāh, the Exalted, preferred that that should be entrusted to one who was illustrious in name, exalted in fame. This indicates the outstanding merit of such a man; it gives evidence of his high rank and distinguishes him from others. Those (things) belonged to the Commander of the Faithful, peace be on him. None of the other people had merit which came near to the merit which we have described nor did any of them share with him (any) of what we have explained.

Examples of what we have mentioned are so numerous that our work in presenting them would lengthen this book, and the speeches would encompass it. It is sufficient for those of intelligence to include what we have set out in the aims which we have outlined.

*****

CHAPTER III

THE MILITARY EXPLOITS OF THE COMMANDER OF THE FAITHFUL

As for armed struggle (*jihād*) by which the rules of Islam were established and by the establishment of which the religious stipulations and laws of the community (*milla*) were settled, the Commander of the Faithful, peace be on him, was so outstanding that his fame is spread among men and reports about him are abundant both among his special followers and the general populace. The learned do not differ on that nor do the specialists in law dispute its truth. The only doubt (which could be raised) about that would be (as a result of) the deliberate neglect of one who did not consider the historical reports. None of those who reflect on the account can reject it except an obstinate liar who has no shame.

The Battle of Badr

An example of that is what he did at the Battle of Badr, which is mentioned in the Qur'ān. It was the first battle in which there was a test (of the Muslims') faith. Fear filled the hearts of a number of Muslims and they wanted to hold back from it out of that fear and dislike, as is shown absolutely in the Explanation (*tibyān* i.e. Qur' ān) where He, may His name be exalted, speaks of them in what He reports of them with full explanation and clarity: *Similarly your Lord brought you out of your house according to the truth while a group of believers were unwilling to (follow you) and were disputing with you about the right course after it had been explained as though they were being driven to death while they were watching.* (VIII 5-6). Concerning the verses connecting that to Allāh's words: *Do not be like those who came out of their houses in insolence and as hypocritical people to stop (them) from the path of Allāh. And Allāh encompasses what they do* (VIII 47) to the end of the *sūra*.

Most accounts of their circumstances in that follow each other; even though the expressions may be different yet their import agrees. The brief outline of the account of this attack is that the polytheists came to Badr intent on battle and determined to gain victory in it because of their vast equipment, their number, supplies and men. At that time the Muslims were a group, few in number. Some of them came (to the battle) unwillingly and showed their reluctance and compulsion. Quraysh challenged them to single combat and called on them to draw up in battle line and to take the field. They suggested that equals (in rank) among them should meet (in battle). The Anṣār delayed coming forward. Indeed, the Prophet, may Allāh bless Him and His Family, stopped them from doing that.[1]

"The people have asked for equals to them," he told them. Then he ordered 'Alī to go out against them. He summoned Ḥamza b. 'Abd al-Muṭṭalib and 'Ubayda b. al-Ḥārith, the pleasure of Allāh be with them, to go forward with him.

When they had drawn up before them, the people did not accept them at first because they were wearing helmets.
"Who are you?" they asked.
They told them their ancestry.
"Noble equals," they replied. Then the battle began between them.

Al-Walīd came out against the Commander of the Faithful, peace be on him. Soon he (i.e. the Commander of the Faithful) killed him. 'Utba came out against Ḥamza, may Allāh be pleased with him, and Ḥamza killed him. Shayba came out against 'Ubayda, may Allāh have mercy on him. Blows were exchanged between them. One of them cut the thigh of 'Ubayda. The Commander of the Faithful, peace be on him, rescued him by striking Shayba with a blow which surprised him and killing him. Ḥamza, may Allāh be pleased with him, participated in that.

The killing of those three was the first (sign) of weakening within (the ranks of) the polytheists. Weakness came upon them and terror by which they were overcome with fear of the Muslims. In that way indications of a Muslim victory were (already) apparent. Then the Commander of the Faithful, peace be on him, came forward (to fight) al-'Āṣ b. Sa'īd b. al-'Āṣ after all (the Muslims) except him had drawn away from him. Soon he had slain him. Ḥanẓala b. Abī Sufyān came against him and he killed him. Ṭu'ayma b. 'Adī came against him and he killed him. After him, he killed Nawfal b. Khuwaylid - he was one of the devils (*shayāṭīn*) of Quraysh. He, peace be on him, continued to slay one of them after another until he had managed (to kill) half of those of them who were killed. There were seventy men (killed) in all, of whom all the Muslims who were present at al-Badr together with three thousand angels who had been sent undertook the killing of half of them while the Commander of the Faithful, peace be on him, undertook the killing of the other half alone with Allāh's help for him, His support, success and victory. Thus victory was brought about at his hands. The matter was finally sealed by the Prophet, may Allāh bless Him and His Family, taking a handful of pebbles and throwing it into their faces while he

1 cf. al-Ṭabarī, I, 1317-8. Ibn Hishām, *Sira*, 443.

said, "May their faces be deformed in ugliness (through the evil eye)." None of them remained without turning their backs in flight. Allāh had been sufficient in battle for the believers through the Commander of the Faithful and his partners in support of religion, who were from the special group of family of the Apostle, peace be on Him and His Family, and those who supported him among the noble angels. As Allāh the Most High said: *Allāh was sufficient in the battle for the believers. Allāh was Strong and Mighty.* (XXXIII 25)

The narrators, both non-Shī'a (*'āmma*) and Shī'a (*khāṣṣa*), confirmed the names of those of the polytheists whom the Commander of the Faithful killed at Badr; (this has been established) with agreement and accord about what they have reported. Among those whom they named were:

1. Al-Walīd b. 'Utba: he, as we have mentioned before, was brave, daring, brazen and murderous; a man whom men were terrified of;
2. Al-'Āṣ b. Sa'īd: he was a very awesome man whom (even) heroes feared and he was the man from whom 'Umar b. al-Khaṭṭab fled - the story of him concerning what we have just mentioned is well known and we will present it later, Allāh willing;
3. Ṭu'ayma b. 'Adī b. Nawfal: he was one of the leaders of the misguided people;
4. Nawfal b. Khuwaylid: he was one of the fiercest in opposition to the Apostle of Allāh, may Allāh bless Him and His Family, and Quraysh used to give him precedence and great position and obey him. He was the one who bound Abū Bakr and Ṭalḥa together in Mecca before the emigration (*hijra*) and tied them with a rope and tortured them night and day so that he might interrogate them about their involvement (*amr*). When the Apostle of Allāh, may Allāh bless Him and His Family, knew of his presence at Badr, he beseeched Allāh that his affair would be sufficient (to destroy) him. He said: "O Allāh, be sufficient on my behalf (to destroy) Nawfal b. Khuwaylid." Thus, the Commander of the Faithful, peace be on him, killed him.
5. Zam'a b. al-Aswad;
6. 'Aqīl b. al-Aswad;
7. Al-Ḥārith b. Zam'a;
8. Al-Naḍr b. al-Ḥārith b. 'Abd al-Dār;
9. 'Umayr b. 'Uthman b. Ka'b b. Taym, the paternal uncle of Ṭalḥa b. 'Ubayd Allāh;
10. 'Uthmān
11. and Mālik, the two sons of 'Ubayd Allāh and brothers of Ṭalḥa b. 'Ubayd Allāh;
12. Mas'ūd b. Abī Umayya b. al-Mughīra;

13. Qays b. al-Fākih b. al-Mughīra;
14. Ḥudhayfa b. Abī Ḥudhayfa b. al-Mughīra;
15. Abū Qays b. al-Walīd b. al-Mughīra;
16. Ḥanẓala b. Abī Sufyān;
17. ʻAmr b. Makhzūm;
18. Abū al-Mundhir b. Abī Rifāʻa;
19. Munabbih b. al-Ḥajjāj al-Sahmī;
20. Al-ʻĀṣ b. Munabbih;
21. ʻAlqama b. Kalda;
22. Abū al-ʻĀṣ b. Qays b. ʻAdī;
23. Muʻāwiya b. al-Mughīra b. Abī al-ʻĀṣ;
24. Lawdhān b. Rabīʻa;
25. ʻAbd Allāh b. al-Mundhir b. Abī Rifāʻa;
26. Masʻūd b. Umayya b. al-Mughīra;
27. Ḥājib b. Sāʼib b. ʻUwaymir;
28. Aws b. al-Mughīra b. Lawdhān;
29. Zayd b. Mulīs;
30. ʻĀsim b. Abī ʻAwf;
31. Sāʻid b. Wahb, ally of the Banū ʻĀmir;
32. Muʻāwiya b. ʻAbd al-Qays;
33. ʻAbd Allāh b. Jamīl b. Zuhayr b. al-Ḥārith b. al-Asad;
34. Al- Sāʼib b. Mālik;
35. Abū al-Ḥakam b. al-Akhnas;
36. Hishām b. Abī Umayya b. al-Mughīra.

That is thirty-six men,[2] excluding those with regard to whose (death) there is some dispute or in which the Commander of the Faithful, peace be on him, participated with others. They are more than half those killed at Badr as we have mentioned.

(Here is) a brief survey of the reports which have come down in explanation of what we have put forward.

[The report which Shu'ba related on the authority of Abū Isḥāq, on the authority of al-Ḥārith b. Muḍarrib, who said:][3]
I heard ʻAlī b. Abī Ṭālib, peace be on him, say:
We came to Badr without there being a horseman among us except al-Miqdād

2 Of these thirty-six names more detailed accounts follow concerning Al-Walīd b. ʻUtba, Al-ʻĀṣ b. Saʻīd, Ṭuʻayma b. ʻAdī and Nawfal b. Khuwaylid. Many of them are reported in the list given by al-Wāqidī, *al-Maghāzī*, I, 148-52, which makes the number killed by ʻAli 22.

3 Same report and *isnād* in al-Ṭabarī, 1291.

b. al-Aswad. We spent the night before Badr and there was not a man among us who did not sleep except the Apostle of Allāh, may Allāh bless Him and His Family. He was standing upright at the trunk of a tree where he performed the ritual prayer and called to Allāh until morning.

[ʻAlī b.Hāshim reported on the authority of Muḥammad b. ʻUbayd Allāh b. Abī Rafīʻ, on the authority of his father, on the authority of his grandfather, Abū Rafīʻ, the retainer of the Apostle of Allāh, may Allāh bless Him and His Family, who said:][4]
When the people awoke on the morning of the day of the battle of Badr, Quraysh drew up their ranks. At their front was ʻUtba b. Rabīʻa and his brother, Shayba, and his son, al-Walīd. ʻUtba called out to the Apostle of Allāh, may Allāh bless Him and His Family, saying: "Muḥammad, send out against us our equal from Quraysh."

Three young men of the Anṣār went forward against them. ʻUtba said to them: "Who are you?" They gave their lineage to him.
"There is no need for us to take part in single combat with you," he replied. "We only seek (to fight) our kinsmen."
"Withdraw to your positions," the Apostle of Allāh, may Allāh bless Him and His Family, ordered the Anṣār. Then he said: "Arise, ʻAlī. Arise, Ḥamza. Arise, ʻUbayda. Fight for your truth with which Allāh sent your Prophet, since they have brought their falsehood to extinguish the light of Allāh."

They arose and arrayed themselves before the people. They were wearing helmets so that they were not recognized.
ʻUtba said to them, "Speak. If you are our equals then we will fight you."
"I am Ḥamza b. ʻAbd al-Muṭṭalib, the lion of Allāh and the lion of His Apostle, may Allāh bless Him and His Family," declared Ḥamza
"A noble equal," said ʻUtba.
"I am ʻAlī b. Abī Ṭālib b. ʻAbd al-Muṭṭalib," declared the Commander of the Faithful, peace be on him.
"I am ʻUbayda b. al-Ḥārith b. ʻAbd al-Muṭṭalib," declared ʻUbayda.
Then ʻUtba told his son al-Walīd: "Arise, al-Walīd."
The Commander of the Faithful, peace be on him, came forward against him. At that time they were both the youngest of the assembled company. They exchanged blows. Al-Walīd's blow missed the Commander of the Faithful, peace be on him, and then he warded off the blow of the Commander of the Faithful, peace be on him, with his left hand and (the blow) cut it off.

---

4 cf. al-Ṭabarī, I, 1317-8, Ibn Hishām, *Sira*, 443, without the verses.

It is related that he (i.e. the Commander of the Faithful) used to mention Badr and the killing of al-Walīd. He would say in his conversation: "It was just as if I was looking at the flashing of the ring on his left hand. Then I struck him with another blow, brought him down and plundered him. I saw he had a robe of saffron and I realised that he had recently been married."

'Utba advanced against Ḥamza, may Allāh be pleased with him, and Ḥamza killed him. 'Ubayda, who was the oldest of the people, marched against Shayba. They exchanged blows and the sharp edge of Shayba's sword struck 'Ubayda's knee and cut it. However, the Commander of the Faithful and Ḥamza rescued him from Shayba and they killed Shayba and carried 'Ubayda away. He died at al-Safrā'.

Hind, the daughter of 'Utba, recited concerning the killing of 'Utba, Shayba and al-Walīd:

> O my eye, profuse with flowing tears, he never withdrew to a better man of Khindif.
> His group and the Banū Ḥāshim and Banū al-Muṭṭalib summoned him at morning.
> They made him taste the blades of their swords. They stripped him after he had perished.

[Al-Ḥasan b. Ḥumayd reported: Abū Ghāssan told us: Abū Ismā'īl 'Umayr b. Bakkār told us on the authority of Jābir, on the authority of Abū Ja'far, peace be on them, who said:]
The Commander of the Faithful, peace be on him, said: "I was amazed at the bravery of the people at Badr. I had killed al-Walīd. Ḥamza had killed 'Utba and I shared with him in the killing of Shayba. Then Ḥanẓala b. Abī Sufyān advanced towards me. When he was near me, I struck him a blow with my sword and his eyes flowed with tears as he cleaved to the ground, dead."

[Abū Bakr al-Hudhalī reported on the authority of al-Zuhrī, on the authority of Ṣāliḥ b. Kaysān, who said:][5]
'Uthmān b. 'Affān passed Sā'īd b. al-'Āṣ and said: "Come with us to the Commander of the Faithful, 'Umar b. al-Khaṭṭab so that we may talk with him." They both went.

Sā'īd reported: As for 'Uthmān, he could take whatever place he wished, but as for me, I had to keep to the side of the people. 'Umar looked towards me and said: "What is (the feeling) towards me which I see in you; as if you felt some

5 A shorter version of this account is given by al-Wāqidī, I, 92.

(animosity) towards me? Do you think that I killed your father? By Allāh, if I had wanted to be his killer and if I had killed him, I would not have made any excuse for killing an unbeliever. However I passed him on the day of Badr and I saw him seeking for battle just as an ox seeks for its mate. His jaws were foaming like a lizard. When I saw that, I became terrified of him and turned aside from him. He said: 'Where are you going, Ibn al-Khaṭṭab?' Then 'Alī directed himself towards him and caught up with him. By Allāh, I remained in my place until he killed him."

'Alī, peace be on him, was present at the assembly (when 'Umar was telling this). He said: "O Allāh, let there be forgiveness; polytheism has gone with what was in it. Islam has wiped out what existed before. Why do you (say that)? You will rouse the people against me."
So 'Umar desisted.

Sā'īd, (later) commented: "Yet it was the only pleasure for me (in the death of my father) that the one who killed him was 'Alī b. Abī Ṭālib."

The people put forward (this story) in another narration.

[Muḥammad b. Isḥāq reported on the authority of Yazīd b. Rūmān on the authority of Urwa b. al-Zubayr:][6]
At the battle of Badr, 'Alī, peace be on him, advanced toward Tu'ayma b. 'Adī b. Nawfal and thrust his spear at him, saying to him: "By Allāh, you will never oppose us concerning Allāh after today."

['Abd al-Razzāq reported on the authority of Ma'mar on the authority of al-Zuhrī, who said:][7]
When the Apostle of Allāh, may Allāh bless Him and His Family knew of the presence of Nawfal b. Khuwaylid at Badr, he said: "O Allāh, be sufficient (to destroy) Nawfal on my behalf."

When Quraysh were routed, 'Alī b. Abī Ṭālib, peace be on him, saw him. He was perplexed, not knowing what to do. He directed himself towards him and struck at him with his sword. He took hold of his shield and pulled it away from him. Then he struck his leg as his armour was covering (the top of his body). He cut it and then gave him a final blow and killed him. When he returned to the Prophet, may Allāh bless Him and His Family, he heard him say: "Who has knowledge of Nawfal?"

6 This extract is not reported by al-Ṭabarī or Ibn Hishām.
7 cf. al-Wāqidī, I, 91-2.

“I have killed him, O Apostle of Allāh,” he, peace be on him, replied.
The Prophet, may Allāh bless Him and His Family, said: “Allāh is greater! Praise be to Allāh who has answered my prayer concerning him.”

(The poet) Usayd b. Abī Iyyās said about the exploits of the Commander of the Faithful, peace be on him, at Badr, in order to urge on the polytheists of Quraysh against him:

> At every meeting there is a purpose which confounds you, a strong youngster who overcomes experienced full-grown horses.
>
> Your abundance comes from God! Do you not deny (it)? Perhaps the noble free man does deny and feels shame.
>
> This is the son of Fāṭima who has destroyed you in slaughter and death with a single blow not with (wild) striking.
>
> They gave him money to avoid his blows - the action of the servile, a contract which brings no profit.
>
> Where were the mature men? Where were all the chiefs (of the people) amid (these) misfortunes? Where was the best of the valley (*al-abṭaḥ*)?
>
> He destroyed them with violent death and blows which he struck as he used his sword whose blade did not (cease) striking (down).

The Battle of Uḥud

The battle of Uḥud came after Badr. During it the standard of the Apostle of Allāh, may Allāh bless Him and His Family, was carried by the Commander of the Faithful, peace be on him, as it had been at Badr. On that day he also carried the banner (*liwā'*): he was noted as the one who carried both the standard and the banner. The same (individual) success was (achieved) by him during this battle as had been (achieved) by him at Badr. However, during it he was outstanding for his noble (suffering) of misfortune, his endurance and his firm footedness when the feet of other men were slipping (backwards). His distress for the Apostle of Allāh, may Allāh bless Him and His Family, was such as no other of the people of Islam had. Allāh killed through his sword (many of) the leaders of the people of polytheism and misguidance. Through him Allāh dispelled the tragedy (of the battle) from His Prophet, peace be on him. Gabriel, peace be on him, spoke to the angels of heaven and earth about his merit in that situation. The Prophet of guidance, peace be on him, set him apart by virtue of his characterising him with what was hidden from ordinary men.

[Of that is what Yaḥyā b. ʻUmāra reported: al-Ḥasan b. Mūsā b. Riyāḥ, retainer of the Anṣār, told me: Abū al-Bakhtarī al-Qurashī:]
The standard and banner of Quraysh were both in the hands of Qusayy b. Kilāb. The standard remained in the hand of the sons of ʻAbd al-Muṭṭalib, the one of them who was present at war used to carry it until Allāh sent His Apostle, may Allāh bless Him and His Family. The standard and the rest of the things came (under the authority of) the Prophet, may Allāh bless Him and His Family. He settled it on the Banū Hāshim. The Apostle of Allāh, may Allāh bless Him and His Family, gave it to ʻAlī b. Abī Ṭālib, at the battle of Waddān; it was the first battle at which the standard was carried in Islam, on behalf of the Prophet, may Allāh bless Him and His Family. It remained with him (i.e. ʻAlī) at the events at Badr -- the greatest victory -- and at the battle of Uḥud. At that time the banner was in the hands of the sons of ʻAbd al-Dār. However, the Apostle of Allāh, may Allāh bless Him and His Family, gave it to Muṣʻab b. ʻUmayr. He was martyred and the banner fell from his hand. The tribes (men) were looking down at him. The Apostle of Allāh, may Allāh bless Him and His Family, seized it and thrust it to ʻAlī b. Abī Ṭālib, peace be on him. On that day he made him combine the standard and the banner and both of them remain to the present day with the Banū Hāshim.

[Al-Mufaḍḍal b. ʻAbd Allāh reported on the authority of Simāk, on the authority of ʻIkrima, on the authority of ʻAbd Allāh b. ʻAbbās, who said:]
Four things were given to ʻAlī b. Abī Ṭālib, peace be on him, which were not given to anyone else: he was the first person, Arab or non-Arab, to pray with the Apostle of Allāh, may Allāh bless Him and His Family; he was the one who carried his banner in every march; he was the one who remained with him at the Battle of Mihrās, that is the Battle of Uḥud; and he was the one who took (his corpse) into his tomb.

[Zayd b. Wahb al Juhnī reported through the following *isnād*: Aḥmad b. ʻAmmār told us: al-Ḥimmānī told us: Sharīk told us on the authority of ʻUthman b. al-Mughīra, on the authority of Zayd b. Wahb,[8] who said: One day we found ʻAbd Allāh b. Masʻūd in a good mood. We asked him if he would tell us about the Battle of Uḥud and how it had been. "Yes," he replied and he carried on the account until he came to the mention of the battle itself. He said:]
The Apostle of Allāh, may Allāh bless Him and His Family, ordered (us): "Go out against them with the name of Allāh."

8 Zayd ibn Wahb's version was probably taken by al-Mufīd from a book written by al-Ḥimmānī. cf. Ṭūsī, *Fihrist*, 148, 361.

We went out and we arrayed ourselves in a long line against them. He positioned fifty men of the Anṣār over the hill-pass. He put one of their number in charge of them and he told them: "Do not leave this position of yours, for if we are going to be killed right up to the last of us, we will be attacked through your position."

Abū Sufyān Ṣakhr b. Ḥarb positioned Khālid b. al-Walīd opposite them. The banners of Quraysh were in (the possession of) Banū 'Abd al-Dār and the banner of the polytheists was in (the hands of) Ṭalḥa b. Abī Ṭalḥa - he was called the leader of the phalanx. The Apostle of Allāh, may Allāh bless Him and His Family, gave the banner of the emigrants (*muhājrīn*) to 'Alī b. Abī Ṭālib, peace be on him. He went forward and stood beneath the banner of the Anṣār. Abū Sufyān came up to the banner-carriers and declared: "Banner-carriers, perhaps you know that the people will only come forward for the sake of their banners. At the battle of Badr, you only came forward for the sake of your banners. (Today) if you think that you will be too weak (to defend) them, give them to us to defend them for you."

Ṭalḥa b. Abī Ṭalḥa became angry and said: "Are you saying this to us? By Allāh, I will lead you with them today to the waters of death." Ṭalḥa was called the leader of the phalanx.

He advanced and 'Alī b. Abī Ṭālib, peace be on him, advanced.
"Who are you?" demanded 'Alī.
"I am Ṭalḥa b. Abī Ṭalḥa," he replied. "I am the leader of the phalanx. Who are you?"
"I am 'Alī b. Abī Ṭālib b. 'Abd al-Muṭṭalib," he answered.

They drew together and blows were exchanged between them. 'Alī b. Abī Ṭālib, peace be on him, struck him on the front of the head. His eyes flowed with tears and he let out a scream, the like of which has never been heard (before or since). The banner fell from his hand. His brother called Mūs'āb seized hold of it but 'Āṣim b. Thābit shot an arrow at him and killed him. Then his brother called 'Uthman seized hold of it. Again 'Āṣim b. Thābit shot an arrow and killed him. Their slave called Ṣawāb, who was one of the fiercest of men, took hold of it. 'Alī, peace be on him, struck his hand and cut it. He took the banner with his left hand and he cut that (too). He took hold of the banner with his chest and both his severed arms. 'Alī, peace be on him, struck him on the crown of his head and he fell prostrate.

The people were put to flight and the Muslims occupied themselves with spoils. When the men at the mountain-pass saw the people plundering, they said: "Those men will take (all) the spoils while we stay (here)."

They asked their leader, 'Abd Allāh b. 'Umar b. Ḥazm: "We want to take part in the plunder like the people are."
"The Apostle of Allāh, may Allāh bless Him and His Family, has ordered me not to leave this position," he replied.
"He ordered you to do that without knowing that the matter would come to what we now see," they told him and went off towards the booty leaving him behind. He remained in his position. Khālid b. al-Walīd attacked and killed him. Then (Khālid) came up behind the Apostle of Allāh, may Allāh bless Him and His Family, making straight for him. He could see the Prophet, may Allāh bless Him and His Family, amid a small troop of his Companions. He said to those with him: "Behold this is the man you want. Your business is with him."

They attacked him as one, striking with swords, thrusting with spears, shooting arrows and hurling stones. The Companions of the Prophet, may Allāh bless Him and His Family, began to fight to (defend) him until seventy of them were killed. The Commander of the Faithful, peace be on him, Abū Dujāna and Sahl b. Ḥunayf supported the people in defending the Prophet, may Allāh bless Him and His Family. The polytheists attacked them. The Apostle of Allāh, may Allāh bless Him and His Family, had been overcome by faintness from (a wound) which he had received. He opened his eyes and saw the Commander of the Faithful, peace be on him.
"'Alī ," he said, "what have the people done?"
"They have broken their pledge and turned their tracks in flight," he answered.
"But these who have shown purposefulness will be sufficient for me (to carry out) my purpose."

The Commander of the Faithful, peace be on him, attacked them and routed them. Then he went back (to the Prophet), who had been attacked from another side. He launched himself against them and routed them. Abū Dujāna and Sahl b. Ḥunayf stood beside him, each with a sword in his hand, in order to defend him. Fourteen of his Companions who had fled came back to him. Among them were Ṭalḥa b. 'Ubayd Allāh and 'Āṣim b. Thābit.

The rest had gone up the hill and people began to cry out throughout Medina: "The Prophet has been killed." As a result of that their spirits abandoned them, and defeated and confused they scattered to right and left.

Hind, the daughter of 'Utba, had urged a savage man to kill the Apostle of Allāh, or the Commander of the Faithful or Ḥamza b. 'Abd al-Muṭṭalib, peace be on them. He had told her: "As for Muḥammad, there is no way I can get to him because his Companions always surround him. In the case of 'Alī, when he fights, he is more wary than a wolf. However, I am quite hopeful with regard to Ḥamza, for when he becomes angry, he does not see what is in front of him."

At that time, Ḥamza could be recognized by an ostrich feather (he wore) on his breast. The savage man lay in wait for him. He reported: "My lance quivered (in my hand) until I was in a good position to hurl it at him. Then it struck him just above the thigh and pierced it. I left him until when he was cold (with death), I went back to him and took my spear from him. Meanwhile the Muslims had been distracted by their flight from (what had happened between) him and me."

Hind had come forward and ordered Ḥamza's stomach to be split open, his liver to be cut out and his body to be mutilated. They cut off his nose and ears. The Apostle of Allāh, may Allāh bless Him and His Family, was also too occupied to be aware of what had happened to him.

*****

[The narrator of the account - Zayd b. Wahb - reported:] I asked Ibn Mas'ūd: "Did the people flee from the Apostle of Allāh, may Allāh bless Him and His Family, so that only 'Alī b. Abī Ṭālib, peace be on him, Abū Dujāna and Sahl b. Ḥunayf remained with him?"
"Ṭalḥa b. 'Ubayd Allāh joined them," he answered.
"Where were Abū Bakr and 'Umar?" I asked.
"They were among those who had turned their backs," he answered.
"Where was 'Uthmān?" I asked.
"He only came three hours after the battle," he replied. The Apostle of Allāh, may Allāh bless Him and His Family, said to him: "Have you brought a petition for (your absence from) it?"
"Where were you?" I (i.e. Zayd) asked (Ibn Mas'ūd).
"I was among those who had turned their backs (in flight)," he said.
"Who told you about this, then?" I enquired.
"'Āṣim and Sahl b. Ḥunayf," was his answer.
"The confirmation of 'Alī in that position is a source of wonder," I said.
"You may well be amazed at that," he said, "for the angels themselves were amazed at it. Didn't you know that Gabriel, peace be on him, said, as he was ascending to heaven: "There is no sword except Dhū al-Fiqār; there is no young man except 'Alī?"
"How is that known about Gabriel, peace be on him?" I asked.
"The people heard a voice crying that, in the sky," was his reply. "They asked the Prophet, may Allāh bless Him and His Family, about it. He told them that

that was Gabriel."

*****

[In the account of 'Imrān b. Ḥusayn, he reported:][9]
At the battle of Uḥud when the people scattered from the Apostle of Allāh, may Allāh bless Him and His Family, 'Alī, peace be on him, came, girding his sword. He stood in front of him and the Apostle of Allāh, may Allāh bless Him and His Family, raised his head and asked: "Why haven't you fled with the people?"
"Apostle of Allāh, would I return to being an unbeliever after I had submitted to Islam?" he answered.

(The Prophet) pointed out to him some of the enemy who had come down from the hill. ('Alī) attacked them and put them to flight. Then, (the Prophet) pointed out to him some more of the enemy. Again he attacked them and put them to flight. The Prophet then pointed out to him another group of the enemy. Yet again he attacked them and put them to flight.

Gabriel, peace be on him, came and said: "The angels are amazed, and we are amazed with them, at the selflessness of 'Alī."
"What could prevent him from being like this?" replied the Apostle of Allāh, may Allāh bless Him and His Family. "He is from me and I am from him."
"And I, Apostle of Allāh, am from you both," said Gabriel.

[Al-Ḥakam b. Ẓuhayr reported on the authority of al-Suddī, on the authority of his father, on the authority of Ibn 'Abbās:][10]
On that day Ṭalḥa b. Abī Ṭalḥa went forward, stood between the two ranks and called out: "Companions of Muḥammad, you claim that Allāh will hurry us towards hellfire through your sword and that we will hurry you towards heaven with our swords. Which of you will come forward to fight me in single combat?"
The Commander of the Faithful, peace be on him, went forward and declared: "By Allāh, today I will not leave you until I have hurried you towards hell-fire with my sword."

The two men exchanged blows. 'Alī b. Abī Ṭālib, peace be on him, struck him on both his legs and cut them. He fell down and was overcome. He said to 'Alī: "I implore you before Allāh and kinship (to leave me), cousin."
Then he withdrew from him to his position. The Muslims said to him: "You have not finished him."
"He implored me by Allāh and kinship (to leave him)," ('Alī) told them, "but he

9 A similar but briefer account in al-Ṭabarī, I, 1402
10 Report from al-Ṭabarī, 1,1395-6.

will never survive after that."

Ṭalḥa died where he was. The good news of that was reported to the Prophet, may Allāh bless Him and His Family. He was delighted with that and said: "This is the captain of the phalanx."

[Muḥammad b. Marwān reported on the authority of 'Umāra, on the authority of 'Ikrima, who said: I heard 'Alī, peace be on him, say:]
When the people fled from the Apostle of Allāh, may Allāh bless Him and His Family, at the battle of Uḥud, I became more worried than I have ever been and I was unable to control myself. I had been in front of him fighting with my sword. I went back to look for him. I could not see him. I said to myself: 'The Apostle of Allāh would not flee.' Yet I could not see him among those who had been killed. I thought he had been taken up, amid us, into heaven. I broke the sheath of my sword and said to myself: 'I will fight with my sword without (ever putting it back into a sheath) until I am killed.' I attacked the enemy and they scattered away from me. Then suddenly (I found that) the Apostle of Allāh, may Allāh bless Him and His Family, had fallen to the ground, unconscious. I stood beside his head. He looked towards me and spoke: "'Alī, what have the people done?" "They have lost their faith, Apostle of Allāh," I answered. "They have turned their backs in flight and surrendered you."

The Prophet, may Allāh bless Him and His Family, looked towards a phalanx (of the enemy) which had approached him. He told me: "Drive this phalanx away from me, 'Alī".
I attacked them with my sword and struck out at them to right and left until they turned their backs in flight.
"'Alī, don't you hear the praise for you in the heavens?" the Prophet, may Allāh bless Him and His Family, asked me.
An angel called Raḍwān was calling out: "There is no sword except Dhū al-Fiqār; there is no young man except 'Alī."
I wept with joy and praised Allāh, all praise be to Him and may He be extolled for His favour.

[Al-Ḥasan b. 'Arafa reported on the authority of 'Umāra b. Muḥammad, on the authority of Sa'd b. Ṭarīf, on the authority of Abū Ja'far Muḥammad b. 'Alī, on the authority of his fathers, peace be on them:]
At the battle of Uḥud an angel called out from heaven: "There is no sword except Dhū al-Fiqār; there is no young man except 'Alī."

[Similarly Ibrāhīm b. Muḥammad b. Maymūn has reported on the authority of

‘Amr b. Thābit, on the authority of Muḥammad b. ‘Ubayd Allāh b. Abī Rafi‘, on the authority of his father, on the authority of his (i.e. Muḥammad’s) grandfather, who said:][11]
“We still hear the Companions of the Prophet say that at the battle of Uḥud a voice called out from heaven: “There is no sword except Dhū al-Fiqār; there is no young man except ‘Alī.”

[Sallām b. Miskīn reported on the authority of Qatāda, on the authority of Sa‘īd b. al-Musayyib, who said:]
If I had seen the position of ‘Alī, peace be on him, at the battle of Uḥud, I would have found him standing at the right of the Apostle of Allāh, may Allāh bless Him and His Family, defending him with his sword when all except him had turned their backs in flight.

[Al-Ḥasan b. Maḥbūb reported: Jamīl b. ‘Ṣāliḥ told us on the authority of Abū ‘Ubayda, on the authority of Abū ‘Abd Allāh Ja‘far b. Muḥammad, on the authority of his fathers, peace be on them, who said:]
At the battle of Uḥud, nine persons held the banner (of Quraysh). ‘Alī b. Abī Ṭālib, peace be on him, killed them down to the last of them and the enemy were put to flight. On that day (the clan of) Makhzūm tried to escape but ‘Alī, peace be on him, destroyed them.

‘Alī, peace be on him, went forward to fight al-Ḥakam b. al-Akhnas. He struck his leg off from half way up his thigh and he died from that.

When the Muslims scattered in that way, Umayya b. Abī Ḥudhayfa b. al-Mughīra advanced. He was in armour and he was declaring: “Today is the day (of vengeance) for Badr.” One of the Muslims opposed him but Umayya b. Abī Ḥudhayfa killed him. ‘Alī b. Abī Ṭālib directed himself towards him and struck him on the head with his sword and it was caught in the middle of his helmet. Umayya struck out with his sword and the Commander of the Faithful, peace be on him, warded off the blow with his leather shield. It (also) got caught there. The Commander of the Faithful, peace be on him, pulled his sword away from his helmet and Umayya also freed his sword from the shield. They both attacked each other again.

‘Alī, peace be on him, reported: “I could see a gap (in his armour, below his arm-pit. I struck at it with my sword and killed him. Then I went away from him.”

---

11 Fuller version in al-Ṭabarī, I, 1402, using the earlier authorities.

When the people fled from the Prophet, may Allāh bless Him and His Family, at the battle of Uḥud and the Commander of the Faithful, peace be on him, stood firm, the Prophet, may Allāh bless Him and His Family, asked him: "Why don't you go with the people?"
"Go and leave you, Apostle of Allāh!" exclaimed the Commander of the Faithful, peace be on him. "By Allāh, I will not leave you until I am killed or Allāh has fulfilled His promise of help to you."
"Know the good news. 'Alī," the Prophet, may Allāh bless Him and His Family, told him. "Indeed Allāh is one who fulfils his promises, and they will never inflict the like of this on us again."

Then he looked towards a troop which had advanced towards him. He said to him: "Attack them, 'Alī."
The Commander of the Faithful, peace be on him, attacked them. He killed Hishām b. Umayya al-Makhzūmi, who was among them, and the people fled.

Another troop advanced. (Again) the Prophet, may Allāh bless Him and His Family, told him: "Attack them." He attacked them and killed 'Amr b. 'Abd Allāh al-Jumaḥī, who was among them. They also fled. Yet another troop advanced and again the Prophet, may Allāh bless Him and His Family, told him to attack them. He attacked them and killed Bishr b. Mālik al-'Āmirī, who was among them. The troop fled.

After that none of them returned and those of the Muslims who had fled began to come back to the Prophet, may Allāh bless Him and His Family. The polytheists withdrew towards Mecca and the Muslims went back to Medina with the Prophet, may Allāh bless Him and His Family. Fāṭima, peace be on her, met him. She had with her a jar of water. He washed his face with it and then the Commander of the Faithful, peace be on him, followed him. Blood covered him from his arm to his shoulder. He had (his sword) Dhū al-Fiqār with him and he gave it to Fāṭima, peace be on her.
"Take this sword," he told her. "It has been true to me today." He began to recite:[12]

> Fāṭima,this sword in not without honour and I am no coward, nor am I blameworthy.
>
> By my life, I have been free from blame in the support (I gave to) Aḥmad (i.e. Muḥammad) and in the obedience (I showed) to a Lord Who knows about (those who perform) the worship (of Him).

---

12 Similar verses in al-Ṭabarī, 1, 1436.

> Remove the blood of the people from it. Indeed it has offered the cup of death to the family of 'Abd al-Dār for them to drink.

"Take it, Fāṭima," the Apostle of Allāh, may Allāh bless Him and His Family, told her. "For your husband has done his duty and through his sword Allāh has killed the leaders of Quraysh."

The biographers of the Prophet (*ahl al-siyar*) mention the dead of the polytheists at Uḥud and the majority were slain by the Commander of the Faithful.

['Abd al-Malik b. Hishām reported: Ziyād b. 'Abd Allāh told us on the authority of Muḥammad b. Isḥāq, who said:]
The standard-bearer of Quraysh at the battle of Uḥud was Ṭalḥa b. Abī Ṭalḥa b. 'Abd al-'Uzzā b. 'Uthmān b. 'Abd al-Dār. He was killed by 'Alī b. Abī Ṭālib. The latter killed his son Abū Sa'īd b. Ṭalḥa and his brother Khālid b Abī Ṭalḥa. He also killed 'Abd Allāh b. Ḥumayd b. Zuhra b. al-Ḥārith b. Asad b. 'Abd al-'Uzzā and he killed Abū al-Ḥakam b. al-Akhnas b. Sharīq al-Thaqafi and al-Walīd b. Abī Ḥudhayfa b. al-Mughīra. He killed the latter's brother, Umayya b. Abī Ḥudhayfa b. al-Mughīra. He also killed Arṭa'a b. Sharḥabīl, Hishām b. Umayya, 'Amr b. 'Abd Allāh al-Jumaḥī and Bishr b. Mālik. He killed Sawāb, the retainer of the Banū 'Abd al-Dār.[13]

His was success. The people came back from their rout to the Prophet, may Allāh bless Him and His Family, (while he was in) the same position in which he had been, defending him apart from them. Allāh, the Most High, sent disgrace down on all of them because of their flight on that day except for him and those of the Anṣār who stood firm with him. They were eight or (as) it has been said four or five. Concerning (the prowess of the Commander of the Faithful in) killing those whom he killed at the battle of Uḥud, his hardship and his noble suffering, al-Ḥajjāj b. 'Alāṭ al-Sulamī recited:

> A man who protects Allāh's people (*ḥizb*) belongs to Allāh -- I mean the son of Fāṭima (i.e. 'Alī), the man with important paternal and maternal uncles.
>
> How two hands acted against him with a speedy thrust when you left Ṭalḥa, lying dead (because of a blow) to his forehead.
>
> You attacked fiercely like a brave man and you scattered them at the foot of the hill when they were descending to the bottom.

13 In the version we have from Ibn Hishām most but not all of these names are included. cf. Ibn Hishām, *Sira*, 610-11.

> You gave your sword a second draught of blood and you did not refuse it while it was thirsty until it had quenched its thirst.

The Campaign against the Banū al-Naḍīr

When the Apostle of Allāh, may Allāh bless Him and His Family, set out against the Banū al-Naḍīr with the intention of besieging them, he set up his tent in the furthest (dry) river bed of the Banū Khaṭma.[14] When it was dark night, a man from the Banū al-Naḍīr shot an arrow at him and hit the tent. The Prophet, may Allāh bless Him and His Family, ordered his tent to be moved to the foot of the mountain, and the Emigrants and Anṣār surrounded him. In the confusion of darkness, they lost the Commander of the Faithful, peace be on him. The people said: "O Apostle of Allāh, we cannot see 'Alī."
He, peace be on him, answered: "I can see him engaged in some enterprise which will bring advantage to your task."

It was not long before ('Alī), peace be on him, came back with the head of the Jew who had shot at the Prophet, may Allāh bless Him and His Family. He was called Gharūr. He threw it down before the Prophet, may Allāh bless Him and His Family. The latter asked him: "How did you do that, Abū al-Ḥasan?"

"I saw this wicked man coming forward bravely," he, peace be on him, answered. "I lay in wait for him. I said to myself: 'What has encouraged him to come out in the middle of the night is that he seeks to catch us unawares.' He advanced with his sword drawn amid a group of nine Jews. I attacked him and killed him. His companions escaped but they are still near. Send me with a group of men and I hope that I will overcome them."

The Apostle of Allāh, may Allāh bless Him and His Family, sent ten men with him. Among them were Abū Dujāna Simāk b. Kharasha and Sahl b. Ḥunayf. They reached them before they could take refuge in the fort and they killed them. They brought back their heads to the Prophet, may Allāh bless Him and His Family. He ordered that they should be thrown in the wells of the Banū Khaṭma. That was the reason for the conquest of the forts of the Banū al-Naḍīr. On that night Ka'b b. al-Ashraf was killed.[15]

The Apostle of Allāh, may Allāh bless Him and His Family, appropriated the

14 Khaṭma has been adopted from al-Wāqidī instead of Ḥaṭma. The following anecdote occurs in al-Wāqidī, *al-Maghāzi*, I, 371-2. al-Wāqidī names the Jew as Ghazūk.

15 In fact Ka'b seems to have been killed before this campaign. al-Wāqidī, dates it the beginning of Rabī' al-Awwal 3 A.H. cf. al-Wāqidī, *al-Maghāzi*, I, 184, and al-Ṭabarī, I. 1368.

property of the Banū al-Naḍīr. It was the first palm grove which the Apostle of Allāh, may Allāh bless Him and His Family, had divided among the earliest Emigrants. He ordered ʻAlī, peace be on him, to take possession of that part of it which was (allocated) to the Apostle of Allāh, may Allāh bless Him and His Family. He made it *ṣadaqa* and it was in (the Prophet's) possession throughout his life. Then it came into the possession of the Commander of the Faithful, peace be on him, after him. It is in the possession of the offspring of Fāṭima to this day.

Concerning the part played by the Commander of the Faithful, peace be on him, in this campaign and his killing of the Jew and bringing the heads of the group of nine to the Prophet, may Allāh bless Him and His Family, Ḥassān b. Thābit recited:

> To Allāh belongs any adversity with which you were tested by the Banū Qurayẓa and the men who came in search.
>
> He destroyed their chief and he brought back ten (heads). Time after time he dashed against them and drove them away.

The Campaign against the Allies (Aḥzāb)

The campaign against the allies took place after the campaign against the Banū al-Naḍīr.[16] A group of Jews including Sallām b. Abī al-Ḥuqayq al-Naḍīrī, Ḥuyayy b. Akhṭab, Kināna b. al-Rabīʻ, Hawdha b. Qays al-Wāʻilī and Abū ʻUmāra al-Wāʻilī together with a number of the Banū Wāʻilī left for Mecca. They went to Abū Sufyān Ṣakhr b. Ḥarb because they knew of his hostility to the Apostle of Allāh, may Allāh bless Him and His Family, and his (desire) to hasten to fight him. They told him about how he (i.e. the Prophet) had treated them and they asked him to help them to fight against them.

Abū Sufyān told them: "I will support you in whatever you want. Therefore go to Quraysh and urge them to make war on him and give them guarantees of help and support in order to root him out."

They went around the leaders of Quraysh and urged them to make war on the Prophet, may Allāh bless Him and His Family. They said to them: "Our hands will be with your hands and we will be with you until we have rooted him out."

16 The first part of this account seems to be summary based on al-Ṭabarī, II, 1463-76, this mainly depends on Ibn Isḥāq, cf. Ibn Hishām, *Sira*, 669-79. However, al-Ṭabarī gives information about the trench bang Salman's idea and does not include the verses of ʻAli which are given by Ibn Hishām. In the translation some slight mistakes in names have been corrected in accordance with al-Ṭabarī and Ibn Hishām's versions.

Quraysh answered: "People of the Jews, you are the people of the first Scripture and of former knowledge. You know the religion which Muḥammad has brought and the religion which we believe in. Is our religion better than his religion or is he more endowed with truth than we are?"
"Indeed, your religion is better than his," they answered them.

Quraysh were encouraged because of the war which they had urged them to against the Apostle of Allāh, may Allāh bless Him and His Family. Abū Sufyān came to them and said to them: "God has given you power over your enemy and these Jews will fight alongside you and they will not part from you until all of them are destroyed or until we extirpate him and those who follow him."

At that time their passion to fight against the Prophet, may Allāh bless Him and His Family, became intense. The Jews left and went to the tribes of Ghaṭafān and Qays 'Aylān. They urged them to make war on the Apostle of Allāh, may Allāh bless Him and His Family. They guaranteed them help and aid and informed them of Quraysh's (desire) to pursue that course.

They assembled together. Quraysh came and their leader at that time, Abū Sufyān Ṣakhr b. Ḥarb. Ghaṭafān came with their leader 'Uyayna b. Ḥiṣn, accompanied by the Banū Fazāra. With the Banū Murra was al-Ḥārith b. 'Awf and Mas'ūd b. Rukhayla b. Nuwayra b. Ṭarīf (came) with his people, the clan of Ashja'. Quraysh gathered with them.

When the Apostle of Allāh, may Allāh bless Him and His Family, heard of the gathering of the allies (*aḥzāb*) against him, and the strength of their desire to fight against him, he consulted his Companions. It was their unanimous view that they should remain in Medina and fight the people if they came against them across the mountain paths. Salmān, may Allāh have mercy on him, suggested to the Apostle of Allāh, may Allāh bless Him and His Family, about a trench. He ordered it to be dug. He himself worked on it as did the Muslims.

The allies advanced against the Apostle of Allāh, may Allāh bless Him and His Family. Their power filled the Muslims with fear and they felt terror at their number and their gathering. They camped near the ditch and remained in their positions for some twenty days without any action taking place between them except for the shooting of arrows and (the throwing of) stones. When the Apostle of Allāh, may Allāh bless Him and His Family, perceived the weakness of spirit of the majority of Muslims as a result of the siege, and their reluctance to fight, he sent to 'Uyayna b. Ḥiṣn and al-Ḥārith b. 'Awf - they were both leaders of Ghaṭafān. He urged to make peace with him, to leave him and to

withdraw with their people from the war against him, on the condition that he would give them a third of the produce of Medina. He consulted Sa'd b. Mu'ādh and Sa'd b. 'Ubāda about the terms he sent to 'Uyayna and al-Ḥārith. They said: "Apostle of Allāh, this situation requires us to adopt this plan because Allāh has ordered you to do what you have done with regard to it and inspiration from Allāh has come to you. Therefore do what seems appropriate to you. If you choose to do this on our behalf, then that is our view on the matter."
"Inspiration from Allāh has not come to me," he, peace be on him, answered. "However, I saw the Arabs united against you (lit., shooting at you from one bow) and they had come from every side and I wanted to break up their attack against you for a while."
"These people and ourselves used to be polytheists and worship idols," said Sa'd b. Mu'ādh. "We did not know of Allāh and we did not worship him. But then we did not feed them with our produce except by invitation or by selling it. Now when Allāh has honoured us with Islam, has guided us with it and has made us strong through you, shall we give them our property? What need have we to do this? By Allāh, we will give them nothing except the sword until Allāh decides between us and them."
"I realise your attitude," replied the Apostle of Allāh, may Allāh bless Him and His Family. "Therefore remain in your belief. Allāh, the Most High, will never desert his Prophet nor hand him over to (his enemy) until He fulfils His promise."

The Apostle of Allāh, may Allāh bless Him and His Family, stood up before the Muslims and urged them to strive against the enemy. He encouraged them and he told them of Allāh's help.

Leading horsemen of Quraysh volunteered to take part in single combat against (Muslim fighters). (They were) 'Amr b. 'Abd Wudd b. Abī Qays b. 'Āmir b. Lu'ayy b. Ghālib, 'Ikrima b. Abī Jahl, Hubayra b. Abī Wahb - (the last two were both from the clan of) Makhzūm - Ḍirār b. al-Khaṭṭāb and Mirdās al-Fihrī. They dressed for battle and went out until they passed the houses of the Banū Kināna. They called out: "Banū Kināna, get ready for battle."

They went on, with their horses hurrying forward, until they stopped at the trench. After they had pondered it, they said: "This is a cunning trick which the Arabs have never used."

They aimed themselves at a place in the trench which was narrow. They struck their horses and they rushed blindly at it. (Their horses) brought them on to the swampy ground between the ditch and (the hill of) Sulay'.

The Commander of the Faithful, peace be on him, came out with a group of Muslims so that they could hold the gap (in their defences) which these men had charged through. 'Amr b. 'Abd Wudd advanced with the group who had come out with him. He raised his standard so that his position could be seen. When he saw the Muslims, he and the cavalry with him stopped.

"Is there anyone who will engage in single combat?" he called out. The Commander of the Faithful, peace be on him, advanced towards him.
"Go back, cousin," 'Amr told him. "I don't want to kill you."
"You have made a promise to God, 'Amr, that no man of Quraysh would give you two courses without you choosing one of them from him," said the Commander of the Faithful, peace be on him.
"Indeed," he replied, "what is that?"
"I summon you to Allāh, His Apostle and to Islam," he said.
"I have no need of that," he answered.
"Then I summon you to fight."
"Go back," he told him, "there was great friendship between me and your father and I don't want to kill you."
"By Allāh, I am willing to kill you as long as you continue to deny the truth," retorted the Commander of the Faithful, peace be on him.
At that he became angry and said: "Will you kill me?"

He dismounted from his horse, hocked it and struck its face until it leapt away. Then he advanced towards 'Alī, peace be on him, with his sword drawn. He brought his sword quickly against him but he got his sword caught in the shield of 'Alī, peace be on him. The Commander of the Faithful, peace be on him, struck a (fierce) blow against him and killed him.

When 'Ikrima b. Abī Jahl, Hubayra b. Abī Wahb and Ḍirār b. al-Khaṭṭāb saw 'Amr lying prostrate they turned their horses and fled until they rushed across the trench without looking at anything.

The Commander of the Faithful, peace be on him, went back to his former position. The spirits of those who had come out to the trench with ('Amr) were full of grief while ('Alī) recited:

> He supported stone idols because of his view which lacked judgement while I supported the Lord of Muḥammad because of true guidance.
>
> I struck him and I left him fallen like the stump of a palm tree between sandy ground and hills.

I refrained from taking his clothes even though if I had fallen, he would have robbed me of my clothes.

O people of the alliance (*aḥzāb*), do not think that Allāh will abandon His religion and His Prophet.

[Muḥammad b. ʻUmar al-Wāqidī reported: ʻAbd Allāh b. Jaʻfar told me on the authority of Abū ʻAwn on the authority of al-Zuhrī, who said:][17]
ʻAmr b. ʻAbd Wudd, ʻIkrima b. Abī- Jahl, Hubayra b. Abī Wahb, Nawfal b. ʻAbd Allāh b. al-Mughīra and Ḍirār b. al-Khaṭṭāb came one day during the campaign of the alliance to the trench. They began to go around it looking for a narrow place along it so that they could cross. They came to an (unguarded) place where they forced their horses to cross. They began to ride their horses in the area between the trench and Sulayʻ.

The Muslims held back: none of them advanced against them. ʻAmr b. ʻAbd Wudd began to call for a single-combat while he chided the Muslims saying:

I have become hoarse through calling to all of you, is there anyone who will come forward to fight in single combat?

All that time ʻAlī was standing ready to go out and fight against him. The Apostle of Allāh, may Allāh bless Him and His Family, ordered him to sit down and wait so that someone else might take action. However, on that day, the Muslims remained motionless as if birds were resting their heads because of the (great) status of ʻAmr b. ʻAbd Wudd and their fear of him, and those with him and those behind him.

After ʻAmr had been calling for battle for a long time and the Commander of the Faithful, peace be on him, started to stand up again, the Apostle of Allāh, may Allāh bless Him and His Family, said to him: "Come close to me, ʻAlī."

He went close to him and (the Prophet) took off his turban from his own head and put it on him and he gave him his sword, saying: "Carry out your task."
Then he said: "O Allāh, give him assistance."

He ran out towards ʻAmr. With him went Jābir b. ʻAbd Allāh al-Anṣāri, may Allāh have mercy on him, so that he might see what happened between the two men. When the Commander of the Faithful, peace be on him, reached ʻAmr, he said to him: "ʻAmr, in the days of ignorance (before the Prophet's mission), you

17 The account follows al-Wāqidī, *al-Maghāzi*, II, 470-72. But the *isnād* given is incorrect. al-Mufīd's account is .shorter.

used to say: 'No one will summon me to three - meaning al-Lāt, al-'Uzzā (and Manāt) - without me accepting them or one of them.'"
"Indeed," he replied.
"I summon you to the testimony that there is no God but Allāh and that Muḥammad is the Apostle of Allāh, and to submit to Allāh, Lord of the worlds," he said.
"Cousin," he answered, "delay this matter from me for a time."
"It would be better for you, if you adopted it," replied the Commander of the Faithful, peace be on him. Then he said, "Here is an alternative."
"What is that?"
"That you go back to where you came from," he replied.
"The women of Quraysh would never accept that," he answered.
"Then here is yet another alternative."
"What is that?"
"That you dismount and fight me," ('Alī) replied.
'Amr laughed and said: "This is not the course that I thought an Arab would desire of me. I am unwilling to kill a noble man like you. Moreover your father was a bosom companion of mine. (Go back, you are only a young man. I only want to fight the two older men (*shaykhayn*) of Quraysh, Abū Bakr and 'Umar.)"[18]
"But I want to fight you," retorted 'Alī, peace be on him.
'Amr became angry and dismounted. He struck his horse in its face so that it went back.

[Jābir, may Allāh have mercy on him, reported:]
The dust rose up around them so that I could not see them. But I heard the words *Allāhu Akbar* (Allāh is greater) coming out of it and I knew that 'Alī, peace be on him, had killed him. His companions fled with the horses jumping over the trench. The Companions of the Prophet, may Allāh bless Him and His Family, hurried forward when they heard the words *Allāhu Akbar*, searching for what these people had done. They found Nawfal b. 'Abd Allāh in the middle of the trench. His horse could not jump out of it. They began to hurl stones at him.

"Death should be nobler than this," he shouted to them. "Let one of you come down to me and fight against me."
The Commander of the Faithful, peace be on him, went down to him, struck him down and killed him.[19]

He followed Hubayra and hit him from behind. Then the binding of his saddle was struck and the armour on (his horse) fell off. 'Ikrima fled and Ḍirār b. al-

18 The two sentences in brackets are not in al-Mufīd's text.
19 In al-Wāqidī's version the rest of the fighting is attributed to al-Zubayr.

Khaṭṭāb made his escape.

Jābir said (of this): I do not know how to describe 'Alī's killing of 'Amr except with the words which Allāh used to tell the story of David and Goliath where He, may His affair be exalted, says: *So by the permission of Allāh, they routed them and David killed Goliath* (II 251).

[Qays b. Rabī' reported: Abū Hārūn al-'Abdī told us on the authority of Rabī'a al-Sa'dī, who said:]
I went to Ḥudhayfa b. al-Yamān and asked him: "O Abū 'Abd Allāh, let us talk about 'Alī, peace be on him, and his great qualities, for the Baṣrans say to us that we exaggerate (the qualities of) 'Alī. Aren't you someone who reports traditions about him?"

Ḥudhayfa answered: "Rabī'a, do not ask me about 'Alī, peace be on him. For, by Allāh in Whose hand is my soul, if all the actions of the Companions of Muḥammad, may Allāh bless Him and His Family, from the time of Allāh giving Muḥammad his mission until this present day were put in one balance of the scales and the actions of 'Alī, peace be on him, were put in the other, 'Alī's actions, peace be on him, would outweigh all their actions."
"This is something which no one could accept either standing or sitting," retorted Rabī'a.

"O vile fellow," declared Ḥudhayfa, "how do you think (otherwise)? Where were Abū Bakr, 'Umar, Ḥudhayfa and all the Companions of Muḥammad, may Allāh bless Him and His Family, on the day 'Amr b. 'Abd Wudd (called them to fight)? He called on them to fight in single combat and all the people drew back in fear except 'Alī, peace be on him. He went forward to fight him and Allāh killed him acting through his hand. By Allāh in Whose hand is Ḥudhayfa, his action on that day was greater in measure than the action of the Companions of Muḥammad, may Allāh bless Him and His Family, until the Day of Resurrection."

[Hishām b. Muḥammad reported on the authority of Ma'rūf b. Kharrabūdh, who said:]
At the battle of the Trench, 'Alī b. Abī Ṭālib recited:

> Was it against me that the horsemen rushed? Tell my companions about me and it.
>
> On that day, my zeal (to defend the Prophet) prevented me from fleeing.
>
> A penetrating sword in the head is not a blunt one.

I destroyed ‘Amr because he became tyrannical, with a sword of Indian iron, (a sword) of pure iron, a sharp cutting (sword).

I went away after I had left him fallen like the stump of a palm tree between sandy ground and hills.

I refrained from taking his clothes even though if I had fallen, he would have robbed me of my clothes.[20]

[Yunūs b. Bukayr reported on the authority of Muḥammad b. Isḥāq:][21]
When ‘Alī b. Abī Ṭālib, peace be on him, had killed ‘Amr, he came towards the Apostle of Allāh, Allāh bless Him and His Family, with a smiling face. ‘Umar asked him: "‘Alī, have you plundered his armour, for there is not any like it among the Arabs?"
"I was ashamed to uncover the private parts of my cousin," answered the Commander of the Faithful, peace be on him,

[‘Umar b. Abī al-Azharī reported on the authority of ‘Amr b. ‘Ubayd on the authority of al-Ḥasan:]
When ‘Alī, peace be on him, killed ‘Amr b. ‘Abd Wudd, he cut off his head, and took it and threw it before the Prophet, may Allāh bless Him and His Family. Abū Bakr and ‘Umar got up and kissed the head of ‘Alī, peace be on him.

[‘Alī b. al-Ḥakīm al-Awdī reported: I Heard Abū Bakr. b. ‘Ayyāsh say:]
‘Alī struck a more powerful blow than any other in Islam - that is the blow (which killed) ‘Amr b. ‘Abd Wudd. He, peace be on him, was struck down by a blow more inauspicious than any struck in Islam - that is the blow of Ibn Muljam, may Allāh curse him.

With regard to (the campaign) against the allies, Allāh the Exalted revealed: *When they came against you from above you and from below you and when your eyes looked away and your hearts were in your throats and you were entertaining doubts about Allāh, then at that place were the believers tested and violently shaken. The Hypocrites and those with sickness in their hearts were saying: Allāh and His Apostle have promised us nothing except deceit.* (XXXIII 10-12) *Allāh relieved the believers from fighting. Allāh was powerful and mighty.* (XXXIII 25)

---

20 The last two verses are reported in the verses on page 65.

21 cf. Guillaumes's translation, *The Life of Muhammad*, (Oxford, 1955), 456, where he translates the following from Ibn Isḥāq on the authority of Ibn Sayyid al-Nāṣ.

Thus he directed against them censure, blame, reproof and a sermon. By (common) consent the only person excluded from the blame was the Commander of the Faithful, peace be on him, since the conquest had been brought about by him and through his hands. His killing of 'Amr and Nawfal b. 'Abd Allāh was the cause of the defeat of the polytheists. The Apostle of Allāh, may Allāh bless Him and His Family, said: "From this moment we will raid them, and they will (no longer) raid us."

[Yūsuf b. Kulayb reported on the authority of Sufyān b. Zayd, on the authority of Qurra and others, on the authority of 'Abd Allāh b. Mas'ūd:]
He ('Abd Allāh b. Mas'ūd) used to recite this verse (XXXIII 25): *Did not Allāh relieve you from fighting (through 'Alī?) Allāh was powerful and mighty.*

About the killing of 'Amr b.'Abd Wudd, Ḥassān b. Thābit, may Allāh have mercy on him, used to recite:

> The young 'Amr b. 'Abd has come close to the flanks of Yathrib. Repayment (for his death) is not expected.
>
> You found our swords drawn, you found our good horses were not deficient.
>
> On the morning of the battle of Badr you saw a band who struck you with a blow which was not weak.
>
> You have come (to a state), 'Amr, when you will (no longer) be summoned to a great campaign, or to the mighty execution of repugnant deeds.[22]

It is said that when the poetry of Ḥassān b. Thābit reached the Banū 'Amīr, one of their young men. answered him. He recited in reply to Ḥassān's boasting and great praise about the Anṣār:

> By the Sacred House of God, you have lied. You did not kill us but it was by the sword of the Hāshimites, so boast on (about nothing to do with yourselves).
>
> By the sword of the son of 'Abd Allāh, Aḥmad (i.e. Muḥammad) and by the arm of 'Alī in the battle, you gained that. So stop.
>
> You did not kill 'Amr b. 'Abd through your courage. But it was a rival like a great old lion.

---

22 cf. Ibn Hishām, *Sira*, 710.

It was 'Alī, whose standing in pride has lasted long. So do not make so many claims against us and look scornful.

At Badr, you came out for battle and the leaders of Quraysh openly held back from you and delayed.

Then when Ḥamza and 'Ubayda came against them and 'Alī came forward brandishing his Indian sword,

They said: "Yes these are truly our equals." So they came forward against them quickly since they wished (for battle) and showed pride.

'Alī circled the field in Hāshimite style. (It was he who) destroyed them when they showed haughtiness and pride.

There is no case for your pride over us with anyone else. There is no case for your proud boasts to be considered and mentioned.

[Aḥmad b 'Abd al-'Azīz reported: Sulaymān b. Ayyūb told us on the authority of Abū al-Ḥusayn al-Madā'inī, who said:]
When 'Alī b. Abī Ṭālib, peace be on him, killed 'Amr b. 'Abd Wudd and the news of his death was given to his sister, she asked: "Who attacked him?"
"'Alī b. Abī Ṭālib," they told her.
She said: "His death can only be considered (as being brought about) at the hand of a noble equal. There is no reason that my tears should cease since I have shed them for him who has killed heroes and has come forward in battle against an equal. His fate was at the hand of a noble equal. I have not heard of a man with more (right to) pride than this man, O Banū 'Amīr."

Then she began to recite:

If the killer of 'Amr had been any other man, I would have wept for ever.

But the killer of 'Amr cannot be charged with any defect. He was a man who was called of old the foremost of the land.

She also recited concerning the killing of her brother and remembrance of 'Alī b. Abī Ṭālib, the blessings and peace of Allāh be on him:

Two lions attacked one another in a narrow field of battle, each of them was a noble and brave equal.

Both of them wanted to tear the souls away from each other in the middle of the battlefield, either by stealth or by fighting.

Both attended the struggle with zeal. No distracting distraction diverted either man from that.

Then 'Alī, go, for you have never gained a victory like this. That is a true statement in which there is no unfairness.

'Alī, vengeance will be mine. Would that I could come upon him, then my blood-vengeance would be complete.

Quraysh have been humiliated after the death of a (noble) horseman. Thus humiliation is what will destroy them and disgrace is all-embracing.

Then she said: "By Allāh, as long as Quraysh do not avenge my brother, the old she-camel will remain unmarried."

The Campaign against the Banū Qurayẓa[23]

When the allies were routed and turned their backs (in flight) from the Muslims, the Apostle of Allāh, may Allāh bless Him and His Family, turned his attention to the Banū Qurayẓa. He sent the Commander of the Faithful, peace be on him, to them with thirty men from (the tribe) of Khazraj. He told him: "See whether Banū Qurayẓa have left their fortresses."

When he looked over their walls, he heard them cursing. He returned to the Prophet, may Allāh bless Him and His Family, and gave him the information. He said: "Leave them. Indeed Allāh will give us power over them, for He who gave you power over 'Amr b. 'Abd Wudd will not desert you. Therefore wait until the people gather before you and tell them of the victory brought through Allāh. Allāh, the Most High, has helped me by (spreading) terror from here to a distance of a month's (travel)."

'Alī, peace be on him, reported: The people gathered before me. I went up close to their walls. One of them shouted out: "The killer of 'Amr has come against you." Another called out: "The killer of 'Amr has come towards you." They began to shout to one another, telling each other about that. Allāh threw terror into their hearts and I heard a reciter say:

23 This account summarises the reports of al-Ṭabarī, I, 1385, and Ibn Hishām, *Sira*, 684-89. However, they do not include the details about 'Alī and the fear he caused, nor his words at the time of the execution, though al-Ṭabarī gives his name as one of the executioners.

'Alī has killed 'Amr.
'Alī has hunted down a hawk.
'Alī has punished a wrongdoer.
'Alī has weakened (their) affair.
'Alī has brought (them) shame.

I said: "Praise be to Allāh Who has given victory to Islam and suppressed polytheism."

The Prophet, may Allāh bless Him and His Family, had said to me when I had set off towards the Baūu Qurayẓa: "Go with the blessing, of Allāh, the Most High. Indeed Allāh has promised you their land and their estates."

I went in the certainty of the help of Allāh, the Mighty and High. I planted the standard at the chief fortress. They received me, while remaining in their fortresses, with curses against the Apostle of Allāh, may Allāh bless Him and His Family.

When I heard them cursing him, I so hated to hear that being said against the Apostle of Allāh, may Allāh bless Him and His Family, that I determined to return to him. Yet he, may Allāh bless Him and His Family, had already appeared and had heard them cursing him. He called out to them: "Brothers of apes and pigs, when we arrive at the court of the people, then how evil will be the morning of those who have been warned."

They replied: "Abū al-Qāsim, you did not use to be an ignorant man nor one who cursed much."

The Apostle of Allāh, may Allāh bless Him and His Family, felt ashamed and went back for a little while. Then he ordered his tent to be pitched opposite their fortresses. The Prophet, may Allāh bless Him and His Family, remained besieging the Banū Qurayẓa for twenty-five days. At last they asked him (for surrender terms), agreeing that they should submit to the judgement of Sa'd b. Mu'ādh. Sa'd decreed the sentence that the men should be killed, the women and children enslaved and their property divided out.

"Sa'd, you have given judgement on them according to Allāh's judgement from above the seven firmaments," the Prophet, may Allāh bless Him and His Family, told him. Then the Prophet ordered their men to be brought - they were nine hundred - and they were taken to Medina. The property was divided out and the women and children were enslaved. When the prisoners were brought to

Medina, they were detained in the houses of the Banū al-Najjār.

The Apostle of Allāh, may Allāh bless Him and His Family, went out to the place which is now the market. Trenches had been dug there. The Commander of the Faithful, peace be on him, was present and with him were the Muslims. He had ordered them to come out. He had earlier told the Commander of the Faithful, peace be on him, that the heads (of the prisoners) should be struck (so that they fell) into the trench. (The prisoners) were brought out in groups. Among them were Ḥuyayy b. Akhṭab and Ka'b b. Asad. At that time they were the leaders of the people. They had said to Ka'b when they were about to be taken to the Apostle of Allāh: "Ka'b, what do you think he will do with us?"

He answered: "You don't seem to understand anything anywhere. Don't you see that the man who summons you will not desist and that whoever goes will not return? By God, (your future) is to be killed."

Ḥuyayy b. Akhṭab was brought out with his two hands tied around his neck. When he looked towards the Apostle of Allāh, may Allāh bless Him and His Family, he said: "By God, I do not blame myself for my hostility to you. Yet whomsoever God deserts, is deserted."

Then he approached the people and said: "People, there is no escape from the order of God. It is written and ordained. It has been decreed that such slaughter is the lot of the Banū Isrā'īl."

Then he stood before the Commander of the Faithful, peace be on him, while saying: "Noble victims are slain by a noble hand."
"Rather," replied the Commander of the Faithful, peace be on him, "the select of the people will kill the evil ones among them and the evil ones among them will kill the select. There will be woe to those whom the select and noble kill and there will be happiness for those whom the wicked unbelievers kill."
"True," he replied, "but do not plunder my robes."
"It would be most despicable of me to do that," he answered.
"You have covered me, may God cover you," he said and stretched out his neck. 'Alī, peace be on him, struck it and he did not plunder him in front of them. Then the Commander of the Faithful, peace be on him, asked those who had brought him: "What was Ḥuyayy saying while he was being led to his death?"

They replied that he was saying:

> By your life, Ibn Akhṭab does not blame himself but whomsoever God deserts is deserted.

> He strove until his soul attained (the maximum) of its exertion, and he has attempted to search for greatness in every disturbing situation.

The Commander of the Faithful, 'Alī, blessings and peace be on him, said:

> He was a man of earnestness, earnestness in his unbelief. He was brought out to us in bonds as he was forcibly pulled along.
>
> I put my sword around his neck with a blow of one who preserves (the truth). He went to the pit of Hell as the captive he was.
>
> That is the place of return for unbelievers, while those who obey the commands of Allāh are the creatures who will dwell in eternal (happiness).

The Apostle of Allāh, may Allāh bless Him and His Family, chose from their women (Rayḥāna, daughter of) 'Amr b. Khunāfa. Of their women, only one was killed. She had thrown a stone at him when he had come in front of the Jews in order to negotiate with them before the war broke out between them. Allāh protected him from that stone.

The conquest of the Banū Qurayẓa and Allāh's victory to the Prophet, may Allāh bless Him and His Family, was brought about through the Commander of the Faithful, and because of those whom he had killed and because of terror which Allāh, the Mighty and High, threw into their hearts with regard to him. This great virtue has already been described among his virtues, peace be on him, just as this quality has already been mentioned in the enumeration of his qualities, peace be on him.

(The Battle of Dhāt al-Salāsil)[24]

(The part played) by the Commander of the Faithful, peace be on him, in the campaign of Wādī al-Raml - it is reported that it was named the campaign of Dhāt al-Salāsil - has been preserved by religious scholars, recorded by jurists, handed down by traditionists (*aṣḥāb al-athār*) and reported by historians (*naqalat al-akhbār*) as being one of the matters which may be attributed to his qualities, peace be on him, and described as one of his outstanding virtues in battle (*jihād*). (The account) has been agreed as a single unit in sense by all men.

---

24 This account is out of place. A fuller version is given, pages 240-244. cf al-Ṭabarī, I, 1604-5 and al-Wāqidī, *al-Maghāzī*, II, 769-71. In their account, first 'Amr b. al-'Āṣ is sent and then Abū 'Ubayda. There is no mention of 'Ali.

The biographers of the Prophet (*aṣḥāb al-siyar*) have reported that one day the Prophet, may Allāh bless Him and His Family, was sitting down when a Bedouin came and squatted in front of him and said: "I have come to advise you."
"What is your advice?" he asked.
"A group of Arabs," he told him, "have plotted to come and attack you at night in Medina." Then he described them to him.

Then (the Prophet) ordered the Commander of the Faithful, peace be on him, to call out: "The prayer is general (*al-ṣalāt jāmi'a*, i.e. all should attend the prayer)." The Muslims gathered and the Prophet went up on to the pulpit. He praised and glorified Allāh. Then he said: "People, there is an enemy of Allāh and of you. (News) has come for you that they will attack you at night in Medina. Who will go to the valley?"

One of the Emigrants stood up and said: "I will go there, Apostle of Allāh."
So he gave him the flag and gathered seven hundred men for him. Then he said to him: "Depart in the name of Allāh."

He arrived before the people at mid-morning. They said to him: "Who is the man?"
"I am a messenger of the Apostle of Allāh," he answered. "Either you declare: There is no God but Allāh alone, Who has no partner and Muḥammad is His servant and His Apostle; or I will strike you down with my sword."

"Go back to your master," they told him, "for we are in such numbers as you could have no power over."
The man returned and informed the Apostle of Allāh about that. The Prophet, may Allāh bless Him and His Family, (again) asked: "Who will go to the valley?"

Another man from the Emigrants stood up and said: "I will go there, Apostle of Allāh." He gave him the standard and he set out. Then he returned exactly as his first colleague had returned. Then the Apostle of Allāh, may Allāh bless Him and His Family, said: "Where is 'Alī b. Abī Ṭālib?"

The Commander of tile Faithful, peace be on him, stood up and said: "I am here, Apostle of Allāh."
"Go to the valley," he told him.
"Yes," he replied.

He had a turban which he could not put on until the Prophet, may Allāh bless Him and His Family, sent him on a difficult mission. He went to the house of

Fāṭima, peace be on her, and he asked her for the turban.
"Where are you going?" she asked. "Where has my father sent you?"
"To Wādī al-Raml," he answered.
She wept in anxiety for him. The Prophet came in while she was still in that state. "Why are you crying?" he said. "Are you afraid that your husband will be killed? No indeed, not if Allāh, the Exalted, wishes (him not to be)."
"Don't deprive me of heaven, Apostle of Allāh," 'Alī, peace be on him, said to him.

Then he set out. With him he took the standard of the Prophet. He went on until he reached people in the evening. He waited until morning and then prayed the morning prayer with his companions. He put them in ranks and leant on his sword as he advanced towards the enemy.

"Men," he called out, "I am the messenger of the Apostle of Allāh to you that you should declare: There is no God but Allāh and Muḥammad is His servant and His Apostle. If you do not, I will strike you down with my sword."
"Go back like your colleagues went back," they said.
"By Allāh, I will not go back until you submit to Islam or I have struck you down with this sword of mine," he answered. "I am 'Alī b. Abī Ṭālib b. 'Abd al-Muṭṭalib."

The people became agitated when they realised who he was. Then they became courageous enough to fight against him, peace be on him. He killed six or seven of them. Then the polytheists fled and the Muslims were victorious. They collected up the booty and he set off back to the Prophet, may Allāh bless Him and His Family.

[It is reported on the authority of Umm Salama, the mercy of Allāh be on her, who said:]
The Prophet of Allāh, may Allāh bless Him and His Family, used to take a siesta in my house. When he woke up frightened by a dream, I told him: "Allāh is He Who will give you neighbourly protection."
"True," he said, "Allāh is the One Who will give me neighbourly protection. But Gabriel, peace be on him, told me that 'Alī is coming."

Then he went out to the people and ordered them to meet 'Alī. The Muslims positioned themselves in two ranks with the Apostle of Allāh, may Allāh bless Him and His Family. When ('Alī) saw the Prophet he dismounted from his horse and bent to (the Apostle's) feet to kiss them. The (Prophet) said to him, peace be on him: "Mount (your horse). Allāh, the Exalted, and His Apostle are pleased with you."

The Commander of the Faithful, peace be on him, wept with joy and went off to his house. The Muslims handed over the booty. Then the Prophet, may Allāh bless Him and His Family, asked some of those who were with him in the army: "What did you think of your commander?"
"We were aware of nothing from him except that he never led us in the prayer without reciting in it: *Say: He is One Allāh* (CXII)," they answered.
"I will ask him about that," said the Prophet, may Allāh bless Him and His Family.

When he came upon him, he asked him, "Why in the statutory prayers, did you only recite *Sūrat al-Ikhlāṣ* (CXII) with them?"
"Apostle of Allāh," he answered, "I loved it."
"Indeed Allāh has loved you as you have loved it," said the Prophet, may Allāh bless Him and His Family. Then he said: "'Alī if it was not for the fact that I am concerned that some factions will say of you what the Christians say of Jesus, son of Mary, I would say of you today words such as (after them) you would never pass a gathering of men without them taking the soil from your feet."

The conquest in this campaign was especially due to the Commander of the Faithful, peace be on him, after others had completely failed in it. 'Alī, peace be on him, was especially singled out for praise for it from the Prophet, may Allāh bless Him and His Family. These are virtues the like of which did not occur in anyone else. Many biographers of the Prophet (*aṣḥāb al-siyar*) have mentioned that it was with regard to this campaign that the *Sūrat al-'Ādiyāt* (the Swift-Runners) (C) was revealed to the Prophet and that it includes the report of the circumstances in which the Commander of the Faithful, peace be on him, acted there.

The Campaign against the Banū al-Muṣṭaliq[25]

Then there are the reports which are well known among religious scholars of his heroism, peace be on him, against the Banū al-Muṣṭaliq. The conquest was due to him in that campaign after men from the Banū 'Abd al-Muṭṭalib had been struck down. The Commander of the Faithful, peace be on him, killed two of the enemy: they were Mālik and his son. The Prophet of Allāh took many prisoners whom he divided out among the Muslims. Among the prisoners captured on that day were Juwayra daughter of al-Ḥārith b. Abī Ḍirār. The

25 'Ali's exploits are reported by al-Ṭabarī, I, 1516, and Ibn Hishām, *Sira*, 729, but in that account he does not have any part in the Prophet's acquisition of Juwayra.

battle-cry of the Muslims during the battle with the Banū al-Muṣṭaliq was: *Ya Manṣūr, amit*. "O He Who is victorious, bring death," The Commander of the Faithful, peace be on him, captured Juwayra and took her to the Prophet, may Allāh bless Him and His Family. Her father came to the Prophet after the rest of the tribe had submitted to Islam and said: "O Apostle of Allāh, my daughter should not be a prisoner because she is a noble woman."
"Go and ask her choice," he told him.
"You are good and kind," he replied.
Then her father went to her and said: "My little child, do not disgrace your tribe."
"I have chosen Allāh and His Apostle," she answered.
"Allāh has now done this for you," her father told her.

It was settled and the Apostle of Allāh freed her and put her in the group of his wives.

(The Expedition to al-Ḥuḍaybiyya)[26]

(The expedition to) al-Ḥuḍaybiyya followed (the campaign against) the Banū al-Muṣṭaliq. At that time the standard was given to the Commander of the Faithful, peace be on him, just as it had been on many occasions before that. His bravery in the ranks of the men on that day both in war and battle has appeared from what was reported and mention of it has become widespread. That was after the pledge of allegiance (*bay'a*) which the Prophet, may Allāh bless Him and His Family, took from his Companions and (they gave) their covenants to remain steadfast. The Commander of the Faithful, peace be on him, was the one who took the women's pledge of allegiance on behalf of the Prophet, may Allāh bless Him and His Family. On that day their pledge of allegiance took the form that he threw a robe between himself and them and he rubbed it with his hand and they made their pledge of allegiance to the Prophet, may Allāh bless Him and His Family, by rubbing the robe. Then the Apostle rubbed the robe of 'Alī, peace be on him.

Other things connected with (the expedition to) al-Ḥuḍaybiyya are (as follows). When Suhayl b. 'Amr saw them and came towards their position, he begged the Prophet, may Allāh bless Him and His Family, for peace. Inspiration came down on the Prophet in answer to that, and that he should make the Commander of the Faithful, peace be on him, his writer on that day and the one who would take down the peace treaty in his handwriting.

The Prophet, may Allāh bless Him and His Family, said to him: "'Alī, write

26 The details of 'Alī's involvement with women's pledge do not seem to be reported by the early histories nor the prophecy of 'Alī's treaty. The other accounts are not recorded by them.

down: In the name of Allāh, the Merciful, the Compassionate."

"This is something which is being written between us and you, Muḥammad," Suhayl b. 'Amr intervened. "Therefore begin with something which we accept and write: In Your name, O God."

The Prophet, may Allāh bless Him and His Family, said to the Commander of the Faithful, peace be on him: "Remove what you have written and write: In Your name, O God."

"If it was not for the fact that I obey you, Apostle of Allāh, I would not remove: In the name of Allāh, the Merciful, the Compassionate," the Commander of the Faithful, peace be on him, replied. Then he removed it and wrote: In Your name, O God.

Then the Prophet, may Allāh bless Him and His Family, told him: "Write: This is what the Apostle of Allāh and Suhayl b. 'Amr have agreed upon."
However Suhayl b. 'Amr again intervened, saying: "If I accepted this description of you in this document which is being made between us, I would have admitted prophethood to you, otherwise by agreeing to that I would be witnessing against myself or at least expressing it with my tongue. Remove this name and write: This is what Muḥammad b. 'Abd Allāh has agreed upon."

"Indeed, by Allāh, he is truly the Apostle of Allāh despite your arrogance," said the Commander of the Faithful, peace be on him.
"Write his name as the condition which must be carried out," retorted Suhayl.
"Suhayl, woe on you, cease from your obstinate behaviour," the Commander of the Faithful, peace be on him, said to him.
"Remove it, 'Alī," the Prophet, may Allāh bless Him and His Family, ordered him.
"Apostle of Allāh," he said, "my hand will not move to remove your name from association with prophethood."
"Then put my hand on it," he said to him.

He did that and the Apostle of Allāh removed it with his own hand. Then he said to the Commander of the Faithful, peace be on him: "You will be asked to do the same and you will agree to it despite any pain (it causes you)."

The Commander of the Faithful, peace be on him, completed the document. When the truce had been completed, the Apostle of Allāh, may Allāh bless Him and His Family, slaughtered his sacrificial victim, which had been destined for

Mecca, where he was.

The system of the organisation of this expedition had been dependent on the Commander of the Faithful, peace be on him. All that took place in it including the pledge of allegiance, the drawing up of the people in ranks for battle and then the truce and the writing of the document, had been due to the Commander of the Faithful, peace be on him. There was in what Allāh had arranged, the sparing of the shedding of blood and the well-being of the position of Islam.

The people have reported of the raid, two virtues with which he was specially singled out, in addition to what we have already mentioned.

We have added these to his great virtues and noble qualities.

[Ibrāhīm b. 'Umar reported on the authority of those men he relies upon, on the authority of Qāyid, the retainer of 'Abd Allāh b. Sālim, who said:]
When the Apostle of Allāh, may Allāh bless Him and His Family, set out on the *'umra* (the minor pilgrimage) of al-Ḥuḍaybiyya, he stopped at al-Juḥfa and did not find any water there. He sent Sa'd b. Mālik with the water-skins. However Sa'd returned with the water-skins after only going a little way. He said: "Apostle of Allāh, I was not able to continue. My legs stopped moving out of fear of the enemy."
"Sit down," the Prophet, may Allāh bless Him and His Family, told him.

Then he sent for another man. He went out with the water-skins but when he reached the place where the first had stopped, he also returned. The Apostle of Allāh asked him: "Why have you returned?"
"Apostle of Allāh," he answered, "by Him Who sent you with the truth as a prophet, I was not able to continue because of my fear."

The Apostle of Allāh summoned the Commander of the Faithful and sent him with the water-skins. Those who were thirsty came out but they were not complaining about his return since they had seen the return of those who had gone before him. 'Alī, peace be on him, went out with the water-skins. Eventually he reached al-Ḥarār and looked for water. Then be brought them back to the Prophet, may Allāh bless Him and His Family. There were shouts of joy for them. When he entered, the Prophet, may Allāh bless Him and His Family, declared: "Allāh is greater (*Allāhu akbar*)," and he prayed for goodness for him.

In this expedition, Suhayl b. 'Amr approached the Prophet and said to him: "Muḥammad, our slaves have joined you, send them back to us."

The Apostle of Allāh was so angry that the anger could be seen in his face. He said: "Men of Quraysh, desist or Allāh will send on you a man whose heart Allāh has examined for faith who will strike your necks according to (the requirements of) religion."

One of those present asked: "Apostle of Allāh, is Abū Bakr that man?"
"No," he answered.
"Then is it 'Umar?" he asked.
"No," he replied, "it is he who is patching sandals within the enclosure." The people hurried to the enclosure to see who the man was and there was the Commander of the Faithful, 'Alī b. Abī Ṭālib peace be on him.

A group of men report this tradition on the authority of the Commander of the Faithful. In it they say that 'Alī, peace be on him, told this story and then he said: "I heard the Apostle say: Whoever vies against 'Alī deliberately, will take as his own a place in Hell-fire."

What the Commander of the Faithful, peace be on him, was repairing was the strap of one of the sandals of the Prophet, may Allāh bless Him and His Family. It had broken and he was patching the place and repairing it.

[Ismā'īl b. 'Alī al-'Ammī reported on the authority of Na'il b. Najīḥ, on the authority of 'Amr b. Shamir, on the authority of Jābir b. Yazīd, on the authority of Abū Ja'far Muḥammad b. 'Ali, on the authority of his father, peace be on them, who said:]
The strap of the sandal of the Prophet, may Allāh bless Him and His Family, had broken. He gave it to 'Alī, peace be on him, to repair. Then he walked with one sandal for the distance of about a bow-shot. He approached his Companions and said: "One among you will fight for the interpretation (of the Qur'ān) as he fought with me for its revelation."
"I am that man, Apostle of Allāh," said Abū Bakr.
"No," he replied.
"I, Apostle of Allāh," said 'Umar.
"No," he replied.
The people desisted and looked at one another. The Apostle of Allāh, may Allāh bless Him and His Family, said: "It is the one who is repairing the sandal." Then he indicated with his hand towards 'Alī b. Abī Ṭālib, peace be on him. "He will fight for the interpretation (of the Qur'ān) when my practice (*sunna*) is abandoned and neglected and the Book of Allāh is distorted and when those who have no right speak of religion, 'Alī, peace be on him, will fight them in order to revive the religion of Allāh, the Exalted."

The Campaign against Khaybar

After al-Ḥuḍaybiyya, there followed the campaign against Khaybar. In that too, beyond any doubt, success was due to the Commander of the Faithful, peace be on him. What has been gathered from the accounts of the reporters makes clear his great merit in this campaign, and uniquely characterizes him in the qualities shared by no other person.

[Yaḥyā b. Muḥammad al-Azdī reported on the authority of Mas'ada b. Yasa' and 'Abd Allah b. 'Abd al-Raḥīm, on the authority of 'Abd al-Mālik b. Ḥishām and Muḥammad b. Isḥāq and other traditionists (*aṣḥāb al-āthār*), who say:][27]

When the Apostle of Allāh, may Allāh bless Him and His Family, drew near to Khaybar, he said to the people: "Halt"

The people halted and he raised his hand towards the sky and said: "O Allāh, Lord of the seven heavens and what they shade, Lord of the seven earths and what they maintain, Lord of the devils and what they lead astray, I ask You for the good of this village and the good of what is in it and I seek refuge with You from its evil and the evil that is in it."

Then he went down under a tree in that place. He stayed there and we stayed there for the rest of that day. On the next day at mid-day, the herald of the Apostle of Allāh, may Allāh bless Him and His Family, summoned us and we gathered before him. There was a man sitting with him. He said: "This man came to me while I was sleeping. He drew my sword and said: 'Muhammad, who can save you from me today?' I told him: 'Allāh will save me from you.' Then he sheathed the sword and has remained sitting here without moving as you see."

"Apostle of Allāh, perhaps something has disturbed his reason," we suggested.

"Yes," said the Apostle of Allāh, may Allāh bless Him and His Family, "leave him."

Then he turned away and did not pay any attention to him.

The Apostle of Allāh, may Allāh bless Him and His Family, besieged Khaybar for more than twenty days. At that time the standard was held by the Commander of the Faithful, peace be on him. He was suffering from pains in his eyes which kept him from the battle (for a time). The Muslims used to attack the Jews in front of their forts and at the sides. One day they overcame the gate but they had

27 In parts it follows Ibn Hishām's account (*Sira*, 567-62) very closely but it omits large portions that do not concern 'Alī and elaborates those that do. According to Ibn Hishām Marḥab is killed by Muhammad b. Maslama. The account of the gate is given in several versions, but according to Ibn Hishām's version it was seven men who could not lift it.

dug a trench around themselves. Marḥab came out on foot to oppose them in battle.

The Apostle of Allāh, may Allāh bless Him and His Family, summoned Abū Bakr and said to him: "Take the standard."
He took it with a number of the Emigrants and they fought without achieving anything. He returned vigorously denouncing the people who had followed him while they were just as vigorously blaming him.

The next day he gave it to 'Umar. The latter went a little way with it and then came back accusing his followers of cowardice while they were also accusing him of cowardice.

Then the Prophet, may Allāh bless Him and His Family, said: "This standard is not for anyone to carry whom they can accuse of cowardice to me. It is for 'Alī b. Abī Ṭālib."
"He has bad eyes," he was told.
"Show him to me and you will show me a man who loves Allāh and His Apostle and whom Allāh and His Apostle love. He takes things up in the right way and he will not flee," he said.

They brought 'Alī b. Abī Ṭālib, peace be on him, leading him to him.
"What is troubling you, 'Alī?" the Prophet, may Allāh bless Him and His Family, asked him.
"Sore eyes which prevent me from seeing and a pain in my head," he answered.
"Sit down," he told him, "and put your head on my thigh."
'Alī, peace be on him, did that and the Prophet, may Allāh bless Him and His Family, prayed for him. He spat some saliva into his hand and rubbed it on his eye and his head. His eyes opened and the pain in the head which he had had was eased. He had said in his prayer: "O Allāh, make the heat and the cold obedient." He gave him the standard; it was a white standard. He said: "Take the standard and set forth with it. Gabriel is with you. Victory is in front of you and terror is spread into the hearts of the enemy. Be aware, 'Alī, that they have found in their Book that the name of the one who will destroy them is Īliyā. When you meet them, say: I am 'Alī, then they will forsake (the field) if Allāh, the Exalted, wishes."

The Commander of the Faithful, peace be on him, reported: I set out with it until I came to the fortress. Marḥab came out. He was wearing a helmet in which a stone had made a hole showing the white of his head. He was reciting:

Khaybar knows that I am Marḥab - the carrier of arms, a hero who has been tested.

I answered:

I am he whom my mother called a lion.
Like a lion of the forests, fierce in strength,
With my sword I will make you weigh the weight of an ear torn off.

We exchanged blows. I came quickly against him and struck him. I cut through (the place where) the hole (was) in the helmet and through his head so that my sword reached his teeth. He fell dead.

In the account it is reported that when the Commander of the Faithful said: "I am 'Alī b. Abī Ṭālib," one of the rabbis of the people called out to them: "I swear by what was revealed to Moses that you are defeated." As a result such terror entered their hearts that they were not able to bear it.

When the Commander of the Faithful, peace be on him, killed Marḥab, those who had gone out with Marḥab withdrew and barred the gate of the fortress to keep him out. The Commander of the Faithful, peace be on him, advanced against it. He worked on it until he opened it. However, most of the people from the other side of the trench did not come across against him. Thus did the Commander of the Faithful, peace be on him, capture the gate of the fortress. Then he used it as a bridge across the trench so that they might go across and conquer the fortress. They seized booty. When they withdrew from the fortress the Commander of the Faithful, peace be on him, took the gate in his right hand and spread it out many metres over the ground. It used to take twenty men to lock that gate.

After the Commander of the Faithful, peace be on him, had brought about the conquest of the fortress and had killed Marḥab and Allāh had granted their property as booty to the Muslims, Ḥassān b. Thābit al-Anṣāri sought permission from the Apostle of Allāh to recite a poem about him.
He told him: "Recite it."
He recited:

'Alī was ashen-eyed, needing medicine, even then he did not find (the help of anyone) to nurse him.

The Apostle of Allāh healed him with saliva. He blessed the healer (*raqī*) and He blessed the healed.

He said: I will give the standard today, to a dauntless man, brave, one who loves the Apostle as a follower.

He loves Allāh and Allāh loves him. Through him Allāh will overcome the fortress, returning it to Allāh.

He distinguished 'Alī by that apart from all other creatures and he named him his helper and his brother.

[The traditionists have reported on the authority of al-Ḥasan b. Ṣāliḥ, on the authority of al-A'mash, on the authority of Abū Isḥāq, on the authority of Abū 'Abd Allāh al-Judalī, who said:]
I heard the Commander of the Faithful, peace be on him, say: "When I broke down the gate of Khaybar, I used it as a shield and I fought against them with it. When Allāh brought about their humiliation and I had made the gate a means of overcoming their fort, I threw it into their trench."
A man asked him: "How were you able to bear the weight of it?"
"It was only like my shield which was in my hands on other occasions," he answered.

The biographers of the Prophet (*aṣḥāb al-siyar*) report that when the Muslims left Khaybar, they tried to carry the gate. It could only be lifted by seventy men. Concerning the Commander of the Faithful, peace be on him, carrying the gate, the poet says:

Indeed a man who carried a huge gate at Khaybar in the campaign against the Jews was supported by great power.

He carried the great gate, a gate which was the door to the restless hearts, while the Muslims and the people of Khaybar were mustered.

He threw it down and it took seventy men to undertake the burden of picking it up again - all of these exerting themselves fully to do it.

At last they picked it up with much effort and difficulty and urging of one another to pick it up again.

One of the Shī'a poets also spoke of this, praising the Commander of the Faithful, peace be on him, and disparaging his enemies, as has been reported by Abū Muḥammad al-Ḥasan b. Muḥammad b. Jamhūr, who said: I recited this to Abū 'Uthmān al-Māzinī:

The Prophet sent with his victorious standard 'Umar b. Ḥantama, the blackest of black. He went forward with it until they came out against him.

Without spirit, he bent, he was filled with fear and he withdrew. He brought back to the Prophet a standard which he had refused (to take forward).

He did not fear the shame of it and the blameworthiness of it.

The Prophet wept for him and criticised him for it.

Then he called for a man, noble of vision, who would go forward. He advanced with it amid a group of men, while (the Prophet) prayed for him.

Surely he would not shun it nor be defeated? He brought the Jews to a sad state of withdrawal when he slaughtered.

The leader of their army, a man with a sharp sword, who struck out fiercely. Then he turned to (the rest of) the people after that and scattered them.

The flies flee and every eagle is a lion. Allāh oppressed them because of His love for the family of Muḥammad

And because of His love of those who support (the family) by shedding blood.

The Conquest of Mecca

The campaign against Khaybar was followed by situations which were not the same as those which had occurred before. We now (briefly) allude to them. The majority of these consisted of missions which the Prophet did not take part in. Nor was their importance the same as it had been before. This was due to the present weakness of the enemy and that some of the Muslims did not need the others. We have passed over the enumeration of these matters even though the Commander of the Faithful, peace be on him, played a great role both in word and deed in all of these events.

Then followed the conquest of Mecca. By it the situation of Islam was strengthened and the religion became powerful by virtue of what Allāh, may He be exalted, (had bestowed) on His Prophet, may Allāh bless Him and His Family. Through it the promise was fulfilled, which Allāh had earlier given in His words, may He be exalted: *When the help of Allāh and the conquest comes, you will see the people enter into the religion of Allāh in group after group* (CX 1-2). And Allāh, the Mighty and High, had said a long time before that: *You will enter the sacred Mosque in safety with your heads shaven or trimmed and without fear* (XLVIII 27).

Eyes were turned towards it and necks were stretched out (in expectancy) of it. Yet the Prophet of Allāh organised that affair by keeping his journey to Mecca secret and by keeping the purpose of his intentions towards the inhabitants of that city hidden. Allāh, the Most High, had demanded that he keep reports of it concealed from the Meccans so that he should surprise them when he entered the city. In the group to whom the secret was confided was the Commander of the Faithful, 'Alī b. Abī Ṭālib, peace be on him. He was the partner of the Apostle of Allāh, may Allāh bless Him and His Family, in the plan. Then the Prophet, may Allāh bless Him and His Family, spread it to a further group. The matter was arranged with regard to it according to circumstances, in all of which the Commander of the Faithful was unique in merit insofar as no other person participated in them to the same extent.

Among (the indications of) that (is the incident that occurred when) Ḥāṭib b. Abī Balta'a - who was from Mecca and had been present at Badr alongside the Apostle of Allāh, may Allāh bless Him and His Family - wrote to the Meccans, informing them of the secret that the Apostle of Allāh, may Allāh bless Him and His Family, was coming against them. Inspiration came to the Apostle of Allāh, informing him of what had been done and of Ḥāṭib's letter being sent to the people (of Mecca). The Apostle of Allāh, may Allāh bless Him and His Family, restored the situation through the Commander of the Faithful, peace be on him. If the situation had not been restored by him, the organisation on whose success the victory of the Muslims depended, would have been put in jeopardy. A report of this story has already been given earlier and there is no need for us to repeat it.[28]

*****

Abū Sufyān came to Medina to renew the treaty between the Apostle of Allāh, may Allāh bless him and grant him peace, and Quraysh, after the incident caused by a group of the Banū Bakr against (the tribe of) Khuzā'a when they had killed some of them. Abū Sufyān intended to restore his leading position among his people. He was afraid of the help of the Apostle of Allāh, may Allāh bless Him and His Family, might give to (al-Khuzā'a). Also he was afraid about what would happen to them (i.e. Meccans) on the day of the conquest. He came to the Prophet and spoke to him about it but he did not give any answer. He left him and met Abū Bakr and caught hold of him. He thought that he could gain his request from the Prophet, may Allāh bless Him and His Family, through him.
"I cannot do that," Abū Bakr answered because he knew that his asking about that would achieve nothing.

28 cf.35-37.

Then Abū Sufyān thought that 'Umar might have the same (influence) as he had previously thought Abū Bakr had had. He spoke to him about it but the latter pushed him away with a roughness and a harshness which would almost have corrupted one's view of the Prophet, may Allāh bless Him and His Family.

He turned aside to the house of the Commander of the Faithful, peace be on him. He asked permission to enter and permission was granted. With (the Commander of the Faithful) were Fāṭima, al-Ḥasan and al-Ḥusayn, peace be on them.

"'Alī," he said, "you are the closest of the people to me in relationship and kin and so I have come to you. Do not send me back as much without hope as I came. Intercede for me with the Apostle of Allāh for what I came for."
"Woe upon you, Abū Sufyān," he replied. "When the Apostle of Allāh, may Allāh bless Him and His Family, has decided on a matter, we cannot speak to him about it."

Abū Sufyān turned to Fāṭima, peace be on her, and said: "Daughter of Muḥammad, can you tell your two sons to give me neighbourly protection among the people? For they are lords of the Arabs to the end of time."
"My sons have not reached the age to grant neighbourly protection among the people," she answered, "and no one will grant neighbourly protection against the Apostle of Allāh, may Allāh bless Him and His Family."

Abū Sufyān was bewildered and felt helpless. Then he went up to the Commander of the Faithful, peace be on him, and said: "Abū al-Ḥasan, I see that matters have become confused as far as I am concerned. (Please,) advise me."
"I cannot see anything which will avail you," the Commander of the Faithful, peace be on him, told him. "However, you are the leader of the Banū Kināna. Therefore arise and grant protection among the people. Then go back to your land."
"Do you think that will help me at all?" he asked.
"No, by Allāh, I do not think so," he answered. "Yet, I can find nothing else."

So Abū Sufyān went and stood in the mosque and called out: "I have come to grant protection among the people."

Then he mounted his camel and departed. When he came back to Quraysh, they asked him: "What (was the situation you left) behind you?"
"I went to Muḥammad, may Allāh bless Him and His Family, and I spoke to him," he told them. "But he gave me no answer. Then I went to Ibn Abī Quḥāfa (Abū Bakr) and I found nothing better from him. Then I met Ibn al-Khaṭṭāb and I

found him harsh and rough without any kindness in him. Then I went to 'Alī and I found him the gentlest of men to me. He advised me to do something, which I did. By Allāh, I do not know whether it will be of any avail to me or not."
"What did he tell you to do?" they asked.
"He told me to grant protection among the people and I did so," he answered.
"Did Muḥammad permit that?" they asked.
"No," he replied.
"By Allāh, the man did no more than play with you," they told him. "It will not be of any use to you."
"No, by Allāh, but I could not find anyone else (to suggest anything)," he answered.[29]

The attitude of the Commander of the Faithful, peace be on him, towards Abū Sufyān was the most correct in terms of the fulfilment of the Muslims' task and for the (success) of the plan. Thus he (Abū Sufyān) brought about for the Apostle of Allāh, may Allāh bless Him and His Family, something, in the attitude of the people, which he would not have been able to achieve, if he had not been able to demonstrate that 'Alī had given Abū Sufyān the truth about his position. Also he achieved this because of his gentleness towards him, so that when he left Medina, he thought that there was some (hope for him). Thus through his departure in those circumstances he ceased from attempting to make a plot by which he might have thrown some disorder into the plan of the Prophet, may Allāh bless Him and His Family. For, if he had left in despair in the way the two men (i.e. Abū Bakr and 'Umar) had filled him with despair, he would have renewed the people's view of fighting against (the Prophet), peace be on him, and of guarding against him in a way which did not occur to them, after Abū Sufyān brought (news of) what he had done to them. For he had stayed in Medina to intrigue to gain his purpose of seeking intercession with the Prophet, may Allāh bless Him and His Family. In that way, he had intended to bring about a situation which would keep the Prophet away from Quraysh and by delaying him from them, (the Prophet) would have missed his opportunity. The success which was brought about through Allāh, the Most High, was connected with the vision of the Commander of the Faithful, peace be on him, insofar as he saw by dealing with Abū Sufyān he would enable the Prophet, may Allāh bless Him and His Family, to occupy Mecca as the latter had intended.

*****

When the Apostle of Allāh, may Allāh bless Him and His Family, ordered Sa'd b. 'Ubāda to enter Mecca carrying the standard, he became aggressive towards the people and showed the anger he felt against them. He entered Mecca shouting:

29 This account follows al-Ṭabarī, I, 1623-4 and Ibn Hishām, *Sira*, 807-808.

"Today is the day of slaughter, the day of capturing any daughter."

Al-'Abbās heard him and asked the Prophet: "Haven't you heard what Sa'd b. 'Ubada is saying? I am afraid that he will attack Quraysh fiercely."
"'Alī," said the Prophet, may Allāh bless Him and His Family, to the Commander of the Faithful, peace be on him, "go to Sa'd and take the standard away from him. You be the one who enters Mecca with it."

The Commander of the Faithful, peace be on him, went up to him and took it from him. Sa'd did not stop him from taking it from him.[30] The loss in this matter which would have been caused by Sa'd, was restored by (the action of) the Commander of the Faithful, peace be on him. The Apostle of Allāh, may Allāh bless Him and His Family, did not regard any of the Emigrants or Anṣār as suitable to take away the standard from the leader of the Anṣār except the Commander of the Faithful, peace be on him. He knew that if anyone else had wanted to do that, Sa'd would have refused him, and in his refusal there would have been caused a disruption of the plan and a dispute between the Anṣār and the Emigrants. Since Sa'd would not have lowered his position for any of the Muslims or for all the people except the Prophet, may Allāh bless Him and His Family, and since it would not be sound judgement for the Apostle of Allāh to take the standard from (Sa'd) himself, he appointed someone who could really take his place and could not be distinguished from him (the Prophet), someone to whom no one else within the group should be shown greater obedience. There was no one else characterised by rank and merit for this except the Commander of the Faithful, peace be on him. In such a quality no one else had a share nor was anyone else his equal. It was a lesson from Allāh, the Most High, and His Apostle, with regard to the attainment of public interest through the despatch of the Commander of the Faithful, apart from anyone else, which indicated his choice for decisive affairs, just as it was a lesson from Allāh with regard to whom He chose for prophethood and the fulfilment of the public good by sending him. This revealed their (i.e. the Prophet and the Commander of the Faithful) being the best of all creatures.

*****

The Apostle of Allāh, may Allāh bless Him and His Family, gave an instruction to the Muslims on setting out for Mecca that they should only kill those who fought against them. He guaranteed the security of those who clung to the veils of the Ka'ba except a group of them who had committed evil actions against him. Among these were Miqyas b. Ṣubāba, Ibn Khaṭal, Ibn Abī Sarḥ and two songstresses who had sung insulting songs about the Apostle of Allāh, may Allāh

30 Cf.37-38.

bless him an his family, and lamentations for the Meccans killed at Badr. The Commander of the Faithful, peace be on him, killed one of the songstresses and the other fled until refuge was found for her. A Persian struck her in al-Abṭah during the rule (*imāra*) of ʻUmar b. al-Khaṭṭāb and killed her. The Commander of the Faithful, peace be on him, also killed al-Ḥuwayrith b. Nufayl b. Kaʻb. He was one of those who had abused the Apostle of Allāh at Mecca.[31] He, peace be on him, learnt that his sister, Umm Hāni', had given refuge to some people from Banū Makhzūm, including al-Ḥārith b. Hishām and Qays b. al-Sā'ib. He, peace be on him, set out for her house wearing an iron helmet. He called: "Send out those to whom you have given refuge."

By Allāh, they began to act out of fear of him just like birds who let their droppings fall (from the sky). Umm Hāni' came out to him and she did not recognize him.

"Servant of Allāh," she said, "I am Umm Hāni', a cousin of the Apostle of Allāh, may Allāh bless Him and His Family. I am the sister of ʻAlī b. Abī Ṭālib, peace be on him. Therefore go away from my house."

"Bring them out," demanded the Commander of the Faithful, peace be on him.
"By Allāh, I will complain about you to the Apostle of Allāh, may Allāh bless Him and His Family," she told him.

Then he took his helmet off his head. She recognized him and she came close to him so that she might embrace him.
"May I be your ransom," she said, "I swore that I would complain about you to the Apostle of Allāh, may Allāh bless Him and His Family."
"Go and make good your oath," he told her. "He is at the top of the valley."

Umm Hāni' reported: I went to the Prophet while he was in his tent washing. Fāṭima, peace be on her, was keeping him veiled (from view). When the Apostle of Allāh, may Allāh bless Him and His Family, heard the sound of my voice, he said: "Welcome to Umm Hāni'."

"By my father and mother (whom I would ransom for) you," I said, "I have come to complain to you of the treatment I have received today from ʻAlī b. Abī Ṭālib."
"Have you given neighbourly protection to those to whom you (are reported to) have given neighbourly protection?" the Apostle of Allāh, may Allāh bless Him and His Family, asked.

31 Ibn Hishām, *Sira*, 820.

Then Fāṭima, peace be on her, said: "You have only come to complain of 'Alī because he caused the enemies of Allāh and of His Apostle to be afraid."

"May Allāh, the Most High, be thanked for the efforts of 'Alī b. Abī Ṭālib," said the Apostle of Allāh, may Allāh bless Him and His Family. "I grant neighbourly protection to those whom Umm Hāni' gave neighbourly protection because of her position through (her brother) 'Alī b. Abī Ṭālib, peace be on him."[32]

When the Apostle of Allāh, may Allāh bless Him and His Family, entered the (Sacred) Mosque, he found there three hundred and sixty idols. Some of them were attached to others by lead.

"Give me a handful of pebbles," he said to the Commander of the Faithful, peace be on him.
The Commander of the Faithful, peace be on him, picked up a handful and gave it to him. Then he threw it at them, saying: "*Say: Truth has come and falsehood has disappeared. Indeed falsehood was ever disappearing.*" (XVII 81).
Every idol fell face downwards. Then he ordered them to be taken out, thrown down and broken.

In the actions of the Commander of the Faithful, peace be on him, which we have mentioned concerning the enemies of Allāh he killed in Mecca, the fear he caused to those who had been traitors and the help which he gave to the Apostle of Allāh, may Allāh bless Him and His Family, in cleansing the (Sacred) Mosque of idols, his great bravery and his ignoring of kinship in obedience to Allāh, the Mighty and High, - all this - is evidence for him being characterised by great merit which no one else shared as we have already said.

*****

In connection with the conquest of Mecca is the despatch of Khālid b. al-Walīd by the Apostle of Allāh, may Allāh bless Him and His Family, to the Banū Ḥudhayfa b. 'Āmir. They were at al-Ghumayṣā'. He was supposed to summon them to Allāh, the Mighty and High. He only sent him because of the hostile connection which existed between him and them. In the Jāhiliyya, they had seized some women from the Banū al-Mughīra and killed al-Fākih b. al-Mughīra, the uncle of Khālid b. al-Walīd, and they had also killed 'Awf b. 'Abd al-Raḥmān b. 'Awf. It was for that reason that the Apostle of Allāh, may Allāh bless Him and His Family, had sent him. He also sent with him 'Abd al-Raḥmān b. 'Awf, who had a similar hostile relationship with them. If it had not been for that, the Apostle of Allāh, may Allāh bless Him and His Family, would not have deemed

32 Ibn Hishām, *Sira*, 820.

Khālid appropriate for command over the Muslims. We have already mentioned matters connected with him insofar as he had opposed the covenant of Allāh and the covenant of His Apostle and he had worked in the service of the practice of the Jāhiliyya; he had put the authority of Islam behind him; he had renounced the Apostle of Allāh through his action and losses caused by him had to be restored by the Commander of the Faithful, peace be on him. We have explained all this earlier, so that there is no need to repeat it here.

The Campaign against Ḥunayn

Then there was the campaign against Ḥunayn when the Apostle of Allāh, may Allāh bless Him and His Family, sought for help, because of the great number of those gathered against him. (The Prophet), peace be on him, went out towards the enemy with ten thousand Muslims. The majority of them thought that they would be victorious when they saw their gathering, their great numbers and their weapons. On that day, Abū Bakr was full of wonder at the great number. He said: "Today we will never be defeated as a result of being few in number."[33]

As it happened the affair turned out the very opposite to what they had thought and Abū Bakr had contributed to this by his wonder at their (great number). However, when they met the polytheists, it was not long before they (the polytheists) put them all to flight so that only ten men remained with the Prophet, nine of them were Hāshimites and the tenth was Ayman b. Umm Ayman. Ayman was killed, may Allāh have mercy on him. Eventually those who had fled began to return to the Apostle of Allāh, may Allāh bless Him and His Family. They returned one by one until they joined one another and there were (sufficient for) an attack on the polytheists. Concerning Abū Bakr's wonder at the great number, Allāh, the Most High, revealed: *At the Battle of Ḥunayn when your great number pleased you, it did not avail you in any way. The earth became too narrow for you (to escape) to the same extent (as before) it had been too wide for you. You turned your backs and fled. Then Allāh sent down calm (fortitude) on His Apostle and the Faithful* (IX 25-26). He means by "the Faithful", the Commander of the Faithful, 'Alī, peace be on him, and those of the Banū Hāshim who remained with him. On that day they were eight, and with the Commander of the Faithful they were nine. Al-'Abbās b. 'Abd al-Muṭṭalib was on the right of the Apostle of Allāh, al-Faḍl b. al-'Abbās was on his left. Abū Sufyān b. al-Ḥārith was holding his saddle at the rear of his mule, while the Commander of the Faithful, peace be on him, stood before him with his sword. Nawfal b. al Ḥārith, Rabī'a b. al-Ḥārith, 'Abd Allāh b. al-Zubayr b. 'Abd al Muṭṭalib and 'Utba and Ma'tib the two sons of Abū Lahab stood around him. All the rest, save those we have

33 al-Wāqidī, *al-Maghāzī*, 111, 890.

mentioned, turned their backs in flight.[34] Concerning this Mālik b. 'Ubāda al-Ghāfiqī recited:

> None consoled the Prophet except the sons of Hāshim in the face of the swords of the battle at Ḥunayn.
>
> The people fled, save for this group of nine. They were calling to the people: Where are you?
>
> Then they stood with the Prophet to face death. They denied us any ornament except shame.
>
> Ayman guarded the trusty one (i.e. Muḥammad) from the people (and died) a martyr, and thus gained (eternal) happiness as a reward.

Al-'Abbās b. 'Abd al-Muṭṭalib recited concerning this situation:

> We, nine, helped the Apostle of Allāh in the battle. The rest who could flee fled and scattered.
>
> Whenever al-Faḍl attacked with his sword against the people, my words (were):
> "Again my son, lest they return"
>
> The nine of us faced death itself because of what is given in the service of Allāh causes no (real) suffering.

(In the first poem) there is a reference to Ayman b. Umm Ayman, may Allāh have mercy upon him.

When the Apostle of Allāh, may Allāh bless Him and His Family, saw the flight of the people from him, he said to al-'Abbās, who was a man with a loud strong voice: "Call to the people and remind them of the covenant."

Al-'Abbās called out at the top of his voice: "People who made the pledge of allegiance at the tree, men of *Sūrat al-Baqara*, where are you fleeing? Remember the covenant which you made to the Apostle of Allāh, may Allāh bless Him and His Family."

However, the people went on and turned their backs (in flight). It was a pitch black night and the Apostle of Allāh was in the valley. The polytheists came

34 Ibn Hishām, *Sira*, 845, and al-Wāqidī, *al-Maghāzī*, III, 900 both include Abu Bakr and 'Umar in the group who remained with the Prophet.

against him from the mountain passes into the valley, and from the sides of the valley, and its narrow defiles, with their swords drawn, and with clubs and stones.

[They reported:] The Apostle of Allāh, may Allāh bless Him and His Family, looked toward the people (turning) part of his face (towards them) in the darkness. And he gave light as if he was the moon on the night of the full-moon. Then he called out to the Muslims: "Where are you who gave your pledge to Allāh (to protect) him?"

The first heard and then others of them. Not a man of them heard but did not fling himself to the ground and crawl down to where they were in the valley. When they met the enemy, they fought against them.

[They reported:] One of the Ḥawāzin approached in front of the people on a red camel with a black standard in his hand fixed on a long spear.[35] Whenever he gained a victory over the Muslims, he would turn them face downward. If any of the people escaped him, he would pass him on to the polytheists behind him and they would follow him.
He was reciting:

> I am Abū Jarwal, there will be no ceasing today until we destroy or are destroyed.

The Commander of the Faithful, peace be on him, directed himself towards him. He struck the buttocks of his camel and brought it down. Then he struck him and overcame him. He recited:

> Now the people know with whom the morrow belonged. In battle I am one who brings disgrace (to others).

The flight of the polytheists began with the killing of Abū Jarwal, may Allāh curse him. Then the Muslims felt rebuked and formed ranks against the enemy. The Apostle of Allāh, may Allāh bless Him and His Family, said: "O Allāh, you have made the first of Quraysh taste defeat, give the last of them pleasure (of victory)."

The Muslims and the polytheists began to fight together. When the Prophet, may Allāh bless Him and His Family, saw them, he put his saddle on my mount so that he might have a view of their group. Then he said:

> Now war has been kindled. I am the Prophet, that is no lie. I am the descendant of ʻAbd al-Muṭṭalib.

35 al-Wāqidī, *al-Maghāzī*, III, 902, gives a briefer account and involves Abū Dujāna with ʻAlī in the killing.

It was very soon after that the (enemy) turned their backs (in flight). The prisoners were brought in bonds to the Apostle of Allāh, may Allāh bless Him and His Family.

When the Commander of the Faithful, peace be on him, killed Abū Jarwal and the people shrank away because of him being killed, the Muslims began to ply them with their swords. The Commander of the Faithful, peace be on him, led them in this so that he killed forty men from these people. Thus was the defeat and the capturing of prisoners brought about at that time.

*****

Abū Sufyān Ṣakhr b. Ḥarb b. Umayya took part in this campaign. He was among the number of those of the Muslims who had fled (at first).

[It is reported on the authority of Mu'āwiya b. Abī Sufyān that he said:] I met my father fleeing with the Meccans of the Banū Umayya. I yelled out to him: "Son of Ḥarb, by Allāh, won't you endure with fortitude alongside your cousin? You have not fought for your religion nor have you faced these bedouin Arabs in order to protect your womenfolk."
"Who are you?" he asked.
"Mu'āwiya," I answered.
"The son of Hind?" he said.
"Yes," I replied.
"May I ransom you with my father and mother," he exclaimed.

Then he stopped and the Meccans gathered with him. I joined them. Then we attacked the people and scattered them. The Muslims continued to fight the polytheists and take them prisoner until day began to break. Then the Apostle of Allāh, may Allāh bless Him and His Family, ordered that none of the people taken prisoner was to be killed.

*****

During the days of the conquest (of Mecca) the tribe of Hudhayl had sent a man called Ibn al-Anza' to spy on the Prophet, may Allāh bless Him and His Family, so that he would gain information about him. He had gone back to Hudhayl with his report. At the battle of Ḥunayn, he was captured. 'Umar b. al-Khaṭṭāb passed by him. When he saw him, he went up to one of the Anṣār and said: "This is the enemy of Allāh, who came to us as a spy. Here he is a prisoner. Kill him."

The man from the Anṣār cut off his head. When the Prophet learnt of that, he disliked it and said: "Didn't I order you not to kill prisoners? Yet after that you killed Jamīl b. Mu'ammar b. Zuhayr while he was a prisoner."

Then the Prophet, may Allāh bless Him and His Family, sent to the Anṣār while he was still angry. He demanded: "What prompted you to kill him when the messenger had come to you (telling you) not to kill any prisoners?"
"We only killed him at the behest of 'Umar," they answered.

The Apostle of Allāh turned away (from them) until 'Umayr b. Wahb spoke to him about forgiving (them).

*****

The Prophet of Allāh made the distribution of the booty of Ḥunayn, particularly among the Quraysh. He gave a generous share to reconcile the hearts of some of them like Abū Sufyān Ṣakhr b. Ḥarb, 'Ikrima b. Abī Jahl, Ṣafwān b. Umayya, al-Ḥārith b. Hishām, Suhayl b. 'Amr, Zuhayr b. Abī Umayya, 'Abd Allāh b. Abī Umayya, Mu'āwiya b. Abī Sufyān, Hishām b. al-Mughīra, al-Aqra' b. Ḥābis, 'Uyayna b. Ḥiṣn and their like.

It is reported that he gave the Anṣār only a small part but that he gave most of it to the people whom we have named. A group of the Anṣār became angry on account of that. The Apostle of Allāh, may Allāh bless Him and His Family, was informed of their words of discontent against him. He summoned them and they gathered. He told them: "Sit down but do not let anyone other than your own people sit with you."

When they were seated the Prophet, may Allāh bless Him and His Family, came out and the Commander of the Faithful, peace be on him, followed him. He sat down in their midst and said to them: "I will ask you about a matter and then you answer me about it".
"Speak, Apostle of Allāh," they said.

"Were you not going astray and then Allāh sent you guidance through me?" he asked.
"Indeed", they answered, "the grace for that belongs to Allāh and His Apostle."

"Were you not on the edge of the pit of Hell-fire and then Allāh rescued you through me?" he asked.
"Indeed", they answered, "the grace for that belongs to Allāh and His Apostle."

"Were you not few and then Allāh made you many through me?" he asked.
"Indeed", they answered, "the grace for that belongs to Allāh and His Apostle."

"Were you not enemies (of each other) and then Allāh reconciled your hearts through me?" he asked.
"Indeed", they answered, "the grace for that belongs to Allāh and His Apostle."

The Prophet fell silent for a short time and then he said: "Will you answer me according to what is in your minds?"
"How else can we answer you?" they said. "Indeed it is our fathers and mothers (who have required) that we answer you by saying that you have outstanding merit, favour and stature over us."

"If you had wanted," he said, "you could have said: You came to us an exile and we gave you refuge. You came to us in fear (of your life) and we protected you. You came to us denounced as a liar and we believed in you."

They raised their voices in weeping. Their shaykhs and leaders stood up before him and kissed his hands and feet. Then they said:
"We are satisfied with Allāh and His Apostle. Here is our wealth (placed) before you. If you wish, divide it among your people. Those of us who spoke earlier (against you), only spoke out of jealousy, deception in the breast and sin in the heart. They had thought that (your action) was taken in anger against them and to reduce them. They seek forgiveness from Allāh for their sins. O Apostle of Allāh, forgive them."

Then the Prophet, may Allāh bless Him and His Family, said: "O Allāh, grant forgiveness to the Anṣār and the sons of the Anṣār, and the sons of the sons of the Anṣār. People of the Anṣār, are you not content that no one except you will return with grace and favour? For when you return (part of) your share (of the rewards of battle) will be (the presence of) the Apostle of Allāh (in your city)."
"Indeed," they replied, "we are content."

The Prophet, may Allāh bless Him and His Family, said: "On that day the Anṣār were my close supporters and my family. If the people had gone along the valley and the Anṣār had gone along a mountain pass, I would have gone along the mountain pass of the Anṣār. O Allāh, grant forgiveness to the Anṣār."

On that day the Apostle of Allāh, may Allāh bless Him and His Family, had given al-'Abbās b. Mirdās four camels. He was angry at this and recited:

> Do you divide my share of the booty and the share of al-'Ubayd between 'Uyayna and al-Aqra'?
>
> At any gathering (of people) neither Ḥiṣn nor Ḥābis would take

precedence over my leader.

I am no less a man than those two. Whoever you put down today will not be raised.

The Prophet, may Allāh bless Him and His Family, learned of what he had said and summoned him to attend him.
"You are the one who spoke these words: Do you divide my share of the booty and the share of al-'Ubayd between al-Aqra' and 'Uyayna," he said.

"No, may my father and mother be a ransom for you, you are not the poet," interrupted Abū Bakr.
"How is that?" he asked.
"Rather he said between 'Uyayna and al-Aqra'," he replied.
"Arise, 'Alī," the Apostle of Allāh, may Allāh bless Him and His Family, told the Commander of the Faithful, peace be on him, "and cut out his tongue for (what) it said."

"By Allāh, because of these words you are harsher with me than at the battle with Khath'am when they came against us in our houses," al-'Abbās b. Mirdās cried out. He caught hold of the hands of 'Alī b. Abī Ṭālib (and said): "Take me away. If I knew anyone who would free me from this, I would summon him. So I say to you, 'Alī, will you be the one who cuts out my tongue?"
"I will only carry out with you what I have been ordered to do," he said.

Al-'Abbās reported: He set off and remained with me until he brought me to the enclosures. He told me: "Count out the numbers between four and a hundred." I said: "May I ransom you with my father and mother. How generous, considerate and learned you are!"

"The Apostle of Allāh gave you four camels," he said, "and thus made you one of the number of the Emigrants. If you wish, just keep them. However, if you wish, take a hundred and be included with the people (who were given) a hundred."
"Advise me," I asked.
"I would advise you to take what the Apostle of Allāh, may Allāh bless Him and His Family, has given you and be satisfied with that," he told me.
"Then I will do so," I said.[36]

When the Apostle of Allāh, may Allāh bless Him and His Family, had

36 Ibn Hishām, *Sira*, 881-3, al-Wāqidī, *al-Maghāzī*, 946-7, without the part 'Ali played in the affair.

distributed the booty at Ḥunayn, a tall man with a lump of skin between his eyes, as a result of much prostration approached him. He greeted him without any specific reference to the Prophet. Then he said: "I have seen what you have done with this booty."
"How do you see it?" he asked.
"I consider that you have gone astray," he said.

At this, the Apostle of Allāh became angry and said: "Shame on you, since I have no injustice, who has it?"
"Shall we not kill him?" the Muslims asked.
"Leave him," he said. "He will have followers who will dart from this religion like the arrow darts from the bow. Allāh will bring about their death at the hand of the man most loved by Him after me."[37]

The Commander of the Faithful, 'Alī b. Abī Ṭālib, peace be on him, killed him among the Khawārij he killed at the battle of al-Nahrawān.

Consideration should be given to the qualities displayed by the Commander of the Faithful, peace be on him, in this campaign. If you ponder them and think about their implications, you will find that he, peace be on him, carried out every outstanding action which took place in it. Thus he is uniquely characterised by qualities which nobody else in the community (*umma*) shares. It was he, peace be on him, who stayed with the Apostle of Allāh when all the rest of the people fled except the small group who remained alongside him, peace be on him. We already have thorough knowledge of his precedence in courage, bravery, fortitude and vigour over al-'Abbās and al-Faḍl, his son, and Abū Ṣufyān b. al-Ḥārith and the rest of the group. (We have this) by the example of his actions on other occasions at which none of them were present. Reports of him are famous concerning his battle with men of equal rank and his killing of heroes. None of these has been known for anything similar to his exploits. No death of an enemy (in battle) is traced back to them by any famous report. Thus it can be realised that their remaining steadfast was through him, peace be on him. If it had not been for him, a crime would have been committed against religion which would not have been set right. By his taking up that attitude and his endurance with the Prophet, may Allāh bless him and grant him peace, the return of the Muslims to the battle was made possible and their encouragement to attack the enemy. His killing Abū Jarwal, the foremost of the polytheists, was the reason for the defeat of the people and the victory of the Muslims. Through the killing by him, peace be on him, of the forty whom he killed, weakness came upon the polytheists and thus he was the cause of the their desertion and anxiety, and the victory of the Muslims.

37 Ibn Hishām, *Sira*, 884-5.

(The Muslims' flight) was contributed to by the lack of judgement of this man (when he caused them to be overconfident) through expressing wonder at their great numbers. (It was this man) who preceded 'Alī to the rank of the caliphate (*khilāfa*) after the Apostle of Allāh, may Allāh bless Him and His Family. Thus he was the cause of their initial defeat, or at least one of the causes. Then it was his colleague who caused prisoners of the enemy to be killed after the Prophet, may Allāh bless Him and His Family, had forbidden them to be killed. Thus he committed a great crime against Allāh, the Exalted, and against His Apostle. (On the other hand, 'Alī) was a help to the Prophet, may Allāh bless Him and His Family, in reconciling the Anṣār, by gathering them together and speaking to them. Religion was strengthened by him and by him was removed fear of discord which overshadowed the people because of the distribution of the booty. Thus he shared with the Apostle of Allāh, may Allāh bless Him and His Family, in that merit which no one else participated in. In the matter of al-'Abbās b. Mirdās, he carried it out in such a way that he was the cause of the strengthening of faith in his heart and the removal of doubts about religion from his soul and his accepting of His Apostle, peace be on him, by obeying his command and being content with his judgement. Then the Apostle of Allāh, may Allāh bless Him and His Family, made him the one who would carry out the judgement on the man who protested against his decision, as a sign of the right of the Commander of the Faithful, peace be on him, in his actions, and in the correctness in his fighting. He called attention to the duty of obedience (to 'Alī) and warned against disobedience (to him). Indeed truth was in his heart and loins and he testified to it by being the best of creatures. This is in contrast to the actions carried out by his rivals who usurped his position. It shows the contradictory nature of their actions and excludes them from merit (leading them) to a low position which would cause such a man to perish, or would almost (cause it). This is apart from the greatness (of 'Alī's actions which are above) the actions of even those loyal men in that campaign and their closeness in the battle which they fought in. By this they are excluded from the praise which we have given to him by virtue of their deficiency which we have described.

Expeditions to Awṭās and al-Ṭā'if

When Allāh, the Exalted, had scattered the gathering of the polytheists at Ḥunayn, they separated into two groups. The Bedouin and those who followed them went to Awṭās while Thaqīf and those who followed them went to al-Ṭā'if. The Prophet, may Allāh bless Him and His Family, sent Abū 'Āmir al-Ash'arī to Awṭās with a group of men which included Abū Mūsā al-Ash'arī. He sent Abū Sufyān Ṣakhr b. Ḥarb to al-Ṭā'if.

Abū ʻĀmir went forward carrying the standard and fought until he was killed protecting it. The Muslims said to Abū Mūsā: "You are the cousin of the commander and he has been killed. So take up the standard so that we might fight before it."

Abū Mūsā took it up and he and the Muslims fought until Allāh gave them victory.

Abū Sufyān, on the other hand, came against Thaqīf and they made a direct attack on him. He was put to flight and he returned to the Prophet, may Allāh bless Him and His Family. He said: "You sent me with men who would not even have been able to lift the buckets of Hudhayl and the Bedouin. They were of no use to me."

The Prophet, may Allāh bless Him and His Family, turned away from him in silence. Then he went, himself, to al-Ṭā'if and laid siege to it. He sent out the Commander of the Faithful, peace be on him, with some horsemen. He ordered him to plunder everything he found and to destroy every idol he found.

He went forward until the horsemen of Khathʻam met him amid a great group. One of their men called Shihāb came forward in the darkness just before dawn. He called: "Is there anyone who will fight me in single combat?"
"Which (of you) will be for him?" the Commander of the Faithful, peace be on him, asked them.
No one rose. So the Commander of the Faithful rose to go against him. Then Abū al-ʻĀṣ b. al-Rabīʻ jumped up and said: "You will be too much for him, Commander of the Faithful."
"Indeed," he replied, "but if I am killed, you take command over the men."

The Commander of the Faithful went forward against him while reciting:

> Duty is required of every leader that he water the straight lance (with blood) or it is broken.

Then he struck him down and killed him. He went along with those horsemen until he had broken the idols. Then he returned to the Apostle of Allāh, may Allāh bless him-and his family, while the latter was besieging the inhabitants of al-Ṭā'if.

When the Prophet, may Allāh bless Him and His Family, saw him, he magnified Allāh for his victory. Then he took him by the hand and went aside with him and spent a long time in confidential talk with him.

['Abd al-Raḥmān b. Ṣubāba and al-Ajlaḥ both report on the authority of Abū al-Zubayr, on the authority of Jābir b.'Abd Allāh al-Anṣārī:]
When the Apostle of Allāh, may Allāh bless Him and His Family, had been alone with 'Alī, peace be on him, on the campaign against al-Ṭā'if, 'Umar b. al-Khaṭṭāb came to him and said: "Why do you take him aside and speak to him alone, apart from us?"

"'Umar," he replied, "I have not made him my confidant. Rather Allāh has made him His confidant."

'Umar opposed him, saying: "This is just the same as you said to us before al-Ḥudaybiyya that we would enter the Sacred Mosque safely if Allāh wished it. Then we did not enter it and we were turned away from it."

"I did not tell you that you would enter it in that year," the Prophet, may Allāh bless Him and His Family, shouted at him.

Later Nāfi' b. Ghaylān b. Ma'tib came out from the fortress of al-Ṭā'if with some horsemen from Thaqīf. The Commander of the Faithful, peace be on him, met him at Baṭn Wajj. There he killed him and the polytheists were put to flight. Terror seized the people and a group of them came down to the Prophet, may Allāh bless Him and His Family, and submitted to Islam. The Prophet's siege had lasted a little more than ten days.

In this campaign Allāh, may He be glorified, also characterised the Commander of the Faithful, peace be on him, with qualities which none of the other people shared. During it, the conquest was brought about at his hands; he killed those men of Khath'am whom he killed apart from anyone else; there occurred the confidential conversation which the Apostle of Allāh, may Allāh bless Him and His Family, attributed to Allāh, may His name be exalted. By this is clearly demonstrated his outstanding merit, his special consideration by Allāh, the Exalted, by which he was separated from the rest of men. The intensity of his opponents' reaction to these events indicates their awareness of his inner significance and Allāh's revelation of the reality of His secret communications with him. In that there is a lesson for those who have minds.

The Expedition to Tabūk and the Commander of the Faithful's Deputising for the Prophet at Medina

With regard to the expedition to Tabūk, Allāh, may His name be exalted, revealed to His Prophet, may Allāh bless Him and His Family, that he should go there himself and summon the people to set out with him. He told him that in the expedition there would be no need for war and there would be no fighting against the enemy since these matters would come to him without the sword. It was a device by which to test and try his Companions' (willingness) to set out, so that in that way they could be distinguished and their secret feelings revealed to him. The Prophet, may Allāh bless Him and His Family, summoned them to set out for the lands of the Byzantine (Empire). However, their fruit had ripened and the heat was oppressive for them. Most of them were slow in obeying him out of a desire for delay, out of greed for their own livelihoods and their improvement, and out of fear of intense heat, of the extent of the distance and of meeting the enemy. But some of them, despite finding it burdensome, arose to set out while others lingered behind.

When the Prophet, may Allāh bless Him and His Family, was ready to go out, he appointed the Commander of the Faithful, peace be on him, as his deputy over his family, his children and his place of emigration. He told him: "'Alī, Medina will only be properly looked after by myself or by you."

He said that because he, peace be on him, knew the wicked intentions of the Bedouin and many of the Meccans, and those around them whom he had attacked and whose blood he had shed. He was concerned that they would seek (to control) Medina when he was away from it and occupied in Byzantine territory. Since there was no one to take his place there, there would be no safety from their treachery, from the corruption they would cause in (Medina) the place of emigration, and from their overreaching themselves to actions which would hurt his family and his successors. He, peace be on him, knew that no one could take his place in terrifying the enemy, guarding the place of emigration and protecting those who were there except the Commander of the Faithful. Thus he clearly appointed him as his deputy, and gave an explicit nomination of him to the Imamate after him.

This is indicated by the account that has made clear that when the Hypocrites learnt that the Apostle of Allāh, may Allāh bless Him and His Family, had appointed 'Alī, peace be on him, as his deputy over Medina, they were envious of him because of that. After (the Prophet's) departure, ('Alī's) position there began to distress them; for they knew that (the city) would be protected and that there would be no opportunity for a man with hostile or covetous intent. That grieved them and they would have preferred ('Alī) to leave with (the Prophet) because of the occurrence of corruption and confusion which they hoped for during the absence of the Apostle of Allāh, may Allāh bless Him and His Family, from Medina and while it would be free of a man to guard it who would cause terror and fear. Therefore they accused him of (seeking) luxury and ease by remaining with the people while those of them who had departed were undergoing hardships, through journeying and (risking) danger. They spread rumours about him, peace be on him, and said: "The Apostle of Allāh, may Allāh bless Him and His Family, did not appoint him as deputy as an act of honour, privilege and love. He only left him behind because of his finding him burdensome."

With this rumour they slandered him like Quraysh had slandered the Prophet by (attributing to him) madness sometimes, and poetry at other times, by (accusing him of) magic at times and of being a pagan soothsayer at others. They knew that (the facts) were opposite and contrary to that, just as the Hypocrites knew that (the facts) were opposite and contrary to the slanders they were spreading against the Commander of the Faithful, peace be on him. The Prophet had specifically recommended the Commander of the Faithful, peace be on him, to the people. He was the most lovable of the people to him, the happiest of them in his view, the most favoured by him, and the closest to him.

When the Commander of the Faithful, peace be on him, learned of the rumours spread by the Hypocrites against him, he wanted to show them to be liars and to reveal their shameful action. So he followed the Prophet, may Allāh bless Him and His Family, and told him: "Apostle of Allāh, the hypocrites are alleging that you left me behind because of finding (me) burdensome and because of hatred."

"Go back to your position, brother," the Prophet said to him. "Medina will only be properly looked after by myself and by you. You are my deputy (*khalīfa*) among my family (*ahl al-bayt*) and in the place of my emigration and my people. Are you not content, 'Alī, that you have the same rank with regard to me as Aaron had with regard to Moses, except that there is no prophet after me?"[38]

This statement by the Apostle of Allāh is his designation of him for the Imamate and his setting him apart from the rest of the people for succession (*khilāfa*). Through it he indicated a merit in him which no one else shared and by it he required for him all the ranks which Aaron received from Moses except those which custom specifies to be required from (natural) brotherhood. He also excluded him from prophethood. Do you not see that (the Prophet), peace be on him, gave him all the ranks of Aaron with the only exceptions which his expressed word and reason would exclude? Everyone who has contemplated

38 Ibn Hishām, *Sira*, 894, omits mentioning that the Prophet appointed 'Ali as his deputy. al-Ṭabarī, I, 1696, says that he actually appointed Siba' b. 'Urfata as his deputy leaving 'Ali responsible for his family.

the meaning of the Qur'ān, who has pondered on the accounts and reports, has realised that Aaron was the brother of Moses, peace be on him, through his father and mother, his partner in his affair, and his helper in his prophethood and in propagating the messages from his Lord Allāh, may He be praised, his loins were strengthened through him and he was his deputy (*khalīfa*) over his people. His (authority) over them was from the Imamate; for the requirement of obedience to him (Moses) was like the Imamate of him (Aaron) and the requirement of obedience to him. He (Aaron) was the most lovable of the people to him (Moses) and the most meritorious of them in his view. Allāh, the Mighty and High, has said, putting words in the mouth of Moses, peace be on him: *My Lord, enlarge my breast for me and let my affair give joy to me. Loosen the knot of my tongue so that they may understand my speech. Make Aaron, my brother, my helper from my family. Strengthen my loins through him and make him a partner in my affair so that we may praise You much and mention You frequently.* (XX 25-34). Allāh, the Exalted, answered his request and gave him his request and desire when He said: *Your request has been granted, Moses.* (XX 36). And Allāh, the Exalted, said, putting the words into the mouth of Moses: *Moses said to his brother Aaron: Be my deputy over my people, be righteous and do not follow the path of the corrupters.* (VII 142).

When the Apostle of Allāh, may Allāh bless Him and His Family, gave 'Alī the same rank with regard to himself as Aaron had with regard to Moses, he required for him by that everything which we could mention except what custom specifies for natural brotherhood, and the exception of prophethood which was expressly stated. This is a virtue which no other creatures shares with the Commander of the Faithful, peace be on him. Nor does anyone else equal him in its significance, nor does anyone come near to it in any circumstance. If Allāh, the Mighty and High, had known that His Prophet, may Allāh bless Him and His Family, would have any need of fighting and support on this expedition, He would not have allowed him to leave behind the Commander of the Faithful, peace be on him, as we have already mentioned. However He realised that the public interest (*maṣlaḥa*) lay in making him his deputy and that ('Alī) taking his place in (Medina) the place of emigration was the best action. (Allāh) had organised creation and religion as He had decreed concerning that and He brought it about as we have outlined and explained.

(The Campaign against 'Amr b. Ma'dīkarib)

When the Apostle of Allāh, may Allāh bless Him and His Family, returned from Tabūk to Medina, 'Amr b. Ma'dīkarib came to him. The Prophet said to him: "Submit to Islam, 'Amr, and then Allāh will protect you from the greatest terror."

"What is the greatest terror, Muḥammad?" he asked. "For I have no fear."
"'Amr," he told him, "it is not as you think and suppose. Indeed there will be one great shout among the people. Not one person will remain who does not attend, nor a living person who does not die, except as Allāh wishes. Then there will be another great shout among them and those who are dead will assemble and all get into ranks. The heavens will split open and the earth will be crushed. The mountains will be cut asunder at the crushing and the fire will hurl the mountains like sparks. No one who has a soul will remain except his heart be stripped bare while he mentions his sins and is occupied with his soul, except as Allāh wishes. Then, where will you be, 'Amr, at this?"

"Indeed I am hearing of a terrible event," said 'Amr.
Then he believed in Allāh and His Apostle. People from his tribe also believed with him and then they returned to their tribe.

'Amr b. Ma'dīkarib looked towards Ubayy d. 'Ath'ath al-Khath'amī. He seized him by the neck and brought him to the Prophet, may Allāh bless Him and His Family.
"Give me back this sinner who has killed my father," he said.
"Islam leaves unavenged acts committed in the Jāhiliyya," replied the Apostle of Allāh, may Allāh bless Him and His Family.

'Amr departed as an apostate. He made a raid on people from the Banū al-Ḥārith b. Ka'b and went on to his own tribe. The Apostle of Allāh, may Allāh bless Him and His Family, summoned 'Alī b. Abī Ṭālib, peace be on him. He put him in charge of some of the emigrants and despatched him to the Banū Zubayd. He sent Khālid b. al-Walīd with a group of Bedouin and ordered him to head against (the tribe of) Ju'fā. When the two men ('Alī and Khālid) met, 'Alī b. Abī Ṭālib, peace be on him, was to be the commander of the people.

The Commander of the Faithful, peace be on him, set out. He put Khālid b. Sa'īd b. al-'Āṣ in charge of his vanguard. Khālid (b. al-Walīd) put Abū Mūsā al-Ash'arī in charge of his vanguard. When Ju'fā heard about the army, they split into two groups. One group went to Yemen and the other group attached themselves to the Banū Zubayd.

The Commander of the Faithful, peace be on him, learnt of that and wrote to Khālid b. al-Walīd: "Stop where my messenger reaches you." He did not stop, so ('Alī) wrote to Khālid b. Sa'īd b. al-'Āṣ: "Intervene so that you stop him." Khālid (b. Sa'īd) met him and stopped him.

The Commander of the Faithful, peace be on him, caught up with him and upbraided him severely for his opposition to his orders. Then he went on until he came upon the Banū Zubayd in a valley called Kisr. When the Banū Zubayd saw him, they said to 'Amr: "How are you, Abū Thawr? When this young man meets you, he will take tribute from you."
"He will know that he has met me," he said.
Then 'Amr went forward and cried out: "Who will meet me in combat?"

The Commander of the Faithful, peace be on him, rose to go against him but Khālid b. Sa'īd also stood up and said: "Abū al-Ḥasan, (I would ransom) you with my father and mother, let me meet him in combat."
"If you consider that you owe any obedience to me, remain in your place," the Commander of the Faithful, peace be on him, told him.

He stayed and the Commander of the Faithful went forward. There was a great clamour. 'Amr was put to flight and his brother and cousin were killed. His wife, Rukāna daughter of Salāma, was taken, and his (other) womenfolk were captured.

The Commander of the Faithful, peace be on him, departed and left Khālid b. Sa'īd behind in charge of the Banū Zubayd to collect their taxes and to provide security for those who, having submitted to Islam, returned to him from their flight. 'Amr b. Ma'dīkarib returned. He asked permission (to visit) Khālid b. Sa'īd and the latter gave him permission. Then he returned to Islam. He spoke to him about his wife and children and he gave them to him.

When 'Amr stood at the door of Khālid b. Sa'īd, he found (there) an animal which had been slaughtered. He gathered the bones of it together and struck them with his sword, cutting through them all. His sword was called Ṣimṣama. When Khālid b. Sa'īd gave 'Amr his wife and children, 'Amr gave him al-Ṣimṣama.

(Earlier) the Commander of the Faithful, peace be on him, had chosen a slave-girl from among the prisoners. Now Khālid b. al-Walīd sent Burayda al-Aslamī to the Prophet, may Allāh bless Him and His Family. He told him: "Get to (the Prophet) before the army does. Tell him what 'Alī, peace be on him, has done in choosing a slave-girl for himself from the *khums* (fifth of the booty that was to go to the Prophet and others, including the family of the Prophet) and bring him dishonour."

Burayda went and came to the door of the Apostle of Allāh. There he met 'Umar al-Khaṭṭāb. The latter asked him about how their expedition had gone and about why he had come. He told him that he had only come to bring dishonour to 'Alī and he mentioned his choosing a slave-girl from the *khums* for himself.

"Carry out what you have come to do," 'Umar told him, "for he (the Prophet) will be angry at what 'Alī, peace be on him, has done on account of his daughter."

Burayda went in to the Prophet, may Allāh bless Him and His Family. He had with him the letter from Khālid with which he had been sent. He began to read it. The face of the Prophet began to change.

"Apostle of Allāh," said Burayda, "if you permitted the people (to act) like this, their *fay'* (booty to be distributed) would disappear."

"Woe upon you, Burayda," the Prophet, may Allāh bless Him and His Family, told him. "You have committed an act of hypocrisy.'Alī b. Abī Ṭālib is allowed to have what is allowed to me from their *fay'*. 'Alī b. Abī Ṭālib, peace be on him, is the best of men for you and your people and the best of those whom I will leave behind after me for the whole of my community. Burayda, I warn you that if you hate 'Alī, Allāh will hate you."

Burayda reported: I wanted the earth to split open for me so that I could be swallowed into it. Then I said: "I seek refuge in Allāh from the anger of Allāh and the anger of the Apostle of Allāh. Apostle of Allāh, forgive me. I will never hate 'Alī and I will only speak good of him."

The Prophet, may Allāh bless Him and His Family, forgave him.

In this expedition, the Commander of the Faithful (demonstrated) qualities which were beyond comparison with the qualities of anyone else. In particular, victory in it was brought about by his hand. It also showed his great merit and his sharing with the Prophet, may Allāh bless Him and His Family, in the *fay'* which Allāh had permitted to the latter. Thus it showed his special designation for something which none of the other people could have and it set him apart by reason of the Apostle of Allāh's love for him and his preference for him which had been hidden to those who had no previous knowledge of it. There is also his warning Burayda and others against hating him and against enmity towards him, and his urging him to love him and accept his authority (*wilāya*). In addition the response to the plot of his enemies in their attempt to vilify him indicates that he was the best (*afḍāl*) of creatures in the view of Allāh, the Exalted, and of him (the Prophet), peace be on him, and the one with the most right for his position (of authority) after him. In himself he was the most special of (the Muslims) with (the Prophet) and the most influential of them with him.

(The Campaign of (Dhāt) al-Salāsil)[39]

Then there was the campaign of (Dhāt) al-Silsila. That was when a Bedouin came to the Prophet, may Allāh bless Him and His Family. He squatted in front of him and said: "I have come to advise you. A group of Arabs have gathered together at Wadī al-Raml and they have plotted to come and attack you at night in Medina." Then he described them to him.

The Prophet, may Allāh bless Him and His Family, ordered the call to be given: "The prayer is general (*al-ṣalāt jāmi'a* i.e. all should attend the prayer)." The Muslims gathered and he went up on to the pulpit. He praised and glorified Allāh. Then he said: "There is an enemy of Allāh and an enemy of yours who has plotted to attack you at night. Who will (go against) them?"

A group of the poor people stood up and said: "We will go against them, Apostle of Allāh. Therefore appoint whoever you wish over us."
He drew lots among them and the lot fell upon eighty from among them and others. He summoned Abū Bakr and said to him: "Take the flag and depart against the Banū Sulaym. They are near al-Ḥarra."

He departed and with him went the people until he drew near their land. There were many stones and trees there and the people (i.e. the Banū Sulaym) were in the middle of the valley and the descent to it was difficult. When Abū Bakr got to the valley, he intended to go down but the people came out against him and put him to flight. They killed a great number of the Muslims and Abū Bakr fled from the people.

When they came to the Prophet, may Allāh bless Him and His Family, he gave the command to 'Umar b. al-Khaṭṭāb and sent him against them. They lay hidden under the stones and trees. When he went to descend, they came out against him and put him to flight.

The Prophet, may Allāh bless Him and His Family, was grieved at this. 'Amr b. al-'Āṣ said to him: "Send me against them, Apostle of Allāh. For warfare is deception and perhaps I can deceive them."
He sent him with a group of men and commissioned him (to carry out the task). When he got to the valley, they came out against him and put him to flight. They

39 cf. footnote 24 referring to pages 74-77.

killed a number of those who accompanied him.

(After this,) the Apostle of Allāh, may Allāh bless Him and His Family, delayed for several days praying (for Allāh's help) against them. Then he summoned the Commander of the Faithful, peace be on him. He gave him the command and said: "I have sent him as one who will attack, not one who will flee." Then he raised his hands to the heavens and said: "O Allāh, if You know that I am Your Apostle, then protect him for me. Act through him, act."
Thus he prayed for the will of Allāh for him.

'Alī b. Abī Ṭālib set out and the Apostle of Allāh, may Allāh bless Him and His Family, went out to say farewell to him. He went with him to the mosque of the allies (*al-aḥzāb*). 'Alī, peace be on him, was riding a shorn-haired bay. He was wearing two Yemenī garments and carrying a spear. The Apostle of Allāh, may Allāh bless Him and His Family, said farewell to him and prayed for him.

He had sent among those who had been sent with him, Abū Bakr, 'Umar and 'Amr b. al-'Āṣ. ('Alī) set off towards Iraq deviating from the (usual) route so that they would think that he was heading with (his men) in another direction. Then he took them along a little known track and brought them along so that he approached the valley from (the direction of) its entrance. When he was near the valley, he ordered those with him to tie up their horses and he made them stop in their place. He said to them: "Do not leave your position." Then he went forward in front of them. He stood at a distance from them.

When 'Amr b. al-'Āṣ saw what he had done, he had no doubt that victory would be his. (Resenting this, he) said to Abū Bakr: "I know that place better than 'Alī, peace be on him. There, there is something which will attack us more fiercely than the Banū Sulaym. There are hyenas and wolves. If they come out against us, I am afraid that they will cut us down. Speak to him to let us go up the valley."

Abū Bakr went forward and spoke to him. He spoke at length but the Commander of the Faithful, peace be on him, did not answer a single word. He went back to them and said: "No, by Allāh, he did not say a single word in reply."

Then 'Amr b. al-'Āṣ said to 'Umar b. al-Khaṭṭāb: "You are more powerful with him."
So 'Umar went and spoke to him. He treated him exactly as he had treated Abū Bakr. He returned to them and told him that he had not answered him.

'Amr b. al-'Āṣ spoke to (the men): "It is not fitting that we should lose our lives.

So come with us up the valley."

"No, by Allāh," retorted the Muslims, "we will not do so. The Apostle of Allāh ordered us to listen to 'Alī, peace be on him, and to obey him. Shall we abandon his command and listen to you and obey you?"

They continued in this manner so that the Commander of the Faithful, peace be on him, felt (a feeling of) pride. He was able to surround the people while they were still unaware. Allāh, the Exalted, gave him power over them.

Sūrat al-'Ādiyāt ḍabḥan (C) was revealed to the Prophet, may Allāh bless Him and His Family. The Prophet, may Allāh bless Him and His Family, announced the news of the victory to his Companions and ordered them to meet the Commander of the Faithful, peace be on him. They went to meet him with the Prophet, may Allāh bless Him and His Family, at their head. The Muslims positioned themselves in two ranks. When ('Alī) saw the Prophet, he dismounted from his horse. The Prophet said to him: "Mount (your horse). Allāh and His Apostle are pleased with you."

The Commander of the Faithful, peace be on him, wept with joy. Then the Prophet, may Allāh bless Him and His Family, said: "'Alī, if it was not for the fact that I am concerned that some factions of my community would say (of you) what the Christians say of the Messiah, Jesus, son of Mary, I would say of you today such as (after them) you would never pass a gathering of men without them taking the soil from under your feet."

Victory in this expedition was entirely due to the Commander of the Faithful after the corruption which had occurred through the others. He was singled out for special praise by the Prophet with regard to it, for virtues which in no way occurred in anyone else. He distinguished him with a rank in which no one else had any share.

CHAPTER IV

THE ROLE OF THE COMMANDER OF THE FAITHFUL IN THE LAST YEAR OF THE PROPHET'S LIFE

(The Deputation of Christians from Najrān and the Contest of Prayer)

When Islam had spread after the conquest (of Mecca) and the raids already described, which followed it, and its authority had become strong, delegations began to visit the Prophet, may Allāh bless Him and His Family. Some of them submitted to Islam while others sought protection so that they might return to their people (to tell) their people about his view towards them. Among those who came in a delegation to him were Abū Ḥāritha, the bishop of Najrān, with thirty of the Christians who included the deputy (*al-'āqib*), the chief (*al-sayyid*) and 'Abd al-Masīḥ. They arrived at Medina at the time of the afternoon prayer. They were wearing robes of silk and crosses.

The Jews approached them and they began to interrogate each other. The Christians said: "You are not believing in anything (correctly)." And the Jews replied to them: "You are not believing in anything (correctly)." Concerning that, Allāh, may He be praised, revealed: *The Jews say that the Christians are not believing in anything (correctly) and the Christians say that the Jews are not believing in anything (correctly)* . . . . etc. to the end of the verse (II 113).

When the Prophet had prayed the afternoon prayer, they came forwards. At their head was the bishop. He said to him: "Muḥammad, what do you say about the Lord, the Messiah?"
"He is a servant of Allāh," replied the Prophet, "whom Allāh chose and he answered Him."
"Do you know, Muḥammad, whether a father caused him to be born?" asked the bishop.
"He was not born as a result of intercourse so he could not have a father," answered the Prophet.
"How can you say that he is a servant who has been created, when you can only consider a servant who has been created to be born as a result of intercourse and so to have a father?" he asked.

Allāh, may He be praised and exalted, revealed these verses in *Sūrat 'Āl 'Imrān* (III) in answer to him: *The likeness of Jesus according to Allāh is like the likeness of Adam. Allāh created him from earth. Then Allāh said to him: "Be." That is the truth from your Lord. Therefore do not be one of those who go beyond the bounds (of reason). If anyone disputes with you concerning him, after knowledge has been given to you, say to him: Come, let us call our sons and your sons, our women and your women, and ourselves and yourselves. Then let us call on Allāh to witness against each other and let us make the curse of Allāh fall on those who lie* (III 59-61).

The Prophet, may Allāh bless Him and His Family, recited it to the Christians and challenged them to a contest of prayer to Allāh (*mubāhala*). He said: "Allāh, the Mighty and High, has informed me that dread torment will come down on him who has spoken falsely after the contest of prayer (*mubāhala*). By this the truth will be distinguished from the false."

The Bishop held a meeting of consultation with 'Abd al-Masīḥ and the deputy. Their unanimous view was to wait until the early morning of the next day. When they both returned to their men, the bishop told them: "Watch Muḥammad tomorrow morning. If he comes out with his children and his family, then be warned against the contest of prayer (*mubāhala*) with him. However, if he comes out with his Companions, then make the contest of prayer with him, for he believes in something other (than the true religion)."

On the next morning, the Prophet, may Allāh bless Him and His Family, came and took 'Alī b. Abī Ṭālib by the hand, while al-Ḥasan and al-Ḥusayn, peace be on them, were walking in front of him and Fāṭima, peace be on her, walked behind him. The Christians came out, at their head their bishop. When the bishop saw that the Prophet, may Allāh bless Him and His Family, was advancing with those who were with him, he asked about them. He was told: "That is his cousin 'Alī b. Abī Ṭālib, who is his son-in-law and the father of his two grandsons and the most lovable of creatures to him. Those children are the sons of his daughter by 'Alī, peace be on him. They are the most lovable of creatures to him. That girl is his daughter, Fāṭima, peace be on her, the dearest of people to him and the closest to his heart."

The bishop looked at the deputy, the chief and 'Abd al-Masīḥ and said: "Have you seen that he has come with the special members of his children and his family so that he may make the contest of prayer with them, trusting in his truthfulness. By God, he would not have come with them while he was afraid that the proof would be against him. Therefore be warned against the contest of prayer with him. By God, if it was not for the position of Caesar (i.e. the Byzantine emperor), I would submit to him. But (now) make peace with him on

what can be agreed between you and him. Return to your land and think about it yourselves."
"Our view conforms with your view," they replied.
"Abū al-Qāsim," the bishop called out, "we will not make a contest of prayer with you but we will make peace with you. Therefore make peace with us as we propose."

So the Prophet made peace with them on the condition (of the payment) of two thousand protective breastplates, each breastplate being forty standard dirham (in value). If they varied in value, it would be taken into account. The Prophet, may Allāh bless Him and His Family, had a document written (laying out the terms) by which he had made peace with them. The document is as follows:

> In the name of Allāh, the Merciful and the Compassionate.
> In terms of gold and silver, produce and slaves, nothing will be taken from them except two thousand protective breastplates, each breastplate being worth forty dirham. If they vary in value, it will be taken into the account. They will pay one thousand of them in the month of Ṣafar and one thousand of them in the month of Rajab. (In addition,) they will provide forty dīnārs for a dwelling house for my agent (*rasūl*), not more than that. Also in every incident that occurs in Yemen, it will be required of them, (that is) of everyone who lives in a permanent settlement (*dhī'adan*), to pay as guaranteed equally (by both parties) thirty breastplates, thirty horses and thirty camels as guaranteed equally (by both parties). They will have the neighbourly protection of Allāh (*jiwār Allāh*) and the protection (*dhimma*) of Muḥammad b. 'Abd Allāh. Whoever of them takes interest after this year will be denied my protection.
>
> This is a document made on behalf of Muḥammad, the Prophet, the Apostle of Allāh, may Allāh bless Him and His Family, and the people of Najrān and their followers.

The people took the document and departed.

In the story of the people of Najrān there is a clear explanation of the outstanding merit of the Commander of the Faithful, peace be on him, in addition to the clear sign of the Prophet, may Allāh bless Him and His Family, and the miracle which indicates his prophethood. Do you not see the Christians' admission of his prophethood, and his convincing them to refrain from the contest of prayer, and making them realise that if they had taken part in such a contest, dread punishment against them would have been permissible? Similarly he, peace be on him, was confident in victory and success over them by the proof (he would bring) against them. Allāh, the Exalted, gave judgement in the verse of the contest of prayer on behalf of the Commander of the Faithful, peace be on him, that he was of the same (station) as the Apostle of Allāh, thus revealing the great extent of his outstanding merit and his equality with the Prophet, the blessings and peace of Allāh be on Him and His Family, in terms of perfection and protection (*iṣma*) from sin. Indeed Allāh made him and his wife and his two sons, who were so close to each other in age, a proof for His prophet and evidence for His religion. He gave textual evidence of the judgement that al-Ḥasan and al-Ḥusayn were his sons and that Fāṭima was his "womenfolk" referred to in the statement and those addressed in the call for the contest of prayer and dispute. This is a merit which no one else of the community shares with them, nor even approaches them in it, nor has anything like it in its significance. It is associated with the outstanding special qualities of the Commander of the Faithful, peace be on him, which we have already mentioned earlier.

The Prophet's Farewell Pilgrimage[1] and the Declaration at Ghadīr Khumm.[2]

Among the stories relating the outstanding merit of the Commander of the Faithful, peace be on him, and giving special emphasis to his virtues, which came after the (visit of the) delegation from Najrān, is that which distinguishes him from all the rest of men - (that is) the Farewell Pilgrimage and the reports of what took place during it. During it the Commander of the Faithful had the most elevated position.

The Apostle of Allāh, may Allāh bless Him and His Family, had sent him, peace be on him, to Yemen to collect the fifth share (*khums*) of their gold and silver and collect the breastplates and other things which the people of Najrān had agreed to pay. He went there to carry out the requests of the Apostle of Allāh, may Allāh bless Him and His Family. In accordance with his instructions and speedily demonstrating his obedience, he performed his duty. The Apostle of Allāh trusted in no one else as he trusted in him for that task. Nor did he consider anyone among the people appropriate to undertake it except him. He made him, peace be on him, occupy a similar position to himself in that. He appointed him as his deputy, in confidence of him and secure in the knowledge that he would carry out the difficult tasks which were imposed upon him.

1 The account concurs with that of Ibn Isḥāq though according to him 'Ali does not bring any sacrificial offering. Nor is 'Umar mentioned by Ibn Isḥāq, cf. Ibn Hishām, *Sira*, 966-968.

2 For a collection of the traditions supporting the account of Ghadir Khumm, cf. al-Balādhurī, *Ansāb al-Ashrāf*, II, 108-111.

Then the Apostle of Allāh, may Allāh bless Him and His Family, decided to go on the pilgrimage and to carry out the duties which Allāh, the Exalted, had decreed. He summoned the people to (join) him and his call went out to the furthest points in the land of Islam. The people began to prepare to set out with him. A great crowd came to Medina from the outskirts, and around, and the area nearby. They began to make preparations to set out with him.

He, may Allāh bless Him and His Family, set out with them with five days remaining in (the month of) Dhū al-Qa'da. He had written to the Commander of the Faithful, peace be on him, about going on the pilgrimage from Yemen but he had not mentioned the kind of pilgrimage he had decided to make.

In fact (the Prophet), peace be on him, had set out as a *qārin* (a pilgrim who would make the lesser pilgrimage (*'umra*) and the greater pilgrimage (*ḥajj*) together without any break in the state of ritual consecration necessary for both pilgrimages), by driving the sacrificial animal with him. He put on the pilgrim garment and entered into the state of ritual consecration (*aḥrama*) at Dhū al-Ḥulayfa. The people did the same with him. He began the ritual call of the pilgrimage (*talbiya*) on the night he reached al-Baydā' which is half-way between the two sanctuaries (of Medina and Mecca). Then he went on to Kirā' al-Ghamīm. The people with him were riding and on foot. Those on foot found the journey arduous. (The hardships of) travelling and tiredness beset them. They complained of that to the Prophet, may Allāh bless him and grant him peace, and asked him if they could be carried by mounts. He told them that he could not find (an animal) for each of them and instructed them to fasten their belts and to mix sand with milk (to rub on their feet). They did that and they found relief in it.

(Meanwhile) the Commander of the Faithful, peace be on him, set out with the soldiers who had accompanied him to Yemen. He had with him the breastplates which he had collected from the people of Najrān. When the Apostle of Allāh, may Allāh bless Him and His Family, was nearing Mecca on the road from Medina, the Commander of the Faithful, peace be on him, was nearing it on the road from Yemen. He went ahead of the army to meet the Prophet, may Allāh bless Him and His Family, and he left one of their number in charge of them. He came up to the Prophet as the latter was looking down over Mecca. He greeted him and informed him of what he had done and of what he had collected and that he had hurried ahead of the army to meet him. The Apostle of Allāh, may Allāh bless Him and His Family, was pleased at that and delighted to meet him.

"'Alī, have you consecrated yourself for the pilgrimage?" he asked him.
"You did not write to me about the way you would consecrate yourself, Apostle

of Allāh," he answered. "I did not know. Therefore I made my intention according to your intention and said: O Allāh, let my intention be the intention of Your Prophet. I have driven thirty-four sacrificial animals with me."

"Allāh is greater (*Allāhu akbar*)," replied the Apostle of Allāh, may Allāh bless Him and His Family. "I have driven sixty-six. You will be my partner in my pilgrimage, my rituals and my sacrifice. Therefore remain in your state of ritual consecration and return to your army. Then hurry with them to me so that we may meet in Mecca, if Allāh, the Exalted, wills."

The Commander of the Faithful, peace be on him, said farewell to him and returned to his army. He met them nearby and found that they had put on the breastplates which they had had with them. He denounced them for that.

"Shame on you!" he said to the man whom he had appointed as his deputy over them. "Whatever made you give them the breastplates before we hand them over to the Apostle of Allāh, may Allāh bless Him and His Family? I did not give you permission to do that."

"They asked me to let them deck themselves out and enter into the state of consecration in them, and then they would give them back to me," he replied.

The Commander of the Faithful, peace be on him, took them off the people and put them back in the sacks. They were discontented with him because of that. When they came to Mecca, their complaints against the Commander of the Faithful, peace be on him, became numerous. The Apostle of Allāh ordered the call to be given among the people: "Stop your tongues (speaking) against 'Alī b. Abī Ṭālib, peace be on him. He is one who is harsh in the interests of Allāh, the Mighty and High, not one who deceives in His religion."

At this the people refrained from mentioning him and they realised the high position he enjoyed with the Prophet, may Allāh bless Him and His Family, and his anger against anyone who wanted to find fault with him.

The Commander of the Faithful, peace be on him, had entered into his state of consecration following the Apostle of Allāh, may Allāh bless Him and his family. Many of the Muslims had set out with the Prophet without driving victims for sacrifice. Allāh revealed: *Complete the greater pilgrimage (ḥajj) and the lesser pilgrimage ('umra)* (II 196). The Apostle of Allāh explained: "The lesser pilgrimage ('*umra*) has been brought into the (rites of the) greater pilgrimage (*ḥajj*) until the Day of Resurrection."

He knitted the fingers of both hands together and then he said: "If I had anticipated the consequence of my commandment, I would not have driven sacrificial victims."

Then he ordered the call to be given: "Those of you who have not driven sacrificial victims, should break your state of consecration so that you only made it to perform the lesser pilgrimage (*'umra*). But those of you who drove sacrificial victims must remain in that state of consecration."

Some of the people obeyed that but others opposed it. Discussions took place among them concerning it. There were some who maintained: "The Apostle of Allāh, may Allāh bless Him and His Family, has dishevelled hair and is dusty; shall we dress in clothes, have intercourse with women and use perfume?" And others said: "Are you not ashamed to come with heads dripping with water from ritual ablutions (after intercourse) while the Apostle of Allāh, may Allāh bless Him and His Family, remains in a state of ritual consecration?"

The Apostle of Allāh denounced those who opposed that and explained: "If I had not driven sacrificial victims, I would have broken my state of ritual consecration and only made it for the lesser pilgrimage (*'umra*). Therefore those of you who have not driven sacrificial victims, should break your state of consecration."

Some of the people withdrew their opposition but others still maintained it. Among those who maintained their opposition to the Prophet, may Allāh bless Him and His Family, was 'Umar b. al-Khaṭṭāb.

The Apostle of Allāh summoned him and asked him: "Why are you still in a state of ritual consecration, 'Umar? Did you drive sacrificial victims?"
"I did not drive any." he replied.
"Then why have you not broken your state of consecration when I told those who had not driven sacrificial victims to break it?" he asked.
"By Allāh, Apostle of Allāh," he answered, "I could not break my state of ritual consecration while you were still in yours."
"You will never believe in it until you die." the Prophet, may Allāh bless Him and His Family, said.

Thus it was that ('Umar) maintained his denial of *mut'at al-ḥajj* (the joining of the lesser pilgrimage and the greater pilgrimage together with an intervening period of a few days when the pilgrim breaks the state of ritual consecration and is allowed all things in normal life). In the time of his leadership, he went up on the pulpit and forbade it once more and threatened punishment for its performance.

When the Apostle of Allāh carried out his rituals of the pilgrimage, he made 'Alī his partner in his sacrifice of animals: Then he began his journey back to Medina. ('Alī) and the Muslims went with him. He came to a place known as Ghadīr Khumm. At that time, it was not a place suitable for a halt because it lacked water and pasturage. However, he, peace be on him, stopped there and the Muslims with him. The reason for his halting at this place was that a revelation had been received by him concerning the appointment of the Commander of the Faithful, 'Alī b. Abī Ṭālib, peace be on him, as successor for the community after him. The revelation concerning that had been received earlier but without the designation of the time (for it to be made public). He had delayed (making it public) until the presence of a time in which he would be secure from any dispute among them concerning it. Allāh, the Mighty and High, had informed him that if he went beyond Ghadīr Khumm, many of the people would separate from his party (heading) for their towns, homes and valleys. Allāh wanted him to gather them together to hear the designation of the Commander of the Faithful, peace be on him, and to confirm the proofs of it to them. Therefore Allāh, the Exalted, revealed: *O Apostle, make known what has been revealed to you from your Lord* (V 67), that is concerning the succession of 'Alī and the designation of the Imamate for him. *If you do not do it, you will not have made known His message. Allāh will protect you from the people* (V 67). Thus He confirms the duty he had concerning that and the fear that had caused him delay and He guarantees to him protection and defence against the people.

The Apostle of Allāh, may Allāh bless Him and His Family, stopped at the place we have mentioned because of what we have described and explained about the command for him to do that. The Muslims stopped around him. It was a scorching day of intense heat. He ordered ('Alī), peace be on him, to go and stand under a great tree that was there and he ordered the travellers to be gathered in that place and to be put in (rows) one after another.

Then he ordered the crier to call out: "The prayer is general (*al-ṣalat jāmi'a* i.e. everybody should gather)." The travellers (all) gathered before him. Most of them wrapped their cloaks (*riḍā'*) around their feet because of the scorching hot ground. When they had gathered, he climbed above the travellers so that he was high above them and he summoned the Commander of the Faithful, peace be on him. He made him come up with him so that he stood on his right. He then began to address the people. He praised and glorified Allāh, and preached most eloquently. He gave the community news of his own death, saying: "I have been summoned and it is nearly the moment for me to answer. The time has come for me to depart from you. I leave behind me among you two things which, if you cleave to them, you will never go astray - that is the Book of Allāh and my offspring from my family (*ahl al-bayt*). They will never scatter (from you) until they lead you to me at the (sacred) waters (of Heaven)."

Then he called out at the top of his voice: "Am I not more appropriate (to rule) you than yourselves?"
"By Allāh, yes!" they answered.

He went on speaking continuously without any interruption and taking both arms of the Commander of the Faithful, peace be on him, and raising them so that the white of his armpits could be seen, he said: "Whoever I am the master (*mawlā*) of, this man, 'Alī, is his master. O Allāh, befriend whoever befriends him, be hostile to whoever opposes him, support whoever supports him and desert whoever deserts him."

Then he, peace be on him, went down. It was the time of the midmorning heat. He prayed two *rak'as*. The sun then began to decline (at mid-day) so the *mu'adhdhin* (the one who calls the prayer) called for the statutory prayer (of mid-day). He led them in the mid-day prayer. Then he, peace be on him (went to) sit in his tent. He ordered 'Alī, peace be on him, to sit in his tent opposite him, and he ordered the Muslims to go in group after group to congratulate him on his position and to acknowledge his command over the faithful. All the people did that. Then he ordered his wives and the rest of the wives of the faithful who were with him to go to him and acknowledge his command over the faithful. They did that.

Among those who were profuse in their congratulations on his position was 'Umar b. al-Khaṭṭāb. He gave a public appearance of great joy at it, saying: "Bravo, bravo, 'Alī, you have become my master and the master of every believing man and woman."

Ḥassān b. Thābit came to the Apostle of Allāh, may Allāh bless Him and his family, and said: "Apostle of Allāh, will you permit me to recite what would please Allāh with regard to this position?"
"Recite in the name of Allāh, Ḥassān," he told him.

He stood on elevated ground. The people spread out to listen to his words and he began to recite:

> On the day of al-Ghadīr he summoned them and made them answer at Khumm. Listen to the Apostle as he calls.

He said: "Who is your master (*mawlā*) and friend (*walī*)?" They answered without showing any signs of opposition:
"Allāh is our master (*mawlā*) and you are our friend (*walī*). You will never find any disobedience from us to you."

He said to him: "Arise, 'Alī, I am content that you should be Imam and guide after me

Whomsoever I am master (*mawlā*) of, this man is his friend (*walī*). Therefore be faithful helpers and followers of him."

There he prayed: "O Allāh, befriend his friend and be hostile to whoever opposes 'Alī."

"May you always be supported by the Spirit of Holiness, Ḥassān," the Apostle of Allāh, may Allāh bless Him and His Family, said to him, "as long as you support us with your tongue."

The Apostle of Allāh made this condition in his prayer because he was aware that his attitude would end in opposition. If he knew that he would have remained sound (in belief) in future circumstances, he would have made the prayer for him absolute. Similar conditions were made by Allāh, the Exalted, in praising the wives of the Prophet. He did not praise them unconditionally because He was aware that some of them would change their condition later from the righteousness which entitled them to praise and honour. Thus He said: *O Wives of the Prophet, you are not like any other women, if you are pious* (XXXIII 32). He did not treat them in that the same way as he treated the family of the Prophet in terms of honouring and praise when they gave their food to orphans, the poor and prisoners. Therefore Allāh, may He be praised, sent down a revelation concerning 'Alī, Fāṭima, al-Ḥasan and al-Ḥusayn, peace be on them, after they had preferred (to give their food rather than have it) themselves despite their own need for it. For Allāh said: *Out of love of Allāh, they feed the poor, the orphan and the prisoner. Indeed we feed you for the sake of Allāh. We do not want reward, nor thanks from you. We only fear our Lord on an inauspicious stern day. Then Allāh will guard them from the evil of that day. He will meet them with joy and splendour. He will reward them with gardens and silk for what they have endured.* (LXXVI 8-12). He positively asserted reward for them unconditionally just as He stipulated conditions for others because He knew of the different circumstances as we have explained.

In the Farewell Pilgrimage, there was (an example) of the outstanding merit of the Commander of the Faithful, peace be on him, by which he was especially characterised as we have explained. In it he was uniquely set apart with the exalted rank in the way we have mentioned. He was the partner of the Apostle of Allāh in his pilgrimage, (and shared his) sacrificial animals and (shared with him) in the rites of the pilgrimage. Allāh, the Exalted, gave him the same intention as (the Prophet), peace be on them both, and agreement in worship. There was revealed concerning his position with (the Prophet), peace be on him, and his exalted station with Allāh, may He be praised, what extols his praise and requires the necessity of obedience to him by other men, by designating him for succession (*khilāfa*), and by making plain through him the call to follow him and forbidding opposition to him, and by the prayer for those who followed him in religion and provided help for him, the prayer against those who opposed him, and the curse against those who came forward in enmity against him. Thus it was demonstrated that he was the best of the creatures of Allāh, the Exalted, the noblest of His creation. This is also one of the things which no one else in the community had any share in, nor was there any substitute for it which might approximate it as is clear to anyone who thinks, and obvious to anyone who knows the significance of reality. May Allāh be He Who is praised.

The Circumstances of the Last Illness and Death of the Prophet[3]

Among the circumstances which were given new significance by the Apostle of Allāh, may Allāh bless Him and His Family, and the events which occurred through the decree and ordinance of Allāh, which confirm his outstanding merit and characterise his exalted rank, are those which occurred after the Farewell Pilgrimage. That was when the (Prophet), peace be on him, realised through the nearness of (the end of) his allotted span (the need to put into effect) what he had already told his community. He, peace be on him, began to make speech after speech among the Muslims, warning them against discord after him and opposition to him. He confirmed his injunction to them to cleave to his *sunna* and those (matters) on which there was agreement and conformity. He urged them to follow his family, to obey them, to support, guard and hold fast to them in religion. He warned them against opposition and apostasy.

Among the things which were mentioned by him, peace be on him, is one which the reporters (of tradition and history) report with agreement and unanimity, that he, peace be on him, said: "People, I am a way-mark for you. You will come to me at the (heavenly) waters. Then indeed I will ask you about the two important things (which I left behind). Take care how you follow me with regard to them,

3 The crucial events around the Prophet's death represent an important feature of the Shī'ite polemic. The following account gives a clear picture of the Shī'ite position.

for the Good and Knowing (Allāh) has informed me that they will never scatter (from you) until they meet me. I asked my Lord for that and He granted it to me. Indeed I have left among you the Book of Allāh and the offspring of my family (*ahl al-bayt*). Do not try to outdo them, for then you will be destroyed. Do not try to teach them, for they are more knowledgeable than you. People, may I not find you, after I (have gone), returning to being unbelievers with some of you striking down others, for then you will meet me with a host like a sea of flowing soldiers. Indeed 'Alī b. Abī Ṭālib, peace be on him, is my brother, my trustee (*waṣī*). After me he will fight for the (true) interpretation of the Qur'ān just like I fought for its revelation."

He, may Allāh bless Him and His Family, used to address meeting after meeting with words like these.

Then he commissioned Usāma b. Zayd b. Ḥāritha. He ordered and urged him to leave with many members of the community for where his father had been killed in the Byzantine (empire). He, peace be on him, decided to send out the foremost of the Emigrants and Anṣār in his army, so that at his death there would not be anyone in Medina who differed about the leadership and who had ambitions to become the leader of the people. In this way he (hoped to) set in order the situation for the man who was to succeed him and to prevent any opponent from opposing him in his right. He gave (Usāma) the command on the condition which we have mentioned and he endeavoured to send them out. He ordered Usāma to leave Medina with his army for al-Jurf, and he urged the people to go out to him and to go with him. He warned them against lingering and dilatoriness in (doing) it.[4]

While matters were in that situation, the illness came upon him of which he (later) died. When he felt the sickness which had befallen him, he took the hand of 'Alī, peace be on him. A group of the people followed him and he headed for (the cemetery of) al-Baqī'. He told those who followed him: "I have been commanded to seek forgiveness for (the souls of) the people of (the cemetery of) al-Baqī'."

They went with him until he stopped in front of them. He, peace be on him, said: "People of the graves, let there be comfort for you in your situation (as opposed to the situation) in which discords have come upon the people like the cutting of the dark night when the first of them will follow the last."

Then he (spent) a long time seeking forgiveness for (the souls of) the people

4 cf. Ibn Hishām, *Sira*, 1006-7 without mentioning Abū Bakr and 'Umar's involvement.

of (the cemetery of) al-Baqī‘. (After this), he approached the Commander of the Faithful, peace be on him, and told him: "Gabriel, peace be on him, used to revise the Qur'ān with me once each year. This year he has revised it with me twice. I can only consider that it is because (the end of) my allotted span of life is at hand." Then he said: "'Alī, I was given the choice between remaining forever amid the treasuries of the world or of (going to) heaven. I have chosen to meet my Lord and (to go to) heaven. When I die, wash me. Cover my nakedness so that no one but a blind man could see it."[5]

He returned to his house and remained there for three days in a weak condition. Then he went out to the mosque, wearing a turban on his head and leaning on the Commander of the Faithful, peace be on him, on his right hand and on al-Faḍl b. al-‘Abbās on his other hand. He went up on the pulpit and sat there. Then he said: "People, the time of my departure from you has come. Whoever has any goods with me, let him come to me so that I may give them to him. Whoever has a debt which I owe him, let him inform me of it. People, between Allāh and any man there is nothing by which (Allāh) will give him better or by which Allāh will keep away from him evil, except works (*al-'amal*). People, by Him who sent me as a prophet with truth, let no one claim nor anyone desire that there should be salvation without works through (Allāh's) mercy. If I had disobeyed, I would have been hurled down (to damnation). O Allāh, have I conveyed (the message)?"

He went down and led the people in a short prayer. He returned to his house. At that time, he was in the house of Umm Salama, may Allāh be pleased with her. He remained there for a day or two. Then ‘Ā'isha came to her to ask her to move him to her house so that she might undertake to nurse him. She had asked the wives of the Prophet about that and they had given her their permission. Thus he, may Allāh bless Him and His Family, was moved to the house in which ‘Ā'isha lived. The illness remained with him for several days and grew more serious.

At the time of the morning prayer, Bilāl came while the Apostle of Allāh, may Allāh bless Him and His Family, was overcome by sickness. (He asked:) "Do I call the prayer, may Allāh have mercy on you?"

The Apostle of Allāh gave him permission to make his call and said: "Let one of the people pray before them, for I am too distracted by (the final hours of) my life."
"Order Abū Bakr," ‘Ā'isha said.
"Order ‘Umar," intervened Ḥafṣa.

5 cf. ibid., 1001, without mentioning ‘Alī.

When the Apostle of Allāh, may Allāh bless Him and His Family, heard their words and saw the eagerness of each of them to exalt her own father and their discord about that, he said: "Have you put the shroud on the Apostle of Allāh while he is still alive? Indeed you are like the mistresses of Joseph."

Then he, peace be on him, rose hurriedly fearing that one of the two men would go forward (to lead the prayers). He had ordered them to go with Usāma and he had had no idea that they would be disobedient. However when he heard what he heard from 'Ā'isha and Ḥafṣa, he knew that they had delayed in (obeying) his command. He hurried to prevent discord and remove doubt. He, blessings and peace be on him, arose despite the fact that he could barely lift himself off the ground through weakness. 'Alī b. Abī Ṭālib, peace be on him, took his hand and al-Faḍl b. al-'Abbās took the other. He leaned on them both and his feet dragged a trail along the ground because of his weakness.

When he came out into the mosque, he found that Abū Bakr had already got to the *miḥrāb*. He indicated with his hand that he should withdraw and Abū Bakr withdrew. The Apostle of Allāh, may Allāh bless Him and His Family, took up his place. He said the "*takbir*" and began the prayer which Abū Bakr had begun before without taking any account of what had already been performed.

After he had said the final greeting of the prayer, he returned to his house. He summoned Abū Bakr, 'Umar and a group of the Muslims who had been present at the mosque. He said: "Did I not order you to go with the army of Usāma?"
"Yes, Apostle of Allāh," they replied.
"Why have you delayed from (carrying out) my order?"
"I had gone out but then I returned so that I might renew my covenant with you," Abū Bakr said.
"Apostle of Allāh, I did not go out because I did not want to ask travellers about you," 'Umar answered.

"Despatch the army of Usāma, despatch the army of Usāma," commanded the Prophet, may Allāh bless Him and His Family. He repeated it three times and then he fainted from the fatigue which had come upon him and the sorrow which possessed him.

He remained unconscious for a short time while the Muslims wept and his wives and the women and children of the Muslims, and all those present raised great cries of lamentation. The Apostle of Allāh, may Allāh bless Him and His Family, recovered consciousness and looked at them. Then he said: "Bring me ink and parchment so that I may write a document for you, after which you will never

go astray."
Again he fainted and one of those present rose to look for ink and parchment.

"Go back," 'Umar ordered him. "He is delirious."

The man went back. (Later) those present regretted the dilatoriness (they had shown) in bringing ink and parchment and rebuked each other. They used to say: "*We belong to Allāh and to Him we will return*, but we have become anxious about our disobedience to the Apostle of Allāh, may Allāh bless Him and His Family."[6]

When he, peace be on him, recovered consciousness, one of them said: "We will not bring you ink and parchment, Apostle of Allāh."
"May Allāh remove him who made you say 'no'," he said. "However, I will appoint a trustee over you in a better way through my family."

Then he turned his head away from the people. They rose to leave but al-'Abbās, al-Faḍl b. al-'Abbās and 'Alī b. Abī Ṭālib and his family, in particular, remained with him.
"If this matter is to be settled upon us after you, then tell us," al-'Abbās asked him. "If you know that we are to be overcome, then give us the decision."
"You are those who will be found weak after me," he answered and then was silent.

The people (rose to leave), weeping with despair at (losing) the Prophet, may Allāh bless Him and His Family. When they had left, he, peace be on him, said: "Send back to me my brother and my uncle (i.e. 'Alī and al-'Abbās)."

They sent for someone to call them and he brought them. When he had them sitting close, he, blessings and peace be on him, said: "Uncle of the Apostle of Allāh, will you accept my testamentary bequest (*waṣī*), fulfil my promise and carry out my religion?"

"Apostle of Allāh, your uncle is an old man with the responsibilities of a large family," answered al-'Abbās. "You vie with the wind in liberality and generosity. You have made promises which your uncle could never fulfil."

Then he turned to 'Alī b. Abī Ṭālib, peace be on him, and said: "Brother, will you accept my testamentary bequest, fulfil my promises, carry out my religion on my behalf and look after the affairs of my family after me?"

6 cf. al-Ṭabarī, I, 1807

"Yes, Apostle of Allāh," he replied.
"Come near me," he told him.

He went near to him and he embraced him. He took his ring from his finger and said: "Take this and put it on your finger."

Then he called for his sword, his breastplate and all his weapons and gave those to him. He looked for a turban which he used to wear around his stomach when he put on his weapons and went out to battle. It was brought to him and he gave it to the Commander of the Faithful, peace be on him. Then he said to him: "Go, 'Alī, in the name of Allāh, to your house."

On the next day, the people were denied access to him as he was seriously ill in bed. The Commander of the Faithful, peace be on him, did not leave him except to (fulfil) some necessities. Then he had to go to attend to some of his affairs. The Apostle of Allāh, may Allāh bless Him and His Family, recovered consciousness and he missed 'Alī. His wives were around him and he said: "Call my brother and my companion." The weakness returned to him and he fell silent.

"Call Abū Bakr," 'Ā'isha said.
Abū Bakr was summoned. He came and sat by his head. When he opened his eyes, he looked at him and then turned his head away from him. Abū Bakr arose and said: "If he had any need of me, he would have communicated it to me."

When he had gone, the Apostle of Allāh repeated his words a second time and said: "Call my brother and my companion."

"Call 'Umar for him," Ḥafṣa said.
'Umar was summoned. When he came and the Apostle of Allāh, may Allāh bless Him and His Family, saw him, he turned his head away from him. So he went away. Then he said: "Call my brother and companion."

"Call 'Alī," said Umm Salama, may Allāh be pleased with her, "for he does not mean anyone else."

The Commander of the Faithful was summoned. When he was close to him, he indicated to him to bend down to him. Then the Apostle of Allāh, may Allāh bless Him and His Family, spoke privately to him for a long time. Then he rose and sat down beside him until the Apostle of Allāh, may Allāh bless Him and His Family, fell asleep.

When he had fallen asleep, ('Alī) went out.
"What did he entrust to you, Abū al-Ḥasan?" the people asked him.
"He taught me of a thousand doors of knowledge and each door opened for me (another) thousand doors," he answered. "He made a bequest to me of what I will undertake (*qā'im*) if Allāh, the Exalted, wishes."

He became critically ill and death was at hand. The Commander of the Faithful, peace be on him, was present with him. When his soul was about to depart, he said: "'Alī, put my head in your lap, for the order of Allāh (for my death) has come. When my soul departs, take it with your hand and rub your face with it. Then point me in the direction of the *qibla*. Carry out my command and pray over me as the first of the people. Do not leave me until you have buried me in my grave. Seek the help of Allāh, the Exalted."

'Alī, peace be on him, took his head and put it in his lap. Then he lost consciousness. Fāṭima, peace be on her, bent down to look into his face. She was weeping and calling to him, saying:

> May he be watered by the white clouds (pouring water) on his face. (He was) the one who cared for orphans and the one who protected widows.

Then the Apostle of Allāh, may Allāh bless Him and His Family, opened his eyes and said in a weak voice: "These are words for your uncle, Abū Ṭālib. Do not recite them. Rather recite: *Muhammad is no more than a messenger: many Were the messenger that passed away before him. If he died or were slain, will ye then Turn back on your heels?* (III 144)."

She wept for a long time. He indicated to her to come close. She went close to him and he whispered something to her which lit up her face. Then he, blessings and peace be on him, died. The right hand of the Commander of the Faithful was under his jaw and his soul passed into it. He raised it to his face and rubbed it with it. Then he put him in the direction (of the *qibla*), closed his eyes, and laid him out on his waist-cloth (*izār*).

The report has been handed down that Fāṭima, peace be on her, was asked: "What did the Apostle of Allāh, may Allāh bless Him and His Family, whisper to you so that by it he made the grief and worry of his death leave you?"
She replied: "He told me that I would be the first of his family (*ahl al-bayt*) to join him and that it would not be a long time for me after him before I would be with him. That made (the grief) go from me."

When the Commander of the Faithful, peace be on him, wanted to wash him, he

summoned al-Faḍl b. al-'Abbās and told him to get water for him to wash him after he had put a cover over his eyes. Then he split open his shirt from before the pocket to the midriff. He washed him, perfumed (his body) and shrouded him, while al-Faḍl passed him the water and helped him. When he had finished washing and preparing his body, he went forward and prayed alone. No one shared in the prayer with him. The Muslims in the mosque were talking about who would lead them in the prayer over him and where he would be buried. The Commander of the Faithful, peace be on him, came out to them and said: "The Apostle of Allāh, may Allāh bless Him and His Family, is our Imam, both alive and dead. Therefore let group after group of you come in and let them pray over him without an Imam and then let them depart. Allāh only took the soul of the Prophet in one place and it would please him for his grave to be there. I will bury him in the room in which he died."
The people accepted that and were pleased with it.

When the Muslims had prayed over him, al-'Abbās b. 'Abd al-Muṭṭalib sent a man to Abū 'Ubayda b. al-Jarrāḥ. He used to dig graves for the Meccans. That was the custom of the Meccans. He also sent to Zayd b. Sahl, who used to dig graves for the Medinans and make a niche in the side of the grave. He summoned them both and said: "O Allāh, choose (one of them) for your Prophet."

The man was found to be Abū Ṭalḥa Zayd b. Sahl and he was told to dig a grave for the Apostle of Allāh, may Allāh bless him and grant him peace. He dug a tomb for him. The Commander of the Faithful, peace be on him, entered it (as did) al-'Abbās b. 'Abd al-Muṭṭalib, al-Faḍl b. al-'Abbās and Usāma b. Zayd, so that they might carry out the burial of the Apostle.

At this, the Anṣār called out from behind the house: "'Alī, we remind you of Allāh and our right today with regard to the Apostle of Allāh lest it should go (from us). Let a man from among us come in so that we may have a share in the burial of the Apostle of Allāh, may Allāh bless Him and His Family."
"Let Aws b. Khawalī come in," he answered.

He was an excellent man, who had taken part in Badr, from the Banū 'Awf of Khazraj. When he came in, 'Alī, peace be on him, told him: "Go down into the grave."

He went down. The Commander of the Faithful put the (body of) the Apostle of Allāh, blessings and peace be on them both, into his hands and lowered it into his grave. When it reached the earth, he told him to come out. He came out and 'Alī, peace be on him, went down into the grave. He uncovered the face of the

Apostle of Allāh, may Allāh bless Him and His Family, and put his cheek on the earth in the direction of the qibla towards his right. Then he put clay soil on him and then poured the earth over him.

That was on Monday with two days remaining in (the month of) Ṣafar in the eleventh year after his emigration, the blessings and peace of Allāh be on him. He was sixty-three years of age.

Most of the people did not attend the burial of the Apostle of Allāh, may Allāh bless Him and His Family, because of the dispute which was taking place between the Emigrants and the Anṣār over the matter of succession (*khilāfa*). Most of them also missed the (funeral) prayer over him on that account as well. Fāṭima began to call out: "How evil has this morning become for him!"
Abū Bakr heard her and said: "Your morning is an evil morning."

The people seized the opportunity of 'Alī b. Abī Ṭālib, peace be on him, being occupied with the Apostle of Allāh, may Allāh bless Him and His Family, and the isolation of the Banū Hāshim from them because of the tragedy which had befallen them with regard to the Apostle of Allāh, may Allāh bless Him and His Family. So they hurried to take control of the affair. What was agreed on was agreed in favour of Abū Bakr because of the dislike of the newly-converted Meccans (*ṭulaqā'*) and (the dislike of) those whose hearts had been reconciled, of delaying the matter until Banū Hāshim had finished.

Thus was the matter settled and (the people) pledged allegiance to Abū Bakr because of his presence at the place. Well-known factors motivated the people to accept this. Among them were their own desires. This book is not the place to mention them and we will explain in detail the discussion about them (elsewhere).

The report is handed down that when what had taken place for Abū Bakr had taken place and those who pledged allegiance to him, had pledged allegiance, a man came to the Commander of the Faithful, peace be on him, while he was arranging the grave of the Apostle of Allāh, may Allāh bless Him and His Family, with a shovel in his hand. He said to him: "The people have pledged allegiance to Abū Bakr. The Anṣār have given up because of their differences and the new Meccan converts (*ṭulaqā'*) have hurried to make their covenant to the man out of fear of your attaining authority."
He put the tip of the shovel on the ground with his hand still on it and answered: *In the name of Allāh, the Merciful, the Compassionate. Do the people reckon that they will abandon saying: 'We believe,' without being guilty of deceit? We have*

tested those before them. Allāh knows those who are truthful and He knows the liar. Do those who do evil deeds consider that they can outdo us? How wrong is their judgement. (XXIX 2-4).

Abū Sufyān came to the door of the Apostle of Allāh, may Allāh bless Him and His Family, while 'Alī and al-'Abbās were zealously attending to the arrangements for him, and he called out:

> Banū Hāshim, the people have no desire for you. Special (to them) are (the clans of) Taym b. Murra and 'Adī.
>
> Yet authority should only be among you and belong to you. Only Abū al-Ḥasan ('Alī) has (a right) to it.
>
> Abū al-Ḥasan, take hold of it with a resolute hand. You are being deprived of the authority which you expected.

Then he called out at the top of his voice : "Banū Hāshim, Banū 'Abd Manāf, are you content that the despicable father of a young camel, the son of a despicable man, should have authority over you? No, by Allāh, if you wish, let me provide horses and men (who will be sufficient) for it."

"Go back, Abū Sufyān," shouted the Commander of the Faithful, peace be on him. "By Allāh, you do not seek Allāh in what you are suggesting. You are still plotting against Islam and those who believe in it. We are busy with the Apostle of Allāh, may Allāh bless Him and His Family. Each person gets what he has earned and he is (only) responsible for (*walī*) the crime he has committed."

Abū Sufyān went to the mosque. There he found the Banū Umayya gathered. He urged them (to take action) in the matter but they did not respond to him.

Discord was general and affliction was everywhere. Evil events had taken place by which Satan gained (greater) power and in which lying and hostile people co-operated. Through their denunciation of it, the people of (true) belief were abandoned. This is the interpretation of Allāh's words: *Beware of discord which especially strikes against those of you who oppress* (VIII 25).

*****

In the outstanding virtues of the Commander of the Faithful, peace be on him, which we have enumerated after what we have already mentioned with regard to the Farewell Pilgrimage, there is evidence which indicates that he, peace be on him, was especially characterised by them in a way that nobody else of mankind shared. Each one of them was a special category (of virtue) which stood in its own right without needing anything else to (explain) its significance.

Surely you realise that his special distinction during the illness of the Prophet, may Allāh bless Him and His Family, up to the time that Allāh, the Exalted, took him, required merit in religion and affinity to the Prophet, may Allāh bless Him and His Family? (This can be seen) through the good deeds which made (the Prophet) rely and depend on him, and set him apart from all the people in order to look after him at (the end of) his life. (Thus you should realise) the special distinction of his love for him which no one else shared with him. (Then there is also) the testamentary bequest (*waṣiyya*) which he made to him after it had been offered to someone else and refused because the burdens of the duties involved in it, and the responsibility of carrying it out and fulfilling the trust (were too heavy) for that other person to carry out. He was characterised by having been brothered with the Apostle of Allāh, may Allāh bless Him and His Family, and by being with him during his illness when he summoned him. In him was deposited the knowledge of religion by which he made him separate from anyone else. He carried out the washing and preparation of his body for (his journey to) Allāh. He said the (funeral) prayer over him before any one else, and he had precedence over them in that through his rank with (the Apostle) and with Allāh, the Exalted. He guided the community as to the manner of the (funeral) prayer over him when the matter was doubtful to them. He showed them the place to bury him despite the difference of opinion that they had had concerning that. They submitted to what he told them to do and considered him (right) in that. Thus through all of that he must be regarded as unique in his merit. Through it he brought to completion the outstanding action for Islam which he had begun at its beginning (and continued) to the death of the Apostle of Allāh, may Allāh bless Him and His Family. As a result of it there occurred for him a consecutive chain of virtues. No blemish entered any of his actions in religion. No aspect of his merit, as we have recorded it, puts any limitation on the ultimate in qualities of faith and in the virtues of Islam. This should also be associated with his marvellous miracles which confounded nature. He is such that there cannot be found an equal to him except for a prophet who has been sent (with a message) and an angel who has been brought into close proximity (with Allāh), and such as are associated with them in the degree of their virtues in the eyes of Allāh, may He be praised. With regard to those who oppose these three categories, traditional knowledge (*'āda*) follows a contrary (path to them) with the agreement of those who have reason (to think), tongues (to speak) and are aware of the traditions (*'ādāt*). We ask Allāh for success and by Him we will be protected from error.

CHAPTER V

LEGAL DECISIONS OF THE COMMANDER OF THE FAITHFUL

As for the reports which have demonstrated his outstanding quality in the legal decisions (he has given) with regard to religion and the laws (he has propounded) for which all the believers were in need, they are too numerous to be counted and too illustrious to be dealt with (properly), as are those which have been confirmed with regard to his precedence in traditional knowledge (*'ilm*), his supremacy over the community in gnosis (*ma'rifa*) and understanding. (There are many reports that) the scholars of the Companions (frequently) used to resort to him in matters which were difficult for them and they would seek his help in them and submit to his judgement concerning them. I will endeavour to put forward a brief summary which will give some indication of the others, if Allāh, the Exalted, wills.

A. (Judgements of the Commander of the Faithful during the Lifetime of the Prophet)

With the regard to this, there are those of his judgements while the Apostle of Allāh, may Allāh bless Him and His Family, was alive which have been reported by the transmitters of tradition from the non-Shī'a (*'āmma*) and from the Shī'a (*khāṣṣa*). In these (the Prophet) guided him and attested to the correctness of the decisions which he gave. He called attention to his goodness and praised him for it. Thus he separated him from the rest of men as a result of his outstanding merit in that. In this way he showed his entitlement to authority after him and the necessity for him to take precedence over others with regard to the position of the Imamate. Similarly, revelation has taken that (matter) within its compass in terms of the evidence for its meaning and what can be understood from the interpretation of its contents. Thus Allāh, the Mighty and High, says: *Is not he who guides you to truth more entitled to be followed than one who does not go aright unless he is guided? For what is wrong with you, how do you judge?* (X 35). Then there is His statement, may He be praised: *Are those who know and those who do not know equal? Only those who possess hearts (ūlū al-albāb) remember* (XXXIX 9). There is the statement by Him, the Mighty and High, in the story of Adam when the angel said: *Are you creating in it one who will spread corruption there and shed blood while we (constantly) repeat Your praise and hallow You? He replied: I know what you do not know. And He taught Adam all the names (or things) and then He presented them to the angels. He said: Tell me the names of these if you are truthful. They answered: May You be praised, we have no knowledge except what You have taught us. You are the One Who knows and the Wise. Then He said: Adam, tell them their names. When he had told them their names, He said to them: Have I not told you that I know the unseen in the heavens and the earth and I know what you are showing and what you are keeping hidden* (II 30-33). Allāh, the Exalted, informed the angels that Adam was more entitled to the vice-regency (*khilāfa*) than they were because He had informed him of the names and he was the most excellent of them in knowledge of things informed (to him). He, may His names be hallowed, (also) said in the story of Ṭālūt: *Their prophet said to them: Allāh has sent Ṭālūt to you as a king. They asked: Shall he have (the right of) kingship over us while we are more entitled to kingship than he is? He has not brought any extent of wealth. He replied: Allāh has chosen him to be over you and has increased him extensively in knowledge and substance. Allāh bestows His kingship on whom He wishes. Allāh is (all) embracing and One Who knows* (II 247).

Thus (Allāh) made the manner of his right to precedence over them, by virtue of what He granted him in the scope of his knowledge and substance, and His having chosen him above all of them. These verses are in agreement with rational evidence that the one who is more knowledgeable has more right in the area of the Imamate than those who do not equal him in knowledge. Thus they also give evidence for the necessity of the precedence of the Commander of the Faithful, peace be on him, over all the rest of the Muslims in the succession (*khilāfa*) of the Apostle of Allāh, may Allāh bless Him and His Family, and in the Imamate of the community because of his precedence, peace be on him, over them in knowledge and wisdom and their falling short of his rank in that.

1. His Judgements in Yemen

Among those reports which have been handed down about his legal decisions, peace be on him, while the Prophet, may Allāh bless Him and His Family, was still alive and present, is the following:
When the Apostle of Allāh, may Allāh bless Him and His Family, wanted to invest him with the office of judge in Yemen and to send him to them so that he might teach them the laws, explain to them what was permitted and forbidden, and judge for them according to the laws of the Qur'ān, the Commander of the Faithful, peace be on him, asked him: "Apostle of Allāh, you are inviting me to (undertake) the office of judge while I am still a young man without knowledge of all (the matters of) judgement."

"Come nearer to me," he told him. He went nearer and he struck him in the chest with his hand and said: "O Allāh, guide his heart and strengthen his tongue."

The Commander of the Faithful reported: "I never doubted in my ability to judge between two men after that occurrence."

When the administrative house (*dār*) in Yemen was occupied by him and he began to take care of the office of judging and giving decisions among the Muslims, which the Apostle of Allāh, may Allāh bless Him and His Family, had entrusted to him, two men were brought before him. Between them was a maidservant over whom both of them had equal rights of possession as a slave. They had both been ignorant of the prohibition of having intercourse with her and had both had intercourse with her in the same month of her menstrual cycle. (They had done this) in the belief that this was permissible, because of their recent acceptance of Islam and their lack of knowledge of the laws which were in the law of Islam (*sharī'a*). The maidservant had become pregnant and given birth to a boy. They were in dispute as to (who was the father).

He drew lots with their names on for the boy. The lot fell upon one of them. He assigned the boy to him but required him to pay half his value as if he had been a slave of his partner. He said: "If I knew that you had both embarked on what you have done after the proof had been given you of it being prohibited, I would have exerted (every effort) to punish you both."

The Apostle of Allāh, may Allāh bless Him and His Family, learned of this case. He accepted it and he acknowledged the judgement on them within Islam. He said: "Praise be to Allāh Who has created among us, the family (*ahl al-bayt*), one who can judge according to the practice and method of David in judging." In that he was referring to judgement according to inspiration (*ilhām*) which would have been taken in the sense of revelation (*waḥy*) and the sending down of a text for it if there had been any explanation of such (an occurrence ever having taken place).

Among the cases brought before him, peace be on him, while he was in Yemen, is the report of (the case in which) a pit was dug for a lion. It fell into it and the people gathered round to look at it. One man was standing on the edge of the pit. His foot slipped and he hung on to another man. That man hung on to a third, and the third to a fourth. They all fell into the pit and were all killed. He, peace be on him, gave the judgement that the first was the prey of the lion and he (and his family) were responsible for the payment of a third of the blood-price for the second. Similarly the second (and his family) were responsible for the payment of a third of the blood-price for the third and the third (and his family) were responsible for the payment of a third of the blood-price for the fourth.

The report of that reached the Apostle of Allāh, may Allāh bless Him and His Family. He said: "Abū al-Ḥasan has given judgement in their regard with the judgement of Allāh, the Mighty and High above (on) His throne."

Then there was brought before him (the case in which) it is reported that a girl was carrying (another) girl on her shoulder in a game. Another girl came along and pinched the girl who was carrying (the other one). She jumped because of being pinched. The girl who was being carried fell and broke her neck. She died. He, peace be on him, judged that the girl who did the pinching was, responsible for a third of the blood-price, the girl who jumped was responsible for (another) third of it and the remaining third was inoperative because the riding of the girl, who broke her neck, on the girl who jumped was in fun.

The report of that reached the Apostle of Allāh, may Allāh bless Him and His Family. He accepted it and testified to the correctness of it.

He, peace be on him, gave judgement on (a case where) a wall had fallen on some people and killed them. Among their number there was a slave-woman and a free woman. The free woman had had a small child, born of a free man, and the slave-woman had had a small child, born of a slave. The free child could not be distinguished from the slave child.

He drew lots between them; he adjudged freedom as belonging to the one of them for whom the lot for freedom was drawn and he adjudged slavery for the one for whom the lot for slavery was drawn. Then he freed (the slave child) and made him retainer (lit. client *mawlā*) (of the free child). In this way he also decided about their inheritance with the decision going in accordance with (the norm for) the free one and his retainer.

The Apostle of Allāh, may Allāh bless Him and His Family, accepted his judgement in this decision and he declared its correctness through his acceptance of it, as we have mentioned and described.

2. A Case outside Yemen during the Life of the Prophet

Reports have been handed down that two men brought a dispute before the Prophet, may Allāh bless Him and His Family, about a cow which had killed a donkey.

"Apostle of Allāh," said one of them, "this man's cow has killed my donkey."
"Go to Abū Bakr," the Apostle of Allāh told them, "and ask him about that."

They came to Abū Bakr and told him their story.
"Why have you left the Apostle of Allāh, may Allāh bless Him and His Family, and come to me?" he asked them.
"He told us to do that," they answered.
"A beast has killed a beast and therefore its owner has no responsibility (for the dead beast)," he said.

They returned to the Apostle of Allāh, the blessing of Allāh be on him, and told him of that. He said to them: "Go to 'Umar b. al-Khaṭṭāb and tell him your story. Ask him for a judgement about that."

They went to him and told him their story. He asked: "Why have you left the Apostle of Allāh and come to me?"
"He told us to do that," they answered.
"Why did he not tell you to go to Abū Bakr?" he asked.
"We were ordered to do that," they told him, "and we went to him."
"What did he say to you about this case?" he enquired.
"He said such and such," they replied.
"My view agrees with Abū Bakr's," he said.

They returned to the Prophet, may Allāh bless Him and His Family, and gave him a report of that. He said: "Go to 'Alī b. Abī Ṭālib so that he may judge between you."

They went to him and told him their story.
"If the cow entered into the stable of the donkey, then the owner (of the cow) must pay the price of the donkey to the owner (of the donkey)," he declared. "But if the donkey entered into the stable of the cow, and (the cow) killed it, the owner (of the donkey) has no payment due from the owner (of the cow)."

They went back to the Prophet, may Allāh bless Him and His Family, and told him about his judgement between them. He, may Allāh bless Him and His Family, said: "'Alī b. Abī Ṭālib, peace be on him, has given judgement between you with the judgement of Allāh, the Exalted." Then he said: "Praise be to Allāh who has created among us, the family (*ahl al-bayt*), one who can give judgement in the manner of David."

Some of the non-Shī'a (*'āmma*) authorities report that this judgement between the two men was made by the Commander of the Faithful, peace be on him, in Yemen.

B. Judgements of the Commander of the Faithful during the Rule of Abū Bakr

(This is) a brief summary of the legal decisions given by (the Commander of the Faithful), peace be on him, during the rule of Abū Bakr. Among these is the account which has been handed down by both non-Shī'a and Shī'a authorities:

A man was brought before Abū Bakr. He had drunk wine, so Abū Bakr wanted to administer the prescribed punishment (*ḥadd*) on him. However the man pleaded: "I drank it without having knowledge that it was forbidden because I grew up among people who regarded it as lawful. I did not know that it was forbidden until now."

Abū Bakr became unable to deliver a decision in the matter. He did not know the way to judge him. Some of those present advised him to seek for information from the Commander of the Faithful, peace be on him, about the decision in that matter. He sent someone to ask him about it.

The Commander of the Faithful advised: "Tell two trustworthy Muslims to go around the gatherings of the Emigrants and Anṣār to ask them whether any of them had recited to (the man) the verse (of the Qur'ān) forbidding (wine) or had reported it to him on the authority of the Apostle of Allāh, may Allāh bless Him and His Family. If two of them give testimony of that, then he should carry out the prescribed punishment on him. If no one can give testimony on that, he should tell him to repent and let him go."

Abū Bakr did that. Not one of the Emigrants and Anṣār gave evidence that they had recited the verse (of the Qur'ān) forbidding (wine) or had reported it to him on the authority of the Apostle of Allāh, may Allāh bless Him and His Family. So he told him to repent and let him go. He submitted to (the authority of) 'Alī in judging it.

*****

They have reported that Abū Bakr was asked about Allāh's words: *Fākihatan wa abbān* (LXXX 31). He did not know the meaning of *al-abb* in the Qur'ān and said: "Any sky which looks down (on me) or any land which holds me up . ... rather what shall I do, if I say something about the Book of Allāh, the Exalted, which I do not know. As for *al-fākiha*, (fruit), we know its meaning but as for *al-abb* Allāh knows better."

The Commander of the Faithful, peace be on him, was informed of that statement of his about it. "May Allāh be praised, did he know that *al-abb* is fresh herbage (*kalā'*) and pasture (*mar'an*) and that His words, *wa fākihatan wa abbān*, are the enumeration by Allāh, the Exalted, of his favours to His creatures through the things which He has provided for them to eat and created for them and their animals; (these are some of) the things by which their spirits are kept alive and their bodies exist."

*****

Abū Bakr was asked about *al-kalāla* (IV 176). He answered: "I will give my opinion about it. If I am right, then it is from Allāh. If I am wrong, then it is from myself and from Satan."

The Commander of the Faithful was informed of that. He said: "What makes him satisfied with opinion in this situation? Did he not know that *al-kalāla* is brothers and sisters from (the same) father and mother, and from just the father and also from the mother in the same way. Allāh, the Mighty and High, said: *If they seek a decision from you, say: Allāh gave a decision to you in terms of the brothers and sisters (al-kalāla). If a man dies without children and he has a sister she shall have half of what he left* (IV 176). He, the Mighty (also) said: *If a man is succeeded by brothers and sisters (al-kalāla) or by a wife while he had a brother or a sister, each one will have a sixth. If there are more than that, then they shall have a third* (IV 12)."

*****

The report is handed down that one of the Jewish rabbis came to Abū Bakr and said: "You are the successor (*khalīfa*) of this community."
"Yes," he replied.
"We find in the Torah that the successors (*khulafā'*) of prophets are the most knowledgeable of the communities," he said. "Therefore tell me about Allāh, the Exalted. Where is He? In heaven or on earth?"
"In heaven on the throne," answered Abū Bakr.
"Then I should consider that the earth is without Him and I should consider according to this statement that He is in one place and not in another," the Jew stated.
"That is doctrine of atheists (*zanādiqa*)," declared Abū Bakr. "Go away from me or I will kill you."

The rabbi turned away in amazement and mockery at Islam. The Commander of the Faithful, peace be on him, met him.

"Jew, I know what you have asked about and did not get an answer for," he said. "We say that Allāh, the Mighty and High, is the whereness of whereness, there is no where for Him. He avoids any place containing Him while He is in every place, without contact with anything and without being next to anything. He encompasses knowledge of what is there and nothing of it is outside His provenance. I am telling you about what is written in one of your books which attests the truth of what I have told you. If you know it, do you believe in it?"
"Yes," replied the Jew.

He said: "Didn't you find in one of your books that Moses, the son of 'Imrān, peace be on him, was sitting down one day when an angel came to him from the East. Moses asked him: 'From where have you come?' It answered: 'From Allāh, the Mighty and High.' Then an angel came to him from the West. He asked: 'From where have you come?' It answered: 'From Allāh, the Mighty and High.' Then another angel came to him and said: 'I have come to you from the Seventh Heaven, from (being with) Allāh, the Mighty and High.' Another angel came to him and said: 'I have come to you from the Seventh Firmament, from (being with) Allāh, the Mighty and High.' Then Moses said: 'May Allāh be praised, no place is without Him and He is not nearer to one place than another.'"

The Jew replied: "I testify that this is the truth and you have more right to (occupy) the place of your Prophet than the one who has control over it."

Reports like these are numerous.

*****

C. Reports of the Judgements of (the Commander of the Faithful) during the Rule of 'Umar b. al-Khaṭṭāb

Among these is what has been handed down by non-Shī'a (*'āmma*) and Shī'a (*khāṣṣa*) authorities concerning the story of Qudāma b. Maẓ'ūn. The latter had drunk wine and 'Umar wanted to carry out the prescribed punishment on him. However, Qudāma had said: "It is not necessary to give me the prescribed punishment because Allāh has said: *There is no crime in what those who have believed and performed good works have tasted as long as they have feared Allāh, believed and performed good works* (V 93)."
So 'Umar withdrew the prescribed punishment.

The Commander of the Faithful, peace be on him, learned of that. He went to

‘Umar and said: “You failed to administer the prescribed punishment on Qudāma for drinking wine.”
“He recited the verse of Qur’ān to me,” said ‘Umar and recited it.

“Qudāma is not one of the people (referred to) in the verse” retorted the Commander of the Faithful, peace be on him. “Nor can anyone use it (as a pretext) for committing actions which Allāh has forbidden. Those who have believed and performed good actions cannot make what is forbidden lawful. Send for Qudāma and make him repent from what he said. If he repents, then administer the prescribed punishment on him. If he does not repent, kill him, for he has abandoned the religion (*milla*).”

Then ‘Umar became aware (of the real situation). Qudāma knew of the discussion and (publicly) showed his repentance and his withdrawal (of his assertion). ‘Umar withdrew the punishment of death but he did not know how he should administer the prescribed punishment on him. He asked the Commander of the Faithful, peace be on him: “Show me how the prescribed punishment (should be administered) on him.”

“Give him the prescribed punishment of eighty (lashes),” he said. “For when the drinker of wine drinks it, he becomes drunk. When he becomes drunk, he talks nonsense. When he talks nonsense, he spreads calumnies.”

Therefore ‘Umar had him given eighty lashes and he gave judgement according to his advice in that matter.

*****

It is reported that during the time of ‘Umar, a man seduced a mad woman. Evidence for that was established against her. Therefore ‘Umar ordered her to be flogged according to the prescribed punishment. She was brought past the Commander of the Faithful (on her way) to be flogged.

“Why is the mad woman of the family of so-and-so being dragged along?” he asked.

“A man seduced her and fled and the evidence for fornication has been established against her. So ‘Umar ordered her to be flogged,” he was told.

“Take her back to him,” he told them, “and ask him: Don’t you know that this is a mad woman and the Apostle of Allāh, may Allāh bless Him and His Family has said: The order (of punishment) should be withheld from the mad person until he recovers. Her reason and her soul have been overcome."

She was taken back to 'Umar and he was told what the Commander of the Faithful, peace be on him, had said. He said: "Allāh has rescued (me) from it. I was almost destroyed through whipping her." And he withdrew the prescribed punishment from her.

******

It is reported that a pregnant woman who had committed adultery was brought before 'Umar. He ordered her to be stoned. The Commander of the Faithful, peace be on him, told him: "Take care that you have a (right to take) action against her, that is not a (right to take) action against what is in her womb. For Allāh, the Exalted, says: *Nor does any bearer of a burden bear the burden of another* (VI 164)."

"I have not lived (to see) a problem with which Abū al-Ḥasan is not (competent to deal)," said 'Umar. Then he asked: "What shall I do with her?"

"Take care of her until she gives birth," he said. "When she has given birth and you have found someone to nurse her child, then administer the prescribed punishment on her." `

Thus was 'Umar relieved of (his cares). In that decision, he relied on the Commander of the Faithful, peace be on him.

******

It is reported that ('Umar) summoned a woman who had been conversing with men at her (house). When his messengers came to her, she was frightened and afraid. She had a miscarriage and her child fell to the ground crying but then died.

'Umar was informed of that. He gathered the Companions of the Apostle of Allāh, may Allāh bless Him and His Family, together and asked them about the law concerning that. They all said: "We consider that you were acting correctly. You only wanted good and there is no (blame for) anything against you in that."

The Commander of the Faithful, peace be on him, was sitting without saying anything about that. 'Umar asked him: "What is your view about this, Abū al-Ḥasan?"
"You have heard what they said," he answered.
"But what is your view?" he insisted.

"The people have said what you heard," he replied.
"I adjure you to give your view," he said.

"If people have (been trying to) come close to you, they have deceived you," he said. "If they thought about their advice then they have disregarded (the fact that) the blood-wit is required of you as the one responsible for the death and you thereby incur the blood-wit (*'āqila*), because the killing of the child was (as a result of) a mistake connected with you."

"By Allāh, you have advised differently from them," he said. "By Allāh, I will not delay until the blood-wit is paid by (my clan) Banu 'Ādī"

The Commander of the Faithful, peace be on him, had brought that about.

*****

It is reported that during the time of 'Umar, two women were disputing over a child. Each of them claimed that it was her child without any proof but no one else contested their claim to it. The decision with regard to that was not clear to 'Umar. He resorted to the Commander of the Faithful, peace be on him, with regard to it.

He summoned the two women and warned them both, making them both afraid. But they both persisted in their dispute and difference. In the face of their both persisting in dispute, he, peace be on him, said: "Bring me a saw."

"What are you going to do?" the two women asked.
"I will cut it into two halves," he said, "and each of you can have a half."

The one remained silent but the other said: "O Allāh, O Allāh, Abū al-Ḥasan, if there is no escape from that, then let her have it."

"Allāh is greater (*Allāhu akbar*)," he said. "This is your son not hers. If it had been her son, she would have had pity on him and been anxious (about him)."

The other woman admitted that the right (to the child) belonged to her colleague and the child was not hers. Thus was 'Umar relieved (of his cares) and he blessed the Commander of the Faithful for the trouble that he had saved him from through (his) judgement.

******

[It is reported on the authority of Yūnus, on the authority of al-Ḥasan:]

A woman was brought before ‘Umar. She had given birth six months earlier and he now intended to stone her. The Commander of the Faithful, peace be on him, said to him: “If you quarrel with the Book of Allāh, I will dispute with you. Allāh, the exalted says: *The (period) of pregnancy and weaning (of a child) is thirty months* (XLVI 15). And He, the High, (also) says: *Mothers suckle their children for two complete years for anyone who wants to carry out (the full period of) suckling* (II 233). When the woman has carried out the suckling for two years, and the (period of) pregnancy and suckling (of the child) is thirty months . .. . At the moment (she has only fulfilled) the responsibility (of suckling) for six months (and therefore cannot be killed).”

‘Umar freed the woman and confirmed the decision concerning that. The Companions acted according to it and the Successors (*al-tābi‘ūn*) (to the Companions) and those who adopted it right up to the present time.

*****

It is reported that witnesses gave evidence against a woman that they had found her at one of the watering places of the Bedouin and a man who was not her husband (*ba‘l*) was having intercourse with her. ‘Umar ordered her to be stoned as she had a husband (*ba‘l*). She declared: “O Allāh, You know that I am innocent.”

“Do you impugn the witnesses as well?” remarked ‘Umar.

“Let them bring her back and let them question her,” said the Commander of the Faithful, peace be on him. “Perhaps she has an excuse.”

She was brought back and questioned about the circumstances (of what she had done). She said: “My family had some camels. I went out with my family’s camels and took with me some water. There was no milk in the camels. A neighbour of ours had camels with him and there was milk in his camels. My water was used up and I asked him to give me a drink. He refused to give me a drink unless I submitted myself to him. I refused. When my life was about to depart I submitted myself to him unwillingly.”

“Allāh is greater (*Allāhu akbar*),” declared the Commander of the Faithful, peace be on him. “*Whoever is compelled (to do something) without desiring (to do it) is not a transgressor and no sin is (counted) against him* (II 173).”

When ‘Umar heard that he freed her.

*****

Among the reports about (the Commander of the Faithful), peace be on him, with regard to the idea of giving judgement, and the soundness of (his) opinion, his guidance of the people to their (true) interests and his realisation of what would be likely to corrupt the people without his informing them of the proper course is the following:

[Shabāba b. Suwār has reported on the authority of Abū Bakr al-Hudhalī, who said: I heard one of our scholars saying:]

The foreigners (*a'ājim*) from Hamdhān, al-Rayy, Iṣfahān, Qūmus and Nahāwand sent letters to each other. They sent messengers to one another (saying): "The king of the Arabs who has brought them their religion and produced their Book has died." They were referring to the Prophet, may Allāh bless Him and his family. "Their king after him was an insignificant king and he has died." They were referring to Abū Bakr. "Another arose after him who has lived longer so that he has reached as far as you in your lands and he has sent his soldiers to attack you." They were referring to 'Umar b. al-Khaṭṭāb. "He will not desist from you until you expel those of his soldiers who are in your land, go against him and attack him in his land. Therefore make an alliance (to do) this and make a covenant (to carry) it (out)."

When the report (of this) came to the Muslims in Kūfa, they sent it to 'Umar b. al-Khaṭṭāb. When the report reached him, he was very afraid on account of it. He went to the mosque of the Apostle of Allāh, may Allāh bless Him and His Family. He went up on the pulpit and praised and glorified Allāh. Then he said: "Men of the Emigrants and the Anṣār, Satan has gathered groups (of men) against you. With them he has dared to attempt to put out the light of Allāh. Indeed the people of Hamdhān, the people of Iṣfahān, the people of al-Rayy and Qūmus, of Nahāwand, despite difference in language, colour and religion, have made a covenant and an alliance to drive your brother Muslims from their land and to come against you and attack you in your land. Give me advice but be brief and not too lengthy in words This is a day for (such advice), after which there will be a day (to speak at greater length)."

They began to consult. Ṭalḥa b. 'Ubayd Allāh stood up - he was one of the orators of Quraysh. He praised and glorified Allāh. Then he said: "Commander of the faithful, affairs have begun to bridle you; times have brought hardship to you; misfortunes have tested you and experiences have taught you. You, the one blessed with authority (*amr*) and fortunate in nature, have been given authority. Therefore you have knowledge, you have been given information and you know it well. You have only avoided (evil) consequences of Allāh's decision as a result of choosing good. So attend to this matter according to your own view and do not avoid that." Then he sat down.

"Speak," 'Umar urged (the people).

'Uthmān b. 'Affān stood up. He praised and glorified Allāh. Then he said: "I think that you should direct the Syrians from Syria and the Yemenīs from Yemen, and that you should go with the inhabitants of these two sanctuaries (Mecca and Medina) and with the people of the two camp towns of Kūfa and Baṣra. Then all the polytheists would meet all the Muslims. Commander of the faithful, you would not seek to survive after the Arabs, nor would you enjoy with any delight the world, nor would you seek refuge from it in a well-fortified fortress. Therefore attend to (the matter) with your own view and do not avoid that." Then he sat down.

"Speak," 'Umar urged (the people).

The Commander of the Faithful, 'Alī b. Abī Ṭālib, peace be on him, spoke praising Allāh until he had finished the introductory praises and he glorified Him and called for blessings on His Apostle, may Allāh bless Him and his family. Then he said: "If you sent the Syrians from Syria, the Byzantines would come against their children. If you sent the Yemenīs from Yemen, the Abyssinians would come against their children. If you sent (the people) from the two sanctuaries, the bedouin would rebel against us on (every) flank and side. Thus the families of Arabs which you leave behind you are more important to you than what is in front of you. As for what you have mentioned of the number of foreigners and your fear of their groupings, we never fought in the time of the Apostle of Allāh, may Allāh bless Him and His Family, with regard to number. We only used to fight with regard to the help (of Allāh). As for what you have been informed of their gathering to come against the Muslims, Allāh is more averse to their coming than you are to it. It is more appropriate for Him to change what He is averse to. When the foreigners look at you, they say (to themselves) that this is the man of the Arabs. If you break him, you break the Arabs and it would be much more difficult for (them to continue) their eager (advance). Thus you united them against yourself and those who did not use to support them are (now) supporting them. However, I consider that you should make them remain in their camp-town and write to the people of Baṣra. Let them divide into three groups. Let one of their groups look after their offspring as guards of them. Let another group undertake (the task of resisting) the people who have made this covenant, to break them up. Let (the third) group go to their brothers as reinforcements for them."

"This is the best view," said 'Umar. "I would like to follow it." Then he began to repeat the words of the Commander of the Faithful, peace be on him, setting it out in admiration of it and as his choice.

[Al-Shaykh al-Mufīd, may Allāh be pleased with him, said:]
Consider, may Allāh support you, this view which was announced with the merit of sound judgement when the thoughtful leaders (*ūlū al-albāb wa-al-'ilm*) were in dispute. Reflect upon the success which Allāh brought to the Commander of the Faithful, peace be on him, in all circumstances and the way the people used to resort to him in difficult matters. Then add that to what has been established of his merit in religion which was not possible for the other prominent people so that they were in need of him because of his knowledge. You will find out about it in the chapter on miracles, which we have already mentioned. May Allāh be the friend of success.

This has been a brief outline of the judgements delivered by (the Commander of the Faithful), peace be on him, during the rule of 'Umar b. al-Khaṭṭāb. There were similar (judgements) during the rule of 'Uthmān b. 'Affān.

D. Reports of the Judgements of the Commander of the Faithful during the Rule of 'Uthmān b. 'Affān.

Among these is the report which non-Shī'a (*'āmma*) and Shī'a (*khāṣṣa*) historians (*naqalat al-āthār*) relate.
An old man married a woman. The woman became pregnant but the old man claimed that he had not had intercourse with her and denounced her pregnancy. The matter was unclear to 'Uthmān. He asked the woman: "Did the old man make you lose your virginity while (you) were a virgin?"
"No," she replied.
"Administer the prescribed punishment on her," ordered 'Uthmān.

"A woman has two orifices," the Commander of the Faithful, peace be on him, interposed, "the orifice for the menstrual flow and the orifice for urine. Perhaps the old man was close to her and his semen managed to flow into her menstrual orifice. Then she became pregnant through him."

He asked the man about that and he answered: "I used to discharge semen while kissing her but without ever going to the extent of making her lose her virginity."

"The pregnancy is due to him," declared the Commander of the Faithful, peace be on him, "and the child is his child. I consider that he should be punished for his (wrongful) denunciation."

'Uthmān carried out his judgement in that and was amazed at him.

*****

They have reported that a man had a concubine and he gave her a child. Then he separated from her and married her to one of his slaves. The master died. She was freed by virtue of her being in the possession of her son. Her son also inherited her husband. The son died and she inherited her husband from her child. They came before 'Uthmān as a result of a dispute. She was claiming: "This is my slave." He was claiming: "She is my wife and I will not release her (from the marriage)."

"This is a difficult problem," said 'Uthmān.

The Commander of the Faithful, peace be on him, was present. He said: "Ask her whether he has had intercourse with her after her inheritance."
"No," she replied.

"If I was aware that he had done that, I would have punished him," he said. "Go. He is your slave without any rights over you. If you wish to keep possession of him, or to free him, or to sell him, that is your right."

*****

They reported that in the time of 'Uthmān a slave woman who was in the process of buying her freedom (*makātiba*) committed fornication. She had already purchased three-quarters of her freedom. 'Uthmān asked the Commander of the Faithful whether he should have her flogged according to the amount (required) for a free woman or the amount required for a slave. He also asked Zayd b. Thābit. The latter said that she should be flogged according to the amount (required) for a slave. "How can she be flogged according to the amount (required) for a slave when she has already purchased three-quarters of her freedom?" asked the Commander of the Faithful, peace be on him. "Should you not whip her according to the amount (required) for a free woman as she is much more of that?"

"If that is the case," said Zayd, "then she ought to inherit according to the amount (required) for a free woman."

"Indeed, that is necessary," replied the Commander of the Faithful, peace be on him.

Zayd was silenced but 'Uthmān disagreed with the Commander of the Faithful, peace be on him. He followed Zayd's statement without paying attention to the proof which had been given to him (by the Commander of the Faithful).

*****

Mentioning further examples such as these would make the book unduly long. However the reports about them are well known.

E. Reports of the Judgements of (the Commander of the Faithful), peace be on him, after the Pledge of Allegiance of the General Populace to him and the Death of 'Uthmān

The traditionists (*ahl al-naql wa ḥamalat al-āthār*) report that a woman gave birth on the bed of her husband to a child who had two heads and bodies attached to one waist. His family were confused as to whether it was one or two. They went to the Commander of the Faithful, peace be on him, to ask him about that so that they might know the law with regard to him. The Commander of the Faithful, peace be on him, told them: "Watch him when he goes to sleep. Then wake up one of the bodies and heads. If they both wake up at the same time, then they are a single human being. If one of them wakes up and the other remains asleep, they are two persons and their rights in inheritance are the rights of two persons."

*****

[Al-Ḥasan b. 'Alī al-'Abdī reported on the authority of Sa'd b. Ṭarīf, on the authority of al-Asbagh b. Nubāta, who said:]
While Shurayḥ was in a session of judgements, a person came to him and said: "Abū Umayya, let me speak to you privately, for I have a (great) need."

He ordered those around him to leave him and they went away. Only his close associates (*khāṣṣa*) who attended him remained. He said: "Say what your need is."

"Abū Umayya," (the person) told him, "I have what men have and what women have. The judgement rests with you about whether I am a man or a woman."

He answered: "I have heard a decision about that from the Commander of the Faithful, peace be on him, which I remember. Tell me from which of the two orifices does your urine come?"
"From them both," answered the person.

"From which does it (finally) finish?" he asked.
"From them both together," was the reply.

Shurayḥ was amazed.

The person said: "I will tell you something (else) about my affair which is (even) more amazing."
"What is that?" asked Shurayḥ.

"My father married me (to a man) on the assumption that I was a woman. I became pregnant from my husband and I bought a slave girl to look after me. I had intercourse with her and she became pregnant from me."

Shurayḥ struck one of his hands against the other in amazement and said: "This is a matter which must be taken before the Commander of the Faithful, peace be on him, for I have no knowledge of the ruling concerning it."

He got up and the person followed him and those present with him. He went in to the Commander of the Faithful, peace be on him. He told the story to him and the Commander of the Faithful, peace be on him, summoned the person. He asked about (the story) which Shurayḥ had told him. (The person) admitted it.

"Who is your husband?" he asked.
"So-and-so b. so-and-so," was the reply, "and he is present in the town."

He had him summoned and asked him about what (the other) had said.
"It is true," he said.

"You have to be braver than a lion-hunter when you face this sort of situation," he said. Then he called Qanbar, his retainer (*mawlā*) and said: "Take this person into a house and with (the person) four just women and order them to strip (the person) naked and to count the ribs after making sure that the pudenda are covered." The man (i.e. Qanbar) said: "Commander of the Faithful, men and women will not be secure from this person."

So (the Commander of the Faithful) ordered that a straw-dealer should cover him with straw and he left him alone in a house. Then he went into it and counted the ribs. There were seven on the left side and eight on the right side. He declared: "This is a man."

He ordered his hair to be cut and that he be dressed in a hat, sandals and a cloak (*riḍā'*). He separated him from his (former) husband.

[Some traditionists reported:] When the person made the claim he made about two orifices, the Commander of the Faithful, peace be on him, ordered two just Muslims to go to an empty house and take the person with them. He ordered two mirrors to be set up one of them facing the pudenda of the person and the other facing the (first) mirror. He ordered the person to show its nakedness by facing the mirror so that the two just men could not see it (directly). He ordered the two just men to look into the mirror facing (the first) mirror. When the two just men realised the truth of what the person had claimed about (having) two orifices, he considered its status (to be established) by counting the ribs. When he declared him to be a man, he ignored his claims of being pregnant as being a mistake and he did not act in accordance with it. He declared the pregnancy of the slave girl as due to him and he associated him with it.

******

They reported that one day the Commander of the Faithful, peace be on him, went into the mosque and found a young man weeping (there) with some people around him. The Commander of the Faithful, peace be on him, asked about it. He said: "Shurayḥ has judged a case against me and he has not done me justice."

"What is (the nature of) your affair?" he asked.
"These people" he said and he indicated a group who were present, "took my father out on a journey with them. They came back but he did not come back. I asked them about him and they said that he had died. I asked them about the money (*māl*) that he had taken with him and they said: 'We do not know of any money.' Then Shurayḥ made them swear an oath and ordered me to stop interfering with them."

The Commander of the Faithful, peace be on him, told Qanbar: "Gather the people and summon the *shuraṭ al-khamīs*."[1]

Then he sat down and summoned the group (to come before him) and the young man with them. He asked him about what he had said and he repeated his claim and began to cry, saying: "By Allāh, I accuse them of (killing) my father, Commander of the Faithful. They tricked him so that they could take him with them out of a desire to (get) his money."

---

1 According to Ahmad b. Abi 'Abd Allāh al-Barqī, the Shurtat al-Khamis were six thousand of 'Alī's followers who had pledged themselves to serve him until death, *al-Rijāl*, (Tehran 1342 A.H. S.), 3. They can be regarded as a combination of bodyguard, police force and front-line soldiers.

Then, the Commander of the Faithful, peace be on him, questioned the people. They told him exactly what they had told Shurayḥ: "The man died and we do not know of any money of his."

Then he looked into their faces and said to them: "What do you think? Do you think that I do not know what you have done with the father of this youth? Then I would have little knowledge."

He ordered them to separate from each other and they separated from each other within the mosque. Each one of them was made to stand next to one of the pillars in the mosque. Next he summoned 'Ubayd Allāh b. Abī Rāfi', his scribe at that time, and told him to sit down. Then he called one of them. He told him: "Tell me on which day did you leave your houses while the father of this boy was with you? And (do it) without raising your voice."
"On such and such a day," he said.
"Write it down," he told 'Ubayd Allāh.
"In which month was it?" he asked.
"In such and such a month," was the answer.
"Write it down," he instructed.
"In which year?"
"In such and such a year."
"Write it down."
'Ubayd Allāh wrote all that down.
"Of what sickness did he die?" he asked.
"Of such and such a sickness."
"In which place did he die?"
"In such and such a place."
"Who washed and shrouded his corpse?"
"So-and-so."
"With what did you shroud him?"
"With such and such."
"Who said the prayer over him?"
"So-and-so."
"Who put him into the grave?"
"So-and-so."
'Ubayd Allāh b. Abī Rāfi' was writing all that down. When he came to the statement about the burial, the Commander of the Faithful, peace be on him, said: "Allāh is greater (*Allāhu akbar*)." (He said it) in a way that the people in the mosque could hear. Then he ordered the man to be taken back to his place.

He summoned another of the men and made him sit close to him. He questioned him in the same way as he had questioned the first man and he gave answers which disagreed with (the answers of) the first man throughout his interrogation. (All the time) 'Ubayd Allāh was writing them down. When he had finished his questioning, he said: "Allāh is greater," in a way that the people in the mosque could hear. He ordered that the two men be taken out of the mosque to the prison but they were to stand and wait at the door.

He summoned the third and questioned him in the same way as he had questioned the first. He gave answers which contradicted what both of them had said and he confirmed that to him. He said: "Allāh is greater." Then he ordered him to be taken out to his two colleagues.

He summoned the fourth of the men. His words were confused and he stuttered. (The Commander of the Faithful) warned him and made him afraid. (The man) confessed that his colleagues had killed the man and taken his money and that they had buried him in such and such a place near Kūfa. The Commander of the Faithful, peace be on him, said: "Allāh is greater." Then he ordered him to be taken to prison.

He summoned one of the men (already questioned) and said to him: "You have claimed that the man died in bed. Yet you killed him. Tell me the truth about your situation, otherwise I will punish you as a warning to the others that I should be told the truth in your case." He confessed to killing the man with a similar confession to his colleague.

Then he summoned the rest (of them) and they confessed the murder. They were at a loss to do anything. Their statements about the man's murder and the theft of his money concurred. He ordered some of his men to go with some of them to the place where they had buried the money and to get it out and hand it over to the young man, the son of the murdered man.

"What do you want (to be done to them) now that you know what they did to your father?" he asked him.

"I want the judgement between us to take place before Allāh, the Mighty and High," he said. "So I will spare their blood in this world."

Therefore the Commander of the Faithful, peace be on him, desisted from carrying out the prescribed punishment for murder but still punished them severely.

"Commander of the Faithful," Shurayḥ asked him, "how (did you manage to come to) this decision?"

He said: "David, peace be on him, passed some boys playing and calling out to one of them, 'Religion is dead.' The boy would then answer them. David, peace be on him, approached them. He said: 'Boy, what is your name?' 'My name is Religion is Dead,' he answered. 'Who gave you this name?' David, peace be on him, asked. He replied: 'My mother.' Then David asked: 'Where is your mother?' He answered: 'In her house.' 'Go with us to your house,' said David. He went with him to her and brought her out of her house. 'Maidservant of Allāh', he said, 'what is the name of your son?' 'His name is Religion is Dead,' she answered. 'Who gave him this name?' David, peace be on him, asked her. 'His father,' she replied. 'What was the reason for that?' he asked. She said: 'He went out on a journey with some people while I was pregnant with this boy. The people came back but my husband did not come back. I asked them about him and they told me that he had died. I asked them about his money and they told me that he did not leave any money. I asked them if he had made any instruction in his will. They said that he had. He had said that I was pregnant and if I bore a girl or a boy, I should name him Religion is Dead. Therefore I named him as I was instructed in his will as I did not wish to oppose him.' David, peace be on him, asked her: 'Do you know the people?' 'Yes,' she replied. He said to her, 'Come with me with these' - meaning the people who were in front of him. Then he had them brought out of their houses. When they were (all) present, he judged them according to this judgement. The murder was proved against them and he got the money from them. Then he said to her: 'Maidservant of Allāh, name this child of yours Religion is Alive.'"

******

It is reported that a woman desired a young man and she tried to seduce him but the young man refused. She went away and got an egg. She put the white (of the egg) on her dress. Then she began to make accusations against the young man and had him brought before the Commander of the Faithful, peace be on him. She claimed: "This young man has treated me shamefully. He has raped me."

She took her dress and showed the white (on it) from the egg, saying: "This is his semen on my dress."

The young man began to cry, pleading and swearing his innocence from her accusations.

"Order someone to heat water until it is very hot," the Commander of the

Faithful, peace be on him, told Qanbar. "Then bring it to me while it is still like that."

The water was brought and he ordered it to be thrown on the woman's dress. They threw it on it and the water collected up the white of the egg and they came together. He ordered it to be taken and given to two of his followers. He said: "Taste it and spit it out."

They tasted it and found that it (tasted like) egg. He ordered the young man to be freed and the woman to be flogged as a punishment for her false accusation.

****

[Al-Ḥasan b. Maḥbūb reported: 'Abd al-Raḥmān b. al-Ḥajjāj told me: I heard Ibn Abī Layla saying:]
The Commander of the Faithful, peace be on him, judged a case which no one had dealt with before. That was that two men had travelled together on a journey. They sat eating together. One of them took out five loaves of bread and the other three. A man passed them and greeted them. They invited him to eat and he sat eating with them. When he had finished eating, he put down eight dirhams, saying: "This is compensation for your food which I have eaten."

The two men began to dispute over it. The one with three loaves said: "This (should be shared) between us, half each."
"Rather I should have five and you should have three," said the one with five loaves.

They came before the Commander of the Faithful, peace be on him, and told him their story. He said: "This is a matter in which meanness and rivalry is not proper. Reconciliation would be better."

"I will only be satisfied by the giving of judgement," said the one who had had three loaves.

"Since you will only be satisfied by the giving of judgement," said the Commander of the Faithful, peace be on him, "you have one of the eight and your companion seven."

"May Allāh be praised," he exclaimed, "how can this matter come to be like that?"

"I have told you," he said. "Didn't you have three loaves?"

"Yes," he answered.

"And your companion had five?"
"Yes."

"That is twenty-four (when multiplied) by three," he said. "So you ate eight, your companion eight and your guest eight. Thus he gave you eight dirhams. Seven of which belong to your companion (as he supplied seven-eighths of the guest's food) and one to you (as you supplied one-eighth of the guest's food)."

The two men departed (reflecting on) the perspicacity of the judgement of their case.

*****

The scholars of (religious) practices (*siyar*) report that during the time of the Commander of the Faithful, peace be on him, four men drank alcohol. They became drunk and began to cut each other with knives. Each of them was wounded. An account of their (action) was brought to the Commander of the Faithful, peace be on him, and he ordered them to be put into prison until they became sober. Two of them died in prison but two survived. The families of the two (dead) men came to the Commander of the Faithful, peace be on him, and demanded: "Give us the right to retaliate against these two men, Commander of the Faithful. For they have killed two of our colleagues."

"How do you know that?" he asked. "Perhaps (the dead men) killed each other."
"We do not know," they answered. "So judge them according to what Allāh has taught you."

He said: "The blood-wit of the two men who were killed is the responsibility of the tribes of the four men after the account has been settled by the payment for the two who are alive of the blood-wit for their wounds."

That was a judgement in a case for which there was no way of establishing the truth other than by it. Don't you see that there was no evidence to distinguish the killer from the killed and no evidence of intention to kill? Therefore the judgement was made according to the rule of accidental killing and on the basis of confusion about (the actions of) the killer and killed.

******

It is reported that six men went down to the Euphrates and dived into it to play. One of them drowned. Two of them testified that the (other) three had made him drown while the three testified that the two made him drown. He, peace be on him, adjudged the division of the blood-wit into fifths on the five. The two were to pay three-fifths according to the amount of testimony against them and the three were to pay two-fifths in accord with the amount of testimony against them.

There was no judgement in that with more right to (be considered) correct than the judgement he, peace be on him, gave.

******

They reported that a man was about to die and he bequeathed part of his wealth without designating it. His heirs differed on that after his (death). They came before the Commander of the Faithful, peace be on him. He told them to exclude one-seventh of the wealth as the bequest and he recited the words of Him, the Exalted: *It has seven gates, each of which is a divided part* (XV 44).

He, peace be on him, judged (a case) concerning a man who, at his death, had made a bequest of a share of his wealth without specifying it. Similarly when he died, the heirs disputed about its significance. His judgement to them was to take out an eighth of his wealth and he recited the words of Allāh, the Exalted: *The ṣadaqat (alms tax) is only for the poor and needy*. (IX 60). There were eight categories for the (*ṣadaqat*) and to each category (he gave) a share of the *ṣadaqat*.

******

He, peace be on him, judged a case concerning a man who made a bequest and said: "Free every slave of mine who has been long in my possession."

When he died, the executor did not know what to do. He asked about that and (the Commander of the Faithful) told him to free every slave (of the man) who had been in his possession for six months.

Then he recited His words, Exalted be His name: *For the moon we have appointed stages until it becomes again like an old dry branch of a palm tree ('urjūn)* (XXVI 39).

It has been established that the branch of a palm tree only becomes similar to the new moon in its strength six months after fruit has been taken from it.

******

He gave judgement concerning a man who had made a vow to fast for a time but without mentioning any definite time. (He told him) to fast for six months and he recited the words of Him, the Mighty and High: *It brings forth its fruit at every season by the permission of its Lord.* (XIV 25)

That was every six months (so the time he interpreted to be equivalent to six months).

*****

A man came to him and said: "Commander of the Faithful, I had some dates. My wife rushed (up to me) and took one of them and put it in her mouth. I vowed that she would never eat it nor spit it out."

He, peace be on him, said: "Let her eat half of it and spit out the other half. Then you will be free of your vow."

******

He, peace be on him, gave judgement concerning a man who struck a woman and she had a miscarriage (when it was still) an embryo. (He ordered him) to pay the blood-wit for it of forty dīnārs and he recited the words of Him, the Mighty and High: *We created man from an essence of clay. Then We made him a drop in a firm abode. Then We formed the drop into an embryo, and We formed the embryo into a clot of blood, and We formed the clot of blood into bones. We clothed the bones with flesh. Then we caused it to grow as a final act of creation. Blessed be Allāh the best of Creators.* (XXIII 12-14). He explained that (the blood-wit for) the drop was twenty dīnārs, for the embryo forty dīnārs, for the clot sixty dīnārs, for the bone before it was established as a creature eighty dīnārs, for the form (of the child) before the soul entered it a hundred dīnārs. If the soul had entered it, then (the blood-wit) was a thousand dīnārs.

*****

This has been a sample of the judgements and difficult decisions pronounced by (the Commander of the Faithful), peace be on him. No one had given judgements on (such cases) before him. Nor did any of the non-Shī'a (*'āmma*) and Shī'a (*khāṣṣa*) know anything about them. His natural disposition (*'itra*) made him able to deal with them. If anyone else had been tested by having to give a decision about them, such a man would have shown his deficiency in (knowing) the truth about them, just as (the Commander of the Faithful) had made it clear.

In this brief outline of the legal decisions (of the Commander of the Faithful) which we have put forward here, there is sufficient for our purposes, if Allāh wills.

CHAPTER VI

MEMORABLE WORDS AND SPEECHES OF THE COMMANDER OF THE FAITHFUL

His Words about Allāh

(This is) a brief account of some of the words of (the Commander of the Faithful), peace be on him, concerning the necessity of knowing Allāh, the Exalted, His unity and the denial of anthropomorphism (*tashbīh*), together with a description of Allāh's justice, the different kinds of wisdom and the evidence and proof of these.

[Abū Bakr al-Hudhalī reported on the authority of al-Zuhrī, on the authority of 'Īsā b. Zayd, on the authority of Ṣāliḥ b. Kaysān:]
The Commander of the Faithful, peace be on him, said, in urging the knowledge of Allāh, may He be praised, and (the acknowledgement) of His unity:
"The first act of worshipping Allāh is to know Him. The basis of knowledge of Him lies in (the acknowledgement of) His Unity. The support for (the acknowledgement of) His Unity is the denial of any comparison of Him, the High, (with man) in terms of stating that human qualities (*ṣifāt*) subsist in Him. (This is) because of the testimony of reason that everyone in whom human qualities subsist is created (*maṣnū'*). Whereas the testimony of reason (requires) that He, the High and Exalted, Who is the Creator (*ṣāni'*), is not created. Through the creation of Allāh which points towards Himself, through reason which establishes the belief in knowledge of Him, through reflection which confirms the proof of His (existence), Allāh has caused His creation to be evidence of Himself. Through it, He has revealed His Majesty. He is One, Unique in His eternity, without partner in His Divinity, without equal in His Divinity. By virtue of the contradictory nature of things which contradict each other, there is knowledge that nothing is contrary to Him. By virtue of the nature of comparability in matters which can be compared, there is knowledge that nothing can be compared to Him."

(The Commander of the Faithful said this) in a speech which, if it was fully reported, would make this book too long.

*****

Among the speeches recorded on his authority, peace be on him, about the denial of any comparison of Allāh (with human qualities) is that which al-Sha'bī reported. He said that the Commander of the Faithful, peace be on him, heard a man saying: "By Him Who is veiled with seven layers (of heaven)." Then he raised his stick towards the sky.

"Woe upon you," he said, "Allāh is too exalted to be veiled from anything and for anything to be veiled from Him. Praise be to Him, Whom no place contains, yet from Whom nothing on earth or in heaven is hidden."

"Shall I redeem my oath, Commander of the Faithful?" the man asked.
"No," he answered, "you did not swear by Allāh. Therefore no atonement for perjury is required of you, for you were only swearing by something else."

*****

The historians (*ahl al-sīra wa-'ulamā al-naqala*) report that a man[1] came to the Commander of the Faithful, peace be on him, and asked: "Commander of the Faithful, tell me about Allāh, the Exalted. Did you see Him when you worshipped Him?"
"I am not one who worships someone whom I have not seen" he answered.

"Then how did you find Him when you saw Him?" he asked.
"Woe upon you," he said, "the eyes do not see Him in terms of human eye-sight. Rather the hearts see Him through the inner realities of faith (*īmān*). (He can be) known through evidence and can be characterised by signs, which cannot be compared to people nor attained through sense perception."

The man went away saying: "Indeed, Allāh knows well how He should deliver His message."

In this account there is evidence that (the Commander of the Faithful) denied the possibility of direct vision of Allāh, the Mighty and High.

*****

[Al-Ḥasan b. Abī al-Ḥasan al-Baṣrī reported:]
A man came to the Commander of the Faithful, peace be on him, after his departure from the battle of Ṣiffīn. He asked him: "Commander of the Faithful, tell me: Was the battle which took place between you and these people a result of the decree and determination of Allāh?"

"You have never gone up a hill nor gone down into a valley without Allāh's

1 *Nahj al-Balāgha*, (Beirut, 1967), I, tradition no. 258. The man is identified as Dhi'bil al-Yamānī. The final part of the speech is slightly different.

decree and determination being present in the action," he answered.

"Then, Commander of the Faithful, I regard (all) my concerns as Allāh's responsibility," he said.
"Why?"

"If the decree and determination of Allāh drive us to act," he said, "then what is the point of rewarding us for obedience and punishing us for disobedience?"
"Fellow," said the Commander of the Faithful, peace be on him, "have you thought that it was a sealed decree and determination? Don't think that. That sort of statement is the doctrine of idolaters, supporters of Satan and opponents of Allāh, the Merciful. (It is such people) and the Majīs with them who have adopted it. Allāh, exalted be His Majesty, gives commands as a matter of free choice (*takhyīr*), and gives prohibitions as a warning (against an action.) He puts the burden on us. He is not obeyed unwillingly nor is He disobeyed as one who can be overcome. He has not created the heavens and the earth and what is between them in vain. *That is the opinion of those who disbelieve. There will be woe from Hell-fire for those who disbelieve.* (XXXVIII 27)."[2]

"What, then, is the decree and determination which you mentioned, Commander of the Faithful?" asked the man.
He answered: "It is the command to obey, the prohibition of disobedience, the provision (to man) to draw near Him and to abandon those who disobey Him, the promise (of reward) and the threat (of punishment), the inspiration (He gives man) to do good and the fear of doing evil (which He arouses in man). All that is the decree of Allāh with regard to our actions and His determination of our deeds. As for anything else (which has been claimed), do not give it any consideration. For the consideration of it will invalidate your action."

"You have dispelled my worries, Commander of the Faithful," said the man. "May Allāh dispel yours." And he began to recite:

> You are the Imam, through obedience to whom we hope for forgiveness from Allāh, the Merciful, on the Day of the Return (to Him). You have explained what was unclear in our religion. May your Lord bounteously reward you with kindness.

*****

This account clarifies, through the words of the Commander of the Faithful, peace be on him, the meaning of (divine) justice and the prohibition of (belief

2 This paragraph, though in a somewhat different order, is the same as *Nahj al-Balāgha*, III, no. 78, 481.

in) the doctrine of determinism (jabr), (in addition to) establishing the wisdom in the actions of Allāh, the Exalted, and denying that there is any futility in them.

His Words about Knowledge (*'Ilm*)

(This is a selection of) some of the words of (the Commander of the Faithful), peace be on him, in praise of (traditional) knowledge (*'ilm*), about the categories of people, the merit of (traditional) knowledge, and about acquiring it and wisdom.

The traditionists (*ahl al-naql*) have reported on the authority of Kumayl b. Ziyād, may Allāh have mercy on him, that he said:[3] One day the Commander of the Faithful took me by the hand in the mosque and led me out of it. When he had gone out into the desert, he breathed a deep sigh and said: "Kumayl, these hearts are containers (of knowledge); the best of them are those which best preserve (the knowledge). Therefore preserve what I say to you. There are three kinds of people: One who knows the Lord (for His own sake), one who acquires knowledge as a means of salvation and low class rabble, followers of every crower, who bend with every breeze. These men do not seek to be illuminated by the light of learning, nor do they resort to any sure authority (*rukn*).

"Kumayl, knowledge is better than wealth. Knowledge guards you while you guard wealth. Wealth is diminished by expenditure while knowledge is increased even by giving it away.

"Kumayl, the love of knowledge is a (kind of) religion which is professed (by a man) and through which he perfects his obedience (to Allāh) during his life and acquires a noble reputation after his death. Knowledge is a judge and wealth is something which is judged.

"Kumayl, those who amass wealth die even as they live while those who possess knowledge will continue to exist for as long as time lasts. Their individual entities will disappear but their images will remain in the hearts (of men).

"Here, indeed is much knowledge," and he pointed to his breast. "If I could come upon men who would carry it (*ḥamala*)... Indeed I came upon such as took it too quickly and (thus) did not protect it. Such a man would use the tools of religion for (success in) the world. He would seek to use the proofs of Allāh and His favours as a means of dominating His friends and His Book. Or (there was

3 cf. *Nahj al-Balāgha*, III, no. 147, 495 ff.

the sort of man) who submitted to the wisdom (of Allāh's knowledge) without having true vision of his own (need for) humility. At the first appearance of any problem, doubt would eat into his heart. Neither this man nor that one (was appropriate). (As each) eagerly sought pleasures and was easily dominated by passions or enamoured of amassing and hoarding wealth, they were not of the kind who would be shepherds of religion. They were both much more like cattle wandering without restraint in search of fodder. Thus in the (living) death of such carriers of knowledge would knowledge itself die.

"O Allāh, indeed the earth will never be without (a man who is) a proof (*ḥujja* i.e. an Imam) of You to Your Creation, whether (he acts) openly in the public eye or secretly out of fear. (In this way) the proofs of Allāh and His signs will not be brought to nought. Where are those men? They are men who are least in number yet greatest in Allāh's esteem. Through them Allāh preserves His proofs (to the world) until they hand them as a trust to their equals and sow them as seeds in the hearts of those like themselves. Through them knowledge has broken into the inner realities of faith and they have found the spirit of certainty to be something gentle and comforting. They have found easy what those who love the easy life have found to be hard and difficult. They are familiar with things which the ignorant distrust. They have travelled through this world with their bodies while their souls have been (always) associated with the Highest Abode. These are the representatives (*khulafā'*) of Allāh on His earth and those who summon His worshippers to His (true) religion".

Then he breathed a deep sigh and said: "Oh, how I long to see them." He took his hand from mine and said to me: "Go now, if you wish."

*****

Among the words of (the Commander of the Faithful), peace be on him, urging people to knowledge (*ma'rifa*), explaining its merit, and the qualities of those who possess knowledge (*'ulamā'*), and (describing) how those who seek knowledge should be, is (this report) of a speech which scholars have handed down in (their) accounts. However, we have omitted the beginning of it, (starting at) his words:

"Praise be to Allāh, Who has guided us from error, Who has given us vision (and kept us away) from blindness, Who has (bestowed) on us the religion of Islam. (It is He) Who has caused prophethood to have been among us and Who has made us good men. He has made our ultimate pinnacle the ultimate pinnacle of prophets. He has made us the best community which has come for men. We enjoin the good and forbid the evil. We worship Allāh and we do not associate anything with Him, nor do we take any master (*walī*) apart from Him.

We are witnesses of Allāh and the Apostle was our witness (of Him). We seek intercession and are given intercession along with those with whom we sought intercession from Him. We ask and our request is granted. He forgives the sins of those whom we pray for. Allāh has elected us. We do not call on any master (*walī*) apart from Him.

"People, help one another to (acts of) good faith and piety. But do not help one another to sin and aggression. Fear Allāh. Indeed Allāh is severe in (His) punishment.

"People, I am the cousin of your Prophet and the closest of you to Allāh and His Apostle. Therefore question me, question me. It is as if knowledge (*'ilm*) has already wasted away among you. When any one who possesses knowledge perishes, then part of his knowledge perishes with him. Those among the people who possess knowledge (*'ulamā'*) are like the full-moon in the sky whose light illuminates the rest of the constellations. Take hold of whatever knowledge appears to you. Beware of seeking it for four reasons: that through it you may vie with (other) possessors of knowledge; or that by it you may quarrel with the ignorant; or that as a result of it you act hypocritically in discussions; or that through it you may disregard the leaders of the people in favour of yourselves becoming leaders. Those who do (good) acts and those who do not will not receive equal punishment from Allāh. May Allāh benefit both us and you by what He has taught us. May (a man who has knowledge) use it only for the sake of Allāh. Indeed He is One Who hears, One Who answers."

*****

Among his statements, peace be on him, about the description of the one who possesses knowledge (*'ālim*) and the training of one who seeks to possess knowledge is what is reported by al-Ḥārith al-A'war. He said: I heard the Commander of the Faithful say: "It is the right of the one who possesses knowledge (*'ālim*) that he should not be questioned too much, nor be required to answer. Nor should he be troubled when he is tired, nor caught hold of by the sleeves when he rises (to leave). No (finger) should be pointed at him with regard to anything which is needed, nor should any secret of his be divulged. No one should speak slander in his presence. He should be given great respect in as much as he has preserved the command of Allāh. The student should only sit in front of him and should not expose him to too much of his company. If a student (seeking) knowledge, or anyone else, comes to him while he is in a group, he should make a general greeting to them all and give particular good wishes to him.

"Let him be respected whether he is present or absent. Let his right be known. Indeed the man who possesses knowledge receives greater reward than the man who fasts, the man who undertakes (other religious duties), the man who strives along the path of Allāh. When the one who possesses knowledge (*'ālim*) dies, a breach is made in Islam which can only be filled by his successor and the one who seeks after knowledge. The angels ask for forgiveness for him and those in heaven and on earth pray for him."

His Words concerning Heresy.

Among his speeches, peace be on him, concerning heretics (*ahl al-bida'*) and those who speak of religion in terms of their own opinion while opposing the way of true believers (*ahl al-ḥaqq*) through what they say, is (the speech) reported by sound traditionists of the non-Shī'a (*'āmma*) and the Shī'a (*khāṣṣa*). The speech opens with the praising of Allāh and blessings on His Prophet, may Allāh bless Him and His Family, (and then goes on)[4]: "My responsibility for what I say is guaranteed and I am answerable for it. It will not wither the corn-seeds which men have sown, nor will roots be parched as a result of it.

"All goodness is within a man who knows his own Ability. Not knowing one's own ability is sufficient ignorance for man. A creature who is most hateful to Allāh is a man whom Allāh, the Exalted, has left to himself, (a man) who is deviating from the true path, (a man) enamoured of words of heresy. (In this heresy) he has become addicted to fasting and prayer. Yet he is seduction to those who are seduced by him, himself going astray from the guidance of those who came before him, and leading into error those who follow him. Thus he bears (responsibility) for the sins of others, being (himself) settled in his own sinfulness. (Such a man) has picked up the refuse of ignorance amid ignorant men without guidance. Unaware of the intense darkness of rebellion, he is blind to guidance. Yet men like himself call him knowledgeable (*'ālim*) while he is not constant in following it even for one complete day. He goes out early and seeks to make much of what is little (regarding it as) better than what is (truly) much, so that when he has quenched his thirst on polluted water and sought to increase (his knowledge) from what is vile, he sits as a judge responsible for the clarification of what is obscure to everyone else. He fears that those who came before him were without his wisdom and that the action of those who come after him will be like the action of those who came before him. If an obscure matter is brought before him, he gives an irrelevant comment on it according to his own opinion and then asserts (that) categorically. Thus he is enmeshed in doubts as if in the spider's web, not knowing whether he is right or wrong. He does not see

4 Part of this speech is the same as *Nahj al-Balāgha*, 1, no. 17, 59ff.

that what is beyond (him) is within the reach (of others). If he made an analogy of one thing with another, he would never regard his opinion as being wrong. If a matter is obscure to him, he conceals it because he knows his own ignorance, deficiency, and the necessity (of hiding it) in order that it cannot be said that he does not know. Therefore he puts himself forward without knowledge. He is one who wanders aimlessly like riders without direction amid the uncertainties of unknown tracts of desert. Never does he excuse himself for what he does not know. Thus he gives a decision without ever having bitten into knowledge with a tooth that can bite. He scatters the traditions like the wind scatters sand. Inheritances (wrongly distributed) weep because of him, blood cries out for vengeance because of him. By his judgements he makes lawful the forbidden parts and forbids those that are allowed. He is invalid when he issues (judgements on cases) which come before him and he does not regret his inadequacy.

"People, it is required of you to obey and to know the one whom there is no excuse to be ignorant of. The knowledge with which Adam, peace be on him, descended, and everything with which the prophets were favoured down to your Prophet, the seal of the prophets, is in the offspring of your Prophet, Muḥammad, may Allāh bless Him and His Family. Where has it brought you? Or rather where are you going, you who are descended from the loins of the men who were on the Ark? This (offspring of the Prophet) is like (the Ark of Noah). Therefore (adhere to them as) you would board it. Just as those who were in it were saved, so those who enter into (association with this family) will be saved through them. I guarantee that by a true oath and I am not one of those who make false claims. Woe on those who hold back, woe again on those who hold back. Haven't you been made aware of what your Prophet, may Allāh bless Him and His Family, said among you, when he said in the Farewell Pilgrimage: 'I leave behind me among you two important things which, if you cleave to them, you will never go astray - that is the Book of Allāh and the offspring from my family (*ahl al-bayt*). They will never scatter from you until they lead you to me at the (sacred) waters (of Heaven)'. Now take care how you oppose me with regard to these two (things). Otherwise there will be dread punishment. Indeed this (agreement with the Book and the family) is a sweet pleasant drink, so drink. But that (opposition) is salty and brackish, so avoid it.'"

His Words about this World and the Next

(Here is an extract from) his words, peace be on him, describing the world and warning against it.[5]

5 *Nahj al-Balāgha*, III, no. 119, 489.

"The world is just like a snake - a soft thing to touch but vicious in sting. Therefore avoid those things which please you in it because of the short length (of time) which they will be with you there. Be as familiar as you can with what is there while being as wary as you can of its possessions. For whenever one who possesses (the world) seeks to take ease from it, it diverts him from it to what is hateful."

*****

(These are some of) his words, peace be on him, regarding getting ready to go to the next world, preparing to meet Allāh, may His Name be exalted, and advice to the people about righteous deeds. The religious scholars report this in the traditions and the historians (*aṣḥāb al-sīra wa-al-āthār*) (also) report it:

Every night when the people were taking to their beds for sleep, he would call out in a voice which could be heard by all the people in the mosque and nearby:[6] "May Allāh have mercy on you, prepare yourselves, for the call has been made among you for you to set out on the journey (to Allāh). Give scant (attention) to staying in this world and turn (to Allāh) with the best provisions you have. For in front of you is a mountain-pass which will be difficult to climb and halting-places full of terror, from which the one who travels (the road) and stops along it has no escape. Through Allāh's mercy, may you be saved from its horrors. After destruction there will be no haughtiness. How sad it will be for the negligent man that his own life will be a proof against him and (the evils of) his days will lead him to the distress which Allāh has made for (those of) us (who are like him). Beware of those who scorn grace and who will not be freed from vengeance after death. We only (exist) through Him and for Him and by virtue of His kind hand. He has power over everything."

*****

(These are some of) his words, peace be on him, concerning shaming the life of this world and seeking to carry out actions for the next world:
"Son of Adam, let not the greatest of your concerns be what happens to you today. For if it passes you by, it was not meant for you. Your concern should be now and on every day which comes to you, that Allāh will provide you with provision for it. You should know that you will never acquire anything beyond your own sustenance, save as one who looks after things on behalf of others. (If) your share (of wealth) in this world is abundant, then soon your heir will take it over and together with him your account on the Day of Resurrection will be lengthy. So be happy with what you have and make provision for the day of your return (to Allāh) which is ahead of you. The journey is long, the appointment is

6 *Nahj al-Balāgha*, I, no. 204, 321.

(on the day of) the Resurrection, the destiny is Heaven or the fire (of Hell)."

*****

Another speech of his, peace be on him, similar to that, is well known among the religious scholars and has been preserved by men of understanding and wisdom.[7] "People, this world has turned its back and made known its departure. The next world has drawn near and given notice of its appearance. Indeed today is (like) the day horses are prepared (for a race) and tomorrow is (like) the day of the race. The destiny of the winner is Paradise while the fate (of the loser) will be Hell-fire. You are amid days of preparations for (men), behind whom the time of death is urging haste. Whoever dedicates his works to Allāh, will not have his hopes destroyed. Whoever allows the works (of the world) to delay him during the days of his preparations prior to the coming of the time of his death, his (worldly actions) will come to naught and his hopes will destroy him. Indeed act (righteously) with regard to both (what you) desire and (what you) fear. If your desire comes to you, thank Allāh and add it to (what you) fear. If (what you fear) befalls you, then be mindful of Allāh and add it to (what you) desire. Allāh has permitted those who do good (to enjoy) goodness. To those who thank Him, He gives increase (of blessings). There is no acquisition better than an acquisition for a day for which stores are stored, (a day) on which great sins are collected together and the intentions (of the heart) concerning them are tested. I have never seen one who aspires to Heaven asleep nor have I seen one who seeks to flee from Hell-fire asleep. One who does not benefit from certainty is harmed by doubt. The one who does not benefit from the presence of his heart and sight (will attain) his (sad) end without them. You have been commanded to set out (to the next world) and have been guided with provisions (for the journey). There are two things which I most fear for you -- the following of passion and the delay (of good actions) caused by hope. For following passion stops one from (attaining) the truth and the delay (of good actions) caused by hope makes one forget about (the need for such actions for) the next world. Indeed the world has set out on a journey away (from us) while the next world has set out on a journey towards (us). Both of them have children (who follow them). Therefore, if you can, be among the children of the next world and do not be among the children of this world. Today is (the day) for good actions without the account (to be settled). Tomorrow is (the day) for the account (to be settled) without (the opportunity for performing) good actions."

His Words about Companions, Ascetics and his Shīʿa

Among the speeches which he, peace be on him, gave, mentioning the choice

7 cf. al-Jāḥiẓ, *al-Bayān wa-al-Tabyīn*, II, 52-53. Elements from this speech are found in *Nahj al-Balāgha*, I, no. 18, 71; no. 176, 110; and no. 41, 83.

companions and ascetics, is that which Ṣaʻṣaʻa b. Sūḥān al-ʻAbdī reported: He said that one day the Commander of the Faithful, peace be on him, prayed the morning prayer with them. When he had said the final greeting (of the prayer) he turned his head toward the *qibla* (i.e. in the direction of Mecca) as he mentioned Allāh. He did not turn to right or left until the sun's (shadow reached) the height of a spear on the wall of that mosque - meaning the Friday-mosque in Kūfa. Then he, peace be on him, turned his head towards us and said:
"I knew upright men in the time of my bosom companion, the Apostle of Allāh, may Allāh bless Him and His Family, who used to spend this night alternating between prostration and kneeling. In the morning they would have dishevelled hair, be dusty, and between their eyes, there would be (a lump) like the knee of the goat (as a result of prostration). When they remembered death, they quivered like trees quiver in the wind. Then their eyes would shed tears until their clothes became wet."

Then he, peace be on him, arose and he was speaking as if the people had remained heedless (of his words).

*****

(These are some of) his words, peace be on him, concerning his sincere Shīʻa. The historians (*naqalat al-āthār*) report that one evening he, peace be on him, left the mosque. It was a moon-lit night. He headed towards the cemetery (*jabbāna*). A group of men followed him, standing behind him. He stopped and said: "Who are you?"
"Commander of the Faithful, we are your Shīʻa," they replied.

He looked steadfastly at their faces and then said: "Why don't I see the mark of the Shīʻa on you?"
"What is the mark of the Shīʻa, Commander of the Faithful?" they asked.

"Yellow faces through staying awake at night," he replied, "bleary eyes through weeping, hunched backs through standing (in prayer), hollow stomachs through fasting, dry lips through prayer, and there is the dust of those who show humility on them."[8]

His Words concerning Death

Among his words, peace be on him, warning and mentioning death is (the speech) which has become well-known. From it (is the following):[9]

8 For the last sentence, cf. *Nahj al-Balāgha*, I, no. 12, 178.
9 cf. *Nahj al-Balāgha*, I, no. 123, 180

"Death is a greedy pursuer. As for the pursued, neither will the one who stays be able to weaken it, nor will the one who flees be able to escape it. Therefore go forward into battle and do not shrink away since there is no escape from death. Even if you are not killed, you will die. By (Allāh), in Whose hand is the life of 'Alī, a thousand sword blows on the head is easier than death in bed."

Concerning that are his words, peace be on him:[10]
"People, you have become targets so that the Fates are shooting arrows down on you. Your properties have been plundered by the blows (of Fortune). Whatever food you have eaten has stuck in your throat. Whatever drink you have drunk has choked you. I testify by Allāh that you will not gain from this world any advantage which you can enjoy except by losing another which you were showing regard for.

"People, we have been created. Therefore be (eager) for eternity and not for transitory existence. For you will travel from one abode to another. So make provision for where you are going and where you will dwell for ever. Peace (be with you)."

Speeches Urging Men to Himself and his Family

(There are) among his speeches, peace be on him, those which urge men (to follow) him, give evidence of his own outstanding merit and of his being deprived of his right, and explain what oppression was committed against him, indicating it and drawing attention to it. (This is) what the Shī'a (*khāṣṣa*) and non-Shī'a (*'āmma*) have reported. It is mentioned by Abū 'Ubayda Ma'mar b. al-Muthanna and others whom the opponents of the Shī'a cannot accuse of (partiality) in their report.[11] The Commander of the Faithful, peace be on him, said at the beginning of the address which he gave after the people's pledge of allegiance to his leadership (had been given) - that was after the murder of 'Uthmān - (the following):
"The ruler should only pay attention to his own soul. (If he pays attention to others) he will be distracted from Heaven and Hell will be in front of him. One who earnestly strives will be saved. One who seeks has hope. One who is remiss will be in Hell-fire. These are three (kinds of person). There are two (more): an angel who flies with his wings and a prophet whom Allāh has taken by his hand. There is no sixth (kind). The one who makes false claims will be destroyed. Those who rush heedlessly (into bad actions) will be made to fall. The right-hand side and the left-hand side lead (men) astray. The middle road is a path on which

10 cf. *Nahj al-Balāgha*, I, no. 145, 202
11 al-Jāḥiẓ, *al-Bayān wa-al-Tabyīn*, II, 50-2.

there still remains the Book, the *sunna* and the reports (*āthār*) of prophethood. Indeed Allāh, the Exalted, has treated the community with two medicines - the whip and the sword. There will be no hesitation by the Imam in applying them. Take cover in your houses and reconcile (the differences) which are between you. (There should be) repentance for what you have done. Whoever makes himself appear (falsely) to support truth will be destroyed. You were in some affairs, (in which you were inclined against me, it was an inclination for which) you had no excuse in my eyes. As for me, if I had wanted to say (it), I would have said: May Allāh forgive what has gone before. The two men (Abū Bakr and 'Umar) came first (in depriving me of my rights).

"Then the third stood like a crow, his concern for his stomach. Woe to him, if his wings have been clipped and his head cut off, it is better for him. Watch me. If you find something to denounce, denounce it. If you recognise it, then hasten (to carry it out). There is truth and falsehood. Each has its supporters. If the false becomes leader, then he will do as (was done) in the past. If truth becomes scarce, then perhaps for a short time it will recede but only to advance again. If your lives returned (to what they were before) you would be happy. I fear that you are now living in an intermediate period (without a prophet). I have only the ability to use reason (*ijtihād*) (to guide you). However, the pious of my family and the good ones of my offspring are the most forbearing of the people when they are young and the most knowledgeable of the people when they are older. We are the family of the House (*ahl al-bayt*), we know our knowledge from the knowledge of Allāh. We judge according to the law of Allāh, and we have taken (knowledge) from the words of the truthful one (i.e. the Prophet). If you follow our pronouncement, you will be guided by our clear vision. If you do not, Allāh will destroy you at our hands. We have the standard of truth. Whoever follows it, will attain it. Whoever delays from it will be drowned. Indeed through us, the vengeance of every believer will be realised. Through us, the rope of humiliation will be removed from your necks. It is through us, not you, that Allāh brings conquest. It is through us, not you, that He sets the seal (on life)."

*****

Another extract from his speech, peace be on him, urging (men) to himself and his family, peace be on him, are his words:

"Allāh singled out Muḥammad for prophethood, and chose him for the mission. He gave him information through inspiration. He set (him) among the people - He set him (there). We, the family of the House (*ahl al-bayt*), have the strongholds of knowledge, the gates of decision and the illumination of authority. Whoever loves us, his faith will benefit him and his works will bring him close (to Allāh). Whoever does not love us, his faith will not benefit him and his works will not bring him close to Allāh, even though he should strive night and day in prayer and fasting."

*****

In addition to that is what is reported by 'Abd al-Raḥmān b. Jundub on the authority of his father, Jundub b. 'Abd Allāh. The latter said: I visited 'Alī b. Abī Ṭālīb, peace be on him, in Medina after the people had given the pledge of allegiance to 'Uthmān. I found him with head lowered and sorrowful. I asked him: "What has come upon your people?"
"Beautiful endurance," he answered.

"Praise be to Allāh!" I said. "By Allāh, you are indeed enduring. Do what you said you would do among the people. Summon them to yourself and inform them that you are the closest and most appropriate of the people by virtue (of your relationship) with the Prophet, may Allāh bless Him and His Family, by virtue of your outstanding merit (*faḍl*) and your priority (in Islam). Ask them to help you against these men who have conspired against you. If ten out of a hundred answer you, you would be a powerful influence with the ten over the hundred. If they approached you, that would be as you would want. If they refused, you could fight them. If you are victorious, then the authority is Allāh's, Who gave it to his Prophet, blessing and peace be on him, and you are more appropriate for it than them. If you are killed in seeking it, then you would be killed as a martyr and you would be more deserving of Allāh's forgiveness and have more right to the inheritance of the Apostle of Allāh, may Allāh bless Him and His Family."

"Jundub," he said, "do you think that ten out of a hundred would pledge allegiance to me?"
"I would hope so," I replied.

"However," he retorted, "I do not expect two men from every hundred. I will tell you why. The people look to Quraysh. Quraysh says that the family of Muḥammad think that they have merit over the rest of the people and that they are the masters (*awliyā'*) of the affair apart from (the rest of) Quraysh. (They say that) if they took charge of it, this authority would never leave them to go to anyone else. Since it is already with others, you should circulate it among yourselves. No, by Allāh, Quraysh will never give this authority to us voluntarily."

"Won't you go back and tell the people what you have just said?" I asked him. "Then summon them to yourself."

"Jundub," he said, "this is not the time for that."

After that, I returned to Iraq. Whenever I used to mention any of his virtues, accomplishments and rights to the people, they would treat me roughly and drive me away until the matter of my words was brought before al-Walīd b. 'Uqba who was our governor at that time. He sent for me and imprisoned me until someone spoke to him about me and then he freed me.

Speeches about those who refrained from Pledging Allegiance to him and those who broke their Pledge.

Among the speeches which he, peace be on him, made when 'Abd Allāh b. 'Umar b. al-Khaṭṭab, Sa'd b. Abī Waqqāṣ, Muḥammad b. Maslama, Ḥassān b. Thābit and Usāma b. Zayd withheld the pledge of allegiance from him is what al-Sha'bī reported:

When Sa'd and the others whom we have named withdrew from the Commander of the Faithful, peace be on him, and withheld their pledge of allegiance, he praised and glorified Allāh. Then he said:[12]

"People, you have pledged allegiance to me in the same way as the pledge was made to those before me. Choice (*khiyār*) only belongs to people before they make their pledge of allegiance. When the pledge of allegiance is made, then they no longer have any choice. It is duty of the Imam to follow the right course and it is the duty of subjects to submit. However, this is a general pledge of allegiance. Whoever turns away from it turns away from the religion of Islam and does not follow the path of its people. Your pledge of allegiance to me was not a random matter (*falta*). My affair and your affair are not one. I want Allāh to be (the ultimate end) for you and you want me in the interests of yourselves. I swear by Allāh that I will give sincere advice to a rival and I will give justice to the oppressed. I have learnt matters about Sa'd, Ibn Maslama, Usāma, 'Abd Allāh and Ḥassān b. Thābit which I dislike. Truth (will be decided) between them and me."

*****

(These are some of) his words, peace be upon him, when Ṭalḥa and al-Zubayr reneged on their pledge of allegiance and set out for Mecca to meet 'Ā'isha to incite (people) against him and to make an alliance opposed to him. The religious scholars have preserved on his authority, peace be on him, that after he had praised and glorified Allāh, he said:[13]

"Allāh sent Muḥammad, may Allāh bless Him and His Family, to all the people.

12 Most of this speech is included in *Nahj al-Balāgha*, I, no. 136, 194.

13 Elements of this speech are in *Nahj al-Balāgha*, I, no. 231, 353 and no. 54, 90.

He made him a mercy for the worlds. He made manifest what he had been ordered to and spread the message of his Lord. The manifestation was carried out through him and that which was split was united in him. Roads were made safe through him and (the shedding of) blood was brought to an end by him. By him reconciliation was brought about between men with feuds and hostility, with hatred in their breasts and malice rooted in their hearts. Then Allāh took him to Himself, as a man to be praised who had not fallen short in the object for which he performed his mission. He had not achieved anything which fell short of his intention. After him there occurred the strife which there was over the leadership. Abū Bakr took control. Then after him (came) 'Umar. Then 'Uthmān took control. When there happened with regard to his affair what you already know, you came to me and said: 'We will pledge allegiance to you.' I said: 'I will not do it.' You said: 'Yes.' I said: 'No.' Then you seized my hand and stretched (yours) out towards it. I tried to withdraw it from you but you tugged at it and you pressed upon me like thirsty camels at the watering pools on a day when they are brought to them, so that I thought that you would kill me and that you would kill each other on my account. Therefore I stretched out my hand and you pledged allegiance to me of your own accord. The first of you to pledge allegiance to me were Ṭalḥa and al-Zubayr; they were acting voluntarily without any compulsion. It was not much later that they asked me to allow them to make the *'umra* (lesser pilgrimage). Allāh knows that they already intended treachery. I made them renew their covenant of obedience to me and (promise) that they would not harm the community with evil deeds. They gave their covenants to me. However, they did not fulfill their promises to me, they reneged on their pledge of allegiance to me and they broke their covenant to me. How surprising it is that they submitted to Abū Bakr and 'Umar yet showed hostility to me. But I am not inferior to either of those two men. If I wanted to, I would say: O Allāh, judge them both for what they have done against my rights and how they have attempted to diminish my authority. Give me victory over them."

*****

Elsewhere, he, peace be on him, spoke in a similar manner, (when) he said, after praising and glorifying Allāh:

"When Allāh, the Exalted, took His Prophet, blessings and peace be on him, we said: We are the family of his House, his group, his inheritors and his close friends and next of kin (*awliyā*), the creatures with most right with regard to him. There is no dispute about his right and authority. While we were in this position, the hypocrites rushed forward and took the authority of our Prophet by force away from us, and gave it to someone else. By Allāh, at that, our eyes all wept and our hearts (grieved). Because of it our breasts became worn (with sorrow) and our souls were afflicted with grief. I was humiliated. But I swear by

Allāh that if it had not been for my fear of division among the Muslims and that most of them would return to unbelief and that religion would have been placed in jeopardy, we would have changed that as far as we could. But now you have pledged allegiance to me and those two men, Ṭalḥa and al-Zubayr, have pledged allegiance to me. Both you and they (have acted) spontaneously and according to (your own) choice. Yet both of them have arisen, heading for Basra to cause division in your unity (*jamā'a*) and to thrust misfortune into your midst. O Allāh, seize them for the way they have deceived this community and for their evil attitude towards the general populace."

Then he said (to the people): "May Allāh have mercy on you, hurry to seek out these two treacherous sinful perjurers before the opportunity of (preventing) the realisation of their criminal activities escapes."

*****

When he was informed of the journey of 'Ā'isha, Ṭalḥa and al-Zubayr from Mecca to Baṣra, he praised and glorified Allāh. Then he said:
"'Ā'isha, Ṭalḥa and al-Zubayr have set out. Each one of the two (men) makes claims for the caliphate separately from his colleague. Ṭalḥa only claims the caliphate because he is the paternal cousin of 'Ā'isha and al-Zubayr only claims it because he is the brother-in-law of her father. By Allāh, if the two are successful in what they intend, then al-Zubayr will execute Ṭalḥa or Ṭalḥa will execute al-Zubayr, this one disputing the (right to) kingship of the other. By Allāh, I know that she is one who rides a camel. She will not stop at any pasturage; she will not go along any mountain path, and she will not be able to stop anywhere except in rebellion against Allāh until her soul and (that of) those with her comes to its final end. A third (of those with her) will be killed, a third will flee, and a third will come back. Ṭalḥa and al-Zubayr know that they are wrong. They are not ignorant. How often does the ignorance of one who knows kill him and the knowledge that he has does not benefit him? By Allāh, the dogs of al-Haw'ab[14] bark at her but does one who reflects interpret and one who ponders ponder? The sinful party has established itself. Where are the good?"

*****

When the Commander of the Faithful, peace be on him, headed for Baṣra, he stopped at al-Rabadha. The last (of the returning) pilgrims met him there. They gathered together to listen to some words from him, while he was still in his tent.

Ibn 'Abbās, may Allāh be pleased with him, reported:[15]

14 There is a tradition that the Prophet warned 'Ā'isha that when she heard these dogs barking she would know that she was doing wrong.

15 cf. *Nahj al-Balāgha*, I, no. 33, 76.

I went to him and found him stitching a sandal. I said to him: "We have a great need (to know) what you will do in order to put right our affairs."

He did not speak to me until he had finished his sandal. He put it next to the other one and then he asked me: "(How much do you) value them?"
"They have no value," I answered.

"More than that," he retorted.
"A fraction of a dirham," I suggested.

He said: "By Allāh, they are more lovable to me than these affairs of yours but for the fact that I must establish (what is) true and ward off (what is) false."

"The pilgrims have gathered together to listen to some of your words," I said. "Would you permit me to address them? If (my words) are good, they will be yours. If they are not, then they will be mine."

"No, I will speak," he answered, and he put his hands on my breast. The palms were rough and hard and it hurt me.
He got up. I seized hold of his clothes and said: "I commend Allāh and kinship to you."
"You should not (bother to) commend them to me," he replied and went out.

They gathered around him. He praised and glorified Allāh. Then he said:
"Allāh sent Muḥammad, may Allāh bless Him and His Family, while there was no one among the Arabs who recited an (Arabic) scripture nor claimed prophethood. He drove the people towards their salvation. By Allāh, I am still driving them towards it. I have not changed, I have altered nothing, I have betrayed nothing until the whole of it has passed away. What is between me and the Quraysh? By Allāh, I fought against them when they were unbelievers and I will fight against them when they bring sedition. This journey of mine (is made) on account of a covenant (made by the Prophet) to me. By Allāh, I will split open the false so that the truth may come out of its sides. Quraysh will not take vengeance on me, for Allāh has chosen us to be over them, and we will bring them under our control."

Then he recited:

> By my life, you continued your drinking of pure milk and your eating of dry dates with yoghourt.
> Yet we bestowed on you the highest rank even though you are not enough (for it). Around you, we give protection in the shield and spear.

*****

When he stopped at Dhū Qār, he took the pledge of allegiance from those who were present. After that he addressed them. He was profuse in his praise and glorification of Allāh and in calling for blessings on the Apostle of Allāh, may Allāh bless Him and His Family. Then he said:
"Affairs which we have (resolutely) endured have taken place earlier; (it was as if) there was a mote in our eyes in surrendering to the authority of Allāh, the Exalted, in matters by which he tested us. There is reward for that, for endurance of them was better than causing division among the Muslims and shedding their blood. We are the family of the House of Prophethood and the offspring of the Apostle, the creatures with the most right to the authority of the (prophetic) mission. (We are) the source of favour by which Allāh initiated this community. This Ṭalḥa and al-Zubayr are not from the family of prophethood nor from the offspring of the Apostle. When they saw that Allāh had restored our right to us after some time, they could not wait for one year, nor even one full month before they launched an attack, following in the footsteps of those before them, so that they might take away my rights and separate the unity (*jamā'a*) of the Muslims from me."

Then he made a prayer against them.

*****

['Abd al-Ḥamīd b. 'Imrān al-'Ijlī reported on the authority of Salama b. Kuhayl, who said:]
When the people of Kūfa met the Commander of the Faithful, peace be on him, at Dhū Qār, they welcomed him and said: "Praise be to Allāh, who has singled us out for (the honour of) granting you neighbourly protection and has honoured us by (enabling us to) support you."

Then the Commander of the Faithful, peace be on him, stood up among them to address them. He praised and glorified Allāh and said:
"People of Kūfa, you are the noblest of the Muslims, the most purposeful of them in following the correct course, the most upright of them in practice, the best of them in (your) participation in Islam, and the best among the Arabs in composition and origin. You are the fiercest of the Arabs in your love for the Prophet, may Allāh bless Him and His Family, and the members of his House. I only came to you out of my trust in you after Allāh because of the fact that you will give your lives against Ṭalḥa and al-Zubayr's renunciation (of their fealty to me), opposition to giving obedience to me, setting out with 'Ā'isha to create discord and taking her from her house until they had brought her to Baṣra. The common and confused people there were seduced. However I have been informed that men of merit and the choice men in religion among them had kept

aloof and have shown their dislike for what Ṭalḥa and al-Zubayr have done."

He, peace be on him, fell silent and the Kūfans declared: "We are your supporters and helpers against your enemy. If you summon us to weaken their (hold) over the people, we would consider that good and we would hope (to do) it."

The Commander of the Faithful, peace be on him, called to them and praised them. Then he said:
"You know, Muslims, that Ṭalḥa and al-Zubayr gave their pledge of allegiance to me, willingly, without compulsion and of their own accord. Then they asked permission from me to go on the lesser pilgrimage (*'umra*). I gave permission to them. However, they went to Baṣra and killed Muslims and committed forbidden actions. O Allāh, they have cut themselves off from me, they have oppressed me and have broken their pledge of allegiance to me, they have gathered the people against me. Therefore, loose what they have bound, do not give (favourable) judgement on anything which they have done well and show them the evil (which will result) from their actions."

*****

Among his speeches, peace be on him, is (the speech he made) when he left Dhū Qār setting out for Baṣra. After praising and glorifying Allāh and calling for blessings on the Apostle of Allāh, may Allāh bless Him and His Family, (he said:)[16]
"Allāh, the Exalted, has imposed the duty of struggling (on his behalf) (*Jihād*). He magnified it and He has made it a means of helping Him. By Allāh, neither the world nor religion will be properly maintained without it.

"Satan has gathered his party and has assembled his cavalry. He has brought doubt and deception into that when matters had been clear and restored.

"By Allāh, they have not blamed me correctly, nor have they done justice between me and themselves. They are demanding (restitution of) a right which they themselves abandoned, and (vengeance for) blood which they themselves shed. Even if I had been in partnership with them in it, they would have had a share in it. But if they have perpetrated it without me, the consequences of it are only theirs. Their greatest argument against me is against themselves. I have my clear vision which has not confused me.

"Indeed it is a wicked group in which there is kin and a scorpion's sting whose vehemence lasts for a long time and the fever from it is possible. They are

16 Elements of this speech are in *Nahj al-Balāgha*, I, no. 10, 53, and no. 22, 63.

being suckled by a mother who is already dry. They revive a pledge of allegiance (i.e. to 'Uthmān) which had already been forsaken by them in order that straying from truth might be restored to the place it (formerly) had. I am not to blame for what was done. I am innocent of (the crime) which was perpetrated.

"How disappointing is such a man to call on you! Who does he call? If he was asked: To whom is your call addressed and to whom do you answer? Who is your Imam and what is the practice (you call for), since falsehood has been removed from its place, his tongue would be silenced about what it had said.

"By Allāh, I shall make a tank overflow for them, from which I alone will draw. They will not be able to go away from it nor will they every be able to drink from it.

"I am content with Allāh's proof against them and His blaming them, since I call to them and ask them to apologise. If they repent and accept (my call), then forgiveness will be given and the right course will have been accepted. There should be no ingratitude to Allāh. If they refuse, I will let them have the edge of the sword. There is sufficiency in it as a healer of a false man and a helper of a believer."

His Words before and after the Battle of the Camel

(This is) from his speech, peace be on him, when he entered Baṣra and gathered his followers, to urge them to the struggle. Among the things he said, was:
"Servants of Allāh, arise against these people, exposing your breasts to battle against them. They have reneged on their pledge of allegiance to me. They have expelled Ibn Ḥunayf, my governor, after grievous blows and violent punishment. They have killed al-Sabābija and retaliated against Ḥakīm b. Jabala al-'Abdī.

"They have killed righteous men and pursued those who escaped to capture them behind every wall and under every hillock. They brought them and executed them in chains. What is their purpose? May Allāh fight them. Indeed they are liars.

"Arise against them and be fierce against them. Hurl yourself against them with endurance and with fore-thought, for you know that you are attacking and fighting them after you have disposed yourselves (to give) the most piercing thrust and the most severe blow and a contest of equals. Any individual among you who feels strong hearted at the (coming) engagement and sees any of his brothers failing should defend his brother who is a benefit to him just as he would defend himself. If Allāh wishes, he would do the same for him.

*****

(This is an extract) from his speech, peace be on him, when Ṭalḥa had been killed and the Baṣrans scattered.[17]

"Through us you were raised to nobility. Through us you broke into a new dawn of light out of darkness like the darkness of a moonless night. Through us you were guided amid darkness. Ears which do not comprehend the severe warning (given them) have become deaf. How does one who is deaf to the loud cries (of Allāh) hear a weaker call (of myself)? The heart which palpitation (out of fear of Allāh) never leaves is strengthened. I have always expected the consequences of treachery from you and I have perceived in you the quality of the deceitful. The garments of religion have concealed me from you but the true nature of my purpose revealed you to me. I established the right way for you where you might recognize it. Yet without a guide, you were digging (aimlessly for the water of truth) and did not find such water.

"Today I am making things unknown to you speak out to you with clarity. The understanding of a man who has kept apart from me, has deserted him. I have never doubted in the truth from the time it was shown to me. The sons of Jacob were provided with the greatest evidence (for the truth) until they disobeyed their father and sold their brother (into slavery). Their repentance came after their confession of guilt, and through seeking the forgiveness of their father and their brother they were forgiven."

*****

Some of his words, peace be on him, spoken on his walking around the corpses (after the Battle of the Camel):

"Here are (members of) Quraysh who have cut off my kinship with them (literally, my nose). Yet my life has been restored. I had come forward to you warning you against seizing hold of the sword but you were like young men: You did not have any (real) knowledge of what you were seeing. However, it was destruction and an evil end. I seek refuge with Allāh from an evil end."

He passed Mu'īd b. al-Miqdād and said: "May Allāh have mercy on the father of this man. If he had been Alive, his judgement would have been better than this man's."

"Praise be to Allāh Who brought him down and made his side the inferior one," said 'Āmmār b. Yāsir. "Indeed, by Allāh, Commander of the Faithful, we do not

17 *Nahj al-Balāgha*, I, no. 4, 51.

esteem those who obstinately resist the truth, whether father or son."

"May Allāh have mercy on you and reward you well for your (adhering to the) truth," replied the Commander of the Faithful, peace be on him.

He passed 'Abd Allāh b. Rabī'a b. Darrāj who was among the slain. He said: "This hopeless man, what brought him out (in revolution)? Was it religion or support for 'Uthmān which brought him out (in revolution)? By Allāh, 'Uthmān had an unfavourable opinion of him and his father."

Then he passed Mu'īd b. Zuhayr b. Umayya and said: "If the sedition had been at the top of the Pleiades, this young man would have grasped at it. By Allāh, he was not there with a (brave) shout. The one who met him told me that he screamed with fear of the sword."

Then he passed Muslim b. Quraẓa and said: "Piety brought this man out (in revolution). Yet by Allāh he asked me to ask 'Uthmān about something which he used to claim (as his) before in Mecca. 'Uthmān gave it to him and said to me: 'If it had not been for you, I would not have given it to him.' Indeed this is what I knew. How sad for the brother of the clan. Then came the time for destruction as a result of helping 'Uthmān."

He went by 'Abd Allāh b. Ḥamīd b. Zuhayr and he said: "This is also one of those who went into battle against us with the claim that he was seeking Allāh by that. Yet he had written letters to me in which he made accusations against 'Uthmān. Then he gave him something and he was satisfied with that."

He went beside 'Abd Allāh b. Ḥakīm b. Ḥizām and said: "This man opposed his father in coming out in revolution even when his father would not help us. For the latter remained loyal in his pledge of allegiance to us even though he had held back (from helping us) and remained at home when he had doubts about the battle. The man who held back from us and the others today is not as blameworthy as he who fought against us is blameworthy."

Then he passed 'Abd Allāh b. al-Mughīra b. al-Akhnas and he said: "This man's father was killed on the day 'Uthmān was killed in his house. He came out in revolt enraged at the killing of his father. He is a young man and he became afraid because of his being killed."

Then he came to 'Abd Allāh b. Abī 'Uthmān b. al-Akhnas b. Sharīq and said: "As for this man, it is just as if I was looking at him. The people had seized their swords as he fled running from the ranks. I turned away from him but he did not listen to the man who called to him until he killed him. This is one of the things which were hidden to the young inexperienced men of Quraysh. They had no knowledge of war. They were deceived and led into error. When they stopped, they were struck down and killed."

He walked on a little way and came to Ka'b b. Sūr. He said: "This is a man who came out against us with the Qur'ān (*maṣḥaf*) around his neck, claiming that he was a supporter of the community and urging the people to what was in (the Qur'ān) without himself knowing what was in it. Then he opened the Qur'ān for a decision at: *Every obstinate tyrant is disappointed* (XIV 15) (which he understood) as meaning Allāh had called (him) to kill me. However, Allāh killed him. Make Ka'b b. Sūr sit." So he was put in a sitting position. Then the Commander of the Faithful, peace be on him, said: "Ka'b, you have now discovered what my Lord truly promised me. Have you found what your Lord truly promised you?" Then he said, "Lay Ka'b to rest."

He came upon Ṭalḥa b. 'Ubayd Allāh and he said: "This is the man who broke the pledge of allegiance to me, the man who produced discord in the community, the man who gathered the people against me, the man who urged them to kill me and kill my offspring. Make Ṭalḥa b. 'Ubayd Allāh sit." So he was put in a sitting position. Then the Commander of the Faithful, peace be on him, said to him: "Ṭalḥa, you have discovered what my Lord truly promised me. Have you discovered what my Lord truly promised you?" Then he said, "Lay Ṭalḥa to rest."

He went on and one of those who was with him said to him: "Commander of the Faithful, were you speaking to Ka'b and Ṭalḥa after they had been killed?"

"By Allāh," he replied, "they heard my words just as the people of Qulayb heard the words of the Apostle of Allāh, may Allāh bless Him and His Family, on the day of the Battle of Badr."

*****

(This is some of) his speech at Baṣra after the defeat of the enemy. After praising and glorifying Allāh, he said:

"Allāh is One Who possesses extensive mercy, eternal forgiveness and Abundant pardon, (as He possesses) dread punishment. He dispenses His mercy and forgiveness to those of His creatures who obey Him and by His mercy those who are rightly guided are guided. He dispenses His vengeance, His severity and His punishment on those of His creatures who are disobedient. After guidance and clear explanations, those who have gone astray should not go astray. What is your view, people of Baṣra? You have reneged on your pledge of allegiance; you have publicly declared yourselves enemies against me."

A man stood up before him and said: "We think better now, for we see you have conquered and are powerful. If you punish us, that (would be because) we have committed a crime. If you forgive us, then forgiveness is more lovable to Allāh, the Exalted."

He said: "I forgive you but beware of sedition. You are the first subjects to have broken the pledge of allegiance and spread sedition in this community."

Then he sat down before the people and they pledged allegiance to him.

*****

He, peace be on him, wrote about the victory to the Kūfans:

In the name of Allāh, the Merciful, the Compassionate,
From the servant of Allāh 'Alī b. Abī Ṭalīb, Commander of the Faithful.
To the people of Kūfa.
Greetings, I commend to you the praise of Allāh, other than Whom there is no God. Allāh is a just arbitrator who does not change what is in people until they change what is in themselves. If Allāh wants evil for a people, there is no escape from it and they do not have a friend other than Him. I will tell you about ourselves and about those whom we went against - (that is) groups of the Baṣrans and the men of Quraysh and others who mixed with them in support of Ṭalḥa and al-Zubayr - and about their breaking of the agreement made with their oaths. I left Medina when news came to me about the men who had set off for (Baṣra), and about their gathering there and what they had done to my governor 'Uthmān b. Ḥunayf. (I went on) until I came to Dhāqān. There I sent al-Ḥasan b. 'Alī, 'Āmmār b. Yāsir and Qays b. Sa'd (to you) and I summoned you to (support) the right of Allāh and His Apostle, may Allāh bless Him and His Family, and my right. Your brothers soon set out to come to me. I went with them until we reached the outskirts (*ẓahr*) of Baṣra. I sought to excuse them through summoning them, and I presented them with proof. I (endeavoured to) diminish the stumbling and slipping caused by the apostates among Quraysh and others. I summoned them to repent from breaking their pledge of allegiance to me and the covenant which they had made to Allāh. They refused (everything) except to fight against me and to fight against those with me, and to persist in their quarrelsome error. I rose against them in battle. Allāh killed those of them who were killed as perjurers and He

drove back those who withdrew to their town. Ṭalḥa and al-Zubayr were killed as a result of their perjury and rebellion. The woman (i.e. 'Ā'isha) was worse for them than the she-camel of Thamūd. They deserted and turned their backs (in flight). They were cut off from all means of protection. When they saw what had happened to them, they asked me to forgive them. I accepted that from them and sheathed the sword from them. I carried out (the requirements of) truth and the *sunna* among them and appointed 'Abd Allāh b. al-'Abbās as governor of Baṣra. Now I am coming to Kūfa, Allāh, the Exalted, willing. I have sent Zahar b. Qays al-Ju'fī to you so that you can ask him and he will tell you about us and them. Truth has brought them back to us and Allāh has been restored to them while they were reluctant. Greetings and the mercy and blessings of Allāh.

*****

Among the words he, peace be upon him, spoke when he came to Kūfa from Baṣra (are the following):
"Praise be to Allāh Who has aided His friend (*walī*), deserted His enemy, Who has given power to the truthful who was entitled and has brought low the false liar. People of the city, it is your duty to show respect to Allāh and obedience to those of the family of Your Prophet to whom Allāh has enjoined obedience. They are more appropriate (*awlā*) to be obeyed than those who make false claims saying, '(Come) to us. (Come) to us.' Such men were pretending to have our merit and were striving against our authority and sought to divest us of our right and keep it away (from us). They have tasted evil misfortune for what they dared (to do) and they will discover the error. (There are) among you men who have desisted from supporting us. I blame them. Desert them and make them hear (words) which they will dislike until they admit their bad behaviour towards us. Then we will see in such men things which we will like."

His Words about the Campaign against Mu'āwiya and the Battle of Ṣiffīn

Among the speeches which he, peace be on him, made when he undertook to set out for Syria to fight Mu'āwiya b. Abī Sufyān (is the following):

After praising and glorifying Allāh and calling for blessings on the Apostle of Allāh, may Allāh bless Him and His Family, (he said):
"Servants of Allāh, fear Allāh and obey Him and your Imam. Righteous subjects are saved by the just Imam. But sinful subjects are destroyed by the sinful Imam. Mu'āwiya has begun to usurp the right which belongs to me, and to break the pledge of allegiance to me, seeking to harm the religion of Allāh, the Mighty

and High. Muslims, you know what the people did before when you came to me seeking for me to be in authority over you, so that you took me out of my house to pledge allegiance to me. I was reluctant with you in order to test your integrity. Then you repeated your words many times and I repeated (my reluctance) with you. You crowded upon me like thirsty camels at their pools of water in your anxiety to pledge allegiance to me so that I was afraid that some of you would kill others. When I beheld this from you, I considered my position and your position. I said: If I do not agree to their request, to undertake authority over them, they will not find anyone among them to take my place and act with my (degree of) justice among them. So I said: By Allāh, that I should rule them while they acknowledge my right and my merit is preferable to me than that they should rule me without acknowledging my right and my merit. Therefore I stretched out my hand to you and you pledged allegiance to me.

"O Muslims, among you are Emigrants and Anṣār and those who follow good practice. I have received from you the covenant of your pledge of allegiance and I respond with my agreement through a covenant and agreement (*mīthāq*) made before Allāh. It was stronger than covenants and agreements made to prophets; (you pledged) that you would support me, listen to my command, obey me, and consult me, that you would fight with me against every tyrant, aggressor or one who deviated, if he deviated. You all gave me that (pledge). I demanded from you all the covenant and promise made before Allāh and (under) the protection of Allāh and His Apostle and you responded to me by (giving me) that. I made Allāh the witness to your (words) and I made some of you witnesses to others. Then I applied the Book of Allāh and the *sunna* of His Prophet, may Allāh bless Him and His Family, among you. Then surprisingly Mu'āwiya b. Abī Sufyān disputes the succession (*khilāfa*) with me and denies me the (right to) the Imamate. He claims that he has more right to it than me, an act of boldness against Allāh and His Apostle concerning something which he has no right to and no argument for. None of the Emigrants have pledged allegiance to him for it, nor have the Anṣār and Muslims submitted to him.

"O men of the Emigrants and Anṣār, people who hear my words, have you made obedience to me something required of yourselves, whether you have pledged allegiance to me as subjects, or I have received a promise from you to accept my words. On that day your pledge to me was more certain than the pledge to Abū Bakr and 'Umar. Therefore why did those who have opposed me not revoke (their pledge) to those two until they had departed, while they have revoked (their pledge to me) and have not carried out the instructions which I was entitled to expect them (to obey) and they have not kept to my commands? Do you now know that the pledge of allegiance to me is required of those of you who are present and those of you who are absent? Who do Mu'āwiya and his followers find fault with in the pledge of allegiance to me and why do they not fulfil it since my close relationship (to the Prophet), my priority (as a Muslim), and my being son-in-law (of the Prophet) makes me more entitled to authority than those who came before me. Have you not heard the words of the Apostle of Allāh, may Allāh bless Him and His Family, at Ghadir concerning my authority (*wilāya*) and my being the one entitled to rule (*mawlā*)?

"Muslims, fear Allāh and rise to battle against Mu'āwiya, the one who has broken his pledge and the unjust man, and (rise) against his unjust followers. Listen to what I recite to you from the Book of Allāh which was sent down to His Prophet, the man He sent (to you), so that you may understand. By Allāh it is a warning to you, so take advantage of Allāh's warning and hold back from disobedience to Allāh. Allāh warned you through (His warning to others) when He said to His Prophet, may Allāh bless Him and His Family: *Have you not considered the leaders of the Banu Isrā'īl after Moses when they said to one of their prophets: Send us a king so that we may fight on the path of Allāh. He replied: Perhaps if fighting was ordained for you, you would not fight. They answered We have no other (idea) than to fight on the path of Allāh and we have been brought out of our houses and our villages. When fighting was ordained for them, they turned their backs except a few of them. Allāh is aware of wrong-doers. Their prophet said to them: Allāh has sent Tālūt to you as a king. They asked: Shall he have (the right of) kingship over us when we are more entitled to kingship than he is? He has not brought any extent of wealth. He said: Allāh has chosen him to be over you and has increased him extensively in knowledge and substance. Allāh gives His kingship to whomsoever He wishes. Allāh is all-embracing, knowing* (II 246-7).

"People, in these verses is an example so that you may learn that Allāh has given the succession (*khilāfa*) and the command after prophets to their progeny. He favoured Tālūt and brought him forward over the people (*jamā'a*) by His choice of him and by increasing him in Abundance of knowledge and substance. Do you think that Allāh has chosen the Banū Umayya over the Banū Hāshim and has increased Mu'āwiya extensively in knowledge and substance? Therefore, servants of Allāh, fear Allāh and strive on His path before His anger takes hold of you for your disobedience. Allāh said: *May those of the Banu Isrā'īl who disbelieved be cursed by the tongue of David and Jesus, son of Mary, because they because they disobeyed and used to exceed the limit. They used not to forbid each other the hateful things (which) they did; certainly evil was that which they did!* (V 77-79) *Only the believers who believe in Allāh and His Apostle and then have not doubted and have striven with their wealth and their lives on the path of*

Allāh, only they are the truthful ones (XLIX 15). *O you who believe, shall I show you a trade which will grant you escape from dread punishment. You should believe in Allāh and His Apostle and you should strive with your property and your lives on the path of Allāh. That is better for you if you would (only) realise it. That will bring forgiveness of your sins and cause you to enter gardens beneath which flow rivers and in the gardens of Eden are beautiful houses. That is the great triumph.* (LXI 10-12).

"Servants of Allāh, fear Allāh and rise to fight on behalf of your Imam. If I had a group of you only the number of the men (who fought) at Badr, when I ordered them, they would obey me. When I urged them to rise, they would rise with me so that with them I could dispense with many of you and hurry to rise in battle against Mu'āwiya and his followers. For it is a required battle."

*****

Among his speeches, peace be on him, (which he delivered) when he heard about Mu'āwiya and the Syrians and the harmful words they were saying, (is the following):

"Praise be to Allāh, the Eternal yet the New. However the sinful men have become my enemy, Allāh becomes their enemy. Are you not amazed that this is a great matter. Indeed sinners, not satisfied and turning aside from Islam and its followers, have deceived some of this community and have filled their hearts with the love of discord. They have inclined their passions towards lying and slander. They have prepared for war against us and have embarked on putting out the light of Allāh. Yet Allāh is the one who terminates His light even though the unbelievers may dislike it. O Allāh, they have rejected the truth, so scatter their army, break up their words and destroy them for their sins. May him whom I have befriended not be humiliated and may him whom I fight against not be made strong."

*****

From his words, peace be on him, urging battle at Ṣiffīn, (are those when he said) after praising and glorifying Allāh:

"Servants of Allāh, fear Allāh, lower your glances and your voices, be sparing in your words, make yourselves ready for battle, dispute and combat, and to pave the way and make the place ready, to be friendly and to be generous. Be strong and mention Allāh much. Perhaps you will be successful. Obey Allāh and His Apostle. Do not dispute with one another, for then you will fail and lose your spirit. Be steadfast. Indeed Allāh is with those who are steadfast. O Allāh, inspire them with steadfastness, grant them victory and make the reward for them great."

*****

Another of his speeches, peace be on him, in the same sense (is the following): "Muslims, Allāh has shown you a trade by which He will grant you an escape from dread punishment and which will bring you great good. It is faith in Allāh and His Apostle and striving on His path. He has made the reward for it forgiveness of sin and beautiful houris in the gardens of Eden. Therefore I told you that He loves those who fight on His path in ranks like a tightly-packed building. Therefore bring forward the man clad in armour and keep back the one who loses (his spirit), bite hard on the teeth. This makes swords stronger (to shield) against the head. Twist the edges of lances; this is a matter for the points of spears. Lower your glances; it is a firmer bond of the brave and surer for (men's) hearts. Deaden your voices; for that is the pursuit of failure and (quiet) is more appropriate for dignity. As for your standard, do not incline it and do not desert it. Only put it in the hands of the brave among you. Those who defend honour and are steadfast at the revelation of truth are the defenders who are right in their opinions and make them public. May Allāh have mercy on any man of you who comforts his brother with his own life and does not leave his opponent with his brother so that his own opponent and his brother's opponent gather against (his brother). For by that he will acquire blame and inferiority will come upon him. Do not expose yourselves to the loathing of Allāh and do not flee from death. Allāh, may He be exalted, says: *Say: Flight will never benefit you if you flee from death or being killed, then you will only enjoy it for a little* (XXXIII 16).

"I swear by Allāh that if you flee from the sword which is at hand, you will not be safe from the sword of the next world. Therefore seek help in steadfastness, prayers, truthfulness of intention. For Allāh, the Exalted, will grant victory after steadfastness (is shown)."

*****

Among his words, peace be on him, (are those) when he passed the standard of the Syrians and the followers of it did not withdraw from the positions (but remained) steadfast to fight the Commander of the Faithful. He said to his followers:
"These men will never withdraw from their positions without a successful attack by which life will be taken (from them) and a blow which will split their heads, chop down their bones and cut off their wrists and hands. (They will not do it) until their brows are beaten down by iron rods and (the blood from) their brows is scattered over chests and their chins. Where are the people of victory? Where are those who seek reward?"

Immediately a group of Muslims rose against them and defeated them.

*****

Among his words, peace be on him, in the same sense (are the following):
"These people have not been acting for truth nor have they responded to the words of an equal, until the vanguard attacks, followed by the front line (*'asākir*), until phalanxes are hurled against them, followed by the reserves (*jalā'ib*), until army after army drives through their land, until the cavalry remains in areas of their land with its reins over their river beds and lands, until raids will be made in every direction and their standards will shake in their hands. A true people will come against them. Their steadfastness will only increase the destruction of those of their killed and dead who will be destroyed in the path of Allāh (by those) renewing obedience to Allāh and anxious to meet Allāh. By Allāh, we were with the Prophet, may Allāh bless Him and His Family, when our fathers, our sons, our brothers and our uncles fought together. That has only served to increase us in faith, submission and endurance in face of the tribulations of suffering and (to increase us) in bravery to fight against the enemy and to scorn fighting anyone except equals. One of our men and one of our enemies will assault each other ferociously and contend with each other to take each other's life. Which one of the two will make his opponent drink the cup of death? At one time it could be for us (to do it) to our enemy, at another for our enemy (to do it) to us. Yet when Allāh beholds our endurance and our faith, He will send down the decrees against the enemy and He will send down victory to us. However, by my life, if we were to give an example like the one you have just given, neither would religion be sustained nor Islam strengthened. I swear by Allāh, that you will lose fresh blood (as a result of your inactivity). So remember what I say."

His Words about the Truce and the Revolt of the Khārijites

Among his words, peace be on him, when his followers had returned from the battle at Ṣiffīn after Mu'āwiya had deceived them by raising copies of the Qur'ān and thus they withdrew from the fight (is the following):
"You have committed an action which has pulled down the power from Islam, reduced its strength and bequeathed (it) weakness and humiliation. When you were successful and your enemy was afraid of being destroyed, for the fighting was crushing them and they felt the pain of wounds, they raised copies of the Qur'ān and called you to (accept) something which was only so that they might turn you away from themselves and bring to an end the battle between you and them and that they might cause the suspicion of death to lay in wait for you. It was deception, trickery. What have you done? You have agreed to what they wanted and have given it to men who only asked for it out of deception. I swear by Allāh, I do not consider you have any guidance after (failing to obey) my views nor any resolution (after failing to follow) my purpose."

*****

Among his words, peace be on him, (spoken) after the writing of the document for a truce and arbitration and the dispute about it among the Iraqīs (are those when) he said:
"By Allāh, I did not consent (to do this) and I did not want you to consent. However you refused everything except giving consent. So I consented. Since I have consented, it is not proper to withdraw after giving consent and to change after acceptance. Indeed we would rebel against Allāh by breaking the covenant and by transgressing its text through abrogating its agreement. Therefore fight against whoever abandons the command of Allāh. As for what you have mentioned about al-Ashtar having abandoned my command to put his signature to the document and being opposed to it, he is not such a man and I have no fear of him doing that. I wish there were two men like him among you. Indeed I wish there was a single man like him among you, who could see in your enemy what he sees. Then your burden would be lightened for me. I hope that he will straighten some of your crookedness for me. I forbade you (from doing) what you did and you disobeyed me. Myself and you are as the man of Hawāzin described:

Am I anything with regard to Ghuzzaya?

If she is mistaken, I am mistaken. If Ghuzzaya are right, I am right."

*****

(The following is) among his speeches to the Khārijites when he returned to Kūfa. He was on the outskirts (of Kūfa) before entering it. After praising and glorifying Allāh and calling for blessings on Muḥammad, His Apostle, may Allāh bless Him and His Family, he said:
"O Allāh, this is a position where whoever succeeds in it, will be more entitled to succeed on the Day of Resurrection and whoever is wrong and commits a crime in it will be blind and lose the path in the next world. I commend Allāh to you. You know that when they raised the copies of the Qur'ān, you said: We will answer their call to the Book of Allāh. I told you then: I know these people better than you. They are not followers of religion nor of the Qur'ān. I have been with them and I have known them as children and as men. They were evil children and they are evil men who seek to exploit your right and your belief. The people have only raised these copies of the Qur'ān before you as a deception, as a sign of weakness and as a trick. You rejected my opinion and said: No, rather you accept (this call) from them. I told you: Remember my words to you and your disobedience of me. Then when you refused everything except to make a truce (*kitāb*). I made the condition on the two arbitrators that they should allow to revive whatever the Qur'ān revives and make obsolete whatever the Qur'ān makes obsolete. None of us can oppose the judgement of anyone who judges

according to what is in the Book. However if (the two arbitrators) rejected that, then we would be exempt from their judgement."

One of the Khārijites said: "Tell us, do you regard the arbitration of men concerning blood (which has been shed) as just?"

"We do not judge men," he, peace be on him, answered. "The Qur'ān judges us. This Qur'ān is only lines of writings between two covers. It does not speak. It is only men who speak it."

Then (the Khārijite) said to him: "Tell us about the time-limit you made in what is between you and them"

He answered: "Let the ignorant learn and let the one who knows be confirmed (in his knowledge). Perhaps Allāh will set right the community during this armistice. Go into your city, may Allāh have mercy on you."

They departed to the last man.

His Words concerning the Syrian Raids after the Truce

(The following is) among the words which he spoke, peace be on him, when Mu'āwiya broke the covenant and sent al-Daḥḥāk b. Qays on a raid against the Iraqīs. 'Amr b. 'Abs b. Mas'ūd had met him and al-Daḥḥāk had killed him and some of his men. After praising and glorifying Allāh, he said:
"People of Kūfa, go out to a good man, to your army. Part of it has been struck down. Therefore go out and fight your enemy. Protect your women if you are men who act."

[The narrator reported:]
They rejected him weakly and he perceived weakness and failure in them. Then he said: "By Allāh, I wish I had one man of them for every eight of you. Woe upon you, go out with me. Then withdraw from me, if it seems good to you. By Allāh, I am not unwilling to meet my Lord as a result of my resolution and perception. In that I would have a spirit which is great and a release from your (malicious) whispering, your ill-treatment and your deceit which is like the deceit of wilful brides and nagging women; whenever they sew one side, they tear the other for their husbands."

*****

(Here is) another of his speeches, peace be on him, summoning the people and finding them slow to go to war. (When) he learnt that Busr b. Arṭa'a had gone to Yemen, (he said)

"People, the beginning of your unseemly talk and your refusal was the loss of the men of influence and authority (*ra'y*) among you. These were men who would meet and speak the truth; they would discuss and follow the just course; they would ask and they would answer. By Allāh, I have summoned a second time and a first, secretly and aloud, at night and by day, in the morning and in the afternoon. Yet my call to you does nothing except increase your flight and (your turning) your backs. Does not warning and a call to guidance bring you benefit?

"Indeed I am one who knows what is of advantage to you and what will straighten your crookedness for me. Yet, by Allāh, I will bring you no (worldly) advantage by the corruption of my soul. Grant me a respite. By Allāh, it is as if you are with a man (i.e. Mu'āwiya) who has come to you, forbidding you and punishing you. Then Allāh will punish him just as He will punish you. Indeed (his actions) are the humiliation of the Muslims and the destruction of religion. Indeed the sons of Abū Sufyān summon (men) to wicked vices and (their call) is answered. I summon you as virtuous and good men and you are deceitful and put me off. This is not the action of pious men."

*****

Another of his speeches, peace be on him, concerning the dilatoriness of those who held back from supporting him, is:[18]

"People, whose bodies are gathered together but whose inclinations are diverse, your words would weaken the firmest of hard-hearted men. Yet your actions would make your doubting enemy full of confidence against you. In your gatherings you say 'such and such' but when the battle comes, you say 'turn aside'. The call of the one who calls you (away) is not strong. The heart of the one who will make you endure uncertainties and weaknesses will not rest. You ask me to delay defending religion. Holding back (from its defence) will not prevent humiliating oppression. Nor will right be achieved except by serious endeavour. What house will you defend after your own house (is destroyed)? With what Imam will you fight after I (am killed)? By Allāh, deluded is the one whom you have deluded. Whoever acquires you, acquires the most deceitful partner. By Allāh, I have come not to believe in your words nor to aspire to your help. May Allāh make a separation between me and you. May He give me in exchange for you those who will be better for me than you. By Allāh. I wish I had for every ten of you, one man from the tribe of Firās b. Ghanam. It would be exchanging dirhams for dīnārs."

*****

18 *Nahj al-Balāgha*, I, no. 29, 72-3. Except for the last sentence.

In a further speech of his, peace be on him, concerning the same idea, after praising and glorifying Allāh, (he said):
"I can only think that these people - meaning the Syrians - will overcome you."
"Why is that, Commander of the Faithful?" they asked.

"I can see their affairs in the ascendancy," he said, "while your fires are dying away. I see them as in earnest while I see you as being weak. I see them as united while I see you as divided among yourselves. I see them obedient to their leader while I see you as disobedient. By Allāh, if they overcome you, you will find them evil masters for you after me. It is as if I was looking at them now. They have become partners of you in your land. They carry off your share of the booty held by the central government to their land. It is as if I was looking at you rustling like lizards without taking your due and without protecting those sacred to Allāh. It is as if I was looking at them killing the righteous men among you and terrorising your reciters of the Qur'ān; they are forbidding you and hindering you; they are bringing other people close to themselves apart from you. If you could see the privation, the selfishness, the blows of the swords and the coming of terror, you would regret and be sorry for your neglect in going to war and you would remember the ease and well-being you had today when the memory will no longer benefit you."

*****

(This is) from his words, peace be on him, when Mu'āwiya b. Abī Sufyān broke the terms of the truce and began to launch attacks against the people of Iraq. He said, after he had praised and glorified Allāh:
"What is (the intention) of Mu'āwiya, may Allāh kill him. He wants me (to involve myself) in a dreadful matter. He wants me to act as he has acted. Then I would have broken my compact and revoked my covenant. He would use that as a proof against me and it would be disgrace against me until the Day of the Resurrection whenever (my name) was mentioned. If it was said to him, 'You began it', he would reply: 'I did not know about (those raids) and I did not order them'. Then some will say, 'He is truthful' and others will say, 'He is lying'. By Allāh, indeed Allāh is the (true) possessor of compassion and great forbearance. Forbearance was shown by many of the first Pharaohs and by those who followed the Pharaohs. If Allāh gives him a respite now, He will never let him escape. He is at the watch-tower looking down on the path he follows. Let him do what seems appropriate to him. We will not break our compact, we will not revoke our covenant. We will not terrorize a man who has submitted, nor one who has made a covenant until the terms of the truce between us are proved to be nothing, if Allāh wishes."

*****

The following is from his speech in another place:
"Praise be to Allāh and peace be on the Apostle of Allāh, may Allāh bless Him and His Family. Indeed the Apostle of Allāh, may Allāh bless Him and his family, was pleased to make me his own brother and he described me as his helper (*wazīr*). People, I am the very nose of guidance and its eyes. Do not keep yourselves isolated from the path of guidance because of the small numbers of those who come to it. Whoever claims that the one who will kill me is a believer (is wrong). It is time which will kill me. Indeed at some time there is an avenger for all blood that is shed. The avenger of our blood, the judge concerning the rights of himself and the right of those who are kin, of orphans, of the poor, and the traveller, is the one who does not fail to get what he searches for and whom no one who flees will escape. *Those who do wrong will be aware of it. By what kind of change shall they be changed* (XXVI 227). I swear by Allāh, Who split the seed and created man, you will be seized by the throat, Banū Umayya, on account of it (i.e. dominion) and you will recognize it in the possession of others and in the house of your enemy after (only) a short while. You will be aware of His prophecy after a time."

*****

This is another speech with the same idea as the previous one. (He said:)
"People of Kūfa, make your preparations to fight against your enemy, Mu'āwiya and his followers."
"Give us a respite, Commander of the Faithful," they said. "He will leave the land."

He said: "By Allāh, Who split the seed and created man, let these people overcome you. It is not because they have greater right than you but because of their obedience to Mu'āwiya and your disobedience of me. By Allāh, all the nations have come to fear the tyranny of their rulers but I have come to fear the tyranny of my subjects. I have appointed to office men from among you and they have been treacherous and betrayed (me). Some have gathered the booty which they were entrusted with for distribution to the Muslims and carried it off to Mu'āwiya while others took it to their own. Thus they have ignored the Qur'ān and have been bold before the Merciful. (It has come to such a state) that if I entrusted anyone with the handle of a whip, he would betray it. You have made me tired."

Then he raised his hand to heaven and said: "O Allāh, I loathe life amid these people, I am weary of hope. Let my companion (i.e. the angel of death) come home so that I may rest from them and they may rest from me. They will never be successful after me."

*****

This is a speech which he, peace be on him, made on another occasion:[19]
"People, I have summoned you to fight against these people and you have not helped. I have asked you to listen and you have not answered. I have given you sincere advice and you have not accepted. You are present and you are like absent people. I have recited to you (Allāh's) wisdom and you have turned aside from it. I have given you eloquent warnings and you have refused them. *It is as if you were scared donkeys who had fled from a lion* (LXXIV 50-51). I urge you to fight against men of oppression and I do not reach the end of my words before I see you scattering from me like the people of Saba' (after the breaking of the dam) in Yemen. You go back to your own councils, you sit in your circles, you coin maxims, you recite poetry. You know the news yet when you leave, you are asking about poetry, ignoring any other kind of knowledge, careless of any other conduct and distracted from fear, you have forgotten the war, the need to prepare for it. Your hearts become empty of any talk of it. You occupy them with diversion and idle (chatter). It is wonderful, completely wonderful. But it is not for me to feel wonder that people have agreed on the wicked plan and to deprive you of your rights.

"People of Kūfa, you are like the mother of Mujālid: She became pregnant and gave birth. Then her husband died and her widowhood was long. Her inheritance was lost to her. By Him Who split the seed and created man, behind you, who are one-eyed and keep turning away, is the hell of the present life which does not remain and does not leave anything. After it are wolves and lions in various packs. So Banū Umayya will inherit from you. Their number from first to last will not treat you with compassion except for one man. It is a tribulation which Allāh has decreed for the community which is inescapable. They will kill your choice men and enslave the wicked among you. They will take out your treasure and your stores even from within the bridal chamber as a punishment for what you have abandoned of your affairs, the goodness of your own souls and your religion.

"People of Kūfa, I tell you of what will happen before it happens so that you may be on your guard against it and warned of it; whoever (of you) will be warned and consider. Sometimes you say that 'Alī is a liar, just like Quraysh said of their Prophet, may Allāh bless Him and His Family, their master, Muḥammad b. 'Abd Allāh, beloved of Allāh. Woe to you, it is I who am accused of lying. May Allāh be exalted, I was the first to worship Him, to believe in His unity. Or (is it) the Apostle of Allāh, may Allāh bless Him and His Family (who is accused of lying)? I was the first who had faith in him, who believed in him, who helped

19 This is a composite speech. It contains elements already reported by al-Mufīd and references to it are scattered throughout *Nahj al-Balāgha.*

him. No, by Allāh, they are deceitful words. You would be better without them. By Him Who split the seed and created man, you will know their news after a time but that will be when your ignorance has brought you to it. Then your knowledge will not benefit you. Disgrace upon you, you mere images, you are not men but dreams of children with the minds of the ladies of the bridal chamber. By Allāh, their bodies are present but their minds are absent from them and their inclinations are diverse. Allāh has not strengthened the support of the one who calls to you (to desert). Nor will the hearts of those who will treat you harshly take rest. There is no joy for anyone who seeks refuge with you. Your words would weaken the firmest of hard-hearted men.

"Yet actions would make your doubting enemy full of confidence against you. Woe upon you, what house will you defend after your own house (is destroyed)? With what Imam will you fight after I (am killed)? By Allāh, deluded is the one whom you have deluded. Whoever acquires you, acquires the most deceitful partner. I have not come to aspire in your help or believe in your words. May Allāh make a separation between me and you. May He give me in exchange for you, those who will be better for me than you. May he give you in exchange for me one who will be worse for you than me. Your Imam obeys Allāh and you disobey him. The Imam of the Syrians disobeys Allāh and they obey him. By Allāh, I wish Mu'āwiya would agree with me to exchange you: it would be exchanging dirhams for dīnārs. He could take ten of you and give me one of them. By Allāh, I wish that I did not know you and that you did not know me. For it is a knowledge that flows with regret. You have wounded my breast with anger, you have brought my affair to nought through your desertion and disobedience so that Quraysh have begun to say: "Alī is a brave man but he has no knowledge of war.' Yet is there anyone among them who has been longer engaged in it than I and are there any of them fiercer in battle than me? I was involved in it when I had not reached twenty and I am still in it now when I am more than sixty. However a man who is not obeyed has no power. By Allāh, I wish that my Lord had taken me from among you to His Paradise. Indeed death is looking down on me. There is nothing preventing the most wicked of (the community) from dyeing (this)" - he put his hand on his head and his beard - "It is a promise which the unlettered Prophet made to me. Whoever makes false statements is lost, whoever is pious and is truthful about the good is saved.

"People of Kūfa, I have summoned you to fight these people at night and during the day, secretly and in public. I have said to you: Attack them before they attack you. Only men who are humiliated are attacked in the ruins of their own home. You rely on one another and desert one another. My words weigh heavily on you. My command is difficult for you. You put it behind you as something to be neglected until attacks have been launched against you and abominations and detestable things appear in your midst which will be with you at night and in the morning. (This is) just as happened to the people of the stories of old (*mathalāt*) before you, where Allāh gave information about haughty tyrannous despots and those weakened by seducers in His words, the Mighty and High: *They slaughter your sons and disgrace your women. In that there is great tribulation from your Lord* (XIV 6). By Him who split the seed and created man, what you were promised has happened to you.

"People of Kūfa, I have remonstrated with you by reminding you of the warning of the Qur'ān, yet I have not benefited you. I have punished you with the whip, yet have not corrected your attitude towards me. I have flogged you with the lash, with which the revealed criminal punishments (*ḥudūd*) are carried out, yet you have not abstained from unlawful things. I know that the only thing suitable for you is the sword but I would not bring about your righteousness at the cost of the destruction of my own soul. However, after me a harder authority will have domination over you. It will not show respect to the old among you, nor be merciful to the children among you. It will not honour the learned among you, nor will it distribute the booty for distribution fairly among you. It will strike you down, humiliate you and kill the wounded among you in battles. It will hinder your path and block you at its door so that it may gorge itself on your strong men, on your weak men. Allāh will only destroy those of you who do wrong. Rarely can one turn one's back on something and then go forward. I think you are in a period (where there is no prophetic help). It is only my duty to give you sincere advice.

"People of Kūfa, I have been tested by two or three among you who are deaf while having ears, who are dumb yet have tongues, who are blind but have eyes, brothers who are not trustworthy at a meeting, brothers who are not reliable in a test. O Allāh! I make them bored and they bore me. I disgust them and they disgust me. O Allāh! Let no commander please them and let them please no commander. Mix their hearts as salt is mixed with water. By Allāh, if I could find an escape from your words and your correspondence, I would use it. I have remonstrated with you for your guidance until life has become distasteful. (Despite) all that you repeat the sneering at my words, fleeing from the truth and deviating to the false. Allāh will not strengthen the religion of those who support (the false). I know that the only thing you do more of for me is to cause me loss. Whenever I order you to fight against your enemy, you lower your heads to the ground and ask me to postpone the defence of the religion which is being nullified. When I say to you in the winter 'give me assistance', you say 'this is (impossible) in such a cold time'. If I say to you in the summer 'give me assistance', you say 'this (is impossible) in such intense heat. Call us when the heat has left us'. All that is fleeing from Heaven since you were unable (to act) because of the heat and the cold, by Allāh, you are more unable because of the heat of sword, much more unable. We belong to Allāh and to Him do we return.

"People of Kūfa, an Arab has come to me to tell me that a man of the tribe of Ghāmid has descended on the people of al-Anbār at night with four thousand men and attacked them as if he was attacking the Byzantines or the Khazars. He killed my governor there, Ḥassān, and with him he killed righteous men of merit, devotion and courage, may Allāh make a home for them in the blessed gardens (of Heaven). Indeed He has declared it to be permitted (for them). I have learnt that a group of Syrians broke in on a Muslim woman and another who was protected by treaty. They tore off her veil and took her scarf from her head, the earrings from her ears, the bracelets from her wrists and legs and upper arms, and the silver-bands and waistwrapper from her legs. She was unable to defend herself except by the repetition of the verse of return to Allāh and by calling out: 'O Muslims'. But no one gave her help. No one gave her assistance. If a believer died in sorrow at this, I would not blame him. On the contrary in my view he would be pious and good. The strangest of all is the gathering of these people in support of their falsehood and your failure to support your truth. You have become a target which is shot at and you do not shoot back. You are attacked and you do not fight back. (The enemy) rebels against Allāh and you are content. May your hands be filled with dust, O men like camels whose masters are absent from them so that as soon as they gather at one side, they begin to split up on the other side."

*****

[Among his speeches complaining of his enemies and defending his rights is the speech reported by al-'Abbās b. 'Abd Allāh al-'Abdī, on the authority of 'Amr b. Shamir on the authority of his narrators, who said:]

We (i.e. the narrators of 'Amr b. Shamir) heard the Commander of the Faithful, peace be on him, say:

"Since Allāh sent Muḥammad, may Allāh bless Him and His Family, I have never seen (a time of) ease. Praise be to Allāh. By Allāh, as a little one I lived in fear. When I was bigger, I fought in battle against the polytheists and made war on the hypocrites until Allāh took His Prophet to Himself. Then tribulations were worse. I have not ceased being careful and cautious. I was afraid that something would happen which would make me rise up. I have seen only good, praise be to Allāh. By Allāh I have not ceased striking with my sword from the time I was a boy until I have become an old man. What gives me endurance for what I am involved in is that all that is for the sake of Allāh and His Apostle. I am hopeful that the Spirit is near at hand. I have seen its threads."

[They reported:]
Only a few days after this speech he, peace be on him, was struck down.

*****

['Abd Allāh b. Bukayr al-Ghamawī reported on the authority of Ḥakīm b. Jubayr, who said: One who was present when 'Alī spoke at al-Raḥaba told us:]
Among the things he said was:
"People, you have refused me. I say, by the Lord of the heavens and the earth, my bosom friend promised me: 'The community will betray you after me'."

[Ismā'īl b. Sālīm reported on the authority of Abū Idrīs al-Awdī, who said:]
I (i.e. Abū Idrīs) heard 'Alī, peace be on him, say: "Among the things which the unlettered Prophet, may Allāh bless Him and His Family, promised me was: 'The community will betray you after me'"

His Words about the Succession and Men's Desertion of him

[Among his words, peace be on him, about the consultative committee (*shūrā*) (for the election of a successor to 'Umar b. al-Khaṭṭāb) at the house is (the conversation) which is reported by Yaḥyā b. 'Abd al-Ḥamīd al-Ḥimmānī, on the authority of Yaḥyā b. Salama b. Kuḥayl, on the authority of his father, on the authority of Abū Ṣādiq, who said:]
When 'Umar made a consultative committee (to elect a successor) consisting of six, he said: "If two make the pledge to one man (of the six) and two to another (of the six), the people must be with the three (i.e. the two men and their candidate) among whom is 'Abd al-Raḥmān (b. 'Awf) and kill the three who do not include 'Abd al-Raḥmān."

The Commander of the Faithful, peace be on him, came out of the house, leaning on the arm of 'Abd Allāh b. al-'Abbās. He said: "Ibn al-'Abbās, the people have opposed you after your Prophet just as they used to oppose your Prophet, may Allāh bless Him and His Family, during his life. By Allāh, nothing will bring them back to the truth except the sword."
"How is that?" Ibn al-'Abbās asked him.

He answered: "Haven't you heard 'Umar's statement: If two make the pledge to one man (of the six) and two to another (of the six), (the people) must be with the three among whom is 'Abd al-Raḥmān and kill the three who do not include 'Abd al-Raḥmān?"

"Yes," replied Ibn al-'Abbās.

"Don't you realise," he went on, "that 'Abd al-Raḥmān is the cousin of Sa'd and 'Uthmān is the brother-in-law of 'Abd al-Raḥmān?"
"Yes," he replied.

"'Umar knew," he said, "that Sa'd, 'Abd al-Raḥmān and 'Uthmān would not differ in their view. Therefore whoever among them they make the pledge of allegiance to, will have two of them (as supporters). Then he ordered that those who oppose them should be killed. He does not care if Ṭalḥa is killed as long as he kills me and al-Zubayr is killed. By Allāh if 'Umar lives, I will make known to him his evil attitude toward us which has existed of old and recently. If he dies there will be a day which will bring him and me together and on which will be the Last Judgement."

*****

['Amr b. Sa'īd reported on the authority of Jaysh al-Kinānī, who said:]
When 'Abd al-Raḥmān struck the hand of 'Uthmān as (a token of) his pledge of allegiance to him on the day of (the meeting at) the house, the Commander of the Faithful, peace be on him, said: "Marriage relationship has made and encouraged you (to do) what you have done. By Allāh what you expected from him is what your colleague (i.e.'Umar) expected from his colleague (i.e. Abū Bakr). May Allāh spread among you the perfumes of death."

*****

[A group of traditionists (*ahl al-naql*) report by a variety of chains of authority (*ṭuruq*) on the authority of Ibn 'Abbās, who said:][20]
I (i.e. Ibn 'Abbās) was with the Commander of the Faithful at al-Raḥaba. I mentioned the caliphate and those who had preceded him. He breathed heavily and said:
"By Allāh, Ibn Abī Quḥāfa (i.e. Abū Bakr) took on its clothes although he was aware that my position with regard to it was like the position of the axle of a mill. The stream (of knowledge) flows from me and the birds cannot rise to (the exaltedness of) my position. I allowed myself to let another robe cover me instead of it and I turned aside from it. I began to consider whether I should attempt to attack (when I would be like a man) with a hand cut off or I should endure the blind darkness (of oppression), in which the old man would grow feeble and the young become white-haired, while 'a believer' would toil until he meets his Lord.

---

20 This is the famous speech known as *al-Shiqshiqiyya*; cf. *Nahj al-Balāgha*, I, no. 3, 48-50.

"I realised that endurance in this was most appropriate. So I endured while all the time there was a mote in my eye and an obstruction in my throat. I could see my inheritance plundered until the time of his death came to him (i.e. Abū Bakr) and he handed it down to 'Umar. How amazing that, while he used to offer to give it up during his life, he should make a bequest (*'aqd*) of it after his death! How eagerly the two divided its two udders between them:

> How different was my time in its saddle and the time of a man of wickedness, my brother Jābīr.

"By Allāh, he (i.e. Abū Bakr) directed it towards a coarse direction (i.e. 'Umar) whose touch was harsh, who was wounding in his roughness. The man in control of it was like the rider of an obstinate camel. If he pulled its reins, he choked it. If he held its reins loosely, he caused it to go at random so that it stumbled frequently and its excuses were few. In the name of Allāh, the people were afflicted with disorderliness, with refractoriness, with constant changes and with obstruction until death came to him. Yet even then he made it (the decision of) a consultative committee consisting of a group among whom he claimed that I was merely one. O Allāh! O what a consultative committee it was when doubt was stirred up against me through (being put alongside) the leading members among them so that I now come to be regarded (as merely an equal) with these men as my equals. However I descended (like a bird) when they descended and I flew like (a bird) when they flew (acting) out of a patience as a result of the long trial (I had endured) and the passage of time. One man (of the group) inclined (against me) because of his jealousy (i.e. Sa'd b. Abī Waqqāṣ). Another man (i.e. 'Abd al-Raḥmān b. 'Awf) favoured his brother-in-law (i.e. 'Uthmān) for other reasons which I will not mention. Eventually the third person (i.e. 'Uthmān) among these people arose lifting his chest from out of his excrement and his trough. His family (i.e. the Umayyads) rushed to devour the treasury of Allāh like the camel devours spring vegetation until its stomach is satiated by it. His actions brought about his death. The action of the people which shocked was that they (came) as messengers to me - like waves of hyenas - asking me that I should give them my acceptance of the pledge of allegiance. They were crowding in on me so that (my two sons) al-Ḥasan and al-Ḥusayn would have been trampled underfoot and my two shoulders pulled apart. Yet when I undertook the affair (of the Caliphate), a group broke their oath of allegiance, another deviated from the truth and others acted wickedly as if they had never heard Allāh say: *That last abode is that which we have made for those who seek nobleness on earth and not corruption. Good health is for those who fear Allāh* (XXVIII 83). Rather, by Allāh, they heard these words and they were aware of them but their own world was more attractive to their eyes and its adornments excited wonder in them.

"By Him who split the seed and created man, if it was not for the presence of those present and the necessity of a proof (*ḥujja*) to man through the existence of such supporters and the fact that Allāh does not give the true possessors of authority it without them being resigned (to it being swallowed) by the over-full bellies of the wrongdoers while the oppressed starve (for their rights) - (if it was not for all that) - I would throw down the reins (of the Caliphate) on to its withers and I would swallow the last with the cup of its beginning. Then in my view, they would find their world scantier than snot from the nose."

A man from the Sawād came before him and handed him a letter. He broke off from his speech.

[Ibn 'Abbās added:]
I have never regretted anything nor felt such distress like the distress I felt at losing the rest of the speech of the Commander of the Faithful, peace be on him. When he had finished reading the letter, I said: "Commander of the Faithful, would you continue your speech from the point which you reached?"

He answered: "In no way, in no way. It was like foam on the camel's mouth (*shiqshiqa*) as it opens its mouth to bellow and then falls silent."

*****

[Mas'ada b. Ṣadaqa reported: I heard Abū 'Abd Allāh Ja'far b. Muḥammad (al-Ṣādiq), peace be on them, say:]
The Commander of the Faithful, peace be on him, addressed the people at Kūfa. He praised and glorified Allāh. Then he said: "I am the master of the white-haired men and in me is an example of what happened to Job. Allāh will gather my family for me just like He gathered his family for Jacob. That will be when the globe turns around - and you have been told - and it goes astray and is destroyed. Indeed, therefore before that put on the garment of endurance and acknowledge your sins to Allāh. You have cast off your sanctity, you have put out your torches. You entrusted your guidance to those who do not even have control over themselves. You have neither ear nor eye, which is (even) weak. By Allāh, the seeker and the sought are thus. If you had not forsaken your task, abandoned support for the truth which is in your midst, and become weak through the weakening power of the false, one who is not like you would not have taken courage at you, and the one who becomes strong against you would not have become strong and (been able) to destroy your obedience and take it away from those of you who had it. You went astray like the children of Isrā'īl went astray in the time of Moses. I speak truly (when I say): Indeed your being astray will be doubled for you after me through your persecution of my sons; it will double the

loss which the children of Isrā'īl suffered. If you have drank and filled yourselves with the illnesses brought about by the authority of the tree cursed in the Qur'ān, you have gathered with the one who calls croakingly (to you) to go astray and have run to answer the false. You have betrayed the one who summons (you) to the truth; you have cut yourselves off from those close to the men who fought (for the Prophet) at Badr and you have joined those of the sons of war who are furthest away (from the Muslims who fought at Badr). Indeed if what they had possessed had melted away, the test for punishment would have been near, the covering would have been revealed and the period would have been brought to an end. Then the threat (of hell) would be near. The stars would have appeared to you from the east and your moon would shine for you like the full moon. Since that is clear, come back to repentance and throw off sin.

"You should be aware that if you are obedient, the rising star of the east will take you along the path of the Apostle of Allāh, may Allāh bless Him and His Family and grant them peace; you would then have treated yourself for deafness and have sought a cure for dumbness; you would have been given sufficient provisions against straying from the path and seeking them (outside it); you would have cast a crushing burden from your necks. Allāh only destroys those who refuse His mercy and forsake His protection: *Those who do wrong will be aware of it. By what kind of change shall they be changed?* (XXVI 227)."

*****

[Mas'ada b. Ṣadaqa reported: I heard Abū 'Abd Allāh Ja'far b. Muḥammad (al-Ṣādiq), peace be on them, say:]
The Commander of the Faithful, peace be on him, addressed the people at Medina. After praising and glorifying Allāh, he said:
"Allāh, the Exalted, never destroyed tyrants except after showing forbearance and giving a respite. He did not rejoin a broken bone of anyone in (all) the nations except after constraint and testing. People, the problems which you have faced in the times which have passed are a lesson. Not every one who has a heart is gifted with sound judgement. Not every one who has ears can hear. Not everyone who looks through an eye can see. Therefore, servants of Allāh, make your view good concerning (the things) which Allāh makes your concern and look at the ruins of those whom Allāh has destroyed because He knew that they were following the practices of the people of Pharaoh. They were people with gardens, with fantasies, with farms and high position. Those are the ruins of those who were oppressors. Indeed it is everlasting hell which will warn the one who sees it of destruction. (It comes) after well-being, joyfulness and temporary security and happiness. To whoever is steadfast, there is the happy end. The final end of affairs belongs to Allāh. How surprising for people with intelligence! How

would they live amid the rolling torrents and how would they gain sustenance without one who was protected a friend and ruler (*walī*) for His community which thirsts in its journey and which desires guidance? For they do not follow the tracks of a prophet, nor do they copy the practice of a testamentary trustee of authority (*waṣī*), nor do they believe in supernatural (things), nor do they turn away from sin. How indeed, while they resort to their own minds in ambiguous matters? Each person among them, being the leader of himself, adopts in (these matters) what he considers appropriate without authorities who are able to follow a just path. They will never increase (in anything) except after violence. Some are kind to each other, and believe one another in disagreement to everything which the Apostle, may Allāh bless Him and His Family, bequeathed, and in deserting whatever he carried out on the authority of the Creator of the heavens and the earths, the Aware, the Knowing. They are people from the darkness of caves of shadows, leaders of bewilderment and doubt. Whoever trusts to himself, will sink into errors. This is so for Allāh has guaranteed the end of this path: *So that whoever is destroyed will be destroyed with proof (which has been given to him) and whoever lives will live with proof. Indeed Allāh is hearing, aware* (VIII 42). What is in greater error than a community which shuns its rulers and turns away from its shepherds. O sorrow, sorrow, the heart is wounded and grief becomes a habit as a result of the actions of our Shī‘a after my death despite the nearness of its love and the intertwining of its friendship. How do some of them kill others and how does their friendship turn to hatred? By Allāh, tomorrow (there is) the family caused to deviate from its root, encamped around a branch, given hope of victory from another direction, expecting spirit from a place other than which it will come. Every group among them will cling to a branch by which they will be taken wherever the branch inclines despite the fact that Allāh - and praise be to Him - will gather them like the scattered clouds of spring, will bring them together and make them heaped together like heavy clouds. He will open gates for them to which they will flow, at (the advice of) their advisor, like torrents of rain where no land can resist it, no dam can stop it and the base of a lofty mountain cannot resist its path. Allāh will plant them in the middle of valleys. He will make springs in the land for them. Through them, He will remove the privation of people and He will make available for them the estates of people so that they will take forcibly what had been taken from them forcibly. Through them, He will pull down columns and through them He will break down the casings of bricks at Iram. He will let them enjoy the stones of olives. By Him Who split the seed and created man, what they possess will melt away after they have had power in the land and high position over men just as tar and lead melt in the fire. Perhaps Allāh will gather my Shī‘a after scattering them because of the evil day of these men. No man has a right to goodness from Allāh. Rather goodness belongs to Allāh and the matter is all (with Him)."

*****

The historians (*naqalat al-āthār*) report that a man from the tribe of Asad stood before the Commander of the Faithful, peace be on him and said to him: "Commander of the Faithful, there is wonder among you, Banū Hāshim, how this authority came to be diverted from you. You are the highest in family and in connection and closeness to the Apostle, may Allāh bless Him and His Family, as well as in understanding of the Book."

The Commander of the Faithful, peace be on him, replied: "Son of a worm, you are unstable and the gap is narrow so that you shoot in a way which is not straight. You have protection through your relationship by marriage and therefore the right to ask. You have sought information so know then that it was preference through which the souls of the people were generous while other souls were niggardly with it. Therefore leave off plundering the rooms which are (already) empty. Pay attention to the disasters concerning the affairs of the son of Abū Sufyān (i.e. Mu'āwiya). Time has made me laugh after it had made me weep. There is no deceit which the people despaired of. By Allāh, through my restraint and my dignity they tried to act in a false way with regard to the nature of Allāh. How very far that is from me. They have mixed drink and dwelling between them and me. If the trials of misfortune are taken from us, I would make them responsible for the truth in its purity. If it is otherwise, do not give yourself sorrows for them and do not console sinful people."

Some of his Words of Wisdom and Warning, Peace be on him

May Allāh have mercy on you, take your (eternal) abode from your transitory (life).
Do not rend your veils before One from Whom even your secrets are not concealed.
Take your hearts out of the world before your bodies are taken from it.
For the next life you were created and in the world you are imprisoned.
When a man dies, the angels ask about what he has brought while the people ask about what he has left behind. By Allāh, your fathers brought some of what was for you. Do not leave behind anything at all, for then you will owe it.
The world is like a poison which the one who does not recognise it eats.

*****

There is no life without religion and there is no death except through the denial of certain truth.
Drink the sweet water. It will wake you from the slumber of rest. Beware of the pestilential torrid winds which bring destruction.

*****

The world is the abode of truth for those who know it and the place of salvation for those who take provisions from it. It is the place to which the inspiration of Allāh has been sent down and the market place of His friends. So trade and gain the profit of heaven.

*****

Similar words were addressed by him, peace be on him, to a man whom he heard blaming the world without knowing what he ought to say about its (true) meaning:

"The world is the place (*dār*) of truth for those who believe in it, and a place which is to be wiped out for those who understand it. It is a place which is full of wealth for those who take their provision from it and the place of prostration for the prophets of Allāh and a place to which His inspiration has been sent down. It is the place of prayer for His angels and the market-place of His friends, in which they gain mercy and in which they earn the profit of Heaven. Who is the man who blames it when it has called out (for men) to keep apart from it and it has cried out (for men) to separate from it, when it has announced its own death? Through its own joy it has yearned for joy. Through its own tribulation it has warned against tribulation, bringing fear, giving warning, trying to turn (men) away and terrify them. O you who blame the world and (yet are one) who is seduced into rushing blindly into it, when did it tempt you to kill your fathers as a test and to sleep with your mothers under the earth? How did it weaken your hand and make your arm sick so that a cure is necessary for them, and doctors prescribe for them and medicines are sought for them without your search bringing them any benefit, without your (seeking) intercession bringing them any intercession? The world has made an example of them for you with your killing and your intercourse so that your weeping will not avail you not will your darlings be of any use to you."

*****

People, take five things from me. For by Allāh if you travelled on a camel for them, you would exhaust it before you found anything like them. No one should hope for anything except from His Lord, nor should one fear (anything) except his sins. The scholar (*'ālīm*), when asked about something he does not know, should not be ashamed to say that Allāh knows. Steadfastness is of the same rank with faith as the head is to the body. He who has no patience has no faith.

*****

Every statement in which Allāh is not mentioned is a vanity. Every silence in which there is no thought (of Him) is carelessness. Every reflection in which there is no consideration (of Him) is an idle pastime.

*****

One who buys his soul and sets it free is not like the one who sells his soul and imprisons it.

*****

The one who gets to the shade first has been exposed to the sun. The one who gets to water first is thirsty.

*****

Good breeding takes the place of a good family.

*****

The man who is abstemious towards the world increases his renunciation of it whenever it increases its manifestation of itself to him.

*****

Affection is the greatest of traps. Knowledge is the noblest of qualities.

*****

If work is an effort then being concerned with avoiding (it) is an act of corruption

*****

The man who goes to the extreme in rivalry commits a sin. The man who falls short in it will be subjected to it.

*****

Forgiveness corrupts the wicked to the same extent as it restores the noble.

*****

Whoever loves noble actions avoids crimes.

*****

Men cast their eyes on a man whose thoughts adorn him.

*****

The ultimate generosity is that you should give what you are able.

*****

There is no distance for one who is present and no nearness for one who is separate.

*****

One of the greatest sins of a man is to be unaware of his faults.

*****

The perfection of moderation is a willingness to accept what is sufficient.

*****

Generosity is perfected through the adoption of noble deeds and the payment of debts.

*****

Nobility is revealed through loyalty to brotherhood in hard times and easy times.

*****

If the sinner is displeased, he slanders. If he is content, he lies. If he is covetous, he wounds.

*****

One who is not more concerned with his reason for what is, will more (inevitably) come to his death.

*****

Put up with an error by your friend for the time of an attack by your enemy.

*****

A good confession wipes out the act of committing a wrong.

*****

What money is spent to make you aware of reforming your character is not wasted.

*****

Acting moderately is easier than acting immoderately and restraint is greater in protection than profligacy.

*****

The evilest of provisions for the return (to Allāh) is the committing of a crime against men.

*****

No benefit is wasted if it is received with thanks. No grace remains if it is received ungratefully.

*****

Time is of two kinds: time you have and time you owe. When you have it don't undervalue it and when you owe it, be steadfast.

*****

Often a mighty man is the humblest of creatures and a humble man is the mightiest of creatures.

*****

Whoever is not tested by affairs is deceived and the one who struggles against the truth is brought down.

*****

If the allotted span of life is known, hope is diminished.

*****

Thankfulness is the ornament of sufficiency and steadfastness is the ornament of tribulation.

*****

The value of each person lies in the good he does.

*****

People are the children of their own good actions.

*****

The person is found under his tongue.

*****

Whoever consults those with understanding is guided correctly.

*****

One who is satisfied with little can do without much. Those who cannot do without much have need of wicked men.

*****

Whoever has sound roots has branches which will bear fruit.

*****

Whoever gives hope to man regards him with awe. Whoever is deficient in the knowledge of anything, shames him.

*****

Part of his speech, peace be on him, describing man are his words: "The most amazing thing in man is his heart. It loves wisdom and its opposite. If hope occurs to it, ambition reduces it. If ambition rouses in it, covetousness destroys it. If despair possesses it, sorrow kills it. If anger occurs to it, rage intensifies it. If it comes near contentment, it forgets to be on guard. If fear takes hold of it, caution (totally) occupies it. If protection is provided for it, heedlessness takes possession of it. If a blessing is renewed for it, (love of) power seizes it. If a tragedy befalls it, violent grief disgraces it. If it acquires wealth, riches make it unjust. If poverty gnaws at it, misfortune (completely) occupies it. If hunger presses upon it, weakness makes it idle. If it has earlier satisfied its stomach to satiety, then every diminution of it is harmful and every increase of it is corrupting."

*****

When Shāhzamān, daughter of Chroesroe was captured, he, peace be on him, asked her: "What did you learn from your father after the Battle of the Elephant?" "I learned from him," she replied, "that he used to say: When Allāh controls a matter, ambitions are brought to nought without Him and when the allotted time comes to an end, death is in view."

"How well your father spoke," he, peace be on him, answered. "Affairs are led towards their destinations until death takes part in their control."

*****

One who followed certain truth and then was struck by doubt, should remain with his certain truth. Indeed certain truth cannot be removed by doubt.

*****

A believer is tired of himself while the people find themselves in comfortable position with regard to him.

*****

The man who is lazy does not love Allāh's truth.

*****

The best kind of worship is steadfastness, silence, and waiting for relief.

*****

Steadfastness is of three types: steadfastness in tragedy, steadfastness against disobedience, and steadfastness in obedience.

*****

Clemency is the helper of the believer. Knowledge is his friend, gentleness his brother, piety his father and steadfastness is the commander of his troops.

*****

Three things (which will earn) the treasures of Heaven are: giving alms secretly, keeping tragedy hidden and keeping sickness hidden.

*****

Feel need for the one whose prisoner you wish to be, dispense with the one whose equal you wish to be and prefer the one whose leader you wish to be.

*****

There is no satisfaction for the licentious, no rest for the envious and no affection for the weary.

*****

He, peace be on him, said to Aḥnaf b. Qays:
"The silent is the brother of the one who gives consent. Whoever is not with us is against us."

*****

Generosity belongs to the nobility of nature but over-generosity is a corruption of creation.

*****

The abandonment of a promise to a friend is the motive for being cut off (from his friendship).

*****

Rumours of anything among the ordinary people are evidence for the beginnings of its existence.

*****

Search out sustenance. It is guaranteed to one who looks for it.

*****

Four kinds of men whose prayer will not be rejected: the prayer of the just Imam for his subjects; the son who is respectful to his father; the father who is respectful to his son; and the oppressed man. Of them Allāh says: By My strength and My majesty, I will support you even after (some) time.

*****

The best kind of wealth is the abandonment of begging. The worst kind of poverty is the clinging to subservience.

*****

Good behaviour lies in protection from destruction. Gentleness is the alleviation of distress.

*****

A man who laughingly acknowledges hissing is better than one who behaves boldly towards Allāh in tears.

*****

If it was not for discussion, the (different) schools of thought would be ignorant.

*****

No tool is more beneficial than intelligence. No enemy is more harmful than ignorance.

*****

One who widens his hopes lessens his effort.

*****

The most grateful of the people is the most satisfied of them. The most ungrateful of them is the most covetous of them.

*****

In such speeches as these wisdom may be gained. We have not included in this chapter of speeches, all of those which have been reported with these ideas from him, lest by that the speeches would become too diffuse and the book become too long. In what we have presented, there is sufficient for those with intelligence.

CHAPTER VII

SOME OF THE MIRACLES OF THE COMMANDER OF THE FAITHFUL

(The following are) some of the signs of Allāh, the Exalted, and His clear proof of the Commander of the Faithful, peace be on him, which indicate his position with regard to Allāh, the Mighty and High, and his special endowment with miracles by which he was set apart from everyone else through the call for obedience to him, to remain steadfast in respecting his authority and closeness to Allāh (*wilāya*), to recognise his rights and the certainty of His Imamate, and to be aware of his protection (from error), perfection and the demonstration of the proof of him.

The Miracle of his Wisdom while still a Boy

Among these are some qualities which make him equal to two of the prophets, apostles and proofs of Allāh to His creatures and about the authenticity and correctness of which there can be no doubt. Allāh, the Mighty and High, said in mentioning Jesus, son of Mary, the spirit (*rūḥ*) and word of Allāh, and the prophet and Apostle of Allāh to His creatures, when He mentioned the story of his mother's conceiving and giving birth to him and the miraculous nature of that: *She said: How can I have a son when no man has ever touched me and I have not been adulterous. He answered: As it (shall be), for your Lord said: That will be easy for Me and We will make him a sign to the people and a mercy from us. It is a matter which is decreed* (XIX 21).

Among the signs of Allāh, the Blessed and Exalted, concerning the Messiah, Jesus, son of Mary, peace be on him, was his speaking in the cradle. By that normal human behaviour was transcended and in it there was great wonder and an illustrious miracle to the minds of men. Among the signs of Allāh concerning the Commander of the Faithful, peace be on him, was the perfection of his intellect, dignity and knowledge of Allāh and His Apostle, His blessing and peace be on Him and His Family, despite his youth and his being in outward form still only a child when the Apostle of Allāh, may Allāh bless Him and His Family, summoned him to believe in him and acknowledge him, and made him responsible for knowing his rights, and recognising his Creator and His unity. (He also) entrusted him with the secrets of His religion, the defence and preservation of it, and the fulfilment of the trust in it. At that time, he, peace be on him, was according to some statements a boy of seven years of age, according to others a boy of nine but according to the majority he was a boy of ten. The perfection of his intellect, peace be on him, (at that age) and the occurrence (in a boy of that age) of the ability to acknowledge Allāh and His Apostle, may Allāh bless Him and His Family, is an illustrious sign from Allāh which transcends normal human behaviour, and thus indicates his position with Him, his special endowment and his being worthy for what he was nurtured for the Imamate of the Muslims, and the proof (of Allāh) to all mankind. In this transcendence of ordinary human behaviour which we have mentioned there is a similarity with Jesus and John the Baptist as we have described. If it was not for the fact that at that (time) he was perfect, complete and (capable of) acknowledging Allāh, the Exalted, the Apostle of Allāh, may Allāh bless Him and His Family, would not have made him responsible to acknowledge his prophethood, nor would he have bound him to believe in himself and to accept his mission, nor would he have summoned him to accept his rights, nor would he have begun his mission with him before every other person except his wife, Khadīja, peace be on her.

Because the Prophet of Allāh, may Allāh bless Him and His Family, entrusted him with his secret which he ordered him to protect and because he set him apart by that from all the other children of his time and endowed him apart from all others as we have mentioned, that indicates that he, peace be on him, was perfect despite his youth, (capable of) acknowledging Allāh, the Exalted and His Prophet, may Allāh bless Him and His Family, before adolescence. This is the meaning of the words of Allāh, the Exalted concerning John the Baptist, peace be on him: *We gave him wisdom while still a boy* (XIX 12). There is no wisdom dearer than knowledge of Allāh, nor more obvious than the knowledge of the prophethood of the Apostle of Allāh, may Allāh bless Him and His Family, nor more celebrated than the ability of rational deduction, nor more discerning than the understanding of speculation (*naẓar*) and consideration and the knowledge of the aspects of elucidation, by which one is able to arrive at the realities of the unknown. If the matter is as we have explained it, it confirms that Allāh, the Exalted, caused ordinary human behaviour to be transcended in the case of the Commander of the Faithful, peace be on him, by an illustrious sign which is equivalent to His two prophets whom the Qur'ān speaks of in its great verses as we have explained.

The Miracle of his Military Prowess

Among the signs of Allāh, the Exalted, concerning the Commander of the Faithful, peace be on him, which transcend ordinary human behaviour is that He never endowed anyone else, with regard to fighting in single combat against one's rivals and against heroes, with what is known about him, peace be on him, in terms of the vast amount of (fighting) which he had to engage in during the course of time. Among those who have engaged in warfare there can only be found men to whom it brings disgrace and who acquire wounds and deformities through it except the Commander of the Faithful, peace be on him. Despite the length of time which he fought against his enemies, he acquired no ugly wound nor was anyone able to do him any harm until there occurred what happened at his assassination by Ibn Muljam, may Allāh curse him. This is a marvel by which Allāh set him apart through this sign and endowed him with illustrious knowledge of its meaning. By that He indicated his position with regard to Him and his being characterised by miracles, the favour of which set him apart from all other men.

Among the signs of Allāh, the Exalted, concerning him, peace be on him, is the fact that there is not mentioned a single contestant during the battles whom he met as an opponent, whom he did not overcome at one time and did not overcome at another time. He did not give any of his enemies a wound unless that man died of it immediately or recovered after a time. No rival escaped from him in battle, no one could escape his blow. For that it is appropriate that there was no doubt about his victory over every rival who came against him and his killing of every hero who fought. This is also among the things by which he, peace be on him, was set apart from all other men and by which Allāh caused ordinary human behaviour to be transcended at every time and occasion. It is among the clear indications of his (position).

Among the signs of Allāh, the Exalted, concerning him is the fact that despite the long period in which he was engaged and occupied in warfare and in which he was tested by the bravery of his enemies and their leaders, and by all the efforts which they made to gather against him and to bring about his death through deceit, he never turned his back and fled from one of them, nor did he weaken in his position or show fear to any of his rivals. He never met any opponent in battle without transfixing him at one time or turning aside from him (to another part of the battle) at another time. He would advance against him immediately and attack him at that time. Since his conduct was as we have described, it confirms what we have mentioned about his being set apart by an illustrious sign and a clear miracle transcending ordinary human behaviour by which Allāh indicated his Imamate and revealed the duty to obey him. By that He set him apart from all mankind.

The Miracle of the Survival of his Reputation and his Family despite Suppression and Oppression

Among the signs and indications of him, peace be on him, by which he was set apart from those who opposed him is the clear appearance of his outstanding qualities to both the Shī'a (*khāṣṣa*) and the general populace (*'āmma*). (This has been sufficient) to force the people to transmit reports of his merits and his qualities endowed by Allāh and for them to be admitted to even by opponents of the proof that there is in them. It has occurred despite the great number who have attempted to deviate from him and oppose him and the great number of occasions they have been prompted to suppress his merit and deny his rights. (It has occurred when) the (control of the) world has been in possession of his rivals and has been turned aside from his friends (*awliyā'*). (Despite this) his opponents who possess authority over the world and the narrators of the people, have not been able to put out his light and to deny his career (*amr*). Allāh has caused ordinary human behaviour to be transcended by spreading his merit and revealing his outstanding qualities, by forcing everyone to recognize that and to admit its truth, and to refute the deceitful attempts of his enemies to conceal his outstanding qualities and to deny his rights so that the proof of him may be brought about and the justification of his rights may be revealed. Because the normal view among those who agree to render his career obscure continues to oppose what we have mentioned, and yet it has not been able to bring that about with regard to the Commander of the Faithful, peace be on him, and the normal view has been transcended, that indicates his being apart from the rest of men through the illustriousness of the sign which we have described.

The report is well-known and widespread on the authority of al-Sha'bī that he used to say:
"I (i.e. al-Sha'bī) used to hear the preachers of the Umayyads curse the Commander of the Faithful, 'Alī b. Abī Ṭālib, peace be on him, on their pulpits." He would raise his finger to the sky and (go on): "I used to hear them praising their ancestors on their pulpits as if they could reveal their corpses."

One day al-Walīd b. 'Abd al-Malik said to his sons: "My sons, your duty is to religion. I do not see that religion has built anything which the world has destroyed. I see that the world has built a building which religion has destroyed. I still hear our followers and the members of our family curse 'Alī b. Abī Ṭālib, peace be on him, suppress his merits and urge the people to hate him. Yet that does not bring the people's hearts anything but closeness (to him). They strive to bring the spirits of the people closer to themselves. Yet that does not bring their hearts anything except (to make the people) more distant from them."

The manner of suppressing the merits of the Commander of the Faithful, peace be on him, of the deception practised by the religious scholars and of their spreading of what seemed authentic to a rational being reached the extent that when a man wanted to report a tradition on the authority of the Commander of the Faithful, peace be on him, he was not able to refer to him either by mentioning his name or his family background. Necessity required him to say: "A man from the Companions of the Apostle of Allāh, may Allāh bless Him and His Family, told me." Or he might say: "A man from Quraysh told me." Some used to say: "Abū Zaynab told me."

'Ikrima reported on the authority of 'Ā' isha in her account of the sickness and death of the Apostle of Allāh, may Allāh bless Him and His Family, that she said in a sentence of it: "The Apostle came out, leaning on two men from his House, one of whom was al-Faḍl b. al-'Abbās." When he (i.e. 'Ikrima) reported that on her authority to 'Abd Allāh b. al-'Abbās, the later asked: "Do you know the other man?"
"No," he replied, "she did not name him."

"That was 'Alī b. Abī Ṭālib, peace be on him," he told him. "'Our mother' would not mention any good of him while she could (avoid it)."[1]

The tyrannical governors would flog anyone who mentioned any good of him. Indeed their heads were cut off for doing that and exposed to the people to make them disassociate themselves from him. The normal course (of events) followed this pattern for it to become accepted that no good should be mentioned of him in any way much less his outstanding merits be mentioned, his qualities be reported and proof of his rights be set out. Yet since the appearance of his merits and the spreading of his qualities has taken place as we have mentioned its being widespread both among the Shī'a (*khāṣṣa*) and the general populace (*'āmma*), and since the compulsion of both enemy and friend to report it is now established, (this) has transcended the normal course of events as far as he is concerned and the nature of the proof of this idea is explained by the illustrious sign (of Allāh) as we have said before.

Another of the signs of Allāh, the Exalted, concerning him, peace be on him, is that no one has suffered such tribulation with regard to his sons and his offspring as he, peace be on him, suffered with regard to his sons and offspring. The fact is that no terror is known to have encompassed the group of children of any prophet, of any Imam, of the king of any period whether pious or profligate like the terror which encompassed the offspring of the Commander of the Faithful, peace be on him. Nor were any so much subjected to being killed, to being pursued from their houses and lands, and to being terrorised as the offspring and

---

1 Same tradition reported in al-Ṭabarī, I, 1800-1, but 'Ikrima is not the authority. 'Abd Allāh b. al-'Abbās explains 'Ā'isha's omission to 'Ubayd Allāh b. 'Abd Allāh.

sons of the Commander of the Faithful were subjected to. The different kinds of severity meted out to them did not occur for any other group of people. They were killed by murderous treachery, by treason and by deception. It was done to most of them during their lifetimes as an example. They were tormented by hunger and thirst until their lives were taken by death. This required them to scatter throughout the land and to become separated from their houses, their families and their countries. (It required) their family background to be kept secret from the majority of the people. The fear surrounding them extended to keeping themselves hidden from those who loved them in addition to their enemies. Their flight extended from their lands to the furthest east and west, to places which lacked civilisation and where the majority of the people were without knowledge of them. They avoided bringing such people close to them and mixing with them, out of fear for their own lives and their offsprings' from the tyrants of those times. All of these are the reasons which should bring about the disruption of their organisation, the pulling out of their roots, and the paucity of their numbers. Yet they, despite everything we have described, are the most numerous offspring of any one of the prophets, the righteous men and the friends (of Allāh). Indeed they are more numerous than the offspring of anyone else among the people. They have extended across the lands through their great number and have become more numerous than the offspring of most men. They have done this despite their marriages within their (family circles) to the exclusion of those outside them and by limiting them to those possessing their own genealogies of the nearer members of the relations. In that the normal practice has been transcended as we have explained. It is proof of the illustrious sign concerning the Commander of the Faithful, peace be on him, as we have already described and explained.

This is something about which there can be no doubt. Praise be to Allāh, Lord of the Worlds.

The Prophecies and Inner Knowledge of the Commander of the Faithful

Among the illustrious signs of Allāh concerning him, peace be on him, and the special characteristic by which he has been set apart, the miraculous nature of which is evidence for his Imamate, for the duty to obey him, and for the confirmation of his proof, are the group of arguments by which Allāh, the Exalted, makes known prophets and apostles, peace be on them, and which He gives as signs of their truthfulness. Of these are the widespread reports of him, peace be on him, concerning the unknown and (foretelling) things which will happen before they happen. He never asserted anything of that without his statement agreeing with the report of the event so that in this way his truthfulness was established. This is one of the most illustrious of the miracles of prophets, peace be on them. Will you not look at the words of Allāh, the Exalted, in which He makes manifest Jesus, son of Mary, peace be on him, through illustrious miracles and signs which indicate his prophethood? *I will tell you what you will eat and what you will store in your houses* (III 49). He, may His name be mighty, made similar miraculous signs for the Apostle of Allāh, may Allāh bless Him and His Family, when he said at the defeat of the Romans' (i.e. Byzantines) horsemen: *Alif Lam mim, Rome has been conquered in the lower lands (of its empire) but in a few years after their defeat they will conquer* (XXX 1-4). The matter turned out just as Allāh, the Mighty and High, had said. He, may His name be mighty, said of those who took part in the Battle of Badr before the battle (occurred): *The groups (of the enemy) will be defeated and they will turn their backs (in flight)* (LIV 45). The matter occurred just as Allāh, the Exalted, had said without there being any difference in it. He, the Mighty and High, said: *Indeed you will enter the Sacred Mosque in safety, if Allāh wills, with your heads shaved or shortened, without fear* (XLVIII 27). The matter took place as Allāh, the Exalted said. He, may He be praised, said: *When the help of Allāh comes and victory, you will see the people entering the religion of Allāh in parties* (CX 1-2). The event occurred as He, the Exalted, described. He, may He be praised, said, giving information about the inner feelings of the Hypocrites: *They say within themselves: If it was not for the fact that Allāh would punish us for what we say* (LVIII 8). Thus He gave information about the inner feelings and the secrets which they kept hidden. He, may the mention of Him be extolled, said concerning the story of the Jews: *Say: O those who have been guided, if you claim that you are friends of Allāh apart from other people, then you should seek death if you are truthful. Yet they do not seek it in an attempt to escape from (the crimes) which their hands have committed. Indeed Allāh is aware of the wrongdoers* (LXII 6-7). The matter happened as Allāh, the Exalted, had said and not one of them dared to seek it. That established (the reliability of the prophet's) reports and by it He made clear his truthfulness. He gave evidence of his prophethood, peace be on him, with similar examples, which, to present in this book, would make it too long.

(The evidence for) this kind (of miracle) by the Commander of the Faithful, peace be on him, is such that it can only be denied through stupidity, ignorance, slander and obstinacy. Can you not see what the reports have made public knowledge, what traditions have been widespread and what everybody hands down about him, peace be on him?

*****

He said before fighting against the three groups after the pledge of allegiance had been made to him: "I have been ordered to fight against those who break their pledges, those who are unjust and those who deviate (from the truth)."

He, peace be on him, fought against them and the matter was just as he had predicted.

He, peace be on him, said to Ṭalḥa and al-Zubayr, when they asked permission to leave to go on the lesser pilgrimage: "By Allāh, you are not going to make the lesser pilgrimage, you are going to Basra."

The matter was as he had said.

He, peace be on him, also said to Ibn 'Abbās when informing him about their asking for permission to go on the lesser pilgrimage: "I have given them permission despite knowing of the treachery they harboured within themselves. I have appealed for the help of Allāh against them. Indeed Allāh, the Exalted, will rebuff their plotting and give me victory against them."

The matter happened as he predicted.

*****

At Dhū Qar, he said while sitting to receive the pledge of allegiance: "Exactly a thousand men will come from the direction of Kufa to pledge themselves to me until death."

[Ibn 'Abbās commented:]
I (i.e. Ibn 'Abbās) was disturbed at that and was afraid that if the number of the people was less or more, the matter would bring failure on us. The anxiety to count them continued to trouble me so that when the first of them came, I began to count them. Their number reached nine hundred and ninety-nine and then the people stopped coming. I said: "We belong to Allāh and to Him we will return. What is the interpretation of what he said!"

As I was thinking that I saw a person coming towards us. He was a man wearing a woollen cloak and he had a sword with him, a shield and (other) weapons. He went up to the Commander of the Faithful, peace be on him, and said: "Stretch out your hand so that I may pledge allegiance to you."

"On what conditions do you make the pledge of allegiance to me?" the Commander of the Faithful, peace be on him, asked him.
"To hear and to obey and to fight before you until I die or Allāh grants you

victory," he replied.

"What is your name?" he asked.
"Uways," he answered.

"You are Uways al-Qaranī," he said.
"Yes," he replied.

"Allāh is greater (*Allāhu akbar*)," he said. "My dear friend, the Apostle of Allāh, may Allāh bless Him and His Family, told me that I would meet a man from his community called Uways al-Qaranī who would be of the party of Allāh and His Apostle, who would die in martyrdom and the number who would gain his intercession was like the number of the tribes of Muḍar and Rabī'a."

[Ibn 'Abbās reported:]
Then, by Allāh, (my anxiety) left me.

*****

Another example of that is what he, peace be on him, said when the Syrians raised copies of the Qur'ān and a group of his followers began to have doubts (about their position) and insisted (that he agree) to making a truce: "Shame on you, this is a deceitful trick. Those people do not really mean (to settle the issue by) the Qur'ān because they are not people (who accept) the Qur'ān. Fear Allāh and carry out your decision to fight against them. If you do not, you will be separated into (different) groups and you will regret it when regret will not bring any advantage."

The matter turned out just as he had predicted. This group of people fell into disbelief after the arbitration (between 'Alī and Mu'āwiya) and they regretted the action which they had previously hastily embarked on and made him accept. They were separated into different groups and destruction came to them soon after.

*****

He, peace be on him, said as he was setting out to fight against the Khārijites: "If it was not for the fact that I am afraid that you would just carry on discussions and abandon (all other) action, I would tell you the decision Allāh has made through the words of His Prophet, peace be on him, concerning those who fight against these people (i.e. against the Khārijites) as a result of seeing them to be misguided. Indeed, among them is a man with a stunted arm who has breasts like the breasts of a woman. They are the wickedest of creatures and the one who fights against them is the closest in relationship to Allāh among His creatures."

The malformation of the man (*mukhdaj*) had not been known to the people. After the battle, he, peace be on him, caused a search to be made for him among those killed saying: "By Allāh, I have not lied nor have I been lied to."

Eventually (his body) was found among those people and his shirt was torn open, On his shoulder there was a swelling like the breast of a woman, on which were hairs. When the hairs were pulled, his shoulder came forward with it. When they were left, his shoulder went back to its position. When he was found, he said: "Allāh is greater. In this there is a warning for anyone who reflects."[2]

*****

[The historians (*aṣḥāb al-sīra*) report in their account on the authority of Jundub b. 'Abd Allāh al-Azdī, who said:]
I (i.e. Jundub b. 'Abd Allāh) took part with 'Alī in the battles of the Camel and Ṣiffīn. I never had any doubts about fighting against those who fought him until I took part in the battle of al-Nahrawān (against the Khārijites). Then doubts came to me about fighting against these people. I said: "It is our reciters of the Qur'ān and our choice men whom we are killing. This matter is dreadful."

In the morning I went for a walk, (taking) some vessels of water with me, until I left the lines (of the army). Then I fixed my spear in the ground, fitted my shield on it and shaded myself from the sun. While I was sitting, the Commander of the Faithful, peace be on him, came along. He said to me: "Brother from (the tribe of) al-Azd, do you have water for ritual purification with you?"
"Yes," I answered and I gave him a vessel.

He went aside so that I could not see him. Then he came back after he had purified himself. He sat down in the shade of the spear. Suddenly a horseman appeared asking for him. I said: "Commander of the Faithful, there is a horseman who wants you."
"Make a sign to him (to come here)," he told me.

I made a sign and he came. He said: "Commander of the Faithful, the people have crossed the river."
"No," he retorted, "they have not crossed."
"Yes, by Allāh, they have crossed," (the man) insisted.
"You are lying," he said.

2 cf. al-Ṭabarī, I, 3383-4.

Then another man came. He said: “Commander of the Faithful, the people have crossed.”
“No,” he replied, “they have not crossed.”

“By Allāh,” (the man) said, “I did not come to you until I saw the standards and the baggage on that side.”
“By Allāh,” he declared, “they have not done so. (What you want) is to kill them and shed their blood.”

Then he arose and I arose with him. I said to myself: “Praise be to Allāh, who has given me insight into this man and enabled me to recognise his affair. He is one of two men: he is either a thorough-going liar or (one given) evidence (for his authority) by his Lord and a covenant by his Prophet. O Allāh, I give You a solemn undertaking which You can ask me about on the Day of Resurrection. If I find that the people have crossed, I will be the first to fight against him, the first to thrust my spear into his eye. If the people have not crossed, then I will go forth with him and fight alongside him.”

We returned to the lines (of the army) and we found that the standards and baggage were as they had been (before).

He took me by the scruff of the neck and pushed me. Then he said: “Brother of (the tribe of) al-Azd, has the matter become clear to you?”
“Yes, Commander of the Faithful,” I replied.

“Your business is with your enemy,” he said.
I killed one man from those people (i.e. the Khārijites) and then I killed another. I and another of them were exchanging blows. I struck him and he struck me. We both fell together. My comrades carried me back. By the time I recovered consciousness, there were none of the people (i.e. the Khārijites) left (there).

This is a famous account which has a wide circulation among the reporters of historical traditions (*āthār*). In it the man tells of his own solemn undertaking towards the Commander of the Faithful, peace be on him, and (what happened) after that. There is no way that it can be rejected or its truthfulness denied. In it (the Commander of the Faithful) provides information about the unknown, gives clear evidence of his knowledge of the inner conscience (of man) and his knowledge of what is in men’s souls. The evidence in it is outstanding which could only be equalled by evidence of a similar nature in terms of the greatness of the miracle and its clear proof.

*****

Of a similar kind are the narrations which have been reported on a wide scale (*tawātur*) about him, peace be on him, announcing his own death before it took place and giving information about the event and the fact that he would leave the world as a martyr through a blow on the head, the blood from which would colour his beard. The event came to happen exactly as he described.

Among the expressions which the reporters report concerning that are his words, peace be on him: "By Allāh, this will be coloured by this." He put his hand on his head and his beard.

(Similarly) there are his words, peace be on him: "By Allāh, it will colour it from above." He indicated his white hair. "The most wretched of the community will not be prevented from colouring it with blood from above."

(Other) of his words, peace be on him are: "The most wretched (of the community) will not be prevented from colouring it with blood from above."

He, peace be on him, (also) said: "The month of Ramaḍān has come to you. It is the lord of the months and the beginning of the year. In it the mill of authority will change. (Next) year, you will make the pilgrimage in one rank (i.e. there will be no Imam). The sign of that will be that I will not be among you."

His followers began to say that he was announcing his own death. He, peace be on him, was struck down on the night of the 19th of the month of Ramaḍān and he died on the night of the 21st of that month.

On the same (subject) is what trustworthy men report about him, peace be on him. During this month he used to break his fast one night with al-Ḥasan, one night with al-Ḥusayn, peace be on them, and one night with 'Abd Allāh b. Ja'far, may Allāh be pleased with him. He never used to have more than three mouthfuls. One of his two sons, al-Ḥasan and al-Ḥusayn, peace be on them, commented on that. He replied: "My son, Allāh's command (to leave the world) is coming and I am enduring hunger (in preparation for it)."

It was only one night or two later when he was struck down.

[The historians (*aṣḥāb al-āthār*) also report:]
Ja'd b. Ba'ja, one of the Khārijites, said to the Commander of the Faithful, peace be on him: "Fear Allāh, 'Ali, for you will die."
"By Allāh," said the Commander of the Faithful, peace be on him. "Rather I will be killed by a blow on this which will colour this." He put his hand on his

head and his beard. "It is a promise which will be fulfilled. Let anyone who lies despair."

(Similarly) there are his words, peace be on him, on the night at the end of which the wretched man struck him. He had set out for the mosque and the geese screeched in his face. The people drove them away from him but he said: "Leave them, they are wailing at death."

*****

In a similar vein is the account which al-Walīd b. al-Ḥārith and others report on the authority of the men (whom they cite):
When the Commander of the Faithful learnt what Busr b. Arṭa'a had done in Yemen, he said: "O Allāh, Busr has sold his religion for the world, so take his reason away. Do not let there remain to him in his religion anything by which he would merit Your mercy. May Busr survive until his mind becomes disordered."

(Later) Busr used to ask for a sword and a sword of wood would be brought to him. He would strike with it until he became unconscious. When he recovered consciousness, he would say: "The sword, the sword." It would be given to him and he would strike with it. He continued like that until he died.

*****

The report of these words of his is also well-known: "After I (am gone) you will be exposed to my being cursed. For they will curse me. If they give you the opportunity to disassociate yourselves from me, do not do so, for I was born for (the service of) Islam. Whoever is given the opportunity to disassociate himself from me, let him (rather) stretch out his neck (for his head to be cut off). The man who does disassociate himself from me will gain neither this world or the next."

That matter turned out as he, peace be on him, described.

*****

There is another report of his words, peace be on him, with the same implication: "People, I have called you to the truth and you turned your backs away from me. I have flogged you and you have made me tired. After me rulers will rule you. They will not be satisfied with this (attitude) from you so that they will torment you with whips and iron. Whoever torments people in this world will be tormented by Allāh in the next. The sign of that will be that the ruler of Yemen will come against you to settle in your midst. A man called Yūsuf b. 'Umar will seize the tax-collectors and those who collect the taxes of the tax-collectors."

That happened as he, peace be on him, predicted.

*****

Then there is the report which the religious scholars recount:
Juwayriyya b. Mishar stood at the gate of the palace.
"Where is the Commander of the Faithful?" he asked.
"Sleeping." was the reply.

"You who are sleeping wake up," he shouted. "For by Him in Whose hands is my soul, a blow will be struck on your head from which your beard will be coloured with blood, as you have told us before."

The Commander of the Faithful, peace be on him, heard that. He called out: "Come, Juwayriyya so that I can discuss with you what you are saying."

He came and (the Commander of the Faithful) said to him: "By Him in Whose hands is my soul, you will be pulled before a rough harsh man. He will cut off your hand and your leg. Then you will be crucified below the tree trunk where an unbeliever (has already been crucified)."

Time went by after that until in the days of Mu'āwiya, Ziyād became governor. He cut off his hand and his leg, then he crucified him on the tree trunk where Ibn Muka'bir (was crucified). It was a long trunk and he was under him.

*****

There is in addition this report:
Maytham al-Tammār was a slave of a woman from (the tribe of) Banū Asad. The Commander of the Faithful, peace be on him, bought him from her and then gave him his freedom.
"What is your name?" he asked him.
"Sālim," he replied.

"The Apostle of Allāh, may Allāh bless Him and His Family, told me that the name which your father gave you in Persian was Maytham," he said.
"Allāh and His Apostle are true and you are true, Commander of the Faithful," he said. "By Allāh that is my name."

"Go back to the name by which the Apostle of Allāh referred to you and leave (the name) Sālim," he told him.

He returned to (the name) Maytham and was given the kunya Abū Sālim. On the same day, 'Alī, peace be on him, told him: "After me, you will be seized and crucified and stabbed by a spear. On the third day your nostrils and mouth will flow with blood which will colour your beard. So wait for that colour (to come). You will be crucified on the gate of the house of 'Amr b. Ḥurayth. You will be the tenth one of ten (crucified) men. You will have the shortest timber among them but you will be the nearest of them to the place for washing. Come so that I may show you the palm-tree on (the timber of) whose trunk you will be crucified."

He showed it to him. Maytham used to go there and pray at it. He used to say: "What a blessed palm-tree you are. I am created for you and you grew up for me."

He continued to frequent it until it was cut down and he knew the place in Kūfa where he would be crucified. He used to meet 'Amr b. Ḥurayth and say to him: "I will be your neighbour, so show neighbourliness to me."
"You want to buy the house of Ibn Mas'ūd or the house of Ibn Ḥakīm," 'Amr used to say, because he did not understand what he meant.

In the year in which he was killed he made a pilgrimage. He visited Umm Salama, may Allāh be pleased with her.
"Who are you?" she asked.
"I am Maytham," he said.

"By Allāh, how often I heard the Apostle of Allāh, may Allāh bless Him and His Family, mention you," she said. "He used to commend you to 'Alī in the middle of the night."

Then he asked her about al-Ḥusayn, peace be on him.
"He is at an estate of his," she said.
"Tell him that I would have liked to greet him and that we will meet before the Lord of the Worlds, if Allāh, the Exalted, wills," he told her.

Umm Salama called for some perfume and she perfumed his beard.
"Soon it will be coloured by blood," she said.

He went to Kūfa and 'Ubayd Allāh b. Ziyād, may Allāh curse him, had him arrested and brought to him. He had been told that that man was one of the closest people to 'Ali, peace be on him.
"For shame, is he not a Persian?" he said.
"Yes," he was told.

"Where is your master?" he asked him.
"He is looking down on every wrongdoer and you are one of the wrongdoers," he answered.

"Despite your foreign accent you say what you mean," he said. "What has your leader told you that I will do to you?"
"He told me that you would crucify me as the tenth one of ten men," he answered. "I will have the shortest timber among them but will be the nearest of them to the place for washing."

"We will oppose him" ('Ubayd Allāh) declared.
"How could you oppose him?" he retorted. "He did nothing but give me information on the authority of the Prophet, may Allāh bless Him and his family, on the authority of Gabriel, peace be on him, on the authority of Allāh, the Exalted. How could you oppose these? I know the place in Kūfa where I will be crucified. I am the first of Allāh's creatures to be bridled in Islam."

He imprisoned him and he imprisoned al-Mukhtār b. Abī 'Ubayda with him.
"You will escape," Maytham told him, "and you will rebel to avenge the blood of al-Ḥusayn, peace be on him. Then you will kill this man who is going to kill us."

When 'Ubayd Allāh called for al-Mukhtār to kill him, a messenger (*barīd*) arrived with a letter for 'Ubayd Allāh from Yazīd, ordering him to free (al-Mukhtār). He freed him and ordered Maytham to be crucified.

A man who met (Maytham) said to him: "Would not something satisfy you rather than this, Maytham?"
He smiled and said, pointing to the palm tree: "I was created for it and it has grown for me."

When he was put on the wood, the people gathered around him at the gate of 'Amr b. Ḥurayth.
"By Allāh he used to say: I will be your neighbour," 'Amr said. After he had been crucified, he ordered a maidservant to sweep under the wood, to sprinkle it with water and to fumigate it.

Maytham began to speak of the virtues of Banū Hāshim and it was reported to Ibn Ziyād: "That slave has insulted you."
"Bridle him," he ordered.

He was the first of Allāh's creatures to be bridled in Islam. Maytham, may Allāh have mercy on him, was killed ten days before al-Ḥusayn came to Iraq. On the third day after his crucifixion, he was stabbed with a spear, and He declared the greatness of Allāh. At the end of that day blood flowed from his mouth and his nose. This is one of the group of reports about the unknown which have been preserved concerning the Commander of the Faithful, peace be on him. Its reputation is extensive and the narration of it is widespread among the religious scholars (*'ulamā*).

*****

[Another such report has been related by Ibn 'Abbās. It has been reported on the authority of Mujālid, on the authority of al-Sha'bī, on the authority of Ziyād b. al-Naḍr al-Ḥārithī, who said:]
I was with Ziyād when Rushayd al-Hijrī was brought to him. Ziyād said to him: "What did your leader say to you?" - meaning 'Alī, peace be on him – "For we will do that to you."
"You will cut off my hands and my legs and then you will crucify me," he answered.

"By Allāh, I will make his word false," declared Ziyād. "Free him."

When he was about to leave, Ziyād said: "By Allāh, we do not find anything wrong with what his leader told him. Therefore cut off his hands and legs and crucify him"

"Wait a moment," Rushayd said to him, "I still have something (to tell) you which the Commander of the Faithful, peace be on him, told me."
"Cut out his tongue," ordered Ziyād.

"Now, by Allāh, is the verification of the words of the Commander of the Faithful, peace be on him," declared Rushayd.

This report has also been handed down by those friendly and those hostile on the authority of men they regard as trustworthy, on the authority of those persons whom we have named. Its content is well known to all the religious scholars. It is one of the group already mentioned of (his) miracles and giving information about the unknown.

*****

[A further account is reported by 'Abd al-Azīz b. Ṣuhayb on the authority of Abū al-'Āliyya, who said: Mazra' b. 'Abd Allāh told me:]
I (i.e. Mazra' b. 'Abd Allāh) heard the Commander of the Faithful, peace be on

him, say: "By Allāh, an army will advance so that when it is at al-Baydā' it will be swallowed up."
"You are telling me about the unknown," I said.

"Remember what I tell you," he said. "By Allāh, what the Commander of the Faithful, peace be on him, tells you, will happen. A man will be taken. He will be killed and crucified between the two sides of the walls of the mosque."
"You are telling me about the unknown," I said.

"The trustworthy, the one protected by Allāh, 'Alī b. Abī Ṭālib, peace be on him, told me," he replied.

[Abū 'Āliyya reported:]
Friday had not come when Mazra' was seized, killed and crucified between the two sides of the wall.

[(Abū 'Āliyya) said: He used to tell me about a third thing but I have forgotten it.]

*****

Yet a further example is reported by Jarīr on the authority of al-Mughīra, who said:]
When al-Ḥajjāj, may Allāh curse him, became governor, he sought for Kumayl b. Ziyād. The latter fled from him. (al-Ḥajjāj) deprived his people of their allowances (*'Aṭā'*). When Kumayl saw that, he said: "I am an old man and my life is nearly finished. It is not right for me to deprive my people of their allowances."

So he went and offered his hand to al-Ḥajjāj. When the latter saw him, he said: "I would have liked to have found a way to get you, myself."
"Don't gnash your teeth at me and don't threaten me," Kumayl replied. "What is left of my life is like mere specks of dust. Therefore give judgement as long as you are a judge. For there is an appointed time to be with Allāh and after death there is the reckoning. The Commander of the Faithful, peace be on him, told me that you would kill me."

"Then that is evidence against yourself," al-Ḥajjāj said to him.
"But the judgement is yours," answered Kumayl.

"Indeed," he retorted, "you were among those who killed 'Uthmān b. 'Affān. Strike off his head."

Then he was executed.

This report is also recorded by the non-Shīʿa (*ʿāmma*) which they report on the authority of men whom they regard as trustworthy. The Shīʿa (*khāṣṣa*) participate in reporting it. Hence it has been included in this section where we mention miracles, proofs and evidence (concerning him).

*****

There is, in addition, the account recorded by the historians (*aṣḥāb al-sīra*) on various authorities:
One day al-Ḥajjāj b. Yūsuf al-Thaqafī said: "I would like to strike down one of the followers of Abū Turāb (derogatory name of ʿAlī). Through his blood, I would get closer to Allāh."
"We know of no one who was a companion of Abū Turāb for a longer time than Qanbar, his retainer," he was told.

He sent in search of him and he was brought.
"Are you Qanbar?" he asked.
"Yes," he replied

"(Your *kunya*) is Abū Hamdān?" he asked.
"Yes," he replied

"Is your master ʿAlī b. Abī Ṭālib?"
"Allāh is my Master," he replied, "and the Commander of the Faithful ʿAlī is the master of my provisions."

"Disassociate yourself from his religion,"he ordered him.
"If I disassociate myself from his religion, will you show me another better than it?" he asked.

"I will kill you," he answered. "So choose what sort of death you prefer."
"I leave that to you," he responded.

"Why?" he asked.
"Because in whatever way you kill me, you will be killed in the same way," he said. "The Commander of the Faithful, peace be on him, told me that my fate would be to be slaughtered unjustly and without right."

Then he ordered him to be slaughtered.

This is also one of the reports which is established with regard to the Commander of the Faithful, speaking about the unknown. It has been included in the section concerning the compelling miracles and outstanding evidence and the knowledge which Allāh specially endowed to His proof among His prophets, apostles and chosen ones, peace be on them. Therefore it follows on from what has been presented before.

*****

[Of a similar kind is the account reported by al-Ḥasan b. Maḥbūb on the authority of Thābit al-Thumālī, on the authority of Abū Isḥāq al-Sabī'ī, on the authority of Suwayd b. Ghafla, (who said):]
A man came to the Commander of the Faithful, peace be on him. He said: "Commander of the Faithful, I have passed through Wadī al-Qarnī and I saw that Khālid b. 'Arfaṭa had died there. I asked forgiveness for him."
"Nonsense!" declared the Commander of the Faithful. "He has not died and he will not die until he leads an army of error whose standard-bearer will be Ḥabīb b. Ḥimāz."

A man from below the pulpit said: "Commander of the Faithful, I belong to your Shī'a and I am one who loves you."
"Who are you?" he asked.
"I am Ḥabīb b. Ḥimāz," he replied.

"Beware," he said, "you will carry (that standard). Indeed you will carry it and you will enter from this gate." He pointed with his hand to the Gate of al-Fīl.

After the death of the Commander of the Faithful, peace be on him, and al-Ḥasan, peace be on him, after that, and the events concerning al-Ḥusayn and his revolt, Ibn Ziyād sent 'Umar b. Sa'd against al-Ḥusayn, peace be upon him. He put Khālid b. 'Arfaṭa in command of the vanguard and he made Ḥabīb b. Ḥimāz the standard-bearer. He went there until he entered the mosque through the gate of al-Fīl.

This is also a widespread report which the traditionists (*ahl al-'ilm*) and the narrators of historical reports (*'āthār*) have not refused to acknowledge. It is widespread among the Kūfans and well known in their circles. Not even two of them have denied it. It belongs to the class of miraculous (knowledge) which we have mentioned.

*****

[Another example is the report of Zakariyyā b. Yaḥyā al-Qaṭṭān, on the authority

of Faḍl b. al-Zubayr, on the authority of Abū al-Ḥakam, who said: I heard our shaykhs and our religious scholars say:]
'Alī b. Abī Ṭālib, peace be on him, preached. In his sermon, he said:
"Ask me before you lose me. But, by Allāh, do not ask me about a group who will lead a hundred astray and which will guide a hundred, otherwise I will tell you about the screecher of that group and the driver of it until the day of Resurrection."

A man rose before him and said: "Tell me how many pieces of hair there are on my head and my beard?"

The Commander of the Faithful, peace be on him, said: "By Allāh, my bosom friend, the Apostle of Allāh, may Allāh bless Him and His Family, told me about what you have asked. For every piece of hair on your beard there is an angel who curses you and for every piece of hair on your beard there is a devil who provokes you. In your house there is a worthless (child) who will kill the (grand) son of the Apostle of Allāh. That will be the proof of the truthfulness of what I have told you. If it was not for the fact that it is difficult to prove what you asked about, I would (simply) have informed you of it. However the proof of (my answer to) that (question) lies in the information I have given about your curse and your cursed worthless (child)."

At that time his son was a small boy still crawling. When the (tragic) events in the affair of al-Ḥusayn, peace be on him, occurred, he took part in killing him. So the event occurred as the Commander of the Faithful had described.

*****

[In the same way Ismā'īl b. Ṣabīḥ reported on the authority of Yaḥyā b. al-Musāwir al-'Abdī, on the authority of Ismā'īl b. Ziyād, who said:]
One day 'Alī, peace be on him, said to al-Barā' b. 'Āzib: "Barā', my son al-Ḥusayn, peace be on him, will be killed while you are alive and you will not help him."

After al-Ḥusayn, peace be on him, was killed, al-Barā' b. 'Āzib used to say: "By Allāh, 'Alī b. Abī Ṭālib, peace be on him, spoke the truth about al-Ḥusayn being killed and my not helping him."
He showed (much) grief and regret about that.

This belongs to what we have mentioned about him giving information about the unknown and the prevailing attitudes of men's hearts.

*****

[Another account is reported by ‘Uthmān b. ‘Īsā al- ‘Amirī on the authority of Jābir b. al-Ḥurr, on the authority of Juwayriyya b Mishar al-‘Abdī, who said:] When we set out with the Commander of the Faithful, peace be on him, to Ṣiffīn. We reached the plains of Karbalā’. He stood at the side of the camp and looked right and left. He cried and he said: “By Allāh, this is the place where the camels will kneel for their riders. This is the place of their fate.”

“Commander of the Faithful, what is this place?” he was asked.
“This is Karbalā’,” he said. “Here people will be killed who will enter heaven without any reckoning (against them).”

Then he went on and the people did not understand the explanation of what he had said until the tragedy of al-Ḥusayn b. ‘Alī, peace be on them, and his followers took place on the plain. Then those who had heard his words recognised the truthfulness of what he had told them.

This has been (a summary) of his knowledge of the unknown and his telling what would happen before it happened. It is clearly miraculous in nature and wonderful knowledge as we have mentioned. Reports conveying the same sense are so numerous that their explanation would make the book unduly long. What we have presented is sufficient for our intention.

His Miraculous Strength at Khaybar

Among his wonderful signs is the ability by which Allāh set him apart and the strength which he specially endowed to him, and the transcendence of normal events through miracles.

Of that kind is that which has been handed down in the historical reports and has become well-known through accounts. The religious scholars have agreed on it and both opponents and friends accept it, (namely) the story of Khaybar and of the Commander of the Faithful, peace be on him, removing the gate of the fortress with his own hand, and laying it on the ground with, his own hand, while it was of such a weight that (it took) not less than fifty men to carry it.

[‘Abd Allāh b. Aḥmad b. Ḥanbal has mentioned that in what he reports on the authority of his transmitter. The latter reported: Ismā‘īl b. Isḥāq, the *qāḍī*, told us: Ibrāhīm b. Ḥamza told us: ‘Abd al-‘Azīz b. Muḥammad told us on the authority of Ḥizām, on the authority of Abū ‘Atīq on the authority of Jābir:]
At the battle of Khaybar, the Prophet, may Allāh bless Him and His Family, gave the standard to ‘Alī b. Abī Ṭālib, peace be on him. After he had prayed for him,

'Alī, peace be on him, began to rush forward while his comrades were telling him to go slowly. He came to the fortress, and pulled away its gate throwing it to the ground. Then seventy of us gathered around it. It was only as a result of their (combined) effort that they could lift the door.[3]

This is an example of the special strength with which Allāh endowed him. Through it the normal (human) qualities were transcended and it became a miraculous sign as we have said before.

THE MIRACLE OF MOVING THE ROCK AND THE WATER UNDER IT

Another example is reported by the historians (*aṣḥāb al-siyar*) and the account of it is widespread among both the non-Shī'a (*'āmma*) and the Shī'a (*khāṣṣa*) so that poets have written verses about it, rhetoricians have compiled sermons on it and men of understanding and learning have reported it. (It is) the story of the monk in the area of Karbalā' and the stone. Its reputation (is such) that it does not need the presentation of its chain of authorities (*isnād*).

[It is that the whole group (of scholars) report.]
When the Commander of the Faithful, peace be on him, headed toward Ṣiffīn, a terrible thirst came on his followers. The water with them had been used up. They began to search for water to right and left but they did not find any trace of it. The Commander of the Faithful, peace be on him, turned off the main road with them and went a little way. A hermitage appeared before them in the middle of the desert. He went with them towards it. When he reached its courtyard, he ordered those (with him) to call for its occupant to come before them. They called him and he came. The Commander of the Faithful, peace be on him, asked him: "Is this residence of yours near water, which will quench the thirst of these people?"

"There is more than six miles between me and water," he answered. "There is no water nearer than that to me. If it was not for the fact that I brought enough water for each month to sustain me, I would be destroyed by thirst."

"Did you hear what the monk said?" the Commander of the Faithful, peace be on him, asked.
"Yes," they answered. "Order us to go to the place which he indicated. Perhaps we will reach water while we still have strength."

"There is no need for you to do that," the Commander of the Faithful, peace

3 This has already been presented, cf 82-86.

be on him, told them. He turned the neck of his mule in the direction of the *qibla* (i.e. towards Mecca) and he directed them to a place near the hermitage. "Uncover the ground in this place," he ordered them.

A group of them went straight to the place and uncovered it with iron shovels. A great shiny rock appeared. They said: "Commander of the Faithful, here is a great rock on which the shovels are useless."

"This rock is over water," he told them. "If it moves from its position, you will find the water."

They struggled to remove it. All the people gathered together and tried to move it but they could find no way to do that. It was too difficult for them. When he, peace be on him, saw that they had gathered together and striven to remove the rock but it was too difficult for them, he put his leg over his saddle until it reached the ground. Then he rolled up his sleeves. He put his fingers under the side of the rock and he moved it. He removed it with his hand and pushed it many yards away. When it had moved from its position, the white (glitter) of water appeared before them. They hurried to it and drank from it. It was the sweetest, coldest and purest water that they had ever drunk from on their journey.

"Get supplies and quench your thirst," he told them.
They did that. Then he went to the rock and took it with his hand and put it back where it had been. He ordered that its traces be removed with earth. The hermit had been watching from on top of his hermitage. When he realised what had happened, he called out: "People, help me down, help me down."

They helped him to get down. He stood in front of the Commander of the Faithful, peace be on him and said: "Man, are you a prophet sent (by Allāh)?"
"No," he replied.

"(Then are you) an angel who is close to Allāh?" he asked.
"No," was the answer.

"Then who are you?" asked (the hermit).
"I am the testamentary trustee of the Apostle of Allāh, Muḥammad b. 'Abd Allāh, the seal of the prophets, may Allāh bless Him and His Family," he replied.

"Stretch out your hand," said the hermit, "so that I may submit to Allāh, the Blessed and Exalted, at your hands."
The Commander of the Faithful, peace be on him, stretched out his hand and told

him: "Make the two-fold testimony."
He said: "I testify that there is no God but Allāh alone without any partner. I testify that Muḥammad is His servant and His Apostle. I testify that you are the testamentary trustee of the Apostle of Allāh, the one with most right among the people to authority after him."

The Commander of the Faithful, peace be on him, made him understand the conditions of being a Muslim and then asked him: "What is it that has prompted you to enter Islam after your long residence in this hermitage in opposition to it?"

"I will tell you, Commander of the Faithful," he said. "This hermitage was built to seek out the one who would remove that rock and then water would come from underneath it. Scholars before me died and they did not attain that (knowledge) but Allāh, the Mighty and High, has provided me with it. We find in one of our books and a prose writer of our scholars that in this land there is a spring with a rock over it. No one knows its place except a prophet or the testamentary trustee of a prophet. He must be a friend of Allāh who calls (men) to truth, whose sign is the knowledge of the place of this rock and his ability to remove it. When I saw you do that, I realised what we had been waiting for. The object of desire had been attained. Today I am a Muslim (converted) at your hands, a believer in your right and your servant (*mawlā*)."

When he heard that, the Commander of the Faithful, peace be on him, wept until his beard became moist with tears. He said: "Praise be to Allāh, by Whom I have not been forgotten. Praise be to Allāh in Whose books I have been mentioned."

Then he summoned the people and told them: "Listen to what your brother Muslim says."
They listened to his words. Then they gave much praise to Allāh and thanks for the blessing which he had bestowed upon them in giving them knowledge of the right of the Commander of the Faithful, peace be on him. Then they went on and the hermit went before him amid a group of his followers until he met the Syrians. The hermit was among a group of those who were martyred there. He, peace be upon him, carried out the prayer over him. He buried him and sought much forgiveness for him. Whenever he was mentioned, ('Alī) would say: "That was my servant (*mawlā*)."

In this report there are (several) kinds of miracle. One of them is knowledge of the unknown, a second is the strength by which normal human capabilities were transcended, and (another) is the distinction (of him) from other men through the confirmation of the message about him in the first Books of Allāh. This is validated by the words of Allāh, the Exalted: *That is their example in the Torah and their example in the Gospels* (XLVIII 29).

Al-Sayyid Ismā'īl b. Muḥammad al-Ḥimyarī, may Allāh have mercy on him, speaks of the same thing in his glorious golden ode:

> During his journey he went by night after the evening prayer to Karbalā' in a procession.
>
> Until he came to one who devoted himself to God on a piece of raised ground. He made his camp on inhospitable land.
>
> O wilderness, it is not (a place) where he meets a living soul other than the wild animals and the balding white haired man (i.e. 'Alī).
>
> He approaches and cries out at it. (The holy man) looks down as he stands, like the defender (looks down) over his bow from a watchtower.
>
> Is there water which can be attained near the position which you have settled at. He answers: There is nothing to drink,
>
> Except at a distance of six miles and the water I have with me (here) between the sandy hill and the vast desert.
>
> He turns the reins towards the flat ground. He uncovers a smooth rock which shines like golden leaf-paste for camels.
>
> He says: Turn it around. If you turn it around, you will see. You will not see if it is not turned around.
>
> They gang together to remove it. It is impossible for them. It is a difficult impossible task which cannot be performed.
>
> When it had weakened them, he stretched a hand towards it -- when the conqueror comes, it is conquered.
>
> It was as if it was a ball of fallen cotton in a skein, which he pushed in a playground.
>
> He gave them sweet delicious water to drink from under it, which was better than the most delicious, the sweetest.

Then when they had all drunk, he put it back and went away. Its position is left alone. It cannot be approached.

Ibn Maymūn added these words concerning that:

The signs for the monk were a miraculous secret there and he believed in the noble born testamentary trustee of authority (*waṣī*).

He died a martyr, truthful in his (statement of) support, most noble of monks who have become fearful (of Allāh).

I mean that the son of Fāṭima is the testamentary trustee of authority. Whoever declares (their belief in) his outstanding merit and his (illustrious) actions does not lie.

He is a man both of whose sides are (descended) from Shem, without any father from Hām, nor a father of a father.

He is one who does not flee and in battle only the striking of his sword dyed red (with blood) can be seen.

His Miraculous Victory over the Jinn

Another example is the tradition which has become well-known about the Apostle of Allāh, may Allāh bless Him and His Family, sending him to the valley of the jinn. Gabriel, peace be on him, had told him that groups of them had gathered to plot against him. (The Commander of the Faithful) took the place of the Apostle of Allāh, may Allāh bless Him and His Family, and through Allāh was sufficient for the believers against the plotting (of the jinn). He repelled them from the believers through his strength by which he was set apart from the rest of them.

[Muḥammad b. Abī al-Sirrī al-Tamīmī reported on the authority of Aḥmad b. al-Faraj, on the authority of al-Ḥasan b. Mūsā al-Nahdī, on the authority of his father, on the authority of Wabira b. al-Ḥārith, on the authority of Ibn al-'Abbās, may Allāh have mercy on him, who said:]
When the Prophet, may Allāh bless Him and His Family, set out against the Banū al-Muṣṭaliq, he avoided the road. Night came and he stopped near a rugged valley. Towards the end of the night, Gabriel, peace be on him, came down to tell him that a group of unbelieving jinn had gone into the valley with the intention of plotting against him, peace be on him, and causing harm to his Companions. He

called for the Commander of the Faithful, peace be on him, and told him: "Go to this valley, those of the jinn who are enemies of Allāh, who want (to attack) you, will come against you. Repel them with the strength which Allāh, the Mighty and High, has given you. You will be protected by the names of Allāh, the Mighty and High, which He has specially endowed you with knowledge of."

He sent with him a hundred men from different groups among the people. He told them: "Stay with him and obey his orders."

The Commander of the Faithful, peace be on him, set out for the valley. When he was near the side of the valley, he ordered the hundred men who had accompanied him to stand close to the side and not to do anything until he gave them permission. He went forward and stood at the edge of the valley. He sought refuge with Allāh from his enemies and he named Allāh, may His name be magnified. He signalled to the people who had followed him to come closer. They came closer and there was a gap between him and them of the distance of a bow-shot. Then he began to go down into the valley when a hurricane arose, which almost made the people fall on their faces because of its violence. They could not keep their feet on the ground because of terror of opposition and terror of what would come upon them. The Commander of the Faithful, peace be on him shouted: "I am 'Alī b. Abī Ṭālib b. 'Abd al-Muṭṭalib, the testamentary trustee of authority (*waṣī*) of the Apostle of Allāh, may Allāh bless Him and His Family, and his cousin. Defy (us) is if you want to." Persons in the form of gipsies appeared before the people who seemed to have torches of fire in their hands and they dried up (all) the sides of the valley. The Commander of the Faithful, peace be on him, penetrated deep into the valley, while reciting the Qur'ān and signalling to right and left with his sword. It was not long before the persons became like black smoke. The Commander of the Faithful, peace be on him, magnified Allāh. Then he climbed back the way he had come down. He stood with the people who had accompanied him. The place became yellow as a result of what had happened to it. The Companions of the Apostle of Allāh, may Allāh bless Him and His Family, said to him: "Abū al-Ḥasan ('Alī), we almost died of fear and anxiety for you because of what you met. It was worse than (anything else) that has happened to us."

"When the enemy showed themselves to me," he told them, "and I shouted the names of Allāh, the Exalted, among them, they became smaller and I knew the terror which had come upon them. Therefore I went into the valley without any fear of them. If they had remained in substantial forms, I would have attacked them to the last one. Allāh was sufficient (protection) against their plotting and He was sufficient (help) for the Muslims against their wickedness. The rest of them will go ahead of me to the Apostle of Allāh, may Allāh bless Him and His Family, in order to (confess that they) believe in him."

The Commander of the Faithful, peace be on him, returned with those who had been with him to the Apostle of Allāh, may Allāh bless Him and His Family. He gave him the news. (The Apostle) was delighted with him and prayed for his well-being. Then he said to him: "'Alī, those whom Allāh filled with fear through you have come ahead of you to me. They submitted to Islam and I accepted their submission."

Then he continued the journey with all the Muslims and they passed through the valley in safety and without fear.

*****

The non-Shī'a (*'āmma*) report that account as well as the the Shī'a (*khāṣṣa*) and they do not refuse to accept it. However, the Mu'tazila because of their inclination to the beliefs of the Brahmins reject it. In addition to that they deny it because of their understanding of traditional reports. However, they are following the methods of atheism in imputing error to the Qur'ān and the reports which it includes about the jinn, their believing in Allāh and His Apostle and the information about them which Allāh gives in the Qur'ān in the *Surat al-Jinn* (LXXII) where they say: *We heard a wonderful recitation (Qur'ān) which gave guidance to righteousness and we believed in it* (LXXII 1-2) to the end of the contents of the *sura* which gives information about them. Since the opposition of the atheists to that is invalidated by the possibility of minds (conceiving) the existence of jinn and of their being made responsible (for their action) and the proof of this is through the Qur'ān and the glorious wonder in it. In the same way it demonstrates the invalidity of the accusation of the Mu'tazila against the report which we have given, (when they accuse it) of being impossible to be sustained by (human) intellects. Insofar as it is reported by two different chains of authority and by two groups to give evidence for two dissimilar attitudes, that is proof of its validity. There is no substance in its rejection by those who deviate from true justice like the Mu'tazila and the determinists (*mujabbara*), nor in the denigration of the necessity of using it which we have mentioned, just as there is no substance in the denial by the atheists, and varieties of agnostics, the Jews, the Christians, the Zoroastrians and the Sabians of the validity of the reports of the miracles of the Prophet, may Allāh bless Him and His Family, such as: the splitting of the moon, the bending of the palm trunk, stones speaking in his hand, the camel complaining, wild calves speaking, the tree moving (to him), water coming from his hands at the place for ritual ablution and feeding great crowds of people. (There are indeed no grounds for them) to denigrate the validity, the truthfulness of their narration and the establishment of the proof of them. Indeed their error in rejecting that, even in finding it weak, is much greater than the error of those who deny the miracles of the Commander of the Faithful, peace be on him, and their proof. Since such things are not hidden to people capable of considering them, there is no need for us to explain their arguments in this place. Since the special nature of the Commander of the Faithful, peace be on him, apart from (the rest of) the people has been established by what we have described as his being separate from all others in the knowledge which we have explained, (this) has made clear the statement of his right to precedence over (the rest of) the community with regard to the position of the Imamate and his right to precedence over them in the place of leadership. (It is further confirmed) by what the Wise Words (i.e. the Qur'ān) contain concerning the story of David and Ṭālūt where He, may His name be exalted, says: *Their prophet said to them: Allāh has sent Ṭālūt to you as a king. They asked: Shall he have (the right of) kingship over us while we are more entitled to kingship than he is? He has not brought any extent of wealth. He replied: Allāh has chosen him to be over you and increased him extensively in knowledge and substance. Allāh bestows His kingship on whom He wishes. Allāh is (all) embracing, one who knows* (II 247). Allāh, the Exalted, gives the proof for Ṭālūt's precedence over the community of his people. (Similarly) He gave him a proof of (being) His friend and the brother of His Prophet in having precedence of the rest of the community through choosing (him to be) over them and adding to him a (great) extent knowledge and substance. That is corroborated by similar things which have corroborated the right of the Commander of the Faithful, peace be on him, through his wonderful miraculous nature, in addition to him being separate from the people through the addition of the great extent of his knowledge and substance. Allāh, may He be praised and exalted, said: *The sign of his kingship is that he will bring you the ark in which there is assurance from your Lord and the rest of what the family of Moses and the family of Aaron left, which the angels brought. In that there is a sign for you if you would believe* (II 248).

The transcendence of ordinary human behaviour by the Commander of the Faithful, peace be on him, lies in the knowledge which we have recounted and other things similar to the transcendency of ordinary human behaviour by Ṭālūt in bringing the ark. This is clear. May Allāh be the bringer of success.

I still find the ignorant and the obstinate among the anti-Shī'a (*nāṣiba*) showing surprise at the report of the Commander of the Faithful, peace be on him, meeting the jinn, and keeping their evil away from the Prophet, may Allāh bless him, his family, and his Companions. They laugh at that and attribute the story to such useless nonsense. They diminish such things concerning reports of similar miracles by him, peace be on him, and say these are forgeries by the Shī'a, and those of them who forge have forged them in order to acquire (prestige) and in order to defend desperately (their beliefs). This is exactly what all the atheists (*zanādiqa*) and the enemies of Islam say about what the Qur'ān mentions with regard to the report of the jinn and their submission to Islam in its words: *We heard a wonderful recitation (Qur'ān) which gave guidance to righteousness and we believed in it* (LXXII 1-2). (They take a similar attitude) about the report of Ibn Mas'ūd concerning the story of the night of the jinn and him seeing them like gipsies. (They also have the same view) of the miracles of the Apostle of Allāh, may Allāh bless Him and His Family. They show surprise at all of these and laugh when they hear the account of them, dispute their authenticity, mock and talk nonsense in a slanderous way in which they conduct themselves against Islam and its followers, regarding as stupid those who believe in it and support it, accusing the followers of Islam of deficiency and ignorance, and forging false stories. Let the people examine the crime which they have committed against Islam by their hostility to the Commander of the Faithful, peace be on him, and their relying on removing his virtues, noble actions and signs by which they resemble the classes of the atheists (*zanādiqa*) and unbelievers through their departure from the roads of (true) proofs into the gates of deviation and ignorance. In Allāh do we seek help.

His Sending back the Sun

Among the wonderful signs which Allāh, the Exalted, has brought forth through the hands of the Commander of the Faithful, 'Alī b. Abī Ṭālib, is one, the reports of which have become widespread among the biographers and historians (*'ulamā' al-siyar wa al-āthār*) and about which the poets have composed verses (namely) when he, peace be on him, sent back the sun (to its earlier position) on two occasions, once during the life of the Prophet and another time after his death.

The account of it being sent back on the first occasion has been reported by Asmā' daughter of 'Umays, Umm Salama, the wife of the Prophet, may Allāh bless Him and His Family, Jābir b. 'Abd Allāh al-Anṣāri, Abū Sa'īd al-Khudrī and a group of the Companions.

One day the Prophet, may Allāh bless Him and His Family, was in his house and 'Ali, peace be on him, was in front of him when Gabriel, peace be on him, came to him to speak privately to him about Allāh. When inspiration closed in upon him, he used the thigh of the Commander of the Faithful, peace be on him, as a pillow. He did not raise his head from it until the sun had set. Thus he compelled the Commander of the Faithful, peace be on him, (to remain) in that position. So he prayed the afternoon prayer sitting, giving a nod (with his head) for his bowing and prostration. When (the Apostle) awoke from his trance, he said to the Commander of the Faithful: "Have you missed the afternoon prayer?"

"I could not pray it standing because of your position, Apostle of Allāh, and the circumstances of hearing inspiration which I was in," he answered.

"Ask Allāh to send the sun back for you so that you may pray it standing at its proper time just as (it was) when you missed being able to do it," he told him. "Allāh, the Exalted, will answer you because of your obedience to Allāh and to His Apostle."

The Commander of the Faithful, peace be on him, asked Allāh to send back the sun. It was sent back for him so that it came into its position in the sky at the time for the afternoon prayer. The Commander of the Faithful, peace be on him, prayed the afternoon prayer at its proper time. Then it set. [Asmā' reported:]
By Allāh we heard it at its setting, screeching like the screech of the saw in wood.

*****

Its being sent back for him after the Prophet, may Allāh bless Him and His Family, was when he wanted to cross the Euphrates at Babylon, many of his followers were occupied in taking their animals and baggage across. He, peace be on him, prayed the afternoon prayer himself with a group who were with him. The people did not finish their crossing and many of them missed the time of the prayer. The people recalled the merit of being together for that (prayer) and they spoke about that. When he heard their talk about it, he asked Allāh to send back the sun so that all his followers might be together to perform the afternoon prayer at its proper time. Allāh, the Exalted, answered him by sending back the sun for him. The horizons became such as they are for the time of the afternoon prayer. When the people had said the final greeting (at the end of the prayer), the sun disappeared and a violent throbbing was heard from it which terrified the people. They became profuse in their glorification of Allāh, in their declarations of His uniqueness, and in seeking forgiveness from him, and in praising Allāh for the favour which he had shown to them.

The reports of that have reached the (distant) horizons and its account is widespread among the people. Concerning that al-Sayyid b. Muḥammad al-Ḥimyarī, may Allāh have mercy on him, recited:

> The sun was sent back for him when he missed the time of the afternoon prayer and sunset had drawn near.

So that its light shone (the same as) at its time for the afternoon. Then it fell like a shooting star.

For him it was sent back another time at Babylon. It has not been sent back for any Arab creature,

Only so that his first (view of it) may be mixed with his later (view of it) and so that it being sent back may be an explanation of a wondrous matter.

The Miracle of Speaking to the Fish

Similar to that is (the account) which the historians (*ahl al-āthār*) report and which has become famous among the Kūfans because of it being widespread among them. Hence the report has spread to other people in other places. The scholars also confirm it. (It is) that the fish talked to him at the Euphrates by Kūfa.

[They report:]
The waters of the Euphrates overflowed and grew so big that the people of Kūfa became anxious about drowning. They resorted to the Commander of the Faithful, peace be on him. He rode out on the mule of the Apostle of Allāh, may Allāh bless Him and His Family, and the people went with him until he reached the banks of the Euphrates. He, peace be on him, dismounted and performed the ritual ablution and prayed alone, by himself, while the people watched him. Then he called on Allāh with prayers which most of them heard. He went towards the Euphrates, leaning on a stick which was in his hand. He struck the surface of the water with it and said: "Abate, with Allāh's permission and His will."

The waters sank so that the fish at the bottom (of the flood) appeared. Many of them greeted him with title of the Commander of the Faithful. However some kinds of fish did not speak. They were eels, a scaleless fish (*marmāliq*) and mud fish (*zumār*). The people were amazed at that and they asked for the reason that the ones who spoke spoke and the ones who were silent were silent. He said: "Allāh made those fish which were ritually pure speak to me and he kept those silent towards me which were forbidden, impure and worse."

This is a widespread report, the fame of which is, through its transmission and narration, like the fame of the wolves speaking to the Prophet, the stones praising Allāh in the palm of his hand, the trunk of the tree bending towards him and the feeding of many with little food. Whoever continues to find fault with ('Alī's miracles) is one who can only find the doubts about it in what the denigrators depend upon, in what we have enumerated of the miracles of the Apostle.

The Commander of the Faithful and the Jinn

The historians (*ḥamalat al-āthār wa ruwāt al-akhbār*) have also reported the story of the snake and the sign and miraculous nature of it which is like the story of the fishes and the abating of the waters of the Euphrates.

[They reported:]
One day the Commander of the Faithful, peace be on him, was making a speech on the pulpit at Kūfa, when a snake appeared at the side of the pulpit and began to climb up until it was near the Commander of the Faithful, peace be on him. The people shook with fear at that and were worried about its purpose and about driving it away from the Commander of the Faithful, peace be on him. He signalled to them to keep away from it. When it reached the raised platform on which the Commander of the Faithful, peace be on him, was standing, he bent down towards the snake and the snake spread itself up towards him so that it could gobble his ear.

The people fell silent and became distraught at that. It made a croaking sound which many of them heard. Then it went down from its position. The Commander of the Faithful moved his lips in a whisper and the snake acted as if it was listening to him. Then it glided away. The ground had swallowed it up. The Commander of the Faithful, peace be on him, went on with his speech and brought it to a close.

When he had finished it and gone down, the people gathered around him, questioning him about the circumstances of the snake and the wonder of it. He told them: "That was not as you had thought. It was only one of the judges of the jinn, whom a case had confused. He came to me to find out from me about it. I informed him about it. He wished me well and departed."

*****

Often the ignorant among the people regard the appearance of jinn in the form of animals which cannot speak as impossible. However, that was well-known by the Arabs, before the mission (of the Prophet) and after it, and reports from people belonging to Islam corroborate it. Nor is it more unlikely than the report which is agreed on by Muslims (*ahl al-qibla*) of the appearance of the Devil to the people in the assembly building in the form of an old man from Najd, and his agreement with them to deceive the Apostle of Allāh, may Allāh bless Him and His Family, and of his appearing to the polytheists at the Battle of Badr in the form of Sarāqa b. Ja'sham al-Madlijī. He, the Exalted, said: *There will be no conqueror of you among the people today. I am one who grants you neighbourly protection* (VIII 48). Allāh, the Mighty and High, said: *When the two groups looked at each other, he turned on his heels and said: I am innocent of you. I see what you do not see. I fear Allāh. Allāh is violent in His punishment* (VIII 48).

All who continue to find fault with the signs which we have mentioned only say about them the same as the atheists and unbelievers among the opponents of religion, say. They find fault with them in the same way as they find fault with the signs of the Prophet in confirmation of his prophethood, and with the validity of the miracles of the Apostle of Allāh, may Allāh bless Him and His Family.

Some other Miracles of the Commander of the Faithful

[Another example is reported by 'Abd al-Qāhir b. 'Abd al-Malik b. 'Atā' al-Ashja'ī on the authority of al-Walīd b. 'Imrān al-Bajalī, on the authority of Jamī' b. 'Umayr, who said:]
'Alī, peace be on him, suspected a man called al-Ghayzār of giving information to Mu'āwiya. He denied that and disputed it. The Commander of the Faithful, peace be on him, said: "Do you swear by Allāh that you have not done so?"
"Yes," he answered and he hurried forward and took the oath.
"If you are a liar," the Commander of the Faithful, peace be on him, told him, "Allāh will blind you."

The Friday had not come when he was brought out blind, being led. Allāh had taken away his sight.

*****

[Of the same kind is what is reported by Ismā'īl b. 'Umayr, who said: Mis'ar b. Kidām told me: Ṭalḥa b. 'Umayra told us:]
'Alī, peace be on him, recited the words of the Prophet to the people: *To whomsoever I am his master (mawlā), 'Alī is his master*. Twelve men from the Anṣār testified to that but Anas b. Mālik was among the people who did not give testimony to it. The Commander of the Faithful, said to him: "Anas."
"At your service," he replied

"What stopped you from testifying?" he asked. "You have heard what they heard."

"Commander of the Faithful," he replied, "I have grown old and I have forgotten."

"O Allāh," the Commander of the Faithful, peace be on him, prayed, "if he is a liar, strike him with leprosy" - [or he said a word for it which is understood by the ordinary people].

[Ṭalḥa reported:]
"I testify before Allāh, I saw a whiteness (of leprosy) between his eyes."

[Similarly Abu Isrā'īl has reported on the authority of al-Ḥakam b. Abī Salmān, the *mu'adhdhin*, on the authority of Zayd b. Arqam, who said:]
'Alī, peace be on him, recited before the people in the mosque and said: "May Allāh adjure to arise any man who heard the Prophet, may Allāh bless Him and His Family, say: *To whomsoever I am his master (mawlā), 'Alī is his master. O Allāh, be a friend to those who befriend him and an enemy to those who are hostile to him.*"

Twelve men, who fought at Badr, stood up, six on the right and six on the left, and they testified to that.

[Zayd b. Arqam added:]
I was among those who heard that but I kept it hidden. Then Allāh took away my sight.

He used to regret failing to give testimony and he used to seek forgiveness from Allāh.

*****

[Another example is what is reported by 'Alī b. Mushir on the authority of al-A'mash, on the authority of Mūsā b. Ṭarīf, on the authority of 'Abāya and (also it is reported on the authority of) Mūsā b. Ukayl al-Numayrī, on the authority of 'Imrān b. Maytham on the authority of 'Abāya. (It is further reported on the authority of) Mūsā al-Wajīhī, on the authority of al-Minhāl b. 'Umar, and on the authority of 'Abd Allāh b. al-Ḥārith, 'Uthmān b. Sa'īd, and 'Abd Allāh b. Bukayr, on the authority of Ḥakīm b. Jubayr: They (all) said:]
We witnessed 'Alī, the Commander of the Faithful, peace be on him, on the pulpit saying: "I am the servant of Allāh, the brother of the Apostle of Allāh. I have inherited the blessing from the Apostle. I have married the mistress of the women of Heaven. I am the master of the testamentary trustees of authority, and those who are the last trustees of the Prophet. No one except me can claim that

without Allāh striking him with evil."

A man from (the tribe of) 'Abs who was sitting in front of the people said: "Who is not good enough to say this. I am the servant of Allāh, the brother of the Apostle of Allāh."

He had not left his place when the Devil caught hold of him and dragged him by his leg to the door of the mosque. His people asked us about him and we said: "Did you know him to be a man of (stupid) risks before this?"

"O Allāh, no," they answered.

[Al-Shaykh al-Mufīd, may Allāh be pleased with him, says:]
The reports about similar things to what we have mentioned are (such) that the book would become too long as a result of them. We have put forward in this book of ours sufficiency in its outline to do without what is similar to them. We ask Allāh for success and we seek help from Him along the path of guidance.

CHAPTER VIII

THE CHILDREN OF THE COMMANDER OF THE FAITHFUL

(This is) an account of the children of the Commander of the Faithful, peace be on him, their number and names, and a selection of reports about them.

The Commander of the Faithful, peace be on him, had twenty-seven children, male and female:

1. Al-Ḥasan
2. Al-Ḥusayn
3. Zaynab the elder
4. Zaynab the younger, who was given the *kunya* Umm Kulthūm.

Their mother was Fāṭima, the blessed, mistress of the women of the worlds, daughter of the master of those sent by Allāh and the seal of the prophets, the Prophet Muhammad.

5. Muḥammad, who was given the *kunya* Abū al-Qāsim.

His mother was Khawla, daughter of Ja'far b. Qays al-Ḥanafī.

6. 'Umar
7. Ruqayya

They were twins. Their mother was Umm Ḥabīb, daughter of Rabī'a.

8. Al-'Abbās
9. Ja'far
10. 'Uthmān
11. 'Abd Allāh

(The last four) were martyrs with their brother al-Ḥusayn on the plain of Karbalā'. Their mother was Umm al-Banīn[1], daughter of Ḥizām b. Khālid b. Dārim.

12. Muḥammad, the younger, who was given the *kunya* Abū Bakr.
13. 'Ubayd Allāh

Both of these were martyrs with their brother al-Ḥusayn on that plain. Their mother was Layla, daughter of Mas'ūd al-Dārimī.

---

1 Her actual name was Fāṭima, daughter of Ḥizām b. Khālid b. Dārim. Because she had four sons, she commonly known as Umm al-Banin ("mother of several sons").

14. Yaḥyā

His mother was Asmā', daughter of 'Umays al-Khath'amī, may Allāh be pleased with her.

15. Umm al-Ḥasan
16. Ramla

The mother of these two was Umm Sa'īd, daughter of 'Urwa b. Mas'ūd al-Thaqafī.

17. Nafīsa
18. Zaynab, the youngest
19. Ruqayya, the younger
20. Umm Hānī'
21. Umm al-Kirām
22. Jumāna, who was given the *kunya* Umm Ja'far.
23. Umāna
24. Umm Salama
25. Maymūna
26. Khadīja
27. Fāṭima

These, the blessings of Allāh be on them, had different mothers.

Among the Shī'a, there are those who mention that Fāṭima, the blessing of Allāh be on her, after the Prophet had a miscarriage with a son, whom the Prophet, may Allāh bless Him and His Family, had (already) named during her pregnancy as Muḥsin.[2] According to this group there were twenty-eight children of the Commander of the Faithful, the blessing and peace of Allāh be on him. Allāh knows and judges best.

---

2 There were many sources that clearly confirm the presence of Mohsen among the children of Fāṭima and 'Alī peace be upon them, this is not confined within the limits of Shī'ite books, Indeed, many of the books of the non-Shī'a (*'āmma*) mention this matter, and they agreed to his existence without comment or hesitation, see: *Al-Kafi*, 6:18/2; *Al-Khisal*, 634; *Tarikh Ya'qubi*, 2:213; *Manaqib* by Ibn Schahrashub, 3:358; *Tarikh al-Ṭabarī*, 5:153; *Tarikh* by Ibn Athir, 3:397; *Ansab al-Ashraf* of al-Baladhiri, 2:189; *al-Asaba* by Ibn Hajar, 3:471; *Lisan al-Mizan* of al-Dahabi, 268; *Mizan al-I'tidal,* 1:139; *al-Qamus al-Muhit* of Firuzabadi, 2:55, and other various sources

PART II

THE LIFE OF THE OTHER IMAMS

CHAPTER I

IMAM AL-ḤASAN B. 'ALĪ

(This is) an account of the Imam after the Commander of the Faithful, peace be on him, the date of his birth, the evidence for his Imamate, the period of his succession, the time of his death, the place of his grave and the number of Children. (It also provides) a brief summary of the reports about him.

The Imam after the Commander of the Faithful, peace be on him, was his son al-Ḥasan, the son of the mistress of the women of the worlds, Fāṭima, daughter of Muḥammad, the Lord of Messengers, may Allāh bless Him and His Family. (Al-Ḥasan's) *Kunya* was Abū Muḥammad. He was born in Medina, on the night of the middle day of the month of Ramaḍān, three years after the *Hijra* (624).

His mother, Fāṭima, peace be on her, brought him to the Prophet, may Allāh bless Him and His Family, on the seventh day in a silken shawl from heaven, which Gabriel had brought down to the Prophet, may Allāh bless Him and His Family. He called him Ḥasan and sacrificed a ram for him (in the ceremony of *'aqīqa*).[1]

[It is reported by a group (of authorities), including Aḥmad b. Ṣāliḥ al-Tamīmī, on the authority of 'Abd Allāh b 'Īsa on the authority of Ja'far al-Ṣādiq b. Muḥammed, peace be on him:]
Al-Ḥasan, peace be upon him, was the most similar person to Apostle of Allāh, may Allāh bless Him and His Family, in form, manner and nobility.

[It is reported by a group (of authorities), including Ma'mar on the authority of al-Zuhrī on the authority of Anas b. Malik, who said:]
No one was like the Apostle of Allāh, may Allāh bless Him and His Family, than Al-Ḥasan b. 'Alī, peace be on them.

[Ibrāhim ibn 'Alī al-Rāfi'ī reported on the authority of his father, on the authority of his grandmother Zainab, dauther of Abū Rāfi'ī, and Shabīb b. Abī Rāfi' al-Rāfi'ī on the authority of those who told him - she said:]
Fāṭima, peace be on her, brought her two sons, al-Ḥasan and al-Ḥussain, peace be on them, to the Apostle of Allāh, may Allāh bless Him and His Family, at the time when he was suffering from the sickness from which he died.

"Apostle of Allāh," she said, "these are your two (grand)sons. Give them something as an inheritance"

1 *'Aqīqa* is a ceremony in which the child's hair is shaved and a sheep sacrificed

"As for al-Ḥasan", he replied, "he has my form and my nobility. As for al-Ḥusayn, he has my generosity and my bravery"

Al-Ḥasan b. 'Alī, peace be on him, was the testamentary trustee (*waṣī*) of the Commander of the Faithful, peace be on him, over his family, his children and his followers. He bequeathed him to look after his position and (the position of) his taxes (*ṣadaqāt*) and he wrote him a covenant (of succession) which is well-known. His testamentary trustee is obvious in terms of the outlines of religion, the essential characteristics of wisdom and good-breeding. A great number of scholars have reported this trusteeship and many of the men of understanding have realised the truth of this through his (attitude to) the world.

Al-Ḥasan's Succession to the Caliphate and his Abdication

When the Commander of the Faithful, peace be on him, died, Al-Ḥasan addressed the people. He reminded them of his right (to authority). The followers of his father pledged allegiance to him in terms of fighting those he fought and making peace with those with whom he made peace.

[Abū Mikhnaf Lūt b. Yaḥyā al-Azdī reported: Ash'ath b. Suwār told me on the authority of Abū Isḥāq al-Sabī'ī and others, who said:][2]
Al-Ḥasan b. 'Alī, peace be upon them, addressed the people towards dawn on the night in which the Commander of the Faithful, peace be on him, died. He praised and glorified Allāh and blessed the Apostle of Allāh, may Allāh bless Him and His Family. Then he said: "There has died tonight a man who was the first among the early (Muslims) in (good) actions. Nor did any later (Muslims) attain his level in (good) actions. He used to fight alongside the Apostle of Allāh, may Allāh bless Him and His Family, and protect him with his own life. The Apostle of Allāh, may Allāh bless Him and His Family, used to send him forward with his standard while Gabriel supported him on his right and Michael supported him on his left. He would not return until Allāh brought victory through his hands. He, peace be on him, has died on this the night on which Jesus, Son of Mary, was taken up (to Heaven), on which Joshua, son of Nūn, the testamentary trustee (*waṣī*) of Moses, peace be on him, died. He has left behind him no gold and silver except seven hundred dirhams of his stipend (*'aṭā'*), with which he was intending to buy a servant for his family." Then tears overcame him and he wept and the people wept with him.

Then he continued: "I am the (grand)son of the one Who brought the good

2 The *isnād* is not as full as Abū al-Faraj al-Iṣfahānī's but the rest of the account follows his, with occasional variations, c.f. *Maqātil al-Ṭālibiyyīn*, 51-70.

news. I am the (grand)son of the warner. I am the (grand)son of the man who, with Allāh's permission, summoned (the people) to Allāh. I am the (grand)son of the light which shone out (to the world). I am of the House, from whom Allāh has sent away abomination and whom Allāh has purified thoroughly. I am of the House for whom Allāh has required love in his Book, when Allāh, the Most High, said: *Say: I do not ask you for any reward except love for (my) near relatives; Whoever earns good, will increase good for hmself* (XLII 23). The good is love for us, the House." Then he sat down.

'Abd Allāh b. al-'Abbās, may Allāh have mercy on him, arose in front of him and said: "People, this is the son of your Prophet, the testamentary trustee (*waṣī*) of your Imam. So pledge allegiance to him"

The people answered him saying: "No one is more loved by us nor has anyone more right to succession (*khilāfa*)."

They rushed forward to pledge allegiance to him as successor. That was on Friday on the eleventh of the month of Ramaḍān in the year 40 A H. (660). Then he assigned (the posts of) the tax collectors and he gave instructions to the governors (or the provinces). He sent 'Abd Allāh b. al-'Abbās to Basra. He took charge of all the matters.

When Mu'āwiya b. Abī Sufyān learnt of the death of the Commander of the Faithful, peace be on him, and the people's pledge of allegiance to his son, al-Ḥasan, peace be on him, he sent a man of Ḥimyar secretly to Kūfa and a man from Banū al-Qayn to Baṣra. They were to write reports to him to undermine affairs for al-Ḥasan, peace be on him. Al-Ḥasan, peace be on him, learned of that. He ordered the Ḥimyarī to be brought out from among (the tribe) of Lakhm in Kūfa. He had him brought out and executed. (Al-Ḥasan) wrote to al-Baṣra, ordering the Qaynī to be brought out from among the Banū Sulaym. He was brought out and executed.

Then al-Ḥasan, peace be on him, wrote to Mu'āwiya:

> You sent men to use deception and to carry out assassinations and you sent out spies as if you want to meet (in battle). That is something which will soon happen so wait for it, if Allāh wills. I have learnt that you have become haughty in a way that no wise man would become haughty. In that you are just as al-Awwal described:
>
> Say to him who desires the contrary of the one who has died:
> Prepare for another like him as if (from the same) root.

> I and the one among us who has died are like the one who goes in the evening so that (the other) may come in the morning.

Mu'āwiya replied to him with his letter, which there is no need to mention. There followed between him and al-Ḥasan, peace be on him, correspondence, messages and disputes regarding the right of al-Ḥasan, peace be on him, to authority, and the unlawful seizure of power of those who came before his father, peace be on him, and of Mu'āwiya's attempt to strip the cousin of the Apostle of Allāh, may Allāh bless Him and His Family, from his authority and of their (the House's) right to it apart from them. (All these) matters would take too long to describe.[3]

Mu'āwiya set off towards Iraq. When he reached the bridge of Manbij, al-Ḥasan, peace be on him reacted. He sent Ḥujr b. 'Adī to order the leaders (*'ummāl*) to set out and to call the people together for war.

They were slow to (answer) him and then they came forward. al-Ḥasan had a mixed band of men: some of them belonged to his Shī'a and to his father's; some of them were members of the *Muhakkima* (i.e. Khārijites) who were influenced by (the desire of) fighting Mu'āwiya with every means (possible); some of them were men who loved discords and were anxious for booty; some of them were doubters; others were tribal supporters who followed the leaders of their tribes without reference to religion.[4]

He set off until he came to Ḥammām 'Umar, then he went on to Dayr Ka'b. He stopped at Sābāṭ, just before the bridge and spent the night there. In the morning, He peace be on him, wanted to test his followers and make their situation clear with regard to obedience to him, so that in that way he might be able to distinguish his friends from his enemies and be in a clear mind (about his position) to meet Mu'āwiya and the Syrians.[5] He ordered the call to be made: "The prayer is a general one (which all should attend) (*al-ṣalāt jāmi'a*)." They gathered and he went up on the pulpit and addressed them. He said: "Praise belongs to Allāh whenever a man praises Him. I testify that there is no God but Allāh whenever a man testifies to Him. I testify that Muḥammad is His servant and His apostle whom He sent with the truth and whom He entrusted with revelation, may Allāh bless Him and His Family. By Allāh, I hope that I shall always be with Allāh's praise and kindness. I am the sincerest of Allāh's

3 A fuller version is given in *Maqātil al-Ṭālibiyyīn*, 53-60.

4 This paragraph is not in *Maqātil al-Ṭālibiyyīn*. It probably represents al-Mufīd's explanation of some reluctance shown by the Kūfans. cf. *Maqātil al-Ṭālibiyyīn*, 61.

5 This sentence appears to be al-Mufīd's explanation and is not in *Maqātil al-Ṭālibiyyīn*

creatures in giving advice to them. I have not become one who bears malice to any Muslim, nor one who wishes evil or misfortune for him. Indeed what you dislike about unity (*jamā'a*) is better for you than what you like about division. I see what is better for you better than you see for yourselves. Therefore do not oppose my commands and do not reject my judgement. May Allāh forgive both me and you and may He guide me and you to that in which there is love and satisfaction."

[He reported:]
The people began to look at one another and asked each other, "What do you think he intends by what he has just said?"
"We think that he intends to make peace with Mu'āwiya and hand over the authority to him" they answered.

"By Allāh, the man has become an unbeliever," they declared and they rushed towards his tent. They plundered him to the extent that they even took his prayer mat from under him. Then 'Abd al-Raḥmān b. 'Abd Allāh b. Ja'āl al-Azdī set on him and stripped his silk cloak from his shoulder. He remained sitting, still girt with his sword but without his cloak. He called for his horse and mounted it. Groups of his close associates and his Shī'a surrounded him and kept those who wanted (to attack) him away from him. He said: "Summon (the tribes of) Rabī'a and Hamdān to me."

They were summoned to him and they surrounded him and defended him, peace be on him, from the people. A mixed group of others went with him (as well). When he was passing through the narrow pass of Sābāṭ, a man of Banū Asad called al-Jarrāḥ b. Sinān caught hold of the reins of his mule. He had an axe in his hand. He cried: "Allāh is greater (*Allāhu akbar*)! You have become a polytheist, Ḥasan, just like your father became a polytheist before."

Then he stabbed him in the thigh. It penetrated right through to the bone. He seized (al-Ḥasan) by the neck and they both fell to the ground. A man from al-Ḥasan's Shī'a called 'Abd Allāh b. Khaṭal al-Ṭā'ī pulled the axe away from his hand and struck him with it in the stomach. Another man called Ẓubyān b. 'Umāra attacked him, struck him upon the nose and killed him. Another man who had been with (al-Jarrāḥ) was caught and killed.

Al-Ḥasan, peace be on him, was carried on a stretcher to al-Madā'in where he was lodged with Sa'd b. Mas'ūd al-Thaqafī. The latter was the governor of ('Alī), the Commander of the Faithful, peace be on him, there and al-Ḥasan had confirmed him in that position.

Al-Ḥasan, peace be on him, was distracted by his own (discomfort) and with treating his wound. (In the meantime) a group of the tribal leaders wrote secretly to Mu'āwiya offering to accept his authority (lit. to listen and obey). They urged him to come to them and they guaranteed to hand over al-Ḥasan, peace be on him, when they got to his camp, or to kill him treacherously.

Al-Ḥasan, peace be on him, learnt of that when a letter came to him from Qays b. Sa'd, may Allāh be pleased with him. He had sent Qays with 'Ubayd Allāh b. 'Abbās (to go on ahead) when he had set out from Kūfa to meet Mu'āwiya and to drive him out of Iraq, and make himself a commander of a unified people (*jamā'a*). He had said to 'Ubayd Allāh: "If you are struck down, then the commander will be Qays b. Sa'd."

Qays b. Sa'd's letter arrived informing him that they had stopped Mu'āwiya at a village called al-Ḥabūbiyya opposite Maskan. Then Mu'āwiya had sent to 'Ubayd Allāh b. 'Abbās, urging him to come to him and offering him a million dirhams, half of which he would give him immediately, and the other half on his entry into Kūfa. 'Ubayd Allāh had slipped away in the night with his close associates to (join) Mu'āwiya's camp. In the morning the people found their leader missing. Qays b. Sa'd, may Allāh be pleased with him, said the prayer with them and took charge of their affairs.[6]

Al-Ḥasan's awareness of the people's desertion of him increased; (as did his awareness) of the corrupt intention of the Muḥakkima (the Khārijites) against him, which they made obvious by cursing him, accusing him of disbelief, and declaring that it was lawful to shed his blood and plunder his property. There remained no one to protect him from his unfortunate predicament except the close associates from his father's Shī'a and his own Shī'a, and they were a group which could not resist the Syrian soldiers.

Mu'āwiya wrote to him about a truce and peace treaty. He also sent him the letters of his followers in which they had guaranteed to kill him treacherously or to hand him over. He offered him as many conditions as he wanted, to answer his (call) for peace and he gave his (sworn) covenant by whose fulfilment everybody's interests would be served. Al-Ḥasan, peace be on him, did not trust him. He was aware of his deception and his attempts at assassination. However he could find no escape from assenting to his demands to abandon the war and bring about a truce because of the weakness of his followers' understanding of his right, their corrupt attitude towards him and their opposition to him. (In addition, he was aware) of the view of many of them in declaring it lawful to

6 This summarises *Maqātil al-Ṭālibiyyīn*, 64-5. The next section is omitted by al-Mufīd.

shed his blood and to hand him over to his rival. (He also knew) of his cousin's desertion (of him) and his joining his enemy, as well as the inclination of the people towards the immediate present and their reluctance (to show concern) for the future.

Therefore he, peace be on him, bound himself (in a treaty) with Mu'āwiya as a result of the confirmation of the proof (of his situation) and with the excuses before Allāh, the Most High, and all the Muslims, of what had taken place among them, He stipulated:

> That the cursing of the Commander of the Faithful, peace be on him, should be abandoned and the practice of using the personal prayer (*qunūt*) in the formal prayer (*ṣalāt*) (as prayer) against him should be set aside;
>
> That his Shī'a, may Allāh be pleased with them, should be given security and that none of them should be exposed to any evil; That each of them who had certain rights should attain those rights.[7]

Mu'āwiya accepted all that and made a treaty with him to observe that. He swore to him that he would fulfil it. When the truce had been concluded, Mu'āwiya went on until he reached al-Nukhayla. That was on a Friday; he prayed the mid-morning prayer (*ḍuḥā al-nahār*) with the people, and he addressed them. In his address, he said: "By Allāh, I have not fought against you to make you pray, nor to fast, nor to make the pilgrimage, nor to pay *zakāt*. Indeed you do that (already). I fought so that I might have power over you and Allāh has given that to me when you were reluctant to (obey) Him. Indeed I have been requested by al-Ḥasan, peace be on him, (to give him) things and I have given things to him. All of them are now under my foot. And from now on I will not fulfil anything."

Then he went on until he entered Kūfa. He resided there for several days. When the pledge of allegiance by its inhabitants had to be carried out, he went up on the pulpit and addressed the people. He mentioned the Commander of the Faithful, peace be on him, and that he had taken from him and from al-Ḥasan, peace be on him, what he had taken.

Al-Ḥasan and Al-Ḥusayn, peace be on them, were present. al-Ḥusayn, peace be on him, rose to reply but al-Ḥasan, peace be on him, took him by the hand and made him sit down. Then he himself, (al-Ḥasan) arose and spoke: "O you who mention 'Alī, I am al-Ḥasan and 'Alī was my father. You are Mu'āwiya and your father was Ṣakhr (Abū Sufyān). My mother was Fāṭima and your mother was Hind. My grandfather was the Apostle of Allāh and your grandfather was Ḥarb.

7 The reasons for the treaty are not included in *Maqātil al-Ṭālibiyyīn* and terms are slightly different. cf. *Maqātil al-Ṭālibiyyīn*, 66-7.

My grandmother was Khadīja and your grandmother was Futayla. May Allāh curse him who tries to reduce our reputation and to diminish our nobility, who does evil against our antiquity and yet who has been ahead of us in unbelief and hypocrisy."

Groups of the people in the mosque shouted out: "Amen, Amen"[8]

When the peace between al-Ḥasan, peace be on him, and Mu'āwiya was concluded in the way we have mentioned, al-Ḥasan, peace be on him, left for Medina. He resided there, restraining his anger, staying close to his house, and awaiting the command of his Lord, the Mighty and High, until Mu'āwiya had completed ten years of his administration. (Then) the latter decided to have the pledge of allegiance given to his son, Yazīd, (as his successor). He communicated secretly With Ju'da, daughter of al-Ash'ath b. Qays - she was the wife of al-Ḥasan, peace be on him - to urge her to poison him. He gave an undertaking to her that he would marry her to his son, Yazīd, and he sent her a hundred thousand dirhams. Ju'da gave him the poison to drink but he lingered on sick for forty days. He passed along his (final) road in the month of Ṣafar in the year 50 A. H. (670). At that time, he was forty-eight years of age. His succession (to the Imamate) had been for ten years. His brother and testamentary trustee (*waṣī*), al-Ḥusayn, peace be on him, undertook the washing and shrouding of his body, and buried him with his grandmother, Fāṭima, daughter of Asad b. Hāshim b. 'Abd Manāf, may Allāh be pleased with her, in (the cemetery of) al-Baqī'.

Reports of the Cause of the Death of al-Ḥasan, Peace be on him, and of Mu'āwiya Poisoning him, the Story of his Burial and the Actions and Statements Concerning that.

'Īsā b. Mihrān reported: 'Ubayd Allāh b. al-Ṣabbāḥ told us: Jarīr told us on the authority of Mughīra, who said:]
Mu'āwiya sent to Ju'da daughter of al-Ash'ath b. Qays: "I will arrange for you to marry my son, Yazīd, on condition that you poison al-Ḥasan."
He, also, sent her a hundred thousand dirhams.

She did that: she poisoned al-Ḥasan, peace be on him. (Mu'āwiya) gave her the money but did not marry her to Yazīd. Instead he gave her a man from the family of Ṭalḥa as a substitute. The latter gave her children. Whenever any argument occurred between them and the clans of Quraysh, they would revile them saying: "Sons of a woman who poisons her husbands."[9]

---

8 For the speeches cf. *Maqātil al-Ṭālibiyyīn*, 68-70.
9 *Maqātil al-Ṭālibiyyīn*, 73.

['Īsā b. Mihrān reported: 'Uthmān b. 'Umar told me: Ibn 'Awn told us on the authority of 'Umar b. Isḥāq, who said:]
I was with al-Ḥasan and al-Ḥusayn, peace be on them, in the house. al-Ḥasan, peace be on him, came in from outside and then went out again. He said: "I have been given poison to drink several times but I have never been given poison like this. A bit of my liver has come out or my mouth and I began to turn it over with a stick I had."

"Who gave you the poison to drink," al-Ḥusayn, peace be on him, asked him, "and what do you want for him? Do you want him killed? If he may remain as he is, then Allāh will be more terrible in His vengeance than you. If he may not remain as he is, then I should like to be free of any blame,"[10]

['Abd Allāh b. Ibrāhīm reported on the authority of Ziyād al-Makhāriqī, who said:]
When death was close to al-Ḥasan, peace be on him, he summoned al-Ḥusayn, peace be on him, and said: "My brother. I am leaving you and joining my Lord. I have been given poison to drink and have spewed my liver into a basin. I am aware of the person who poisoned me and from where I have been made a subject to this deceitful action. I will oppose him before Allāh, the Mighty and High. Therefore by the right I have with regard to you, say nothing about that and wait for what Allāh, the Mighty and High, will decide concerning me. When I have died, shut my eyes, wash me and shroud me. Then carry me on my bier to the grave of my grandfather, the Apostle of Allāh, may Allāh bless Him and His Family, so that I may renew my covenant with him. After that take me to the grave of my grandmother, Fāṭima, daughter of Asad, may Allāh be pleased with her, and bury me there. My brother, the people will think that you intend to bury me with the Apostle of Allāh, may Allāh bless Him and His Family. For that reason, they will gather to prevent you from doing it. I swear by Allāh that you should not shed even your blood into the cupping-glass in (carrying out) my command."

Then he made his testamentary bequests to his family and his children. (He gave him) his heirlooms and the things which the Commander of the Faithful, peace be on him, had bequeathed to him when he had made him his successor, had declared him worthy to occupy his position, and had indicated to his Shī'a that he was his successor, and set him up as their sign-post after himself.

When he passed on his (final) journey, al-Ḥusayn, peace be on him, washed and shrouded his (body). Then he carried him on his bier. Marwān and those of the

10 *Maqātil al-Ṭālibiyyīn*, 74.

Banū Umayya who were with him had no doubt that they would try to bury him beside the Apostle of Allāh, may Allāh bless Him and His Family. They gathered together and armed themselves. When al-Ḥusayn, peace be on him, approached the tomb of the Apostle of Allāh, may Allāh bless Him and His Family, with (the body of al-Ḥasan) so that he might renew his covenant with him, they came towards them with their group. 'Ā'isha had joined them on a mule and she was saying: "What is there between you and me that you should allow someone I don't want to, to enter my house?"

Marwān began to recite:

O Lord, battle is better than ease.

(Then he went on:) "Should 'Uthmān be buried in the outskirts of Medina and al-Ḥasan be buried alongside the Prophet, may Allāh bless Him and His Family? That will never be while I carry a sword."

Discord was about to occur between the Banū Umayya and the Banū Hāshim. Ibn 'Abbās hurried to Marwān and said to him: "Go back to where you came from, Marwān. Indeed we do not intend to bury our companion with the Apostle of Allāh, may Allāh bless Him and His Family. But we want him to be able to renew his covenant with him by visiting him. Then we will take him back to his grandmother, Fāṭima, and bury him alongside her according to his last instructions concerning that. If he had enjoined that he should be buried alongside the Prophet, may Allāh bless Him and His Family, you know that you would be the least able to deter us from that. However, he, peace be on him, was much too aware of Allāh and His Apostle and the sacredness of his tomb to bring bloodshed to it as others have done (who) have entered it without his permission."

Then he went to 'Ā'isha and said to her: "What mischief you bring about, one day on a mule and one day on a camel! Do you want to extinguish the light of Allāh and fight the friends (*awliyā'*) of Allāh? Go Back! You have been given assurance against what you fear and have learned what you wanted (to know). By Allāh, victory will come to this House, even if it is after some time."

al-Ḥusayn, peace be on him, said: "By Allāh, if there had been no injunction to me from al-Ḥasan, peace be on him, to prevent bloodshed and that I should not even pour blood into a cupping-glass in (carrying out) his command, you would have known how the swords of Allāh would have taken their toll from you. You have broken the agreement which was made between you and us. You have ignored the conditions which we made with him for ourselves."

Then they went on with (the body of) al-Ḥasan, peace be on him, and they buried him in (the cemetery of) al-Baqī‘ beside his grandmother, Fāṭima daughter of Asad b. Hāshim b. ‘Abd Manāf, may Allāh be pleased with her.

An Account of the Number and Names of the Children of al-Ḥasan b. ‘Alī, Peace be on them, and an Extract from the Reports about them.

Al-Ḥasan b. ‘Alī, Peace be on him, had fifteen children, both male and female:

1. Zayd b. al-Ḥasan

and his two sisters :

2. Umm al-Ḥasan
3. Umm al-Ḥusayn

Their mother was Umm Bashīr daughter of Abū Mas‘ūd ‘Uqba ‘Amr b. Tha‘laba al-Khazrajī

4. Al-Ḥasan b. al-Ḥasan

His mother was Khawla daughter of Manẓūr al-Faẓārī.

5. ‘Umar b. al-Ḥasan

and his two brothers

6. Al-Qāsim
7. ‘Abd Allāh

Their mother was a slave-wife (*umm walad*).

8. Abd al-Raḥmān b. al-Ḥasan

His mother was a slave-wife (*umm walad*).

9. Al-Ḥusayn b al-Ḥasan, who was nicknamed the one with the broken tooth (*al-athram*)

and his brother:

10. Talḥa b. al-Ḥasan

and their sister:

11. Fāṭima daughter of al-Ḥasan

Their mother was Umm Isḥāq daughter of Ṭalḥa b. ‘Ubayd Allāh al-Taymī

12. Umm ‘Abd Allāh
13. Fāṭima
14. Umm Salama
15. Ruqayya

These were daughters of al-Ḥasan, peace be on him, by various mothers.

*****

As for Zayd b. al-Ḥasan, peace be on him, he was in charge of the (proportion of) taxes (*ṣadaqāt*) given to the Apostle of Allāh, may Allāh bless Him and His Family. He was the oldest (of the children) and was noble in worth, generous in character, unusual in spirit and great in piety. The poets praised him and people came to him from far and wide to seek his favour.

The historians (*aṣḥāb al-sīra*) related that Zayd b. al-Ḥasan was in charge of the (proportion of) taxes (*ṣadaqāt*) given to the Apostle of Allāh, may Allāh bless Him and His Family. However when Sulaymān b. 'Abd al-Malik came to authority, he wrote to his governor in Medina:

> When this letter of mine comes to you, dismiss Zayd from (control over) the taxes (*ṣadaqāt*) of the Apostle of Allāh, may Allāh bless Him and His Family, and give them to so-and-so son of so-and-so - he was a man from his (i.e. Sulayman's) clan. Give him (all) the help he seeks from you. Greetings.

However, when 'Umar b. 'Abd al-'Azīz succeeded, (another) letter came from him:

> Zayd b. al-Ḥasan is the leader (*sharīf*) of the Banū Hāshim and the oldest of them. When this letter of mine comes to you, restore (control of) the taxes of the Apostle of Allāh, may Allāh bless Him and His Family, to him. Give him (all) the help he seeks from you. Greetings.

Concerning Zayd b. al-Ḥasan, Muḥammad b. Bashīr, the Khārijite, recited:

> When the son of the chosen one comes down the valley-stream, he drives away its drought and makes its sticks green with vegetation.
>
> Zayd is the spring of the people in every winter season when their rains and thunder have come.
>
> (He is) meek before those who seek the blood-price just as if he was a sun amid darkness as if its stars were joined to him.

Zayd b. al-Ḥasan died when he was ninety years of age. A group of poets composed elegies for him, mentioning their loss of him and his outstanding merit. Among these elegies is that of Qudāma b. Mūsā al-Jumaḥī who said:

> If the earth had been deprived of Zayd's person, kindness and goodness would have been absent from it.

If the guarantee of the dust of the grave has come upon him, then he has been covered by it while he, the departed, was praised for his action.

The One Who listens to a humble request knows that he only seeks good from Him and so He will return (good to him).

He was not loquacious but he undertook his journeying to search for good wherever you wanted (it).

If a lowly servant was remiss, he would urge him on to praise his fathers and grandfathers.

(He was one of the) generous givers to servants and (one of) those who sides with kinsmen, (one of the) lions in endurance in the face of misfortunes.

When a mighty one with many ancestors is removed, they have a praiseworthy inheritor to succeed as would be desired.

When a lord from among them dies, another noble lord arises who builds and fortifies them after him.

(Further) examples of this would make the book too long.

Zayd b. al-Ḥasan, may Allāh have mercy on him, departed from this world without claiming the Imamate, nor do anyone of the Shī'a or anyone else make the claim for it on his behalf. The fact is that the Shī'a are of two types - Imāmī and Zaydī. The Imāmī bases the Imamate on nominations (*nuṣūṣ*) and these do not exist for the sons of al-Ḥasan, peace be on him, with their agreement: not one of them claimed that for himself while there was any doubt with regard to it. The Zaydī regards the Imamate, after 'Alī, al-Ḥasan and al-Ḥusayn, peace be on them, as belonging (to the one who makes) a claim for it and (embarks on) war (*jihād*). However, Zayd b. al-Ḥasan, may Allāh have mercy on him, submitted to the Banū Umayya and accepted the actions performed by them. His attitude was (that of) precautionary dissimulation (*taqiyya*) towards his enemies and reconciliation and blandishment towards them. According to the Zaydī movement, this is contrary to the signs of the Imamate as we have explained.

The Hashwiyya adhere to the Imamate of the Banū Umayya and do not consider the Imamate as belonging to the children of the Apostle of Allāh, may Allāh bless Him and His Family, in any circumstance. The Mu'tazila only consider the Imamate as belonging to those who hold their view of withdrawal (*i'tizāl*) and those whose agreement (*'ahd*) is made through a consultative body (*shūrā*) and election (*ikhriyār*). As we have mentioned before, Zayd was far from (conforming to) these conditions. The Khārijites do not consider the Imamate of anyone whom the Commander of the Faithful, peace be on him, appointed whereas Zayd followed both his father and his grandfather without any dispute.

*****

Al-Ḥasan b. al-Ḥasan, peace be on him, was noble, a leader, a man of merit and piety. He was in charge of the (proportion of) taxes (*ṣadaqāt*) give to the Commander of the Faithful, peace be on him, while he (al-Ḥasan) was alive, until al-Ḥajjāj b. Yūsuf, as they report.

[Al-Zubayr b. Bakkār has reported:]
Al-Ḥasan b. al-Ḥasan was in charge of the (proportion of) taxes (*ṣadaqāt*) of the Commander of the Faithful, peace be on him, while he was alive. One day al-Ḥajjāj b. Yūsuf came in a procession - at that time he was governor of Medina. Al-Ḥajjāj said to him: "Bring 'Umar b. 'Alī into (association) with you in the *ṣadaqāt* of your father. He is your uncle and a survivor of your family."

"I will not change the conditions laid down on me," al-Ḥasan told him, "nor will I bring anyone else into (association) in it, who need not be brought in."

"Then I will bring him into association with you," retorted al-Ḥajjāj.

However, al-Ḥasan b. al-Ḥasan withdrew it from him when al-Ḥajjāj was distracted (with other matters). Then he went to 'Abd al-Malik. He came to him and stood at his door seeking permission (to enter). Yaḥyā b. (Umm) al-Ḥakam passed him. When Yaḥyā saw him, he turned towards him, greeted him and asked him about his reason for coming. (Al-Ḥasan) told him.
"I will try to favour you with the Commander of the faithful," Yaḥyā said - he was referring to 'Abd al-Malik.

When al-Ḥasan b. al-Ḥasan went in to 'Abd al-Malik, the latter welcomed him and questioned him kindly. Al-Ḥasan's hair had grown white quickly. Yaḥyā b. (Umm) al-Ḥakam was in the gathering.
"Your hair has grown white quickly, Abu Muḥammad," 'Abd al-Malik said to (al-Ḥasan)
"The whitenes of his half would not prevent him from carrying out the desires of the Iraqis, Commander of the faithful." said Yaḥyā, "should their riders come to him to inspire him with desire for the caliphate."

Al-Ḥasan b. al-Ḥasan went to him and said: "Shame on you! By Allāh, the gift that I ask for is not as you have said. But we, the members of the House, grow white (in our hair) quickly."

'Abd al-Malik had been listening. He came towards him and asked: "Come on, why have you come?"
(Al-Ḥasan) told him about what al-Ḥajjāj had said.

"He has no right to do that," ('Abd al-Malik) said. "I will write to him a letter which he will not ignore."

He wrote to him and gave gifts to al-Ḥasan b. al-Ḥasan and treated him generously. When he left him, Yaḥyā b. (Umm) al-Ḥakam met him. Al-Ḥasan reproached him for his bad testimony. He said to him: "What was it that you promised me?"
"Stop that," retorted Yaḥyā. "He still fears you. If I had not made him fear you, he would not have carried out your request and thus was I able to help you."

Al-Ḥasan b. al-Ḥasan had been present with his uncle, al-Ḥusayn. peace be on him, at the battle on the banks (of the Euphrates). When al-Ḥusayn, peace be on him, was killed and the rest of his family had been taken prisoner, Asmā' b. Khārija had come to him and taken him from among prisoners. She had said: "By Allāh, don't ever let him go to Ibn Khawla."
"Let him go to Abū Ḥassān, the son of his sister" said 'Umar b. Sa'd.

It was said that he was captured when he had received a wound from which he was (later) cured.

It is reported that al-Ḥasan b. al-Ḥasan sought to become engaged to one of two of the daughters of his uncle, al-Ḥusayn, peace be on him.
"Choose, my son," al-Ḥusayn, peace be on him, told him, "the one of them which is preferable to you."

Al-Ḥasan became shy and could not make a choice in answer. So al-Ḥusayn, peace be on him, said: "I have chosen my daughter, Fāṭima, for you. Of the two, she is the most like my mother, Fāṭima, daughter of the Apostle of Allāh, may Allāh bless Him and His Family."

Al-Ḥasan b. al-Ḥasan died when he was thirty-five years of age, may Allāh have mercy on him. His brother, Zayd b. al-Ḥasan was still alive but he appointed his brother on his mother's side, Ibrāhīm b. Muḥammad b. Ṭalḥa, as his trustee. When al-Ḥasan b. al-Ḥasan, may Allāh be pleased with him, died, his wife, Fāṭima, daughter of al-Ḥusayn b. 'Alī, peace be on them, pitched a tent at his tomb and she used to stand in prayer at night and fast during the day. She was like a houri of heaven in her beauty. At the beginning of the new year, she said to her retainers: "When the night becomes dark, pull down the tent. "

Then when the night became dark, she heard a voice saying: "Have they found what they had lost?" She answered: "Nay, they have despaired so they have reversed things."

Al-Ḥasan b. al-Ḥasan passed away without making any claim for the Imamate. Nor was any claim for it made on his behalf, just as we have described in the case of his brother, Zayd, may Allāh be pleased with him.

*****

As for 'Umar, al-Qāsim and 'Abd Allāh, sons of al-Ḥasan b. 'Alī, peace be on them, they died as martyrs in front of their uncle, al-Ḥusayn b. 'Alī, peace be on them, on the banks (of the Euphrates) - may Allāh be pleased with them and grant them satisfaction and reward their bravery on behalf of religion and Islam and His family.

'Abd al-Raḥmān b. al-Ḥasan went on a pilgrimage with his uncle, al-Ḥusayn, peace be on him, and he died at al-Abwā' while still in a pilgrim state (*muḥrim*), may Allāh have mercy on him.

Al-Ḥusayn b. al-Ḥasan, known as 'the one with the broken tooth' (*al-athram*) had great merit but there was no other record of him with regard to that.

Ṭalha b. al-Ḥasan was an excellent man.

*****

CHAPTER II

IMAM AL-ḤUSAYN B. 'ALĪ

(This is) an account of the Imam after al-Ḥasan b. 'Alī, peace be on him, (giving) the date of his birth, the evidence of his Imamate, the age he reached, the period of his succession (*khilāfa*), the time and cause of his death, the place of his grave, the number of his children. (It also provides) a selection from the (historical) reports about him.

The Imam after al-Ḥasan b. 'Alī was his brother, al-Ḥusayn b. 'Alī, (who was) the son of Fāṭima, daughter of the Apostle of Allāh, may Allāh bless Him and His Family, through the designation (*naṣṣ*) of his father and grandfather, peace be on them, and the testamentary bequest (*waṣiyya*) of his brother, al-Ḥasan, peace be on him. His *kunya* was Abū 'Abd Allāh.

He was born in Medina, on the fifth of Sha'bān in the year 4 A.H. (626). His mother, Fāṭima, peace be on her, brought him to the Apostle of Allāh. The latter was delighted with him and named him Ḥusayn. He sacrificed a ram on his behalf in the rite of *'aqīqa*. On the testament of the Apostle of Allāh, he and his brother are the two lords of the youth of Heaven, and by unanimous agreement, they were the grandsons of the Prophet of Mercy.

Al-Ḥasan b. 'Alī, peace be on them, was like the Prophet, may Allāh bless Him and His Family, from his head to his chest, while al-Ḥusayn was like him from his chest to his feet. They were the two dear ones of the Apostle of Allāh among all his family and children.

[Zādhān reported on the authority of Salmān, may Allāh be pleased with him:]
I heard the Apostle of Allāh, may Allāh bless Him and His Family, say concerning al-Ḥasan and al-Ḥusayn, peace be on them: "O Allāh, I love both of them. Therefore love them and love whoever loves them:" Then he said: "Whoever loves al-Ḥasan and al-Ḥusayn, is one whom I love. Whomever I love, Allāh loves, and whomever Allāh loves, He will cause to enter Heaven. Whoever hates them, I hate and Allāh hates. Whomever Allāh hates, He will cause to enter the Fire." Then he said: "These two sons of mine are my two plants of sweet basil (to sweeten) the world."

[Zirr b. Ḥubaysh reported on the authority of Ibn Mas'ūd:]

While the Prophet, may Allāh bless Him and His Family, was praying, al-Ḥasan and al-Ḥusayn came and stood behind him. When he raised his head, he took them tenderly (into his arms). When he resumed (his prayers), they resumed (theirs). Then when he had finished, he sat one on his right knee and the other on his left knee and said: "Whoever loves me, should love these two. They, peace be on them, are the two proofs (*ḥujjatay Allāh*) of Allāh of His Prophet in the contest of prayer (*mubāhala*). After their father, the Commander of the Faithful, they are the two proofs of Allāh (*ḥujjatay Allāh*) to the community concerning religion (*dīn*) and belief (*milla*)."

[Muḥammad b. 'Umayr has reported on the authority of his teachers (*rijāl*) that Abu 'Abd Allāh (i.e. Imam Ja'far al-Ṣādiq), peace be on him, said:][1]
Al-Ḥasan, peace be on him, said to his companions: "Allāh has two cities - one in the east and the other in the west - in which Allāh's creatures are never interested in disobeying Him. Yet, by Allāh, Allāh's proof to His creatures, both in those two and between them, is no other than myself and my brother, al-Ḥusayn."

A narration of the same kind is reported from al-Ḥusayn b. 'Alī, peace be on them, when he said to the followers of Ibn Ziyād on the day of deprivation: "What is the matter with you that makes you help each other against me? Or (don't you see) if you kill me, you kill Allāh's proof to yourselves? No, by Allāh, there is not between Jābilqā and Jabirsā a son of a prophet through whom Allāh provides proof to you other than myself." He meant by Jābilqā and Jabirsā, the two cities which al-Ḥasan, peace be on him, had mentioned.

One of the conclusive pieces of evidence (*burhān*) of the perfection of both of them, peace be on them, and the proof of Allāh's special regard for them both, after what we have mentioned of the contest of prayer of the Prophet, may Allāh bless Him and His Family, (in which he used) them both, is the pledge (*bay'a*) which the Apostle of Allāh made, to them, when he never made any (other) pledge to a child. The Qur'ān also brings down the positive statement of the reward of Heaven to them both because of their works, despite the outward state of childhood in which they were. It did not bring down that to any other like them. Allāh said in *Sūrat Hal ātā* (*Insan*) (known also as *Sūrat al-Dahr*) (LXXVI 8-12): *And they give food out of love for Him to the poor and the orphan and the captive. We only feed you for Allāh's sake; we desire from you neither reward nor thanks. Surely we fear from our Lord a stern, distressful day. Therefore Allāh will guard them from the evil of that day and cause them to meet with ease and happiness. And reward them, because they were patient, with*

1 Al-Kāfī (Tehran, 1388A.H.) I,462, tradition no.5. Al-Kulayni's *isnād* has been shortened as has the tradition.

garden and silk. This statement is general to them, peace be on them, with their father and their mother. The tradition contains their assertion of that and their awareness of it; both of which indicate that the illustrious verse was about the two of them and (that) the greatest proof (*ḥujja*) to creatures was through them both. In the same way the report about the Messiah, peace be on him, speaking in the cradle was a proof of his prophethood and Allāh's special regard for him through miraculous acts (*karāma*) which indicated his place and position with Allāh with regard to merit (*faḍl*).

The Apostle of Allāh, may Allāh bless Him and His Family, had made clear his Imamate and the Imamate of his brother before him through designation (*naṣṣ*) when he said: "These two sons of mine are Imams who will experience difficulties."

The testamentary bequest (*waṣiyya*) of al-Ḥasan, peace be on him, to him indicated his Imamate, just as the testamentary bequest of the Commander of the Faithful, peace be on him, to al-Ḥasan, peace be on him, indicated his Imamate just as the testamentary bequest of the Apostle of Allāh, may Allāh bless Him and His Family, to the Commander of the Faithful, peace be on him, indicated his Imamate after himself.

According to what we have (just) mentioned the Imamate of al-Ḥusayn, peace be on him, was confirmed after the death of his brother al-Ḥasan, peace be on him, and the obedience of all creatures to him was binding, although he did not summon them to (follow) him because of precautionary dissimulation (*taqiyya*) which he was following and because of the truce which existed between him and Mu'āwiya b. Abī Sufyān and the need to fulfil it. In that he followed the same course as his father the Commander of the Faithful, peace be on him, in terms of the establishment of his Imamate after the Prophet, may Allāh bless Him and His Family, despite (his own) silence (about it), and also of the Imamate of his brother after the truce despite (his) abstention (from politics) and (his) silence. In that they were acting according to the practices (*sunan*) of the Prophet of Allāh, may Allāh bless Him and His Family, when he was blockaded in al-Shi'b and when he escaped Mecca as an emigrant by hiding in a cave and he was hidden from his enemies.

*****

When Mu'āwiya died, the period of the truce came to an end. (It was this) which had prevented al-Ḥusayn, peace be on him, from calling (people) to (follow) him. Then he made public his (claim to) authority as far as was possible. Time after time he explained his right (to authority) to those who were ignorant of it until followers gathered around him. Then he, peace be on him, urged (them) to take up the struggle (*jihād*) and prepared for battle.

Then with his children and the people of his house (*ahl baytihi*), he set out from the sanctuary of Allāh (Mecca) and the sanctuary his Apostle (Medina) towards Iraq because of the help that was sought from him by the members of his Shī'a who had urged him (to come) against the enemies. His paternal cousin, Muslim b. 'Aqīl, may Allāh be pleased with him, had preceded him and had satisfied him of the (sincerity of their) call to Allāh and of (their) pledge of allegiance to him to take part in the struggle. For the people of Kūfa had pledged their allegiance to him (Muslim) to (do) that, and had promised (to do) it and had guaranteed help and advice to him and had given their trust and contract to him. However it was not long before they broke their pledge, deserted him and handed him over. Then he was killed in their midst without them (trying) to stop it. (Furthermore) they went out to (make) war against al-Ḥusayn. They besieged him, peace be on him, prevented him from returning to Allāh's land (i.e. Mecca) and they used force against him in such a way that he could find no one to help him, and no place of refuge from them. They prevented him from getting water from the Euphrates so that they might gain power over him. Then they killed him. He, peace be on him, died, (a man desperately) thirsty, yet still striving and showing fortitude, (a man) forced to be detained, (a man) oppressed. The pledge of allegiance to him was revoked. The respect due to him was ignored. The covenant to him was not fulfilled nor the responsibility of the agreement made with him honoured. (He died) a martyr as his father and brother, peace be on them, had done before him.

The Account of the Martyrdom of al-Ḥusayn

(This is) a selection of the reports which give the reason for his (putting forward) his call (to follow him), and (which tell) of the pledge of allegiance which the people gave to strive (for him), with a brief account of his affair in setting out and (of) his death.

[What al-Kalbī, al-Madā'inī and other historians (*aṣḥāb al-sīra*) have reported:][2] When al-Ḥasan, peace be on him, died, the Shī'a in Iraq began to make plans. They wrote to al-Ḥusayn, peace be on him, about removing Mu'āwiya and giving the pledge of allegiance to him. However, he refused them and pointed out that there was an agreement and contract between himself and Mu'āwiya which he could not break until the period (of the contract) came to an end.

2 In fact the account follows Ibn al-Kalbī's account as reported by al-Ṭabarī, II, 216-381. Al-Ṭabarī uses three versions, but al-Mufīd follows the version of Ibn al-Kalbī, only once adopting another reading. In places al-Kalbī's version is summarised by al-Mufīd, parts of it are omitted, but by and large al-Mufīd faithfully follows that version.

However, when Mu'āwiya died, he would examine that (matter).[3]

When Mu'āwiya did die - and that was halfway through the month of Rajab in the year 60 A.H. (680) - Yazīd wrote to al-Walīd b. 'Utba b. Abī Sufyān, who was in Medina (acting) on behalf of Mu'āwiya, instructing him to get al-Ḥusayn, peace be on him, to pledge allegiance to him and to allow him no delay in (doing) that. Therefore, al-Walīd sent in the night to al-Ḥusayn, peace be on him, and summoned him (to attend). Al-Ḥusayn, peace be on him, was aware of what he wanted and so he called a group of his retainers (*mawāli*) and ordered them to carry arms.

"Al-Walīd has summoned me (to come to him) at this time (of night)," he told them. "I cannot be sure that he might not burden me with a matter I may be unwilling to respond to, he is an unpredictable man, so remain with me. When I go to him, sit at the door. If you hear my voice raised, come in to prevent him from (doing anything to) me."

Al-Ḥusayn, peace be on him, went to al-Walīd, and Marwān b. al-Ḥakam was with him. Al-Walīd gave him news of the death Mu'āwiya and al-Ḥusayn, peace be on him, replied with the formula: "*We belong to Allāh and to Him we will return.*" Then (al-Walīd) read out Yazīd's letter and his order to get the pledge of allegiance from him.

"I do not see that my pledge of allegiance to Yazīd in private would be sufficient," al-Ḥusayn, peace be on him, said. "(Wouldn't you prefer me) to give it in public so that the people are aware?"
"Indeed," agreed al-Walīd.

"So see what you think about that in the morning," suggested al-Ḥusayn, peace be on him.
"Go, then, in the name of Allāh but come to us when the people gather," said al-Walīd

"By Allāh," interrupted Marwān, "if al-Ḥusayn leaves you now without giving the pledge of allegiance, you will never have the same power over him until there is a great number of slain men between you and him. Imprison the man and don't let him leave you until he has paid homage (to Yazīd), or you have executed him."
At that, al-Ḥusayn jumped up and said: "O son of foreign woman, would you

3 This explanation is, rather surprisingly, not included in al-Ṭabarī's version, for such letters cf. al-Balādhurī, *Ansāb al-Ashrāf*, II, 151-2

or he kill me? By Allāh, you are a liar." With that he went out and walked away accompanied by his retainers until he reached his house.

"You disobeyed me," Marwān told al-Walīd. "No, by Allāh, he will never give you the same opportunity over his life."
"Then blame someone other than yourself, Marwān." replied al-Walīd. "Indeed, You had chosen for me something which would have involved the destrucion of my own faith. By Allāh, I would not want all the worldly wealth and dominion which the sun rises and sets over, (if it involved) killing al-Ḥusayn. Glory be to Allāh, should I kill al-Ḥusayn because he said 'I will not swear allegiance'? By Allāh, I do not think that on the Day of Resurrection a man who is (responsible) for the blood of al-Ḥusayn (will weigh) little in the scales of Allāh."

"If this is your opinion, then you have acted correctly in what you did," said Marwān, without commending him for his view.

Al-Ḥusayn, peace be on him, spent that night at his house. It was the night of Saturday (i.e. Friday night) when there were three days left in the month of Rajab, in the year of 680. Al-Walīd b. 'Utba was occupied with sending to Ibn al-Zubayr about the pledge of allegiance to Yazīd, and with his refusal (to come) to them. Ibn al-Zubayr left Medina at night heading for Mecca. In the morning al-Walīd sent men after him - he sent (a party of) eighty horsemen under the command of a retainer (*mawlā*) of the Banū Umayya. They pursued him but did not catch up with him, so they returned.

Towards the end of Saturday he sent men to al-Ḥusayn, peace be on him, to bring him to pledge allegiance to al-Walīd on behalf of Yazīd b. Mu'āwiya. Al-Ḥusayn, peace be on him, said to them: "Come in the morning. Then you will (have time to) consider (the situation) and so shall we."

They left him that night without insisting upon him (attending). He, peace be on him, left under (cover of the) night, - it was the night of Sunday (i.e. Saturday night) with two days left in the month of Rajab - and he headed towards Mecca accompanied by his sons, his brother's (al-Ḥasan's) sons and his brothers. There was most of the House except for Muḥammad b. al-Ḥanafiyya, may Allāh have mercy on him.

When the latter had heard of his decision to leave Medina he did not know where he was intending to go. He said: "My brother, you are the most lovable of people to me and the dearest of them to me. I could not give advice to any creature except to you while you are more entitled to it. Avoid giving your pledge of allegiance to Yazīd b. Mu'āwiya and (avoid) the towns while you can. Then send your messengers to the people and summon them to (follow) you. If the people pledge allegiance to you, I praise Allāh; if the people agree upon someone other than you, Allāh will not make your religion nor your reason deficient on that account, nor will He remove your manliness and outstanding merit because of it. Yet I am afraid that you will enter one of these towns and the people will differ with each other: a group will be for you and another against you. They will fight and you will be a target for the first of their spears. Then, the best of all this community, in person, in father and in mother would be the one in it, whose blood was most terribly exposed and whose family most humiliated,"

"Where should I go, brother?" asked al-Ḥusayn, peace be on him.
"(Go and) stay at Mecca," he answered, "if that base is secure for you, it will be a means for (gaining power). However, if it becomes dangerous for you, then you can take to the deserts and the mountain peaks, and move from place to place so that you may see how the people's attitude to the affair develops. Your best judgement will be made when you are facing matters directly."

"Brother," replied (al-Ḥusayn), "you have given advice and shown your concern. I hope that your judgement is correct and successful."

Al-Ḥusayn, peace be on him, set of for Mecca reciting: *Then he left it out of fear while he kept on the lookout. He said: My Lord, save me from the unjust people* (XXVIII 21). He kept to the high road and members of his House suggested: "If you had avoided the high road, like Ibn al-Zubayr did, the search (party) could not follow you."
"No, by Allāh," he replied, "I will not leave it until Allāh judges what He will judge."

When al-Ḥusayn, peace be on him, entered Mecca, his entry occurred on the night of Friday (i.e. Thursday), 3rd (of the month) of Sha'bān. As he entered, he recited: *And when he set our towards Madyan, he said: Perhaps my Lord will guide me in the right pat*h (XXVIII 22).

Then he stayed there and its inhabitants began to visit him frequently, as did those who had to come to make the lesser pilgrimage and (other) people from far and wide. Ibn al-Zubayr had settled himself there, near the Ka'ba, where he used to stand in prayer and perform the circumambulation (*ṭawāf*). He came to visit him, peace be on him, with the (others) who came to visit him. He used to come to him at intervals of two consecutive days, and sometimes between the two-day intervals. He (al-Ḥusayn) was the most troublesome of Allāh's creatures to Ibn al-Zubayr, who realised that the people of Ḥijāz would not pledge allegiance to him as long as al-Ḥusayn, peace be on him, was in the land. He was more capable of (commanding) the people's obedience than him, and was more respected.

*****

The Kūfans learnt of the death of Mu'āwiya, may the pit of Hell be for him, and spread rumours about Yazīd. They (also) came to know of the news of the refusal of al-Ḥusayn, peace be on him, to give (Yazīd) the pledge of allegiance, (as well as) what the attitude of Ibn al-Zubayr had been, and (how) both of them had left for Mecca. The Shī'a in Kūfa gathered in the house of Sulaymān b. Ṣurad al-Khuzā'ī. (There) they discussed the death of Mu'āwiya, and praised and glorified Allāh (for that).

"Mu'āwiya is dead." announced Sulaymān b. Ṣurad. "Al-Ḥusayn has withheld giving his pledge of allegiance to the people (i.e. the Umayyads) and has gone to Mecca. You are his Shī'a and the Shī'a of his father. If you know (in your hearts) that you will be his helpers and fighters against his enemy, and that our lives will be given on behalf of him, then write to him and tell him of that. But if you fear failure and weakness, do not tempt the man (to risk) his own life."

"No," they declared, "indeed we will fight his enemy and our lives will be given on behalf of him."

"Then write to him," he told them. They wrote to him:

> In the Name of Allāh, the Merciful, the Compassionate,
> To al-Ḥusayn b. 'Alī, peace be on them,
>
> From Sulaymān b. Ṣurad, al-Musayyib b. Najaba, Rifā'a b. Shaddād al-Bajalī, Habīb b. Muẓāhir, and the believers and Muslims of his Shī'a among the Kūfans.
>
> Greetings, we praise Allāh before you, other than Whom there is no deity. Praise be to Allāh Who has broken your enemy, the obstinate tyrant who had leapt upon this community, stripped it of its authority, plundered its *fay'* (booty for distribution) and seized control of it without its consent. Then he had killed the choice members of it and had preserved the wicked members of it. He had made the property of Allāh a state (divided) among its tyrants and wealthy. He was destroyed as Thamūd were destroyed. (Now) there is no Imam over us. Therefore come; through you, may your Allāh unite us under truth. Al-Nu'mān b. Bashīr is in the governor's palace and we do not gather with him for the Friday (service). Nor do we

accompany him (out of the mosque) for the festival service. If we learn that you will come to us, we will drive him away until we pursue him to Syria, if Allāh, the Exalted, wills.

They despatched the letter with ʻAbd Allāh b. Musmaʻ[4] al-Hamdānī and ʻAbd Allāh b. Wālin. They ordered them to go quickly. They hurried off and came to al-Ḥusayn, peace be on him, at Mecca on the 10th of the month of Ramaḍān. Two days after sending them with the letter, they sent Qays b. Mushir al-Ṣaydāwī and ʻAbd Allāh and ʻAbd al-Raḥmān - the two sons of Shaddad al-Arḥabī[5] - and ʻUmāra b. ʻAbd Allāh al-Salūlī[6] to al-Ḥusayn, peace be on him. With them they took about one hundred and fifty letters,[7] (some written) by one man individually, (others by groups) of two and four. They (the Kūfans) delayed a further two days and then sent Ḥāni' b. Ḥāni' al-Sabiʻī and Saʻīd b. ʻAbd Allāh al-Ḥanafī (with another letter in which) they had written:

In the Name of Allāh, the Merciful, the Compassionate,
To al-Ḥusayn b. ʻAlī, peace be on them,
From the believers and Muslims of his Shīʻa. Make haste. The people are waiting for you. They have no opinion (of any man) except you. Therefore, speed, speed! And then again speed, speed!
Greetings.

Shabath b. Ribʻī, Ḥajjār b. Abjar, Yazīd b. al-Ḥārith b. Ruwaym, ʻUrwa b. Qays,[8] ʻAmr b. al-Ḥajjāj al-Zubaydī and Muḥammad b. ʻAmr al-Taymī[9] wrote (a further letter which said):

The dates have grown green; the fruit has ripened. Therefore if you want to, come to an army which has been gathered for you.
Greetings.

When all the messengers gathered together with him, he read the letters and asked the messengers about the people. (Then) he wrote (an answer and sent it) with Ḥāni' b. Ḥāni' al-Sabiʻī and Saʻīd b. ʻAbd Allāh al-Ḥanafī, who were the last two messengers.

In the name of Allāh, the Merciful, the Compassionate,

From al-Ḥusayn b ʻAlī,
To the leaders of the believers and the Muslims.

---

4 Sabuʻ in al-Ṭabarī, II, 234.
5 The two sons are one in al-Ṭabarī, II, 234.
6 ʻUbayd in al-Ṭabarī, II, 234.
7 Thirty-five in al-Ṭabarī, II, 234.
8 ʻAzra in al-Ṭabarī, II, 234.
9 Muḥammad b. ʻUmayr al-Tamīmī in al-Ṭabarī, II, 234.

Hāni' and Sa'īd have brought me your letters; they are the last two of your messengers who have come to me. I have understood everything which you have described and mentioned. The (main) statement of your great men is: "There is no Imam over us. Therefore come; through you, may Allāh unite us under truth and guidance." I am sending you my brother, Muslim b. 'Aqīl, who is my cousin and my trustworthy (representative) from my House. If he writes to me that the opinion of your leaders and of the men of wisdom and merit among you is united in the same way as the messengers who have come to me have described and as I have read in your letters, I will come to you speedily, Allāh willing. For by my life, what is the Imam except one who judges by the Book, one who upholds justice, one who professes the religion of truth, and one who dedicates himself to the essence of Allāh.

Greetings.

Al-Ḥusayn, peace be upon him, summoned Muslim b. 'Aqīl and despatched him with Qays b. Mushir al-Ṣaydāwī and 'Umāra b. 'Abd Allāh al-Salūlī, and 'Abd Allāh and 'Abd al-Raḥmān, the sons of Shaddād al-Arḥabī. He enjoined him to be pious before Allāh and to conceal his affair, and to act in a kindly way. If he saw that the people were united and had committed themselves to an agreement, he should speedily inform him of that.

Muslim, the mercy of Allāh be on him, departed until he came to Medina. There he prayed in the Mosque of the Apostle of Allāh, may Allāh bless Him and His Family, and said farewell to the dearest members of his family. Then he hired two guides. These two set out with him, but they missed the way and got lost. Both were struck by severe thirst and were unable to continue the Journey. They indicated the path to him after it again appeared clear to them. Muslim carried on along the path and the two guides died of thirst. Muslim b. 'Aqīl, the mercy of Allāh be on them both, wrote (a letter) from the place known as al-Maḍīq (and sent it) with Qays b. Mushir:

I set out from Medina with two guides and they missed the way and got lost. Both were overcome by thirst and soon died. But we kept going until we came to water. we were only saved at the last moment of our lives. That water is in a place called al-Maḍīq in a low valley. I have taken this as a bad omen for my mission. If you consider it so, you could relieve me and send another in my place.

Greetings.

Al-Ḥusayn, peace be upon him, wrote (back):

I am afraid that your urging me in the letter to relieve you from the task

which I sent you on is only cowardice. Therefore go on with your task which I gave you.
Greetings.

Muslim read the letter, he said: "It is not for myself that I am afraid." So he continued (once more) until he came to a well belonging to (the tribe of) Ṭayyi'. He stayed there (the night) then as he rode off (he saw) a man hunting. He saw him shoot a fawn as it came into his sight, and kill it. Muslim said: "(Thus), will we kill our enemies, Allāh Willing."

He went on until he entered Kūfa. There he stayed in the house of al-Mukhtār b. Abī 'Ubayda. which is called today the house of Muslim b. al-Musayyib. The Shī'a began to come regularly to (see) him . Whenever a group of them gathered together with him, he would read the letter of al-Ḥusayn, peace be upon him, and they would weep. The people pledged allegiance to him (on behalf of al-Ḥusayn) to the extent that eighteen thousand men made such a pledge to him. Therefore Muslim wrote to al-Ḥusayn, peace be upon him, informing him of the pledge of allegiance to him of the eighteen thousand and urging him to come.

The Shī'a began to visit Muslim b. 'Aqīl so frequently that his place (of residence) became well-known. Al-Nu'mān b. Bashīr, who had been Mu'āwiya's governor of Kūfa and had been confirmed in office by Yazīd, knew of his whereabouts. He went up on the pulpit and after praising Allāh said: "Servants of Allāh, fear Allāh and do not rush into rebellion and discord. For in that men will be destroyed, blood will be shed, and property will be plundered. I do not combat anyone who does not combat me, nor do I disturb those of you who remain quiet. I do not oppose you, nor do I apprehend (you merely) on grounds of suspicion, accusation or hearsay. However, if you turn your faces away from me, violate your pledge of allegiance and oppose your Imam, by Allāh, other than Whom there is no deity, I will strike you with my sword as long as its hilt remains in my hand, even though I do not have any of you to help me. Yet I hope that those among you who know the truth are more numerous than those whom falsehood will destroy."

'Abd Allāh b. Muslim b. Rabī'a[10] al-Ḥaḍramī, an ally of the Banū Umayya stood before him and said: "O governor, what you see can only be adequately dealt with by violence; for the view which you hold about what (should be done) between you and your enemy is that of the weak,"
"I would prefer to be one of the weak (while remaining) in obedience to Allāh than to be one of the mighty (while at the same time being) in rebellion against

10 Ibn Sa'īd in al-Ṭabarī, II, 238.

Allāh," answered al-Nu'mān. Then he went down (from the pulpit).

'Abd Allāh b. Muslim went out and wrote the (following) letter to Yazīd b. Mu'āwiya:

> Muslim b. 'Aqīl has come to Kūfa and Shī'a have pledged allegiance to him on behalf of al-Ḥusayn b. 'Alī b. Abī Ṭālib, peace be on them. If you have any need for Kūfa, then send it a strong man, who will carry out your orders and act in the same way as you would against your enemy. Al-Nu'mān b. Bashīr is a weak man, or he is acting like a weak man.

'Umāra b. 'Uqba wrote to him in a similar vein, as did 'Umar b. Sa'd b. Abī Waqqāṣ. When the letters reached Yazīd, he summoned Sarjūn, a retainer (*mawlā*) of Mu'āwiya and asked (him): "What is your view (of the fact) that Ḥusayn has sent Muslim b. 'Aqīl to Kūfa to receive pledges of homage on his behalf? I have (also) learnt that Nu'mān is weak, and had other bad reports of him. Who do you think that I should appoint as governor of Kūfa?"

Now Yazīd was angry with 'Ubayd Allāh b. Ziyād so Sarjūn answered him, "Do you think if Mu'āwiya was alive and advising you, that you would take his advice?"
"Yes," he answered.

Sarjūn produced a (letter of) appointment for 'Ubayd Allāh b. Ziyād (as governor) of Kūfa and said: "This is the advice of Mu'āwiya, which he ordered before he died. So join the two cities of Baṣra and Kūfa (under the authority) of 'Ubayd Allāh."

"I'll do that," replied Yazīd. "I'll send the letter of authority (which my father wrote) for 'Ubayd Allāh b. Ziyād to him."

After this he summoned Muslim b. 'Amr al-Bāhilī and he sent him to 'Ubayd Allāh with the following (letter):

> My Shī'a among the people of Kūfa have informed me that Ibn 'Aqīl is there gathering units in order to spread rebellion among the Muslims. Therefore, when you read this letter of mine, go to Kūfa and search for Ibn 'Aqīl as if you were looking for a bead until you find him. Then bind him (in chains), kill him or expel him.
> Greetings.

In this way he gave him authority over Kūfa. Muslim b. 'Amr went to 'Ubayd Allāh at Baṣra and brought him the authorisation and the letter. 'Ubayd Allāh ordered that preparations should be made immediately and that the departure for Kūfa would take place on the next day. He himself left Baṣra after he had made his brother, 'Uthman, his deputy. He took with him Muslim b. 'Amr, Sharīk b. al-A'war al-Ḥārithi, together with his entourage and household.

When he reached Kūfa, he was wearing a black turban and he was veiled. News of al-Ḥusayn's departure had reached the people and they were expecting his arrival. When they saw 'Ubayd Allāh, they thought that he was al-Ḥusayn. He (i.e. 'Ubayd Allāh) did not pass a group of people without them greeting him. They were saying: "Welcome, son of the Apostle of Allāh, your arrival is a happy (event)."

He saw in their welcoming of al-Ḥusayn something which (greatly) troubled him. Muslim b. 'Amr said, when their number had become so great (that) they were delaying them: "This is the governor 'Ubayd Allāh b. Ziyād."

He went on so that he was approaching the (governor's) palace at night. With him was (still) a great crowd who had gathered round him and who did not doubt that he was al-Ḥusayn. Al-Nu'mān b. Bashīr had (the palace) bolted against him and against his entourage. One of those with him called on him to open the door to them. But al-Nu'mān, still thinking that be was al-Ḥusayn, went up to the balcony and called down: "I invoke Allāh before you, unless you withdraw (from me), by Allāh, I will not hand over my office (*amana*) to you but I have no wish to fight you."

(Ibn Ziyād) did not answer him. But he went closer while al-Nu'mān was hanging over the balcony of the palace. Then he began to say to him: "Open, you have not opened yet and you have already had a long night (in which you have slept instead of governing)."[11]

A man behind him heard this and withdrew to the people from Kūfa who had followed (Ibn Ziyād) (believing) him to be al-Ḥusayn. He said: "O people, it is Ibn Murjāna,[12] by Him other than Whom there is no deity." Al-Nu'mān opened the door for him and he entered. They slammed the door in the faces of the people and they dispersed.

In the morning the call was made among the people: "*Al-ṣalāt jāmi'a* (the prayer

11 Al-Mufīd omits Ibn al-Kalbī's account of 'Ubayd Allāh's entry into Kūfa as given by al-Ṭabarī, II, 242, and gives 'Umar b. Shabba's cf. al-Ṭabarī, II, 243. This suggests that al-Mufīd got his version of Ibn al-Kalbī from al-Ṭabarī.

12 Reference to Ibn Ziyād by his mother's name.

is a general prayer which all should gather for)." The people gathered and he went out to them. He praised and glorified Allāh and said. "The Commander of the faithful (Yazīd) has appointed me to be in charge of your town and your frontier-station and the distribution of your booty (*fay'*). He has ordered me to give justice to the oppressed among you, to be generous to those of you who are deprived, and to treat the obedient among you with generosity like a good father, but to use the whip and the sword against those who abandon my commands and oppose my appointment. Let each man protect himself. True belief (*sidq*) should declare itself on your behalf, not the threat of punishment (*wa'īd*)."

Then he went down, he took the group leaders (*'arīfs*) and (some of) the people forcibly and he said: "Write to me about the strangers, those among you who supported the Commander of the Faithful (i.e. 'Alī b. Abī Ṭālib), those among you who support the Ḥarūriyya (i.e. Khārijites), and the trouble-makers whose concern is discord and turmoil. Whosoever of you makes these lists for us will be free from harm. But those of you who do not write anyone, will have to guarantee that there is no opponent in his group (*'irāfa*) who will oppose us, and no wrongdoer who will try to wrong us. Anyone who does not do so, will be denied protection and his blood and his property will be permitted to us. Any group leader (*'arīf*) in whose group is found anyone with partisanship for the Commander of the Faithful, who has not been reported to us, will be crucified at the door of his house, and I will abolish the pay (*'aṭā'*) of that group (*'irāfa*)."

When Muslim b. 'Aqīl heard of the coming of 'Ubayd Allāh to Kūfa, of the speech he had made and his treatment of the *'arīfs* and (other) people, he left the house of al-Mukhtār and went to the house of Hāni' b. 'Urwa and went in (to stay) there. The Shī'a began to visit Hāni's house secretly to keep it hidden from 'Ubayd Allāh and they enjoined that it should be kept secret.

Ibn Ziyād summoned a retainer (*mawlā*) of his called Ma'qil. "Take three thousand dirhams," he told him, "and look for Muslim b. 'Aqīl and search out his followers. If you get hold of one or a group of them, give them these three thousand dirhams. Tell them to use it to help in the war against your enemy. Let them know that you are one of them. For if you give it to them, they will be sure of you and have confidence in you, and they will not keep any of their information from you. So go (looking) for them and continue until you find where Muslim b. 'Aqīl is staying and you have met him."

He did that. He came (to a place where) he sat near Muslim b. 'Awsaja al-Asadī in the great mosque. The latter was praying, and he (Ma'qil) heard some people saying that this (was one of those who) had pledged allegiance to al-Ḥusayn. He went up and sat right next to him until he had finished praying.

“O servant of Allāh,” he said, “I am a Syrian whom Allāh has blessed with love for the House and love for those who love them.”

He pretended to weep (in front of) him. Then he continued: “I have three thousand dirhams with which I want to meet a man from them (the House) whom I have learnt has come to Kūfa to receive pledges of allegiance on behalf of the son of the daughter of the Apostle of Allāh, may Allāh bless Him and His Family. I have been wanting to meet him but I have not found anyone who will direct me to him and I don’t know the place (where he is staying). While I was sitting (here), I heard a group of the faithful saying that this is a man (i.e. Muslim b. ‘Awsaja) who is acquainted with this House. Therefore I have come to you so that you may take this money from me and introduce me to your leader (*ṣāḥib*); for I am one of your brethren and someone you can trust. If you wish, you may receive my pledge of allegiance to him before my meeting him.”

“I thank Allāh for you meeting me,” replied (Muslim) b. ‘Awsaja, “and it gives me great joy to get (you) what you desire, and that Allāh should help the House of His Prophet, peace be on them, through you. Yet the people’s knowledge of my (connection) with this affair before it is finished troubles me, because of (my) fear of this tyrant and his severity.”

“It would be better (if) you took the pledge of allegiance from me (now),” Ma‘qil told him. So he took his pledge of allegiance and testaments heavily supported by oaths that he would be sincere and keep the matter concealed. He (Ma‘qil) gave him whatever would make him content in that way.

“Come to visit me at my house for (a few) days,” said (Muslim b. ‘Awsaja). “for I will seek permission for you (to visit) your master.”

He began to go to visit him frequently with the people (i.e. the other members of the Shī‘a) and sought permission for him (to visit). Permission was given and Muslim b. ‘Aqīl received (Ma‘qil’s) pledge of allegiance. He told Abū Thumāma al-Ṣā’idī to take the money from him. The latter was the one who collected money from them and what could be used to help each other, and he used to buy their arms. He was a perceptive man and one of the knights (*fāris*) of the Arabs and one of the notables of the Shī‘a.

That man (i.e. Ma‘qil) began to visit them regularly. He was the first to enter and the last to leave, in order to become acquainted with (everything of) their affairs which Ibn Ziyād wanted. He used to keep him informed about that at regular intervals.

Hanī' b. 'Urwa began to fear for himself and he stopped attending Ibn Ziyād's assembly (*majlis*). He pretended to be sick. Ibn Ziyād asked those who did attend, "Why is it I don't see Hanī'?"
"He is sick." they replied.

"If I had been informed of his illness, I would have paid him a sick visit," said Ibn Ziyād. Then he summoned Muḥammad b. al-Ash'ath, Asmā' b. Khārija and 'Amr b. al-Ḥajjāj al-Zubaydī. Ruwayḥa,[13] daughter of 'Amr was married to Hānī' b. 'Urwa; she was the mother of Yaḥyā b. Hānī'.
"What prevents Hānī' from coming to visit us?" he asked them.
"We don't know," they replied, "but it is said that he is sick"

"I have learnt," replied (Ibn Ziyād), "that he is better and that he sits at the door of his house. Go and tell him that he should not abandon his duty towards us. For I do not like one of the Arab nobles like him to ill-treat me,"

They went until they stood before his (house) in the evening. He was sitting at his door.
"What is stopping you from seeing the governor?" they asked. "For he has mentioned you and said that if he had been told you were ill, he would have paid you a sick-visit."
"An illness has stopped me," he answered.

"He has been informed." they said. "that you sit at the door of your house every evening. He finds you tardy and tardiness and churlish behaviour are things which the authorities will not tolerate. We adjure you to ride with us."

He called for his clothes and got dressed. Then he called for a mule and rode (with them). When he got near the palace, he began to feel some apprehension. He said to Ḥassān b. Asmā' b. Khārija,
"Nephew, by Allāh, I fear this man. What do you think?"'
"Uncle, by Allāh, I do not fear anything for you. Why do you invent a reason (for blame) against yourself?" he answered, for Ḥassān did not know why 'Ubayd Allāh had sent for him. (So) Hānī' went on until he came to 'Ubayd Allāh b. Ziyād. With him was a group (of people).

When he looked up, 'Ubayd Allāh said (to himself): "The fool's legs have

13 Rua in al-Ṭabarī, II, 250.

brought him to you." Then, when Hānī' had drawn near Ibn Ziyād, who had the *qāḍī* Shurayḥ, with him, Ibn Ziyād turned towards him and recited:

> I want is friendship but he wants my death.
> The one who makes excuses to you is one of your own bosom friends from the tribe of Murād.[14]

He was referring to his earlier kindness and gentleness to him (Hānī').
"What is that, governor?" asked Hānī'.
"Yes, Hānī', what are these matters which you have been plotting in your house against the Commander of the faithful and the general community of the Muslims?" asked Ibn Ziyād. "You have brought Muslim b. 'Aqīl and taken him into your house. You have gathered arms and men for him in houses around you. You thought that was hidden from me."

"I have not done that and Muslim is not with me," he replied.
"Oh yes (you have)," was the answer.

After the argument between them had gone on for some time and Hānī' persisted in contradicting and denying (the accusations), Ibn Ziyād summoned that spy, Ma'qil. He came and stood before him.
"Do you know this man?" (Ibn Ziyād) asked him.
"Yes," he replied.

At that (moment) Hānī' realised that he had been a spy against them and had brought (Ibn Ziyād) all their information. For a moment he was bewildered, and then his spirit returned to him.
"Listen to me," he said. "and believe what I say. I swear by Allāh that I do not lie. By Allāh, I did not summon him to my house. I did not know anything about his business until he came to me asking to stay with me. I was too ashamed to refuse him. As a result of that, the duty of giving (him) protection fell upon me. Therefore I gave him lodging and refuge. Then his affair developed as you have been informed. If you wish, I will give you strongly sworn testaments that I will not do you any harm and danger. And I will come to you and put my hand in your hand. If you wish, I will give you a guarantee which will be in your hand until I return to you. Then I will go to him and order him to leave my house for wherever in the land he wants to go. Then he will leave his right of protection."

"You will never leave me unless you bring him," answered Ibn Ziyād.
"No, by Allāh. I will not bring him to you," (the other) declared.

---

14 This verse is also supposed to have been recited by 'Alī concerning Ibn Muljam.

After the argument between them had gone on for some time, Muslim b. ʻAmr al-Bāhilī rose (to speak). There was no other Syrian or Baṣran in Kūfa except him.

"May Allāh make you prosper, governor," he interjected. "(please) leave me with him (for a time) so that I can speak to him." He arose and took him (Hānī') aside from Ibn Ziyād. They were (standing) where he could see them and when they raised their voices, he could hear what they were saying.

"I adjure you before Allāh, Hānī'," said Muslim, "you are killing yourself and bringing tribulation on your clan. By Allāh, I hold you too precious to be killed. This man is the cousin of (your) tribe so they will not fight against him, nor harm him. Therefore give him (i.e. Muslim b. ʻAqīl) to them (the authorities). There will be no shame and failure for you by that for you would only be handing him over to the authorities."

"By Allāh, indeed there would be shame and disgrace for me," answered Hānī', "were I to hand over one who has come under my protection and is my guest, while I am still alive and sound. I can hear; I see well; I have a strong arm and many helpers. By Allāh, if I was the only one without any helper, I would not hand him over until I had died on his behalf."

He began to shout at him saying: "By Allāh, I will never hand him over to him."

Ibn Ziyād heard that. "Bring him to me," he said. They brought him. "Either bring him to me or I will have your head cut off," demanded Ibn Ziyād.
"Then there will be much flashing (of swords) around your house," replied Hānī', thinking that his clan would prevent him (from being killed).

"Come near me," demanded (Ibn Ziyād). He came nearer and Ibn Ziyād struck his face with his cane and went on beating at his nose, forehead and cheeks so that he broke his nose and the blood flowed from it on to his face and beard and the flesh of his forehead and cheeks was sprinkled over his beard. Eventually the cane broke. Hānī' stretched out his hand towards the hill of the sword of one of the armed attendants but the man pulled it away and prevented him.

"You have been behaving like one of the Ḥarūrī (i.e. Khārijites) all day long!" yelled Ibn Ziyād, "so your blood is permitted to us. Take him away!"

They took him and threw him into one of the rooms in the building. They locked the doors on him. He had told them to put guards on him and that (also) was done. However Ḥassān b. Asmā' arose and said: "Are (we) messengers of treachery now? For you told us to bring the man to you. Yet when we brought him to you, you smashed his nose and face, and his blood flowed on his beard. Then you claimed that you would kill him."

"You will be for it here (and now)," cried 'Ubayd Allāh and he ordered him to be struck, shaken and pushed aside.
"We are satisfied with the governor's attitude on our behalf and against (those of) us (who are wrong): the governor is only punishing (those who are wrong)," declared Muḥammad b. al-Ash'ath.

However when it was reported to 'Amr b al-Ḥajjāj and he learnt that Hānī' had been killed, he advanced with Madhḥij and surrounded the palace. He had a great crowd with him.
"I am 'Amr b. al-Ḥajjāj" he called out "and these are the knights of Madhḥij, and their leading men. We have not broken away from obedience, nor have we separated from the community."

It had been reported to them that their colleague had been killed and they regarded that as a great crime. 'Ubayd Allāh was told that Madhḥij were at the gate. He told the *qāḍī* Shurayḥ: "Go in to their colleague, look at him and then go out and inform them that he is still alive and has not been killed."

Shurayḥ went in and looked at him. When Hānī' saw Shurayḥ he said, with blood flowing down his beard: "Oh Allāh! Oh you Muslims! Has my clan been destroyed? Where are the people of religion? Where are the people of the town?" When he heard the tumult at the door of the palace he said: "I think those are the voices of Madhḥij and my group of the Muslims. If ten of them got in, they would be able to rescue me."

After Shurayḥ had listened to what he had to say, he went out to them and told them: "When the governor learnt about your attitude and your statements concerning your colleague, he ordered me to go and see him. I went and I saw him. Then he ordered me to meet you and inform you that he is still alive and that the report that he had been killed was false."

"Praise be to Allāh since he has not been killed," answered 'Amr b. al-Ḥajjāj and his colleagues. Then they went away,

'Ubayd Allāh b. Ziyād went out and went up on the pulpit. (He had brought) with him the nobles of the people, his bodyguard (*shuraṭ*) and his entourage. He said "O people, seek refuge in obedience to Allāh and your Imams. Do not cause division, for you will be destroyed, humiliated, killed or harshly treated and deprived. Your brother is he who speaks the truth to you. He who warns is excused."

After he had finished, he was about to go down but had not gone from the pulpit, when the look-outs at the date-sellers' gate of the mosque rushed in yelling; "Muslim b. 'Aqīl has come!"

'Ubayd Allāh quickly went into the palace and locked the gates.

['Abd Allāh b. Ḥāzim reported:]
By Allāh, I was Ibn 'Aqīl's messenger at the palace to see what was done to Hānī'. When he was beaten and imprisoned I mounted my horse and was the first to enter the house to bring information of him to Muslim b. 'Aqīl. There the women of Murād had gathered and they were crying out; "O tears of grief for him! O bereavement of him!"

I went in to see Muslim and gave him the news of him (Hānī'). He ordered me to summon his supporters. The houses around him were full of them; there were four thousand men there. He told his messengers to cry out: "O victorious, kill!" so I cried out; "O victorious, kill". Then the Kūfans gathered and assembled before him. Muslim, may Allāh have mercy on him, appointed leaders over the quarters, over the tribes of Kinda, Madhḥij, Tamīm, Asad, Muḍar and Hamdān. The people had answered the call and gathered, except for a few who had delayed so that the mosque and the market place were full of people. They were full of enthusiasm until the evening. 'Ubayd Allāh's situation was grim. All his energy was concentrated on holding the door, for he only had thirty members of his bodyguard with him in the palace, twenty nobles of the people, and his family and entourage. The nobles who had not been with him began to come to him through the door which adjoined the building of the Romans. Then those of the nobles who were with Ibn Ziyād began to look down on them (the people outside). (These) were looking at them, while they hurled stones at them and cursed them and abused 'Ubayd Allāh and his father. Ibn Ziyād summoned Kathīr b. Shihāb and ordered him to go out among those of Madhḥij who obeyed him and to go round Kūfa and make the people desert Ibn 'Aqīl; he should make them afraid of (the possibility of) war and threaten them with the punishment of the authorities. Then he ordered Muḥammad b. al-Ash'ath to go out among those of Kinda and Ḥaḍramawt who obeyed him; he should raise a standard which would guarantee security to those people who came to him. He gave similar instructions to al-Qa'qā' al-Dhuhlī, Shabath b. Rib'ī al-Tamīmī, Ḥajjār b. Abjar al-'Ijlī and Shamīr b. Dhī al-Jawshan al-'Āmirī. He kept the rest of the nobles of the people with him, not wishing to be without them because of the small number of people who were with him. Kathīr b. Shihāb went out (and began) making the people desert Muslim. Muḥammad b. al-Ash'ath went out until he reached the houses of the Banū 'Umāra. Ibn 'Aqīl sent 'Abd al-Raḥmān b. Shurayḥ al-Shibāmī to Muḥammad b. al-Ash'ath from the mosque. When Muḥammad b. al-Ash'ath saw the great number of those who had come to him (Muslim), he lingered where he was (i.e. he did not carry out Ibn Ziyād's instructions). Then he - Muḥammad b. al-Ash'ath - Kathīr b. Shihāb, al-Qa'qā' al-Dhuhlī and Shabath b. Rib'ī began to make the people withdraw from their close adherence to Muslim for they made them afraid of the authorities so that a great number of their tribesmen and others gathered to them and they went to Ibn Ziyād through the house of the Romans. The tribesmen went in with them.

"May Allāh make the governor prosperous," said Kathīr b. Shihāb, "you have many of the nobles of the people with you, (as well as) your bodyguard, family and servants. Let us go out against them."

'Ubayd Allāh refused but he gave Shabath b. Rib'ī a standard and he sent him out. The people with Ibn 'Aqīl remained numerous until evening.

Their situation became strong. 'Ubayd Allāh sent for the nobles and he assembled them. They (went up to the roof to) look down on the people. They offered additional (money) and kind treatment to those who would obey and they terrified the disobedient with (threats of) dispossession and (dire) punishment. They told them that the army from Syria was coming against them. Kathīr b. Shihāb spoke until the sun was about to set. He said: "O people, stay with your families. Do not hurry into evil actions. Do not expose yourselves to death. These are the soldiers of the Commander of the faithful Yazīd, who are approaching. The governor has given Allāh a promise that if you persist in fighting him and do not go away by nightfall, he will deprive your children of their (right to a) state allotment of money (*'ata'*) and he will scatter your solders in Syrian campaigns. He will make the healthy among you responsible for the sick and those present responsible for those who are absent until none of those rebellious people will remain who has not tasted the evil consequences of what their hands have earned."

The (other) nobles spoke in a similar vein. After the people had heard what they had to say, they began to disperse. Women began to come to their sons and brothers (saying): "Go, the people will be enough (without) you". Men were going to their sons and brothers and saying: "Tomorrow the Syrians will come against you. What are you doing causing war and evil? Come away." Thus (a man) would be taken away or would leave. They continued to disperse so that by the time evening came and Muslim b. ‘Aqīl prayed the evening prayer, he had only thirty men with him in the mosque. When he saw that it was evening and he only had that group with him, he left the mosque and headed for the gates of Kinda. He reached the gates with only ten of them (left) with him. When he left the gate, there was no one with him to guide him. He looked around but could see no one to guide him along the road, to show him to his house and to give him personal support if an enemy appeared before him.

He wandered amid the lanes of Kūfa without knowing where he was going until he came to the houses or the Banū Jabala of Kinda. He went on until he came to a door (at which was) a woman called Ṭaw‘a. She had been a slave-wife (*umm walad*) of al-Ash‘ath b. Qays and he had freed her. She had, then, married Usayd al-Ḥaḍramī and had borne him (a son called) Bilāl. Bilāl had gone out with the people and his mother was standing al the door waiting for him.

Ibn ‘Aqīl greeted her and she returned the greeting.
“Servant of Allāh, give me water to drink,” he asked her. She gave him a drink and he sat down. She took the vessel inside and then came out again.

“Servant of Allāh, haven’t you had your drink?” she asked.
“Yes,” was the answer

“Then go to your people,” she said. But he was silent. She repeated it but he was still silent. A third time she said: “Glory be to Allāh, servant of Allāh. get up - may Allāh give you health - (and go) to your people. For it is not right for you to sit at my door and I will not permit you to do it.”

(At this) he got up and said: “Servant of Allāh, I have neither house nor clan in this town. Would you (show) me some generosity and kindness? Perhaps I will be able to repay it later on.”

“What is it, Servant of Allāh?” she asked.
“I am Muslim b ‘Aqīl” he replied. “These people have lied to me, incited me (to action) and then abandoned me.”

“You are Muslim,” she repeated.
“Yes,” he answered.

“Come in,” she said and he was taken into a room in her house but not the room she used. She spread out a carpet for him and offered him supper but he could not eat.

Soon her son returned. He saw her going frequently to and fro between the rooms and exclaimed: "By Allāh, the number of times which you have gone into and come out of that room this evening, makes me suspect that you have something important (there)."

"My young son, forget about this," she answered.
"By Allāh, tell me," he replied.

"Get on with your own business and don't ask me about anything," she retorted. However he persisted until she said: "My young son, don't tell any of the people anything about what I am going to tell you."

"'Indeed." he answered and she made him take an oath. When he swore (not to do) that, she told him. He went to bed without saying anything.

After the people had deserted Muslim b. 'Aqīl, a long time passed for Ibn Ziyād without him hearing the voices of the supporters of Ibn 'Aqīl as he had heard them before. He told his followers to look down at them and see whether they could see any of them. They looked down and did not see anyone. Then he told them to see whether they were in the shadow and were lying in ambush for them. They removed the (bamboo) roof covers of the mosque and began to lower the torches of fire in their hands, and to look. Sometimes the torches gave light for them and sometimes they did not give (as much) light for them as they would have wished. They let down the torches and sticks of cane tied with rope on which was fire. They were let down until they reached the ground. They did this in (place in which was) the deepest darkness, (as well as) those parts which were closer and those which were in between. They (also) did that in the darkness around the pulpit. When they saw that there was nothing, they informed Ibn Ziyād that the people had dispersed. Then he opened the gateway which (went) into the mosque. He came out and went up on the pulpit. His followers had come out with him. He told them to sit for a little while before the night prayer. He ordered 'Amr b. Nafī' to call out that there would be no guarantees of security for any man of the bodyguard, the *'arīfs*, the supporters and the fighters who prayed the night prayer (anywhere) except in thc mosque. Not an hour passed before the mosque was full of people. After ordering his caller (to call for prayer), he rose for the prayer. His guard rose behind him but he told them to guard him against anyone coming in (to try) to assassinate him. After praying with the people, he went up on the pulpit. When he had praised and glorified Allāh, he said. "Ibn 'Aqīl, stupid and ignorant (man as he is) has attempted the opposition and rebellion which you have seen. There will be no security from Allāh for a man in whose house we find him. Whoever brings him, will have the reward for his blood. Fear Allāh, you servants of Allāh, and keep to obedience and your pledge of allegiance. Do not do (anything which will be) against yourselves. Ḥusayn b. Numayr, your mother will lose you, if any of the gates of the lanes of Kūfa is open or this man gets away. And you do not bring him to me. I give you authority over the houses of the inhabitants of Kūfa. Send lookouts (to inspect) people on the roads. Tomorrow morning clear out (the people from) the houses and search them thoroughly so that you bring me this man."

Al-Ḥusayn b. Numayr was in charge of the bodyguard and was of the Banū Tamīm. After this Ibn Ziyād went back into the palace. He gave ʻAmr b. Ḥurayth his standard and put him in charge of the people. In the morning he held an assembly and gave permission for the people to come to him. Muḥammad b. al-Ashʻath approached.

"Welcome to one of those whose loyalty is above suspicion," he said to him and sat him by his side.

That same morning the son of that old woman went to ʻAbd al-Raḥmān b. Muḥammad b. al-Ashʻath and told him about Muslim b. ʻAqīl being with his mother. ʻAbd al-Raḥmān went to his father who was with Ibn Ziyād. He went to him and Ibn Ziyād learned his secret.
"Get up and bring him to me immediately," said Ibn Ziyād to (Muḥammad b. al-Ashʻath), poking a cane into his side. He sent (ʻAmr b.)[15] ʻUbayd Allāh b. ʻAbbās al-Sulamī with him, together with seventy men from the tribal group of Qays.

They went to the house where Muslim b. ʻAqīl was. When the latter heard the beating of horses' hooves and the voices of men, he knew that it was him whom they had come for. He went out against them with his sword (drawn) as they rushed blindly towards the house. He fell upon them and struck them with his sword so that he drove them away from the house. They repeated the attack, and Muslim counter-attacked in the same way. He and Bakr b. Ḥumrān al-Aḥmarī exchanged blows and Bakr struck Muslim's mouth, cutting his top lip and slicing down to the lower lip to knock out two of his teeth. Muslim struck him a terrible blow on the head and repeated it again, cutting a nerve along his shoulder with a blow which almost reached his stomach. When the people saw that, they (went up and) looked down on him (Muslim) from the tops of the houses, and began to hurl stones at him and to light canes of wood with fire which they threw from the top of the house. When he saw that, he went out against them into the lane with his sword unsheathed.

15 ʻAmr supplied from al-Ṭabarī, II, 263.

"You can have my guarantee of security," said Muḥammad b. al-Ash'ath. "don't kill yourself."

But he continued to fight against them saying:

> I swear I will only be killed as a free man, although I see death as something horrible,
>
> Or it makes the cold a bitter heat and deflects the ray of the sun (for ever).
>
> Every man one day will meet an evil, I fear that I will be cheated and deluded.

"You will not be cheated, deluded or deceived," replied Muḥammad b. al-Ash'ath. "These people (ie. the Banū Umayya) are your cousins and they will not fight against you or strike you."

He had been hurt by stones and weakened by the fighting. He was out of breath and he was propping his back up against the wall of that house. Ibn al-Ash'ath repeated the offer of security to him.
"Am I granted security?" he said.
"Yes," he replied and he said to the people who were with him, "he is given security by me."

"Yes," replied the people, except ('Amr b.) 'Ubayd Allāh b. al-'Abbās al-Sulamī. "I have neither she-camel or camel in this (i.e. I will have nothing to do with it)," he said and he turned aside.

"If you will not grant me security," declared Muslim, "I will not put my hand in yours."

A mule was brought and he was put on it. They gathered around him and pulled his sword away. At that he was in despair for his life and his eyes filled with tears. "This is the first betrayal," he cried.
"I hope no harm will come to you," called out Muḥammad b. al-Ash'ath.

"Is it only hope?" he retorted as he wept. "Where then is your guarantee of security? Indeed We belong to Allāh and to Him we will return."
"One who has sought for the like of what you have sought for, should not weep when there befalls him what has befallen you," 'Amr b. 'Ubayd Allāh b. al-'Abbās goaded him.

"I would not weep for myself," he replied, "nor would I grieve for my own death, even though I have not the slightest desire for destruction. But I am weeping for my family who are coming to me, I am weeping for al-Ḥusayn and the family of al-Ḥusayn, peace be on them."

Then he went closer to Muḥammad b. al-Ash'ath and said: "O servant of Allāh, by Allāh, I see that you are unable to grant me a guarantee of security. Yet do you have the goodness to be able to send one of your men with my message so that it will get to al-Ḥusayn? For I have no doubt that he has already set out towards you, or will be setting out soon with his House. (This messenger) would say: 'Ibn 'Aqīl has sent me to you. He is a prisoner in the hands of the people, and he does not expect to see evening before he is killed; and he says: Return, may my father and mother be your ransom, with your House and do not let the Kūfans tempt you, for they were the followers of your father and he desired to leave them even through death and murder. The Kūfans have lied to you. A liar has no judgement'."

"By Allāh, I will do that," replied Ibn al-Ash'ath, "and I will inform Ibn Ziyād that I have given you a guarantee of security."

Ibn al-Ash'ath went with Ibn 'Aqīl to the door of the palace. He asked permission to enter. Permission was given him and he went in (to see) Ibn Ziyād. He gave a report about Ibn 'Aqīl and Bakr's blow against him, and about his own guarantee of security to him.

"What (is this about) you and a guarantee of security?" demanded 'Ubayd Allāh, "as if we sent you to guarantee him security when we only sent you to bring him."
Ibn al-Ash'ath fell silent.

While Ibn 'Aqīl remained at the palace door, his thirst had become severe. At the palace door there were people sitting waiting for permission to enter. Among them were 'Umāra b. 'Uqba b. Abī Mu'ayt, 'Amr b. Ḥurayth, Muslim b. 'Amr and Kathīr b. Shihāb. There was a jug of cold water placed at the doorway.
"Give me a drink of that water:' asked Muslim
"See how cold it is." replied Muslim b. 'Amr. "but by Allāh you will never taste a drop of it until you taste the heat of Hell-fire"
"Shame on you whoever you are!" cried Ibn 'Aqīl.
"I am the one who recognized the truth when you denied it; who was sincere to his Imam when you deceived him; who was obedient to him when you opposed him. I am Muslim b. 'Amr al-Bāhilī"

"Your mother has been bereft of a son" replied Ibn 'Aqīl. "How coarse you are, how rough, how hard your heart is. Man of Bāhila, you are more appropriate for the heat of Hell-fire and to remain there forever, than I am."

He sat down, propping himself against a wall. 'Amr b. Ḥurayth sent one of his boys to bring a jug with a napkin and cup. He poured water into it and told him to drink. But whenever he went to drink, the cup filled with blood so that he was not able to drink. He did that once and then twice. When he made as if to drink for the third time, his tooth fell into the cup,
"Praise be to Allāh." he said, "if it had been a provision granted to me (by Allāh), I could have drunk it "

Ibn Ziyād's messenger came out and ordered him to go to (see) him. He went in but did not greet him as governor.
"Don't you greet the governor?" demanded the guard.
"If he wants my death, what is (the point of) my greeting him with words of peace?" he replied. "if he did not want my death, my greetings (of peace) to him would be profuse."

"By my life, you will be killed," declared Ibn Ziyād.
"So be it," he replied.

"Indeed, (it will)."
"Then let me make my will to one of my fellow tribesmen"
"Do (so)."

Muslim looked those sitting with 'Ubayd Allāh. Among them was 'Umar b. Sa'd b. Abī Waqqāṣ. He said to him " 'Umar, there is kinship between you and me and I have need of you. So you could carry out what I need of you. But it is secret."
'Umar refused to listen to him.
"Why do you refuse to consider the need of your cousin?" asked 'Ubayd Allāh.

So 'Umar got up with him and sat where Ibn Ziyād could watch both of them.
"I have a debt in Kūfa," said Muslim. "I borrowed seven hundred dirhams when I came to Kūfa. Sell my sword and armour and pay the debt for me. When I have been killed, ask Ibn Ziyād to give you my corpse and bury it. Send to al-Ḥusayn, peace be on him, someone to send him back. For I have written to him telling him that the people are with him and now I can only think that he is coming,"

"Do you know what he said to me, governor?" 'Umar said to Ibn Ziyād. "He mentioned these things"

"The faithful would not betray you," said Ibn Ziyād to (Muslim), "But the traitor was confided in. As for what you have, it is yours, and we will not prevent you from doing with it what you like. As for the body when we have killed it, we do not care what is done with it. As for al-Ḥusayn, if he does not intend (harm) to us, we will not intend (harm) to him."

Then Ibn Ziyād said: "Ibn 'Aqīl, you came to the people while they were all (united) and you scattered them and divided their opinions so that some of them attacked others"

"No," replied Ibn 'Aqīl, "I did not come for that but (because) the people of the town claimed that your father had killed their best men, shed their blood and appointed governors among them like the governors of Choesroe and Caesar. We came to enjoin justice and to urge rule by the Book."

"What are you (to do) with that, you great sinner?" cried Ibn Ziyād. "Why did you not do that among the people when you were drinking wine in Medina?"

"Me, drink wine! By Allāh, Allāh knows you are not speaking the truth, and have spoken without any knowledge, for I am not like what you have said. It is you who are more correctly described as drinking wine than me, (you) who lap the blood of Muslims and kill the life whose killing Allāh has forbidden and (you are one) who sheds sacred blood on behalf of usurpation, enmity and evil opinion while he (Yazīd) enjoys himself and plays as if he had done nothing."

"You great sinner (*fāsiq*)," shouted Ibn Ziyād, "your own soul made you desire what Allāh prevented you from having (i.e. authority) (because) Allāh did not regard you as worthy of it."

"Who is worthy of it, if we are not worthy of it?' asked Muslim

"The Commander of the faithful, Yazīd," answered Ibn Ziyād.

"Praise be to Allāh," called out Muslim. "We will accept Allāh's judgement between us and you in every circumstance."

"May Allāh kill me, if I do not kill you in such a way as no one in Islam has (ever) been killed before," retorted Ibn Ziyād.

"You are the person with the most right to commit crimes of innovation in Islam which have not been committed before," Muslim replied, "for you will never abandon evil murder, wicked punishment, shameful practice and avaricious domination to anyone (else)."

Ibn Ziyād began to curse him, and to curse al-Ḥusayn, 'Alī and 'Aqīl, peace be on them, while Muslim did not speak to him.

"Take him up to the top of the palace," ordered Ibn Ziyād. "and cut off his head, (throw it to the ground) and make (his body) follow it (to the ground)."

"By Allāh," said Muslim. "if there was any (real) kinship between you and me, you would not kill me."

"Where is the man whose head Ibn 'Aqīl struck with (his) sword?" asked Ibn Ziyād. Then Bakr b. Ḥumrān al-Aḥmarī was summoned and he told him: "Climb up, and you be the one who cuts his head off."

He went up with him. He (Muslim) said: "Allāh is greater (*Allāhu Akbar*)." He sought forgiveness from Allāh and prayed for blessings on the Apostle, saying: "O Allāh, judge between us and a people who have enticed us, lied against us and deserted us."

They (took) him to a part which overlooked where the shoemakers are today. His head was cut off (and thrown down) and his body was made to follow his head. Muḥammad b. al-Ash'ath, then approached 'Ubayd Allāh b. Ziyād and spoke to him of Hāni' b. 'Urwa. He said: "You know of the position of Hāni' in the town and of his House in the clan. His people know that I and my colleague brought him to you. I adjure you before Allāh, hand him over to me for I would not like (to face) the enmity of the town and his family."

He promised to do that but then afterwards something occurred to him and he ordered Hāni' (to be) taken (immediately) to the marketplace and (his head) cut off.

Hāni' was taken in chains until he was brought to a place where sheep were sold. He began to shout "O Madhḥij! There is no one from Madhḥij for me today! O Madhḥij, where is Madhḥij?"

When he realised that no one was going to help him, he pulled his hand and wrenched it free of the chain, crying: "What is there, stick, knife, stone or bone, with which a man can defend his life?"

(At this) they jumped upon him and tied the chain (more) tightly. He was told to stretch out his neck but he answered: "I am not so liberal with my life and I will not help you (to take) my life."

A Turkish retainer (*mawlā*) of 'Ubayd Allāh called Rashīd struck him with a sword but it did not do anything.

"To Allāh is the return. O Allāh to Your mercy and Your paradise," called out Hāni'. Then (Rashīd) struck him with another blow and killed him.

Concerning Muslim b. 'Aqīl and Hāni' b. 'Urwa, may Allāh have mercy upon them, 'Abd Allāh b. al-Zubayr al-Asadī said:[16]

> If you do not know what death is, then look at Hāni' in the market-place and Ibn 'Aqīl:
>
> (Look at) a hero whose face has been covered with wounds and another who fell dead from a high place.
>
> The command of the governor struck them (down) and they became legends for those who travel on every road.
>
> You see a corpse whose colour death has changed and a spattering of blood which has flowed abundantly;
>
> A young man who was (even) more bashful than a shy young woman, was more decisive than the polished blade of a two edged sword.
>
> Is Asmā' riding in safety a mount which moves at walking pace while Madhḥij urged him to seek vengeance
>
> And Murād wander around him? Are all of them in fear of the questioner and the questioned?
>
> If you do not avenge your two brothers, then be harlots satisfied with little.

When Muslim and Hāni' were killed, the mercy of Allāh be on them, 'Ubayd Allāh b. Ziyād sent their heads with Hāni' b. Abī Ḥayya al-Wādi'ī and al-Zubayr b. al-Arwaḥ al-Tamīmī to Yazīd b. Mu'āwiya. He ordered his secretary (*kātib*) to write to Yazīd about what had happened to Muslim and Hāni'. The secretary who was 'Amr b. Nāfi' – wrote but he was very wordy (in his style). He was the first to be wordy in writing letters. When 'Ubayd Allāh saw the letter, he disliked it.

"What is this prolixity and this excess?" he asked.

"Write:

> Praise be to Allāh, Who exacted the dues of the Commander of the faithful and has given him sufficient provisions against his enemy. I (am writing to) inform the Commander of the faithful that Muslim b. 'Aqīl took refuge in the house of Hāni' b. 'Urwa al-Murādī. I set look-outs and spies on them, concealed men against them, I tricked them until I brought them out. Allāh gave me power over them. Thus I came upon

16 Al-Ṭabarī reports that the verses are also attributed to al-Farazdaq, II, 266.

them and had them executed. I have sent their heads to you with Hāni' b. Abī Ḥayya al-Wādi'ī and al-Zubayr b. al-Arwaḥ al-Tamīmī. They are both people who are attentive and in obedience to you, and of sincerity. Let the Commander of the faithful ask them about whatever of the affair he may wish; for they have knowledge and truth.
Farewell. Greetings."

Yazīd b. Mu'āwiya wrote (back):

You have not gone beyond what I wanted. You have acted with the decisive action I wanted. You have launched into the attack with the violence of man who has control of his emotion. You have satisfied me, been sufficient for (the task) and corroborated my view of you and my opinion of you. I have summoned your two messengers and questioned them, and talked to them. I found them in their views and merit as you had mentioned. Receive them both with kindness on my recommendation. I have been informed that al-Ḥusayn has set out for Iraq. Therefore set look-outs and watches, be vigilant and detain suspicious (characters). Put to death (any who are) accused and write to me about any news which occurs. Allāh, the Exalted, wishing.

Muslim b. 'Aqīl's (attempted) rising in Kūfa was on Tuesday, 8th of Dhū al-Ḥijja in the year 60 A.H. (680). He, may Allāh have mercy on him, was killed on Wednesday, 9th of Dhū al-Ḥijja, the Day of 'Arafa. Al-Ḥusayn, the blessings of Allāh be on him, set out from Mecca to Iraq on the day of Muslim's (attempted) rising in Kūfa, that is the Day of *Tarwiya*,[17] after staying in Mecca for the rest of Sha'bān, the month of Ramaḍān, Shawwāl and Dhū al-Qa'da, and eight days of Dhū al-Ḥijja. In his stay in Mecca, peace be on him, a number of Ḥijāzīs and Baṣrans had gathered around him, joining themselves to his household and his retainers.

When he determined on journeying to Iraq, He made the circumambulation of the (sacred) House and the ritual running between al-Ṣafā and al-Marwa.[18] Then he left the state of consecration (for the pilgrimage) (after) he had performed the lesser pilgrimage (*'umra*) because he was not able to perform the greater pilgrimage (*ḥajj*). Through fear of being apprehended in Mecca, and being taken to Yazīd b. Mu'āwiya, He, peace be upon him, had set out early with his House, his sons and those of his Shī'a who had joined him

17 The Day of 'Arafa is the day when the pilgrims assemble on Mount 'Arafa for the pilgrimage. The Day of *Tarwiya* is the day before it when the pilgrims collect water from the well of Zamzam.

18 These are the rituals of the *'umra*, lesser pilgrimage, but they also form part of the ritual of the greater pilgrimage.

[As it has been reported to us:]
News of Muslim's (capture and death) had not yet reached him because (it had only happened) on the day he set out.

[It is reported that al-Farazdaq, the poet, said.]
I made the pilgrimage with my mother in the year 60 A. H. (680). I was driving her camel when I entered the sanctuary. (There) I met al-Ḥusayn b. 'Alī, peace be on them, leaving Mecca accompanied by (some men carrying) swords and shields.
"Whose caravan is this?" I asked.
"al-Ḥusayn b. 'Alī's, peace be on them." was the reply. So I went up and greeted him.

"May Allāh grant you your request and (fulfil) your hope in what you want, by my father and mother, son of the Apostle of Allāh," I said to him. "But what is making you hurry away from the pilgrimage?"
"If I did not hurry away, I would be apprehended," he replied. Then he asked me; "Who are you?"
"An Arab," I answered and he did not question me (about myself) any further.

"Tell me about the people you have left behind you," he asked.
"You have asked a good (question)," I answered. "The hearts of the people are with you but their swords are against you. The decision comes from Heaven and Allāh does what he wishes."

"You have spoken truly of the affair belonging to Allāh," he replied. "*Every day He (is involved) in (every) matter* (LV, 29). If fate sends down what we like and are pleased with, we praise Allāh for His blessings. He is the One from Whom help should be sought in order to give thanks to Him. However, although fate may frustrate (our) hopes, yet He does not destroy (the souls of) those whose intention is the truth and whose hearts are pious."

"True, Allāh brings you what you wish for (ultimately) and guards you against what you are threatened by," I said. Then I asked him about matters concerning vows and pilgrimage rites. He told me about them and then moved his mount off, saying farewell, and so we parted.

When al-Ḥusayn b 'Alī, peace be on them, left Mecca, Yaḥyā b. Sa'īd b. al-'Āṣ met him with a group (of men). They had been sent to him by 'Āmr b. Sa'īd.

"Come back from where you are going," they ordered. But he refused (to obey) them and continued. The two groups came to blows and hit at each other with whips. However al-Ḥusayn and his followers resisted fiercely. Al-Ḥusayn continued until he got to al-Tan'īm. There he met a camel-train which had come from Yemen. He hired from its people (additional) camels for himself and his followers to ride.

Then he said to the owners (of the camels): "Whoever (of you) wants to come with us to Iraq, we will pay his hire and enjoy his company and whoever wants to leave some way along the road we will pay his hire for the distance he has travelled."

Some of the people went with him but others refused. 'Abd Allāh b. Ja'far sent his sons, 'Awn and Muḥammad, after him, and he wrote a letter to him which he gave to them. In it, he said:

> I ask you before Allāh (to return) if you have set out when you see my letter. For I am very concerned because the direction in which you are heading will have within it your destruction, and the extirpation of your House. If you are destroyed today, the light of the land will be extinguished; for you are the (standard) of those who are rightly-guided and the hope of the believers. Do not hurry on your journey as I am following this letter.
> Greetings.

'Abd Allāh, then went to 'Amr b. Sa'īd and asked him to write to al-Ḥusayn (offering him) a guarantee of security, and (promising) to favour him, so that he would return from where he was going. 'Amr b. Sa'īd wrote a letter in which he offered him favour and a guarantee of security for himself. He dispatched it with his brother Yaḥyā b. Sa'īd. Yaḥyā b. Sa'īd went after him (as did) 'Abd Allāh after dispatching his sons. The two handed ('Amr's) letter to him and strove (to persuade) him to return.

"I have seen the Apostle of Allāh, may Allāh bless Him and His Family, in my sleep," answered (al-Ḥusayn) "and he ordered me (to do) what I am carrying out."
"What was that vision?" they both asked.
"I have not told anyone of it," he answered, "and I am not going tell anyone until I meet my Lord, the Mighty and Exalted."

When 'Abd Allāh b. Ja'far despaired of (persuading) him, he told his sons, 'Awn and Muḥammad, to stay with him, to go with him a to struggle on behalf of him. He returned with Yaḥyā b. Sa'īd to Mecca.

Al-Ḥusayn, peace be on him, pressed on swiftly and directly towards Iraq until he reached Dhāt 'Irq.

When 'Ubayd Allāh b. Ziyād had learnt of the journey of al-Ḥusayn, peace be on him, from Mecca to Kūfa, he had sent al-Ḥusayn b. Numayr, the commander of the bodyguard (*shurta*) to station himself at al-Qādisiyya and to set up a (protective) link cavalry between the area of al-Qādisiyya to Khaffān and the area al-Qādisiyya to al-Quṭquṭāniyya. He informed the men that al-Ḥusayn was heading for Iraq .

When al-Ḥusayn, peace be on him, reached al-Ḥājiz (a hill above) Baṭn al-Rumma, he sent Qays b. Mushir al-Ṣaydāwi - some say it was his brother-in-nurture, 'Abd Allāh b. Yuqṭur - to Kūfa.[19] For He, peace be upon him, had not yet learnt the news of the fate Ibn 'Aqīl. He sent a letter with him:

> In the Name of Allāh, the Merciful, the Compassionate
> From al-Ḥusayn b. 'Alī
>
> To his brother believers and Muslims,
> Greetings to you, I praise Allāh before you, other than whom there is no deity. Muslim b. 'Aqīl's letter came to me, informing me of your sound judgement and the agreement of your leaders to support us, and to seek our rights. I have asked Allāh to make your actions good and reward you with the greatest reward. I set out to you from Mecca on 8th of Dhū al-Ḥijja, the day of *Tarwiya*. When my messenger reaches you, be urgent and purposeful in your affairs, for I am coming to you Within the (next few) days.
> Greeting and the mercy and blessings of Allāh.

Muslim had written to al-Ḥusayn seventeen days before he was killed and the Kūfans had written to him: "Here you have a hundred thousand swords. Do not delay."

Qays b. Mushir went towards Kūfa with the letter. However, When he reached al-Qādisiyya, al-Ḥusayn b. Numayr apprehended him and sent him to 'Ubayd Allāh b. Ziyād.
"Go up on the pulpit." 'Ubayd Allāh b. Ziyād ordered him. "and curse the liar, al-Ḥusayn b. 'Alī, peace be on him"

Qays went up on the pulpit and praised and glorified Allāh. Then he said:

19 Al-Ṭabarī reports two separate accounts concerning these two individuals, II, 289 and 293. As they both meet similar ends, al-Mufīd's surmise seems reasonable.

"People, this man, al-Ḥusayn b. 'Alī, the best of Allāh's creatures, the son of Fāṭima, the daughter of the Apostle, may Allāh bless Him and His Family and grant them peace, (is nearby). I am his messenger to you. Answer him."

Then he cursed 'Ubayd Allāh b. Ziyād and his father and prayed for forgiveness for 'Alī b. Abī Ṭālib and blessed him. 'Ubayd Allāh ordered him to be thrown from the top of the palace. They threw him and he was smashed to pieces.

[It is (also) reported:]
He fell on the ground in chains and his bones were crushed and there only remained to him his last breath. A man called 'Abd al-Malik b. 'Umayr al-Lakhmī came to him and cut his throat. When he was told that that had been a shameful (thing to do) and he was blamed for it, he said: "I wanted to relieve him (of his suffering)."

(While this had been going on) al-Ḥusayn, peace be on him, had left Ḥājiz in the direction of Kūfa until he came to one of the watering (places) of the Arabs. There was 'Abd Allāh b. Mutī' al-'Adawī, who was staying there. When he saw al-Ḥusayn, peace be on him, he got up and said to him: "(May I ransom) my father and mother for you, son of the Apostle of Allāh, what has brought you (here)?" He brought him (forward) and helped him to dismount.

"It is a result of the death of Mu'āwiya as you would know," replied al-Ḥusayn, peace be on him. "The Iraqis have written to me urging me to (come to) them"
"I remind you, son of the Apostle of Allāh, (of Allāh) and the sacredness of Islam, lest it be violated. I adjure you before Allāh (to think) about the sacredness of Quraysh. I adjure you before Allāh (to think) about the sacredness of the Arabs. By Allāh, if you seek that which is in the hands of Banū Umayya, they will kill you, If they kill you, they will never fear anyone after you. Then it will be the sacredness of Islam which is violated, and the sacredness of Quraysh and the sacredness of the Arabs. Don't do it! Don't go to Kūfa! Don't expose yourself to Banū Umayya!!"

Al-Ḥusayn, peace be on him, insisted on continuing his journey. (In the meantime) 'Ubayd Allāh b. Ziyād had ordered (the area) which was between Wāqiṣa and the roads to Syria and Baṣra to be occupied (so that) they should not let anyone enter, nor anyone leave (Kūfa).

However, al-Ḥusayn, peace be on him, went on without knowing anything (of that) until he met some Arabs. He asked them (about the situation) and they told him: "No, by Allāh, we don't know (anything about it) except that we cannot get

into or out of (Kūfa)."
He continued on his journey.

[A group of Fazāra and Bajīla reported (the following account). They said:]
We were with Zuhayr b. al-Qayn al-Bajalī when we came from Mecca. (Although) we were travelling alongside al-Ḥusayn, peace be on him, there was nothing more hateful to us than that we should stop with him at a halting place. (Yet) when al-Ḥusayn, peace be on him, travelled and halted, we could not avoid halting with him. Al-Ḥusayn halted at the side (of the road) and we halted at the (other) side (of the road). While we were sitting, eating our food, a messenger of al-Ḥusayn, peace be on him, approached, greeted us and entered (our camp).

"Zuhayr b. al-Qayn," he said, "Abū 'Abd Allāh al-Ḥusayn, peace be on him, has sent me to you (to ask) you to come to him."

Each man of us threw away what was in his hands (i.e. threw up his hand in horror): it was (as surprising) as if birds had alighted on our heads.
"Glory be to Allāh," (Zuhayr's) wife said to him, "did the son of the Messenger of Allāh send for you? Then aren't you going to him? If you went to him, you would hear what he had to say. Then you could leave him (if you wanted to)."

Zuhayr b. al-Qayn went (across) to him. It was not long before he returned to announce that he was heading east. He ordered his tent (to be struck) and (called for) his luggage, mounts and equipment. His tent was pulled down and taken to al-Ḥusayn, peace be on him, then he said to his wife: "You are divorced, go back to your family, for I do not want anything to befall you except good."

Then he said to his companions: "Whoever wants to follow me (may do so), otherwise he is at the end of his covenant with me (i.e. released from obedience to follow Zuhayr as the leader of his tribal group). I will tell you a story (of something which happened to me once): We were raiding a rich land. Allāh granted us victory and we won (a lot of) booty. Salmān al-Fārsī, the mercy of Allāh be on him, said to us: 'Are you happy with the victory which Allāh has granted you and the booty you have won?' We said: 'Yes.' Then he said: 'Therefore when you meet the lord of the young men of the family of Muḥammad be happier to fight with them than you are with the booty which you have obtained today.' As for me, I pray that Allāh may be with you."

He remained among the people with al-Ḥusayn until he was killed.

['Abd Allāh b. Sulaymān and al-Mundhir b. Musham'ill both from Asad,

reported:]
When we had finished the pilgrimage, there was no concern more important to us than to join al-Ḥusayn, peace be on him, on the road, so that we might see what happened in his affair. We went along trotting our two camels speedily until we joined him at Zarūd. As we approached, there we (saw) a man from Kūfa who had changed his route when he had seen al-Ḥusayn, peace be on him. Al-Ḥusayn, peace be on him, had stopped as if he wanted (to speak to) him, but (the man) ignored him and went on. We went on towards the man. One of us said to the other: "Come with us to ask this man if he has news of Kūfa."

We came up to him and greeted him. He returned out greeting.
"From which (tribe) do you come, fellow?" we asked.
"(I am) an Asadī," he answered.
"We also are Asadīs," we said. "Who are you?"
"I am Bakr b. so and so," he answered and we told him our lineage.
"Tell us of the people (you have left) behind you?" we asked.
"Yes," he replied, "I only left Kūfa after Muslim b. 'Aqīl and Hāni' b. 'Urwa had been killed. I saw them being dragged by their legs into the market-place."

We went on to join al-Ḥusayn, peace be on him, and we were travelling close to him until he stopped at al-Tha'labiyya in the evening. We caught up with him when he stopped and we greeted him. He returned our greeting.
"May Allāh have mercy on you," we said, "we have news. If you wish, we will tell it to you publicly or if you wish, secretly."

He looked at us and at his followers.
"There is no veil for these men," he answered .
"Did you see the rider who whom you were near, yesterday evening'?"
"Yes," he answered. "I had wanted to question him ."
"We have got the news from him and spared you (the trouble of) questioning him," we said. "He was a man from our (tribe), of sound judgement, honesty and intelligence. He told us that he had only left Kūfa after Muslim and Hāni' had been killed, and he had seen them being dragged by their legs into the market-place."
"We belong to Allāh and to Him we shall return; may Allāh have mercy on them both." said al-Ḥusayn and he repeated that several times

"We adjure you before Allāh." we exhorted him. "for your own life and for your house that you do not go from this place, for you have no one to support you in Kūfa and no Shī'a. Indeed we fear that such men (will be the very ones who) will be against you."

"What is your opinion," he asked, looking towards the sons of 'Aqīl, "now that Muslim has been killed?"
"By Allāh," they declared, "we will not go back until we have taken our vengeance or have tasted (the death) which he tasted."
Al-Ḥusayn, peace be on him, came near us and said. "There is nothing good (left) in life for these men."

Then we knew that his decision had been taken to continue the journey.
"May Allāh be good to you," we said.
"May Allāh have mercy on you both," he answered.

Then his followers said to him: "By Allāh, you are not the same as Muslim b. 'Aqīl. If you go to Kūfa, the people will rush to (support) you."

He was silent and waited until daybreak. Then he ordered his boys and servants to get a lot of water, to give (the people) to drink and more for the journey. They set out (once more) and went on to Zubāla. News of 'Abd Allāh b. Yuqṭur reached him. He took out a written statement to the people and read it to them:

> In the name of Allāh, the Merciful, the Compassionate,
> News of the dreadful murder of Muslim b. 'Aqīl, Hāni' b. 'Urwa, and 'Abd Allāh b. Yuqṭur has reached us. Our Shī'a have deserted us. Those of you who would prefer to leave us, may leave freely without guilt.

The people began to disperse from him to right and left until there were only left with him those followers who had come with him from Medina, and a small group of those who had joined him. Al-Ḥusayn had done that because he realised that the Arabs who had followed him had only followed him because they thought that he was going to a land where the inhabitants' obedience to him had already been established. And he did not want them to accompany him without being (fully) aware of what they were going to.

At dawn, he ordered his followers to provide themselves with water and with extra (supplies of it). Then they set out until they passed Baṭn al-'Aqaba. He stopped there and was met by a shaykh of the Banū 'Ikrima called 'Amr b. Lawdhān.
"Where are you heading?," he asked.
"Kūfa," replied al-Ḥusayn, peace be on him.
"I implore you before Allāh," exhorted the shaykh, "why are you going there? You won't come to anything there except the points of spears and the edges of swords. If those who sent for you were enough to support you in battle and

had prepared the ground for you, and you came to them, that would be a wise decision. However, in the light of the situation as it has been described I don't think that you ought to do it."

"Servant of Allāh," he answered, "wise decisions are not hidden from me. Yet the commands of Allāh, the Exalted, cannot be resisted. By Allāh, (my enemies) will not leave me till they have torn the very heart from the depths of my guts. If they do that, Allāh will cause them to be dominated and humiliated until they become the most humiliated of the factions among nations."

He, peace be on him, went on from Baṭn al-'Aqaba until he stopped at Sharāf (for the night). At dawn he ordered his boys to get water and more (for the journey). Then he continued from there until midday. While he was journeying, one of his followers exclaimed: "Allāh is greater (*Allāhu akbar*)!"
"Allāh is greater (*Allāhu akbar*)!" responded al-Ḥusayn, peace be on him. Then he asked: "Why did you say *Allāhu akbar*?"
"I saw palm-trees," answered the man.
"This is a place in which we never see a palm-tree," a group of his followers asserted.
"What do you think it is then?" asked al-Ḥusayn, peace be on him.
"We think it is the ears of horses," they answered.
"By Allāh, I think so too," he declared. Then he said: "(So that) we can face them in one direction (i.e. so that we are not surrounded), we should put at our rear whatever place of refuge (we can find)."

"Yes," (lit. we)[20] said to him, "there is Dhū Ḥusam over on your left. If you reach it before them, it will be (in) just (the position) you want." So he veered left towards it and we went in that direction with him. Even before we had had time to change direction the vanguard of the cavalry appeared in front of us and we could see them clearly. We left the road and when they saw that we had moved off the road, they (also) moved off the road towards us. Their spears looked like palm branches stripped of their leaves and their standards were like birds' wings. al-Ḥusayn ordered his tents (to be put up) and they were erected. The people came up; (there were) about one thousand horsemen under the command of al-Ḥurr b. Yazīd al-Tamimī. (It was) during the heat of midday (that) he and his cavalry stood (thus) facing al-Ḥusayn, peace be on him. Al-Ḥusayn, peace be on him, and his followers were all wearing their turbans and their swords (ready to fight).

20 Mufīd has switched into the first person narrative of an eye-witness accouont as presented by Ibn al-Kalbī. cf. al-Ṭabarī, II, 296

"Provide (our) people with water and let them quench their thirst and give their horses water to drink little by little." al-Ḥusayn ordered his boys. They did that and they began filling their bowls and cups and took them to the horses. When a horse had drunk three or four or five draughts, the water was taken away and given to another horse until they had all been watered.

['Ali b. al-Ta'ān al-Muḥāribī reported:]
I was with al-Ḥurr on that day, I was among the last of his followers to arrive. When al-Ḥusayn, peace be on him, saw how thirsty both I and my horse were, he said: "Make your beast (*rāwiya*) kneel." I thought *rāwiya* meant water-skin so he said: "Cousin, make your camel (*jamal*) kneel." I did so. Then he said: "Drink." I did so, but when I drank, water flowed from my water-skin.

"Bend your water-skin," said al-Ḥusayn. I did not know how to do that. He came up (to me) and bent it (into the proper position for drinking). Then I drank and gave my horse to drink.

Al-Ḥurr b. Yazīd had come from al-Qādisiyya. 'Ubayd Allāh b. Ziyād had sent al-Ḥusayn b. Numayr and ordered him to take up (his) position at al-Qādisiyya. Then al-Ḥurr had been sent in advance with one thousand horsemen to meet al-Ḥusayn.

Al-Ḥurr remained positioned opposite to al-Ḥusayn, peace be on him, until the time for the midday prayer drew near. Al-Ḥusayn, peace be on him, ordered al-Ḥajjāj b. Masrūq to give the call to prayer. When the second call to prayer immediately preceding the prayer (*iqāma*) was about (to be made) al-Ḥusayn came out (before the people) dressed in a waist-cloth (*izār*) and cloak (*ridā'*) and wearing a pair of sandals. He praised and glorified Allāh, then he said: "People, I did not come to you until your letters came to me, and they were brought by your messengers (saying), 'Come to us for we have no Imam. Through you may Allāh unite us under guidance and truth.' Since this was your view, I have come to you. Therefore give me what you guaranteed in your covenants and (sworn) testimonies. If you will not and (if you) are (now) averse to my coming, I will leave you (and go back) to the place from which I came,"

They were silent before him. Not one of them said a word. "Recite the *iqāma*." he said to the caller for prayer (*mu'adhdhin*) and he recited the *iqāma*.

"Do you want to lead your followers in prayer?" he asked al-Ḥurr b. Yazīd.
"No," he replied, "but you pray and we will pray (following the lead of) your prayer."

Al-Ḥusayn, peace be on him, prayed before them. Then he returned (to his tent) and his followers gathered around him. Al-Ḥurr went back to the place where he had positioned (his men) and entered a tent which had been put up for him. A group of his followers gathered around him while the rest returned to their ranks, which they had been in and which now they went back to. Each of them held the reins of his mount and sat in the shade (of its body).

At the time for the afternoon (*'aṣr*) prayer, al-Ḥusayn, peace be on him, ordered his followers to prepare for departure. Then he ordered the call to be made, and the call for the *'aṣr* prayer was made, and the *iqāma*. Al-Ḥusayn, peace be on him, came forward, stood and prayed Then he said the final greeting (of the prayer) and turned his face towards them (al-Ḥurr's men). He praised and glorified Allāh and said: "People, if you fear Allāh and recognise the rights of those who have rights, Allāh will be more satisfied with you. We are the House of Muḥammad and as such are more entitled to the authority (*wilāya*) of this affair (i.e. the rule of the community) over you than these pretenders who claim what does not belong to them. They have brought tyranny and aggression among you. If you refuse (us) because you dislike (us) or do not know our rights, and your view has now changed from what came to us in your letters and what your messengers brought, then I will leave you."

"By Allāh," declared al-Ḥurr, "I know nothing of these letters and messengers which you mention."
"'Uqba b Sim'ān," al-Ḥusayn, peace be on him, called to one of his followers, "bring out the two saddle-bags in which the letters to me are kept,"

He brought out two saddle-bags which were full of documents, and they were put before him.
"We are not among those who wrote these letters to you." said al-Ḥurr, "and we have been ordered that when we meet you we should not leave you until we have brought you to Kūfa to 'Ubayd Allāh."
"Death will come to you before that (happens)," al-Ḥusayn, peace be on him, told him. Then he ordered his followers, "Get up and get mounted."

They got mounted and (then) waited until their women had been mounted.
"Depart," he ordered his followers.

When they set out to leave, the men (with al-Ḥurr) got in between them and the direction they were going in. "May Allāh deprive your mother of you," said al-Ḥusayn, peace be on him, to al-Ḥurr, "what do you want?"
"If any of the Arabs other than you were to say that to me," retorted al-Ḥurr,

"even though he were in the same situation as you, I would not leave him without mentioning his mother being deprived (of him), whoever he might be. But by Allāh there is no way for me to mention your mother except by (saying) the best things possible."

"What do you want?" al-Ḥusayn, peace be on him, demanded.
"I want to go with you to the governor, 'Ubayd Allāh," he replied.
"Then by Allāh I will not follow you."
"Then by Allāh I will not let you (go anywhere else)."

These statements were repeated three times, and when their conversation was getting more (heated) al-Ḥurr said: "I have not been ordered to fight you. I have only been ordered not to leave you until I come with you to Kūfa. If you refuse (to do that), then take any road which will not bring you into Kūfa nor take you back to Medina, and let that be a compromise between us while I write to the governor, 'Ubayd Allāh. Perhaps Allāh will cause something to happen which will relieve me from having to do anything against you. Therefore take this (road) here and bear to the left of the road (to) al-'Udhayb and al-Qādisiyya."

Al-Ḥusayn, peace be on him, departed, and al-Ḥurr with his followers (also) set out travelling close by him, while al-Ḥurr was saying to him: "Al-Ḥusayn, I remind you (before) Allāh to (think of) your life; for I testify that you will be killed if you fight."
"Do you think that you can frighten me with death?" said al-Ḥusayn, peace be on him. "Could a worse disaster happen to you than killing me? I can only speak (to you) as the brother of al-Aws said to his cousin when he wanted to help the Apostle of Allāh, may Allāh bless him and grant Him and His Family peace. His cousin feared for him and said: 'Where are you going, for you will be killed?' but he replied:

> I will depart for there is no shame in death for a young man, whenever he intends (to do what is) right and he strives like a Muslim,
>
> (Who) has soothed righteous men through (the sacrifice of) his life, who has scattered the cursed and opposed the criminal.
>
> If I live, I will not regret (what I have done) and if I die, I will not suffer. Let it be enough for you to live in humiliation and be reviled."

When al-Ḥurr heard that he drew away from him. He and his follower, travelled on one side (of the road) while al-Ḥusayn, peace be on him, travelled on the other, until they reached 'Udhayb al-Hijānāt. Al-Ḥusayn, peace be on him, went on to Qaṣr Banī Muqātil. He stopped there and there a large lent had (already) been erected.

"Whose is that?" he asked.
"That belongs to 'Ubayd Allāh b. al-Ḥurr al-Ju'fī," he was told.
"Ask him to come to me," he said.

The messenger went to him and said: "This is al-Ḥusayn b. 'Alī, peace be on them, and he asks you to come to him."
"We belong to Allāh and to Him we shall return," said 'Ubayd Allāh. "By Allāh, I only left Kūfa out of dread that al-Ḥusayn, peace be on him, would enter Kūfa while I was there. By Allāh, I do not want to see him, nor him to see me."

The messenger returned to him (al-Ḥusayn). Al-Ḥusayn, peace be on him, rose and went over to him. He greeted him and sat down. Then he asked him to go with him. 'Ubayd Allāh b. al-Ḥurr repeated what he had said before and sought to excuse himself from what he was asking him (to do).

"If you are not going to help us," al-Ḥusayn, peace be on him, said to him. "then be sure that you are not one of those who fight against us. For, by Allāh, no one will hear our cry and not help us without being destroyed."

"As for that (fighting against you)," he replied, "it will never happen, If Allāh, the Exalted. wishes."

Then al-Ḥusayn, peace be on him, left him and continued to his camp. Towards the end of the night, he ordered his boys to get provisions of water. Then he ordered the journey (to continue). He set out from Qaṣr Banī Muqātil.

['Uqba b. Sim'ān reported:]
We set out at once with him and he became drowsy while he was on his horse's back. He woke up, saying: "We belong to Allāh and to Him we will return. Praise be to Allāh, Lord of the worlds."

He did that twice or three times, then his son, 'Ali b. al-Ḥusayn approached him and asked: "Why are you praising Allāh and repeating the verse of returning to Him?"
"My son," he answered, "I nodded off and a horseman appeared to me, riding a horse and he said: 'Men are travelling and the fates travel towards them.' Then I knew it was our own souls announcing our deaths to us."

"Father," asked (the youth), "does Allāh regard you as evil? Are we not in the right?"
"Indeed (we are)," he answered, "by Him to Whom all His servants must return."
"Father," said (the youth), "then we need have no concern, if we are going to die righteously."
"May Allāh give you the best reward a son can get for (his behaviour towards) his father," answered al-Ḥusayn, peace be on him.

In the morning, he stopped and prayed the morning prayer. Then he hurried to remount and to continue the journey with his followers, veering to the left with the intention of separating from (al-Ḥurr's men). However al-Ḥurr b. Yazīd came towards him and stopped him and his followers (from going in that direction) and he began to (exert pressure to) turn them towards Kūfa, but they resisted him. So they stopped (doing that) but they still accompanied them in the same way until they reached Nīnawā, (which was) the place where al-Ḥusayn, peace be on him, stopped. Suddenly there appeared a rider on a fast mount, bearing weapons and carrying a bow on his shoulder, coming from Kūfa. They all stopped and watched him. When he reached them, he greeted al-Ḥurr and his followers and did not greet al-Ḥusayn and his followers. He handed a letter from 'Ubayd Allāh b. Ziyād to al-Ḥurr. In it (was the following):

> When this letter reaches you and my messenger comes to you, make al-Ḥusayn come to a halt. But only let him stop in an open place without vegetation. I have ordered my messenger to stay with you and not to leave you until he brings me (news of) your carrying out my instructions.
> Greetings.

When al-Ḥurr had read the letter, he told them: "This is a letter from the governor 'Ubayd Allāh. He has ordered me to bring you to a halt at a place which his letter suggests. This is his messenger and he has ordered him not to leave me until I carry out the order with regard to you." .

Yazīd (b. Ziyād) b. al-Muhājir al-Kindī who was with al-Ḥusayn, peace be on him, looked at the messenger of Ibn Ziyād and he recognized him.
"May your mother be deprived of you." he exclaimed, "what a business you have come to!"
"I have obeyed my Imam and remained faithful to my pledge of allegiance," (the other man) answered.
"You have been disobedient to your Lord and have obeyed your Imam in bringing about the destruction of your soul," responded Ibn al-Muhājir. "You have acquired (eternal) shame (for yourself) and (the punishment of) Hell-fire. What a wicked Imam your Imam is! Indeed Allāh has said: *We have made them*

Imams who summon (people) to Hell-fire and on the Day of Resurrection they will not be helped. (XXVIII 41) Your Imam is one of those."

Al-Ḥurr b. Yazīd began to make the people stop in a place that was without water and where there was no village.
"Shame upon you, let us stop at this village or that one," said al-Ḥusayn, peace be on him. He meant by this, Nīnawā and al-Ghādiriyya, and by that, Shufayya.
"By Allāh, I cannot do that," replied (al-Ḥurr), "for this man has been sent to me as a spy."

"Son of the Apostle of Allāh," said Zuhayr b. al-Qayn, "I can only think that after what you have seen, the situation will get worse than what you have seen. Fighting these people, now, will be easier for us than fighting those who will come against us after them. For by my life, after them will come against us such (a number) as we will not have the power (to fight) against"
"I will not begin to fight against them," answered al-Ḥusayn.

That was Thursday, 2nd of (the month of) Muharram in the year 61 A.H. (680). On the next day, 'Umar b. Sa'd b. Abī Waqqāṣ set out from Kūfa with four thousand horsemen He stopped at Nīnawā and sent for 'Urwa b. Qays al-Aḥmasī[21] and told him: "Go to him (al-Ḥusayn) and ask him: What brought you, and what do you want?"

'Urwa was one of those who had written to al-Ḥusayn, peace be on him, and he was ashamed to do that. The same was the case with all the leaders who had written to him, and all of them refused and were unwilling to do that. Kathīr b. 'Abd Allāh al-Sha'bī stood up - he was a brave knight who never turned his face away from anything - and said: "I will go to him. By Allāh, if you wish, I will rush on him."
""I don't want you to attack him." said 'Umar, "but go to him and ask him what has brought him."

As Kathīr was approaching him, Abū Thumāma al-Ṣā'idī saw him and said to al-Ḥusayn, "May Allāh benefit you, Abū 'Abd Allāh, the wickedest man in the land, the one who has shed the most blood and the boldest of them all in attack, is coming towards you."
Then (Abu Thumāma) stood facing him and said: "Put down your sword."
"No, by Allāh," he replied, "I am only a messenger. If you will listen to me, I will tell you (the message) which I have been sent to bring to you. If you refuse,

21 'Azra in al-Ṭabarī. II,309. The same difference is maintained concerning the letter. cf. 304, footnote 9.

I will go away."

"I will take the hilt of your sword," answered (Abu Thumāma), "and you can say what you need to."
"No, by Allāh, you will not touch it," he retorted.

"Then tell me what you have brought and I will inform him for you. But I will not let you go near him, for you are a charlatan."

They both (stood there and) cursed each other. Then (Kathīr) went back to 'Umar b. Sa'd and told him the news (of what had happened). 'Umar summoned Qurra b. Qays al-Ḥanẓalī and said to him: "Shame upon you Qurra, go and meet al-Ḥusayn and ask him what brought him and what he wants."

Qurra began to approach him. When al-Ḥusayn, peace be on him, saw him approaching. he asked: "Do you know that man?'

"Yes," replied Ḥabīb b. Muẓāhir, "he is from the Ḥanẓala clan of Tamīm. He is the son of our sister. I used to know him as a man of sound Judgement. I would not have thought that he would be present at this scene."

He came and greeted al-Ḥusayn, peace be on him. Then he informed him of 'Umar b. Sa'd's message.

"The people of this town of yours wrote to me that I should come," answered al-Ḥusayn, peace be on him. "However, if now you have come to dislike me, then I will leave you."

"Shame upon you, Qurra," Ḥabīb b. Muẓāhir said to him, "will you return to those unjust men? Help this man through whose fathers Allāh will grant you (great) favour."

"I will (first) return to my leader with the answer to his message," replied Qurra, "and then I will reflect on my views."

He went back to 'Umar b. Sa'd and gave him his report.
"I hope that Allāh will spare me from making war on him and fighting against him," said 'Umar and then he wrote to 'Ubayd Allāh b. Ziyād:

> In the name of Allāh, the Merciful, the Compassionate. I am (writing this from) where I have positioned myself, near al-Ḥusayn, and I have asked him what brought him and what he wants. He answered: 'The people of

> this land wrote to me and their messengers came to me asking me to come and I have done so. However if (now) they have come to dislike me and (the position) now appears different to them from what their messengers brought to me, I will go away from them.'

[Ḥassān b. Qā'id al-'Absī reported:]
I was with 'Ubayd Allāh when this letter came to him, he read it and then he recited:

> Now when our claws cling to him, he hopes for escape but he will be prevented (now) from (getting) any refuge.

He wrote to 'Umar b. Sa'd:

> Your letter has reached me and I have understood what you mentioned. Offer al-Ḥusayn (the opportunity) of him and all his followers pledging allegiance to Yazīd. If he does that, we will then see what our judgement will be.

When the answer reached 'Umar b. Sa'd, he said: "I fear that 'Ubayd Allāh will not accept that I should be spared (fighting al-Ḥusayn)."

(Almost immediately) after it, there came (another) letter from Ibn Ziyād (in which he said): "Prevent al-Ḥusayn and his followers from (getting) water. Do not let them taste a drop of it just as was done with 'Uthmān b. 'Affān."

At once 'Umar b. Sa'd sent 'Amr b al-Ḥajjāj with five hundred horsemen to occupy the path to the water and prevent al-Ḥusayn and his followers from (getting) water in order that they should (not) drink a drop of it. That was three days before the battle against al-Ḥusayn, peace be on him.

'Abd Allāh b. al-Ḥusayn al-Azdī, who was numbered among Bajīla, called out at the top of his voice: "Ḥusayn, don't you see that the water is as if in the middle of heaven. By Allāh, you will not taste a drop of it until you die of thirst."

"O Allāh, make him die of thirst and never forgive him," cried al-Ḥusayn, peace be on him.

[Ḥumayd b. Muslim reported:]
By Allāh, later I visited him when he was ill. By Allāh, other than whom there is no deity, I saw him drinking water without being able to quench his thirst, and then vomiting. He would cry out, "The thirst, the thirst!" Again he would drink water without being able to quench his thirst, again he would vomit. He would

then burn with thirst. This went on until he died, may Allāh curse him.

When al-Ḥusayn saw the extent of the number of troops encamped with ʻUmar b. Saʻd, may Allāh curse him, at Nīnawā in order to do battle against him, he sent to ʻUmar b. Saʻd that he wanted to meet him. The two men met at night and talked together for a long time. (When) ʻUmar b. Saʻd went back to his camp, he wrote to ʻUbayd Allāh b. Ziyād, may he be cursed.

> Allāh has put out the fire of hatred, united (the people) in one opinion (lit. word), and set right the affairs of the community. This man, al-Ḥusayn, has given me a promise that he will return to the place which he came from, or he will go to one of the border outposts - he will become like any (other) of the Muslims, with the same rights and duties as them; or he will go to Yazīd, the Commander of the Faithful, and offer him his hand and see (if the difference) between them (can be reconciled). In this (offer) you have the consent (to what you have demanded) and the community gains benefit.

When ʻUbayd Allāh read the letter, he said: "This is the letter about a sincere man who is anxious for his people."

"Are you going to accept this from him," demanded Shamir b. Dhī al-Jawshan, jumping up, "when he has encamped on your land nearby? By Allāh if he was a man from your land and he would not put his hand in yours, whether he was in a position of power and strength (or) whether he was in a position of weakness and impotence you would not give this concession, for it would be (a mark) of weakness. Rather let him and his followers submit to your authority. Then if you punish them, (it will be because) you are the (person) most appropriate to punish, and if you forgive them, you have the right (to do so)."

"What you have suggested is good," replied Ibn Ziyād. "Your view is the correct view. Take this message to ʻUmar b. Saʻd and let him offer al-Ḥusayn and his followers (the opportunity of) submitting to my authority. If they do that, let him send them to me in peace. If they refuse, he should fight them. If he (ʻUmar b. Saʻd) acts (according to) my instructions, then listen to him and obey him. However if he refuses to fight them then you are the commander of the army (lit. people), attack him, cut his head off and send it to me."

Then he wrote to ʻUmar b. Saʻd:

> I did not send you to al-Ḥusayn for you to restrain yourself from (fighting) him, nor to idle the time away with him, nor to promise him peace and preservation (of his life), nor to make excuses for him, nor to

be an intercessor on his behalf with me. Therefore see that if al-Ḥusayn and his followers submit to my authority and surrender, you send them to me in peace. If they refuse, then march against them to fight them and to punish them; for they deserve that. If al-Ḥusayn is killed, make the horses trample on his body, both front and back; for he is a disobedient rebel, and I do not consider that this will be in any way wrong after death. But it is my view that you should do this to him if you kill him. If you carry out your command concerning him, we will give you the reward due to one who is attentive and obedient. If you refuse, then we withdraw (the command of) our province and army from you and leave the army to Shamir b. Dhī al-Jawshan. We have given him our authority.
Greetings.

Shamir b. Dhī al-Jawshan brought the letter to 'Umar b Sa'd. After he had brought it and read it, 'Umar said to him: "Shame upon you, what is this to you? May Allāh never show favour to your house. May Allāh make abominable what you have brought to me! By Allāh, I did not think that you would cause him to refuse what I had written to him, and ruin for us a matter which we had hoped to set right. Al-Ḥusayn will not surrender, for there is a spirit like (his) father's in his body."

"Tell me what you are going to do," demanded Shamir. "Are you going to carry out the governor's command and fight his enemy or are you going to leave the command of the army to me?"

"No, (there is going to be) no advantage to you. I will carry that out instead of you. You take command of the foot-soldiers."

'Umar b. Sa'd prepared to (do battle with) al-Ḥusayn, peace be on him, on the night of Thursday, 9th of the month of Muḥarram. (In the meantime) Shamir went out and stood in front of the followers of al-Ḥusayn, peace be on him.
"Where are my sister's sons?" he demanded. Al-'Ābbās, Ja'far, 'Abd Allāh and 'Uthmān, sons of 'Alī b. Abī Ṭālib, peace be on him, came forward.

"What do you want?" they asked
"Sons of my sister, you are guaranteed security," he said.
"Allāh curse you and curse the security which you offer without offering it to the son of the Apostle of Allāh," the young men replied.

"Cavalry of Allāh, mount and announce the news of Heaven (i.e. death)," 'Umar b. Sa'd called out and the people mounted and he approached (the supporters of al-Ḥusayn) after the afternoon (*'aṣr*) prayer

Meanwhile, al-Ḥusayn, peace be on him, was sitting in front of his tent dozing with his head on his knees. His sister heard the clamour (from the enemy's ranks). She came up to him and scid, "My brother, don't you hear the sounds which are getting nearer?"

"I have just seen the Apostle of Allāh, may Allāh bless him and grant him peace, in my sleep," said al-Ḥusayn, peace be on him, as he raised his head. "He said to me: 'You are coming to us'."

His sister struck at her face and cried out in grief.
"You have no (reason) to lament, sister," al-Ḥusayn, peace be on him, told her. "Be quiet, may Allāh have mercy on you."

Then he turned to al-'Abbās b. 'Alī: "Brother, the enemy have come, so get ready, but first, al-'Abbās, you, yourself, ride out to meet them, to talk to them about what they have (in mind) and what appears (appropriate) to them and to ask about what has brought them (against us)"

Al-'Abbās went towards them with about twenty horsemen, among whom was Zuhayr b. al-Qayn.
"How do you see (the situation)?" he asked. "What do you want?"
"The command of the governor has arrived that we should offer you (the opportunity of) submitting to his authority, otherwise we (must) attack you," they answered.
"Do not hurry (to do anything) until I have gone back to Abu 'Abd Allāh (al-Ḥusayn) and told him what you have said," al-'Abbās requested.

They stopped (where they were) and told him: "Go to him and inform him, and tell us what he says to you."

Al-'Abbās went galloping back to al-Ḥusayn, peace be on him, to give him the information. While his companions remained exchanging words with enemy, trying to test them and dissuade them from fighting against al-Ḥusayn, peace be on him, (al-'Abbās) told him what the enemy had said.

"Go back to them," he, peace be on him, said, "if you can, delay them until the morning and (persuade) them to keep from us during the evening. Then, perhaps, we may be able to pray to our Lord during the night to call upon Him and seek His forgiveness. He knows that I have always loved His formal prayer, the recitation of His Book and (making) many invocations to Him, seeking His forgiveness."

Al-'Abbās went back to the people, and returned (after) being with them, accompanied by a messenger on behalf of 'Umar b. Sa'd, who had said: "We will grant you a day until tomorrow. Then if you surrender, we will send you to our governor, 'Ubayd Allāh b. Ziyād but if you refuse we will not leave you (any longer)."

(After) he departed towards the evening al-Ḥusayn gathered his followers around him.

['Alī b. al-Ḥusayn, Zayn al-'Ābidīn. reported:]
I went near to hear what he would say to them (even though) at that time I was sick. I heard my father say to his followers: "I glorify Allāh with the most perfect glorification and I praise Him in happiness and misfortune. O Allāh, I praise You for blessing us with prophethood, teaching us the Qur'ān and making us understand the religion. You have given us hearing, sight and hearts, and have made us among those who give thanks (to You). I know of no followers more loyal and more virtuous than my followers nor of any House more pious and more close-knit than my House. May Allāh reward you well on my behalf. Indeed, I do not think that there will be (any further) days (left) to us by these men. I permit you to leave me. All (of you) go away with the absolution of your oath (to follow me), for there will be no (further) obligation on you from me. This is a night (whose darkness) will give cover to you. Use it as a camel (i.e. ride away in it)."

His brothers and sons, the sons of his sisters and the sons of 'Abd Allāh b. Ja'far said: "We will not leave you to make ourselves continue living after your (death). Allāh will never see us (do) such a thing."

Al-'Abbās b. 'Alī, peace be on them, was the first of them to make this declaration. Then the (whole) group followed him, (all) declaring the same thing.

"Sons of 'Aqīl," said al-Ḥusayn, "enough of your (family) has been killed. So go away as I have permitted you "
"Glory be to Allāh." they replied, "what would the people say? They would say that we deserted our Shaykh, our lord, the sons of our uncle, who was the best of uncles; that we had not shot arrows alongside them, we had not thrust spears alongside them, we had not struck swords alongside them. (At such an accusation) we do not know what we would do. No, by Allāh, we will not

do (such a thing). Rather we will ransom you with our lives, property and families. We will fight for you until we reach your destination. May Allāh make life abominable (for us) after your (death)."

Then Muslim b. 'Awsaja arose and spoke: "Could we leave you alone? How should we excuse ourselves before Allāh concerning the performance of our duty to you? By Allāh, I will stab them with my spear (until it breaks), I will strike them with my sword as long as the hilt is in my hand. If I have no weapon (left) to fight them with, I will throw stones (at them). By Allāh we will never leave you until Allāh knows that we have preserved through you (the company of His Apostle) in his absence. By Allāh, if I knew that I would die and then be revived and then burnt and then revived, and then scattered, and that would be done to me seventy times, I would never leave you until I met my death (fighting) on your behalf. So how could I do it when there can only be one death, which is a great blessing which can never be rejected?"

Zuhayr b. al-Qayn, may Allāh have mercy on him, spoke: "By Allāh, I would prefer to be killed and then recalled to life; and then be killed a thousand times in this manner; and that in this way Allāh, the Mighty and Exalted, should protect your life and the lives of these young men of your House."

All his followers spoke in similar vein, one after the other. Al-Ḥusayn, peace be on him, called (on Allāh to) reward them well and then went back to his tent.

['Alī b. al-Ḥusayn, peace be on them, reported:]
I was sitting on that evening (before the morning of the day) in which my father was killed. With me was my aunt, Zaynab, who was nursing me when my father left to go to his tent. With him was Juwayn, the retainer (*mawlā*) of Abū Dharr al-Ghiffarī, who was preparing his sword and putting it right. My father recited:

> Time, shame on you as a friend! At the day's dawning and the sun's setting.
>
> How many a companion or seeker will be a corpse! Time will not be satisfied with any substitute.
>
> The matter will rest with the Mighty One, and every living creature will have to journey along my path.

He repeated it twice or three times. I understood it and realised what he meant. Tears choked me and I pushed them back. I kept silent and knew that tribulation had come upon us. As for my aunt, she heard what I heard – but she is a woman and weakness and grief are part of the qualities of women; she could not control herself, she jumped up, tearing at her clothes and sighing, and went to him.

"Then I will lose (a brother)," Zaynab said to him. "Would that death deprived me of life today, (for) my mother, Fāṭima, is dead, and my father, 'Alī and my brother, al-Ḥasan, peace be on them (all)."
"O sister," al-Ḥusayn said to her as he looked at her with his eyes full of tears. "don't let Satan take away your forbearance. (Remember:) If the sandgrouse are left (alone) at night, they will sleep (i.e. let nature take its course)."

"O my grief, your life will be violently wrenched from you and that is more wounding to my heart and harsher to my soul," she lamented, and then she struck at her face. She bent down to (the hem of) her garment and (began to) tear it. Then she fell down in a faint.

Al-Ḥusayn, peace be on him, got up and bathed her face with water. Then he said to her: "Sister, fear Allāh and take comfort in the consolation of Allāh. Know that the people on the earth will die and the inhabitants of heaven will not continue to exist (for ever). For everything will be destroyed except the face of Allāh Who created creation by His power (*qudra*); He sends forth creatures and He causes them to return; He is unique and alone. My grandfather was better than me, My father was better than me and my mother was better than me. I and every muslim have an ideal model in the Apostle of Allāh, may Allāh bless Him and His Family."

By this and the like he tried to console her and he said: "Sister, I swear to you – and I (always) keep my oaths – that you must not tear your clothes, nor stratch your face, nor cry out with grief and loss when I am destroyed."

Then he brought her and made her sit with me. He went out to his followers and ordered them to bring their tents (much) closer together so that the tent pegs came within the area of each other's tents, and so that if they remained among their tents, the enemy could only approach (them), from one side (for there would be) tents behind them, and to their right and left. Thus (the tents completely) surrounded them except for the one way which the enemy could come against them.

(After that) he, peace be on him, returned to his place and spent the whole night in performing the prayer, and in calling on Allāh's forgiveness and in making invocations. In the same way, his followers performed the prayers, made invocations and sought Allāh's forgiveness.

[Al-Ḍaḥḥāk b. 'Abd Allāh reported]
(A contingent of) 'Umar b. Sa'd's (continually) passed us keeping watch over us while al-Ḥusayn, himself recited: "*Let not those who disbelieve think that our giving them a delay is better for their souls. We give them a delay only that they might increase their wickedness. They shall have a disgraceful punishment. Allāh does not leave the believers in the situation you are in until He has made the evil distinct from the good.*" (III 178-179)

A man called 'Abd Allāh b. Samīr, (who was) among those horsemen heard that. He was given to much laughter, and was a brave fighter, a treacherous knight and a noble. He cried out : "By the Lord of the Ka'ba. we are the good, we have been distinguished from you."
"O terrible sinner," cried Burayr b. Ḥuḍayr. "has Allāh made you one of the good?"
"A curse on you, whoever you are" he shouted back.
"I am Burayr b.Ḥuḍayr," he replied. And they both cursed each other.

In the morning al-Ḥusayn, peace be on hin, mobilised his followers after the morning prayer. He had with him thirty-two horsemen and forty foot-soldiers. He put Zuhayr b. al-Qayn in charge of his right wing and Ḥabib b. Muẓāhir in charge of his left wing, and he gave his standard to his brother, al-'Abbās. They positioned themselves with the tents al the rear. He ordered (the) firewood and cane which was behind the tents to be left in a ditch which had been dug there and to be set on fire, fearing that they would attack them from the rear.

'Umar b. Sa'd began the morning of that day - it was Friday, or Saturday as some say - by mobilising his followers. He went out with the men with him towards al-Ḥusayn, peace be on him. 'Amr b. al-Ḥajjāj was in command of his right wing, Shamir b. Dhī al-Jawshan of the left Wing, 'Urwa b. Qays was in command of the cavalry, Shabath b. Rib'i of the foot-soldiers. He gave his standard to Durayd, his retainer (*mawlā*).

['Alī b. al-Ḥusayn, Zayn al-'Ābidīn, peace be on them, reported:]
When the cavalry began to approach al-Ḥusayn, he raised his hands and said: "O Allāh, it is You in Whom I trust amid all grief. You are my hope amid all violence. You are my trust and provision in everything that happens to me, (no matter) how much the heart may seem to weaken in it, trickery may seem to diminish (my hope) in it, the friend may seem to desert (me) in it, and the enemy may seem to rejoice in it. It comes upon me through You and when I complain to You of it, it is because of my desire for You, You alone. You have comforted me in (everything) and have revealed its (significance to me). You are the Master

of all grace, the Possessor of all goodness and the Ultimate Resort of all desire."

When the enemy began to move around the tent of al-Ḥusayn, peace be on him, they saw the ditch behind and the fire burning the firewood and cane which had been thrown in it. (At this) Shamir b. Dhī al-Jawshan called out at the top of his voice: "Al-Ḥusayn, are you hurrying towards the fire (of Hell) before the Day of Resurrection?"
"Who is that?" asked al-Ḥusayn, peace be on him. "(It sounds) like Shamir b. Dhī al-Jawshan?"
"Yes, (it is)," they told him.
"Son of a goat-herdess, you are more worthy to be burnt by that." he retorted.

Muslim b. ʻAwsaja wanted to shoot an arrow at him, but al-Ḥusayn, peace be on him, stopped him from (doing) that. "Let me shoot at him," he asked, "for he is a wicked sinner, one of the enemies of Allāh, and the great tyrants. (Now) Allāh has made it possible (to kill) him."
"Do not shoot at him," ordered al-Ḥusayn, peace be on him, "for I am unwilling to begin (the fighting) against them."

Then al-Ḥusayn called for his mount and mounted it. He called out at the top of his voice: "O people of lraq,"- and most of them (began to) listen to him - "people, listen to my words and do not hurry (to attack me) so that I may remind you of the duties you have towards me and so that (by telling you the true circumstances) I may free myself from any blame in (your attacking me). If you give me justice, you will become happier through that. If you do not give me justice of your own accord (as individuals), *then agree upon your affairs (with your associates); let not your affairs be in darkness toyou. Then carry (it) out against me and do not reflect (any further)* (X 71). *Indeed my guardian is Allāh, Who created the Book; He takes care of the righteous* (VII 196.)"

Then he praised and glorified Allāh, and mentioned what Allāh is entitled to. He called for blessings on the Prophet, may Allāh bless Him and His Family, and on the angels and (other) prophets. No speaker has ever been heard before or after him more eloquent in his speech than he was. He continued: "Trace back my lineage and consider who I am. Then look back at yourselves and remonstrate with yourselves. Consider whether it is right for you to kill me and to violate the honour of my womenfolk. Am I not the son of the daughter of your Prophet, of his testamentary trustee (*waṣī*) and his cousin, the first of the believers in Allāh and the man who (first) believed in what His Apostle, may Allāh bless Him and His Family, brought from his Lord? Was not Ḥamza, the lord of the martyrs, my uncle? Was not Jaʻfar, the one who flies in Heaven, my uncle? Have you not heard the words of the Apostle of Allāh, may Allāh bless Him and His Family, concerning myself and my brother: 'These are the two lords of the youths of the inhabitants of heaven?' Whether you believe what I am saying - and it is the truth, for by Allāh I have never told a lie since I learnt that Allāh hated people (who told) them - or whether you regard me as a liar, there are among you those who, if you asked them, would tell you: Ask Jābir b. 'Abd Allāh al-Anṣārī, Abū Sa'īd al-Khudrī, Sahl b. Sa'd al-Ṣā'idī, Zayd b. Arqam and Anas b. Mālik to tell you that they heard these words from the Apostle of Allāh, may Allāh bless Him and His Family, concerning myself and my brother. Is there not (sufficient) in this to prevent you shedding my blood?"

"If I understand what you are saying," interrupted Shamir b. Dhī al-Jawshan, "then I only worship Allāh (very shakily) on the edge."

"I think that you worship Allāh (very shakily) on seventy edges," said Ḥabib b. Muẓāhir "For I testify that you are right. You do not understand what he is saying. For Allāh has impressed (ignorance) upon your heart."

"If you are in any doubt about this," al-Ḥusayn, peace be on him, told them, "you are in doubt that I am the Son of the daughter of your Prophet. By Allāh there is no son of a prophet other than me among you and among the peoples from East to West. Shame on you, are you seeking retribution from me for one of your dead whom I have killed, or for property of yours which I expropriated, or for a wound which I have inflicted?"

They did not say anything to him. They he called: "Shabath b. Rib'ī, Ḥajjār b. Abjar, Qays b. al-Ash'ath, Yazīd b. al-Hārith, didn't you write: 'The fruit has ripened; the dates have grown green; come to an army which has been gathered for you?'"

"We don't know what you are talking about," said Qays b. al-Ash'ath. "Submit to the authority of your kinsmen (the Umayyads). They have never treated you with anything but what you liked. "

"By Allāh, I will never give you my hand like a man who has been humiliated; nor will I flee like a slave," said al-Ḥusayn, peace be on him. Then he called out, "O Servants of Allāh, *I take refuge in my Lord and your Lord from your stoning* (XLIV 20) *I take refuge in my Lord and your Lord from every haughty man who does not believe in the Day of Reckoning* (XL 27) .

He made his mount kneel and ordered 'Uqba b. Sim'ān to tie its reins. They

(the Kūfans) began to advance towards him (al-Ḥusayn). When al-Ḥurr b. Yazīd perceived that the people were determined to fight al-Ḥusayn, peace be on him, he said to 'Umar: "Are you going to fight this man?"
"Yes," he replied, "it will be a terrible battle, the least part of which will be heads falling and severed hands flying (through the air)."

"Haven't you any other way of getting what you want?"
"If the matter rested with me," answered 'Umar, "I would do (anything else), but your governor has refused (any alternative)."

Al-Ḥurr went and stood apart from the people. With him was a man from his tribe called Qurra b. Qays.
"Qurra, have you watered your horse, today?" he asked.
"No."
"Do you want to Water it?"

[Qurra reported (later):]
I thought that he (al-Ḥurr) was going to leave the battle, and did not want to be present at it but was unwilling to be seen when he (left). So I said: "I have not watered it and I was going to water it." Then I left him where he was. By Allāh, If he had told me what he was intending to do, I would have gone with him to al-Ḥusayn, peace be on him.

He (al-Ḥurr) began gradually to draw closer to al-Ḥusayn.
"What do you want, Ibn Yazīd?" asked Muhājir b. Aws, but he did not answer. (Instead) a great shudder came over him.

"Your behaviour is suspicious," said Muhājir. "By Allāh, I have never seen you act like this before. If I was asked who was the bravest of the Kūfans, I would not (normally) neglect (to mention) you. What is this I see in you, (today)?"

"By Allāh, I am giving my soul the choice between Heaven and the fire (of Hell)," answered al-Ḥurr. "By Allāh, I will not choose anything before Heaven, even though I am cut to pieces and burnt"

(With that) he whipped his horse and (galloped over) and joined al-Ḥusayn, peace be on him.

"May I be your ransom, son of the Apostle of Allāh?" he said. "I was your companion who stopped you from returning. I accompanied you along the road and made you stop in this place. But I did not think that the people would refuse to respond to what you have offered them and that they would ever come to this position (which they have now come to) with regard to you. By Allāh, if I had known that they would finish up (by doing) what I am seeing (them do) to you, I would not have committed what I have committed against you. I repent to Allāh for what I have done. Will you accept my repentance?"

"Yes," replied al-Ḥusayn, peace be on him, "Allāh will forgive you. So get down,"
"You will have (no) horseman better than me, (nor), while I am on foot, any foot-soldier," he said. "I will continue fighting on foot to the (bitter) end."
"Do so," replied al-Ḥusayn, peace be on him. "May Allāh grant you mercy (though) what He has revealed to you."

He advanced, in front of al-Ḥusayn, peace be on him, and called out: "People of Kūfa, your mother(s) will be deprived of their sons and tears will come to their eyes. Have you summoned this righteous man (to come to you), then, when he has come to you, have you handed him over (to his enemies)? Did you claim that you would fight with your own lives for him, and then have you begun to attack him in order to kill him? You have laid hold of his life; you have seized his throat; you have encircled him on every side in order to prevent him returning to Allāh's broad land (i.e. the Ḥijāz). He has come into your hands like a prisoner who no longer has the power to use his own life and cannot defend it against harm. You have prevented him, his womenfolk, his children and his people from (getting) the water of the Euphrates which Jews, Christians and Majians may drink, and which the pigs and dogs of Sawād drink. They (al-Ḥusayn's family) are likely to die of thirst. How wickedly you have treated the offspring left by Muḥammad. May Allāh not give you water to drink on the Day of Thirst."

Some of the foot-soldiers attacked him by shooting arrows at him. He went and stood in front of al-Ḥusayn, peace be on him.

"Durayd." 'Umar b. Sa'd called out, "bring forward your standard (for us)."
He brought it forward. ('Umar) put an arrow in his bow and let it fly. He said, "(All of you) be witnesses of who was the first to shoot."

The people began to shoot at each other and to come forward (for single combat). Yasār, retainer (*mawlā*) of Ziyād b. Abī Sufyān, came forward (from 'Umar's army). 'Abd Allāh b. 'Umayr (al-Kalbī) came forward (from al-Ḥusayn's ranks) to meet him .

"Who are you?" Yasār asked him, and (Ibn al-Kalbī) gave him his lineage.

"I do not know you," (Yasār) answered. "Let Zuhayr b. al-Qayn or Ḥabīb b. Muẓāhir come out against me."
"Son of a prostitute, you wanted to do single combat with one of the people," retorted 'Abd Allāh b. 'Umayr (al-Kalbī).

With that (Ibn al-Kalbī) struck him with his sword until he had quietened him. While he was occupied with striking against him, Sālim, retainer (*mawlā*) of 'Ubayd Allāh b. Ziyād, attacked him (Ibn al-Kalbī). Al-Ḥusayn's followers cried out (in warning): "The (other) servant is closing in on you!" (Ibn al-Kalbī) did not notice (Sālim) until the latter was upon him. With his left arm he warded off Sālim's blow but the fingers of his hand were cut off. Then he turned on (Sālim) and struck him and killed him. After (thus) killing them both, (Ibn al-Kalbī) came forward and recited:

> If you do not know me, I am Ibn al-Kalbī: I am a man of bitterness and anger, I am not a weakling in the face of disaster.

'Amr b. al-Ḥajjāj, with the Kūfans under his command, launched an attack on the right wing of the supporters of al-Ḥusayn, peace be on him. When they drew near, the followers of al-Ḥusayn, peace be on him, knelt down and pointed their spears at them. The (attackers') horses would not come forward against the spears and they swung round to retreat. The followers of al-Ḥusayn, peace be on him, began to shoot arrows at (the enemy), killing some of them and wounding others.

'Abd Allāh b. Ḥawza, one of the Banū Tamīm, approached al-Ḥusayn's camp and the people called out to him, "Where are you going, may your mother be deprived of you?"
"I am (in the right) advancing to a merciful Lord and an intercessor who is listened to (i.e. the Prophet)," he answered.
"Who is that?" al-Ḥusayn, peace be on him, asked his followers.
"Ibn Ḥawza al-Tamīmī," he was told.
"O Allāh, drive him into the fire!" (al-Ḥusayn) exclaimed. With that his horse upset him in its stride and fell. His left leg was stuck in the stirrups and his right leg was free. Muslim b. 'Awsaja attacked him and struck his right leg and cut it off. The horse galloped off (dragging) him (along) and his head struck every stone and clod of earth until he died. Allāh hurried his soul to (Hell) fire. (More) fighting then broke out and more men were killed.

Al-Ḥurr b. Yazīd attacked the followers of 'Umar b. Sa'd and (as he did so), he recited the words of 'Antara:

> With my charger's neck and breast thrust forward I will launch myself at them again and again until (the beast) is clothed in blood.

Yazīd b. Sufyān, from Banū al-Ḥārith (of Tamīm), came forward to meet him. Soon al-Ḥurr killed him.

(In the meantime) Nāfi‘ b. Hilāl came forward, declaring:
I am the son of Hilāl. I believe in the religion of ‘Alī.

Muzāhim b. Ḥurayth came against him, crying, "I follow the religion of ‘Uthmān."
"Rather you follow the religion of Satan," Nāfi‘ replied and attacked and killed him.

"You stupid fellows." ‘Amr b. al-Ḥajjāj cried out to (his) men, "don't you realise whom you are fighting? (These) knights of the town are people who are seeking death. Don't let any of you go forward to fight them in single combat. They are only few and their time is running out. If you only threw stones at them, you would kill them (eventually)."

"True, you've come to the right conclusion," ‘Umar b Sa‘d said to him. Then he sent (the message) to the commanders that none of their men should fight in single combat.

‘Amr b. al-Ḥajjāj and his men launched an attack against al-Ḥusayn, peace be on him, from the direction of the Eupharates. They fought together fiercely for a time. Muslim b. ‘Aswaja was struck down, may Allāh have mercy on him, (but) ‘Amr and his men withdrew. When the dust settled, (al-Ḥusayn's followers) found Muslim stretched out dying. Al-Ḥusayn, peace he on him, walked towards him and he was on the point of death.

"Muslim, may Allāh have mercy on you" said (al-Ḥusayn). "*of them (the believers) is he who has accomplished his vow, and of them is he who waits; they have not changed at all*" (XXXIII 23).

Ḥabīb b. Muẓāhir approached and said, "Muslim, your death is hard for me to bear but I bring you good news of Heaven (where you are going)."
"May Allāh bring you good news too," replied Muslim in a weak voice.
"Even if I knew that I would follow you at this very moment. I would still like you to appoint me to carry out everything which concerns you."

Then the people came again against al-Ḥusayn, peace be on him. Shamir b. Dhī al-Jawshan attacked with his left wing (and thrust at) (al-Ḥusayn's) left wing, but they stood firm against him and forced him away (with their spears). Al-Ḥusayn, peace be on him, and his followers were attacked on every side but the followers of al-Ḥusayn fought fiercely. Then their cavalry began to attack and even though they were only thirty-two horsemen, they did not attack any side of the Kūfan cavalry without putting it to flight.

When ʻUrwa b. Qays saw that - he was in command of the Kūfan cavalry - he sent word to ʻUmar b. Saʻd: "Don't you see what my cavalry is receiving today from this small number (of men)? Send the foot-soldiers and archers against them."

He sent the archers against them. Al-Ḥurr b Yazīd's horse was lamed. He dismounted and began to shout:

> You have tamed my (horse) but I am the son of freedom and braver than a manned lion.

He struck out against them with his sword but a great number came against him. Ayyūb b. Musarriḥ and another of the Kūfan horseman shared in killing him.

The followers of al-Ḥusayn, peace be on him, continued to fight fiercely against the enemy until it was midday. When al-Ḥusayn b. Numayr – he was in command of the archers – perceived the steadfastness of the followers al-Ḥusayn, peace be on him, he advanced against his supporters with five hundred archers so that they showered the followers of al-Ḥusayn, peace be on him, with arrows. They continued shooting at them until they had lamed (most of) their horses and wounded some of their men. Then they moved against them and a fierce battle was fought between them for some time. Shamir b. Dhī al-Jawshan (also) attacked them with his followers but Zuhayr b. al-Qayn with ten of the followers of al-Ḥusayn (counter) attacked and drove them away from the tents. Shamir b. Dhī al-Jawshan turned back against them but (some) of his men were killed and the rest retreated to their positions. (The number) of killed was apparent among the followers of al-Ḥusayn, peace be on him, because of the fewness of their number while it was not so apparent among the followers of ʻUmar b. Saʻd because of their great number. The battle (continued to be) fought fiercely and desperately. The number killed and wounded among the followers of Abū ʻAbd Allāh al-Ḥusayn, peace be on him, continued to grow until the sun began to decline. Al-Ḥusayn and his companions prayed the prayer according to the rite of the prayer of fear.

Ḥanẓala b. Saʻd al-Shibāmī advanced in front of al-Ḥusayn, peace be on him, and called out "People of Kūfa, *O people I fear for you the same (that happened) on the Day of Parties. I fear for you on the Day of Summoning.* (XL 30, 32). O people, do not kill al-Ḥusayn *for Allāh will destroy you with punishment. He who forges a lie will be disappointed* (XX 61)."

He advanced and fought until he was killed, may Allāh have mercy on him. After that, Shawdhab, retainer (*mawlā*) of Shākir, went forward, (after saying): "Greetings, Abū 'Abd Allāh and may Allāh store his mercy and blessings for you." He fought until he was killed, may Allāh have mercy on him.

Then came 'Ābis b. Shabīb al-Shākirī. He greeted al-Ḥusayn, peace be on him, and fought until he was killed. Each man of (al-Ḥusayn's) followers continued to go forward and be killed until there only remained with al-Ḥusayn, peace be on him, the members of his own House.

His son, 'Alī b. al-Ḥusayn, peace be on them, whose mother was Layla daughter of Abū Murra b. 'Urwa b. Mas'ūd al-Thaqafī, was (the next) to advance. He was one of the most handsome men of the time. On that day he was nineteen years of age. He attacked the enemy declaring:

> I am 'Alī b. al-Ḥusayn b. 'Alī. By the House of Allāh, we are those rightly (endowed) with the Prophet.
>
> By Allāh, the son of a spurious son will not judge us. I will strike with my sword in defence of my father,
>
> I will strike with the blow of a Hāshimī, a Qurayshī,

He did that several times, and the Kūfans were afraid to kill him. Then Murra b. Munqidh al-'Abdī saw him. He said: "May the felonies of the Arabs come on me, if he gets past me doing the same as he has been doing, (and) if I do not deprive his mother of him."

('Alī b. al-Ḥusayn) continued to attack the enemy as he had been doing but then Murra b, Munqidh came against him and stabbed him. He was struck down and the enemy fell upon him, cutting him with their swords. Al-Ḥusayn, peace be on him, went out until he stood over him and said: "May Allāh kill (the) people who killed you, my son. How foolhardy they are against the Merciful and in violating the sacredness of the family of the Apostle, may Allāh bless Him and His Family."

His eyes filled with tears and he said: "There will (only) be dust on the world after you."

Zaynab, the sister of al-Ḥusayn, peace be on him, came hurrying out, crying: "My brother. my nephew!"

She came up and threw herself on (her dead nephew). Al-Ḥusayn raised her head and then led her back to the tent. He told his young (sons); "Carry your brother back."

They carried him and put him before the tent which they had been fighting in front of. (Then) one of 'Umar b. Sa'd's men called 'Amr b. Ṣubayḥ shot an arrow at 'Abd Allāh b. Muslim b. 'Aqīl. 'Abd Allāh put his hand to guard his brow. The arrow struck his hand and penetrated through his brow, and riveted the hand to it. He was not able to move it when another man came down on him with a spear, thrust it into his heart, and killed him.

'Abd Allāh b. Quṭba al-Ṭā'ī attacked 'Awn b. 'Abd Allāh b. Ja'far b. Abī Ṭālib and killed him.

'Āmir b. Nashhal al-Tamīmī attacked Muḥammad b. 'Abd Allāh b. Ja'far b. Abī Ṭālib and killed him.

'Uthmān b. Khālid al-Hamdānī launched himself against 'Abd al-Raḥmān b. 'Aqīl b. Abī Ṭālib, and killed him.

[Humayd b. Muslim reported:]
It was like that among us (i.e. many of al-Ḥusayn's supporters had been killed by 'Umar b. Sa'd's army) when a young lad came out against us. His face was young like the first splinter of the new moon and he carried a sword. He was wearing a shirt and a waistcloth (*izār*) and a pair of sandals, one of whose straps was broken. 'Umar b. Sa'd b. Nufayl al-Azdī said to me: "Let me attack him." I said; "Praise be to Allāh, what do you want to do that for? Leave him. While even one of the family of al-Ḥusayn remains, that will be enough to take vengeance on you for his (death)." But he insisted: "By Allāh, let me attack him." So he rushed against him and did not turn back until he had struck his head with his sword and split it in two. The young lad fell face downwards and he called out: "O uncle!"

At this, al-Ḥusayn, peace be on him, showed himself just like the hawk shows itself. He launched into attack like a raging lion and struck 'Umar b. Sa'd b. Nufayl with his sword. That man tried to fend off the blow with his arm but his arm was cut off from the elbow, and he gave a great shriek (of pain) which was (even) heard by the people in the camp. As al-Ḥusayn, peace be on him, turned away from him, the cavalry of Kūfa attacked in order to save him but they (only succeeded) in trampling him to death beneath the horses' hooves, and the dust rose.

I saw al-Ḥusayn, peace be on him, standing by the head of the young lad, looking at his feet and al-Ḥusayn, peace be on him was saying: "May the people who have caused your death perish. For the one who will oppose them on the Day of Resurrection on your behalf will be your grandfather ('Alī, or great-grandfather, i.e. the Prophet)." Then he continued: "By Allāh, it is hard on your uncle that you called him and he did not answer you, or rather he answered but your cry was (too late) to help you. For by Allāh, those who kill his relatives are many but those who help him are few." Then he carried him in his arms. It is just as if (even now) I am looking at the two legs of the boy making marks (as they trail) on the ground. He took him and put him with his son. 'Alī b. al-Ḥusayn, peace be on them both, and the other members of the household who had been slain. I asked about the boy and was told that he was al-Qāsim b. al-Ḥasan b. 'Alī b. Abī Ṭālib, peace be on them.

Then al-Ḥusayn, peace be on him, sat in front of the tent. He brought his son. 'Abd Allāh b. al-Ḥusayn, peace be on him, who was (just) a baby and sat him on his knee. But one of the Banū Asad shot an arrow which slaughtered the child. Al-Ḥusayn, peace be on him, caught the child's blood in the palm of his hand. When his palm was full, he poured (the blood) on to the ground and said: "O Lord, if it be so that You have kept the help of Heaven from us, then let it be because (Your purpose) is better than (immediate help). Take vengeance on these people who are (such) oppressors." Then he carried the child and laid him with the (other) members of his household who had been slain.

(Just then) 'Abd Allāh b. 'Uqba al-Ghanawī shot an arrow at Abu Bakr b. al-Ḥasan b. 'Alī, peace be on them, and killed him. When al-'Abbās b. 'Alī saw the number of his family who had been killed, he said to his brothers on his mother's side - 'Abd Allāh, Ja'far and 'Uthmān: "My brothers through my mother, go forward so that I may see that you have remained true to Allāh and His Apostle. For you have no children (to defend)."

'Abd Allāh, may Allāh have mercy on him, advanced and fought fiercely He exchanged blow with Hāni' b. Shabīb al-Ḥadrāmī and Hāni' killed him. After him Ja'far went forward and Hāni' also killed him. Khawalī b. Yazīd al-Aṣbaḥī, may Allāh curse him, went against 'Uthmān who had taken the place of his brother. He fired an arrow at him and brought him down. One of the Banū Dārim attacked him (while he was down) and cut off his head.

The group then launched an attack against al-Ḥusayn, peace he on him, and cut off his access to his camp. His thirst became severe, and he set off towards the dam, trying to reach the Euphrates. In front of him was his brother, al-'Abbās. However, the cavalry of Ibn Sa'd, may Allāh curse him, blocked his route. Among these was a man from the Banū Dārim: he said to (the cavalry): "Woe upon you! Prevent him from reaching the Euphrates, don't let him get water."

Then al-Ḥusayn, peace be on him, cried nut: "O Allāh, I am thirsty." The Dārimī became angry and shot an arrow at him which lodged in his throat. Al-Ḥusayn, peace be on him, pulled out the arrow and held his hand below his throat. Both his palms were filled with blood which he shook away, then he said: "O Allāh, I complain to You about what is being done to the son of the daughter of Your Prophet." Then he returned to his position, while his thirst had become (even more) severe.

Meanwhile the people had surrounded al-'Abbās and cut him off from (al-Ḥusayn). Single-handed he began to attack them until he was killed, may Allāh have mercy on him.The two who took part in killing him were Zayd b. Warqā al-Ḥanafī and Hakīm b. al-Ṭufail al-Shabsī, after he had been covered with wounds and could not move.[22]

When al-Ḥusayn, peace be on him, came back from the dam to his tents, Shamir b. Dhī al-Jawshan advanced towards him with a group of his followers and surrounded him. The fastest of them was a man called Mālik b. al-Nusayr al-Kindī. He cursed al-Ḥusayn, peace be on him, and struck him on the head with his sword. (Al-Ḥusayn) was wearing a cap. (The sword) went through it right into his head and made it bleed. The cap was filled with blood

Al-Ḥusayn, peace be on him, said to him: "May you never eat or drink with your right hand! May Allāh gather you (on the Day of Judgement) with those people who are wrong-doers." Then he threw away the cap and called for a cloth which he tied around his head. Then he called for another cap, put it on and bound it (in place).[23]

Shamir b. Dhī al-Jawshan and those who were with him had withdrawn from him to their (earlier) positions. After a short delay they came again against him and surrounded him. 'Abd Allāh b. al-Ḥasan b. 'Alī, peace be on them, came out against them, he was only a boy, not yet mature enough to leave the women. He rushed forward until he stood beside his uncle, al-Husayn, peace be on him. Then

22 The account of al-'Abbās' death is missing from al-Ṭabarī.
23 This attack and the account of the cap are also missing from al-Ṭabarī.

Zaynab, the daughter of ʻAlī, peace be on him, came after him to stop him, and al-Ḥusayn, peace be on him, told her to stop him. However he refused (to take any notice of her) and determinedly prevented her (from taking him away). He said: "By Allāh, I will not leave my uncle."

(At this) Abjar[24] b. Kaʻb rushed towards al-Ḥusayn, peace be on him. With sword (in hand), the young lad said to him: "Woe upon you, you son of an impure woman, are you trying to kill my uncle?" Abjar struck at him with his sword. The boy tried to fend off (the blow) with his arm. The sword cut through (his arm) to the skin (on the other side). There was the arm hanging (by the skin). The boy cried out: "O my mother!" Al-Ḥusayn took hold of him and embraced him. He said to him: "My nephew, try to bear what has come to you and be comforted with the news that Allāh will unite you with your righteous ancestors." Then al-Ḥusayn, peace be on him, raised his hand and said: "O Allāh, even as You have made life pleasant for them for a time, divide them into factions and make them follow the ways of factions and let their rulers never be pleased with them. They summoned us so that they might support us and then they became hostile to us and killed us."

The foot-soidiers launched an attack from right and left against those who were left with al-Ḥusayn, peace be on him, until only a group of three or four remained with him. When al-Ḥusayn, peace be on him, saw that, he called for of pair of dazzling Yemenī trousers (*sarāwīl*). He tore them and put them on. He tore them so that he should not have been plundered after he had been killed. When al-Ḥusayn, peace be on him, was killed, Abjar b. Kaʻb set on him, plundered him of the trousers and left him naked. After that the two hands of Abjar b. Kaʻb, may Allāh curse him, became so dry in the summer that they were like sticks and then soaking wet in the winter so that they sprinkled drops of water and pus, until Allāh destroyed him.

When nobody except a group of three members of his family was left with al-Ḥusayn, peace be on him, he moved against the people, while the three protected him until (all) three were killed. Al-Ḥusayn, was left alone. Despite being weighed down by wounds in his head and body, he began to strike against them with his sword and they scattered to right and left, away from him.

Then Ḥumayd b. Muslim said: "By Allāh, I have never seen such persistence. His sons have been killed, and the members of his household and his followers, yet he is still as brave as ever and he has not allowed his spirits to leave him. When the soldiers attack him, he fights back with his sword and scatters them to

24 Baḥr in al-Ṭabarī, II, 363.

right and left of him like goats when a wolf comes upon them."

When Shamir b. Dhī al-Jawshan realised (the position), he called for the cavalry and they came up at the rear of the foot-soldiers. He ordered the archers to shoot at (al-Ḥusayn) and they showered him with arrows until he became (quilted with arrows) like a hedgehog (is with spikes).

He drew back from them and they stood facing him. His sister, Zaynab, came to the door of the tent and called out to 'Umar b. Sa'd b. Abī Waqqāṣ: "Woe unto you, 'Umar. Is Abū 'Abd Allāh being killed while you (stand by and) watch?" But 'Umar did not answer. Then she called out: "Woe upon you (all), is there not a Muslim among you?" But no one answered.

Then Shamir b. Dhī al-Jawshan shouted at the foot soldier and the cavalry: "Why are you waiting for the man? May your mothers be deprived of you!" So they attacked him from every side.

Zur'a b. Sharīk struck him on the left shoulder-blade and cut into it. Another of them struck him on the shoulder. He fell prostate on his face. Sinān b. Anas al-Nakha'ī stabbed him with a spear and killed him. Khawalī b. Yazīd al-Aṣbaḥī hurried to him and bent down to cut off his head but he trembled (too much). Shamir[25] said to him: "May Allāh crush your arm, why are you trembling?" Then Shamir bent down and decapitated him. He lifted the head (and handed it) to Khawalī saying: "Take it to the commander 'Umar b. Sa'd".

Then they began to plunder (the body of) al-Ḥusayn, peace be on him. Isḥāq b. al-Ḥayāt al-Ḥaḍrāmī, may Allāh curse him, took his shirt. Abjar b. Ka'b, may Allāh curse him, took his trousers. Akhnas b. Marthad, may Allāh curse him, took his turban. One of the Banū Dārim took his sword. They plundered his saddle and his camel and they looted his womenfolk.[26]

[Ḥumayd b. Muslim reported:]
By Allāh, I did not see one of his women or daughters or the women of his family who did not have her clothes ripped from her back, taken away and removed from her forcibly. Then we came to 'Alī b. al-Ḥusayn, peace be on them both. He was stretched out on a bed and he was very ill. Shamir had a group of foot-soldiers with him and they asked him, "Shall we kill this sick one?" I said: "Praise be to Allāh, will boys be killed (too)? This is only a youth even though he is what he is." And I went on (arguing) until I had moved them away from him.

25 Sinān in al-Ṭabarī, II, 366

26 The names of the plunderers and the plundered objects are different in al-Ṭabarī, II, 366.

Then ʻUmar b. Saʻd arrived and the women cried out and wept in his face. He ordered his followers: "None of you should enter the tents of these women nor disturb this sick boy." The women asked him to return what had been taken from them so that they could clothe themselves again. So he commanded that whoever had taken any of their belongings should return them to them. But by Allāh, none of them returned anything. He then entrusted charge of the main tent and the tents of the women to a group (of men) who were with him. He said: "Guard (the women) so that none of them may leave and do not harm them."

After this, he returned to his tent and called out to his followers: "Who will volunteer (to go) to al-Ḥusayn and make his horse trample on (al-Ḥusayn's body)?" Ten volunteered. Of these, Isḥaq b Hayyat and Akhnas b. Marthad trampled on (the body of) al-Ḥusayn with their horses until they had broken and bruised his back. ʻUmar b. Saʻd despatched on that day - it was the day of ʻAshūrā', - the head of al-Ḥusayn, peace be on him, with Khawalī b. Yazīd al-Aṣbaḥī and Ḥumayd b. Muslim al-Azdī, to ʻUbayd Allāh b. Ziyād. Then he ordered the heads of the remainder of his followers and members of his House (who had been slain) to be cut off. There were seventy-two heads. He sent Shamir b. Dhī al-Jawshan, Qays b. Ashʻath and ʻAmr b. al-Ḥajjāj with these. They journeyed until they brought them to Ibn Ziyād. He (ʻUmar b Saʻd) remained there for the rest of that day, and the next day until just after midday. Then he summoned the people for the journey, and set out towards Kūfa. He took with him the daughters and sisters of al-Ḥusayn, peace be on him, together with ʻAlī b. al-Ḥusayn, peace be on him. The latter was still sick with a dysentery and was almost on the point of death .

When Ibn Saʻd departed, some of Banū Asad, who had been staying at al-Ghāḍiriyya went to al-Ḥusayn, peace be on him, and his followers. They performed the funeral prayer over them. Then they buried al-Ḥusayn at the place where his tomb still is, and they buried his son ʻAlī. b. al-Ḥusayn al-Asghar (the younger) at the foot of the body. They dug around the area next to the two feet of al-Ḥusayn, peace be on him, for the martyrs from his House and his followers. They gathered them together and buried them all together. However, they buried al-ʻAbbās b. ʻAlī, peace be on them both, in the place where he was killed, on the road to al-Ghāḍiriyya, where his tomb still is.[27]

When the head of al-Ḥusayn, peace be on him, arrived and after Ibn Saʻd arrived on the next day (bringing) with him the daughters and household of al-Ḥusayn, peace be on him, Ibn Ziyād sat before the people in the governor's palace. He had given the people a general summons and had ordered them to be present (to

27 These details are not given by al-Ṭabarī.

see) the head. He put it in front of him, and he began to look at it with a smile. In his hand he had a cane and he began to poke at the teeth with it.

When Zayd b. Arqam, a companion of the Prophet who was (then) an old man, saw him poking at the teeth with the cane, he said: "Take your cane away from those two lips. For, by Allāh, other than Whom there is no deity, I have seen the lips of the Apostle of Allāh, may Allāh bless Him and His Family, touch those two lips countless times"
(with that) he began to weep.

"Does Allāh make your eyes weep?" asked Ibn Ziyād. "Or are you weeping because of Allāh's victory? If it was not for the fact that you are an old man who has become silly and your mind has left you, I would have cut off your head."

Zayd b. Arqam stood up in front of him and went to his house. (Meanwhile) the family of al-Ḥusayn, peace be on him, was brought before Ibn Ziyād. Zaynab, the sister of al-Ḥusayn, peace be on him, came in the middle of the group, pretending not to be herself; she was wearing her dirtiest clothes. She went and sat in a corner of the palace and her maids crowded her.

"Who is that woman who has gone to the side and has sat in a corner with her women?" Ibn Ziyād demanded but Zaynab did not answer. He repeated the question about her a second time.

"This is Zaynab, daughter of Fāṭima, the daughter of the Apostle of Allāh, may Allāh bless him and grant him peace," one of her women told him.

"Praise be to Allāh Who has disgraced you, killed you and revealed the false nature of your claims," said Ibn Ziyād as he came towards her.

"Praise be to Allāh Who has favoured us with His Prophet, Muḥammad, may Allāh bless Him and His Family," answered Zaynab "and He has purified us completely from sin. He only disgraces the great sinner and reveals the false nature of the profligate. Such men are not among us, praise be to Allāh"

"How do you consider Allāh has trealed your House?" asked Ibn Ziyād.

"Allāh decreed death for them and they went forward (bravely) to their resting places," Zaynab replied. "Allāh will gather you and us together. You will plead your excuses to Him and we will be your adversaries before Him."

Ibn Ziyād became enraged and burnt with anger.

"Governor," intervened 'Amr b. Ḥurayth, "She is only a woman and women are not responsible for anything that they say. Do not blame her mistakes."

"Allāh has healed my soul from your tyranny and the rebellion of your House," he said to her.

Zaynab, peace be on her, became weak and wept.

"By my life," she cried out to him, "You have killed the mature ones (of my family); you have pierced my family; you have cut down my young branches; and you have pulled out my root. If this heals you, then you have been healed."

"By my life," declared Ibn Ziyād, "this is a woman who makes poetry. Your father was a poet."

"What has a woman to do with poetry?" she answered. "Indeed I have (things) to distract me from poetry but my heart causes me to say what I am saying."

'Alī b. al-Ḥusayn, peace be on them, was presented to him.
"Who are you?" he asked.
"I am 'Alī b. al-Ḥusayn," he answered.

"Didn't Allāh kill 'Alī b. al-Ḥusayn?"
"I have a brother who is also called 'Alī," answered 'Alī, peace be on him, "the people killed him."
"Rather Allāh killed him," affirmed Ibn Ziyād.

"*Allāh receives the souls at the time of their death*" (XXXIX 42).
"How dare you answer me like that!" shouted Ibn Ziyād angrily, "and that will be the last of you because of (your) answer to me. Take him away and cut his head off!"

Zaynab, his aunt, clung on to him, pleading: "O Ibn Ziyād. haven't you had enough of our blood?"
Then she clung on to him and said : "By Allāh, I will not leave him. If you kill him, kill me with him."

Ibn Ziyād looked at her and at him, and said, "How wonderful is family relationship! I think she wants me to kill her with him. Leave him, for I see him (now) for what he is."

He rose from his assembly to leave the palace and go to the mosque. He went up on the pulpit. He praised and glorified Allāh, then he said: "Praise be to Allāh Who has revealed the truth and the followers of the truth, and has given victory to the Commander of the faithful, Yazīd, and his party, and has killed the liar who is the son of a liar and his Shī'a."

At this 'Abd Allāh b. 'Afīf al-Azdī, who had been one of the Shī'a of the Commander of the Faithful (i.e. 'Alī b. Abī Ṭālib) stood in front of him and shouted: "O enemy of Allāh, you are the liar and your father and (the man) who appointed you and his father. O Ibn Murjāna, you kill the sons of Prophets and take the place of men of truth on the pulpit."
"Get him for me," ordered Ibn Ziyād.

The soldiers seized him but he gave the battle cry of al-Azd. Seven hundred of them (quickly) gathered and took him away from the soldiers.

At night Ibn Ziyād sent someone to get him out of his house. He was executed and crucified in al-Sabkha, may Allāh have mercy on him.

The (next) morning 'Ubayd Allāh b. Ziyād sent the head of al-Ḥusayn, peace be on him, (to Yazīd) after it had been taken through all the streets and tribes of Kūfa.

[It is reported from Zayd b. Arqam:]
It was brought past, it was stuck on a spear and I was in a room in my (house). As it was opposite me I heard it recite: "*Or do you think that the Companions of the Cave and the inscription were among Our wonderful signs.*" (XVIII 9). My flesh shuddered and I called out. "O son of the Apostle of Allāh, your head is miraculous, miraculous."[28]

When they had finished taking it around Kūfa and had brought it back to the palace door, Ibn Ziyād gave it to Zaḥar b. Qays and he (also) gave him the heads of his companions. He despatched him to Yazīd b. Mu'āwiya and he sent with him Abū Burda b. 'Awf al-Azdī, and Ṭāriq b. Abī Ẓubyān al-Azdī together with a group of Kūfans, to take them to Yazīd b. Mu'āwiya in Damascus.

['Abd Allāh b. Rabī'a al-Ḥimyarī reported:]
I was with Yazīd b. Mu'āwiya in Damascus when Zaḥar b. Qays brought the

28 This account is not in al-Ṭabarī.

head to him.

"Woe upon you! What is behind you? What have you got?" demanded Yazīd. "O Commander of the faithful," he replied, "I bring good news of Allāh's victory and support. Al-Ḥusayn b. 'Alī, peace be on them, came against us with eighteen men of his House and sixty of his Shī'a. We went out to meet them and we asked them to surrender and submit to the authority of the governor, 'Ubayd Allāh b. Ziyād, or to fight. They chose to fight rather than to surrender. We attacked them as the sun rose and surrounded them on every side. Eventually (our) swords took their toll of the heads of the people and they began to flee without having any refuge (to go to). They (tried to) take refuge from us on the (open) hills and in the hollows, like the doves seek refuge from a hawk. By Allāh, Commander of the faithful, it was nothing but the slaughtering of animals for slaughter. (It was only the time taken by) the sleep of a man taking his siesta (before) we had come upon the last of them. There were their naked bodies, their blood-stained clothes their faces thrown in the dust. The sun burst down on them, the wind scattered (dust) over them; their visitors were (scavenging) eagles and vultures."

Yazīd looked down for a time, then he raised his head and said: "I would have been satisfied with your obedience (to my orders) without this killing of al-Ḥusayn, peace be on him. If it had been me who had accompanied him, I would have let him off (such a fate)."

After 'Ubayd Allāh b. Ziyād had despatched the head of al-Ḥusayn, he ordered the women and the young boys to be made ready for travelling. He ordered 'Alī b. al-Ḥusayn, peace be on them, to be chained with a chain around his neck. Then he despatched them, to follow the heads, with Muḥaffir b. Tha'laba al-'Ā'idhī and Shamir b. Dhī al-Jawshan. They set out with them until they caught up with the people with the head. 'Alī b. al-Ḥusayn did not speak a word to any of the people who had the head on that Journey. Eventually they reached (their destination). When they reached the door of Yazīd's (palace), Muḥaffir b. Tha'laba raised his voice and shouted: "Here is Muḥaffir b. Tha'laba who has brought the Commander of the faithful these vile profligates."

'Alī b. al-Ḥusayn,[29] peace be on him, answered him. "What did the mother of Muḥaffir give birth to more evil and more grievous (than him)?"

When the heads were put in front of Yazīd and among them was the head of al-Ḥusayn, peace be on him, Yazīd recited:

We will split the skull of proud men (who come) against us; they were

29 Yazid in al-Ṭabarī, II, 376.

very disobedient and oppressive.

Yaḥya b. al-Ḥakam, the brother of Marwān b. al-Ḥakam recited:

On the bank (of the river) a great army met him who is closer in kinship (to Yazīd) than Ibn Ziyād (is), the man with a false lineage.

The offspring of Sumayya has acquired status, while the offspring of the daughter of the Apostle of Allāh is (given) none.

Yazīd struck his hand against the chest of Yaḥya b. al-Ḥakam and shouted, "Be quiet!"

Then he said to 'Alī b. al-Ḥusayn, peace be on them: "Son of al-Ḥusayn, your father cut (the bond of) kinship with me and showed ignorance of my rights, trying to deprive me of my position of authority. (Now) Allāh has treated him in the way you have seen."

"*No misfortune strikes the earth nor yourselves unless it has been written in a book before We bring it into existence; that is easy for Allāh.*" (LVII 22) replied 'Alī b. al-Ḥusayn.

"Answer him," Yazīd urged his son, Khalīd. However Khalīd did not know what to say in reply. So Yazīd answered: "Say rather: *whatever misfortunes has struck you is because of what your hands have earned. And (Allāh) forgives much*" (XLII 30)."

He summoned the women and the children and they were made to sit in front of him. What he saw was dreadful.

"May Allāh detest Ibn Murjāna," he said: "If there had been (any bond of) kinship between him and you, he would not have done this to you; he would not have sent you in this state."

[Fāṭima, daughter of al-Ḥusayn, peace be on him, reported:]
When we sat before Yazīd, he showed pity on us. An Aḥmar of the Syrians stood up and said to Yazīd; "Commander of the faithful, give me this one."

He meant me. (Then) I was a pretty young girl. I shuddered for I thought that that would be allowed to them. I caught hold of the skirt of my aunt Zaynab and she told (me) that that would not happen. She said to the Syrian: "By Allāh, you are a liar. By Allāh, you are (too) lowly born! Such a thing is not for you nor for him (to decide)."

"You are a liar," Yazīd cried out angrily. "That is for me (to decide). If I wish to do anything, I can do it."

"No, by Allāh," she replied, "Allāh would only let you do that if you left our faith and professed belief in another (religion)."

"It is me," screamed Yazīd, distraught with anger. "whom you are treating in this (way). It is your father who has left the religion, and your brother."

"I am led by the religion of Allāh, the religion of my father and the religion of my brother," she answered, "and (it is what) you are led by, and your grandfather and your father, if you are a Muslim."
"Enemy of Allāh, you lie," he shouted.

"You are a Commander of the faithful, (yet) you vilify unjustly and you have become oppressive with your authority," she answered.

(At this) he was ashamed and became silent.

"Give me that girl," repeated the Syrian.
"Be a bachelor," Yazīd said to him, "May Allāh strike you dead!"

Then he ordered the women to be lodged in a house on (the) banks (of the river). With them (also he sent) their brother, 'Alī b. al-Ḥusayn, peace be on them. (Later) a house was set aside for them, which was attached to Yazīd's own house. They resided (there) for several days. (After a short time) he summoned al-Nu'mān b. Bashīr and told him to make preparations to take these women back to Medina. When he was about to despatch them, he summoned 'Alī b. al-Ḥusayn, peace be on them. He took him aside.

"Allāh curse Ibn Murjāna," he said. "If I had been with your father, he would never have asked me for a favour without me granting him it; I would have protected him from death with all my power. But Allāh has decreed what you have seen. Write to me from Medina and everything that you need will be yours."

He presented clothes to him and to his family. He sent with them in the group (of men under the command) of Nu'mān b. Bashīr, a messenger, who brought him (al-Nu'mān) the order to set out with them in the night; and that they should go in front of him but they should never be out of his sight. When they stopped, he should go aside from them and he and his followers should separate around them like a group of guards over them. He should (only) keep away from them when any person of their group wanted to wash or perform a need, so he (or she) would not be ashamed.

(The messenger) set off with them amid the group of al-Nu'mān. (Al-Nu'mān) continued to stay close to them along the road but he was kind to them as Yazīd had instructed him and he looked after them until they entered Medina.

*****

After Ibn Ziyād had despatched the head of al-Ḥusayn, peace be on him, to Yazīd, he went to 'Abd al-Malik b. Abī al-Hārith[30] al-Sulamī and told him, "Go to 'Amr b. Sa'id b. al-'Āṣ in Medina and give him the good news of the killing of al-Ḥusayn (peace be on him)."

['Abd al-Malik reported:]
I rode my mount and went towards Medina. (On the way) one of Quraysh met me.
"What is the news'?" he asked.
"The news is for the governor, (then) you will hear it ," I answered.
"We belong to Allāh and to Him we will return," he said. "By Allāh, al-Ḥusayn, peace be on him, has been killed."

When I went to 'Amr b. Sa'id, he asked: "What is your purpose?"
"What will please the governor." I answered, "Al-Ḥusayn, peace be on him, has been killed."
"Go out and announce his being killed," he told me.

I announced (it). I have never heard such wailing as the wailing of the Banū Hāshim in their houses for al-Ḥusayn b. 'Alī, peace be on him, when they heard the announcement of his death. I went back (in) to 'Amr b. Sa'id. When he saw me, he smiled at me and laughed. Then he quoted a verse of 'Amr b. Ma'dīkarib:

> The women of Banū Ziyād raised a great lament like the lamentation of our women mourning (after the battle) of al-Arnab.

"This lamentation is in return for the lamentation for 'Uthmān," 'Amr exclaimed. Then he went up on the pulpit and informed the people about the killing of al-Ḥusayn b. 'Alī, and he summoned (them to obey) Yazīd b. Mu'āwiya. (After that) he went down.

---

30 Al-Ḥārith in al-Ṭabarī, II, 383

One of the retainers (*mawālī*) of 'Abd Allāh b. Ja'far b. Abī Ṭālib, peace be on him, went to him and announced the news of the killing of his two sons and he said that we (all return) to Allāh.

"This is what we have through al-Ḥusayn b. 'Alī, peace be on them," said Abū Salāsil, the retainer (*mawlā*) of 'Abd Allāh.

"O son of an obscene (woman)," exclaimed 'Abd Allāh b. Ja'far, taking off his shoe (to strike him). "Are you saying this of al-Ḥusayn, peace be on him? If I had been present with him, I would have preferred not to leave him and to be killed with him. By Allāh, I would not have withheld those two from him and I take consolation from what befell them in that these two were struck down with my brother and cousin, consoling him and enduring with him."

He went forward to those who were sitting with him and said: "Praise be to Allāh, Who has (made life hard for me) through the death of al-Ḥusayn. For I did not console al-Ḥusayn with my own hands, my two sons consoled him."

Umm Luqmān, the daughter of 'Aqīl b. Abī Ṭālib, may Allāh have mercy on them, came out crying when she heard the news of the death of al-Ḥusayn, peace be on him. With her were her sisters Umm Hāni', Ramla and Zaynab, daughters of 'Aqīl b. Abī Ṭālib, may Allāh have mercy on them. She wept for her (relatives) slain on the bank and she recited:

> What would you say if the Prophet asked you: What have you, the Last of the (religious) communities, done with my offspring and my family after my departure from them? They are prisoners and slain and have been stained with their own blood
>
> What sort of reward is this for my advice to you, that you should oppose me by doing evil to my blood relations?

On the night of the day upon which 'Amr b. Sa'id had given the public notice of the killing of al-Ḥusayn b 'Alī, peace be on them, in Medina, in the middle of the night the Medinans heard a voice calling out. They listened to the voice but they did not see any person. (The voice called out:)

> O men who ignorantly killed al-Ḥusayn, hear the news of punishment and chastisement:
>
> All the people of heaven, prophets, angels and slain, prosecute you.
>
> You have been cursed by the tongue of the son of David and (that) of

Moses and (that) of the master of the Gospels

THE NAMES OF THE MEMBERS OF THE HOUSE WHO WERE KILLED WITH AL-ḤUSAYN IN THE PLAIN OF KARBALĀ.

There were seventeen souls. In addition to al-Ḥusayn b. ʿAlī, peace be on them both:

1. Al-ʿAbbās.
2. ʿAbd Allāh.
3. Jaʿfar.
4. ʿUthmān.

(These were all) sons of the Commander of the Faithful, peace be on them, and their mother was Umm al-Banīn.

5. ʿAbd Allāh.
6. Abū Bakr.

(Both of these were) sons of the Commander of the Faithful, peace be on them and their mother was Laylā, daughter of Masʿūd al-Thaqafī.

7. ʿAlī.
8. ʿAbd Allāh.

(These were) two sons of al-Ḥusayn b. ʿAlī, peace be on them both.

9. Al-Qāsim
10. Abū Bakr
11. ʿAbd Allāh.

(These were) sons of al-Ḥasan b. ʿAlī, peace be on them.

12. Muḥammad.
13. ʿAwn.

(They were) two sons of ʿAbd Allāh b. Jaʿfar b. Abī Ṭālib, may Allāh be pleased with them all

14. ʿAbd Allāh.
15. Jaʿfar.
16. ʿAbd al-Raḥmān.

(They were) sons of ʿAqīl b. Abī Ṭālib, may Allāh be pleased with them.

17. Muḥammad.

(He was) the son of Abū Saʿid b ʿAqīl b. Abī Ṭālib, may Allāh have mercy on them all.

These seventeen souls, all members of Banū Hāshim, may Allāh be pleased with them all, included brothers of al-Ḥusayn, peace be on him and them, sons of his brother and sons of his two uncles, Ja'far and 'Aqīl.

They were all buried at the feet of al-Ḥusayn, peace be on him, at the scene of his martyrdom. A trench was dug for them, they were all put in it, then the earth was flattened over them. (That is all of them) except al-'Abbās b. 'Alī, peace be on them both. He was buried at the place where he was killed, by the dam on the road to al-Ghāḍiriyya. His grave is clearly distinguishable but that is not the case with the graves of his brothers and his family whom we named after (him). A visitor may only visit their graves at the tomb of al-Ḥusayn, peace be on him, if he directs his greetings to them towards the ground at the feet of al-Ḥusayn. 'Alī b. al-Ḥusayn, peace be on them both, is among their number; it is said that he is the one of them who is buried nearest to al-Ḥusayn, peace be on him.

The followers of al-Ḥusayn, peace be on him and the mercy of Allāh be on them, who were killed with him, were buried nearby. We are not able to find out accurate details about (the whereabouts of) their corpses. However, we have no doubt that that ground covers them, may Allāh be pleased with them, make them happy and let them dwell in the Gardens of Paradise.

A Sample of the Outstanding Virtues of al-Ḥusayn b. 'Alī, Peace be on Him, the Merit in Visiting (His Grave) and Mention of His Tragedy

[Sa'id b. Rāshid reported on the authority of Ya'lā b. Murra, who said:]
I heard the Apostle of Allāh, may Allāh bless Him and His Family, say: "Ḥusayn is from me and I am from Ḥusayn. Allāh loves whoever loves him. Ḥusayn is indeed an (outstanding) grandson among grandsons."[31]

[Ibn Lahī'a reported on the authority of Abū 'Awāna (with an interrupted chain of authorities) (*rafa'ahu*) back to the Prophet, may Allāh bless him and his family:]
The Apostle of Allāh said: "Al-Ḥasan and al-Ḥusayn, peace be on them, are the ornaments of the throne (of Heaven). Indeed Heaven, itself, said, 'O my Lord, You have filled me with weak and poor inhabitants.' Allāh, the Exalted, replied to it: 'Are you not content that I have adorned your corners with al-Ḥasan and al-Ḥusayn, peace be on them?' Then it swaggered as a bride swaggers with happiness."

---

31 cf. al-Balādhurī, *Ansāb al-ashraf*, III, 142

['Abd Allāh b. Maymūn al-Qaddāḥ reported on the authority of Ja'far b. Muḥammad al-Ṣādiq, peace be on them, who said:]
Al-Ḥasan and al-Ḥusayn, peace be on them, were wrestling in front of the Apostle of Allāh, may Allāh bless Him and His Family.

"Ḥasan, catch hold of Ḥusayn," said the Apostle of Allāh, may Allāh bless Him and His Family.

"Apostle of Allāh, are you encouraging the big one against the little one?" said Fāṭima, peace be on her.

"It is Gabriel, peace be on him, who is saying to al-Ḥusayn: Ḥusayn, catch hold of al-Ḥasan," replied the Apostle of Allāh, may Allāh bless Him and His Family.

[Ibrāhīm b. al-Rāfi'ī reported on the authority of his father, on the authority of his grandfather, who said:]
I saw al-Ḥasan and al-Ḥusayn, peace be on them, walking to the pilgrimage. They did not pass a rider who did not dismount and walk too. It became arduous for some of them. They said to Sa'd b. Abī Waqqāṣ: "Walking is arduous for us. We would prefer to ride but these two young lords (*sayyid*) are walking."

"Abū Muḥammad," said Sa'd to al-Ḥasan, peace be on him, "walking is hard on a group of those with you. Yet the people cannot make themselves feel better by riding when they see you two walking. If you rode, (it would be easier for them)."

"We will not ride," replied al-Ḥasan, peace be on him. "We have pledged ourselves to walk to the Sacred House of Allāh on our feet. However, we will turn aside from the road."
They both went aside from the people.

[Al-Awzā'ī has reported on the authority of 'Abd Allāh b. Shaddād, on the authority of Umm al-Faḍl, daughter of al-Ḥārith:]
She visited the Apostle of Allāh, may Allāh bless Him and His Family and said: "Apostle of Allāh, I have had a strange dream during the night."
"What was it?" he asked.

"It was terrible," she said.
"What was it?" he repeated.

"I saw (something) like a piece of your body cut up and put in my lap," she answered.

"You have seen well," said the Apostle of Allāh, may Allāh bless Him and His Family. "Fāṭima will give birth to a boy when she is sitting on your lap (to give birth)."

[She reported:] Fāṭima did give birth to al-Ḥusayn, peace be on him, and he was in my lap just as the Apostle of Allāh, may Allāh bless Him and His Family, had said. One day I took him to the Prophet, may Allāh bless Him and His Family, and I put him in his lap. His gaze turned away from me. Behold, both the eyes of the Apostle of Allāh, may Allāh bless Him and His Family, were flowing with tears. I said: "(May I ransom you) with my father and mother, Apostle of Allāh, what is the matter with you?"

"Gabriel, peace be on him, came to me," he said. "He told me that my community will seek to kill this son of mine and he brought me dust made red by his (blood)."[32]

[Simāk reported on the authority of Ibn al-Mukhāriq on the authority of Umm Salama, may Allāh be pleased with her, who said:]
One day while the Apostle of Allāh, may Allāh bless Him and His Family, was sitting down, and al-Ḥusayn was sitting on his knee, his eyes suddenly filled with tears. I said to him: "Apostle of Allāh, why do I see you weeping, may I be your ransom?

"Gabriel, peace be on him, came to me," he said. "He consoled me for the death of my son, al-Ḥusayn, and he told me that a group of my community will kill him. May Allāh never let them have infercession from me."[33]

[It is reported with another chain of authorities on the authority of Umm Salama, may Allāh be pleased with her, that she said:]
One evening the Apostle of Allāh left us and was away for a long time. He came back, he was dishevelled and dusty and his hand was holding (something). I said to him: "Apostle of Allāh, why do I see you dishevelled and dusty?"

He said: "I have just been on a night journey to a place in Iraq called Karbalā'. There I saw the death of my son, al-Ḥusayn, and a group of my children and the members of my family (*ahl al-bayt*). I could not stop (myself) from gathenng (some of) their blood and here it is in my hand."
He opened his hand and said: "Take it and look after it."

I took it. It was like red soil. I put it in a phial, fastened its top and kept it. When

32 cf. Ibn al-A'tham, IV, (Hyderabad, 1971), 211-2.
33 cf. Ibn al-A'tham, IV, 213.

al-Ḥusayn, peace be on him, left Mecca on his way to Iraq, I look out that phial every day and night. I used to smell it and look at it. Then I would weep for his fate. On the 10th of (the month of) al-Muḥarram, the day on which al-Ḥusayn, peace be on him, was killed, I took it out. At the beginning of the day it was in its usual condition, but at the end of the day, behold, it was fresh blood. I shrieked (with grief) and wept. Then I restrained my anger out of fear that the enemies (of the family of the Prophet) in Medina would hear and would hurry to rejoice at their misfortune. I have kept it secret up to the present time, even to the day when the messenger bringing the news of his death came to announce it. Then what I had seen was proved.[34]

It is reported that one day the Prophet, may Allāh bless Him and His Family, was sitting down. Around him were 'Alī, Fāṭima, al-Ḥasan and al-Ḥusayn, peace be on them. He asked them: "How would you feel If when you were killed, your tombs were scattered around (the country)?"
"Will we die an (ordinary) death or will we be killed?" al-Ḥusayn, peace be on him, asked.

"Rather you will be killed unjustly, my little son, and your brother will be killed unjustly," he answered. "Your offsprihg will be scattered over the land."

"Apostle of Allāh, who will kill us?" asked al-Ḥusayn, peace be on him.
"The evil men among the people." he said.

"Will anyone visit (our graves) after we are killed?" he asked.
"Yes, my little son," he told him. "a group (*ṭā'ifa*) of my community will gain my benificence and favour through visiting (your graves). On the Day of Resurrection, I will bring them to the place so that I may take them by the arms and save them from its terrors and sorrows."

['Abd Allāh b. Sharīk al-'Āmirī reported:]
I heard the followers of 'Alī say when 'Umar b. Sa'd went through the gate of the mosque: "There is the killer of al-Ḥusayn b. 'Alī, peace be on him." That was some time before he was killed.

[Sālim b. Abī Ḥafṣa reported:]
'Umar b. Sa'd said to al-Ḥusayn: "Abū 'Abd Allāh, stupid people have come to me claiming that I will kill you."

"They are not stupid," al-Ḥusayn, peace be on him, told him. "They are men who

34 cf. Ibn al-A'tham, IV, 212-4.

dream (of the future). Yet it pleases me that you will not enjoy the land of Iraq for long after me."

[Yūsuf b. 'Abīda reported: I heard Muḥammad b. Sīrīn say:]
Such a redness which was in the sky was never seen except after the killing of al-Ḥusayn b. 'Alī, peace be on him.

[Sa'd al-Iskāf reported: Abū Ja'far, peace be on him, said:]
The killer of Yaḥyā b. Zakariyyā (John the Baptist) was a son born out of wedlock. The killer of al-Ḥusayn b. 'Alī was a son born out of wedlock. The sky only went red for those two.

[Sufyān b. 'Uyayna reported on the authority of 'Alī b. Zayd, on the authority of 'Alī b. al-Ḥusayn, peace be on them, who said:]
We set out with al-Husayn, peace be on him. We did not stop at any halting-place without him setting off from there by (first) mentioning Yaḥyā b. Zakariyyā and his death. He would say: "There was a day - and it was a day of the humiliation of the world before Allāh - when the head of Yaḥyā b. Zakariyyā was given to one of the prostitutes of the Banū Isrā'īl."

Reports have already been presented (which show) that none of the killers of al-Ḥusayn, peace be on him, and his followers, may Allāh be pleased with them, managed to avoid being killed or suffering tribulation in such a way as put them to shame before their death.

*****

Al-Ḥusayn, peace be on him, came to his death on Saturday, the 10th of (the month of) al-Muḥarram in the year 61 A.H. after the (time for) the mid-day prayer. (He was) killed wrongfully, while thirsty, always showing fortitude but forced to be detained, as we have already explained. His age on that day was fifty-eight years. Of these, he spent seven with his grandfather, the Apostle of Allāh, may Allāh bless Him and His Family, thirty-seven with his father, the Commander of the Faithful, peace be on him, and forty-seven with his brother, al-Ḥasan, peace be on him. The period of his succession (to the Imamate) after his brother was eleven years. He, peace be on him, used to use henna and a black dye (*katam*). When he, peace be on him, was killed, the dye came off (the beard on) his two cheeks.

*****

Many reports have come down about the great merit (to be acquired) by visiting his (grave), indeed of it being necessary for everyone who accepts the Imamate of al-Ḥusayn, peace be on him, (as being bestowed on him) by

Allāh, the Mighty and High.

It is reported from al-Ṣadiq Ja'far b Muḥammad, peace be on him, that he said: "Visiting the grave of al-Ḥusayn, peace be on him, is equal to a hundred acceptable pilgrimages and a hundred acceptable lesser pilgrimages (*'umra*)."

The Apostle of Allāh, may Allāh bless Him and His Family, said: "Whoever visits the grave of al- Ḥusayn, peace be on him, after the latter's death, will have heaven (as his reward)."

Reports of this kind are numerous and we have given sufficient detail of them in our book *Manāsik al-mazār* "The rites of Visitations"

*****

The Children of al-Ḥusayn b. 'Alī, Peace be on them

Al-Ḥusayn, peace be on him, had six children:

1. 'Alī b. al-Ḥusayn al-Akbar (the elder).

His *kunya* was Abū Muḥammad and his mother was Shāhzanān, daughter of Choesroe Yazdigard.

2. 'Alī b. al-Ḥusayn al-Aṣghar (the younger).

He was killed with his father on the banks (of the Euphrates) as has already been mentioned earlier. His mother was Laylā daughter of Abū Murra b. 'Urwa b. Mas'ūd al-Thaqafī.

3. Ja'far b. al-Ḥusayn, peace be on him.

He had no survivors. His mother was a woman of (the tribe of) Qudā'a and he died during the lifetime of al-Ḥusayn.

4. 'Abd Allah b. al-Ḥusayn.

He was killed while still a baby child with his father. An arrow came, while he was in his father's arms, and killed him. Mention of that has already come earlier also.

5. Sukayna, daughter of al-Ḥusayn, peace be on him.

Her mother was Rabāb, daughter of Imru' al-Qays b. 'Adī of Kalb of Ma'd. She was also the mother of 'Abd Allah b. al- Ḥusayn, peace be on him.

6. Fāṭima, daughter of al-Ḥusayn, peace be on him.

Her mother was Umm Ishāq, daughter of Talḥa b. 'Ubayd Allāh of Taym.

CHAPTER III

IMAM 'ALĪ B. AL-ḤUSAYN

(This is) an account of the Imam after al-Ḥusayn b. 'Alī, peace be on them, the date of his birth, the evidence for his Imamate, the age he reached, (together with) the period of his succession, the time and cause of his death, the place of his grave, the number of his children and a selection from the reports about him.

The Imam after al-Ḥusayn b. 'Alī, peace be on them, was his son, Abū Muḥammed 'Alī b al-Ḥusayn Zayn al-'Ābidīn, peace be on them. He also had the *kunya* Abū al-Ḥasan.

His mother was Shahzanān daughter of Yazdigard b. Shahriyār b. Choesroe. Her name was also said to be Shahrbānawayh. The Commander of the Faithful, peace be on him, had appointed Ḥurayth b. Jābir al-Ḥanafī over part of the eastern provinces. The latter had sent to him two daughters of Yazdigard b. Shahriyār b. Choesroe. Of these he had given his son al-Ḥusayn, peace be on him, Shahzanān and she bore him Zayn al-'Ābidīn ('Alī b al-Ḥusayn), peace be on him. He had given the other to Muḥammad b. Abī Bakr and she bore him al-Qāsim b. Muḥammad b. Abī Bakr, so that these two (Zayn al-'Ābidīn and al-Qāsim) were maternal cousins.

'Alī b al-Ḥusayn, peace be on them, was born in Medina in the year 38 A.H. (658/9). He lived with his grandfather, the Commander of the Faithful, peace be on him, for two years, with his uncle, al-Ḥasan, peace be on him, for twelve years, and with his father, al-Ḥusayn, peace be on him, for twenty-three years. After his father, he lived a further thirty-four years and he died in Medina in the year 95 A.H. (713/4). At that time he was fifty-seven years of age. His Imamate was for thirty-four years. He was buried in al-Baqī' with his uncle, al-Ḥasan b. 'Alī, peace be on them.

His Imamate was confirmed in several ways. One of these was that he was the most meritorious (*afḍal*) of the creatures of Allāh, the Most High, after his father in traditional knowledge (*'ilm*) and practice (*'amal*). The Imamate belongs to the most meritorious (*afḍal*) to the exclusion of the less meritorious (*mafḍūl*) by rational proofs. Among these there was the fact that he was more appropriate for authority by virtue of his father, al-Ḥusayn, peace be on him, and more entitled to his position after him through his merit and lineage. The one who was entitled through the last Imam has more right to his position than anyone else through the evidence of the verse of next of kin (*dhū al-arḥām*) and the (Qur'ānic) story of Zacharia, peace be on him.[1]

Another of (the facts which confirms his Imamate) is the necessity according to reason of the Imamate existing in every age. The claim of every (other) claimant to the Imamate during the time of 'Alī b. al-Ḥusayn, peace be on them, was invalid and the impossibility of there being any time without an Imam is confirmed by him (being the Imam). Another (of the facts which confirms his Imamate) is the fact that the Imamate is established in the offspring (*'itra*) (of the family of 'Alī) exclusively by rational deduction and by a report on the authority of the Prophet, may Allāh bless Him and His Family. Invalidity of the arguments of those who claim it for Muḥammad b. al Ḥanafiyya,[2] may Allāh be pleased with him, through him (also) belonging to the offspring is established by the absence of the designation of it to him. Therefore it is established that it belongs to 'Alī b al-Ḥusayn, peace be on them, since there was no claim for it for any other member of the offspring (of the family) except Muḥammad, may Allāh be pleased with him; his exclusion from it was on account of what we have already mentioned.

Another (of the facts which confirmed his Imamate) was the designation of the Apostle of Allāh, may Allāh bless Him and His Family, of him for the Imamate, in the tradition which is related concerning the tablet (*lawḥ*) which Jābir reported on the authority of the Apostle of Allāh, may Allāh bless Him and His Family. Muḥammad b. 'Alī al-Bāqir, peace be on them, (also) related it on the authority of his father, on the authority of his grandfather, on the authority of Fāṭima, daughter of the Apostle of Allāh, may Allāh bless Him and His Family.

His grandfather, the Commander of the Faithful, peace be on him, designated him during the life-time of his father, al-Ḥusayn, peace be on him, according to the reports which include that. The testamentary bequests (*waṣiya*) (were made) by his father, al-Ḥusayn b. 'Alī, peace be on him, and they were deposited with Umm Salama for him. He received them when his father died. His father made the request (for these) from Umm Salama, the sign of the Imamate of the one who should request them among men.[3] This part may be known by the

1 The verse of *dhū al-arḥām* refers to Qur'ān XXX, 6. The relevant part reads. *those who have a relationship of kinship (ūlū al-arḥām) are more entitled (to inherit) from one another according to the Book of God than the believers and the Emigrants*. On the story of Zacharia. cf. Qur'ān III, 37-41 and XIX, 2-11. The story stresses the idea of succession through the family.

2 In particular the Imamate of Muḥammad b. al Ḥanafiyya was maintained by al-Mukhtār b. Abī 'Ubayd, who led a revolt in Kūfa on his behalf.

3 cf. al-Kāfī, I, 304, tradition no. 3, but other traditions in al-Kāfī suggest that these things were in the hands of Fāṭima, his daughter, cf. al-Kāfī, I, 363-4.

examination of the reports and we do not intend in this book to speak about its significance for we will study it thoroughly separately.

A Brief Survey of the Reports about 'Alī b al-Ḥusayn, Peace be on them.

[Abū Muḥammad al-Ḥasan b. Muḥammad b. Yaḥyā informed me: my grandfather (Yaḥyā b. al-Ḥasan) told us: Idrīs b. Muḥammad b. Yaḥyā b. 'Abd Allāh b. Ḥasan b. Ḥasan, 'Aḥmad b. 'Abd Allāh b. Mūsā, and Ismā'īl b. Ya'qūb, all told me: 'Abd Allāh b. Mūsā told us on the authority of his father (Musa b. 'Abd Allāh), on the authority of his grandfather ('Abd Allāh b. al-Ḥasan), who said:]
My mother, Fāṭima, daughter of al-Ḥusayn, peace be on him, used to tell me to sit with my maternal uncle, 'Alī b al-Ḥusayn, peace be on them. I never sat with him without rising with some good which I had derived from him, whether it was fear of Allāh which occurred in my heart when I realised (what) fear of Allāh (was) or some traditional knowledge (*'ilm*) which I acquired from him.

[Abū Muḥammad al-Ḥasan b. Muḥammad al-'Alawī informed me on the authority of his grandfather (Yaḥyā b. al-Ḥasan), on the authority of Muḥammad b. Maymūn al-Bazzāz, who said: Sufyān b. 'Uyayna informed us on the authority of Ibn Shihāb al-Zuhrī, who said:]
'Alī b al-Ḥusayn, peace be on them, who was the best Hāshimī we ever met, said: "Love us, for it is love for Islam. May your love for us never cease even if it becomes a public disgrace."

[Abū Mu'ammar reported on the authority of 'Abd al-'Azīz Abū Ḥāzim who said:]
I heard my father say: "I have never seen a Hāshimī more meritorious (*afḍal*) than 'Alī b al-Ḥusayn."

[Abū Muḥammad al-Ḥasan b. Muḥammad b. Yaḥyā informed me: my grandfather (Yaḥyā b. al-Hasan) told me Abū Muḥammad al-Anṣārī told me: Muḥammad b. Maymūn al-Bazzāz told me: al-Ḥasan b. 'Alwān told us on the authority of Abū 'Alī Ziyād b. Rustum, on the authority of Sa'īd b. Kulthūm who said:]
I was with al-Ṣādiq Ja'far b. Muḥammad, peace be on them. He mentioned the Commander of the Faithful, 'Alī b. Abī Ṭālib, peace be on him, and praised and extolled him with (praise) which he was worthy of. Then he said: "O Allāh, 'Alī b. Abī Ṭālib, peace be on him, never ate anything forbidden in this world until he passed along his (final) road. Two alternatives were never presented to him, when Allāh would be pleased with both, without him taking the more religious of

them. No dispute occurred about the Apostle of Allāh, may Allāh bless Him and His Family, without him being summoned as a reliable authority. No one else of this community was able to do the work of the Apostle of Allāh, may Allāh bless Him and His Family; for if he enjoined (such a) man (as 'Alī) to work, his position would be between Heaven and Hell, hoping for the reward of the former and fearing the punishment of the latter. He freed a thousand slaves with his own money in his desire to seek the face of Allāh and to escape the fire of Hell, (money) which he had laboured for with his own hands and for which his own brow had sweated, even though it had been to provide his family with oil, vinegar and dates. He did not have (many) clothes except white cotton fabrics since when there was any sleeve left over his arm, he called for scissors and cut it off.

None of 'Alī's children or his family was more like him and nearer to him in manner of dress and understanding than 'Alī b al-Ḥusayn, peace be on them. (One day) his son, Abū Ja'far, (Muḥammad al-Bāqir), peace be on them, came to him. He had carried out in worship what no one had ever carried out. He saw that his colour had gone yellow from weeping all night; his eyes had used up all their water from being awake all night; his forehead was bruised and his nose squashed from prostrating; and his legs and feet were swollen from standing in prayer.

Abū Ja'far, peace be on him, reported: "I could not control myself from weeping when I saw him in that state and I wept, may Allāh have mercy on him. Behold, he was thinking and he turned to me a short time after I had come and said: 'My son, give me some of those parchments in which there is the (practice of) worship of 'Alī b. Abī Ṭālib, peace be on him'."

"I gave them to him and he read something from them for a while. Then he let them go from his hand in exasperation and said: 'Who is strong enough to perform the worship of 'Alī b. Abī Ṭālib, peace be on him?"

[Muḥammad b. al-Ḥusayn reported: 'Abd Allāh b. Muḥammad al-Qurashī told us:]
When 'Alī b al-Ḥusayn, peace be on them, used to perform ritual ablutions, his skin would turn yellow,
"What is it that has afflicted you?" his family asked him.
"Don't you know Whom you are preparing to stand before?" he asked

['Amr b. Shamir reported on the authority of Jabīr al-Ju'fī, on the authority of Abū Ja'far, peace be on him:]

'Alī b al-Ḥusayn, peace be on them, used to pray a thousand *rak'as* during the day and the night. The wind would bend (his body) forward like an ear of corn.

[Sufyān al-Thawrī reported on the authority of 'Ubayd Allāh b. 'Abd al-Raḥmān b. Mawhib:]
The great merit (*faḍl*) of 'Alī b al-Ḥusayn, peace be on them, was mentioned to him but he replied: "It is sufficient for us that I should be one of the righteous members of our people"

[Abū Muḥammad al-Ḥasan b. Muḥammad informed us on the authority of his grandfather (Yaḥyā b. al-Ḥasan), on the authority of Salama b. Shabīb, on the authority of 'Ubayd Allāh b. Muḥammad al-Taymī who said: I heard a shaykh from (the tribe of) 'Abd al-Qays say: Ṭāwus said:]
I (i.e. Ṭāwus) went into the *ḥijr* one night and there was 'Alī b al-Ḥusayn, peace be on them. He had come in and was standing praying. He prayed as Allāh had wished then he prostrated. I asked a righteous man from the family of goodness whether I might listen to his prayer.
I heard him saying during his prostration:

> Your little servant is at Your courtyard;
> Your miserable one is at Your courtyard:
> Your poor one is at Your courtyard;
> Your beggar is at Your courtyard.

(Ṭāwus added:) I have never prayed with these words at any tribulation without me being freed from it.

[Abū Muḥammad al-Ḥasan b. Muḥammad informed us on the authority of his grandfather (Yaḥyā b. al-Ḥasan), on the authority of Aḥmad b. Muḥammad al-Rāfi'ī, on the authority of Ibrāhīm b. 'Alī, on the authority of his father ('Alī b. Abī Rāfi'), who said:)
I (i.e. 'Alī b. Abī Rāfi') made the pilgrimage with 'Alī b al-Ḥusayn, peace be on them. The camel carrying him was moving slowly. He pointed toward it with his stick and then said: "Woe if there was no retaliation (in the next world)!" And he moved his hand away from it.

[With this chain of authorities:]
'Alī b al-Ḥusayn, peace be on them, made the pilgrimage on foot and he took twenty days to travel from Medina to Mecca.

[Abū Muḥammad al-Ḥasan b. Muḥammad informed me: my grandfather (Yaḥyā b. al-Ḥasan) told us: 'Ammār b. Abān told us: 'Abd Allāh b. Bukayr told us on

the authority of Zurāra b. A'yan who said that:]
He (Zurāra b. A'yan) heard a voice calling in the middle of the night: "Where are those who abstain with regard to this world out of desire for the next?" A voice called out in answer from the region (of the cemetery) of al-Baqī' - he heard its voice without seeing the person - "Such a man is 'Alī b al-Ḥusayn, peace be on them."

['Abd al-Razzāq reported on the authority of Ma'mar on the authority of al-Zuhrī, who said:]
I have never seen any of that House, meaning the House of the Prophet, may Allāh bless Him and His Family, more meritorious (*afḍal*) than 'Alī b al-Ḥusayn, peace be on them.

[Abū Muḥammad al-Ḥasan b. Muḥammad informed me: my grandfather (Yaḥyā b. al-Ḥasan) told me: Abū Yūnus Muḥammad b. Aḥmad told us: my father and another of our companions told me:]
A young man from Quraysh was sitting in an assembly with Sa'īd b. al-Musayyib and saw 'Alī b al-Ḥusayn, peace be on them.

"Who is that, Abū Muḥammad?" the Qurashī asked Sa'īd b. al-Musayyib.
"That is the lord of worshippers (*'ābidīn*), 'Alī b al-Ḥusayn b. 'Alī b. Abī Ṭālib, peace be on them," he answered.

[Abū Muḥammad al-Ḥasan b. Muḥammad informed me: my grandfather (Yaḥyā b. al-Ḥasan) told me: Muḥammad b. Ja'far and others told me:]
A man from his House stood in front of 'Alī b al-Ḥusayn, peace be on them, and made him listen to him and cursed him. However, he did not reply. When (the man) had gone away, he said to those who were sitting with him: "You heard what that man said? I want you to come with me so that you may hear from me my reply to him."
"We will do that," they replied, "we wanted you to answer him while we were speaking (together),"

He took his shoes and went, while reciting: *Those who restrain their anger, and those who forgive the people, Allāh loves those who do good.* (III 134).
Then we knew that he would not say anything to him.

He went along until he came to the house of that man who had screamed at him. "This is 'Alī b al-Ḥusayn," they told him,

He came rushing out towards us with evil intent. He had no doubt that ('Alī b al-

Ḥusayn) had come to him to repay him for some of the evil which he had given him.

"Brother," said 'Alī b al-Ḥusayn, "you were standing proudly over me and you said this and that. If you have said what is (really) in my (character), I seek Allāh's forgiveness for it. If you have said what is not in my character, may Allāh forgive you",
The man kissed him between the eyes and replied: "Yes, I said what was not in your character, may I be worthy of it (i.e. Allāh's forgiveness)".

[The narrator of the account added:] The man was al-Ḥasan b. al-Ḥasan, may Allāh be pleased with him.

[Al-Ḥasan b. Muḥammad informed me on the authority of his grandfather (Yaḥyā b. al-Ḥasan) who said: A Shaykh from Yemen, who was some ninety years old, told me: A man called 'Ubayd Allāh b. Muḥammad informed me: I heard 'Abd al-Razzāq say:]
A maid-servant of 'Alī b al-Ḥusayn began to pour water for him so that he might perform the ritual ablutions for prayer. The maidservant became faint and the jug dropped from her hand and struck him. He raised his head towards her and the maidservant said to him: "Allāh, the Most High, says: *Those who restrain their anger.*"
"I have restrained my anger." he replied.

"*And those who forgive the people.*" she went on.
"May Allāh forgive you," he said.

"*Allāh loves those who do good.*" she said.
"Go, you are a free woman before the face of Allāh, the Mighty and High," he answered.

[Al-Wāqidī reported: 'Abd Allāh b. Muḥammad b. 'Umar b. 'Alī, peace be on him, told me:]
Hishām b. Ismā'īl used to harm our neighbourhood. 'Alī b al-Ḥusayn, peace be on them, received severe hardship from him. When he was dismissed, al-Walīd ordered that he should be made to stand before the people. 'Alī b al-Ḥusayn, peace be on them, walked past him and greeted him. 'Alī b al-Ḥusayn, peace be on them, had come especially so that no one should harm him.

It is reported that 'Alī b al-Ḥusayn, peace be on them, called his slave twice and the latter did not answer him. At the third time, he answered.

"Didn't you hear my voice?" asked ('Alī b al-Ḥusayn).
"Yes," was the reply.

"What was on your mind so that you did not answer me?" he asked.
"I was safe (from any harm) from you," he answered.

"Praise be to Allāh," he said, "Who has caused my slave to be safe (from any harm) from me."

[Abū Muḥammad al-Ḥasan b. Muḥammad b. Yaḥyā informed me: my grandfather (Yaḥyā b. al-Ḥasan) told me: Ya'qūb b. Yazīd told us: Ibn Abī 'Umayr told us on the authority of 'Abd Allāh b. al-Mughīra, on the authority of Abū Ja'far al-A'shā, on the authority of Abū Ḥamza al-Thumālī, on the authority of 'Alī b al-Ḥusayn, peace be on them, who said:]
I (i.e. 'Alī b al-Ḥusayn) went out until I came to that wall and leaned against it. There was a man wearing two white garments who was looking at me directly in the face. Then he said: "'Alī b al-Ḥusayn, why do I see you sorrowful and sad? Is your sorrow on account of the world, since Allāh provides for both the pious and the profligate?"
"I am not sad on account of that, though it is as you say." I replied.

"Is it on account of the next world, for it is a true promise that there conquering angels will give judgement?" he asked.
"I am not sad on account of that, though it is as you say," I answered.

"Then why are you sad?" he asked.
"I am fearful of the discord (caused) by Ibn al-Zubayr," I replied.

He laughed and said: "'Alī b al-Ḥusayn, have you ever seen anyone who trusted in Allāh and Allāh was not sufficient for him?"
"No," I replied.

"'Alī b al-Ḥusayn," he said, "have you ever seen anyone who feared Allāh without Allāh saving him?"
"No," I replied.

"'Alī b al-Ḥusayn." he asked, "have you ever seen anyone ask (for something) of Allāh without Allāh giving it to him?"
"No," I replied. Then I looked and suddenly there was no one there.

[Abū Muḥammad al-Ḥasan b. Muḥammad informed me: my grandfather

(Yaḥyā b. al-Ḥasan) told us: Abū Naṣr told us: 'Abd al-Raḥmān b. Ṣāliḥ told us: Yūnus b. Bukayr told us on the authority of Ibn Isḥāq, who said:]
There was in Medina such and such a family. Their provisions used to come to them without them asking for them. They did not know from where they came to them. However, when 'Alī b al-Ḥusayn, peace be on them, died, they stopped (receiving) those.

[Abū Muḥammad al-Ḥasan b. Muḥammad informed me: my grandfather (Yaḥyā b. al-Ḥasan) told me: Abū Naṣr told us: Muḥammad b. 'Alī b. 'Abd Allāh told us: my father told me: 'Abd Allāh b. Hārūn told us: 'Umar b. Dīnār told me:]
Death was close to Zayd b. Usāma b. Zayd and he began to weep. "What makes you weep?" asked 'Alī b al-Ḥusayn, peace be on them.

"What makes me weep," he said, "is the fact that I owe fifteen thousand dīnārs and I have not left anything to fulfil the debt for them."
"Do not weep," 'Alī b al-Ḥusayn, peace be on them, told him, "they are my debt now and you are free of them." So he paid them for him.

[Hārūn b. Mūsā reported: 'Abd al-Malik b. 'Abd al-'Azīl told us:]
When 'Abd al-Malik b. Marwān succeeded to the caliphate, he returned the (proportion of) taxes (*ṣadaqāt*) given to the Apostle of Allāh, may Allāh bless Him and His Family, to 'Alī b al-Ḥusayn, peace be on them, and also (the proportion of) taxes (*ṣadaqāt*) given to 'Alī b. Abī Ṭālib, peace be on him. They were both written down (in the *dīwān* as going to 'Alī b al-Ḥusayn). 'Umar b. 'Alī went to 'Abd al-Malik and complained to him on behalf of himself. 'Abd al-Malik replied, "I can only use the words of Ibn Abī al-Ḥuqayq:

> Indeed when claims of desire are put forward, the listener listens to the speaker.
>
> The people wrestle with their hearts but we are judging with a just and decisive judgement.
>
> We do not make the false true, nor do we deny the true in favour of the false.
>
> We fear that we would make our minds foolish and we would spend (our) time with those without repute.

[Abū Muḥammad al-Ḥasan b. Muḥammad informed me: my grandfather (Yaḥyā b. al-Ḥasan) told me: Abū Ja'far Muḥammad b. Ismā'īl told us:]
'Alī b al-Ḥusayn, peace be on them, made the pilgrimage and the people were

shouting about his comely disposition and looking at him. They began to question each other: “Who is that? Who is that?”

(They were doing this) in magnification of him and in exaltation of his rank. Al-Farazdaq was there and he composed the following, saying:

> This is he whose ability the valley (of Mecca) recognises, and whom the (Sacred) House recognises (as do) the sanctuary and the area outside the sanctuary (*al-ḥill*).
>
> This is the son of the best of all Allāh's servants This is the pure pious man, the pure eminent man.
>
> When he comes to touch the corner of the wall of the Ka‘ba, it almost grasps the palm of his hand.
>
> He takes care to be modest and he is protected from his terror. He only speaks when he smiles.
>
> None of mankind has within their souls such primacy as he does nor such grace as he does.
>
> Whoever knows Allāh, knows his friend (*walī*). Religion is from the House of this man.
>
> When Quraysh saw him, their spokesmen told of the outstanding qualities of this man which indicate (his) nobility.

[Abū Muḥammad al-Ḥasan b. Muḥammad informed me: my grandfather (Yaḥyā b. al-Ḥasan) who said: Dāwud b. al-Qāsim told us: Al-Ḥusayn b. Zayd told us on the authority of his uncle, ‘Umar b. ‘Alī, on the authority of his father ‘Alī b al-Ḥusayn, peace be on them:]
(‘Alī b al-Ḥusayn) used to say; “I have never seen similar preference (given to) a prayer (than this prayer). The worshipper will never pray without an answer coming to him on every occasion.”

It was one of the prayers learned from him, peace be on him, when it was learned that Musrif b. ‘Uqba[4] was heading towards Medina.

> My Lord, however much favour You have bestowed upon me, my thanks to You for it have been little. However much testing You have given me,

4 Musrif b. ‘Uqba is Muslim b. ‘Uqba, who attacked Medina and Mecca for Yazīd against Ibn al-Zubayr. He was nicknamed *Musrif* which means “one who acts outrageously.”

my endurance in the face of it has been little. O He who receives little thanks from me for His favour, let Him not deprive me. O He Who receives little endurance from me when He tests me, let Him not desert me. O Possessor of unceasing kindness! O Possessor of incalculable favours, bless Muḥammad and the family of Muḥammad; ward off the evil (of man) from me so that I may find protection through You amid (man's) slaughter. I seek refuge with You from (man's) evil.

Musrif b. 'Uqba came to Medina. It was said that he did not have any hostility towards 'Alī b al-Ḥusayn, peace be on them. He greeted him, honoured him, was generous to him and gave gifts to him.

The account from another source is that when Musrif b. 'Uqba came to Medina, he sent for 'Alī b al-Ḥusayn, peace be on them. The latter went to him. When he came to him, he honoured him and said: "The Commander of the faithful (i.e. Yazīd) has enjoined me to show goodness and generosity towards you, to distinguish you from the others."

So he treated him very well. Then he said to those who were around him: "Saddle my mule for him."[5] Then he said to him: "Go to your family. I see that we have filled them with fear when we made you come to us. If that with which we might increase your gift according to your right, were in our hands, we would give it to you."

"Do not apologise for the ruler (*amīr*) to me," said 'Alī b al-Ḥusayn, peace be on them and rode away.

"That is the best of men," said Musrif to those who were sitting with him. "There is no evil in him because of his position and rank from the Apostle of Allāh, may Allāh bless Him and His Family."

The account has been reported that one day 'Alī b al-Ḥusayn, peace be on them, was in the mosque of the Apostle of Allāh, may Allāh bless Him and his family, when he heard some people describing Allāh in terms of His creation. He became fearful and frightened of that. He rose and went to the tomb of the Apostle of Allāh, may Allāh bless Him and His Family. He stood before it and raised his voice to talk to his Lord. He said in his conversation to Him:

My Allāh. Your power has been shown but the form of Your Majesty has not been shown. They are ignorant of You and they try to estimate You on the basis of what You are not, and they make comparisons with You.

5 cf. al-Ṭabarī, II, 420-1.

> O my Allāh, I renounce those who seek to discover You through human comparisons. My Allāh, there is nothing like You, and they have not become aware of You. It is clear that the favour which they have is their evidence for You, if they would (choose to) know You in Your creation, My Allāh, I am free from the fact that they should give You (these characteristics). Indeed they have pictured You according to Your creation. Thus they do not know You and have adopted some of Your signs as (if they were their) Lord. In that way they have attempted to describe You. May You be exalted, O my Allāh, above the pictures of You of those who try to describe You in human terms.

This has been a sample of the accounts which are given about the virtues of Zayn al-'Ābidīn, peace be on him.

Non-Shī'a (*'āmma*) jurists report countless traditions in the religious sciences on his authority. Sermons, prayers, (details of) the merits of the Qur'ān, accounts of the laws of what is permitted and forbidden, and the raids (*maghazī*) and battles (*ayyām*) (during the time of the Prophet) have been recorded on his authority. He was famous among the religious scholars. If we attempted to give a full explanation of that, the book would be greatly lengthened by it and we would spend too much time on it. The Shī'a have reported his signs, miracles and clear proofs, which this place is not big enough to include mention of. The presence (of these reports) in their books which they have compiled may compensate for not putting them in this book. Allāh is He Who grants success to what is correct.

An Account of the Children of 'Alī b al-Ḥusayn, Peace be on them

Fifteen children were born to 'Alī b. al-Ḥusayn, peace be on them.

1. Muḥammad.

His kunya was Abū Ja'far al-Bāqir and his mother was Umm 'Abd Allāh, the daughter of al-Ḥasan b. 'Alī b. Abī Ṭālib, peace be on him.

2. 'Abd Allāh
3. Al-Ḥasan
4. Al-Ḥusayn

Their mother was a slave-wife (*umm walad*).

5. Zayd
6. 'Umar

(Both were born) from a slave-wife.

7. Al-Ḥusayn the younger (*al-aṣghar*)
8. ʻAbd al-Raḥmān
9. Sulaymān

Their mother was a slave-wife (*umm walad*).

10. ʻAlī

He was the youngest of the children of ʻAlī b. al-Ḥusayn, peace be on them.

11. Khadīja

The mother of both of these was a slave-wife.

12. Muḥammad the younger

His mother was a slave-wife.

13. Fāṭima
14. ʻAlīyya
15. Umm Kulthūm

Their mother was a slave-wife.

CHAPTER IV

IMĀM MUḤAMMAD B. 'ALĪ AL-BĀQIR

(This chapter will give) an account of the Imam after 'Alī b al-Ḥusayn, peace be on them, the date of his birth, the evidence for his Imamate, the age he reached, the period of his succession, the time and cause of his death, the place of his grave, the number of his children, and a summary of the reports about him.

Al-Bāqir Muḥammad b. 'Alī b al-Ḥusayn, peace be on them, was out of (all) his brothers the successor of his father, 'Alī b al-Ḥusayn, his testamentary trustee (*waṣi*), and the one who undertook (*qā'im*) the office of Imam after him. He surpassed all of them through his outstanding merit (*faḍl*) in traditional knowledge (*'ilm*), asceticism and leadership. He was the most renowned of them, the one among them who was most esteemed by both non-Shī'a (*'āmma*) and Shī'a (*khāṣṣa*), and the most able of them. None of the sons of al-Ḥasan and al-Ḥusayn, peace be on them, showed the same ability in knowledge of religion, traditions, the sunna, the knowledge of the Qur'ān and the life of the Prophet (*sīra*), and the techniques of literature, as Abu Ja'far (Muḥammad al-Bāqir) showed. The surviving companions (of the Prophet), the leading members of the next generation (*tābi'ūn*) and the leaders of the Muslim jurists reported the principal features (*ma'ālim*) of religion on his authority. By virtue of his outstanding merit he became a signpost (of knowledge) to his family. Proverbs were coined about him and reports and verses were written to describe him.

Concerning him al-Quraẓi says:

> O (you) who split open (*Bāqir*) knowledge (making it available) to the people of piety and the best of those who seek to answer the call of the Exalted.

Mālik b. A'yan al-Juhnī said in praise of him, peace be on him:

> When the people seek for knowledge of the Qur'ān, Quraysh rely upon him.
>
> If someone asked where is the son of the daughter of the Prophet, you would gain through him the wide branches (of knowledge):
>
> (You are like) stars which shine for night-travellers, (you are) like mountains which have inherited vast knowledge.

He, peace be on him, was born in Medina, in 57 A.H. (676/7). He died in 114 A.H. (732) at the age of fifty-seven. He was a (leading) member of the Hāshimite family within the Hāshimites. He was a (leading) descendant of 'Alī among the descendants of 'Alī. He was buried in (the cemetery of) al-Baqī' in (Medina) the city of the Apostle, may Allāh bless Him and His Family.

[Maymūn al-Qaddāḥ reported on the authority of Ja'far b. Muḥammad, on the authority of his father, peace be on them:]
I (i.e. al-Bāqir) visited Ja'far b. 'Abd Allāh al-Anṣari, may Allāh be pleased with him. I greeted him and he returned my greeting. Then he said to me. "who are you?" - That was after he had lost his sight.
"Muḥammad b. 'Alī b. al-Ḥusayn, peace be on them," I answered.

"My young child, come close to me," he said. I went closer and he kissed my hand. Then he stooped down to my foot and kissed that. I turned away from him. Then he said to me: "The Apostle of Allāh, may Allāh bless Him and His Family, recites his greeting to you:'

"Peace and Allāh's mercy and blessings be on the Apostle of Allāh." I said. "How is that, Jābir?"
He told me: "One day I was with him when he said to me: 'Jābir, perhaps you will live until you meet one of my descendants called Muḥammad b. 'Ali b. al-Ḥusayn, peace be on them, on whom Allāh will bestow light and wisdom. Then recite to him my greetings.'"[1]

In the testamentary bequest (*waṣiyya*) which the Commander of the Faithful, peace be on him, made to his children, mention was made of Muḥammad b. 'Ali b. al-Ḥusayn and of his trusteeship. The Apostle of Allāh, may Allāh bless him and his famly, named him and caused him to be known as the one who split open (religious) knowledge (*'ulūm*) as the narrators of tradition (*aṣḥāb al-āthār*) report.[2]

Thus it is reported on the authority of Jābir b. 'Abd Allāh in a direct (*mujarrad*) tradition: The Apostle of Allāh, may Allāh bless Him and His Family, said to me: "It will happen that you will live until you meet one of my children descended from al-Ḥusayn, peace be on him, called Muḥammad, who will spilt wide open knowledge of religion. When you meet him, recite my greeting to him."

The Shī'a give an account of the tablet which Gabriel, peace be on him, brought

1 A similar tradition is reported with a different *isnād* in *al-Kāfī*; cf. *al-Kāfī*, I, 304, tradition no. 4.
2 cf. *al-Kāfī*, I, 469-470, tradition no. 2.

down to the Apostle of Allāh, may Allāh bless Him and His Family, from heaven. (The Apostle) gave it to Fāṭima, peace be on her. In it are the names of the Imams after (the Apostle) and in it is Muḥammad b. 'Ali, the Imam after his father.[3]

The Shī'a also reported that Allāh, the Mighty and High, sent down to His Prophet, the blessings and peace of Allāh be on him, a document sealed with twelve seals. He ordered him to give it to the Commander of the Faithful, peace be on him, and to tell him to break the first seal, and he should act according to what is in (that part of the document). At the time of his death, he should pass it to his son, al-Ḥasan, peace be on him, and tell him to break the second seal and act according to what is in (that part of) the document. At the time of his death he should pass it to his brother al-Ḥusayn, peace be on him. He should tell him to break the third seal and act according to what is below it. Then at his death, he should pass it to his son, 'Alī b al-Ḥusayn al-Akbār (the elder) and he should instruct him in a similar way. Then Muḥammad should pass it to his son right down to the last of the Imams.

They report also numerous designations (*nuṣūṣ*) of him for the Imamate after his father on the authority of the Prophet, may Allāh bless Him and His Family, on the authority of the Commander of the Faithful and on the authority of al-Ḥasan, al-Ḥusayn and 'Alī b al-Ḥusayn, peace be on them.

The people report (accounts) of his outstanding virtues and accomplishments which would be too numerous to include. We will mention what will be sufficient in meaning for our purposes, if Allāh wills.

[Al-Sharīf Abu Muḥammad al-Ḥasan b. Muḥammad informed me: My grandfather (Yaḥyā b. al-Ḥasan) told me: Muḥammad b. al-Qāsim al-Shaybānī told us: 'Abd al-Raḥmān b. Ṣāliḥ al-Azdī told us on the authority of Abū Mālik al-Juhnī on the authority of 'Abd Allāh b. 'Atā' al-Makkī who said:]
I have never seen the scholars with anyone so much younger than them as I saw them with Abu Ja'far Muḥammad b. 'Alī b al-Ḥusayn, peace be on them. I have seen al-Ḥakam b. 'Utayba, despite his eminence among the people, conduct himself before him as if he was a young boy conducting himself before his teacher.

*****

Whenever Jābir b. Yazīd al-Ju'fī reported anything on his authority, peace be on him, he used to say: "The trustee of the trustees (of the Apostle) and the heir of the knowledge of the prophets, Muḥammad b. 'Alī b al-Ḥusayn, peace be on

3 cf. *al-Kāfī*, I, 527-8. tradition no. 3.

them, told me."

[Makhūl b. Ibrāhīm reported on the authority of Qays b. al-Rabī', who said: I asked Abū Isḥāq al-Sabī'ī about rubbing the two shoes (in the ritual ablution), he said:]
I used to tell people to rub the two shoes (in the ritual ablution instead of rubbing the feet) until I met a man from the Banū Hāshim, whose like I have never seen - Muḥammad b. 'Alī b. al-Ḥusayn, peace be on him. I asked about the rubbing and he forbade me to do it. He said: "The Commander of the Faithful, peace be on him, never used to rub (the shoes). He used to say: 'The Book (which does not mention the practice) comes before (the introduction of the practice of) rubbing the shoes.'"

[Abū Isḥāq added : I have never rubbed them since he forbade me to do it. And Qays b. al-Rabī' said: I have never rubbed them since I heard Abū Isḥāq.]

[Al-Sharīf Abū Muḥammad al-Ḥasan b. Muḥammad informed me: My grandfather (Yaḥyā b. al-Ḥasan) told me on the authority of Ya'qūb b. Yazīd, who said: Muḥammad b. Abī 'Umayr told us on the authority of 'Abd al-Raḥmān b. al-Ḥajjāj, on the authority of Abū 'Abd Allāh (Ja'far al-Ṣādiq), peace be on him, who said:]
Muḥammad b. Munkadir used to say: "I did not use to think that the like of 'Alī b. al-Ḥusayn, peace be on them, could leave a successor because of the outstanding merit of 'Alī b al-Ḥusayn, peace be on them, until I saw his son, Muḥammad b. 'Alī. I wanted to advise him but he advised me."

My companions asked me: "What did he warn you of?" I told them: I went out to one of the suburbs of Medina at a time when it was hot. There I met Muḥammad b. 'Alī, peace be on him. He was a well built man and he was leaning on two servant boys. Either they were black slaves of his or they were retainers of his. I said to myself: Here is a venerable leader (*shaykh*) of Quraysh out at this time and in these circumstances seeking worldly (advantage). I must warn him. So I approached him and greeted him. He returned my greeting with anger. The sweat was pouring down him.

I said: "May Allāh remove you, a venerable leader of Quraysh, out at this time in these circumstances seeking worldly (advantage). If death came upon you while you were in this condition (what would you do)?"

He made the two servant-boys let go of his hand and held himself up. Then he said: "By Allāh, if death came upon me while I was in this condition, it would come upon me while I am (fulfilling) an act of obedience to Allāh, by which I make myself withdraw from you and from the (rest of the) people. I would only fear death if it came upon me while I was performing an act of disobedience against Allāh."

Then I replied: "May Allāh have mercy on you, I wanted to warn you and you have warned me."

[Al-Sharīf Abū Muḥammad al-Ḥasan b. Muḥammad informed me: My grandfather (Yaḥyā b. al-Ḥasan) told me A *shaykh* from the people of al-Rayy, who was very old, told me: Yaḥyā b 'Abd al-Ḥamīd al-Ḥimmānī told me on the authority of Mu'āwiya b. 'Ammār al-Duhnī, on the authority of Muḥammad b. 'Alī b al-Ḥusayn, peace be on them:]
(Muḥammad b. 'Alī was asked) about Allāh's words: *Ask the people of remembrance (ahl al-dhikr) if you do not know* (XVI 43).
He said: "We are the people of remembrance (ahl al-dhikr)."

The *shaykh* from al-Rayy said: I asked Muḥammad b. Muqātil about these (words). He spoke about them according to his opinion and he said: "The people of remembrance (*ahl al-dhikr*) are all the religious scholars (*'ulamā'*)."

I mentioned that to Abū Zur'a. He was astounded at his words. Then I put before him what Yaḥyā b 'Abd al-Ḥamīd had told me. He said: "Muḥammad b. 'Alī, peace be on them, speaks the truth. They are the people of remembrance (*ahl al-dhikr*). By my life, Abū Ja'far, peace be on him, is one of the greatest scholars (*'ulamā'*)."

*****

Abū Ja'far, peace be on him, recounted reports of the beginnings of history (*mubtada'*) and reports of the prophets. Stories of the campaigns of the Prophet (*maghāzī*) were written on his authority. (Men) followed the practices of the Prophet (*sunan*) on his authority and relied on him with regard to the rites of the pilgrimage which he reported on the authority of the Apostle of Allāh, may Allāh bless Him and His Family. They (also) wrote a commentary of the Qur'ān on his authority. Both the Shī'a (*khaṣṣa*) and the non-Shī'a (*'amma*) report traditions on his authority. He debated with the exponents of individual reasoning (*ahl al-ārā'*) and the people learnt a great deal of theology (*'ilm al-kalām*) from him.

*****

[Al-Sharīf Abū Muḥammad al-Ḥasan b. Muḥammad informed me: My grandfather (Yaḥyā b. al-Ḥasan) told me: Al-Zubayr b. Abī Bakr told me: 'Abd

al-Raḥmān b. 'Abd Allāh al-Zuhrī told me.]
Hishām b 'Abd al-Malik made the pilgrimage. He went into the Sacred Mosque leaning on the arm of Sālim, his retainer. Muḥammad b. 'Alī b. al-Ḥusayn, peace be on them, was sitting in the mosque.

"Commander of the faithful," Sālim said to (Hishām). "there is Muḥammad b. 'Alī b. al-Ḥusayn"
"The man for whom the people of Iraq are ready to revolt?" he asked.
" Yes," replied (Sālim).
"Go to him," (Hishām) told him, "and say to him: The Commander of the faithful (i.e. Hishām) asks you: What is it that the people eat and drink until Allāh has finished judging them on the Day of Resurrection?"

Abū Ja'far Muḥammad, peace be on him, replied: "The people will gather on (earth which will be) like a loaf of pure bread. There, there will be rivers branching out. They will eat and drink until the account (with Allāh) is settled."

Hishām realised that (Abū Ja'far Muḥammad) had overcome him. So he said: "Allāh is greater. Go to him and say to him: (Hishām) says to you: What will keep men away from food and drink on that day?"

"Those in the fire of Hell will be too occupied," replied Abū Ja'far, peace be on him, "but they will say to those who have not been distracted from it: *Bestow upon us water and some of what Allāh has provided for you* (VII 50)."

Hishām fell silent and did not reply.

*****

Reports have come down that Nāfi' b. al-Azraq[4] came to Muḥammad b. 'Alī, peace be on them, and sat before him to ask him questions about what was permitted and what forbidden. Abū Ja'far, peace be on him, said in the course of his answer: "Say to these deviators (from the true course): How did you make separation from the Commander of the Faithful ('Alī), peace be on him, lawful when you had earlier shed your own blood on his behalf and in obedience to him and (you were then close) to Allāh through helping him? Then they will answer you: He allowed arbitration with regard to the religion of Allāh. Say to them: Allāh, the Exalted, allowed arbitration in the law (*sharī'a*) of His Prophet, may Allāh bless Him and His Family, between two of His creatures. For He said:

4 Nāfi' b. al-Azraq, a prominent Khārijite, was killed in 65 A.H., so this discussion would have to take place when Muḥammad al-Bāqir was only eight. The discussion concerns the reasons for the Khārijite revolt after the Battle of Ṣiffīn.

Send an arbitrator from his family and an arbitrator from her family if they want reconciliation (to take place) between them with the agreement of Allāh (IV 35). The Apostle of Allāh, may Allāh bless Him and His Family, appointed Sa'd b. Mu'ādh as an arbitrator over the tribe of Qurayẓa. He judged them according to what Allāh had accomplished. Did you not know that the Commander of the Faithful, peace be on him, ordered the arbitrators only to judge according to the Qur'ān and not to go beyond it? He stipulated the rejection of any of the laws of men which opposed the Qur'ān. They said to him: 'You have appointed as arbitrator over yourself, men who will judge you.' He replied: 'I have not appointed a creature as an arbitrator. I have only made the Book of Allāh an arbitrator'. Therefore where do the deviators find the wrong-doing in the matter of arbitration by the Qur'ān, when he stipulated the rejection of whatever opposed it, unless they are persisting in a false accusation?"

"By Allāh", said Nāfī' b. al-Azraq, "these are words which I have never heard before and which have never occurred to my mind. It is the truth, Allāh willing."

*****

The scholars report that 'Amr b. 'Ubayd came to visit Muḥammad b. 'Alī b. al-Ḥusayn, peace be on them, to test him with questions. He said: "May I be your ransom, what is the meaning of the words of Him, the Exalted: *Do not those who disbelieve realise that the heavens and the earth were ratq and we made them fitq?* (XXI 30) What is this *ratq* and this *fitq*?"

"The heaven was *ratq* (means) that no rain came down from it," answered Abū Ja'far, peace be on him. "and the earth was *ratq* (means) that no plants came out of it."

'Amr stopped. He could not find any opposition. He went away but then came back.

"May I be your ransom," he said, "tell me of the words of Him, the Mighty and High: *On whomsoever My anger alights, he falls (to disaster)* (XX 81). What is the anger of Allāh. the Mighty and High?"

"The anger of Allāh, 'Amr, is His punishment," replied Abū Ja'far, peace be on him. "Whoever thinks that anything changes Allāh, is an unbeliever."

*****

In addition to what we have described of his merit in knowledge (*'ilm*), headship and leadership and the Imamate, there was the obvious excellence (of the man) to both the Shī'a (*khaṣṣa*) and the non-Shī'a (*'amma*). He was recognised by all for his nobleness and well-known for generosity and kindness through the abundance of his help to the poor and his moderate temperament.

[Al-Sharīf Abū Muḥammad al-Ḥasan b. Muḥammad informed me: My grandfather (Yaḥyā b. al-Ḥasan) told me: Abū Naṣr told us: Muḥammad b. al-Ḥusayn told me: Aswad b. 'Āmir told us: Ḥayyan b. 'Alī told us on the authority of al-Ḥasan b. Kuthayyir, who said:)
I (i.e. al-Ḥasan b. Kuthayyir) complained to Abū Ja'far Muḥammad b. 'Alī, peace be on them, of (my) need and the uselessness of brothers.
"Shame on the brother," he said, "(who is) a brother who looks after you when you are rich and separates from you when you are poor."

Then he ordered his servant-boy to take out a pouch in which were seven hundred dirhams.
"Spend this," he told me, "and when you have used it, tell me."

[Muḥammad b. al-Ḥusayn reported: 'Abd Allāh b. al-Zubayr told us: They told us on the authority of 'Amr b. Dīnār and 'Abd Allāh b. 'Ubayd b. 'Umayr, who said:]
We (i.e., 'Amr b. Dīnār and 'Abd Allāh b. 'Ubayd) never met Abū Ja'far Muḥammad b. 'Alī, peace be on them, without him giving us money, gifts and clothes. He used to say: "This is something which had been prepared for you before you met me."

[Abū Nu'aym al-Nakha'ī reported on the authority of Mu'āwiya b. Hishām on the authority of Sulayman b. Qarm, who said:]
Abū Ja'far Muḥammad b. 'Alī, peace be on them, used to pay us five hundred dirhams to six hundred dirhams to a thousand dirhams as gifts. He never tired of bestowing generosity on the brethren, and on those who came to visit him, and on those who placed their hopes and trust in him.

It is reported on his authority, on the authority of his fathers, peace be on them, that the Apostle of Allāh, may Allāh bless Him and His Family, used to say: "The best of works are three: Looking after brothers with money, giving the people justice on your own account; and mentioning Allāh in every circumstance."

[Isḥāq b. Manṣūr al-Salūlī reported: I heard al-Ḥasan b. Ṣāliḥ say:]
I (al-Ḥasan b. Ṣāliḥ) heard Abū Ja'far Muḥammad b. 'Alī peace be on them, say: "There is not anything that can be mixed with anything better than clemency (mixed) with knowledge."

It is reported on his authority, peace be on him, that he was asked about traditions which he put forward and did not support with a chain of authorities. He said: "If I report a tradition without giving it a chain of authorities, then my chain of authorities for it is in fact my father on the authority of my grandfather on the authority of his father, on the authority of his grandfather, the Apostle of Allāh, may Allāh bless Him and His Family, on the authority of Gabriel, peace be on him, on the authority of Allāh, the Mighty and High."[5]

He, peace be on him, (also) used to say: "The people cause us great trouble. We summon them but they do not answer us. If we abandoned them, they would be guided by no one."

He, peace be on him, used to say: "What is it that the people hate in us who are the family of the House of Mercy, the Tree of Prophethood, the Source of Wisdom, (the people) frequented by angels and (those upon whom) inspiration descended?"

He, peace be on him, died and left behind seven sons. Each of his brothers had great merit, even though they did not attain his merit because of his position with regard to the Imamate, because of his rank with Allāh with regard to closeness and love (*wilāya*), and because of his position with regard to succession (*khilāfa*) of the Prophet, may Allāh bless Him and His Family. The period of his Imamate and of his undertaking the position of his father in the succession (on behalf of) Allāh, the Mighty and High, over His servants was nineteen years.

An Account of His Brothers and an Extract from the Reports about Them

'Abd Allāh b. 'Alī b. al-Ḥusayn, peace be on them, the brother of Abū Ja'far Muḥammad, peace be on him, was in charge of the endowments (*ṣadaqāt*) of the Apostle of Allāh, may Allāh bless Him and His Family, and the endowments (*ṣadaqāt*) of the Commander of the Faithful, peace be on him. He was a man of merit and a jurist. He reported many traditions on the authority of his fathers, on the authority of the Apostle of Allāh. The people told traditions on his authority and also gave historical reports (*āthār*) on his authority.

Among these is:
[Ibrāhīm b. Muḥammad b. Dāwud b. 'Abd Allāh al-Ja'farī reported on the authority of 'Abd al-'Azīz b. Muḥammad al-Darāwardī, on the authority of 'Umāra b. Ghuzayya, on the authority of 'Abd Allāh b. 'Alī b. al-Ḥusayn, peace

5 A similar tradition is reponed in *al-Kāfī*, I , 53, tradition no. 14, on the authority of Ja'far al-Ṣādiq

be on them:]
He (ʻAbd Allāh b. ʻAlī b. al-Ḥusayn) said: The Apostle of Allāh, may Allāh bless Him and His Family, said: "The meanest of men is one whom when my name is mentioned by him is unwilling to ask for Allāh's blessing on myself and my family."

[Zayd b. al-Ḥasan b. ʻĪsā reported: Abū Bakr b. Abī Uways told us on the authority of ʻAbd Allāh b. Simʻān, who said: I met ʻAbd Allāh b. ʻAlī b. al-Ḥusayn, peace be on them, and he told me on the authority of his father, on the authority of his grandfather, on the authority of the Commander of the Faithful, peace be on him:]
(The Commander of the Faithful) used to have the right hand of the thief cut off for the first theft. If he stole again, he would have his left leg cut off. If he stole a third time, he would put him in prison for life.

*****

ʻUmar b. ʻAlī b. al-Ḥusayn, peace be on them, was a man of merit and of high-standing. He was in charge of the endowments (*ṣadaqāt*) of the Apostle of Allāh, may Allāh bless Him and His Family, and the endowments (*ṣadaqāt*) of the Commander of the Faithful, peace be on him. He was pious and Allāh-fearing.

[Dāwud b. al-Qāsim has reported: Al-Ḥusayn b. Zayd said :]
I (Ḥusayn b. Zayd) saw my uncle, ʻUmar b. ʻAlī b. al-Ḥusayn, peace be on them, stipulate to those who wanted to buy (produce from) the endowments of ʻAlī that if they made a hole in such and such a wall, he would not stop anyone from entering it to take it from there.

[Al-Sharīf Abū Muḥammad informed me: My grandfather told me: Abu al-Ḥasan Bakkār b. Aḥmad al-Azdī told us: Al-Ḥasan b. al-Ḥusayn al-ʻUranī told us on the authority of ʻAbd Allāh b. Jarīr al-Qaṭṭān, who said:]
I (ʻAbd Allāh b. Jarīr al-Qaṭṭān) heard ʻUmar b. ʻAlī b. al-Ḥusayn, peace be on them, say: "The one who is excessive in his love for us is like the one who is excessive in his hatred of us. We have a right (to authority) through our relationship with our Prophet, blessing and peace be on him. It is a right which Allāh has given us. Therefore whoever abandons it, abandons (something which is) great. Grant us the position which Allāh has granted us. Do not say things about us which do not exist concerning us. If Allāh punished us, then it would be for our sins. If Allāh has mercy on us, then it is because of His mercy and favour."

*****

Zayd b. ʻAlī b al-Ḥusayn, peace be on them, was the outstanding brother after Abū Jaʻfar, peace be on him, and the one with the most merit. He was a devout worshipper, pious, a jurist, Allāh-fearing and brave. He came out in revolt with the sword to enjoin the good and forbid the evil and to demand vengeance for al-Ḥusayn, peace be on him.

[Al-Sharīf Abū Muḥammad al-Ḥasan b. Muḥammad informed me: My grandfather (Yaḥyā b. al-Ḥasan) informed him on the authority of al-Ḥasan b. Yaḥyā, who said: Al-Ḥasan b. al-Ḥusayn told us on the authority of Yaḥyā b. Musāwir, on the authority of Abū al-Jarūd Ziyād b. al-Mundhīr, who said:]
I (Abū al-Jarūd) went to Medina. When I began to ask about Zayd b. ʻAlī, peace be on him, I was told: "That man is an ally of the Qur'ān,"

[Hishām b. Hishām reported:]
I (Hishām) asked Khālid b. Ṣafwān about Zayd b. ʻAlī, peace be on him, when (Khālid) was reporting traditions on his authority.
"Where did you meet him?" I asked.
"At al-Ruṣāfa." he answered.

"What kind of man was he?" I asked.
"(He was) just as you have been told." he said. "He would weep out of fear of Allāh until his tears became mixed with his running nose."

Many of the Shīʻa believed in his Imamate. The reason for their belief was because of his coming out (in revolt) with the sword calling on support for the one who is acceptable from the family of Muḥammad, may Allāh bless Him and His Family. Therefore they thought that he intended that for himself. However that was not his intention because he knew of the right of his brother, peace be on him, to the Imamate before him, and of his bequest of trusteeship (*waṣiyya*) at his death to Abū ʻAbd Allāh (i.e. Jaʻfar al-Ṣādiq), peace be on him.

The reason for Abū al-Ḥasan Zayd b. ʻAlī, may Allāh be pleased with him, coming out (to revolt) is also more than his determination which we have already mentioned, to seek (vengeance) for the blood of al-Ḥusayn, peace be on him. He had visited Hishām b. ʻAbd al-Malik. Hishām had gathered the Syrians for him and ordered them to press around him in the assembly so that it was not possible for him to come close to him. Zayd said to him: "None of the servants of Allāh are above being warned to show fear towards Allāh, nor can any of them be excluded from showing fear towards Allāh. I am warning you to show fear towards Allāh, Commander of the faithful (i.e. Hishām). So show fear towards Him,"

"You are the one who thinks yourself entitled to the caliphate," Hishām replied to him. "and (you are) the one who hopes for it. But that is not for you. You have no mother. (At least) your mother was only a servant-girl."

"I do not know anyone greater in rank with Allāh than a prophet whom He has sent," retorted Zayd, "(Yet such a prophet) was the son of a servant-girl. So if he had been unable to carry out His purpose, He would not have sent him. (That prophet) was Ismā'īl b. Ibrāhīm (Ishmael, son of Abraham), peace be on them. Prophethood is greater in rank with Allāh than the mother of the caliphate, Hishām. Furthermore, a man should not be ignored whose father is the Apostle of Allāh, may Allāh bless Him and His Family, and who is the son of 'Alī b. Abī Ṭālib, peace be on him."

Hishām jumped up from his assembly. He summoned his servant and said: "Don't let this man spend the night in my camp"

Zayd left saying that he would never have forced anyone to take up the sword if they had not humiliated him. When he arrived at Kūfa, its inhabitants gathered around him and they soon pledged allegiance to fight on his behalf. Then they broke their pledge to him and handed him over. He, may Allāh have mercy on him, was killed and his body (was left) hanging on a cross among them for four years. None of them denounced it, nor did they help him with hand or tongue.

When he was killed, the full report of that was sent to Abū 'Abd Allāh al-Ṣādiq, peace be on him. He was very sad when it became clear to him (what had happened). He set apart a thousand dīnārs of his own money for the families of those of (Zayd's) followers who were killed with him.

That is reported by Abū Khālid al-Wāsiṭī. He said: Abū 'Abd Allāh, peace be on him, handed me a thousand dīnārs and told me to divide it among the families of those killed with Zayd. Four dīnārs of this reached the family of 'Abd Allāh b. al-Zubayr, the brother of Fuḍayl al-Rassān.

His death was on Monday on the 2nd of (the month) of Ṣafar in the year 120 A.H. At that time he was forty-two years of age.

*****

Al-Ḥusayn b. 'Alī b. al-Ḥusayn, peace be on them, was a man of merit and pious. He reported many traditions on the authority of his father 'Alī b. al-Ḥusayn, peace be on them, and his aunt Fāṭima, daughter of al-Ḥusayn, peace be on him, and his brother, Abū Ja'far, peace be on him.

[Aḥmad b. ʻĪsā reported: My father told us:]
I (ʻĪsā) used to see al-Ḥusayn b. ʻAlī b. al-Ḥusayn, peace be on them, pray. I would say: "He will not put down his hand until his prayer for all creatures is answered."

[Ḥarb b. al-Ṭaḥḥān reported: Saʻīd, the follower of al-Ḥasan b. Ṣālih, told me:]
I (Saʻīd) never saw anyone with greater fear (of Allāh) than al-Ḥasan b. Ṣālih until I went to Medina and saw al-Ḥusayn b. ʻAli b. al-Ḥusayn, peace be on them. I have never seen greater fear (of Allāh) than his. (It is) as if he had been taken into the fire (of Hell) and then taken out of it because of the intensity of his fear.

[Yaḥyā b. Sulaymān b. al-Ḥusayn reported on the authority of his uncle, Ibrāhīm b. al-Ḥusayn, on the authority of his father, al-Ḥusayn b. ʻAlī b. al-Ḥusayn, peace be on them, who said:]
Ibrāhīm b. Hishām al-Makhzūmī was a governor of Medina. He used to gather us (the family of the Prophet) every Friday near the pulpit. Then he would attack ʻAlī, peace be on him, and curse him. One day I (Al-Ḥusayn b. ʻAlī b. al-Ḥusayn) was present. The place was very full so I was close to the pulpit. I dozed off and saw (in a dream) that the grave had opened and out of it had come a man in a white cloak. He said to me: "O Abu ʻAbd Allāh (i.e. al-Ḥusayn b. ʻAlī b. al-Ḥusayn), does not what this man is saying make you sad?"
"By Allāh, yes," I replied.
"Open your eyes," he told me, "and see what Allāh is doing with him."

Behold, as he mentioned (the name) ʻAlī, he was thrown from the pulpit and died, may, Allāh curse him.

An Account of the Children of Abū Jaʻfar Muḥammad b. ʻAlī, Peace be on him, their Number and their Names.

We have mentioned earlier that Abū Jaʻfar, peace be on him, had seven children.

1. Abū ʻAbd Allāh Jaʻfar b. Muḥammad, peace be on them.

He was given his *kunya* by his (father).

2. Abd Allāh b. Muḥammad, peace be on him.

Their mother was Umm Farwa, daughter of al-Qāsim b. Muḥammad b. Abī Bakr.

3. Ibrāhīm
4. ʻUbayd Allāh

Both died young. Their mother was Umm Hakīm, daughter of Asīd b. al-Mughīra al-Thaqafī.

5. ʻAlī
6. Zaynab

Both were born of a slave-wife.

7. Umm Salama

She was born of a slave-wife.

No one considered the Imamate to belong to any of the children of Abū Jaʻfar Muḥammad, peace be on him, except specifically Abū ʻAbd Allāh Jaʻfar b. Muḥammad, peace be on them. His brother, ʻAbd Allāh, may Allāh be pleased with him, used to point to him for his outstanding merit and righteousness..

It is reported that he (ʻAbd Allāh) came upon one of the Banū Umayya, and the latter wanted to kill him. ʻAbd Allāh, may Allāh have mercy on him, said: "Don't (try to) kill me, for Allāh will be my support against you. Leave me and Allāh will be a support to you"

He meant by that that he was one of those who could intercede with Allāh and that he would do so. However, the Umayyad said to him: "You are not there (in heaven where you can ask Allāh's help)."

He made him drink poison and he killed him.

CHAPTER V

IMAM JA'FAR B. MUḤAMMAD AL-ṢĀDIQ

This is an account of the Imam who was in charge (*al-qā'im*) after Abū Ja'far Muḥammad b. 'Alī, peace be on them, (including) who his mother was, the date of his birth, evidence for his imamate, his age, the period of his succession (to the Imamate), the time of his death, the place of his grave, the number of his children and a brief outline of the reports about him.

Al-Ṣadiq Ja'far b. Muḥammad b. 'Alī b. al-Husayn, peace be on them, was out of all his brothers (the one who was) the successor (*khalīfa*) of his father, Muḥammad b. 'Alī, peace be on them, his testamentary trustee (*waṣi*), who was in charge of the Imamate (*al-qā'im bi-al-imāma*) after him. He stood out among their group for his great merit (*faḍl*); he was the most celebrated, the greatest in rank and the most illustrious of them in (the eyes) of both the non-Shī'a (*'āmma*) and Shī'a (*khāṣṣa*). The people transmitted on his authority the religious sciences which travellers carried with them (around many countries) and thus his fame was spread throughout the lands. The learned scholars have transmitted on the authority of no other member of the House (*ahl al-bayt*) as much as they have transmitted on his authority. None of them met as many of the reporters of traditions (*ahl al-āthār wa-naqalat al-akhbār*) as he did, nor did the latter transmit on their authority to the same extent as they transmitted on the authority of Abū 'Abd Allāh (Ja'far b. Muḥammad), peace be on him. The specialists in tradition (*aṣḥāb al-ḥadīth*) have gathered together the names of those who narrated on his authority, who were reliable despite differences in views and doctrines and they were four thousand men. The clear evidence for his Imamate, peace be on him, was such that it overcame (men's) hearts and silenced (the attempts of) an opponent to denigrate it with doubts.

He was born in Medina in the year 83 A.H. (702) and he, peace be on him, died in (the month of) Shawwāl in the year 148 A.H. (765) at the age of sixty-five. He was buried in (the cemetery of) al-Baqī' alongside his father, his grandfather and his (great-great) uncle, al-Ḥasan, peace be on them. His mother was Umm Farwa, the daughter of al-Qāsim b. Muḥammad b. Abī Bakr. His Imamate, peace be on him, lasted for thirty-four years. His father, Abū Ja'far (Muḥammad b. 'Alī), peace be on him, clearly gave him the trusteeship (of the Imamate) and gave him an explicit designation (*naṣṣ jalī*) for the Imamate.

*****

[Muḥammad b. Abī 'Umayr reported on the authority of Hishām b. Sālim on the authority of Abū 'Abd Allāh, Ja'far b. Muḥammad, peace be on them, who said:][1]
When my father was near to death he said: "Ja'far I give testamentary enjoinment to you (to treat) my followers well."

"May I be your ransom," I replied, "by Allāh, I will make them (know their religion so well) that any man among them in the country will not (have to) ask anyone (for advice)."

*****

[Abān b. 'Uthmān reported on the authority of Abū al-Ṣabbāḥ al-Kinānī, who said:][2]
Abū Ja'far Muḥammad, peace be on him, looked towards his son, Abū 'Abd Allāh Ja'far, peace be on him, and said (to us): "Do you see that man? He is one of those of whom Allāh, the Mighty and High, said: *We wish to grant a favour to those who have been humiliated in the land and we will make them Imams and inheritors* (XXVIII 5).

*****

[Hishām b. Sālim reported on the authority of Jabir b. Yazīd al-Ju'fī:][3]
Abū Ja'far Muḥammad, peace be on him, was asked about the one who would take charge (*al-qā'im*) (of the Imamate) after him. He tapped Abū 'Abd Allāh Ja'far, peace be on him, with his hand and said: "By Allāh, this is the man among the family of Muḥammad, peace be on them, who will take charge (*al-qā'im*) (of the Imamate)."

*****

['Alī b. al-Ḥakam reported on the authority of Ṭāhir, a follower of Abū Ja'far Muḥammad, peace be on him, who said:][4]
I was with (Abū Ja'far Muḥammad), peace be on him, when Ja'far, peace be on him approached, Abū Ja'far, peace be on him, said, "Here is the best of creatures."

*****

[Yūnus b. 'Abd al-Raḥmān reported on the authority of 'Abd al-A'lā, a retainer of the family of Sām, on the authority of Abū 'Abd Allāh Ja'far, peace be on

1 *Al-Kāfī*, I, 306, tradition no. 2. Al-Kulaynī's *isnād* has been shortened.
2 *Al-Kāfī*, I, 306, tradition no. 1. Al-Kulaynī's *isnād* has been shortened.
3 *Al-Kāfī*, I, 307, tradition no. 7. Al-Kulaynī's *isnād* has been shortened.
4 *Al-Kāfī*, I, 306, tradition no. 4. Al-Kulaynī's *isnād* has been shortened.

him, who said:][5]
My father, peace be on him, entrusted to me (everything) which was there. When he was near to death, he said: "Call witnesses for me." I summoned four men from Quraysh, among them Nāfi', retainer of 'Abd Allāh b. 'Umar. (My father said:) "Write this testimony which I bequeath (like) Jacob did to his sons:

> *My sons, Allāh has chosen the religion for you. So do not die except as Muslims.* (II 132). Muḥammad b. 'Alī makes this last testimony to Ja'far b. Muḥammad. He orders him to shroud him in the cloak in which he used to perform the Friday prayer, to put on him his turban, to make his grave a square, to raise it the height of four fingers above the ground and to take his shabby clothes away from him at his burial.

Then he said to the witnesses: "Depart, may Allāh have mercy on you."
"Father" I said to him (after they had gone), "what was in this that there had to be witnesses for it?'
"My son," he answered, "I was unwilling for you to be overcome and for it to be said that no testimony had been made for him. I wanted you to have proof."

*****

Reports with the same meaning as this account are numerous. The narration of the report of the tablet (*lawḥ*) with the designation of him, peace be upon him, for the Imamate has already been mentioned. The rational proofs which have been mentioned earlier that the Imam can only be the most outstanding person in merit (*al-afḍal*) also indicate his Imamate, peace be on him, because of the clear demonstration of his outstanding merit in religious knowledge (*'ilm*), in asceticism, and in practice above all his brothers, the members of his uncle's family and the rest of the people of his time. The evidence for the invalidity of the Imamate of those who were not protected (from error) like the prophets (were protected) and the clear demonstration of the lack of protection of those others who claimed the Imamate during his lifetime, together with their deficiency in (attaining) complete knowledge of religion, clearly indicates his Imamate. For there must be an Imam who is protected (from error) at all times as we have mentioned before.[6] The people tell of the clear signs from Allāh which were performed by him, peace be on him, which indicate his Imamate, his true right and the invalidity of the statements of those who claimed the Imamate on behalf of others.

*****

Among those is the report about him which the reporters of history (*naqalat*

5 *Al-Kāfī*, I, 307, tradition no. 8. Al-Kulaynī's *isnād* has been shortened.
6 Al-Mufīd has not dealt thoroughly with this subject in this book.

al-āthār) recount about him with al-Manṣūr.[7] Al-Manṣūr ordered Rabī' to bring Abū 'Abd Allāh, Ja'far, peace be on him, to him. He brought him. When al-Manṣūr saw him, he said: "May Allāh kill me, if I don't kill you. You are attempting to harm my authority and you are seeking treachery against me."

"By Allāh, I am not," retorted Abū 'Abd Allāh (Ja'far), peace be on him, "Nor do I want to. If you have been told so, then it is by a liar. However, even if I had done so, then Joseph was treated badly and he forgave, Job suffered tribulation and he was patient, and Solomon received gifts and he gave thanks. These men were prophets and your lineage goes back to them."

"Indeed," replied al-Manṣūr, "Come up here." He went up and then (al-Manṣūr) continued: "So-and-so has informed me about what you have been saying."
"Bring him, Commander of the faithful," he replied, "so that he may confront me with that."

He had the man whom he had mentioned brought and asked him: "Did you (really) hear what you reported about Ja'far, peace be on him?"
"Yes," he replied.
"Make him swear to that," said Abū 'Abd Allāh (Ja'far), peace be on him.
"Do you swear to that?" demanded al-Manṣūr.
"I do," he replied.

"Say: May I be outside Allāh's power and strength and may I seek refuge in my own power and strength (if I lie that) Ja'far, peace be on him, did such and such and said such and such," said Abū 'Abd Allāh (Ja'far), peace be on him.

(The man) paused for a moment and then made the oath. It was only a moment later that his leg was struck.

"Drag him by his leg and take him out, may Allāh curse him," ordered Abū Ja'far (al-Manṣūr).

Al-Rabī' reported: When Ja'far b. Muḥammad, peace be on them, went in to see al-Manṣūr, I saw his lips moving. As he moved them, al-Manṣūr's anger (gradually) became quietened, so that when he approached him, he was pleased with him. When Abū 'Abd Allāh (Ja'far) peace be on him, came out from Abū Ja'far (al-Manṣūr) I followed him and said to him: "This man was the angriest

7 There are several earlier versions of Ja'far's meeting with the second 'Abbāsid Caliph. The account in *Al-Kāfī*, II, 562-3 is similar but does not mention the witness and gives a different prayer. In *Maqātil al-Ṭālibiyyīn*, 350-3 there is a report of the meeting.

of men towards you. When you went in, you were moving your lips as you went in and when you moved them his anger quietened. With what (words) were you moving them?"

"The prayer of my (great) grandfather, al-Ḥusayn b. 'Alī, peace be on them," he replied.
"May I be your ransom," I said, "what is this prayer?"

He told him:

> O my Provision in time of hardship, O my Help in the face of disaster, guard me with Your Eye which never sleeps, surround me with Your impenetrable fortress.

Al-Rabī' reported: I learned that prayer and I never fell into hard times without saying it and it relieving me.

(At that time) I said to Ja'far b. Muḥammad, peace be on them: "Why did you stop the slanderer from (merely) swearing by Allāh?"
"I was reluctant that Allāh should see him praising His unity and glorifying Him," he answered, "for then He would show forebearance towards Him and delay his punishment. Therefore I made him swear in the way you heard and Allāh struck him fiercely."

*****

It is reported that Dāwud b. 'Alī b. 'Abd Allāh b. 'Abbās killed al-Mu'allā b. Khunays, a retainer of Ja'far b. Muḥammad, peace be on them, and took his property. Ja'far, peace be on him, went to him while he was pulling at his cloak.

"You have killed my retainer and taken his property," (Ja'far) said to him. "Do you know that a man may sleep when he has suffered the loss of a child but he may not sleep when he is at war? I will pray to Allāh against you."
"Do you threaten us with your prayer?" he retorted as if he was ridiculing his words.

Abū 'Abd Allāh (Ja'far), peace be on him, went back to his house and spent the whole night standing and sitting. Then, at dawn he was heard saying in his private prayer:

> O Possessor of mighty strength, O Possessor of fierce enmity, O Possessor of power before which all Your creatures are humble, give me satisfaction against this tyrant and take vengeance on him for me.

It was not an hour before voices were raised in screeching (lamentation) and it was announced that Dāwud b. 'Alī had just died.[8]

*****

Abū Baṣīr reported: I visited Medina and I had a young slave-girl with me. I had intercourse with her and then I went to the baths. But I met some of our colleagues of the Shī'a who were heading towards Ja'far b. Ṣādiq, peace be on them. I was afraid that they would get there before me and I would miss visiting him so I went with them to the house. When I stood before Abū 'Abd Allāh (Ja'far), peace be on him, he looked at me and said: "Abū Basir, don't you know that the houses of prophets and the children of prophets are not suitable places to enter for those who are ritually impure?"

I was ashamed and said: "Son of the Apostle of Allāh, I met out companions and I was afraid that I would miss visiting you with them. I will never do the same thing again," and I left.

*****

There are innumerable reports about him concerning signs and revealing the unknown similar to those which we have mentioned, which would take too long to recount.

*****

He, peace be on him, used to say: "Our knowledge is of what will be (*ghābir*), of what is past (*mazbūr*), of what is marked in hearts (*nakt fī al-qulūb*), and of what is tapped into ears (*naqr fī al-asmā'*). We have the red case (*jafr*), the white case, and the scroll of Fāṭima, peace be on her, and we have (the document called) *al-jāmi'a* in which is everything the people need."

He was asked to explain these words and he said: "*Ghābir* is knowledge of what will be; *mazbūr* is knowledge of what was; what is marked in the hearts (*nakt fī al-qulūb*) is inspiration; and what is tapped into the ears (*naqr fī al-asmā'*) are words of angels; we hear their speech but we do not see their forms. The red case (*jafr*) is a vessel in which are the weapons of the Apostle of Allāh, may Allāh bless Him and His Family. It will never leave us until the one (destined) among us members of the House, to arise (*qā'im*), arises. The white case (*jafr*) is a vessel in which are the Torah of Moses, the Gospels of Jesus, the Psalms of David and the (other) Books of Allāh. The scroll of Fāṭima, peace be on her, has in it every event which will take place and the names of all the rulers until the

8 cf. *Al-Kāfī*, II, 557, but the prayer is different. Al-Kashshī gives several versions. *Ma'rifat al-Rijāl*, (Mashhad, 1348 A.H.S.) paras. 707, 708. 710, 711, 713.

(last) hour comes. (The document called) *al-jāmi'a* is a scroll seventy yards long which the Apostle of Allāh, may Allāh bless Him and His Family, dictated from his own mouth and 'Alī b. Abī Ṭālib, peace be on him, wrote in his own handwriting. By Allāh, in it is everything which people need until the end of time, including even the blood-wit for wounding, and whether a (full) flogging or half a flogging (is due).[9]

*****

He, peace be on him, used to say: "My traditions are my father's traditions; my father's traditions are my grandfather's traditions; my grandfather's traditions are the traditions of 'Alī b. Abī Ṭālib, the Commander of the Faithful; the traditions of 'Alī the Commander of the Faithful are the traditions of the Apostle of Allāh, may Allāh bless Him and His Family; and the traditions of the Apostle of Allāh, may Allāh bless Him and His Family, are the word of Allāh, the Mighty and High".[10]

*****

[Abū Ḥamza al-Thumālī has reported on the authority of Abū 'Abd Allāh (Ja'far), peace be on him:]
I heard Abū 'Abd Allāh Ja'far say: "We have the tablets of Moses, peace be on him, and we have the rod of Moses, peace be on him. We are the heirs of prophets."[11]

*****

[Mu'āwiya b. Wahb reported on the authority of Sa'īd al- Simmān:][12]
I was with Abū 'Abd Allāh Ja'far b. Muḥammad, peace be on them, when two of the Zaydīs visited him. They asked him: "Is there among you an Imam whom it is a duty to obey?"
"No," he replied.

"Reliable men have told us on your authority that you claim to be him," they retorted. They named some people and said: "These are men of piety and distinction. They are among those who do not lie."

Abū 'Abd Allāh, peace be on him, became angry and said: "I have not told them that."
When the two men saw the anger on his face, they left.

9 This seems to be a composite tradition ofthe traditions contained in *Al-Kāfī*, I, 238-242. The description of the different kinds of knowledge is similar to *Al-Kāfī*, I, 264.

10 This tradition is given in *Al-Kāfī*, I, 53.

11 *Al-Kāfī*, I, 231, tradition no. 2. Al-Kulaynī's *isnād* has been shortened.

12 *Al-Kāfī*, I. 232, tradition no. 1. Al-Kulaynī's *isnād* has been shortened.

"Do you know those two?" he asked me.
"Yes," I replied, "they are from the people of our market. They are Zaydīs and they claim that 'Abd Allāh b. al-Ḥasan has the sword of Apostle of Allāh, may Allāh bless Him and His Family."

"They are liars, may Allāh curse them," he said. "By Allāh, 'Abd Allāh b. al-Hasan has never seen it either with both his eyes or even with one of them. O Allāh, not even his father has seen it unless he saw it with 'Alī b. al-Ḥusayn, peace be on him. If they are truthful, (ask them) what is the sign in the hilt and what is the mark on its blade. I have the sword of the Apostle of Allāh, may Allāh bless Him and His Family. I have the standard of the Apostle of Allāh, may Allāh bless Him and His Family, and his breast-plate, his armour and his helmet. If they are truthful (ask them) what is the mark on the breast-plate of the Apostle of Allāh, may Allāh bless him and grant him peace. Indeed the victorious standard of the Apostle of Allāh is with me, as are the tablets and rod of Moses. I have the ring of Solomon, the son of David, and the tray on which Moses used to offer sacrifice and I have (knowledge) of the (greatest) name (of Allāh) which when the Apostle of Allāh, may Allāh bless Him and His Family, used to put it between the Muslims and the polytheists no arrow from the polytheists could reach the Muslims. I have the same as what the angels brought. We have the weapons in the same way that the Banū Isrā'īl had the ark of the covenant. Prophecy was brought to any house in which the ark of the covenant was present; the Imamate will be brought to which ever of us receives the weapons. My father dressed in the armour of the Apostle of Allāh, may Allāh bless him and grant him peace, and it made marks on the ground. I put it on and it was (like) it was (for my father). The one (destined to) rise up (*qā'im*) from among us, will fill it (so that it fits him exactly) when he puts it on, if Allāh wishes."

['Abd Al-A'lā b. A'yan reported:][13]
I heard Abū 'Abd Allāh (Ja'far) peace be on him, say: "I have the weapons of the Apostle of Allāh, may Allāh bless Him and His Family, but I will never fight with them." Then he said: "These weapons are protected, for if they were entrusted to the wickedest of Allāh's creatures, he would become the best of them." Then he said, "This matter (i.e. the carrying of the Prophet's arms in war) belongs to the man, for whom (horses') reins will be twisted (as men ride in support of him). When Allāh wills it, he will be brought out (into the open). Then people will say: 'Who is this who has appeared?' Allāh will give him support (to have power) over his subjects."

*****

['Umar b. Abān reported:]

13 *Al-Kāfī*, I, 234. tradition no. 2. Al-Kulaynī's *isnād* has been shortened.

I asked Abū 'Abd Allāh (Ja'far) peace be on him, about what the people were saying that Umm Salama, the mercy of Allāh be on her, had been handed a sealed scroll. He said: "When the Apostle of Allāh, may Allāh bless him and grant him peace, died, 'Alī, peace be on him, inherited his knowledge, his weapons and what there was. Then that went to al-Ḥasan, peace be on him, then to al-Ḥusayn, peace be on him."

"Did it go to 'Alī b. al-Ḥusayn, peace be on them, after that, then to his son and now has it come to you?" I asked.
"Yes," he replied.

*****

The reports with the same meaning are numerous. However, those of them which we have given will be sufficient to indicate what we are trying to show, Allāh willing.

An Extract from the Accounts of Abū 'Abd Allāh Ja'far b. Muḥammad al-Ṣadiq, Peace be on them, and from his Words.

I found (this written) in the handwriting of Abū al-Faraj 'Alī b. al-Ḥusayn b. Muḥammad al-Iṣfāhānī, in the text of his book known as *Maqātil al-Ṭalibiyīn* (the Martyrdoms of (the family of Abū) Ṭālib):[14]

'Umar b. 'Abd Allāh al-'Atkī informed me:
'Umar b. Shabba told us: Al-Faḍl b. 'Abd al-Raḥmān al-Hāshimī and Ibn Dāja told us:
Abū Zayd ('Umar b. Shabba) (also) told me: 'Abd al-Raḥmān b. 'Amr b. Jabala told me: Al-Ḥasan b. Ayyūb, retainer (*mawlā*) of the Banū Numayr told me, on the authority of 'Abd al-A'lā b. A'yan:
Ibrāhīm b. Muḥammad b. Abī al-Kirām al-Ja'farī told me, on the authority of his father:
Muḥammad b. Yaḥyā told me on the authority of 'Abd Allāh b. Yaḥyā:
'Īsā b. 'Abd Allāh b. Muḥammad b. 'Umar b. 'Alī told me on the authority of his father:
The account of some of them has been introduced into the account of the rest (as follows):
A group of the Banū Hāshim met at al-Abwā'. Among them were Ibrāhīm b. Muḥammad b. 'Alī b. 'Abd Allāh b. 'Abbās and Abū Ja'far al-Manṣūr, Ṣāliḥ. b. 'Alī, 'Abd Allāh b. al-Ḥasan, with his two sons Muḥammad and Ibrāhīm, and Muḥammad b.'Abd Allāh b. 'Amr b. 'Uthmān.

14 *Maqātil al-Ṭalibiyīn*, 205

Ṣāliḥ. b. ʻAlī addressed (them): "You know that you are the ones towards whom the people turn their eyes and that Allāh has brought you together in this place. Therefore give a pledge of allegiance to one from among you, which you should give to him with (genuine dedication) of yourselves. Bind yourselves so that Allāh may bring victory, for He is the best bringer of victory."

ʻAbd Allāh b. al-Ḥasan praised and glorified Allāh. Then he said: "You know that this son of mine is the *Mahdī*. Therefore come, let us pledge allegiance to him."

"Why are you deceiving yourselves?" demanded Abū Jaʻfar. "By Allāh you know that there is no one else to whom the people would take greater strides nor greater speed to answer than they would to this man," meaning Muḥammad b. ʻAbd Allāh.

"True," they said, "this is he whom we acknowledge." So they all pledged allegiance to Muḥammad and took him by the hand.

[ʻĪsā reported:]
ʻAbd Allāh b. al-Ḥasan's messenger came to my father, saying: "Come to us. We are gathered for an (important) affair." He sent (information) about that to Jaʻfar b. Muḥammad, peace be on them.

[Others, not including ʻĪsā, reported:]
ʻAbd Allāh b. al-Ḥasan said to those present: "You don't want Jaʻfar (here), for we fear that he would cause dissension among you in your affair."

[ʻĪsā b. ʻAbd Allāh b. Muḥammad reported:]
My father sent me to see what they had gathered for. So I went to them. (Jaʻfar b. Muḥammad, peace be on them, sent Muḥammad b. ʻAbd Allāh al-Arqaṭ b. ʻAli b. al-Ḥusayn. We went to them). Muḥammad b. ʻAbd Allāh (b. al-Ḥasan)[15] was praying on a folded carpet from a saddle.

"My father has sent me to you," I told them, "to ask you why you have gathered together."
"We have gathered (here)," ʻAbd Allāh b. al-Ḥasan said, "to pledge allegiance to the *Mahdī*, Muḥammad b. ʻAbd Allāh."

[They (i.e. the other authorities) reported:]
Jaʻfar b. Muḥammad, peace be on them, arrived and ʻAbd Allāh b. al-Ḥasan

15 What is between brackets has been omitted by al-Mufi'd but is included from *Maqātil al-Ṭalibiyīn*, 207.

made room for him beside him. He repeated what he had said before. However, Ja'far said: "Don't do it. The time (for the *Mahdī*) has not yet arrived. If you - meaning 'Abd Allāh - consider that this son of yours is the *Mahdī*, he is not, nor is this the time for him (i.e. the *Mahdī*). Because you are one of our most revered elders we will not forsake you in favour of pledging allegiance to your son, even if you only intend him to rise in anger in Allāh's cause, to command the good and prohibit the evil."

'Abd Allāh became angry and said: "I know that (the facts are) the opposite of what you are saying. By Allāh, Allāh has not acquainted you with (knowledge of) His unseen world. Rather it is envy for my son which prompts you to this (attitude)."

"By Allāh, it is not that which prompts me," replied (Ja'far) "but this man, his brothers and his sons." Then he tapped with his hand on the back of Abū al-'Abbās and he tapped with his hand on the shoulder of 'Abd Allāh b. al-Ḥasan.

"By Allāh, it (i.e. the caliphate) is not for you nor for your two sons," (Ja'far) told him, "but it is for them (i.e. the 'Abbāsids). Your two sons will be killed." He got up and leaning on the arm of 'Abd al-'Azīz b. 'Imran al-Zuhrī, he continued, "Do you see the owner of the yellow cloak?" - meaning Abū Ja'far (al-Manṣūr).
"Yes," he replied.
"By Allāh," he said, "we have a foreboding that he (Abū Ja'far) will kill him (Muḥammad b. 'Abd Allāh)."
"Will he kill Muḥammad?" 'Abd al-'Azīz asked him.
"Yes," he replied.

*****

['Abd al-'Azīz reported:]
I said to myself, "By the Lord of the Ka'ba, he is envious of him." But then, by Allāh, I had not left this world before I saw him (Abū Ja'far) kill both of them.

*****

When Ja'far said that, the people arose and separated. 'Abd al-Ṣamad and Abū Ja'far followed him and asked him, "Abū 'Abd Allāh, do you really say this?"
"Yes," he replied, "by Allāh I say it and I know it."

*****

[Abū al-Faraj reported: 'Alī b. al-'Abbās al-Maqāni'ī told me: Bakkār b. Aḥmad informed us: al-Ḥasan b. al-Ḥusayn, on the authority of 'Anbasa b. Bijād[16] al-

16 Correct name from Ibn Dāwud, 264.

'Abīd told us:]
Whenever Ja'far b. Muḥammad, peace be on them, saw Muḥammad b. 'Abd Allāh b. al-Ḥasan, his eyes would flow with tears and then he would say: "(I would sacrifice) my life for him. The people say that (he is the *Mahdī* while) he is to be killed. He is not in the Book of 'Alī, peace be on him, as one of the caliphs of this community."[17]

This (second report) is a famous report just like the one before it. The historians do not differ on the accuracy of both of them. They both (clearly) give evidence for the Imamate of Abū 'Abd Allāh al-Ṣādiq, peace be on him. Indeed miracles were performed by him in order that he might make known things which were unknown and show the existence of things before they came to be, just as prophets, peace be on them, used to make (such things) known. That was one of their signs and indications of their prophethood, and their truthfulness (in speaking) about their Lord, the Mighty and Exalted.

*****

[Abū al-Qāsim Ja'far b. Muḥammad b. Qūlawayh told me on the authority of Muḥammad b. Ya'qūb al-Kulaynī, on the authority of 'Alī b. Ibrāhīm b. Hāshim, on the authority of his father, on the authority of a group of his men (i.e. teachers), on the authority of Yūnus b. Ya'qūb, who said:][18]
I was with Abū 'Abd Allāh (Ja'far), peace be on him, when a Syrian came to him. He said: "I am a scholar (*ṣāḥib*) of theology, jurisprudence, and the laws of inheritance. I have come to dispute with your followers."

"Is your theology from the Apostle of Allāh, may Allāh bless Him and His Family, or from yourself?" Abū 'Abd Allāh (Ja'far), peace be on him, asked.
"Partly from the Apostle of Allāh, may Allāh bless Him and His Family, and partly from myself," replied (the other man).

"Then are you a partner of the Apostle of Allāh, may Allāh bless Him and His Family?" enquired Abū 'Abd Allāh (Ja'far).
"No," he answered.

"Have you heard inspiration (*waḥy*) (direct) from Allāh?"
"No," he replied.

"Is obedience to you required as is obedience to the Apostle of Allāh, may Allāh

17 What is between brackets is omitted by al-Mufīd but is included from *Maqātil al-Ṭalibiyīn*, 208.
18 *Al-Kāfī*, I, 171-3.

bless Him and His Family?"
"No," was the answer.

Abū 'Abd Allāh, peace be on him, turned to me and said: "Yūnus b. Ya'qub, this man has contradicted himself before he has begun (the real business) of discussing." Then he said: "Yūnus, if you were good at theology, you should speak to him."

[Yūnus remarked:]
How sad it was, for I said to him: "May I be your ransom, I have heard you forbid (taking part in) theology and say: Woe to the theologians who say that this follows and that this does not follow; that this is entailed and that this is not entailed; that this we accept as rational and this we do not accept as rational."

"I only said," Abū 'Abd Allāh, peace be on him remarked, "woe to them, if they abandon what I say and adopt their own wishes." Then he told me: "Go out to the door and look for any of the theologians you can see, and bring them in."

I went out and found Ḥumrān b. A'yan who was good at theology, and Muḥammad b. al-Nu'mān al-Aḥwāl, who was a theologian, and Hishām b. Sālim and Qays b. al-Māṣir, both theologians. I brought them (all) in to him. After he had settled us in the assembly - we were in the tent of Abū 'Abd Allāh at the top of a mountain on the edge of the sanctuary (of Mecca) (*ḥaram*) and that was (a few) days before the days of the pilgrimage, Abū 'Abd Allāh, peace be on him, put his head out of the tent. There appeared at that moment a camel dashing along. He cried out: "Hishām, by the Lord of the Ka'ba!"

We thought that it was Hishām, one of the sons of 'Aqīl, who loved him greatly. But behold, it was Hishām b. al-Ḥakam who came. He still only had the first traces of his beard on his face. All of us there were older than him. Abū 'Abd Allāh, peace be on him, made room for him and said: "(Here is) one who helps us with his heart, his tongue and his hand."

He told Ḥumrān: "Debate with the man" - meaning the Syrian. Ḥumrān debated with him and overcame him. Then (Abū 'Abd Allāh) said: "O Ṭāq, debate with him." So Muḥammad b. al-Nu'mān debated with him and overcame him. Next he said: "Hishām b. Sālim, debate with him." So they both argued together. He then told Qays b. Māṣir to debate with him and he did so. Abū 'Abd Allāh, peace be on him, began to smile at their discussion as the Syrian sought to escape in front of him. He told the Syrian: "Debate with this lad" - meaning Hishām b. al-Ḥakam.

"Yes," replied the Syrian and said, "lad, ask me about the Imamate of this man" - meaning Abū 'Abd Allāh, peace be on him.

Hishām was so angry that he trembled but then he said: "Fellow, does your Lord look after His creatures or do they look after themselves?"
"Indeed," replied the Syrian, "my Lord looks after His creatures."

"What does He do to look after their religion for them?"
"He gives them duties and provides them with proof (*ḥujja*) and evidence for the things which He has required of them. He removes any weaknesses they might have about that."

"What is the evidence which He has established for them?" Hishām asked him.
"It is the Apostle of Allāh, may Allāh bless Him and His Family," the Syrian answered.

"What after the Apostle of Allāh?" enquired Hishām.
"The Book and the *sunna*."

"Do the Book and the *sunna* benefit us today in our differences so that the differences are removed from us and we are able to agree?" asked Hishām.
"Yes," replied the Syrian.

"Then do we differ from you," retorted Hishām, "so that you have come to us from Syria to dispute with us? You claim that personal judgement (*ra'y*) is the method (of establishing the practices) of religion while you acknowledge that personal judgement does not bring people who differ together in one doctrine."

The Syrian was silent as if he was thinking. So Abū 'Abd Allāh, peace be on him, asked him: "Why aren't you debating?"
"If I say: We do not differ," he answered, "I would be (merely) being obstinate. If I say: the Book and the *sunna* remove our differences, I would be wrong because the two bear (different) interpretations. However, I could use the same argument against him."

"Ask him, then," Abū 'Abd Allāh, peace be on him, told him. "You will find him competent."

So the Syrian asked Hishām: "Who looks after His creatures, their Lord or themselves?"
"Indeed their Lord looks after them," replied Hishām.

"Does He establish for them someone who will harmonise their doctrine, remove their differences and explain the true from the false to them?" demanded the Syrian.
"Yes," replied Hishām.

"Who is that?" asked the Syrian.
"At the beginning of the *sharī'a*, it was the Apostle of Allāh but after the Prophet, blessings and peace be on him, it was someone else."

"Who is it other than the Prophet, may Allāh bless Him and His Family, who takes his place (*al-qā'im maqāmahu*) in being His (i.e. Allāh's) proof?" the Syrian asked.
"Now or before?" Hishām responded.

"At the present time," answered the Syrian.
"This man who is sitting here," said Hishām - meaning Abū 'Abd Allāh. "He is the one to whom you travelled; he is the one who tells us about heaven and is the inheritor from father and grandfather."

"How would I have knowledge of (the truth of) that?" asked the Syrian.
"Ask him about anything which occurs to you," Hishām told him.

"You have stopped (any) excuse of mine but I do have a question," the Syrian declared.
"I will dispense with your questioning," Abū 'Abd Allāh, peace be on him, told him. "I will tell you about your travel and your journey. You left on such and such a day. Your road was such and such. You passed so and so and such and such (a man) passed you."

Every time he told him anything about his affair, the Syrian would say: "True, by Allāh." Then the Syrian said to him: "At this moment I have submitted (*aslamtu*) to Allāh."

"Rather at this moment you have faith (*āmanta*) in Allāh," said Abū 'Abd Allāh, peace be on him. "*Islām* (submission to Allāh) is before *īmān* (faith in Allāh). On the basis of the former (*Islām*) they arrange inheritance and marriage: on the basis of faith (*īmān*) men are rewarded."

"True," replied the Syrian, "at this moment I testify that there is no God but Allāh, that Muḥammad is the Apostle of Allāh, may Allāh bless Him and His Family, and that you are the (present) trustee (*waṣi*) (of Allāh) among the trustees (appointed by Allāh)."

Abū 'Abd Allāh approached Ḥumrān and said: "Ḥumrān, conduct theology on the basis of traditional knowledge (*āthār*) and you will be correct." He turned to Hishām b. Sālim and said: "You want to use traditional knowledge but you don't know it" Then he turned to al-Aḥwal and said: "You are a man who uses *qiyās* and is evasive, a man who refutes falsehood with falsehood, even though your false argument is stronger." Then he turned to Qays b. Māṣir and said: "When you debate, the nearer you are to truth and traditions (*khabar*) on the authority of the Prophet, the further you are from it: you mix up the truth with what is false. A little truth suffices for much which is false. You and al-Aḥwal are skilful (verbal) gymnasts."

[Yūnus b. Ya'qūb remarked:] By Allāh, I thought he would say to Hishām something close to what he had said to them.
Then he said: "Hishām, you are hardly likely to fall, for you tuck in your legs (like a bird): when you are about to fall to the earth, you fly. Therefore a person like you should debate with the people. Guard against slipping and intercession will be behind you."

*****

This report, together with what it contains of rational proof and evidence for the Imamate, also includes the content of the two previous reports' evidence of the miraculous ability of Abū 'Abd Allāh, peace be on him. It agrees with them in the (full) significance of proof.

*****

[Abū al-Qasim Ja'far b. Muḥammad al-Qummī informed me on the authority of Muḥammad b. Ya'qūb al-Kulaynī, on the authority of 'Alī b. Ibrāhīm b. Hashim, on the authority of his father on the authority of 'Abbās 'Amr al-Faqīmī:][19]
Ibn Abī al-'Awjā', Ibn Ṭālūt, Ibn al-A'mā and Ibn al-Muqaffa' with a group of Zindiqs were gathered in the Sacred Mosque during the season of the pilgrimage. Abū 'Abd Allāh Ja'far b. Muḥammad, peace be on them, was there giving legal decisions to the people, explaining the Qur'ān to them and answering their questions with arguments and proofs. The group said to Ibn Abī al-'Awjā': "Can you induce this man sitting here to make a mistake and question him about what would disgrace him in front of those who are gathered around him? For you can see the fascination of the people for him; he is (supposed to be)

19 The tradition in this form does not seem to appear in *al-Kāfī* despite the inclusion of al-Kulaynī's name in the *isnād.* However cf. Ibn Bābawayh, *Kitāb al-Tawḥīd.* (Tehran 1387 AH) 253-4.

the great scholar of his time."

"Yes," replied Ibn Abī al-'Awjā'. He went forward and the people moved aside. He said: "Abū 'Abd Allāh, gatherings for discussion are things to be taken care of. Everyone who has a cough must cough, so will you permit me to ask a question?"
"Ask, if you want to," Abū 'Abd Allāh, peace be on him, answered him.

Then Ibn Abī al-'Awjā' asked him: "For how long will you tread on this threshing-floor and go round this stone? For how long will you worship this house made of bricks and mud and amble around it like a camel when it is scared? Whoever thinks about this and considers it, realises that it is the action of an unintelligent and unthinking man, so explain (it) as you are the principal exponent (lit. head and hump) of this affair, and your father was its founder and support."

"Those whom Allāh leads astray and whose hearts He blinds find the truth unwholesome and will never taste its sweetness," retorted al-Ṣādiq, peace be on him. "The devil is the friend and lord of such a man. He will lead him to the watering places of destruction and never let him come from them. This is a house where Allāh's creatures seek to worship Him in order that their obedience in coming to it may be well known. Therefore He has urged them to magnify it and to visit it and He has made it the place of His prophets and the direction of prayer for those who pray to Him. It is a part of Paradise and a path which leads to His forgiveness. It is set up at the seat of perfection and at the meeting point of majesty and glory. Allāh created it over two thousand years before the earth was laid out. The most worthy to be obeyed in what He orders and to have His prohibitions refrained from is Allāh the Creator of souls and forms."

"You have only spoken and referred (me) to someone who is not present, Abū 'Abd Allāh," retorted Ibn Abī al-'Awjā'".

"Shame on you," retorted al-Ṣādiq, peace be on him. "How could One Who is present with His creatures and closer to them than a vein in the neck, Who hears their words and knows their secrets, be someone who is not present."

"Is He in every place or isn't He?" asked Ibn Abī al-'Awjā'. "If He is in Heaven, how can He be on earth? And if He is on earth, how can He be in Heaven?"

"You described something which is created," retorted Abū 'Abd Allāh, peace be on him, "which when it moves from one place, and when another place is occupied by it, and when (the former) place is without it, then, in the place which it has come to, it does not know what happens in the place in which it was. As for Allāh, the Mighty, (the Dignified, the Ruler, the Judge,)[20] there is no place without Him and no place occupied by Him. He is not nearer to one place than He is to another. In that way the traces of Himself (which He gives) bear witness to Him and His actions give evidence for Him. He whom He has sent with precise signs and clear proofs, Muḥammad, may Allāh bless Him and His Family, has brought us this (form of) worship. If you have any doubts about any of His commandments, ask about it and I will explain it to you."

Ibn Abī al-'Awjā' became stupified and did not know what to say. He left his presence and said to his companions: "I asked you to find me some wine (to enjoy myself with) and you threw me on to a burning coal."

"Shut up," they told him. "You have disgraced us by your bewilderment. We saw no one today more humiliated than you in his discussion."

"Are you saying this to me?" he replied. "He is (only) the son of a man who shaved the heads of those whom you see." He indicated with his hand towards the people gathered for the pilgrimage.

[It is reported:][21]
One day Abū Shākir al-Daysānī stood in a discussion group of Abū 'Abd Allāh, peace be on him, and said: "You are one of the shining stars, your fathers were wonderful full moons and your mothers were graceful discreet women. Your lineage is the most noble of lineages. When learned men are mentioned, it is for you that the little finger is bent (i.e. he is the first to be counted). So tell me, O bountiful sea, what is the evidence for the creation of the world?"

"The easiest evidence for that is what I will show you (now)," answered Abū 'Abd Allāh, peace be on him. Then he called for an egg and put it in the palm of his hand. "This is a compact protective container; inside it is the thin (substance of an) egg which is surrounded by what could be compared with fluid silver and melted gold. Do you doubt that?"
"There can be no doubt about that," replied Abū Shākir.

"Then it splits open showing a form like (for example) a peacock," continued Abū 'Abd Allāh, peace be on him. "Has anything entered into it other than what

20 What is between brackets is omitted by al-Mufīd and included from Ibn Bābawayh, *Kitāb al-Tawḥīd*, 253-4.
21 This tradition is reported by Ibn Bābawayh, *Kitāb al-Tawḥīd*, 292-3.

you knew (to be there already)?"
"No," he replied.

"This is the evidence for the creation of the world."
"You have explained, Abū 'Abd Allāh," he said, "and you have made it clear. You have spoken and brought improvement. You have described it and spoken concisely. You knew that we would not accept anything which we could not realise with our eyes, or hear with our ears, or taste with our mouths, or smell with our noses, or touch with our skin."

"You have mentioned the five senses," said Abū 'Abd Allāh, peace be on him, "but they will not bring any benefit in rational deduction except as evidence, just as darkness cannot be removed without light."

He, peace be on him, means by that that the senses without reason will never lead to the understanding of things which are not present, and that what he had shown with regard to the creation of the form was a concept whose recognition (*'ilm*) was based on sense-perception.

*****

(The following is an example) of what has been recorded on his authority, peace be on him, concerning the necessity of knowing Allāh the Most High and His religion: He said: "I have found the knowledge of all the people (encompassed) by four things:

1. You should know your Lord;
2. You should know what He has done for you;
3. You should know what He wants from you;
4. You should know what would make you abandon your religion.

These four divisions include (all) the requirement of things which should be known because the first thing that a man should do is to know his Lord, may His Majesty be exalted. When he knows that he has a Lord, it is necessary that he must know what He has done for him. When he knows what He has done for him, he knows of His blessings. When he knows of His blessings, it is necessary that he should thank Him. When he wants to carry out his thanks, he must know what He wants so that he may obey Him in his actions. Since obedience to Him is necessary, it will be necessary for him to know what would cause him to abandon his religion so that he might avoid it, and in that way keep pure his obedience to his Lord and his thanks for His blessings."

*****

(This is an example) of what was recorded on his authority peace be on him, concerning the unity of Allāh and the denial of anthropomorphism.

He said to Hishām b. al-Ḥakam: "Allāh, the Exalted, should not be compared to anything, nor should anything be compared to Him. Whatever comes to the imagination is other than Allāh."

(The following is an example) of what was recorded on his authority, peace be on him, concerning his words on justice: He said to Zurāra b. A'yan: "Zurāra, shall I give you a summary of (the doctrine of) decree (*qaḍā*) and destiny (*qadar*)?" "Yes, may I be your ransom," replied Zurāra.

"When it is the Day of Resurrection and Allāh has gathered His creatures together, He will ask them about what He enjoined upon them but He will not ask them about what He had decreed for them."

*****

(This is an example) of what was recorded on his authority concerning wisdom and exhortation.
He said: "Not everyone who intends something is able to do it. Not everyone who is able to do something will be granted success in it. Not everyone who is granted success in something will do it in the right place. When intention, ability, success and correctness come together, there happiness is perfected."

*****

(This is an example) of what has been recorded of him, peace be upon him, urging consideration of Allāh's religion and the acquisition of knowledge about the friends (*awliyā'*) of Allāh.
He said: "Give close consideration to things which you cannot afford to ignore, be true to yourselves and fight against your (inclinations) so that you may find out those things which it is inexcusable not to know. These are the basic elements of Allāh's religion. If a man ignores them, he will gain no benefit (no matter) how intense is his striving in pursuit of the outward form of worship. On the other hand, no harm will come to a man who knows them and abides by them with moderation (in his behaviour). There is no way for anyone except through the help of Allāh, the Mighty and High."

*****

(The following is an example) of what has been recorded on his authority, peace be on him, urging repentance:
He said: "To delay repentance is to be heedless; to lengthen the time of putting

off (religious duties) is (to create) confusion (in one's mind); to attempt to justify oneself before Allāh is (to bring about one's own) destruction; persisting in sin makes (a person) feel secure from Allāh's devising. *Only people who are lost feel secure from Allāh's devising.* [VII 99]"

*****

The reports about what has been recorded on his authority, peace be on him, concerning knowledge, wisdom, asceticism, exhortation and all the branches of learning are too numerous to be enumerated in one speech or to be included in one book. What we have set out is enough for the purpose of what we intended. Allāh is the bringer of success for what is right.

*****

(The poet) al-Sayyid Ismā'īl b. Muḥammad al-Ḥimyarī, may Allāh have mercy on him, withdrew from the doctrine of the Kaysaniyya[22] which he had professed, when he was informed of Abū 'Abd Allāh's peace be on him, denial of this doctrine and of his prayers for him and he (returned) to the system of the Imamate. He said of him, peace be on him:

> O (you) who ride a tall, strong camel to Medina, on which (you) cross every broad land,
>
> If Allāh guides you, you will look to Ja'far. So speak to the friend (*walī*) of Allāh, the son of the man who was well-educated (in the learning of Allāh):
>
> Friend of Allāh and son of the friend of Allāh, I repent before the Merciful and then I return
>
> To you from the wrong which I used to hold while I was constantly striving against all who obviously expressed (the truth).
>
> Yet my words concerning the son of Khawla[23] were not meant to be rebellious against the offspring of the celebrated one.
>
> Rather they were spoken on the authority of the trustee (*waṣī*) of Muḥammad - and he was not a liar when he said
>
> That the master of the affair (*wali al-amr*) would disappear without being

22 The Kaysaniyya believed in the Imamate of Muḥammad b. al-Ḥanafiyya. They held that he had not died and that he was in occultation until he would return as the *Mahdī*.

23 Muḥammad b. al-Ḥanafiyya's mother.

seen for years like a man afraid.

The possessions of the missing man will be distributed as if his concealment were in the high heaven.

Say, "No," and the truth is what you say, and what you say is final without me adding any fanaticism.

I testify to my Lord that your words are a proof (*ḥujja*) to all creatures, whether obedient or sinful,

That the master of the affair (*wali al-amr*) and the one who will arise (al-qā'im) whom my soul (now) looks towards and who excites it to joy,

That He will have concealment (*Ghayba*) where it is inevitable that he will conceal himself. May Allāh bless him as one who will be concealed.

He will delay for a time then his authority will come to dominate and he will fill all (the lands) from East to West with Justice.

In this poetry there is clear evidence for the withdrawal of al-Sayyid, may Allāh have mercy on him, from the beliefs of the Kaysaniyya, and for his holding the doctrine of the Imamate of al-Ṣadiq, peace be on him. (There is also evidence) for the existence of a clear call on the part of the Shī'a during the time of Abū 'Abd Allāh to (accept) his Imamate and to hold the doctrine of the concealment of the leader (for the rest) of time (*ṣāhib al-zamān*), the blessings and peace of Allāh be on him. This (poem) is a clear indication of (al-Sayyid's belief) and it is a clear statement of (the doctrine of) the Twelver-Imamites (*Imāmiyya ithna 'ashariyya*).

The Number of Abū 'Abd Allāh Ja'far's Children, their Names and an Extract of the Reports about them.

Abū 'Abd Allāh, peace be on him, had ten children. They were

1. Ismā'īl
2. 'Abd Allāh
3. Umm Farwa

The mother of these (three) was Fāṭima, daughter of al-Ḥusayn b. 'Alī b. al-Ḥusayn.

4. Mūsā

5. Isḥāq
6. Muḥammad

(all of these three were born) to a slave-wife

7. Al-'Abbās
8. 'Alī
9. Asmā'
10. Fāṭima

They had different mothers.

*****

Ismā'īl was the eldest of his sons. Abū 'Abd Allāh loved him very much, and was very kind to him. Some of the Shī'a used to think that he would take charge (of the Imamate) (*qā'im*) after his father and would be his successor after him, since he was the oldest in years and because of his father's inclination towards him and compassion for him. However, he died at al-'Arḍ during the life-time of his father, peace be on him, and he was carried on the shoulders of men to his father in Medina and he was buried in (the cemetery) of al-Baqī'.

It is reported that Abū 'Abd Allāh, peace be on him was very grieved and saddened by his (death). He led his litter barefoot and without a cloak. He ordered his litter to be put on the ground many times before he was buried, and he uncovered (Ismā'īl) face and looked at it.

His intention in doing that was to establish the fact of (Ismā'īl) death to those who had thought that he was to succeed after him, and to remove from them any mistaken belief with regard to him (still) being alive.

When Ismā'īl, may Allāh have mercy on him, died, those of his father's followers who had thought and believed in Ismā'īl Imamate after his father, abandoned that doctrine. However, a small group maintained that (Ismā'īl) was still alive (and was the successor). This group was not from the close associates of his father (*khāṣṣa*) nor from those who report on his authority. Such men (who held Ismā'īl to be still alive) were distant and extremists.

When al-Ṣādiq, peace be on him, died, a group of the latter then moved across to declare the Imamate of Mūsā b. Ja'far, peace be on him, after his father, peace be on him. The rest divided into two (main) divisions. One of them withdrew from the doctrine that Ismā'īl was still alive and maintained the Imamate of his son Muḥammad b. Ismā'īl because of their view that the Imamate had belonged to Ismā'īl (as successor) and that a son has more right to the Imamate than a brother has. The other group maintained their position that he was still alive. However, today, they are extremely rare and there is not any knowledge of anyone of them who can be pointed out. Both these groups are called the Ismāʻīlyya. Those of them who are known now, are the ones who claim that the Imamate after Ismāʻīl belonged to his son and the sons of his son to the end of time,

*****

ʻAbd Allāh b. Jaʻfar was the eldest of his brothers after Ismāʻīl but he did not have a position of honour with his father similar to the rest of his father's sons. He was suspected of opposing his father's teaching and it is said that he used to mix with the Hashwiyya and was inclined towards the beliefs of the Murji'a. He claimed the Imamate after his father and argued that he was the eldest of the surviving brothers. A group of the followers of Abū ʻAbd Allāh, peace be on him, followed him in his declaration. Later most of them went back to the doctrine of the Imamate of his brother, Mūsā, peace be on him, when they perceived the weakness of his claim, and the strength of the authority of Abū al-Ḥasan (i.e. Mūsā), peace be on him, together with the evidence for the right of the latter and the clear proofs of his Imamate. However, a small number of them, continued in their belief and professed the Imamate of ʻAbd Allāh b. Jaʻfar. They are the sect which is nick-named al-Faṭḥiyya. This name is only attached to them because of their doctrine of the Imamate of ʻAbd Allāh, for he was flat-footed (*afṭaḥ*) in both feet. It is (also) said that they were called that because of the propagandist for the Imamate of ʻAbd Allāh was called ʻAbd Allāh b. Afṭaḥ.

*****

Isḥāq b. Jaʻfar was one of the men of merit, righteousness, piety and striving (after Allāh) (*ijtihād*). The people relate traditions and reports on his authority. When Ibn Kāsib used to relate a tradition on his authority, he used to say:
"The reliable satisfactory authority, Isḥāq b. Jaʻfar has told me."

Isḥāq used to uphold the Imamate of his brother, Mūsā b. Jaʻfar, peace be on him, and he reported on the authority of his father the designation (*naṣṣ*) of the Imamate on his brother, peace be on him.

*****

Muḥammad b. Jaʻfar was generous and brave. He used to fast on alternate days. However, he held Zaydī views concerning coming out (in rebellion) with the sword.

[It is reported on the authority of his wife, Khadīja, daughter of ʻAbd Allāh b. al-Ḥusayn, who said:]

Muḥammad never left us on any day with a cloak without coming back after having put it (on someone else).[24] Every day he used to slaughter a ram for his guests. He led a revolt against al-Ma'mūn in the year 199 A.H. (814/5) in Mecca. The Jarūdiyya branch of the Zaydīs followed him. 'Īsā al-Jalūdī came to fight against him. He dispersed (Muḥammad's) groups, captured (Muḥammad) and sent him to Ma'mūn. When he reached al-Ma'mūn, the latter treated him with kindness, made him sit close beside him, and gave him the best of gifts. He resided with (al-Ma'mūn) in Khurasān and rode to him in the procession of his kinsmen. al-Ma'mūn put up with (things) from him which a ruler does not (usually) put up with from his subjects.

However, it is (also) reported that al-Ma'mūn refused to allow him to ride to him with a group of the descendants of Abū Ṭālib, who had revolted against al-Ma'mūn in the year 200 A.H. (815/6) and to whom he had given security. The decree came to them: "Do not ride with Muḥammad b. Ja'far. Ride with 'Abd Allāh b. al-Ḥusayn." However, they refused to ride and stayed in their houses. Then the decree came: "Ride with whomever you prefer." So when they rode to al-Ma'mūn, they rode with Muḥammad b. Ja'far and then they departed when he did.

[Mūsā b. Salama has mentioned:]
(News) came to Muḥammad b . Ja'far and he was told: "The servants of the man with two offices[25] have beaten your servants over a dispute about firewood which they had bought." He went out wrapping himself in two cloaks and (taking) with him a thick stick. He was reciting verse, saying: "Death is better than living in humiliation." The people followed him until he struck the servants of the man with two offices and took the wood away from them. News (of this) got back to al-Ma'mūn and he sent to the man with two offices and told him: "Go to Muḥammad b. Ja'far, peace be on him, apologise to him and give him power to decide what to do against your (servants)." The man with two offices came to Muḥammad b. Ja'far.

[Mūsā b. Salama reported:]
I was sitting with Muḥammad b. Ja'far when he came. (Muḥammad) was told: "Here is the man with two offices."
"He will only sit on the ground," he declared and he and those with him took the carpet which was in the house and threw it aside. There was only the cushion on which Muḥammad b. Ja'far was sitting left in the house.

24 cf. *Maqātil al-Ṭalibiyīn*, 538.
25 The man with two offices (i.e. military and civil administration) was al-Faḍl b. Sahl.

When the man with two offices entered, Muḥammad made room for him on the cushion. However, he refused to sit on it and sat on the ground. He apologised to him and gave him power to decide what to do with his servants.

Muḥammad b. Ja'far died in Khurāsān (while he was still) with al-Ma'mūn. Al-Ma'mūn rode to attend his (funeral). He met them as they were bringing him out. He looked at the litter, got down, and walked between the two poles of (the litter). He remained between them until it was put down. Then he went forward and said the prayer over him. Then he (helped to) carry it until he went down into the grave. He remained there until (they) began to erect (the tomb) over it. Then he went out of it and stood at the grave until the burial was complete.

'Ubayd Allāh b. al-Ḥusayn spoke to him and called out to him, "Commander of the faithful, you have become weary today, wouldn't you prefer to ride?".
"These are bonds of kinship which have been cut for two hundred years," replied al-Ma'mūn.

[It is reported on the authority of Ismā'īl b. Muḥammad b. Ja'far, who said :]
I said to my brother who was at my side while al-Ma'mūn was standing at the grave: "If we told him (al-Ma'mūn) about the venerable man's debts, we would not find anyone closer than him at this time." Then we began (to mention them) to Ma'mūn.

"How much debt did Abū Ja'far (i.e. Muḥammad b. Ja'far) leave?" he asked.
"Fifteen thousand dīnār," I told him.
"Allāh has relieved him of his debt," he said. "To whom did he make his will?"
"To his son called Yaḥyā in Medina," we answered.
"He is not in Medina," he said. "He is in Egypt and we are aware of him being there. However, we are unwilling to let him know about (our knowledge) of his departure from Medina so that that should not harm him as a result of his knowledge of our dislike of his departure from there"

*****

'Alī b. Ja'far, may Allāh be pleased with him, was an important narrator of traditions, correct in method, with intense piety and great merit. He stayed close to his brother Mūsā, peace be on him, and reported many traditions on his authority

*****

Al-'Abbās b. Ja'far, may Allāh have mercy on him, was a man of outstanding merit.

*****

Mūsā b. Ja'far, peace be on them, was the most distinguished, the greatest in rank, and the one most hailed by the people of the sons of Abū 'Abd Allāh, peace be on him. In this no one was seen who was more generous than him, kinder in spirit and companionship. He was the person most given to worship and the most pious and distinguished, the most knowledgeable in jurisprudence of the people of his time. The members of his father's Shī'a agreed on the doctrine of his Imamate, on the greatness of his right and on submitting to his authority. They have reported on the authority of his father numerous designations (*naṣṣ*) of the Imamate on him, and indications of him (being given) the succession. They took the guidelines of their religion from him. They report clear signs and miracles from him through which he has established proof of himself and the correctness of the doctrine of his Imamate.

CHAPTER VI

IMĀM MŪSĀ AL-KĀẒIM

This is an account of the Imam who was in charge (*al-qā'im*) after Abū 'Abd Allāh Ja'far b. Muḥammad, peace be on them, (describing) who gave birth to him and the date of his birth. (It includes) the evidence for his Imamate, the age he reached and the period of his succession (*khilāfa*), his death, its cause, the place of his grave, the number of his children and a brief outline of the reports about him.

As we have mentioned before, the Imam after Abū 'Abd Allāh Ja'far, peace be on him, was Abū al-Ḥasan Mūsā b. Ja'far, the righteous worshipper (of Allāh), peace be on him, because the qualities of outstanding merit and perfection were gathered in him, because of the designation (*naṣṣ*) by his father of the Imamate (being) for him, and his clear indication of it being his.

His birth took place at al-Abwā' in the year 128 A.H. (745/6). He, peace be on him, died in the prison of al-Sindī b. Shāhik in Baghdād on the 6th of (the month of) Rajab in the year 183 A.H. (799). He was then fifty-five years of age. His mother was a slave-wife named Ḥamīda al-Barbariyya. The period of his succession and occupying the office of the Imamate after his father, peace be on them, was thirty-five years. His *kunyas* were Abū-Ibrāhīm, Abū al-Ḥasan and Abū 'Alī. He is known as al-'Abd al-Ṣālīḥ (the pious worshipper of Allāh) and also he is described as al-Kāẓim (the restrained), peace be on him.

The Designation (*Naṣṣ*) of (Imam Mūsā) for the Imamate by his Father, Peace be on them.

Among the *shaykhs* of the followers of Abū 'Abd Allāh, peace be on him, his special group (*khāṣṣa*), his inner circle and the trustworthy righteous legal scholars, may Allāh have mercy on them, who report the clear designation of the Imamate by Abū 'Abd Allāh Ja'far peace be on him, for his son, Abū al-Ḥasan Mūsā, peace be on him, are: al-Mufaḍḍal b. 'Umar al-Ju'fī, Mu'ādh b. Kathīr, 'Abd al-Raḥmān b. al-Ḥajjāj, al-Fayḍ b. al-Mukhtār, Ya'qūb al-Sarrāj, Sulaymān b. Khālid, Safwān al-Jammāl, and others whom it would make the book too long to mention.

(That designation) is also reported by his two brothers, Isḥāq and 'Alī, sons of Ja'far, peace be on him. They were men of merit and piety and (therefore reliable witnesses) in so far as two such men did not differ on it.

[Mūsā al-Ṣayqal reported on the authority of al-Mufaḍḍal b. ʻUmar al-Juʻfī, may Allāh have mercy on him, who said:][1]
I (i.e. al-Mufaḍḍal b. ʻUmar al-Juʻfī) was with Abū ʻAbd Allāh (Jaʻfar), peace be on him. Abū Ibrāhīm Mūsā, peace be on him, came in. He was still a boy. Abū ʻAbd Allāh Jaʻfar, peace be on him, said to me "Indicate to those of your Companions whom you trust that the position of authority belongs to him Mūsā."

[Thubayt reported on the authority of Muʻādh b. Kathīr, on the authority of Abū ʻAbd Allāh Jaʻfar:][2]
I (i.e. Muʻādh b. Kathīr) said to (Jaʻfar): "I ask Allāh, Who provided your father with you for this position, to provide you with one of your offspring for the same position before your death."
"Allāh has done that," he answered.

"May I be your ransom, who is it?" I asked.
He indicated al-ʻAbd al-Ṣālīh (the pious worshipper of Allāh) (i.e. Mūsā) to me. He was asleep.
"This one who is sleeping," he said. He was at that time a boy.

[Abū ʻAlī al-Arrajanī reported on the authority of ʻAbd al-Raḥmān b. al-Hajjāj, who said:][3]
I (i.e. ʻAbd al-Raḥmān b. al-Hajjāj) visited Jaʻfar b. Muḥammad, peace be on them, in his house. He was in such-and-such a room in his house which he used as a prayer-room. He was praying there. On his right hand was Mūsā b. Jaʻfar, peace be on them, following his prayer.

"May Allāh make me your ransom," I said, "you know how I have dedicated my life to you and (you know of) my service to you. Who is the master of the affair (*walī al-amr*) after you?"
He said: "Abd al-Raḥmān, Mūsā has put on the armour and it fitted him."
"After that, I have no further need of anything," I replied.

[Abd al-Aʻlā reported on the authority of al-Fayḍ b. al-Mukhtār, who said:][4]
I (i.e. al-Fayḍ b. al-Mukhtār) said to Abū ʻAbd Allāh Jaʻfar, peace be on him: "Take my hand away from the fire (of Hell). Who is (the Imam) for us after you?" Abū Ibrahim (Mūsā) entered - at that time he was a boy. Then (Jaʻfar) said: "This is your leader (*ṣāḥib*). Keep close to him."

1 *Al-Kāfī*, I, 308, tradition no. 4. Al-Kulaynī's *isnād* has been shortened.
2 *Al-Kāfī*, I, 308, tradition no. 2. Al-Kulaynī's *isnād* has been shortened.
3 *Al-Kāfī*, I. 308, tradition no. 3. Al-Kulaynī's *isnād* has been shortened. Al-Arrajānī is al-Kulaynī's reading of the name.
4 *Al-Kāfī*, I, 307, tradition no. 1. Al-Kulaynī's *isnād* has been shortened.

[Ibn Abī Najrān reported on the authority of al-Manṣūr b. Ḥāzim, who said:][5]
I (i.e. al-Manṣūr b. Ḥāzim) said to Abū 'Abd Allāh, peace be on him: "(May I ransom you) with my father and mother. There is a great coming and going among men about (the succession). Since that is so, who is it?"

"Since that is so," replied Abū 'Abd Allāh, peace be on him, "he is your leader." He tapped the right shoulder of Abū al-Ḥasan (Mūsā). He was at that time, as far as I know, about five years old. 'Abd Allāh b. Ja'far was sitting with us.

[Ibn Abī Najrān reported on the authority of 'Īsā b. 'Abd Allāh b. Muḥammad b. 'Umar b. 'Alī b. Abī Ṭālib, on the authority of Abū 'Abd Allāh Ja'far, peace be on him:][6]
I (i.e. 'Īsā b. Muḥammad) asked (Ja'far): "If something happened - may Allāh not make me see such a thing - who should I follow?"
(Ja'far) pointed to his son, Mūsā.
"If anything happened to Mūsā, who should I follow?" I asked.
"His son," he replied.
"If anything happened to his son?"
"Then his son."
"If something happened to him," I went on, "and he left a big brother and a small son?"
"His son; it is always thus," he answered.

[Al-Faḍl reported on the authority of Ṭāhir b. Muḥammad on the authority of Abū 'Abd Allāh Ja'far, peace be on him:][7]
I (i.e. Ṭāhir b. Muḥammad) saw (Ja'far) blaming his son, 'Abd Allāh, and warning him. He was saying: "What stops you from being like your brother? By Allāh, I see the light in (Mūsā's) face."

"Why is that?" asked 'Abd Allāh. "Is not my father and his father one and the same? Is not my origin and his origin one and the same?"
"He is from my soul and you are my son," replied Abū 'Abd Allāh Ja'far, peace be on him.

[Muḥammad b. Sinān reported on the authority of Ya'qūb al- Sarrāj, who said:][8]
I (i.e. Ya'qūb al- Sarrāj) visited Abū 'Abd Allāh Ja'far, peace be on him. He was standing by the head of Abū al-Ḥasan, Mūsā, peace be on him, who was in

5 *Al-Kāfī*, I, 309, tradition no. 6. Al-Kulaynī's *isnād* has been shortened.
6 *Al-Kāfī*, I, 309, tradllion no. 7. Al-Kulaynī's *isnād* has been shortened.
7 *Al-Kāfī*, I, 310, tradition no. 10. Al-Kulaynī's *isnād* has been shortened.
8 *Al-Kāfī*, I, 310, tradition no. 11. Al-Kulaynī's *isnād* has been shortened.

the cradle. He began to play with him for a long time. I sat down until he had finished. Then I stood up before him. He told me: "Approach your master (*mawlā*) and greet him."

I went near him and greeted him and he replied to me eloquently. Then he told me: "Go and change the name of your daughter which you gave her yesterday. For it is a name which Allāh dislikes."
A daughter had been born to me and I had named her al-Ḥumayrā'.[9]

"Pay attention to the command which he gave you," Abū 'Abd Allāh Ja'far, peace be on him, told me. So I changed her name.

[Ibn Miskān reported on the authority of Sulaymān b. Khālid, who said:][10]
One day Abū 'Abd Allāh Ja'far, peace be on him, called for Abū al-Ḥasan Mūsā while we were with him. He told us: "It is your duty (to follow) this man after me. By Allāh, he is your leader after me."

[Al-Washshā' reported on the authority of 'Alī b. al-Ḥusayn, on the authority of Ṣafwān al-Jammāl, who said:][11]
I (i.e. Ṣafwān al-Jammāl) asked Abū 'Abd Allāh Ja'far, peace be on him, about the leader of this affair (*ṣāḥib al-amr*) (after him). He said: "The leader of this affair is one who does not fool and play."

Abū al-Ḥasan Mūsā, peace be on him, approached. He was still small. He had a calf (destined) for Mecca and was saying to it: "Prostrate yourself to your Lord."

Abū 'Abd Allāh Ja'far, peace be on him, took him by the hand and embraced him saying: "May I ransom with my father and mother (you) who do not fool and play."

[Ya'qūb b. Ja'far al-Ju'fī reported: Isḥāq b. Ja'far al-Ṣādiq, peace be on him, told us:][12]
One day I (i.e. Isḥāq) was with my father (Ja'far) when 'Alī b. 'Umar b. 'Alī asked him: "May I be your ransom, to whom shall we and the people turn after you?"
He answered: "To the owner of two yellow clothes and two locks of hair. He who is coming out of the door to you."

---

9 Ḥumayrā' was one of the names by which 'Ā'isha, wife of the Prophet, was known.
10 *Al-Kāfī*, I, 310, tradition no. 12. Al-Kulaynī's *isnād* has been shortened.
11 *Al-Kāfī*, I, 311, tradition no. 15. Al-Kulaynī's *isnād* has been shortened.
12 *Al-Kāfī*, I, 308, tradition no. 5. Al-Kulaynī's *isnād* has been shortened.

We did not wait long before two (little) hands appeared pulling the two doors so that they opened. In before us came Abū Ibrāhīm Mūsā, peace be on him. He was still a boy and was wearing two yellow garments.

[Muḥammad b. al-Walīd reported: I heard 'Alī b. Ja'far b. Muḥammad al-Ṣādiq, peace be on them, say:]
I (i.e. 'Alī b. Ja'far) heard my father, Ja'far b. Muḥammad, peace be on them, say to a group of his close associates and followers: "Treat my son, Mūsā, peace be on him, with kindness. He is the most meritorious (*afḍal*) of my children and the one who will succeed after me. He is the one who will undertake (*qā'im*) my position. He is Allāh's proof (*ḥujja*) to all His creatures after me."

'Alī b. Ja'far remained firmly loyal to his brother Mūsā, peace be on him, devoted to him, and enthusiastic in taking the outlines of religion from him. He has a famous (book) *Masā'il* (questions) in which he relates the answers he heard from (Mūsā), peace be on him.

The reports of what we have mentioned are too numerous to be explained and described fully.

An Extract of the Proofs, Signs, Indications and Miracles which Abū al-Ḥasan Mūsā (presented).

[Abū al-Qāsim Ja'far b. Muḥammad b. Qulawayh informed me, on the authority of Muḥammad b. Ya'qūb al-Kulaynī, on the authority of Muḥammad b. Yaḥyā, on the authority of Aḥmad b.Muḥammad b. 'Īsā, on the authority of Abū Yaḥyā al- Wāsiṭī, on the authority of Hishām b. Sālim, who said:][13]
I (i.e. Hishām b. Sālim) and Muḥammad b. Nu'mān (known as) Ṣāḥib al-Ṭāq were in Medina after the death of Abū 'Abd Allāh, peace be on him. The people had agreed that 'Abd Allāh b. Ja'far was the leader of the affair (*ṣāḥib al-amr*) after his father. We went to visit him and the people were with him. We questioned him about how much poor-tax (*zakat*) had to be paid.
"Five dirhams on two hundred dirhams," he answered.
"How much on a hundred dirhams?" we asked.
"Two and a half dirhams," he answered.
"By Allāh, you are declaring the doctrine of the *Murji'a*," we said.
"By Allāh," he retorted, "I do not know the doctrine of the *Murji'a*."

We, Abū Ja'far al-Aḥwal (i.e. Muḥammad b. Nu'mān) and myself, left, wandering without knowing where to go. We sat in one of the lanes in Medina

13 *Al-Kāfī*, I, 351 tradition no. 7.

weeping. We did not know where we should go or to whom we should turn. We spoke about (joining) the Murji'ites, the Qadarites, the Mu'taẓilites, and the Zaydites. We were in this situation when I saw a venerable man whom I did not know. He indicated to me with his hand. I was afraid that he was one of the spies of (the 'Abbāsid caliph) Abū Ja'far al-Manṣūr. There were spies in Medina for him (to find out) who the people agreed on to succeed Ja'far. Then that man (i.e. the Imam) would be captured and executed. I was afraid that that man was one of them.

"Go aside," I said to al-Aḥwal, "I am afraid for myself. You be careful. He only wants me. He does not want you. Leave me, for you will lead (him) to yourself." (Al-Aḥwal) went some distance away from me and I went over to the venerable man. That was because I thought that I would not be able to escape from him. As I followed him, I was certain of my own death until he brought me to the door of Abū al-Ḥasan Mūsā, peace be on him. Then he left me and went away. There was a servant at the door. He said to me: "Come in, may Allāh have mercy on you."

I went in. There was Abū al-Ḥasan Mūsā, peace be on him. He spoke to me before (I could speak): "To me, to me; not to the Murji'ites, nor to the Qadarites, nor to the Mu'taẓilites, nor to the Zaydites."
"May I be your ransom," I replied, "your father has gone."
"Yes," he answered.
"He has left through death," I said.
"Yes," he retorted.
"Then who is in charge of the people after him?" I asked.
"If Allāh wills, He will guide you to that man," he answered.
"May I be your ransom," I said, "your brother 'Abd Allāh claims that he is the Imam after his father."
"'Abd Allāh intends that Allāh should not be worshipped (properly)," he declared.
"May I be your ransom, who is in charge of us after him?" I asked (again).
"If Allāh wills, He will guide you to that man," he repeated.
"May I be your ransom, are you him?" I questioned.
"I am not saying that," he replied.

I thought to myself that I had not used the correct method of questioning. So I said to him: "May I be your ransom, do you have an Imam over you?"
"No," he replied. Something came to me which only Allāh knew with regard to honouring and showing respect (to Mūsā). So I said to him: "May I be your ransom, may I question you like I used to question your father?"
"Question," he said. "You will be informed but do not spread (the answer)

around. For if you do spread it around, then slaughter will take place."

I questioned him. Indeed he was like a sea (of knowledge) which could not be exhausted. I said to him: "May I be your ransom, the Shīʻa of your father is lost (without a leader). May I put this matter to them and summon them (to follow) you? For you have taken (a promise of) secrecy from me."

"Tell those of them whose righteousness you are familiar with," he said, "but take (a promise of) secrecy from them. For if it gets spread around, there will be slaughter," and he pointed to his neck with his hand.

I left him and met Abū Jaʻfar al-Aḥwal.
"What happened to you?" he asked.
"Guidance," I said and I told him the story.

Then we met Zurāra and Abū Basīr. They went to him, listened to his words and questioned him. They asserted his Imamate. We met wave after wave of the people. Everyone who went to him, declared (his Imamate) except for the group of ʻAmmār al-Sābāṭī. Abd Allāh persisted in his claim but only a few of the people came to him.

[Abū al-Qāsim Jaʻfar b. Muḥammad b. Qulawayh informed me on the authority of Muḥammad b. Yaʻqūb on the authority of ʻAlī b. Ibrāhīm on the authority of al- Wāfiqī who said:][14]
I (al-Wāfiqī) had an uncle called al-Ḥasan b. ʻAbd Allāh. He was an ascetic and one of the most pious people of his time. The authorities were wary of him because of his earnestness and his vigour towards religion. Sometimes he would approach the authorities concerning enjoining the good and forbidding the evil because of something which had angered him. They accepted that because of his righteousness. The state of affairs continued until one day he went into the mosque. There was Abū al-Ḥasan Mūsā, peace be on him. He beckoned to him and (my uncle) went to him.

(Mūsā) said to him: "'Abū ʻAlī, nothing is more pleasing to me and gives me greater joy than the way you behave. Despite that, you do not have true knowledge (*maʻrifa*). Seek for true knowledge."
"May I be your ransom," he said to him, "what is true knowledge?"
"Go so that you may learn," he told him. "Seek out traditions."
"From whom?" he asked.

14 *Al-Kāfī*, I, 352, tradition no. 8. Al-Wāfiqī is al-Kulaynī's reading. He gives the full name as Muḥammad b. so-and-so Wāfiqī.

"From the jurists of Medina," he answered, "and then bring the additions to me."

He went and wrote down (what he learnt). Then he came and read to him. However (Mūsā) invalidated all of it. He told him: "Go and learn."

The man was concerned about (his own attitude to) his religion. He continued to search for 'Abū al-Ḥasan until he went to (visit) an estate of his. On the road he met him. He said to him: "May I be your ransom, I have sought for you (by begging) Allāh. Guide me to what is necessary for me to know."

Then 'Abū al-Ḥasan, peace be on him, informed him about the authority and rights of the Commander of the Faithful, peace be on him, and what it was necessary for him to know. (He told him of) the authority of al-Ḥasan, al-Ḥusayn, 'Alī b. al-Ḥusayn, Muḥammad b 'Alī and Ja'far b. Muḥammad. Then he was silent.
(Al-Ḥasan) said to him: "May I be your ransom, who is the Imam today?"
"If I tell you," he answered, "will you come close to me?"
"Yes," he replied.
"I am he," he said.
"Is there anything by which this could be proved?" he asked.
"Go to that tree," he said - and he pointed towards one of the trees of Umm Ghaylān, "and tell it that Mūsā b. Ja'far tells you to draw near."

[He reported:] I went to it and I saw it furrow through the ground until it stopped in front of him. Then he indicated to it to go back and it went back.

He went up to him and cleaved to silence and worship. No one ever saw him talking after that.

[Ahmād b. Miḥrān reported on the authority of Muḥammad b. 'Alī, on the authority of Abū Baṣīr, who said:]
I (i.e. Abū Baṣīr) said to Abū al-Ḥasan Mūsā b. Ja'far, peace be on them: "May I be your ransom, by what is the Imam known?"

"By special characteristics," he answered. "The first of them is something by which preference has been given him by his father and an indication (has been made) by his (father) that he should be proof (*ḥujja*) (to the world). When he is asked (anything), he can answer it. If (a person) holds back from speaking to him, he may begin (the conversation) by telling him what will happen tomorrow and speaking to each person in his own tongue."

Then he said: "Abū Muḥammad (i.e. Abū- Baṣīr) I will give you a sign before you rise to go."

I did not wait long before a man from the people of Khurāsān entered. The Khurāsānī spoke to him in Arabic and Abū al-Ḥasan, peace be on him, answered him in Persian.

"By Allāh, what prevented me speaking to you in Persian was that I thought you were not fluent in it," the Khurāsāni said to him.
"Praise be to Allāh," he replied, "if I was not fluent enough to reply to you, I would not have the merit over you, by which I am entitled to the Imamate."

Then he said: "Abū Muḥammad, no speech of the people is hidden from the Imam, nor the language of birds, nor the speech of anything which has a soul."

['Abd Allāh b. Idrīs reported on the authority of Ibn Sinān, who said:]
One day al-Rashīd sent some robes to 'Alī b. Yaqṭīn to honour him. Among their number was a black woollen cloak adorned with gold like the robes of kings. 'Alī b. Yaqṭīn dispatched those robes to Mūsā b. Ja'far, peace be on them. Among their number he (also) sent that cloak. He added some money which he had already prepared specifically for him as the fifth of his money (*khums* - tax for the Imams) which he was going to pay him. When that reached Abū al-Ḥasan Mūsā, peace be on him, he accepted the money and the robes but returned the cloak by the hand of the messenger to 'Alī b. Yaqṭīn. He wrote to him: "Keep it and do not let it leave your hands. For an event will occur to you because of it when you will have the need of it with him (al-Rashīd)." 'Alī b. Yaqṭīn was suspicious about it being returned to him and did not understand the reason for that. Some time later, 'Alī b. Yaqṭīn changed (his attitude) towards a servant who had a special position with him and he left his service. The servant knew about 'Alī b. Yaqṭīn's inclination towards Abū al-Ḥasan Mūsā, peace be on him. He was acquainted with the money, garments and other things ('Alī) had sent to (Mūsā) on every occasion. He (went and) informed on him to al-Rashīd. He told (al-Rashīd) that ('Alī) maintained the Imamate of Mūsā b. Ja'far and paid him a fifth of his money each year, and also that he had given him the cloak with which the Commander of the faithful (al-Rashīd) had honoured him at such-and-such a time. Al-Rashīd burned with anger and was furious. He declared: "I will expose this situation. If the matter is as you say, his life will be destroyed."

He immediately sent for 'Alī b. Yaqṭīn to be brought. When he appeared before him, he said: "What have you done with the cloak which I bestowed upon you?"

"Commander of the faithful," ('Alī) replied, "I still have it in a sealed chest and there I keep perfume with it. In the mornings I open it and look at it to gain blessings from it. I kiss it and then put it back in its place. Every night I do the same thing."
"Bring it, immediately," he ordered.

"Yes, Commander of the faithful," he answered. He summoned one of his servants and told him: "Go to such-and-such a room in my house. Take the key for it from my custodian and open it. Open such-and-such a box and bring me the sealed chest which is in it."

It was not long before the servant returned with the chest still sealed. He put it before al-Rashīd and told him to break the seal and open it. When he opened it, he saw the cloak in it folded and laid out in perfume.

Al-Rashīd's anger became pacified and he said to 'Alī b. Yaqṭīn: "Return it to its place and go away righteously. I will never disbelieve you again on the word of an informer."

He ordered a magnificent gift to be sent after him and he had the informer flogged with a thousand lashes. After he had been flogged about a hundred lashes, he died.

[Muḥammad b. Ismā'īl reported on the authority of Muḥammad b. al-Faḍl, who said:]
The tradition concerning rubbing the two feet (*masḥ al-rijlayn*) in the ritual ablution (*wuḍū'*) was a subject of dispute among our companions - whether (it should be done) from the toes to the ankles or from the ankles to the toes. 'Alī b. Yaqṭīn wrote to Abū al-Ḥasan Mūsā, peace be on him: "May I be your ransom, our companions are in dispute over rubbing the feet. If you would think fit to write to me in your own handwriting what my practice should be with regard to it, I would carry it out, Allāh, the Exalted, willing."

Abū al-Ḥasan Mūsā, peace be on him, wrote back to him: "I have understood what you have mentioned about the dispute concerning ritual ablution. What I order you to do with regard to that is: you should rinse your mouth three times; you should sniff water into your nostrils three times; you should wash your face three times; you should rub between the interstices of the hair of your beard; you should wash your arms from the finger to the elbows; you should rub the whole of your head and the outside and inside of your ears; you should wash your feet up to the ankles three times. Do not transgress that for anything else."

When the letter came to 'Alī b. Yaqṭīn, he was surprised at the details he had given in it which were different from what the group had agreed upon. He said: "My master (*mawlā*) knows better what he has said and I will obey his command."

He used to practise it in his ablution and was in conflict with the practice of all the Shī'a out of submission to the command of Abū al-Ḥasan, peace be on him.

Information was given to al-Rashīd against 'Alī b. Yaqṭīn and he was accused of being a Rāfiḍite,[15] who is opposed to (al-Rashīd). Al-Rashīd said to one of his close associates: "Much talk is coming to me about 'Alī b. Yaqṭīn, and the suspicion of him being in opposition to me and being of Rāfiḍite leanings. Yet I cannot see any deficiency in his service to me. I have examined him several times and have not been able to find any suspicious thing about him. I would like to examine his (position) without him being aware of it and thus being able to guard himself against me."

He was told: "Commander of the faithful, the Rāfiḍite oppose the general view (*jamā'a*) with regard to ritual ablution and reduce its form. They do not accept washing the feet. Therefore examine him - without his knowledge - on his practice in ritual ablution."
"Yes," he replied, "this method will reveal his views."

He left it for a while. Then when 'Alī was away at his house doing some work, he came at the time for prayer. 'Alī b. Yaqṭīn was alone in one of the rooms of the house in order to perform his ablution and prayer. Al-Rashīd stood behind the wall where he could see 'Alī b. Yaqṭīn without him seeing him. He ('Alī) called for water for the ablution. He rinsed his mouth out three times; he sniffed water into his nostrils three times; he washed his face three times; he rubbed between the interstices of his beard; he washed his arms to the elbows three times; he rubbed his head and his ears; and he washed his feet three times.

Al-Rashīd watched him. When he saw him do that, he could not contain himself from looking down on him from a position where ('Alī) could see him and calling to him: "'Alī b. Yaqṭīn, those who claim that you are one of the Rāfiḍite are liars."

Thus ('Alī's) situation with (al-Rashīd) was restored. A letter came to him from Abū al-Ḥasan, peace be on him: "Beginning from now 'Alī b. Yaqṭīn, you will perform the ablution as Allāh ordered it. Wash your face once as is mandatory

15 A Rāfiḍite, one of the names for the Shi'a.

and another time (as a voluntary act) within the ablution; similarly wash your arms from the elbows and rub the front of your head and the outer part of your feet with the remnants of the dampness from the ablutionary water (on your hands). What was feared for you has now been removed. Greetings."

['Alī b. Abī Ḥamza al-Baṭāyinī reported:]
One day Abū al-Ḥasan Mūsā, peace be on him, left Medina for one of his estates outside the town. I (i.e. 'Alī b. Abī Ḥamza) accompanied him. He, peace be on him, was riding on a mule and I was on a donkey of mine. As we were going along one of the paths, a lion blocked our way. I stared at it in terror but Abū al-Ḥasan, peace be on him, went forward without worrying about it. I saw the lion become subdued and mutter before Abū al-Ḥasan, peace be on him. Abū al-Ḥasan, peace be on him, stood as if he was listening to the muttering. The lion put its paw on the saddle of his mule. My soul trembled at that and I was absolutely terrified. Then the lion turned away to the side of the road. Abū al-Ḥasan turned his face toward the *qibla* (direction of Mecca) and began to pray. He moved his lips in such a way that I could not understand him. Then he indicated to the lion with his hand that it should go. The lion muttered for a long time and Abū al-Ḥasan said: "Amen, amen."

The lion went away until it disappeared from our sight. Abū al Ḥasan, peace be on him, went straight on and I followed him. When we were far from the place, I came up to him and said: "May I be your ransom, what was that business of the lion? By Allāh, I was frightened for you and surprised at its attitude towards you."
"He came out to complain of the difficulty his lioness was having in giving birth," Abū al-Ḥasan, peace be on him, told me. "He asked me to ask Allāh to make it easier for her and I did that for him. He asked whether (I knew) in my heart if she would bear a male and I told him that. Then he told me: 'Go in the protection of Allāh. Allāh will never impose on you, nor on your offspring, nor on any of your Shī'a, any trouble from wild beasts.' I said: Amen."

Reports of this kind are numerous. What we have set out of them is sufficient according to the scheme which has been set out, through the grace of Allāh, the Exalted.

A Sample of his Virtues, Outstanding Qualities and Merits by which he was distinguished from others

Abū al-Ḥasan Mūsā, peace be on him, was the most religious of the men of his time, the most knowledgeable in law, the most generous and the noblest in spirit.

It is reported that he used to pray supererogatory prayers throughout the night so that he would make them extend until the morning-prayer, then continue them until the sun rose. He would remain prostrating himself before Allāh without raising his head from prayer and praising Allāh until the sun came near to descending (from its midday zenith). Frequently when he used to pray he would say:

> O Allāh, I ask of you ease at death and forgiveness on the Day of Reckoning.

He would repeat that. Another of his prayers, peace be on him, was:

> How great is sin to You. Therefore let forgiveness seem good to You.

He used to weep so much out of fear of Allāh that his beard would be wet with tears. He was the kindest of men to his family and his kin. He used to search out the poor of Medina during the night and take them a basket, in which was money, flour and dates. He would bring that to them without them knowing in any way that it was from him.

[Al-Sharīf Abū Muḥammad al-Ḥasan b. Muḥammad b. Yaḥyā informed me: My grandfather Yaḥyā b. al-Ḥasan b. Ja'far told us: Ismā'īl b. Ya'qūb told us: Muḥammad b. 'Abd Allāh al-Bakrī told us.]
I (i.e Muḥammad b. 'Abd Allāh) came to Medina to ask for repayment of a debt and it made me weary. I said (to myself): "If I had gone to Abū al-Ḥasan Mūsā, peace be on him, and complained to him."So I went to him at Naqmā at his estate. He came out to me. With him was a servant carrying a basket in which there was some chopped-up meat. He had no one else with him. He ate and I ate with him. Then he asked me what I wanted. So I told him my story. He went inside and it was only a short time before he came out to me. He told his servant to go and then he stretched out his hand towards me. He gave me a purse in which was three hundred dīnārs. Then he arose and turned away. I mounted my animal and went away.

[Al-Sharīf Abū Muḥammad al-Ḥasan b. Muḥammad on the authority of his grandfather (Yaḥyā b. al-Ḥasan), on the authority of another of his colleagues and teachers, (who said:)][16]
A man from the family of 'Umar b. al-Khaṭṭāb was in Medina trying to harm Abū al-Ḥasan Mūsā, peace be on him. Whenever he saw (Abū al-Ḥasan) he would curse him and curse 'Alī, peace be on him. One day some of those who used to attend his gatherings said to him: "Let us kill this sinner."

16 The same story is reported in *Maqātil al-Ṭālibiyyīn*, 499-500. Yaḥyā b. al-Ḥasan is the source.

He forbade them from (doing) that most firmly and rebuked them severely.

He asked about the descendant of 'Umar and was told that he had a farm on the outskirts of Medina. He rode out to him and found him at his farm. As he entered the farm with his donkey, the descendant of 'Umar cried out: "Do not tread on my sown land."

Yet Abū al-Ḥasan, peace be on him, continued to tread on it with his donkey until he reached him. He dismounted and sat with him. He greeted him with a smile and laughed at him.
"How much have you paid to sow your land?" he asked.
"One hundred dīnārs," (the other man) answered.
"How much do you hope to acquire from it?"
"I do not know the unknown," was the reply.
"I only asked you about what you hope it would bring you," retorted (Abū al-Ḥasan).
"I hope that it will bring me two hundred dīnārs," he answered.

Abū al-Ḥasan took out a purse in which was three hundred dīnārs and said: "This is (the price) of what you have sown in its present condition (i.e. what you have spent to sow it and what you hope to gain from it.) May Allāh provide you with what you hope for from it."

The descendant of 'Umar kissed his head and asked him to forgive his (former) hasty words about him. Abū al-Ḥasan, peace be on him, smiled at him and went away.

In the evening he went to the mosque and found that descendant of 'Umar sitting there. When the latter saw him, he called out: "Allāh knows best where to put his (prophetic) mission."

His companions jumped (in surprise) towards him and said to him: "What is the story (behind what you say), for you used to speak quite differently from this."

"You have heard what I have said now," he replied and began to speak on behalf of Abū al-Ḥasan, peace be on him. They opposed him and he opposed them.

When Abū al-Ḥasan returned to his house, he said to those who attended his gatherings and who had asked about killing the descendant of 'Umar: "Which was better - what you wanted or what I wanted? I put right his attitude to the extent which you have now become acquainted with. I was sufficient for the evil that was in him."

A group of the traditionalists (*ahl al-'ilm*) mention that Abū al-Ḥasan, peace be on him, always used to travel with two hundred to three hundred dīnārs to give away. The purses of Mūsā, peace be on him, were proverbial.

[Ibn 'Ammār and other narrators record:][17]
When al-Rashīd set out to go on the pilgrimage and was approaching Medina, the leading men among the inhabitants met him. Mūsā b. Ja'far, peace be on them, came out to (al-Rashīd's group) on a mule.

"What! Is this the animal on which you will meet the Commander of the faithful" al-Rabī' asked him. "If you were seeking (something) on it, you would not obtain it and if you were being sought (while you were) on it, you would not escape."

"It is beneath the vanity of horses and above the lowliness of asses and the best of matters are those which are moderate," he replied.

When Hārūn al-Rashīd entered Medina, he went to pay a visitation to (the tomb of) the Prophet, may Allāh bless Him and His Family. The people went with him. Al-Rashīd went forward to the tomb of the Apostle of Allāh, may Allāh bless Him and His Family, and said: "Greetings to you, Apostle of Allāh! Greetings to you, cousin." He was seeking to show his proud position over the others by that. But then Abū al-Ḥasan, peace be on him, went forward to the tomb and said: "Greetings to you, Apostle of Allāh! Greetings to you, father."

(The expression on) al-Rashīd's face changed and the anger in it became transparently obvious.

[Abū Zayd reported: 'Abd al-Ḥamīd told me:]
Muḥammad b. al-Ḥasan asked Abū al-Ḥasan Mūsā, peace be on him, about attending al-Rashīd while they were in Mecca.

"Is it permitted of the person consecrated as a pilgrim (*muḥrim*) to be shaded (from the sun) by his camel train?" (Muḥammad b. al-Ḥasan) asked him.
"It is not permitted for him if there is any choice available for him," Mūsā, peace be on him, told him.

"Is it permitted for him to walk in the (natural) shade by choice?" Muḥammad

17 The same story about the mule on the same authority is in *Maqātil al-Ṭālibiyyīn*, 484-489.

b. al-Ḥasan asked.
"Yes," replied Mūsā.

Muḥammad b. al-Ḥasan laughed at that. Abū al-Ḥasan Mūsā, peace be on him, said: "Does the *sunna* of the Prophet, may Allāh bless Him and His Family, surprise you and are you scoffing at it? The Apostle of Allāh, may Allāh bless Him and His Family, took advantage of the (natural) shade during his state of ritual consecration (*iḥrām*) and walked in the (natural) shade while he was consecrated for the pilgrimage (*muḥrim*). The laws of Allāh, Muḥammad, are not subject to analogy. Anyone who makes analogies of some of them on the basis of others, has strayed from the straight path."

Muḥammad b. al-Ḥasan was silent and did not ask any more questions.

The people have reported traditions on the authority of Abū al-Ḥasan Mūsā, peace be on him, and they have become very numerous; for, as we have said before, he was the most knowledgeable in the law during his time, and the most versed in the Book of Allāh, the best of them in voice for recitation of the Qur'ān. Whenever he recited, those who were listening to his recitation, would become sad and weep.

The people in Medina named him "the ornament of those who spend nights in prayer" (*mutahajjidīn*). He was also called al-Kāẓim (the one who holds back) because of his restraint of anger and the patience (which he showed) in the face of the acts of the oppressors right up until the time he died, murdered in their prison and bonds.

Report about the Reason for him Being Killed and a Sample of the Accounts about that

The reason for al-Rashīd detaining Abū al-Ḥasan Mūsā, peace be on him, imprisoning him and killing him is (contained in what is mentioned in the following tradition).

[Aḥmad b. 'Ubayd Allāh b. 'Ammār reported on the authority of 'Alī b. Muḥammad al-Nawfalī on the authority of his father; and Aḥmad b. Muḥammad b. Sa'īd (reported); and Abū Muḥammad al-Ḥasan b. Muḥammad b. Yaḥyā: on the authority of their teachers, who said:][18]
The reason for the arrest of Mūsā b. Ja'far, peace be on them, was that al-Rashīd had put his son in the care of Ja'far b. Muḥammad b. al-Ash'ath and Yaḥyā. b.

18 cf. *Maqātil al-Ṭālibiyyīn*, 484-489.

Khālid b. Barmak was jealous of that. He said (to himself): "If the caliphate passes on to (the son), my dominion and that of my son will be destroyed." Therefore he deceived Ja'far b. Muḥammad - and the latter used to maintain the belief in the Imamate - so that he managed to gain access to him and establish friendly relations with him. His visits to his house were frequent and he became acquainted with his affairs, which he would report back to al-Rashīd and he used to add to these reports that which would make (al-Rashīd) feel hatred towards him.

One day (Yaḥyā. b. Khālid) asked some of those he trusted: "Would you discover for me a member of the family of Abū Ṭālib who is not in comfortable circumstances, and then he would let me know what I need?"

He was directed towards 'Alī b. Ismā'īl b. Ja'far b. Muḥammad. Yaḥyā. b. Khālid took him some money. Mūsā, peace be on him, was friendly with 'Alī b. Ismā'īl b. Ja'far b. Muḥammad and he used to bring him gifts and treat him well.

Yaḥyā. b. Khālid sent to ('Alī b. Ismā'īl) requesting him to visit al-Rashīd and drawing his attention to the kind treatment which he had given him. So he decided to do that. Mūsā, peace be on him, was concerned and summoned 'Alī.
"Where are you going, cousin?" he asked.
"Baghdād," was the reply.
"Why are you doing that?" he enquired.
"I am in debt and I am poor," he answered.
"I will pay your debt and act for you and carry out (what you need)," Mūsā, peace be on him, told him.

He did not pay attention to that and began to set about (preparations for his) departure. Abū al-Ḥasan, peace be on him, asked him to come and said to him: "Are you leaving?"
"Yes," he replied, "I must do that."
"Look, cousin," he said to him, "fear Allāh and do not give away any confidences against my children."
He ordered him to be given three hundred dīnārs and four thousand dirhams.

(When he stood up in front of him, Abū al-Ḥasan Mūsā, peace be on him, spoke to those who were present: "By Allāh, he will strive against my blood and he will confide against my children."

"May Allāh make us your ransom," they said to him, "did you know this from his state when you were giving him gifts and being generous to him?"

"Yes," he said, "my father told me on the authority of his ancestors, on the authority of the Apostle of Allāh, may Allāh bless Him and His Family, that when kin cut themselves away, then they should be brought back, for if they cut themselves away, Allāh will cut them off. I wanted to bring him back after he had cut himself off from me for if he cuts me off, Allāh will cut him off.)[19]

'Alī b. Ismā'īl set out until he reached Yaḥyā. b. Khālid. He gave him news of Mūsā b. Ja'far, peace be on him, and (Yaḥyā. b. Khālid) reported to al-Rashīd and added additional material to it. Then he took him to al-Rashīd. The latter asked him about his uncle and he gave information against him to (al-Rashīd). He told him that money was being brought to him from east and west and that he had bought an estate named al-Yasīr for thirty thousand dīnārs. Its (former) owner had said when he had brought him the money: "I will not accept this kind of currency. I will only accept such-and-such a kind of currency." Then he ordered that money be brought and then he gave thirty thousand dīnārs of the currency whose coinage he had asked for.

Al-Rashīd listened to that from him and then ordered him to be given two hundred thousand dirhams, with which he sought to make a living in one of the areas. He chose one of the provinces of the east.

His messengers were sent to bring the money and he waited there for its arrival. One day he went into the toilet, when he was suffering from dysentery and as a result of it the whole of his stomach came out. He fell down. They tried to put it back but they could not. He was aware of his situation when the money was brought to him while he was in the pangs of death. He said: "What can I do with it? I am about to die."

That year al-Rashīd went on the pilgrimage. He began it at Medina and there he had Abū al-Ḥasan Mūsā, peace be on him, arrested. It is reported that when he came to Medina, Mūsā, peace be on him, received him with a group of the nobles. They had gone out to meet him and then Abū al-Ḥasan, peace be on him, had gone on to the mosque as was his custom. Al-Rashīd waited until night and then went to the tomb of the Apostle of Allāh, may Allāh bless him and his family. He said: "Apostle of Allāh, I apologise to you for something I want to do. I want to imprison Mūsā b. Ja'far because he is intending to bring division into your community and to cause the shedding of its blood."

Then he ordered him to be taken from the mosque and brought before him. He had him put in chains and called for two awnings to be brought. He had (Abū

19 What is between brackets is not in *Maqātil al-Ṭālibiyyīn*.

al-Ḥasan) put in one of them on a mule and he had the other awning put on another mule. The two mules left his house carrying the two awnings which were closed. With each one went cavalry. The cavalry divided and some of them went with one of the two awnings on the road to Baṣra and the other on the road to Kūfā. Al-Rashīd only did that in order to confuse the people about what had happened to Abū al-Ḥasan, peace be on him. He ordered the men who were with the awning in which was Abū al-Ḥasan to hand him over to ʻĪsā b. Ja'far b. al-Manṣūr, who was governor of Baṣra at that time.

He was handed over to him and he kept him in detention with him for a year. (Then al-Rashīd wrote to him demanding (Abū al-Ḥasan's) blood. ʻĪsā b. Ja'far summoned some of his close associates and trusted colleagues and sought their advice about what al-Rashīd had written to him. They advised him to hold back from doing that and to ask to be excused from it. ʻĪsā b. Ja'far wrote to al-Rashīd saying:

> The affair of Mūsā b. Ja'far and his stay under my detention has been going on for a long time. I have become well-acquainted with his situation. I have set spies on him throughout this period and I have not found him (do anything except) open his mouth in worship. I set someone to listen to what he said in his prayers. He has never prayed against you or against me. He has never mentioned us with malice. He does not pray for himself except for forgiveness and mercy. Either you send someone whom I can hand him over to or I will let him free. I am troubled at detaining him.

It is reported that one of the spies of ʻĪsā b. Ja'far reported to him that frequently he used to hear him say in his prayers while he was detained:

> O Allāh, You know that I used to ask you to give me free time to worship You. O Allāh, you have done that. To You be praise.)[20]

Al-Rashīd directed that he should be handed over by ʻĪsā b. Ja'far and taken to Baghdād. There he was handed over to al-Faḍl b. al-Rabīʻ. He remained with him a long time. Then al-Rashīd wanted him to carry out some matter in (Abū al-Ḥasan's) affair and he refused. So he wrote to him to hand over to al-Faḍl b. Yaḥyā. He received him from the former. (He put him in one of the rooms of one of his houses and set a watch over him. He, peace be on him, was occupied in worship; he used to keep the whole night alive with formal prayer, recitation of the Qur'ān, personal prayer and effort. He would fast most days. His face never turned away from the *miḥrāb* (which showed the direction of prayer towards Mecca.))[21]

20 The section between brackets is not in *Maqātil al-Ṭālibiyyīn*. However, there is a brief mention of ʻĪsā's letter.

21 The section between brackets is not in *Maqātil al-Ṭālibiyyīn*.

Al-Faḍl b. Yaḥyā made him comfortable and treated him with honour. That was communicated to al-Rashīd while he was at al-Raqqa. He wrote to him denouncing him for making Mūsā, peace be on him, comfortable and ordering him to kill him. He held back from doing that and would not carry it out. At that al-Rashīd became very angry. He summoned Masrūr, the servant, and told him: "Go by the messenger-service (*barīd*) immediately to Baghdād. Then go directly to Mūsā b. Ja'far. If you find him in comfort and ease, then deliver this letter to al-'Abbās b. Muḥammad and order him to submit to what is in it."

He handed another letter to him for al-Sindī b. Shāhik, ordering him in it to obey al-'Abbās b. Muḥammad. Masrūr set out and arrived at the house of Al-Faḍl b. Yaḥyā without anyone knowing what he wanted. Then he went to Mūsā, peace be on him, and found him as al-Rashīd had been informed. He went directly to al-'Abbās b. Muḥammad and al-Sindī b. Shāhik. He delivered the two letters to them.

The people did not wait long before the messenger went running to Al-Faḍl b. Yaḥyā. He rode back with him. He went along perplexed and shocked until he reached al-'Abbās b. Muḥammad. Al-'Abbās called for whips and two small platforms (*'aqābayn*) to be brought.

Then he ordered al-Faḍl to be stripped. Al-Sindī flogged (al-Faḍl) in front of (al-'Abbās). (Al-Faḍl) left with his colour changed completely from what it had been when he entered. He began to greet the people to right and to left.

Masrūr wrote to al-Rashīd with the news and the latter ordered that Mūsā, peace be on him, should be handed over to al-Sindī b. Shāhik. Al-Rashīd had a large assembly. He said: "People, al-Faḍl b. Yaḥyā has disobeyed me and opposed (giving) the obedience due to me. You have seen me curse him so you curse him."

The people cursed him from every side until the room and the building shook with the (sound of) cursing him.

The news reached Yaḥyā b. Khālid. He rode to al-Rashīd and entered by another door from that which the people used so that he came to him from behind without him being aware. Then he said: "Commander of the faithful, look at me." Al-Rashīd heard him with great fear, he said: "Al-Faḍl is only a young man and I will take care of him for you in the way you would wish."

(Al-Rashīd's) face brightened and he went forward to the people saying: "Al-

Faḍl disobeyed me in something and I have protected myself against him. Now he has repented and returned to obeying me. Therefore now take him as a friend."

"We are the friends of those you befriend and the enemies of those whom you are against," they answered. "We have made him our friend."

Yaḥyā b. Khālīd departed on the messenger-service and reached Baghdād. There the people were disturbed and spreading disquieting rumours. He gave the impression that he had come to improve the administration of the Sawād and to look into the affairs of the tax-collectors. He occupied himself with some of those matters for a few days. Then he summoned al-Sindī b. Shāhik and gave him his instructions with regard to (Mūsā). (He carried out his instructions. What he commissioned al-Sindī to do was to kill him, peace be on him, with poison which he put in the food he brought him. It is said that he put it in dates. (Mūsā) ate some of them and then felt the effect of the poison. He remained for three days in a fever from it and died on the third day.)[22]

When Mūsā died, al-Sindī b. Shāhik brought the jurists and notable men of Baghdād in (to see) him. Among them were al-Haytham b. 'Adī and others. They saw that there was no mark of any wound on him, nor (any evidence) of strangulation. (Al-Sindī) made them give testimony that he had died normally. They testified to that. He was taken out and he was put on the bridge at Baghdād. Then an announcement was made: "This man Mūsā b. Ja'far, peace be on him, has died. So come and look at him"

The people began to come and look into (Mūsā's) face while he was dead. For a group had claimed during the life of Mūsā that he was the awaited Imam (*al-Muntaẓar*) who would continue to undertake the Imamate for the rest of time (*al-qā'im*). They made his imprisonment the period of absence (*al-ghayba*) which had been reported concerning the last Imam (*al-qā'im*).[23] Yaḥyā b. Khālid ordered it to be announced at his death: "This is Mūsā b. Ja'far whom the Rāfiḍites claim is the last Imam (*al-qā'im*) who will not die. So (come and) look at him." The people saw that he was dead. Then he was carried away and buried in the cemetery of Quraysh at the Tin Gate. This cemetery had been used for Banū Hāshim and the nobles of the people for a long time.

It is reported that when he was about to die, he asked al-Sindī b. Shāhik to bring him his retainer (*mawlā*) from Medina who was staying at the house of al-'Abbās b. Muḥammad at the cane-market (*mashra'at al-qaṣb*). The latter should wash

---

22 What is between brackets is not in *Maqātil al-Ṭālibiyyīn*. The method of killing is different.
23 These are al-Mufīd's comments.

and shroud his body. (Al-Sindī) did that.

Al-Sindī (later) reported:
I (i.e. al-Sindī) asked him to permit me to shroud him but he refused. He said: "I am a member of the House (of the Prophet). The giving of dowries for our women, the performing of pilgrimages on behalf of those of us who have not made the pilgrimage, and the shrouding of our dead can only be performed by one of our retainers (*mawlās*) who is pure. I already have my shroud and I want the washing and preparation (of my body) to be carried out by my retainer so-and-so."

That was done for him.

An Account of the Number of his Sons and an Extract from the Reports about them

Abu al-Ḥasan Mūsā, peace be on him, had thirty-seven children, male and female. They were:

1. 'Alī b. Mūsā al-Riḍā, peace be on them.
2. Ibrāhīm
3. al-'Abbās
4. al-Qāsim

(Their mothers) were slave-wives (*ummahāt awlād*).

5. Ismā'īl
6. Ja'far
7. Hārūn
8. al-Ḥasan

(Their mother) was a slave-wife.

9. Aḥmad
10. Muḥammad
11. Ḥamza

(Their mother) was a slave-wife.

12. 'Abd Allāh
13. Isḥāq
14. 'Ubayd Allāh
15. Zayd
16. al-Ḥasan
17. al-Faḍl

18. al-Ḥusayn
19. Sulaymān

(Their mothers) were slave-wives.

20. Fāṭima the elder
21. Fāṭima the younger
22. Ruqayya
23. Ḥakīma
24. Umm Abīhā
25. Ruqayya the younger
26. Umm Ja'far
27. Lubāba
28. Zaynab
29. Khadīja
30. 'Aliyya
31. 'Āmina
32. Ḥasana
33. Burayḥa
34. 'Ā'isha
35. Umm Salama
36. Maymūna
37. Umm Kulthūm

(Their mothers) were slave-wives.

The most outstanding and celebrated of the children of Abū al-Ḥasan Mūsā, peace be on him, the greatest of them in rank, the most learned and the one in whom was gathered the most merit was Abū al-Ḥasan 'Alī b. Mūsā al-Riḍa, peace be on him.

*****

Aḥmad b. Mūsā was noble, exalted and pious. Abu al-Ḥasan Mūsā, peace be on him, used to love him and showed him preference. He gave him his estate known as al-Yasīra. It is said that Aḥmad b. Mūsā, may Allāh be pleased with him, freed a thousand slaves.

[Al-Sharīf Abū Muḥammad al-Ḥasan b. Muḥammad b. Yaḥyā reported: My grandfather (Yaḥyā b. al-Ḥasan) told me: I heard Ismā'īl b. Mūsā say:]
My father (Mūsā) went out with his children to one of his properties - he named the property but Abū al-Ḥasan Yaḥyā forgot the name. We were in that place and with Aḥmad b. Mūsā were twenty of my father's servants and retinue. If Aḥmad stood up, they stood up with him. If Aḥmad sat down they sat down with him.

After that my father looked at him with a (loving) concern which could not be ignored. We did not depart until Ahmad went before us.

*****

Muḥammad b. Mūsā was a man of merit and righteousness.

[Abū Muḥammad al-Ḥasan b. Muḥammad b. Yaḥyā reported: My grandfather (Yaḥyā b. al-Ḥasan) told me: Hāshimiyya, a woman retainer of Ruqayya, daughter of Mūsā, said:]
Muḥammad b. Mūsā was a man of (continual) ritual ablution and prayer. Throughout the night, he used to perform ritual ablutions and pray. The sound of water pouring (for ablution) would be heard and he would pray for some of the night. Then he would be silent for an hour and then sleep. He would, then, rise and again the sound of water being poured for the ablution would be heard. Then he would again pray for some of the night. He would continue in this way until it was morning. I never saw him without remembering the words of Allāh, the Exalted: *They used to sleep only a little of the night* (LI 17).

*****

Ibrāhīm b. Mūsā was brave and noble. During al-Ma'mūn's time he was invested with the governorship of Yemen by Muḥammad b. Zayd b. 'Alī b. al-Ḥusayn b. Abī Ṭālib, peace be on them, to whom Abū Sarāyā had pledged allegiance at Kūfā. He went there and conquered it. He resided there for a time until what happened to Abū Sarāyā happened. Then a safe-conduct was given to him by al-Ma'mūn.

Each of the sons of Abu al-Ḥasan Mūsā had great merit and well-known rank. However, al-Riḍa was the foremost of them in merit as we have mentioned.

CHAPTER VII

IMĀM 'ALĪ B. MŪSĀ AL-RIḌĀ

(This chapter gives) an account of the Imam who undertook (the office) (*qā'im*) after Abū al-Ḥasan Mūsā, peace be on him, from among the latter's children, (tells of) the date of his birth, the evidence for his Imamate, his age, the length of his succession, the time and cause of his death, the place of his grave, and the number of his children, and (it gives) a brief outline of the reports about him.

The Imam who undertook (the office) (*qā'im*) after Abū al-Ḥasan Mūsā b. Ja'far, peace be on them, was his son, Abū al-Ḥasan 'Alī b. Mūsā al-Riḍā, peace be on them, because of his merit over all his brothers and the members of his House (*ahl baytihi*), because of the knowledge, forbearance and piety which he showed, and which the Shī'a (*khāṣṣa*) and the non-Shī'a (*'āmma*) agreed on with regard to him and recognised him for, and because of the nomination of him for the Imamate after (his father) by his father, peace be on him, and his indication of that (belonging) to him apart from the rest of his brothers and members of his House.

He, peace be on him, was born in Medina in the year 148 A.H. (765). He died in Ṭūs in the land of Khurāsān in the month of Ṣafar in the year 203 A.H. (818). At that time he was fifty-five years of age. His mother was a slave-wife called Umm al-Banīn. The period of his Imamate and his undertaking the succession after his father was twenty years.

Reports of His Nomination (*Naṣṣ*)

Among those of his coterie and trustworthy authorities, and men of piety, traditional knowledge and jurisprudence of his Shī'a, who report the nomination of al-Riḍā 'Alī b. Mūsā, peace be on them, for the Imamate by his father and his indication of him for that (are the following): Dāwud b. Kathīr al-Raqqī, Muḥammad b. Ishāq b. 'Ammār, 'Alī b. Yaqṭīn, Nu'aym al-Qābūsī, al-Ḥusayn b. al-Mukhtār, Ziyād b. Marwān, al-Makhzūmī, Dāwud b. Sulaymān, Naṣr b. Qābūs, Dāwud b. Zurbī, Yazīd b. Sulayṭ and Muḥammad b. Sinān.

[Abū al-Qāsim Ja'far b. Muḥammad b. Qulawayh informed me on the authority of Muḥammad b. Ya'qub, on the authority of Aḥmad b. Mihrān; on the authority of Muḥammad b. 'Alī, on the authority of Muḥammad b. Sinān, and Ismā'īl b. Ghiyath al-Qaṣrī, on the authority of Dāwud al-Raqqī, who said:][1]

1 *Al-Kāfī*, I, 312, tradition no. 3.

I (i.e. Dāwud al-Raqqī) said to Abū Ibrāhīm (Mūsā), peace be on him: "May I be your ransom, I have grown old. So take my hand and save me from hell-fire. Who is our leader (*ṣāḥib*) after you?"
"This is your leader after me," he said and pointed to his son, Abū al-Ḥasan (al-Riḍā), peace be on him.

[Abū al-Qāsim Ja'far b. Muḥammad informed me on the authority of Muḥammad b. Ya'qūb al-Kulaynī, on the authority of al-Ḥusayn b. Muḥammad, on the authority of al-Mu'allā b. Muḥammad, on the authority of Aḥmad b. Muḥammad b. 'Abd Allāh, on the authority of al-Ḥasan, on the authority of Ibn Abū 'Umayr, on the authority of Muḥammad b. Isḥāq b. 'Ammār, who said:][2]
I (i.e Muḥammad b. Isḥāq b. 'Ammār) said to Abū al-Ḥasan the first (i.e. Mūsā), peace be on him: "Show me from whom I will take (instruction in) my religion."

"This son of mine, 'Alī," he said. "My father took my hand and took me to the tomb of the Apostle of Allāh, may Allāh bless Him and His Family. He said to me that Allāh, may His name be exalted, had said: *I make you a khalīfa on earth* (II 30), and that when Allāh, the Exalted, says anything, carry it out."

[Abū al-Qāsim Ja'far b. Muḥammad informed me on the authority of Muḥammad b. Ya'qūb, on the authority of Muḥammad b. Yaḥyā, on the authority of Aḥmad b. Muḥammad b. 'Īsā, on the authority of al-Ḥasan b. Maḥbūb, on the authority of al-Ḥusayn b. Nu'aym al-Ṣaḥḥāf, who said:][3]
I (i.e. al-Ḥusayn b. Nu'aym), Hishām b. al-Ḥakam and 'Alī b. Yaqṭīn were in Baghdād. 'Alī b. Yaqṭīn said:
I (i.e. 'Alī b. Yaqṭīn) was with al-'Abd al-Ṣāliḥ (i.e. Mūsā), peace be on him, and he said: "This 'Alī is the lord of my children and I have given him my *kunya* (i.e. both were called Abū al-Ḥasan)."

[In another narration:] Hishām struck his face with the palm of his hand and said: "Shame on you, how could you say that?"
"By Allāh, I heard it from him, just as I have said it," replied 'Alī b. Yaqṭīn.
"Then, by Allāh, the authority is for him after (Mūsā)," said Hishām.

[Abū al-Qāsim Ja'far b. Muḥammad informed me on the authority of Muḥammad b. Ya'qūb, on the authority of a number of Companions, on the authority of Aḥmad b. Muḥammad b. 'Īsā, on the authority of Mu'āwiya b. Ḥukaym on the authority of Nu'aym al-Qābūsī, on the authority of Abū al-Ḥasan Mūsā:][4]

2 *Al-Kāfī*, I, 312, tradition no 4.
3 *Al-Kāfī*, I, 311, tradit ion no. 1.
4 *Al-Kāfī*, I, 311, tradition no. 2.

(Abū al- Ḥasan Mūsā) said: "My son 'Alī, the eldest of my children, is the one most preferred by me and the one most loved by me. He examined the leather case (*jafr*) with me. Only a prophet or the testamentary trustee (*waṣī*) of a prophet may examine it."

[Abū al-Qāsim Ja'far b. Muḥammad informed me on the authority of Muḥammad b. Ya'qūb, on the authority of Aḥmad b. Mihrān, on the authority of Muḥammad b. 'Alī, on the authority of both Muḥammad b. Sinān and 'Alī b. al-Ḥakam, on the authority of al-Ḥusayn b. al-Mukhtār, who said:][5]
The ordinances (*alwāḥ*) came to us from Abū al-Ḥasan Mūsā, peace be on him, while he was in prison: "My testament (*'ahd*) to the eldest of my sons is that he should do such-and-such. As far as so-and-so is concerned, do not give him anything until you meet me or Allāh decrees death for me."

[With the same chain of authorities (*isnād*) on the authority of Aḥmad b. Mihrān, on the authority of Muḥammad b. 'Alī, on the authority of Ziyād b. Marwān al-Qandī, who said:][6]
I (i.e. Ziyād b. Marwān al-Qandī) visited Abū Ibrāhīm (Mūsā), peace be on him. With him was Abū al-Ḥasan ('Alī al-Riḍā), his son. (Mūsā) said to me: "Ziyad, this is my son, so-and-so. His writing is my writing, his words are my words, his messenger is my messenger, and whatever he says, (the truth) is in what he says."

[With the same chain of authorities (*isnād*) on the authority of Aḥmad b. Mihrān, on the authority of Muḥammad b. 'Alī, on the authority of Muḥammad b. al-Fuḍayl, who said: al-Makhzūmī told me, and his mother was one of the descendants of Ja'far b. Abī Ṭālib, peace be on him:][7]
Abū al-Ḥasan Mūsā, peace be on him sent to us and we gathered. Then he said: "Do you know why I have summoned you?"
"No," we answered.
"Witness that this son of mine is my testamentary trustee (*waṣī*) and the one who will superintend my affair, my successor after me. Whoever has a debt (to be collected) from me, let him collect it from this son of mine. Whoever I have made a promise to, let him get its fulfilment from him. Whoever has to meet me, will only do so through his correspondence."

[With the same chain of authorities (*isnād*) on the authority of Muḥammad b. 'Alī, on the authority of Abū 'Alī al-Khazzāz, on the authority of Dāwud b. Sulaymān who said:][8]

5 *Al-Kāfī*, I, 312-3, rradition no. 8.
6 *Al-Kāfī*, I, 312, tradition no. 6.
7 *Al-Kāfī*, I, 312, tradition no. 7.
8 *Al-Kāfī*, I, 313, tradition no. 11.

I (i.e. Dāwud b. Sulaymān) said to Abū Ibrāhīm (Mūsā), peace be on him: "I am afraid that something may happen and I will not (be able to) meet you. So tell me who the Imam is after you."
"My son so-and-so," he said meaning Abū al-Ḥasan (al-Riḍā), peace be on him.

[With the same chain of authorities (*isnād*) on the authority of Ibn Mihrān, on the authority of Muḥammad b. 'Alī, on the authority of Sa'īd b. Abī al-Jahm, on the authority of Naṣr b. Qābūs, who said:][9]
I (i.e. Naṣr b. Qābūs) said to Abū Ibrāhīm (Mūsā), peace be on him: "I have asked your father who would be after him and he told me that you would be. Therefore when Abū 'Abd Allāh (Ja'far al-Ṣadiq), peace be on him, died, the people went to right and left while I and my companions declared (our support) for you. Therefore tell me which of your children will be (the Imam) after you."
"My son, so-and-so," he said.

[With the same chain of authorities (*isnād*) on the authority of Muḥammad b. 'Alī, on the authority of al-Ḍaḥḥāk b. al-Ash'ath, on the authority of Dāwud b. Zurbī who said:][10]
I (i.e. Dāwud b. Zurbī) brought some money to Abū Ibrāhīm (Mūsā), peace be on him. He took some of it and left some of it.
"May Allāh set you right," I said, "why have you left it with me?"
"The one who will be in charge of this authority (*ṣāḥib hādhā al-amr*) will ask you for it," he told me.

When the news of his death came, Abū al-Ḥasan al-Riḍā. peace be on him, sent to me and asked me for that money and I paid it to him.

[With the same chain of authorities (*isnād*) on the authority of Aḥmad b. Mihrān, on the authority of Muḥammad b. 'Alī, on the authority of 'Alī b. al-Ḥakam, on the authority of 'Abd Allāh b. Ibrāhīm b. 'Alī b. 'Abd Allāh b. Ja'far b. Abī Ṭālib, on the authority of Yazīd b. Sulayṭ in a long tradition (*hadīth*) on the authority of Abū Ibrāhīm Mūsā, peace be on him:][11]
(Mūsā) said in the year in which he died: "I will be taken in this year and the authority (*amr*) will belong to my son 'Alī, who is named after two 'Alīs. The first 'Alī is 'Alī b. Abī Ṭālib and the second 'Alī is 'Alī b. al-Ḥusayn, the blessings of Allāh be on them. He (i.e. 'Alī al-Riḍā) has been given the understanding, forbearance, knowledge, help, love, piety and religion of the first and tribulation, and endurance in the face of adversity of the second."

---

9 *Al-Kāfī*, I, 313, rradition no. 12.
10 *Al-Kāfī*, I, 313, tradition no. 13.
11 *Al-Kāfī*, I, 313-16, tradition no. 14.

[(This) was in a long tradition]
[Abū al-Qāsim Ja'far b. Muḥammad informed me on the authority of Muḥammad b. Ya'qūb, on the authority of Muḥammad b. al-Ḥasan, on the authority of Sahl b. Ziyād, on the authority of Muhammad b. 'Alī, on the authority of 'Ubayd Allāh b. al-Marzubān, on the authority of Ibn Sinān, who said:][12]
I (i.e. Muḥammad b. Sinān) visited Abū al-Ḥasan Mūsā, peace be on him, the year before he went to Iraq. 'Alī, his son, was sitting in front of him. He looked at me and said: "Muḥammad, this year there will be some disturbance but do not be worried by that."
"May Allāh make me your ransom, what will that be?" I asked him, for he had filled me with anxiety.
"I will go to this despot," he answered, " but he will not receive any evil from me nor from the one who will be after me."
"May Allāh make me your ransom, what will happen?" I asked.
"Allāh leads astray the oppressors," he told me, "and Allāh does what he wishes."
"May Allāh make me your ransom, what is this?" I said.

"Whoever wrongs the right of this son of mine and denies his Imamate after me is like those who wronged 'Alī b. Abī Ṭālib, peace be on him, and denied his right after the Apostle of Allāh, may Allāh bless Him and His Family," he replied.

" If Allāh supports me in my life, may I submit to his right and declare (my belief in) his Imamate," I said.
"True, Muḥammad," he said. "Allāh will support you during your life and you will submit to his right and declare (your belief in) his Imamate, and the Imamate of the one who will be (Imam) after him."
"Who will that be?" I asked.
"His son, Muḥammad," he answered.
I said: "(I give) consent (*riḍā*) and submission to him."

A Sample of the Proofs concerning him and the Reports about him.

[Abū al-Qāsim Ja'far b. Muḥammad informed me on the authority of Muḥammad b. Ya'qūb, on the authority of Muḥammad b. Yaḥyā, on the authority of Aḥmad b. Muḥammad, on the authority of Ibn Maḥbūb, on the authority of Hishām b. Aḥmad, who said:][13]
Abū al-Ḥasan the first (Mūsā), peace be on him, said to me: "Did you know that one of the people from al-Maghrib has come?"

12 *Al-Kāfī*, I, 319, tradilion no. 16.
13 *Al-Kāfī*, I, 486-7, tradition no. 1.

"No," I answered.
"Indeed," he said, "a man from the people of al-Maghrib has come to Medina. So come with us."

He rode off and I rode with him until we came to the man. There he was, a man of al-Maghrib. He had with him slave-girls.
"Show us your wares," I told him .

He showed us seven good slave-girls. But all the time Abū al-Ḥasan, peace be on him, was saying: "I have no need of those." Then he told him, "Show us something else."
"I have nothing except a sick slave-girl," he replied
"What is (wrong) with you (not) to offer her (for sale)," he said.

The man refused and went away. On the next day (Abū al-Ḥasan Mūsā) sent for me and told me: "Ask him how much is the maximum he wants for her. Whatever he says, tell him that you will take her."
I went to him and he said: "I would not take less than such-and-such a sum."
"I will take her," I said.
"She is yours," he replied. "But tell me about the man who was with you yesterday."
"He was a man from the Banū Hāshim," I told him .
"Which Banū Hāshim?" he asked .
"I don't have more (information) than this," I answered.

Then he said: "I will tell you that when I bought her, from a remote area of al-Maghrib, a woman from *ahl al-kitāb* (the people of the Book, i.e. Jews and Christians) met me and asked me who this maidservant was whom I had with me. I told her that I had bought her for myself, but she said it was not appropriate that she should be with the like of me. It is fitting that this slave-girl should be with the best person on earth, for she will soon give birth to a son such as has not been born in the east or the west."

I took her to Abū al-Ḥasan (Mūsā). It was not long afterwards that she gave birth to al-Riḍā, peace be on him.

[Abū al-Qāsim Ja'far b. Muḥammad informed me on the authority of Muḥammad b. Ya'qūb al-Kulaynī on the authority of Muḥammad b. Yaḥyā, on the authority of Aḥmad b. Muḥammad, on the authority of Ṣafwān b. Yaḥyā who said:][14]
When Abū Ibrāhīm (Mūsā), peace be on him, died and Abū al-Ḥasan al-Riḍā,

14 *Al-Kāfī*, I, 487, tradition no. 2.

peace be on him, spoke, we were afraid for him. He was told: "You have made public a great matter and on account of that, we fear for you from this tyrant (i.e. al-Rashīd)."
"Let him try as hard as he can." he answered. "He will find no way to harm me."

[Abū al-Qāsim Ja'far b. Muḥammad informed me on the authority of Muḥammad b. Ya'qūb, on the authority of 'Alī b. Muḥammad, on the authority of Ibn Jamhūr, on the authority of Ibrāhīm b. 'Abd Allāh, on the authority of Aḥmad b. 'Ubayd Allāh, on the authority of al-Ghiffārī, who said:][15]
A man from the family of Abū Rāfi', the retainer of the Apostle of Allāh, may Allāh bless Him and His Family, called so-and-so, had me in his debt. He demanded payment from me and insisted on my paying him. When I realised that, I prayed the morning prayer in the mosque of the Apostle of Allāh, may Allāh bless Him and His Family, and I set out to see al-Riḍā, peace be on him, On that day, he was in the valley of al-'Arīd. When I got near his door, he came out on a donkey. He was wearing a shirt and a cloak (*ridā'*). When I looked at him, I felt ashamed before him. When he reached me, he stood and looked at me. I greeted him - it was the month of Ramaḍān. I said: "May I be your ransom, your retainer so-and-so has me in his debt. By Allāh, he has spread reports of me around."

By Allāh, I was thinking to myself, that he would tell him to leave me alone. By Allāh, I had not told him how much I owed nor had I given specific details about anything. He told me to sit down until he came back. I was still there at the time when I prayed the sunset prayer. I had been fasting and I had become troubled and wanted to leave. Suddenly he came. There were (a crowd of) people around him.

Beggars were begging from him and he was giving them alms. Then he retired from them and went into his house. He came out and called me. I rose and went in with him. He sat down and I sat down with him. I began to talk to him about Ibn Musayyib (the governor of Medina). Often I used to tell him about him. When I had finished, he said to me: "I don't think that you have eaten yet""
"No," I replied.

He called for food for me and it was put in front of me. He told the servant to eat with me. The servant and I had our fill of food. When we had finished, he said: "Raise the cushion and take what is under it"

I raised it and there were (many) dīnārs, I took them and put them in my sleeve.

15 *Al-Kāfī*, I, 487-8, tradition no. 4. The man from the family of Abū Rāfi' is identified as Ṭays.

He told four of his slaves to accompany me to my house. I said to him: "May I be your ransom, the spy of Ibn Musayyib (the governor of Medina) will be sitting (there) and I would hate him to see me while I was with your slaves."
"True," he said, "may Allāh direct you with guidance."

Then he told them that they should leave whenever I sent them back. When I was near my house and I could see it, I sent them back. I went to my house and called for a lamp. I examined the dīnārs and there were forty-eight dīnārs. I only owed the man twenty-eight dīnārs. Among them was a dīnār which shone greatly. Its beauty delighted me and I picked it up and took it nearer the lamp. On it was clearly engraved: "The debt to the man is twenty-eight dīnārs and the rest is yours."

No, by Allāh, I had not informed him of the precise amount of my debt.

[Abū al-Qāsim informed me on the authority of Muḥammad b. Ya'qūb on the authority of 'Alī b. Ibrāhīm. on the authority of his father, on the authority of some of his colleagues, on the authority of Abū al-Ḥasan al-Riḍā, peace be on him:][16]
He (ie al-Riḍā) left Medina to make the pilgrimage in the year in which Hārūn made the pilgrimage. He came to a mountain called Fāri' on the left of the road. Abū al-Ḥasan (al-Riḍā), peace be on him, looked at the mountain and said: "Fāri', the one who destroys (a resting place in you) will be cut limb from limb."

We did not know what that meant. When Hārūn reached that place he stopped there. Ja'far b. Yaḥyā went up the mountain and ordered a resting-place to be set up for him. On his return from Mecca, Ja'far b. Yaḥyā went back up the hill and ordered it to be destroyed. When he got to Iraq, Ja'far b. Yaḥyā was cut limb from limb.

[Abū al-Qāsim Ja'far b. Muḥammad informed me on the authority of Muḥammad b. Ya'qūb, on the authority of Aḥmad b. Muḥammad, on the authority of Muḥammad b. al-Ḥasan, on the authority of Muḥammad b. 'Īsā, on the authority of Muḥammad b. Ḥamza b. al-Haytham, on the authority of Ibrāhīm b. Mūsā. who said:][17]
I (ie Ibrāhīm b. Mūsā) kept worrying Abū al-Ḥasan al-Riḍā about something I needed from him and he would promise me (that I would get it). One day he set out to meet the governor of Medina. I went with him. He reached the vicinity of the palace of so-and-so, and stopped there under some trees. I stopped with him.

16 *Al-Kāfī*, I, 488, tradition no. 5.
17 *Al-Kāfī*, I. 488. tradit ion no. 6.

There was no one else with us. I said to him: "May I be your ransom, the festival is drawing near and, by Allāh, I don't even possess a dirham."

He scratched the earth vigorously with his whip, Then he struck it with his hand and took out of it an ingot of gold. Then he said: "Use this but keep secret what you have seen ."

[Abū al-Qāsim Ja'far b. Muḥammad informed me on the authority of Muḥammad b. Ya'qūb, on the authority of al-Ḥusayn b. Muḥammad, on the authority of Mu'alla b. Muḥammad, on the authority of Musāfir, who said:][18]
I (i.e. Musāfir) was with Abū al-Ḥasan al-Riḍā, peace be on them, at Mina. (Al-Faḍl b.) Yaḥyā b. Khālid passed by and covered his face (to escape) from the dust. al-Riḍā peace be on him, said: "Wretched ones who do not know what will happen to them during this year!" Then he added: "The most surprising (thing will be what happens to) Harūn. The two of them (i.e. (Al-Faḍl b.) Yaḥyā b. Khālid and Harūn) will be like these two." Then he joined his two fingers together.

[Musāfir reported:]
By Allāh, I did not understand the meaning of his statement until we buried (Harūn) together with (al-Faḍl).

*****

Al-Ma'mūn had sent for a group of the family of Abū Ṭālib and had them brought to him from Medina.[19] al-Riḍā 'Alī b. Mūsā, peace be on them, was among them. They were taken along the road to Baṣra until they were brought there. The man in charge of their journey was known as ('Īsā) al-Julūdī. He brought them to al-Ma'mūn and the latter put them in a house. He put al-Riḍā 'Alī b. Mūsā, peace be on them, in a house and showed him hospitality and great respect. Then al-Ma'mūn sent for him, (saying): "I want to rid myself of the caliphate and vest the office in you. What is your opinion?"

al-Riḍā, peace be on him, refused this offer, saying: "I seek refuge for you with Allāh from such words, and that anyone should hear of it, Commander of the faithful"

Al-Ma'mūn repeated (the offer) in a letter, which said: "If you refuse what 1 have offered you, then you must accept being the heir after me."

18 *Al-Kāfī*, I, 491, tradition no. 9. This account is in the second half of the tradition.

19 Elements of this account are in *Maqātil al-Ṭālibiyyīn*, 562-3. The version of Yaḥyā b. al-Ḥasan who is one of the authorities for Abū al-Faraj's composite account may be the version al-Mufīd is using.

al-Riḍā refused him vigorously. Al-Ma'mūn summoned him. He was alone with al-Faḍl b. Sahl, the man with two offices (i.e. military and civil). There was no one else in their gathering. (al-Ma'mūn) said to (al-Riḍā): "I thought it appropriate to invest authority over the Muslims in you and to relieve myself of responsibility by giving it to you."

"Allāh! Allāh!" replied al-Riḍā, peace be on him. "Commander of the faithful, I have no ability or power for that."
"Then I will designate you as successor after me," retorted al-Ma'mūn.
"Commander of the faithful, exempt me from that."

Then al-Ma'mūn spoke to him as if threatening him for his refusal. In his speech, he said: "'Umar b. al-Khaṭṭāb made a committee of consultation (*shūrā*) (to appoint a successor). Among them was your fore-father, the Commander of the Faithful, 'Alī b. Abī Ṭālib. ('Umar) stipulated that any of them who opposed the decision should be executed. So there is no escape for you from accepting what I want from you. I will ignore your rejection of it."

"I will agree to what you want of me as far as succession is concerned," answered al-Riḍā, peace be on him, "on condition that I do not command, nor order, nor give legal decisions, nor judge, nor appoint, nor dismiss, nor change anything from how it is at present."
Al-Ma'mūn accepted all of that.

[Al-Sharīf Abū Muḥammad al-Ḥasan b. Muḥammad informed me: My grandfather (Yaḥyā b. al-Ḥasan) told us: Mūsā b. Salama told me:]
I (i.e. Mūsā b. Salama) was in Khurāsān with Muḥammad b. Ja'far. I heard that the man with two offices (i.e. al-faḍl b. Sahl, who was in charge of the military and civil administration) had gone out one day saying: "How fantastic, I have seen a wonder. Ask me what I have seen?"
They asked him: "What have you seen, may Allāh set you right?"

"I have seen al-Ma'mūn, the Commander of the faithful," he answered, "saying to 'Alī b. Mūsā: 'I will invest you with the affairs of the Muslims. I relieve myself of my responsibility and make it yours.' Then I saw 'Alī b. Mūsā saying: 'Commander of the faitful. I have no ability or power for that'. I have never seen the caliphate more abandoned than that. The Commander of the faithful deprives himself of it and offers it to 'Alī b. Mūsā. Then 'Alī b. Mūsā rejects it and refuses it."

[A group of historians (*aṣḥāb al-akhbār*) and biographers (*ruwat al-siyar*) of the

times of the caliphs report:][20]
al-Ma'mūn wanted the agreement (*'aqd*) of al-Riḍā 'Alī b. Mūsā and he considered that matter for himself. He summoned al-Faḍl b. Sahl into his presence and informed him about what he had decided upon concerning that. He told him to meet with his brother, al-Ḥasan b. Sahl, about that matter. The two met in his presence. Al-Ḥasan began to become distressed with him for that and to make him aware (of the disadvantages) of taking the position out of his own family and (giving it) to him.

Al-Ma'mūn told him: "I have promised Allāh that if I succeed in giving up the caliphate, I would leave it for the most meritorious (*afḍal*) of the family of Abū Ṭālib. I do not know anyone more meritorious than this man on the face of the earth."

When al-Ḥasan and al-Faḍl saw his determination to do that, they held back their opposition to it. He sent them to al-Riḍā, peace be on him, and they offered that to him. He refused but they persisted until he accepted. They returned to al-Ma'mūn and informed him of (al-Riḍā's) acceptance. He was delighted with that. On Thursday he held a meeting for his personal entourage (*khāṣṣa*). Al-Faḍl b. Sahl came and informed (them) of al-Ma'mūn's decision concerning 'Alī b. Mūsā, peace be on him, and that he had appointed him his successor and named him al-Riḍā (consent). He ordered them to dress in green and to come back next Thursday for the pledge of allegiance and receive a year's rations.

On that day, the people rode in their respective ranks - the military commanders, the chamberlains, the judges and the others all wearing green. Al-Ma'mūn was seated and he had had two great cushions placed for al-Riḍā peace be on him, so that he would have the same kind of seat and covers. He seated al-Riḍā, peace be on him, on them; he was dressed in green and wearing a turban and a sword. Then al-Ma'mūn ordered his son, 'Abbās b. al-Ma'mūn, to be the first of the people to make the pledge of allegiance to him. al-Riḍā, peace be on him, moved his hand and hit his own face with the back of it and their faces with the palm.

"Stretch out your hand for the pledge of allegiance," al-Ma'mūn demanded. "The Apostle of Allāh, may Allāh bless Him and His Family, used to make the pledge in this way when the people pledged allegiance to him," retorted al-Riḍā, peace be on him. "His hand would be above their hands."

Ten thousand dirhams were laid out. Orators and poets rose and began to mention the great merit of al-Riḍā, peace be on him, and the part played by al-Ma'mūn

20 The following account follows much more closely *Maqātil al-Ṭālibiyyīn*, 562-5.

in his affair. Then Abū 'Abbād summoned al-'Abbās b. al-Ma'mūn. He Jumped up and approached his father. He kissed his hand and the latter ordered him to sit down. Then Muḥammad b. Ja'far b. Muḥammad was summoned.
"Rise," al-Faḍl b. Sahl told him.

He rose and went towards al-Ma'mūn but he did not kiss his hand. He was told to go and take his gift. Then al-Ma'mūn called to him: "Go back, Abū Ja'far, to your seat."

Then Abū 'Abbād began to call individual 'Alīds and 'Abbāsids and give them their gifts until the money was all used up. After that al-Ma'mūn told al-Riḍā. peace be on him: "Address the people and speak to them."

He praised and glorified Allāh. Then he said: "We have a right due to us from you through the Apostle of Allāh and you also have a right due to you from us through him. If you carry out your duty to us, then it is necessary for us to carry out our duty to you."

Nothing other than this is mentioned of him at this gathering. Al-Ma'mūn ordered a dirham to be struck with the name of al- Riḍā, peace be on him, upon it.

(Al-Ma'mūn) married Isḥāq b. Mūsā b. Ja'far to the daughter of his paternal uncle, Isḥāq b. Ja'far b. Muḥammad. He told him to lead the pilgrimage for the people and to speak of the position of al-Riḍā as heir apparent in every town (he passed through).

[Aḥmad b Muḥammad b. Sa'īd reported: Yaḥyā b. al-Ḥasan al-'Alawī told me: One who heard 'Abd al-Ḥamīd[21] preach in that year on the pulpit of the Apostle of Allāh, may Allāh bless Him and His Family, in Medina, said:]
He said in his prayer: "The heir apparent of the Muslims is 'Alī b. Mūsā b. Ja'far b. Muḥammad b. 'Alī b. al-Ḥusayn b. 'Alī, peace be on them, He has six fathers who are the best men who ever drank the rain water from the clouds."

[Al-Madā'ini mentioned on the authority of his authorities:]
When al-Riḍā 'Alī b. Mūsā, peace be on them sat in the robes of the heir apparent, orators and poets stood before them. The standard shook above his head .

[Then al-Madā'ini mentioned on the authority of one of the close associates of al-Riḍā, peace be on him, who was present, that he said:]

21 'Abd al-Jabbar b. Sa'īd in *Maqātil al-Ṭālibiyyīn*, 565.

On that day I (i.e. a close associate of al-Riḍā) was in front of him. He looked at me while I was feeling happy about what had happened. He signalled me to come closer, I went closer to him and he said so that no one else could hear: "Do not occupy your heart with this matter and do not be happy about it. It is something which will not be achieved."

Among the poets who came to him, was Di'bil b. 'Alī al-Khuzā'i, may Allāh have mercy on him. When he visited him, he said: "I have composed an ode and have bound myself not to recite it to anyone before you."

He told him to sit down until the gathering around him had decreased. Then he said: "Come now."

So he recited his ode to him, the opening of which is:

> Schools of verses of the Qur'ān are without recitation,
> The place of inspiration is (like) courtyards without people.

(He recited the poem) to the end. When he had finished reciting it, al-Riḍā stood up and went into his room. Then he sent a servant out to him with a silken purse in which was six hundred dīnārs. He told the servant to tell him: "Use this to help you on your journey and forgive us ."

"No, by Allāh," replied Di'bil, "I do not want this. I have not come for it. But tell him: Give me one of your robes."

He gave the purse back to the servant and the servant gave it back to al-Riḍā, peace be on him, and (al-Riḍā) said: "Take it (back)."
However, (al-Riḍā) also sent one of his robes to (Di'bil) and he went off until he came to Qumm. When (the people there) saw the robe, they offered him a thousand dīnārs for it. He refused them, saying: "By Allāh, not even a piece of cloth from it is sufficient for a thousand dīnārs." Then he left Qumm. However. they followed him and waylaid him and took the robe. So he went back to Qumm and spoke to them about it. They said: "There is no way (for you) to get it. However, if you want, here is a thousand dīnārs."
"And a piece of cloth from it?" he asked.
They gave him a thousand dīnārs. .

['Alī b. Ibrāhīm reported on the authority of Yāsir, the servant and al-Rayyān b. al-Ṣalt][22]
At the time of the festival, when the agreement for al-Riḍā, peace be on him,

22 *Al-Kāfī*, I, 488-490, tradition no. 7. the first part of the tradition has been omitted.

to assume the position of heir apparent had been made, al-Ma'mūn sent to him about the procession for the festival, the prayer before the people and the sermon to them. Al-Riḍā, peace be on him, sent back to him (a message saying): "You know about the conditions made between us (for me) to enter into this affair. Therefore excuse me from saying the prayer before the people."
"I only intend by that that the people's heart should be assured and that they should know your great merit," al-Ma'mūn replied.

The messengers went back and forth between them over that matter. When al-Ma'mūn insisted that al-Riḍā should do it, the latter sent to him (a message saying): "If you had excused me, I would have preferred it. However, since you have not excused me. I will go out as the Apostle of Allāh, may Allāh bless Him and His Family, went out and the Commander of the Faithful, 'Alī b. Abī Ṭālib, peace be on him."

"Go out as you wish," replied al-Ma'mūn. Then he ordered the military commanders, the chamberlains and the people to go to the door of al-Riḍā, peace be on him, early in the morning.

The people sat (waiting) for Abū al-Ḥasan (al-Riḍā), peace be on him, in the roads and on the roof-tops. Women and children gathered to wait for him to come out. All the military commanders and the soldiers went to his door and waited on their mounts until the sun rose. (Then) Abū al-Ḥasan (al-Riḍā), peace be on him, washed and put on his clothes. He put on a white turban of cotton. One end of it he made hang on his breast and the other between his shoulders. Then he rubbed himself with a little perfume. He took his staff in his hand and said to his retainers: "Do whatever I do."

They went on in front of him. He was barefoot and had tucked his trousers half-way up his leg, and his (other) clothes were tucked in. He walked a little way. Then he raised his head towards heaven and said: "Allāh is greater (*Allāhu akbar*)" and his retainers repeated it with him. Then he went on until he stood at the door. When the military commanders and the soldiers saw him (coming) in that way, they all dismounted from their animals to the ground. The best of them in these circumstances were those who had a knife with which they could cut the leather strap of their sandals and could take them off and go barefoot.

Al-Riḍā, peace be on him, said at the door: "Allāh is greater (*Allāhu akbar*)", and the people repeated it with him

It seemed to us that the sky and the walls were answering him and that Merv shook with weeping and clamour. When they saw Abū al-Ḥasan (al-Riḍā) and heard him magnifying Allāh and al-Ma'mūn was informed of that, al-Faḍl b. Sahl, the man with two offices (military and civil), told him: "Commander of the faithful, if al-Riḍā reaches the place of prayer for the festival in this way, the people will break out in rebellion. We are all afraid for our lives. So send instructions to him to go back."

Al-Ma'mūn sent (a message) to him (which said): "We have put an excessive burden on you and we have made you very tired. We do not want you to experience any hardship. Therefore, go back and let someone pray with the people in the usual manner."

Abū al-Ḥasan (al-Riḍā), peace be on him, called for his boots and put them on. Then he mounted and went back.

The situation of the people was full of discord on that day about their prayer and whether it had not been properly performed.

[Abū al-Qasim Ja'far b. Muḥammad informed me, on the authority of Muḥammad b. Ya'qūb, on the authority of 'Alī b. Ibrāhīm, on the authority of Yāsir, who said:][23]
When al-Ma'mūn decided to leave Khurāsān for Baghdād, al-Faḍl b. Sahl, the man with two offices (military and civil), went with him and we went with Abū al-Ḥasan al-Riḍā, peace be on him. A letter came to al-Faḍl b. Sahl from his brother, al-Ḥasan b. Sahl, while we were at one of the halting-places (which said): "I have been investigating the (future of the coming) year. I have found in it that during such-and-such a month on Wednesday you will experience the heat of the iron blade (stuck into you) and the heat of the fire. I think that you, the Commander of the faithful and al-Riḍā should go to the baths on that day and should be cupped and that you should pour the blood over your body in order to remove the evil (of that day)."

The man with two offices (military and civil) (i.e. al-Faḍl b. Sahl) wrote to al-Ma'mūn and asked him to ask Abū al-Ḥasan (al-Riḍā), peace be on him, to do that. Al-Ma'mūn wrote to Abū al-Ḥasan (al-Riḍā), peace be on him, to ask him about it. Abū al-Ḥasan (al-Riḍā), peace be on him answered: "I will not go into the baths tomorrow."

Al-Ma'mūn sent the letter twice again and Abū al-Ḥasan (al-Riḍā), peace be on him, wrote to him: "I will not go into the baths tomorrow. Last night, I had

23 *Al-Kāfī*, I. 490-1, traditIon no. 8.

a vision of the Apostle of Allāh, may Allāh bless Him and His Family. He told me: "Alī, do not go into the baths tomorrow.' Therefore, Commander of the faithful, I do not think that it would be wise for you and al-Faḍl to go into the baths tomorrow."

Al-Ma'mūn wrote back to him: " You are right, Abū al-Ḥasan (al-Riḍā) and the Apostle of Allāh, may Allāh bless Him and His Family, is right. I will not go into the baths tomorrow. However, al-Faḍl will make up his own mind."

[Yāsir reported]
In the evening when the Sun had set, al-Riḍā, peace be on him, said to us: "Say: We seek refuge with Allāh from the evil which comes tonight."

We continued to repeat that. After al-Riḍā, peace be on him, had performed the morning prayer, he told me: "Go up to the roof and listen whether you can discover something."

When I went up I heard a cry. It became more frequent and increased in intensity. Yet we did not experience anything. We were still there. Al-Ma'mūn came in by the door which connected his house to the house of Abū al-Ḥasan (al-Riḍā), peace be on him, saying: "My lord, Abū al-Ḥasan, may Allāh lengthen your life (as a result of the loss of) al-Faḍl. He went into the baths and some people came in upon him with swords and killed him. Of those who attacked him, three were apprehended. One of them was al-Faḍl's cousin by his mother's sister, the son of the man with two pens (i.e. he held two vizierates)."

The soldiers, the military commanders gathered and al-Faḍl's men gathered at the gate of al-Ma'mūn. They said: "He (i.e. al-Ma'mūn) has assassinated him." They reviled him and demanded his blood. They brought fire to set the gate alight.

Al-Ma'mūn said to Abū al-Ḥasan (al-Riḍā), peace be on him: "My lord, would you consider going out to them and quietening them down so that they go away."

"Yes," replied Abū al-Ḥasan (al-Riḍā), and mounted. He told me: "Yasir, mount." I mounted.When we went out of the house, I looked at the people. They had crowded around him. He indicated to them with his hand that they should depart.

[Yāsir reported:]
By Allāh. the people began to fall over each other. He did not point to one of them, except that man ran away and departed directly.

[Abū al-Qasim Ja'far b. Muḥammad informed me, on the authority of Muḥammad b. Ya'qūb, on the authority of Mu'allā b. Muhammad, on the authority of Musāfir, who said:][24]
When Hārūn b. al-Musayyib wanted to attack Muḥammad b. Ja'far, Abū al-Ḥasan al-Riḍā, peace be on him, said to me (i.e. Musāfir): "Go and tell him (Muḥammad b. Ja'far): 'Do not go out tomorrow, you will be put to flight and your companions will be killed.' If he asks you from where you learnt this, tell him that you saw it in a dream."

I went to him and told him: "Do not go out tomorrow. If you go out tomorrow, you will be put to flight and your companions will kill you."
"Where did you learn this?" he asked me.
"I saw it in my sleep," I replied.
"The slave only dreams when he has not washed his buttocks," he retorted. Then he went out and was put to flight and his companions were killed.

*****

An Extract from the Reports about the Death of al-Riḍā 'Alī b. Mūsā, Peace be on them, and about its Cause

Whenever al-Riḍā 'Alī b. Mūsā, peace be on them, was alone with al-Ma'mūn, he used to give him many warnings; he would endeavour to make him fear Allāh and show him the foul crimes he had committed during his caliphate. Al-Ma'mūn would pretend to accept it but inside him he began to hate it and find it difficult to bear. One day al-Riḍā, peace be on him, visited al-Ma'mūn and saw him performing the ablutions for prayer. A servant was pouring water on to his hand. "Commander of the faithful, don't let anyone participate in your act of worship to your Lord," he, peace be on him, told him.

Al-Ma'mūn sent the servant away and finished his ablutions by himself. However, that increased his rage and anger. Also, al-Riḍā, peace be on him, used to disparage al-Ḥasan and al-Faḍl b. Sahl before al-Ma'mūn whenever the latter mentioned the two; he would describe them both in the same terms and would (encourage him) not to listen to their advice. They were both aware of that and they began to seek favour for themselves with (al-Ma'mūn) against (al-Riḍā); they would mention anything which might isolate al-Riḍā from al-Ma'mūn and make the latter fear the people's attitude towards him. They continued in this way until they had changed (al-Ma'mūn's) opinion of (al-Riḍā) and made him act to kill him.

24 *Al-Kāfī*, I, 490, tradition no. 9. Al-Ḥusayn b. Yaḥyā - al-Kulaynī's informant - has been omitted from the *isnād*. Only the first half of the tradition is reported. The second half was given earlier

It happened one day that (al-Riḍā) and al-Ma'mūn ate together. al-Riḍā fell ill from the food and al-Ma'mūn pretended to be sick.[25]

[Muḥammad b. 'Alī b. Ḥamza mentioned on the authority of Manṣūr b. Bashīr. on the authority of his brother 'Abd Allāh b. Bashīr, who said:][26]
Al-Ma'mūn ordered me (i.e 'Abd Allāh b. Bashīr) to grow my finger-nails longer than was usual and not to let anyone know of that. I did so. Then he summoned me. He brought out for me something like tamarind and said "Knead these all together with your hand."

After I had done so, he stood up and left me. He went to al-Riḍā, peace be on him. and said: "What is your news?"
"I hope that I am well," was the reply.
"Today, I am also well, praise be to Allāh," al-Ma'mūn said. "Has one of the servants come to you today?"
"No," he answered.

Al-Ma'mūn was angry and called out to his servants. Then he said: "Take some pomegranate juice now. It is one of the things one should not do without."
Then he called me and said to me: "Squeeze it with your own hand."

I did so and al-Ma'mūn gave it to al-Riḍā, peace be on him, to drink with his own hand. That was the cause of his death. It was only two days later when he, peace be on him, died.

[It is mentioned on the authority of Abū al-Ṣalt al-Harawī, who said:]
I (i.e. Abū al-Ṣalt al-Harawī) went into al-Riḍā, peace be on him. Al-Ma'mūn came out from his room. He said to me: "Abū al-Ṣalt, they have done it." Then he began to declare the unity of Allāh and to magnify Him.

[It is reported on the authority of Muḥammad b. al-Jahm that he said:]
al-Riḍā used to like grapes. He (al-Ma'mūn) got some for him and had needles prodded into them at the place of their storks. I (Muḥammad b. al-Jahm) took them from him and they were brought to (al-Riḍā) and he ate them, while he was ill with the illness which we have already mentioned. It was said that that was caused by the subtlest of poisons.

*****

When al-Riḍā, peace be on him, died, al-Ma'mūn kept his death secret for a day

25 cf. *Maqātil al-Ṭālibiyyīn*, 565-6
26 *Maqātil*, 566-7.

and a night. Then he sent to Muḥammad b. Ja'far al-Ṣadiq, peace be on him, and a group of the family of Abū Ṭālib who were with him. When they came into his presence, he announced the news of al-Riḍā's death to them. He wept and gave an appearance of intense grief and pain. He showed them al-Riḍā (whose) body was healthy (even in death), saying: "My brother, it is hard on me to see you in this state. I had hoped that I would go before you. However, Allāh refused (everything) except what He wanted."

Then he ordered his body to be washed, shrouded and perfumed. He went out with the bier carrying it until he reached the place where it was to be buried and buried it there. The place was the house of Hārūn b. Quḥṭaba in a village called Sanābād near Nawqān in the area of Ṭūs. There was the tomb of Hārūn al-Rashīd and the tomb of Abū al-Ḥasan (al-Riḍā) is in front of it in its direction towards Mecca (*qibla*).

al-Riḍā 'Alī b. Mūsā died without leaving any child we know of, except his son, the Imam after him, Abū Ja'far Muḥammad b. 'Alī, peace be on them. At the time of his death, his son was seven years old and a few months.

CHAPTER VIII

IMĀM MUḤAMMAD B. 'ALĪ AL-JAWĀD

(This chapter gives) will deal with the Imam after Abū al-Ḥasan 'Alī b. Mūsā al-Riḍā, peace be on them; (including) the date of his birth, the evidence for his Imamate, the period of his succession and his age. (It will also mention) his death and the cause of it, the place of his grave, the number of his children and an outline of the reports about him.

The Imam after al-Riḍā 'Alī b. Mūsā, peace be on them, was his son Muḥammad b. 'Alī al-Riḍā, peace be on them, by virtue of his nomination and indication by his father. Outstanding merit attained perfection in him. He, peace be on him, was born in the month of Ramaḍān, in the year 195 A.H. (811) at Medina and he died in Baghdād in the month of Dhū al-Qa'da in the year 220 A.H.(835). At that time he was twenty-five years of age. The period of his succession and his Imamate after his father was seventeen years. His mother was a slave-wife (*umm walad*) called Sabīka, she was a Nubian.

An Outline of the Nomination and Indication of Abū Ja'far Muḥammad b. 'Alī for the Imamate by his Father

Among those who report the nomination for the Imamate by Abū al-Ḥasan 'Alī b. Mūsā al-Riḍā, peace be on him, of his son Abū Ja'far (al-Jawād), peace be on him, are: 'Alī b. Ja'far b. Muḥammad al-Ṣādiq, peace be on them, Ṣafwān b. Yaḥyā, Mu'ammar b. Khallād, al-Ḥusayn b. Bashshār, Ibn Abī Naṣr al-Bizanṭī, Ibn Qayāmā al-Wāsiṭī, al-Ḥasan b. al-Jahm, Abū Yaḥyā al-Ṣan'ānī, al-Khayrānī and Yaḥyā b. Ḥabīb al-Zayyāt. (These are some names) in a group so numerous that to mention them would make the book unduly long.

[Abū al-Qāsim Ja'far b. Muḥammad informed me on the authority of Muḥammad b. Ya'qūb, on the authority of 'Alī b. Ibrāhīm b. Hāshim, on the authority of his father and of 'Alī b. Muḥammad al-Qāsānī, on the authority of Zakariyyā b. Yaḥyā b. al-Nu'mān al-Baṣrī, who said: I heard 'Alī b. Ja'far b. Muḥammad telling al-Ḥasan b. al-Ḥusayn b. 'Alī b. al-Ḥusayn: In his account he (i.e. 'Alī b. Ja'far) said:][1]
Allāh gave Abū al-Ḥasan al-Riḍā, peace be on him, victory when his brothers and uncles treated him unjustly. [Then he gave a long account until he came to:] I (i.e. 'Alī b. Ja'far) arose and seized the hand of Abū Ja'far Muḥammad b. 'Alī

1 *Al-Kāfī*, I, 322-3, tradition no. 14, gives the full tradition.

al-Riḍā and I said to him: "I testify that before Allāh, the Mighty and High, you are my Imam."

Al-Riḍā, peace be on him, wept and said: "Uncle, did you not hear my father saying: The Apostle, may Allāh bless Him and His Family, said to my father (i.e. 'Alī b. Abī Ṭālib): The son of the best of the beautiful Nubian maid-servants will be among his descendants. (He will be) pursued, exiled, deprived of his father. His grandson will be the Imam who goes into occultation. It will be said that he has died or had been killed or any such excuse."
"True, may I be your ransom," I said.

[Abū al-Qāsim Ja'far b. Muḥammad informed me on the authority of Muḥammad b. Ya'qūb, on the authority of Muḥammad b. Yaḥyā on the authority of Aḥmad b. Muḥammad, on the authority of Ṣafwān b. Yaḥyā, who said:][2]
I (i.e. Ṣafwān b. Yaḥyā) said to al-Riḍā, peace be on him: "We used to ask you before Allāh gave you Abū Ja'far (about your son) and you would say: 'Allāh will give me a son.' Now Allāh has given him to you and we are delighted with him. We ask Allāh never to show us the day (of your death) but if something happened, to whom (will the Imamate belong)?"

He pointed to Abū Ja'far with his hand while he was standing in front of him. I said: "May I be your ransom, this is a child of three years old."

"That does not harm him," he replied. "Jesus gave evidence (of his mission) when he was less than three years old."

[Abū al-Qāsim Ja'far b. Muḥammad informed me on the authority of Muḥammad b. Ya'qūb, on the authority of Muḥammad b. Yaḥyā on the authority of Aḥmad b. Muḥammad b. 'Īsā, on the authority of Mu'ammar b. Khallād, who said:][3]
I (i.e. Mu'ammar b. Khallād) heard al-Riḍā, peace be on him, say when I mentioned something: "What need have you for that? Here is Abū Ja'far, whom I have brought into my meetings and whom I have made to be my successor." Then he added: "We are the family of the House. Our young inherit from our old, like one feather (on a wing) followed by the next."

[Abū al-Qāsim Ja'far b. Muḥammad informed me on the authority of Muḥammad b. Ya'qūb, on the authority of a number of his colleagues, on the authority of Aḥmad b. Muḥammad on the authority of Ja'far b. Yaḥyā on the authority of Mālik b. Ashyam. on the authority of al-Ḥusayn b. Bashshār. who said:][4]

2 *Al-Kāfī*, I, 321, tradition no. 10.
3 *Al-Kāfī*, I, 320, tradition no. 2.
4 *Al-Kāfī*, I, 320, tradition no. 4.

Ibn Qayāmā al-Wāsiṭī wrote a letter to Abū al-Ḥasan al-Riḍā, peace be on him, in which he asked: "How will you provide an Imam when you have no son?"

Abū al-Ḥasan al-Riḍā, peace be on him, replied to him: "What tells you that I will have no son? By Allāh, few days and nights will pass before Allāh provides me with a male child who will distinguish the truth from the false."

[Abū al-Qāsim Ja'far b. Muḥammad told me on the authority of Muḥammad b. Ya'qūb, on the authority of some of his colleagues, on the authority of Muḥammad b. 'Alī, on the authority of Mu'āwiya b. Ḥukaym, on the authority of Ibn Abī Naṣr al-Bizanṭī, who said:][5]
Ibn al-Najāshī asked me (i.e. Ibn Abī Naṣr): "Who is the Imam after your (present) leader?"

I wanted to ask him (i.e . the present Imam) so that I might know. Therefore I went to visit al- Riḍā, peace be on him. And I mentioned it to him. He said to me: "The Imam will be my son. Does a man seem bold who says, 'My son', when he does not have a son?"

At that time Abū Ja'far, peace be on him, had not been born but not many days passed before he was born.

[Abū al-Qāsim Ja'far b. Muḥammad told me on the authority of Muḥammad b. Ya'qūb, on the authority of Aḥmad b. Mihrān. on the authority of Muḥammad b. 'Alī, on the authority of Ibn Qayāmā al-Wāsiṭī, - he was a Waqifite - who said][6]
I (i.e. Ibn Qayāmā) visited 'Alī b. Mūsā (al-Riḍā) peace be on them, and asked him: "Can there be two Imam?"
"No" he replied, "unless one is silent (*ṣāmit*)."

"How is it then that you do not have a silent (Imam)?" I asked.
"Indeed," he said, "Allāh will bring one who will confirm the truth and those who hold it and deny the false and those who hold it. "

At that time he did not have a child but a year later Abū Ja'far (al-Jawād), peace be on him, was born to him.

[Abū al-Qāsim Ja'far b. Muḥammad told me on the authority of Muḥammad b. Ya'qūb, on the authority of Aḥmad b. Mihrān, on the authority of al-Ḥasan b. al-Jahm, who said:][7]

5 *Al-Kāfī*, I, 320, tradition no. 5.
6 *Al-Kāfī*, I, 321, tradition no. 7.
7 *Al-Kāfī*, I, 321, tradition no. 8.

I (i.e. al-Ḥasan b. al-Jahm) was sitting with Abū al-Ḥasan (al-Riḍā), peace be on him. He called for his son who was small and put him to sit on my lap. He told me to strip him and take off his shirt. I took it off. Then he told me to look between the shoulders. I looked and there on one of his shoulders was something like a seal within the flesh. Then he said to me: " Do you see this? A similar mark was in this place on my father, peace be on him."

[Abū al-Qāsim Ja'far b. Muḥammad, peace be on him, informed me on the authority of Muḥammad b. Ya'qūb, on the authority of Aḥmad b. Mihrān, on the authority of Muḥammad b. 'Alī, on the authority of Abū Yaḥyā al-Ṣan'ānī, who said:][8]
I (i.e. Abū Yaḥyā al-Ṣan'ānī) was with Abū al-Hasan (al- Riḍā), peace be on him. His son Abū Ja'far (al-Jawād), peace be on him, was brought and he was still a child. (Al-Riḍā) said: "This child, who has been born, is greater than any child born to our Shī'a."

[Abū al-Qāsim Ja'far b. Muḥammad informed me on the authority of Muḥammad b. Ya'qūb on the authority of al-Ḥasan b. Muḥammad, on the authority of al-Khayrānī, on the authority of his father, who said:][9]
I (i.e al-Khayrānī's father) was standing in front of Abū al-Hasan al-Riḍā, peace be on him, in Khurāsān. Someone asked him: "My lord, if something happens, to whom (will authority belong)?"
"To Abū Ja'far (al-Jawād), my son," he replied.

The speaker indicated that the age of Abū Ja'far was too young. So Abū al-Hasan (al-Riḍā), peace be on him, replied: "Allāh, may He be praised, sent Jesus, son of Mary, to be an apostle, a prophet, the bringer of a revealed law (*sharī'a*), to begin (his mission) when his age was younger than that of Abū Ja'far (aJ-Jawād), peace be on him."

[Abū al-Qāsim Ja'far b. Muḥammad informed me on the authority of Muḥammad b. Ya'qūb on the authority of 'Alī b. Muḥammad, on the authority of Sahl b. Ziyād, on the authority of Muḥammad b. al-Walīd, on the authority of Yaḥyā b. Ḥabīb al-Zayyāt, who said: Someone who was sitting with Abū al-Hasan (al-Riḍā), peace be on him, told me:][10]
When the people got up, Abū al-Hasan (al- Riḍā), pcace be on him, said to them: "Meet Abū Ja'far (al-Jawād) and greet him."

---

8 *Al-Kāfī*, I, 321. tradition no. 9.
9 *Al-Kāfī*, I, 322, tradition no. 13.
10 *Al-Kāfī*, I, 320, tradition no. 1.

When the people got up, he turned to me and said: "May Allāh have mercy on Mufaḍḍal (b, 'Umar), since he would have been satisfied without this (explanation)."

An Extract from the Reports, Proofs and Miracles of Abū Ja'far (al-Jawād), Peace be on him.

Al-Ma'mūn had a great affection for Abū Ja'far (al-Jawād), peace be on him, because of the great merit he saw in him despite his age, because of his attainment in philosophy and literature and because of his intellectual maturity which none of the scholars of the time equalled. Therefore (al-Ma'mūn) married him to his daughter Umm al-Faḍl. (Abū Ja'far al-Jawād) took her to Medina with him. Al-Ma'mūn was generous in his honouring and extolling of him and giving him rank and position.

[Al-Ḥasan b. Muḥammad b. Sulaymān reported on the authority of 'Alī b. Ibrāhīm b. Hāshim, on the authority of his father, on the authority of al-Rayyān b. Shabīb, who said:]
When al-Ma'mūn wanted to marry his daughter Umm al-Faḍl to Abū Ja'far Muḥammad b. 'Alī (al-Jawād), peace be on them, this news reached the 'Abbāsid (family), and shocked them and they were greatly concerned at this. They were afraid that the affair (of the caliphate) would finish up with him as it had done with al-Riḍā, peace be on him. They were very concerned about that. He met the close members of his family and they said to him: "Commander of the faithful, we adjure you before Allāh against persevering in this plan you have decided upon, of marrying the son of al-Riḍā (to your daughter). For we are afraid that you will take away from us power which Allāh has made our possession, and strip away what He has clothed us in. You know what is between us and these people, both of old and recently, and the policy of the rightly-guided caliphs before you to isolate them and belittle them. We were (greatly) afraid of your action with al-Riḍā until Allāh was sufficient for us in that task. O Allāh, do not bring back to us that pain from which we had escaped. Turn aside from your opinion about the son of al-Riḍā and turn towards someone you think appropriate from your own family to the exclusion of anyone else."

Al-Ma'mūn replied: "You are the cause of (any friction) there is between yourselves and the family of Abū Ṭālib. If you treated these people justly, they would be much closer to you. As for what those who were before me have done to them, it was an act against kinship and I seek Allāh's protection from it. By Allāh, I do not regret the arrangement of succession which I made with al-Riḍā. I had asked him to undertake the affair and I was (ready to) give it up but he refused. The decision of Allāh was a decree which had been decreed. As for Abū Ja'far (al-Jawād), I have chosen him because of his superiority to all men of merit in knowledge and merit despite his youth, and as a result of his miraculous nature in that. I hope that he shows the people what I know to be in him, and then they will understand why I hold this view with regard to him."

"This young man, even though he has amazed you, needs direction," they told him. "He is still a boy without knowledge and understanding. Therefore act with circumspection towards him so that he may become educated and may gain understanding in religion. Then, after that do what you think appropriate."

"Shame on you!" he retorted. "I know this young man in (comparison with) you. He is from the family of the House whose knowledge is from Allāh, of those who love Him and are inspired by Him. His ancestors were always rich in the knowledge of religion and literature far (beyond) the populace which lacked the range of (their) perfection. If you wish, examine Abū Ja'far (al-Jawād) so that he may make clear to you his condition as I have described"

"We consent to examine him, Commander of the faithful, both for you and for ourselves," they answered. "So let us assign someone to question him, in your presence, about some matter of jurisprudence. If he gets the answer to it correct, there will be no opposition from us to his affair and it will demonstrate, both to the elite and to the public, the sound view of the Commander of the faithful. However, if he fails in that, we will have been able to give protection in a serious matter with regard to this idea."

"It is your affair and it (will take place) whenever you want to do it," al-Ma'mūn told them.

They left him and agreed to ask Yaḥyā b. Aktham. He was, then, the (outstanding) *qāḍī* of the time and he would be able to ask a question which (Abū Ja'far al-Jawād) would not be able to answer. They promised him precious valuables to do that. They returned to al-Ma'mūn and asked him to choose a day for their meeting. He complied with their request. They gathered on the agreed day and with them came Yaḥyā b. Aktham. Al-Ma'mūn ordered a seat of honour to be put for Abū Ja'far (al-Jawād), peace be on him, and leather pillows to be put on it for him. That was done. Abū Ja'far (al-Jawād), peace be on him, came out. At that time he was a boy of nine years and a few months. He sat down amid the leather pillows and Yaḥyā. b. Aktham sat opposite him. The people stood in their rank while al-Ma'mūn was sitting in a seat of honour attached to Abū Ja'far's, peace be on him.

"Commander of the faithful, do you permit me to question Abu Ja'far?" Yaḥyā b. Aktham asked al- Ma'mūn.
"Seek permission from him for that," al-Ma'mūn replied to him.

Then Yaḥyā b. Aktham went forward to him and said: "May I be your ransom, do you permit me to question (you)?"
"Ask if you want to," Abū Ja'far (al-Jawād), peace be on him, told him.

"May Allāh make me your ransom," said Yaḥyā. "what would you say about a *muḥrim* (a person in a state of ritual purification for pilgrimage) who killed an animal while hunting?"

"Did he kill it in the area not sanctified or in the sanctuary?" asked Abū Ja'far (al-Jawād), peace be on him. "Did the *muḥrim* do the killing knowingly or in ignorance, deliberately or by mistake? Was the *muḥrim* free or a slave, young or old, inexperienced in killing or practised? Was the animal hunted, winged or otherwise, little or big? Was the man obstinate in his action or regretful? Was the killing of the hunted animal at night or during the day? Was he in a state of ritual consecration for the lesser pilgrimage (*'umra*) or the greater pilgrimage (*ḥajj*) when he did the killing?"

Yaḥyā b. Aktham became bewildered. Inability and indecision were clear on his face. He began to stutter so that all the people at the assembly were aware of his predicament.

"Praise be to Allāh for this blessing and the success of my judgement," said al-Ma'mūn. Then he looked at the members of his family and said: "Do you recognise now what you used to deny?"

He went up to Abū Ja'far, peace be on him, and asked him: "Will you address us, Abū Ja'far?"
"Yes, Commander of the faithful," he repiled.
"May I be your ransom," al-Ma'mūn said, "address us on your own account and I am pleased with you on my account. I will marry you to Umm al-Faḍl, my daughter, even though these people object."

Abū Ja'far (al-Jawād), peace be on him, said: "Praise be to Allāh in confessing His blessing. There is no god except Allāh, unique in His unity. Blessings be upon Muḥammad the lord of His creatures and upon the pure ones from his family. It is the favour of Allāh to His creatures that He has enriched them with the permitted apart from the forbidden." Then he quoted: "*Marry*

the unmarried among you. And the righteous of your slaves and handmaidens. If they are poor, Allāh will enrich them out of His bounty. Allāh is (all) encompassing, Knowing (XXIV 32). Thus it is that Muḥammad b. 'Alī b. Mūsā will become betrothed to Umm al-Faḍl, the daughter of the servant of Allāh, al-Ma'mūn. He has bestowed as a dowry for her the dowry of his (distant) grandmother, Fāṭima, daughter of Muḥammad, which is five hundred good dirhams. Will you marry him to her for that dowry which has been mentioned, Commander of the faithful?"
"Yes," replied al-Ma'mūn, "I will marry you, Abū Ja'far (al-Jawād), to Umm al-Faḍl, my daughter, for the dowry which has been mentioned. Do you accept the marriage?"
"I accept it and I consent to it," replied Abū Ja'far (al-Jawād), peace be on him.

Al-Ma'mūn ordered the people to sit in the ranks of courtiers and public.

[Al-Rayyān reported:]
It was not long before we heard voices, like the sounds of sailors in their songs. Suddenly (there appeared) slaves pulling a boat made of silver, tied to ropes of silk on carts filled with perfume. Al-Ma'mūn ordered the beards of the courtiers to be daubed with the perfume. Then it passed on to the general populace and they perfumed themselves with it. Tables were set up and the people ate. Gifts were brought out for all the people in accordance with their position. When the people departed and only some of the courtiers remained, al-Ma'mūn said to Abū Ja'far (al-Jawād), peace be on him: "May I be your ransom, would you consider telling us the law (*fiqh*) concerning the aspects into which you divided the killing of an animal by a *muḥrim* so that we may learn and benefit by it?'

"Yes," replied Abū Ja'far (al-Jawād), peace be on him. "If he had killed the animal outside sacred ground and it was winged and large, (an atonement of) a sheep would have been necessary for him. If he had struck it down in the sanctuary, the penalty required of him would be doubled. If he killed a young bird outside sacred ground, then (an atonement of) a lamb which had been weaned off milk would have been required of him. If he had killed it in the sanctuary, then he would have been required (to sacrifice) a lamb and the value of the young bird. As for wild animals, if it was the wild ass, he would have been required (to sacrifice) a cow. If it was an ostrich, the sacrifice of a camel would have been necessary for him. If it had been a deer, then a sheep would have been necessary. If he had killed any of those in the sanctuary, the penalty would have been a doubled sacrifice offered in the Ka'ba. If the *muḥrim* had struck down anything which required a sacrifice to be made for it and his state of ritual consecration was for the greater pilgrimage (*ḥajj*), he would sacrifice it at Mina. If his state of ritual consecration was for the lesser pilgrimage (*'umra*), he would sacrifice it in Mecca. The penalties for hunting by one who knows (it to be forbidden) and by one who is ignorant (of that) are the same. If he did it deliberately, it is a sin. He is absolved of its (sinfulness), if it is by mistake. The free man is responsible for the payment of his own atonement while the master is responsible for the payment of his slave's. There is no atonement necessary for a child while it is necessary for an adult. Anyone who regrets his action will escape the punishment of the Hereafter through his regret and anyone who is obstinate will be required to receive punishment in the Hereafter."

"You have done well, Abū Ja'far (al-Jawād), and Allāh has adorned you," al-Ma'mūn said to him. "Now would you see fit to question Yaḥyā as he questioned you?"

"May I question you?" Abū Ja'far (al-Jawād), peace be on him, asked Yaḥyā. "May I be your ransom," he answered, "that is up to you but if you know the answer of what you ask me, then I will gain the benefit of it from you."

Abū Ja'far (al-Jawād), peace be on him, said: "Tell me about a man who looked at a woman at the beginning of the day, and his looking at her was forbidden to him. Yet as the morning continued, she was allowed to him. At noon she became forbidden to him yet in the afternoon she was permitted to him. At sunset she was forbidden to him but when the night came she was allowed to him. In the middle of the night she was forbidden to him but at dawn she was permitted to him. What was the state of this woman and why was she permitted and forbidden to him at different times?"

"Allāh has not guided me to the answer of this question and I do not know the approach to it," Yaḥyā b. Aktbam told him. "Would you think it appropriate to benefit us with it?"

"This woman is a slave-girl of a man among the people." said Abū Ja'far (al-Jawād), peace be on him. "A foreigner looked at her at the beginning of the day and then his looking at her was forbidden to him. As the morning continued he bought her from her owner and she became permitted to him. At noon, he gave her her freedom and then she was forbidden to him. In the afternoon he married her and then she was permitted to him. At sunset he parted from her according to the disapproved formula (*ẓihār*) - You are to me like my mother's flesh (*ẓihr*) - and then she was forbidden to him. At night he made atonement for the (*ẓihār*) and she was permitted to him. Halfway through the night, he divorced her with the first declaration of the three-fold divorce and she was forbidden to him. At dawn he renounced it and she was permitted to him."

Then al-Ma'mūn went forward towards those of his family who were present and said to them: "Is there anyone among you who could answer questions in the way this answer (has been given) or expatiate on the answer which has just been given?"
"No, by Allāh," they replied. "Indeed the Commander of the faithful knows better about the decisions he makes."

"Shame on you," he said to them. "This House has been singled out among creatures for the outstanding merit which you have seen. Even youthfulness in years does not prevent them from attaining perfection (of intellect). Don't you realise that the Apostle of Allāh, may Allāh bless Him and His Family, began his mission by calling on the Commander of the Faithful, 'Alī b. Abī Ṭālib, to follow him when he was only a boy of ten years? And the latter accepted Islam from him and judged his (actions) by it? He did not call on anyone else of his age (to accept Islam) (Again) al-Ḥasan and al-Ḥusayn, peace be on them, gave the pledge of allegiance when they were only boys of less than six. He did not require the pledge of allegiance from any boy except those two. Do you not realise now the special way Allāh has singled out these people? They are offspring who follow one another so that the last of them carries out what the first of them did."
"True, Commander of the faithful," they replied and then the people rose.

On the next day, the people came and Abū Ja'far (al-Jawād), peace be on him, came. The military leaders, the chamberlains, the Courtiers and the general public came to greet al-Ma'mūn and Abū Ja'far (al-Jawād), peace be on him. Three trays of silver were brought out. On them were nuggets of musk and kneaded saffron. In the middle of the nuggets were pieces of parchment on which was written considerable wealth, annual income and estates. Al-Ma'mūn ordered them to be scattered among the Courtiers. Everyone into Whose hand fell a nugget would take out the piece of parchment in it. He would seek (fulfilment) from him and he would grant it. Bags containing ten thousand dirhams were put down and their contents scattered among the military leaders and others. The people departed and they were rich as a result of the gifts and the salaries. Al-Ma'mūn gave alms to all the poor and he continued to be generous to Abū Ja'far (al-Jawād), peace be on him. and to magnify his position throughout his life, and he recommended him to his children and all his family.

*****

[The people reported:]

Umm al-Faḍl wrote to her father from Medina, complaining about Abū Ja'far (al-Jawād), peace be on him saying: "He has slave-girls in his possession and he makes me jealous."

Al-Ma'mūn wrote to her: "My little daughter, we did not marry you to Abū Ja'far (al-Jawād), peace be on him, so that we should forbid him what is permitted. Do not mention what you have mentioned again after this."

When Abū Ja'far (al-Jawād), peace be on him, set out from Baghdād. after leaving al-Ma'mūn, and (taking) Umm al-Faḍl with him and heading for Medina, he came to the street where the Kūfan Gate was, and with him were the people who had come to say farewell to him. He went to the house of al-Musayyib and stayed there. He went into the mosque. In its courtyard, there was a lote-tree which had not borne any fruit. He called for a jug of water and performed the ritual ablution at the roots of the lote-tree. He, peace be on him. stood up and performed the sunset prayer with the people. In the first (*rak'a* of the prayer) he recited the *sūra* "The Opening" (I) and the *sūra* "The Victory" (CX). In the second (*rak'a*) he recited: "Sincerity" (CXII). During it he made the personal prayer (*qanūt*) before his bowing. Then he prayed the third (*rak'a*) and made the declaration of faith (*shahāda*) and the final salutation. He sat for a short time remembering Allāh, may His name be exalted. He stood up without sitting on his heels to make any superogatory prayer. Then he prayed the customary additional prayer of four *rak'as*, and sat back on his heels to make superogatory prayers. He made two prostrations of thanks and then he departed. When the people went to the lote-tree, they saw that it was bearing good fruit. They were amazed at that. They ate from it and found sweet lotes without stones. They said farewell to him and he departed at that time for Medina.

He remained there until al-Mu'taṣim made him travel to Baghdād at the beginning of the year 220 A.H./835. He resided there until he died at the end of the month Dhū al-Qa'da in the same year. He was buried behind his grandfather Abū al-Ḥasan Mūsā, peace be on him.

[Abū al-Qāsim Ja'far b. Muḥammad told me on the authority of Muḥammad b. Ya'qūb on the authority of Aḥmad b. ldrīs, on the authority of Muḥammad b. Ḥassan, on the authority of 'Alī b. Khālid, who said:][11]
I (i.e. 'Alī b. Khālid) was at al-'Askar (Sāmarrā') and I was told that there was a man in prison who had been brought in chains from the direction of Syria. They said that he had pretended to be a prophet. I went and persuaded the gate-man until I was able to go to him. There (I found him) a man of understanding and intellect. I asked: "Fellow, what is your story?"

11 *Al-Kāfī*, I, 492-3, tradition no 1.

"I was (just) a man in Syria," he said, "who used to worship Allāh, the Exalted. in the place in which it was said that the head of al-Ḥsayn, peace be on him, was placed. One night I was in my place facing the *miḥrāb*, mentioning Allāh, the Mighty and the High when I saw a person standing in front of me. I looked towards him and he told me to get up. I got up with him and he walked with me a little way. Suddenly we were in the mosque of Kūfa. He asked me: 'Do you know this mosque?' I answered: 'Yes, this is the mosque of Kufa.' He said: 'Let us pray.' I prayed with him. Then he left and I left with him. He walked with me a little way. Suddenly we were in the mosque of the Apostle, may Allāh bless Him and His Family. He greeted the Apostle and prayed and I prayed with him. Then he went out and I went out with him. He walked a little way. Suddenly we were in Mecca. He made the circumambulation of the (Sacred) House and I made it with him. Then he went out and walked a little way. Suddenly we were (back) in the place in which I used to worship Allāh in Syria. The person disappeared from my sight and I was left amazed and dazed at what I had seen.

"The next year I saw that person again. I rejoiced (to see) him. He called me and I answered him. He did as he had done in the previous year. When he was about to leave me in Syria, I said to him: 'I ask you by the truth which I estimate you to have through what I have seen from you, will you tell me who you are?' He said: 'I am Muḥammad b. 'Alī b. Mūsā b. Ja'far, peace be on them.'

"I told one of those who came to me, this report of him (about this) and he brought a charge against me of that to Muḥammad b. 'Abd al-Malik al-Zayyāt. He sent for me, arrested me and put me in chains. He took me to Iraq and I was imprisoned as you see now. I was charged with being a cheat."

I said to him: "I will raise your story with Muḥammad b. 'Abd al-Malik al-Zayyāt."
"Do so," he told me.

I wrote his story and I explained his part in it and I sent it to Muḥammad b. 'Abd al-Malik al-Zayyāt. (It was sent back with) an answer written on it: "Tell the one who in one night took you from Syria to Kūfa, from Kūfa to Medina, from Medina to Mecca and then took you back from Mecca to Syria to take you from your prison."

['Alī b. Khālid reported:]
That troubled me for his affair. I felt ashamed and went away saddened for him. On the next day I went early to the prison to tell him the situation and to encourage him to be steadfast and patient. I found soldiers, guards, warders

and a great crowd of people hurrying to and fro. I asked about the situation and was told: "The man brought from Syria who had pretended to be a prophet disappeared yesterday from the prison. We do not know whether the earth has swallowed him or the birds have snatched him away."

This man - meaning ʻAlī b. Khālid - was a Zaydī and then maintained the Imamate when he saw that and his faith became sound.

[Abū al-Qāsim Jaʻfar b. Muḥammad told me on the authority of Muḥammad b. Yaʻqūb on the authority of al-Ḥusayn b. Muḥammad. on the authority of Muʻallā b. Muḥammad, on the authority of Muḥammad b. ʻAlī, on the authority of Muḥammad b. Ḥamza, on the authority of Muḥammad b. ʻAlī al-Hāshimī, who said:][12]
I (i.e. Muḥammad b. ʻAlī al-Hāshimī) visited Abū Jaʻfar Muḥammad b. ʻAlī, peace be on him, early on the morning of his wedding with the daughter of al-Ma'mūn. During the night I had taken medicine. I was the first person to visit him on that morning. I was seized by a thirst but did not like to ask for water. Abū Jaʻfar (al-Jawād), peace be on him, looked at my face and said: "I see that you are thirsty."
"Yes," I replied.
"Servant, bring us water," he said.

I said to myself at that time that they would bring him poisoned water and I was grieved at that. The servant approached and with him was the water. (Al-Jawād) smiled into my face and said: "Servant, give me water."

He gave him the water and he drank it. Then he gave me the water and I drank it. I was with him a long lime and I became thirsty again. He called for water. He did the same as he had done on the first occasion and drank and then gave it to me, smiling.

[Muḥammad b. Ḥamza added: Muḥammad b. ʻAlī al-Hāshimī said to me:] By Allāh, I think that Abū Jaʻfar (al-Jawād) knew what was in men's souls just as the Rāfidites claim.

[Abū al-Qāsim Jaʻfar b. Muḥammad told me on the authority of Muḥammad b. Yaʻqūb on the authority of a number of his companions, on the authority of Aḥmad b. Muḥammad, on the authority of al-Hajjāl and ʻAmr b ʻUthmān, on the authority of a man from Medina, on the authority of al-Miṭrafī, who said:][13]
Abū al-Ḥasan al-Riḍā, peace be on him, died while owing me (i.e. al-Miṭrafī)

12 *Al-Kāfī*, I, 495-6, tradition no. 6.
13 *Al-Kāfī*, I, 497, tradition no. 11.

four thousand dirhams. No one knew about it except myself and him. Abū Ja'far (al-Jawād), peace be on him, sent for me on the next day to come to him. On the next day, I went to him. He said to me: " Abū al-Ḥasan al-Riḍā, peace be on him, died while owing you four thousand dirhams."
"Yes," I answered.

He lifted up the prayer-mat which was under him. Behold under it were (a number of) dīnārs. He gave them to me and their amount was at that time equivalent to four thousand dirhams.

[Abū al-Qāsim Ja'far b. Muḥammad told me on the authority of Muḥammad b. Ya'qūb, on the authority of al-Ḥusayn b. Muḥammad, on the authority of Mu'allā b. Muḥammad, who said:][14]
The death of his father occurred while Abū Ja'far (al-Jawād) was still a young man. I (i.e. Mu'allā b. Muḥammad) examined his size in order to describe his stature to our companions. He sat still and then said: " Mu'allā, Allāh has given proof for the Imamate in the same way as He gave proof for prophethood. For He said: *We gave him the law while still a boy* (XIX 12)".

[Abū al-Qāsim Ja'far b. Muḥammad told me on the authority of Muḥammad b. Ya'qūb on the authority of 'Alī b. Muḥammad, on the authority of Sahl b. Ziyād, on the authority of Dāwud b. al-Qāsim al- Ja'fari, who said:][15]
I (i.e. Dāwud b. al-Qāsim al-Ja'fari) visited Abū Ja'far (al-Jawād), peace be on him. I had with me three pieces of parchment without names on them and I was doubtful about (whose they were) and as a result I was grieved. He took one of them and said: "This is the parchment of Rayyān b. Shābib." Then he took the second of them and said: "This is the parchment of so-and-so."
"Yes," I replied.

I looked at him in surprise. He smiled and took the third. He said: "This is the parchment of so-and-so."
"Yes, may I be your ransom," I replied.

He gave me three hundred dīnārs and told me to take them to one of his uncles. He said: "He will say to you: Show me an artisan who will sell me furniture. Show him one."

I took the dīnārs to him and he said to me: "Abū Hāshim, show me an artisan who will sell me furniture."

14 *Al-Kāfī*, I, 494. tradition no. 4. Al-Kulaynī's version is slightly longer and the eye-witness 'Alī b. Asbāṭ is missing from al-Mufīd's version.
15 *Al-Kāfī*, I, 495, tradition no. 5.

"Yes," I said.

[Abū Hāshim reported:]
A camel-driver spoke to me on the road and asked me to discuss with (al-Jawād) the introduction of one of his companions into his affairs. I visited (al-Jawād) to speak with him and I found him eating. With him was a group of people so that I could not speak with him.

He said to me: "Eat, Abū Hāshim."
He put in front of me the food from which he had eaten and then said to me: "Begin without questioning. Servant, see to the camel-driver whom Abū Hāshim has brought to us and join him to your group."

[Abū Hāshim reported:]
One day I went into an orchard with (al-Jawād). I said to him: "May I be your ransom, I have a desire to eat clay. Pray to Allāh for me."
He was silent. Some days later he said to me: "As from now, Abu Hāshim, Allāh has taken away (your desire) to eat clay from you."

[Abū Hashim reported:]
Today nothing is more hateful to me than it.

*****

Reports conveying these ideas are numerous. What we have given is sufficient for our purpose, if Allāh wills.

The Death of Abū Ja'far (al-Jawād), Peace be on him, its Cause, the Place of his Grave and the Account of his Children

He died in Baghdād. The reason for that was that al-Mu'ṭasim made him leave Medina. So he came to Baghdād, two days before the end of the month of al-Muḥarram in the year 220 A.H. (835). He died there in the month of Dhū al-Qa'da in the same year. It was said that he died as a result of poisoning but in my view no report has established that, and I bear witness to that. He was buried in the cemetery of Quraysh behind his grandfather, Abū al-Ḥasan Mūsā b. Ja'far, peace be on them. He died at the age of twenty-five and some months. He was described as "the chosen one" and "the one who has given pleasure (to Allāh)"

He left among his children 'Alī, his son, the Imam after him, and Mūsā, and his two daughters Fāṭima and Imāma. There were no other male children except those we have mentioned.

CHAPTER IX

IMĀM 'ALĪ B. MUḤAMMAD AL-HĀDĪ

(This is) an account of the Imam after Abū Ja'far Muḥammad b. 'Alī, peace be on him, (describing) the date of his birth, the evidence of his Imamate, and (giving) a survey of the reports about him, the period of his Imamate and the age he reached. (It also) records his death, the reason for it, the place of his grave, the number of his children and a selection of reports about him.

The Imam after Abū Ja'far, peace be on him, was his son, Abū al- Ḥasan 'Alī b. Muḥammad, peace be on them, by virtue of the qualities of the Imamate, which were united in him, and the complete nature of his outstanding merit (*faḍl*). The fact is that no one could succeed to the position of his father except him because of the corroboration of his father's nomination of him to the Imamate and the (clear) indication of his father of his succession. He was born at Ṣurya in Medina, the city of the Apostle, in the middle of the month of Dhū al-Ḥijja in the year 212 A.H. (828). He died at Sāmarrā' in the month of Rajab in the year 254 A.H. (868). At that time he was forty-one years and some months. Al-Mutawakkil had made him come from Medina to Sāmarrā' with Yaḥyā b. Harthama b. A'yan, where he resided until he died. The period of his Imamate was thirty-three years. His mother was a slave-wife called Sumāna.

An Extract from the Reports of his Nomination for the Imamate and of his being Indicated for Succession

[Abū al-Qāsim Ja'far b. Muḥammad informed me on the authority of Muḥammad b. Ya'qūb, on the authority of 'Alī b. Ibrāhīm, on the authority of his father, on the authority of Ismā'īl b. Mihrān, who said:][1]
When Abū Ja'far (al-Jawād) left Medina for Baghdād on the first of the two occasions in which he did so, I (i.e. Ismā'īl b. Mihrān) said to him at his departure: "May I be your ransom, I am afraid for you with regard to this situation. To whom does the affair (of the Imamate) belong after you?"
He turned his face towards me, laughing, and said to me: "It is not as you think this year."

When he was summoned to al-Mu'taṣim, I went to him and said: "May I be your ransom, you are outside (our normal reach). To whom does this affair belong after you?"

1 *Al-Kāfī*, I, 232, tradition no. 1.

He wept until his beard became damp. Then he turned to me and said: "On this occasion when there is fear for me, (it should be known that) the affair (of the Imamate) after me belongs to my son, 'Alī."

[Abū al-Qāsim Ja'far b. Muḥammad informed me on the authority of Muḥammad b. Ya'qūb, on the authority of al-Ḥusayn b. Muḥammad, on the authority of al-Khayrānī, on the authority of his father:][2]
I (i.e. al- Khayrānī's father) was close to the door of Abū Ja'far, peace be on him, to be of service in whatever I was entrusted. Aḥmad b. Muḥammad b. 'Īsā al-Ash'arī used to come at daybreak at the end of each night to learn about the news of the illness of Abū Ja'far, peace be on him. There was a messenger who used to go between Abū Ja'far and (me) al-Khayrānī (that is, the reporter of the tradition at the door). When he came Aḥmad would rise and the messenger would speak privately with (me).

[Al- Khayrānī reported:]
One night, (the messenger) came out. Aḥmad b. Muḥammad b. 'Īsā rose from his seat. The messenger spoke privately to me and Aḥmad wandered around. He stopped when he could hear the conversation. The messenger said: "Your master (*mawlā*) sends you his greetings and tells you: 'I am dying and the affair (of the Imamate) will go to my son, 'Alī. You should treat him after me in the same way as you treated me after my father.'"

Then the messenger departed and Aḥmad returned to his place.
"What did he say to you?" he asked.
"It's all right," I answered.
"I heard what he said", he asserted and repeated what he had heard.
"Allāh has forbidden what you have done," I told him, "because Allāh says: *Do not spy* (XLIX 12). Since you have heard, remember the testimony. Perhaps we will need it one day but beware of revealing it until the (appropriate) time for it."

When morning came, I wrote the text of the message in ten letters. I sealed them and gave them to ten of our leading colleagues. I said: "If death comes upon me before I ask you for them, open them and acquaint yourselves with what is in them."

When Abū Ja'far (al-Jawād), peace be on him, died, I did not leave my house until I knew that the leaders of the group had gathered at Muḥammad b. al-Faraj's (house) to discuss the affair (of the Imamate). Muḥammad b. al-Faraj had written to me to inform me of their meeting with him, saying: "If it was not for

2 *Al-Kāfī*, I, 324, tradition no. 2.

the fear of publicity, I would come to you with them. It would be better for you to ride out (to us)."

I rode out and went to him. I found the people gathered with him. We went through the door. I found that most of them were in a state of perplexity.
"Who of you have the letters?" I asked. "Those who are present, take out those letters."

They took them out.
"This is what you have been ordered (to do)." I told them.

Some of them said: "We would prefer that someone else had been with you in this matter to confirm these words."

"Allāh will give you what you want," I told them. "Here is Abū Ja'far al-Ash'arī (i.e. Aḥmad b. Muḥammad b. 'Īsā) who will testify to my hearing this message. Question him."

The people questioned him and he held back from giving his testimony. I called upon him to take an oath (of destruction, *mubāhila*). He was frightened of that and then admitted: "I heard that. (Such a communication) is a great honour for a man, which I would have preferred to have gone to an Arab. But as a result of the challenge to an oath (of destruction), there is no way of concealing testimony."

It was not long then before the people submitted to Abū al-Ḥasan ('Alī al-Hādī), peace he on him.

*****

Reports of this kind are so very numerous that our task in presenting them would make the book unduly long. As a result of the agreement of the group (*'isāba'*) on the Imamate of Abū al-Ḥasan ('Alī al-Hādī), and of the absence of any who claimed it other than him at his time so that there might have been some doubt in the matter, there is no need to present the reports of the nominations of his being preferred.

A Survey of the Evidence for Abū al-Ḥasan 'Alī b. Muḥammad (al-Hādī), Peace be on him, Reports about him, his Proof and his Explanations

[Abū al-Qāsim Ja'far b. Muḥammad informed me on the authority of Muḥammad b. Ya'qūb, on the, authority of al-Ḥusayn b. Muḥammad, on the authority of

Mu'alla b. Muḥammad, on the authority of al-Washshā', on the authority of Khayrān al-Asbāṭī, who said:][3]
I (i.e. Khayrān al-Asbāṭī) went to Abū al-Ḥasan 'Alī b. Muḥammad (al-Hādī), peace be on them, at Medina. He asked me: "What is the news of al-Wāthiq?"
"May I be your ransom," I replied, "I left him in good health, but while I am one of the closest people in contact with him, my (last) contact with him was ten days ago."
"The Medinans say that he has died," he told me.

When he told me that "the people" were saying (that), I knew that he meant himself. Then he asked me: "What has Ja'far (i .e. al-Mutawakkil) been doing?"
"I left him in the wretchedest of predicaments in prison," I said.
"He is now in control of affairs," he told me.

"What has Ibn Zayyāt been doing?" he asked me.
"The people are with him and the authority is his authority," I answered.
"Now it is unlucky for him," he said. Then he fell silent. He said to me: "There is no escape from the decrees and ordinances of Allāh, Khayrān. Al-Wāthiq has died. Ja'far al-Mutawakkil sits (on the throne) and Ibn al-Zayyāt has been killed."

"When, may I be your ransom?" I asked.
"Six days after your departure," he said.

[Abū al-Qāsim Ja'far b. Muḥammad informed me on the authority of Muḥammad b. Ya'qūb, on the, authority of 'Alī b. Muḥammad, on the authority of Ibrāhīm b. Muḥammad al-Ṭāhirī, who said:][4]
Al-Mutawakkil became ill with boils which appeared on him. He was on the point of death. No one dared to touch him with a knife (to cut them away). His mother vowed that if he was preserved she would give a great deal of wealth from her fortune to Abū al-Ḥasan 'Alī b. Muḥammad (al-Hādī), peace be on them. Al-Fatḥ b. Khāqān said to him: "If you sent to this man - meaning Abū al-Ḥasan ('Alī b. Muḥammad al-Hādī), peace be on him - and ask him, perhaps he will have the description of something by which Allāh will bring ease to you."
"Send to him," he ordered.

The messenger departed. He returned and said: "Take the dregs of the fat from a sheep. Mix it with rose-water and put it on the boils. It will be beneficial, if Allāh permits."

---

3 *Al-Kāfī*, I, 497. tradition no. 1.

4 *Al-Kāfī*, I, 499-500. tradition no. 4. The names in the *isnād* have been corrected according to al-Kulaynī and what comes later in the account.

Those who were present with al-Mutawakkil began to scoff at his words. Al-Fatḥ said to them: "There will be no harm in trying out what he said. By Allāh, I hope there is advantage in it."

The fat was brought, mixed with rose-water and put on the boils. They opened out. Out came what had been in them. The mother of al-Mutawakkil was overjoyed at the news of his health. She sent ten thousand dīnārs under her seal to Abū al-Ḥasan ('Alī b. Muḥammad al-Hādī). Al-Mutawakkil was now cured of his illness. Some days later al-Baṭḥa'ī went to al-Mutawakkil to report lies about Abū al-Ḥasan ('Alī b. Muḥammad al-Hādī). He said. "He has money and weapons."

Al-Mutawakkil sent Sa'īd, the chamberlain, to go unexpectedly to him at night and seize what money and weapons he could find with him and bring (them) to him.

[Ibrāhīm b. Muḥammad reported: Sa'īd, the chamberlain, said to me (i.e. Ibrāhīm b. Muḥammad):]
I (Sa'īd, the chamberlain) went to the house of Abū al-Ḥasan (al- Hādī) at night. I had a ladder with me. I climbed up it on to the roof. I went down some stairs in the darkness. I did not know where I was in the house. Then Abū al-Ḥasan (al- Hādī) called to me from the house: "Sa'īd, (stay) where you are until a candle is brought to you." Soon a candle was brought and I went down, I found him wearing a woollen cloak and a hat of wool. His prayer mat was on the floor in front of him. He was facing the *qibla* (i.e. the direction of Mecca). He said to me: "In front of you are the rooms."

I went into them and searched them but I did not find anything in them. However, I did find a purse of ten thousand dirhams sealed with the seal of the mother of al-Mutawakkil and a bag sealed with her (seal). Then Abū al-Ḥasan (al-Hādī) said: "In front of you is the prayer mat."

I lifted it up and found a sword in a cloth sheath. I took that and went to (al-Mutawakkil). When he saw the seal of his mother on the purse of ten thousand dīnārs, he sent for her. She came to him and he asked her about the purse of ten thousand dīnārs. One of the servants of the courtiers informed me that she said: "When you were ill, I vowed that if you recovered, I would send him ten thousand dīnārs from my wealth and I sent them to him. This is my seal on the bag. He has not disturbed it nor opened the other bag."

There were four hundred dīnārs in the (other) bag. (al-Mutawakkil) ordered anotther purse of ten thousand dīnārs to be added to the (existing) purse and told me: "Carry that to Abū al-Ḥasan (al-Hādī), peace be on him, and take back to him the sword and the bag with its contents."

I carried them to him. I felt ashamed in front of him and I said to him: "Master, it grieves me to have entered your house without your permission but I was ordered (to do it)."

He said to me. "*Those who do wrong will be aware of it. By what kind of change shall they be changed* (XXVI 227)."

[Abū al-Qāsim Ja'far b. Muḥammad informed me on the authority of Muḥammad b. Ya'qūb, on the authority of al-Ḥusayn b. Muḥammad, on the authority of al-Mu'allā b. Muḥammad, on the authority of Aḥmad b. Muḥammad b. 'Abd Allāh, on the authority of 'Alī b. Muḥammad al-Nawfalī, who said: Muḥammad b. al-Faraj al-Rukhkhajī told me:][5]
Abū al-Ḥasan (al-Hādī), peace be on him, wrote to him (i.e. Muḥammad b. al-Faraj al-Rukhkhajī): "Muḥammad, get your affairs in order and take precautions for yourself."

[Muḥammad b. al-Faraj reported:]
My affairs were in order and I did not know what he meant by what he had written to me until a messenger came for me and took me from Egypt chained in iron and seized everything I possessed. I remained in prison for eight years. Then (another) letter came to me from him while I was in prison: "Muḥammad b. al-Faraj, do not go in the area of the western part of Sāmarrā'."
I read the letter and said to myself: "Abū al-Ḥasan (al- Hādī), peace be on him, writes this to me while I am in prison. This is indeed strange."

It was only a few days later that I was set free, my bonds were undone and I was released. After my release, I wrote some requests to him to ask Allāh to restore my estate to me. He wrote to me: "Your estates will be restored to you but it would not harm you if your estates were not restored to you ."

['Alī b. Muḥammad al-Nawfalī reported:]
When Muḥammad b. al-Faraj al-Rukhkhajī went to al-'Askar (Sāmarrā'), (al-Hādī) wrote to him about the restoration of his estates to him. However, the letter did not arrive before he died.

['Alī b. Muḥammad al-Nawfalī reported:]

5 *Al-Kāfī*, I, 500, tradition no. 5.

Aḥmad b. al-Khaḍīb wrote to Muḥammad b. al-Faraj to go al-'Askar (Sāmarrā'). He wrote to Abū al-Ḥasan (al-Hādī), peace be on him, to ask his advice. Abū al-Ḥasan (al-Hādī), peace be on him, wrote to him: "Go there, for there you will find relief."
It was not long after that he died.

[Aḥmad b. (Muḥammad) b. 'Īsā reported: Abū Ya'qūb said:]
I (i.e. Abū Ya'qūb) saw Muḥammad b. al-Faraj one evening before his death at al-'Askar (Sāmarrā'). He went into the presence of Abū al-Ḥasan (al-Hādī), peace be on him. The latter looked at him with an efficacious look. On the following day Muḥammad b. al-Faraj fell sick. I went to pay a sick visit to him some days after his illness. He told me that Abū al-Ḥasan (al-Hādī), peace be on him, had sent him a cloak and he showed it to me wrapped under his head.

[Abū Ya'qūb added:]
By Allāh, he was shrouded in it.

[Aḥmad b. Muḥammad b. 'Īsā mentioned: Abū Ya'qūb told me:][6]
I (i.e. Abū Ya'qūb) saw Abū al-Ḥasan (al-Hādī), peace be on him, with Aḥmad b. al-Khaḍīb. They were both travelling together but Abū al-Ḥasan (al-Hādī), peace be on him, was not keeping up with him.
"May I be your ransom, hurry," Ibn al-Khaḍīb said to him.
"You will be the first," Abū al-Ḥasan (al-Hādī), replied to him.

It was only four days later that the stocks were put on the legs of Ibn al-Khaḍīb and he was killed.

Ibn al-Khaḍīb had harassed him with requests for the house in which he had settled. He asked him to move from it and give it to him. Abū al-Ḥasan (al-Hādī), peace be on him, sent to him: "Let me keep a place for you with Allāh, for you will not remain long with it."

Allāh took him during those days.

[Al-Ḥusayn b. al-Ḥasan al-Ḥasanī reported: Abū al-Ṭayyib Ya'qūb b. Yāsir told me:][7]
Al-Mutawakkil used to say: "Shame on you, the affair of the son of al-Riḍā (i.e. al-Hādī) baffled me. I used to try to make him drink with me and be my intimate friend but he refused. I tried to find an opportunity in this respect but I did not find one."

6 *Al-Kāfī*, 500-1, tradition no. 6. Al-Kulaynī's *isnād* has been shortened.
7 *Al-Kāfī*, I, 502, tradition no. 8.

One of those with him said to him: "If you did not find in the son of al-Riḍā the attitude you wanted, there is his brother, Mūsā, who is a reveller and a musician; he eats and drinks, he loves and divorces. Bring him and make him well-known. The reports will start to spread about that with regard to the son of al-Riḍā and the people will not be able to distinguish between him and his brother. Those who come to know (Mūsā) will accuse his brother of the same actions."
"Write to bring him in honour," he ordered.

He was brought in (great) honour and al-Mutawakkil sent forward all the Banū Hāshim and the military leaders to meet him. The people travelled alongside. He ordered that when he arrived there an estate should be given to him and (a house) built for him on it. Wine-merchants and dancers should be sent to it. He presented (him) with gifts and gave him (great) honours. He set apart a luxurious house for him, which was suitable for him to visit in.

When he had bestowed (all this generosity) on Mūsā, Abū al-Ḥasan (al-Hādī), peace be on him, met (Mūsā) at the bridge of Waṣīf - it is a place where people used to meet before. He greeted him and paid him his due. Then he said: "This man has brought you to disgrace you and lessen your (dignity). Do not admit to him that you have ever drunk wine. Fear Allāh, my brother, lest you commit that which is forbidden."

"He only invited me for this and there is no trick against me," Mūsā replied,
"Do not diminish your rank and be disobedient to your Lord," he told him. "Do not do what will mar you. His only purpose is to destroy you."

Mūsā refused (to listen to) him. Abū al-Ḥasan (al-Hādī) repeated his words and warning while the other persisted in his opposition. When he saw that he would not agree, he said: "As for the assembly which you want to meet him in, you and he will never meet."

For three years Mūsā continued to go early every day to the door of al-Mutawakkil and he would be told that he was busy that day. He would go in the evening and he would be told that he was drunk. He would go early in the morning and he would be told that he had taken medicine. This continued for three years until al-Mutawakkil was killed and he never met him to drink with him.

[Muḥammad b. 'Alī reported: Zayd b. 'Alī b. al-Ḥusayn b. Zayd informed me:][8] I (i.e. Zayd) was sick and the doctor visited me one night. He prescribed a

8 *Al-Kāfī*, I, 502, tradition no. 9.

medicine for me and that I should take it before dawn at such and such a time each day. It was not possible for me to obtain it at night. The doctor left through the door and in came a follower of Abū al-Ḥasan (al-Hādī), peace be on him, at the very same time. With him was a bag in which was that exact medicine. He said to me: "Abū al-Ḥasan sends you greetings and says to you: Take this medicine at such and such a time each day."

I took it and drank it and I recovered.

[Muḥammad b. 'Alī added:]
Zayd b. 'Alī said to me; "Muḥammad, where are the extremists (*ghulāt*) as a result of this account?"

The Account of the Coming of Abū al-Ḥasan (al- Hādī), Peace be on him, from Medina to al-'Askar, His Death there and the Cause of it, the Number of his Children and a Survey of the Reports about him.

The reason for Abū al-Ḥasan (al-Hādī), peace be upon him, leaving Medina for Sāmarrā' was that 'Abd Allāh b. Muḥammad was put in charge of war and prayer in Medina, the city of the Apostle, may Allāh bless Him and His Family. He told lies to Al-Mutawakkil with the intention of harming him. Abū al-Ḥasan (al- Hādī), peace be upon him, learnt of his lying and wrote to al-Mutawakkil, mentioning 'Abd Allāh b. Muḥammad's unfair treatment of him and the lies with which he had slandered him. Al-Mutawakkil sent his answer to his letter, in which he summoned him to come to al-'Askar (Sāmarrā') as an act of courtesy both in word and deed. The text of the letter has been preserved;[9] it is:

> "In the name of Allāh, the Merciful, The Compassionate. . . The Commander of the faithful, being aware of your rank, caring for your close relationship (with him), judging matters which are appropriate for the circumstances of you and your House, confirms your dignity and their dignity, gives security to you and them, requiring by that the consent of his Lord and the performance of what is stipulated with regard to you and them. The Commander of the faithful has seen it as appropriate to dismiss 'Abd Allāh b. Muḥammad from his appointment over war and prayer in Medina, the city of the Apostle, may Allāh bless Him and His Family, because he was ignorant of your rights, as you have mentioned, and took no account of your rank when he suspected you and attributed to you a matter in which the Commander of the faithful knew of your innocence, and of the truthfulness of your intentions through your piety and your words. You have not rendered yourself worthy when you suspected his

9 *Al-Kāfī*, I, 501, tradition no. 7.

(i.e, the Commander of the faithful's) request (to come to Sāmarrā'). The Commander of the faithful has appointed Muḥammad b. al-Faḍl over what (the other man) used to administer. He has ordered him to honour and respect you, to carry out your orders and views and by that to be close to Allāh and to the Commander of the faithful. However the Commander of the faithful is anxious to be close to you and to see you. If you would come to visit him and reside with him as long as you want, then come, you and those whom you choose of your House, your retainers and your coterie, at your leisure and ease. You would travel when you wanted, stop when you wanted and go how you wanted. If you liked Yaḥyā b. Harthama, the retainer of the Commander of the faithful, and the soldiers with him would travel with you and make the journey (with you). The decision about that is up to you. Ask Allāh for a decision so that you may come to the Commander of the faithful. None of his brothers, his children, his family and his courtiers are as sympathetic to you as he is. No one is more praiseworthy in their treatment of you than him. No one among them is kinder to you, nor are any of them more respectful to you, nor more compassionate to you than he will be to you. Greetings and the mercy and blessings of Allāh be on you."

Ibrāhīm ibn al-'Abbās wrote (this letter) in the month of Jumādā al-Ākhira in the year 243 A.H. (857). When the letter reached Abū al-Ḥasan (al-Hādī), peace be upon him, he made preparations for the journey. Yaḥyā ibn Harthama accompanied him until he reached Sāmarrā'. When he arrived there, al-Mutawakkil provided him with what was necessary at that time. He stayed in an inn called the Inn of al-Sa'ālīk. He resided there for a day. Then al-Mutawakkil gave him a house for himself and he moved there.

[Abū al-Qāsim Ja'far b. Muḥammad informed me on the authority of Muḥammad b. Ya'qūb, on the authority of al-Ḥusayn b. Muḥammad, on the authority of Mu'āllā b. Muḥammad, on the authority of Aḥmad b. Muḥammad b. 'Abd Allāh on the authority of Muḥammad b. Yaḥyā on the authority of Ṣāliḥ b. Sa'īd, who said:][10]

"I (i.e. Ṣāliḥ b. Sa'īd) visited Abū al-Ḥasan (al-Hādī), peace be upon him, on the day of his coming to Sāmarrā'. I said to him: "May I be your ransom, in every matter they are only concerned to extinguish your light and to diminish you so that they have put you to stay in this hideous inn - the Inn of al-Sa'ālīk."

"Here you are Ibn Sa'īd," he said, and indicated with his hand. Suddenly I was amid pleasant gardens and flowing rivers and gardens in which were perfumed plants and beautiful maidens like veiled pearls. My sight became confused and

10 *Al-Kāfī*, I, 498, tradition no. 2

my amazement was great. He said to me: "This is where we are. This belongs to us, Ibn Sa'īd. We are not in the Inn of al-Sa'ālīk."

*****

Abū al-Ḥasan (al- Hādī), peace be upon him, resided for a time at his residence in Sāmarrā' publicly honoured. Yet al-Mutawakkil endeavored to make him fall into a trap but he was not able to do that. The reports of him with (al-Mutawakkil) in which there are signs and indications of his (Imamate) are so numerous that it would make the book too long to mention them. If we attempted to present them, we would have to abandon the purpose we set for ourselves.

Abū al-Ḥasan (al-Hādī), peace be upon him, died in Rajab in the year 254 A.H. (868) in his house in Sāmarrā'. Among the children he left behind is Abū Muḥammad al-Ḥassan, his son who was the Imam after him, al-Ḥussein, Muḥammad, Ja'far and his daughter, 'Ā'isha. He resided in Sāmarrā' for ten years and some months until his death. He died at the age of forty-one as we have mentioned before.

CHAPTER X

IMAM AL-ḤASAN B. ʿALĪ AL-ʿASKARĪ

(In this chapter there will be) an account of the Imam undertaking the office (*al-qā'im*) after Abū al-Ḥasan ʿAlī b. Muḥammad (al-Hādī), peace be on them. (It will give) the date of his birth, the evidence for his Imamate and his nomination by his father, his age, and the period of his succession. (It will) mention his death, the place of his grave and a survey of reports about him.

The Imam after Abū al-Ḥasan ʿAlī b. Muḥammad (al-Hādī), peace be on them, was his son Abū Muḥammad al-Ḥasan b. ʿAlī (al-ʿAskarī) by virtue of the occurrence in him of the qualities of outstanding merit, and by his precedence over the rest of the people of his time in terms of knowledge, asceticism, perfection of reason, infallibility (*ʿisma*), bravery, nobility and the great number of his works which brought him close to Allāh, may His name be extolled, all of which required his Imamate and necessitated his leadership. In addition (he was the Imam) because of the nomination of him by his father and the latter's indication of him for the succession.

He was born in Medina in the month of Rabīʿ al-Ākhir in the year 232 A.H. (846). He, peace be on him, died on Friday 8th of the month of Rabīʿ al-Awwal in the year 260 A.H. (873). At that time he was twenty-eight years of age. He was buried in his house at Sāmarrā'. (It was) the house in which his father, peace be on him, was buried. His mother was a slave-wife called Ḥadīth. The period of his succession (to the Imamate) was six years.

A Survey of the Reports put forward concerning his Nomination by his Father, Peace be on them, and the Indication of him for the Imamate after him

[Abū al-Qāsim Jaʿfar b. Muḥammad informed me on the authority of Muḥammad b. Yaʿqūb, on the authority of ʿAlī b. Muḥammad, on the authority of Muḥammad b. Aḥmad al-Nahdī, on the authority of Yaḥyā b. Yasār al-ʿAnbarī, who said:][1] Abū al-Ḥasan ʿAlī b. Muḥammad (al-Hādī), peace be on him, made his testamentary bequest to his son four months before his death. He indicated that the affair (of the Imamate) would belong to him after himself. He made me (i.e. Yaḥyā b. Yasār al-ʿAnbarī) and a group of servants (*mawālī*) witness that.

1 *Al-Kāfī*, I, 325, tradition no. 1.

[Abū al-Qāsim Ja'far b. Muḥammad informed me on the authority of Muḥammad b. Ya'qūb, on the authority of 'Alī b. Muḥammad, on the authority of Ja'far b. Muḥammad al-Kūfī, on the authority of Bashshār b. Aḥmad al-Baṣrī, on the authority of 'Alī b. 'Umar al-Nawfālī, who said:][2]
I (i.e. 'Alī b. 'Umar al-Nawfālī) was with Abū al-Ḥasan (al-Hādī), peace be on him, in the courtyard of his house. Muḥammad, his son, passed us and I said to (al-Hādī): "May I be your ransom, is this our leader after you?"
"No," he replied, "your leader after me is al-Ḥasan."

[With the same chain of authorities (*isnād*), on the authority of Bashshār b. Aḥmad, on the authority of 'Abd Allāh b. Muḥammad al-Iṣfahānī, who said:][3]
Abū al-Ḥasan (al-Hādī), peace be on him, said to me (i.e. 'Abd Allāh b. Muḥammad al-Iṣfahānī): "Your leader after me is the one who will say the prayer over me (at my funeral)."

We did not know that it would be Abū Muḥammad (al-'Askarī) before that. But after his death Abū Muḥammad (al-'Askarī) came out and said the prayer over him.

[With the same chain of authorities (*isnād*), on the authority of Bashshār b. Aḥmad, on the authority of Mūsā b. Ja'far b. Wahb, on the authority of 'Alī b. Ja'far, who said:][4]
I used to attend Abū al-Ḥasan (al-Hādī), peace be on him. When his son, Muḥammad, died, he said to al-Ḥasan (al-'Askarī): "My son, give thanks to Allāh, for Allāh has made an (important) matter (rest) in you."

[Abū al-Qāsim Ja'far b. Muḥammad informed me on the authority of Muḥammad b. Ya'qūb, on the authority of al-Ḥusayn b. Muḥammad, on the authority of Mu'allā b. Muḥammad, on the authority of Aḥmad b. Muḥammad b. 'Abd Allāh b. Marwān al-Anbarī. who said:][5]
I (i.e. 'Abd Allāh b. Marwān al-Anbarī) was present at the death of Abū Ja'far Muḥammad b. 'Alī. Abū al-Ḥasan (al-Hādī) came. A chair was put for him and he sat on it. The members of his House were around him. Abū Muḥammad (al-'Askarī), his son, peace be on him, was standing at the side. When the affairs (concerned with the death) of Abū Ja'far were finished. he turned to Abū Muḥammad (al-'Askarī), peace be on him and said: "My son, give thanks to Allāh, the Exalted, for He had made an (important) matter (rest) in you."

---

2 *Al-Kāfī*, I, 325-6, tradition no. 2 Al-Mufīd's *isnād* has been corrected.
3 *Al-Kāfī*, I, 326, tradition no. 3.
4 *Al-Kāfī*, I, 326. tradition no. 4.
5 *Al-Kāfī*, I, 326, tradition no. 5.

[Abū al-Qāsim Ja'far b. Muḥammad informed me on the authority of Muḥammad b. Ya'qūb, on the authority of 'Alī b. Muḥammad, on the authority of Muḥammad b. Aḥmad al-Qalānisī, on the authority of 'Alī b. al-Ḥusayn b. 'Amr, on the authority of 'Alī b. Mahziyār, who said:][6]
I (i.e. 'Alī b. Mahziyār) said to Abū al-Ḥasan (al-Hādī), peace be on him: "If an event takes place and I seek refuge in Allāh (from that), to whom (does the Imamate belong)?"

"My nomination (*'ahd*) is to the eldest of my (surviving) sons," he said, meanmg al-Ḥasan, peace be on him.

[Abū al-Qāsim Ja'far b. Muḥammad informed me on the authority of Muḥammad b. Ya'qūb, on the authority of 'Alī b. Muḥammad, on the authority of Abū Muḥammad al-Astarābādī, on the authority of 'Alī b. 'Amr al-'Aṭṭār, who said:][7]
I visited Abū al-Ḥasan (al-Hādī), peace be on him, while his son Abū Ja'far (Muḥammad) was still alive. I thought that he was the successor after him. I said to him: "May I be your ransom, who is the specified one among your sons?" "Do not specify anyone until my command comes to you," he said.

I wrote to him later about who would have the affair (of the Imamate). He wrote to me: "(It belongs) to the eldest of my (surviving) sons."

[Abū al-Qāsim Ja'far b. Muḥammad informed me on the authority of Muḥammad b. Ya'qūb, on the authority of Muḥammad b. Yaḥyā and another, on the authority of Sa'd b. 'Abd Allāh, on the authority of a group of the Banū Hāshim, among whom was al-Ḥasan b. al-Ḥusayn al-Afṭas:][8]
They (i.e. the group of Banū Hāshim) were present on the day in which Muḥammad b. 'Alī b. Muḥammad died, in the courtyard of the house of Abū al-Hasan (al-Hādī), peace be on him, and the people were sitting around him.

[They said:]
We estimated that there were a hundred and fifty men from the family of Abū Ṭālib, the Banū 'Abbās and Quraysh, excluding his retainers and the rest of the people. Then al-Ḥasan b. 'Alī (al-'Askarī), peace be on them, looked at (us). He had come wearing a coat rent (with grief). He stood at his right and we did not recognise him. Abū al-Ḥasan (al-Hādī), peace be on him, looked at him after he had been standing for an hour and said to him: "My son, give thanks to Allāh, for he has made an (important) matter (rest) in you."

6 *Al-Kāfī*, I, 326, tradition no. 6.
7 *Al-Kāfī*, I, 326, tradition no. 7.
8 *Al-Kāfī*, I, 326-7. tradition no. 8.

Al-Ḥasan (al-'Askarī) wept and repeated the formula - We belong to Allāh and to Him we return. Then he said: "Praise be to Allāh, Lord of the worlds. To Him do I request the perfection of His bounty upon us. We belong to Allāh and to Him we return."
We asked about him and we were told: "That is al-Ḥasan b. 'Alī, his son."

We reckoned him to be twenty years of age or the like at that time. On that day we knew him and we understood that (al-Hādī) had indicated him for the Imamate and to take his place.

[Abū al-Qāsim Ja'far b. Muḥammad informed me on the authority of Muḥammad b. Ya'qūb, on the authority of 'Alī b. Muḥammad, on the authority of Isḥāq b. Muḥammad, on the authority of Muḥammad b. Yaḥyā, who said:][9]
I visited Abū al-Ḥasan (al-Hādī), peace be on him, after the death of his son, Abū Ja'far, and paid my condolences to him. Abu Muḥammad (al-'Askarī), peace be on him, was sitting (with him). Abū Muḥammad wept and Abū al-Ḥasan (al-Hādī), peace be on them, approached him and said: "Allāh has made succession (rest) with you from Him. Therefore praise Allāh."

[Abū al-Qāsim (Ja'far b. Muḥammad) informed me on the authority of Muḥammad b. Ya'qūb, on the authority of 'Alī b. Muḥammad, on the authority of Isḥāq b. Muḥammad, on the authority of Abū Hāshim al-Ja'farī, who said:][10]
I (i.e. Abū Hāshim al-Ja'farī) was with Abū al-Ḥasan (al-Hādī), peace be on him, after the death of his son, Abū Ja'far (Muḥammad). I was thinking to myself that I wanted to say that they were both - I mean Abū Ja'far (Muḥammad) and Abū Muḥammad (al-'Askarī), peace be on him - like Abū al-Ḥasan Mūsā, peace be on him, and Ismā'īl, the two sons of Ja'far b. Muḥammad (al-Ṣadiq), peace be on them. Indeed the former two's story was like the latter two's story. Abū al-Ḥasan (al-Hādī) approached me before I could speak and said: "Yes, Abū Hāshim, Allāh has revealed (His will) concerning Abu Muḥammad (al-'Askarī) after Abū Ja'far (Muḥammad) (has suffered) what no one could have known, just as He revealed (His will) concerning Mūsā after the death of Ismā'īl revealed his state. It is just like you were saying to yourself. Even though the falsifiers may dislike it, my son Abū Muḥammad (al-'Askarī) is the successor after me. He has the knowledge which is needed. He has the equipment of the Imamate."

[With the same chain of authorities (*isnād*) on the authority of Isḥāq b. Muḥammad, on the authority of Muḥammad b. Yaḥyā b. Darriyyāt, on the authority of Abū Bakr al-Fahfakī, who said:][11]

9 *Al-Kāfī*, I, 327, tradition no. 9.
10 *Al-Kāfī*, I, 327, tradition no. 10.
11 *Al-Kāfī*, I, 327-8 tradition no.11. Al-Mufīd's *isnād* has been corrected.

Abū al-Ḥasan (al-Hādī), peace be on him, wrote to me (i.e. Abū Bakr al-Fahfakī): "Abū Muḥammad, my son, is the soundest of the family of Muḥammad in excellence and the firmest of them as a proof. He is the eldest of my (surviving) sons. To him is the Imamate directed and our laws. Whatever you used to ask me about, ask him. He has (everything) which is needed."

[With the same chain of authorities (*isnād*) on the authority of Isḥāq b. Muḥammad, on the authority of Shāhawayh b. 'Abd Allāh, who sald:][12]
Abū al-Ḥasan (al-Hādī), peace be on him, wrote to me (i.e. Shāhawayh b. 'Abd Allāh) in a letter (in reply to a letter where) I wanted to ask about the successor after (the death of) Abū Ja'far (Muḥammad), peace be on him, and I had become anxious because of that. (He wrote:) "Do not be anxious. Allāh does not lead people astray after He has guided them until He has made clear to them what they should fear. Your leader after me is Abū Muḥammad (al-'Askarī), my son. He has (everything) which they need. Allāh brings forward whatever He wishes and delays whatever He wishes. *We do not cause a verse to be abrogated or forgotten without providing a better one or the like of it* (II 106). In this is a clear explanation and convincing proof for one who has a watchful mind."

[Abū al-Qāsim (Ja'far b. Muḥammad) informed me on the authority of Muḥammad b. Ya'qūb, on the authority of 'Alī b. Muḥammad, on the authority of a man who mentioned it, on the authority of Muḥammad b. Aḥmad al-'Alawī, on the authority of Dāwud b. al-Qāsim (Abū Hashim) al-Ja'farī, who said:][13]
I (i.e. Dāwud b. al-Qāsim Abū Hashim al-Ja'farī) heard Abū al-Ḥasan (al-Hādī), peace be on him, say: "The successor after me is al-Ḥasan, peace be on him. But how will it be for you with regard to the successor after the successor?"
"May Allāh make me your ransom, why?" I asked.
"You will not see his person," he said, "nor will the mentioning of his name be permitted to you."
"Then how will we refer to him?" I enquired.
"Say 'the proof from the family of Muḥammad'," he told me.

*****

Reports of this kind are so numerous that they would (unduly) lengthen the book.

A Survey of the Reports about Abū Muḥammad (al-'Askanī, Peace be on him, his Virtues, Signs and Miracles.

[Abū al-Qāsim Ja'far b. Muḥammad informed me on the authority of

12 *Al-Kāfī*, I, 328. tradition no. 12
13 *Al-Kāfī*, I, 328, tradition no. 13

Muḥammad b. Ya'qūb, on the authority of al-Ḥusayn b. Muḥammad al-Ash'arī and Muḥammad b. Yaḥyā and others, who said:][14]
Aḥmad b. 'Ubayd Allāh b. al-Khāqān was in charge of estates (*ḍiyā'*) and the land-tax in Qumm. During his assembly one day the 'Alawites (i.e. family of 'Alī) and their beliefs were mentioned. He was violently anti-Shī'a and far away from (favouring) the House, peace be on them. He said: I have not seen or known in Sāmarrā' a man from the 'Alawites like al-Ḥasan b. 'Alī b. Muḥammad b. 'Alī al-Riḍā in his manner, his quietness, his self-restraint, his nobility and his greatness in the eyes of all the House (*ahl al-bayt*) and the Banū Hāshim, so that they gave him precedence over those older than him and those of importance. His situation is the same with the military commanders, the ministers and the common people. I remember that one day I was standing beside my father - and it was the day of his assembly for the people - when his chamberlains came in. They told him that Abū Muḥammad (al-Ḥasan al-'Askarī), the descendant of al-Riḍā was at the door. He said in a loud voice: "Give him permission to enter." I was amazed at what I had heard from them at their daring to give a man his *kunya* (i.e. to call him Abū -) in the presence of my father. For in front of him only a caliph was given his *kunya*, or an heir-apparent or a man whose authority (entitled him) to be given his *kunya*. A brown man entered. He was well-built, handsome, with an excellent physique and young in years. He had dignity and a fine appearance. When my father looked at him, he rose and walked some steps towards him. I have not known him do this to any other member of Banū Hāshim and the military commanders. When he was near him, he embraced him, kissed his face and breast. He took him by his hand and sat him down on his prayer-mat which he had been sitting on. He sat beside him facing him and began to speak to him and to use the honorific expression - may I be your ransom. I was amazed at what I saw. Then the chamberlain entered and said al-Muwaffaq had come. When al-Muwaffaq visited my father, his chamberlains and the special men among his military commanders preceded him and erected between the assembly of my father and the door two curtains until he came and left. My father continued to face Abū Muḥammad (al-'Askarī) until he saw the servants of the court. Then he said to him: "If you please, may I be your ransom." Then he said to his chamberlains: "Take him behind two curtains so that this man does not seem him" - meaning al-Muwaffaq. Then he stood up and my father stood up and embraced him and he went. I said to my father's chamberlains and servants: "Shame on you, who is this man whom you have called by his *kunya* in the presence of my father and with whom my father has behaved in this manner?" They said: "This is an 'Alawite called al-Ḥasan b. 'Alī who is known as Ibn al-Riḍā (ie. a descendant of al-Riḍā)." I grew more astonished. I continued, (in a way) which indicates anxiety, to think about his affair and my

14 *Al-Kāfī*, I, 503-6. tradition no. 1

father's affair and what I had seen until it was night. It was his custom to say the late night prayer and then to sit and consider what plans he needed to make and whom he should raise to (positions of) authority. After he had prayed and sat down, I went and sat before him. No one else was with him and he said to me: "Aḥmad, you want something?"
"Yes, father," I replied, "if you will permit me, I will ask you about it."
"You have my permission," he answered.
"Father, who was the man to whom, this morning, I saw you give (so much) respect, honour and glory - using the phrase - may you ransom him with yourself and your parents?"

"My son, that was the Imam of the Rāfiḍites, al-Ḥasan b. 'Alī who is known as Ibn al- Riḍā," he replied. Then he was silent for a time and I was silent. Then he said: "My son, if the Imamate was to be taken from our caliphs, the Banū 'Abbās, none of the Banū Hāshim would be more entitled to it than him because of his great merit, his self-restraint, his modesty, his asceticism, his devotion (to Allāh), his high morality and his righteousness. If you had seen his father, you would have seen a good, noble, excellent man."

I grew more anxious, thoughtful and distressed at my father and what I had heard from him concerning (that man). I had seen his behaviour towards him. My sole concern after that was to seek out information about him and to study his affair. I did not ask anyone from the Banū Hāshim, the military commanders, the secretaries, the judges, the religious jurists and the rest of the people without finding that he was given by them eminence, greatness, distinguished position, kind words and precedence. (This was) over all his House and scholars. His rank was so magnified to me since I never saw a friend or an enemy of his except that he had good words and praise for him.

One of the Ash'arites who was present at (my father's) assembly asked him: "Have you any information about his brother, Ja'far, and how his position was?"

"Who is Ja'far," he said "that he should be asked about or compared with al-Ḥasan? He is a public sinner, a profligate, a winebibber. He is one of the least worthy men whom I have seen, the most shameful in himself and insignificant in himself."

Yet he came to authority and to have followers at the time of al-Ḥasan b. 'Alī's death. What I found surprising in him and did not think that he would do was this. When (al-Ḥasan) was ill, he sent to my father that Ibn al-Riḍā was ill. He (my father) rode to the Caliph's palace. Then he returned quietly with five close trusted servants of the Commander of the faithful. Among them was Naḥrīr. He ordered them to stay at al-Ḥasan's house and to investigate reports about him and his condition. He sent to a number of medical specialists and ordered them to go to him and to supervise him morning and night. Two or three days later, he was informed that he was weak. He ordered the medical specialists to stay at his house. He sent to the chief *qāḍī* (judge) and made him attend his assembly. He told him to choose ten men who were trustworthy in religion, piety and in loyalty. He sent them to the house of al-Ḥasan, peace be on him, and ordered them to stay with him day and night. They remained there until he died, peace be on him. When the news of his death spread around, Sāmarrā' became one uproar. The markets were empty. Banū Hāshim, the military leaders, the secretaries, the judges, the attestators and the rest of the people (all) rode to his funeral. On that day Sāmarrā seemed like the (day of) Resurrection. When they had finished the preparations for him, the authorities sent to Abū 'Īsā b. al-Mutawakkil and ordered him to say the (funeral) prayer over him. When the bier was put down for the prayer (to be said) over it, Abu 'Īsā came up to it. He uncovered (al-Ḥasan's) face and showed it to the Banū Hāshim, both the 'Alawites and the 'Abbāsids, the military leaders, the secretaries, the judges and the attestators. He said: "This is al-Ḥasan b. 'Alī b, Muḥammad b. al-Riḍā, peace be on them. He has died. He departed from life on his bed. So-and-so and so-and-so attended him from among the servants of the Commander of the faithful, so-and-so and so-and-so from among the judges, and so-and-so and so-and-so from among the medical specialists."

Then he covered (al-Ḥasan's) face and said the prayer over him and ordered him to be taken (to be buried). After he had been buried, Ja'far b. 'Alī, his brother, came to my father and said: "Give me the rank of my brother and I will let you have twenty thousand dīnārs each year."

My father repelled him roughly and made him hear what was (even) unpleasant to me. He said to him: "You fellow, you ignorant one, the Caliph, may Allāh make his life long, has unsheathed his sword against those who claim that your father and your brother were Imams in order to bring them back from that (view). He has not succeeded in this. If you were an Imam in the eyes of the Shī'a of your father and your brother, you would have no need of the Caliph to give you their rank, nor of anyone else. If you do not have this position according to them, you will not gain it through us."

At that my father dismissed him and humiliated him. He ordered that he should be excluded and he never gave him permission to enter until he died.

We had gone out while he was still in that situation. The authorities were demanding an investigation for clues about the son of al-Ḥasan b. ʻAlī at that time. They did not find any means of (finding out about) that. Yet his Shīʻa persist in maintaining that when he died, he left a son who would take his place in the Imamate.

[Abū al-Qāsim Jaʻfar b. Muḥammad informed me on the authority of Muḥammad b. Yaʻqūb, on the authority of ʻAlī b. Muḥammad, on the authority of Muḥammad b. Ismāʻīl b. Ibrāhīm b. Mūsā b. Jaʻfar, who said:][15]
Abū Muḥammad (al-Ḥasan al-ʻAskarī), peace be on him, wrote to Abū al-Qāsim Isḥāq b. Jaʻfar al-Zubayrī about twenty days before the death of al-Muʻtazz: "Keep to your house until the event takes place."

When Burayha was killed, (Abū al-Qāsim Isḥāq) wrote to him: "The event has taken place. What do you command me to do?"
(Al-Ḥasan al-ʻAskarī) wrote (back) to him: "This was not the event. It is another event."
Then there happened to al-Muʻtazz what happened.

[(Muḥammad b. Ismāʻīl) added:]
He wrote to another man that Muḥammad b. Dāwud would be killed ten days before his murder. On the tenth day he was killed.

[Abū al-Qāsim Jaʻfar b. Muḥammad informed me on the authority of Muḥammad b. Yaʻqūb, on the authority of ʻAlī b. Muḥammad b. Ibrāhīm, known as Ibn al-Kurdī, on the authority of Muḥammad b. ʻAlī b. Ibrāhīm b. Mūsā b. Jaʻfar, who said:][16]
Circumstances became difficult for us and my father (ʻAlī b. Ibrāhīm b. Mūsā) said to me: "Come with me to this man - meaning Abū Muḥammad (al-Hasan al-ʻAskarī) - for he has been described as being generous."
"Do you know him?" I asked.
"I do not know him," he answered, "nor have I ever seen him."

We set off. While my father was on the road, my father said to me: "What we need is that he should order for us five hundred dirhams: two hundred dirhams for clothing, two hundred dirhams for flour and a hundred for expenses."
I said to myself: "Would that he would order for me three hundred dirhams: one hundred dirhams to buy a donkey with, one hundred dirhams for expenses and one hundred dirhams for clothing. Then I could go to al-Jabal."

---

15 *Al-Kāfī*, I, 506, tradttion no. 2.
16 *Al-Kāfī*, I, 506-7, tradition no. 3.

When we came to the door, his servant came out to us: "Enter 'Alī b. Ibrāhīm and his son, Muḥammad ."
We entered and he greeted us. He said to my father: "'Alī, what has kept you from us until this time?"
"My lord," he answered, "I have been ashamed to meet you in these circumstances."

When we left him, his servant came to us and gave my father a purse. He said: "This is five hundred dirhams: two hundred for clothing, two hundred for flour and a hundred for expenses."
He gave me a purse and said: "This is three hundred dirhams. Use one hundred for the price of a donkey, one hundred for clothing and one hundred for expenses. But do not go to al-Jabal. Go to Suwār."

[Muḥammad b. Ibrāhīm al-Kurdī added:]
He (i.e. Muḥammad b. 'Alī) went to Suwār and married a woman there. His income today is two thousand dīnārs but he still believes in the Waqf (i.e the last Imam was Mūsā). I (i.e. Muḥammad b. Ibrāhīm al-Kurdi) have said to him: "Shame on you, do you need anything clearer than that?"
"True," he replied, "however we hold a doctrine which has been passed down through our (family)."

[Abū al-Qāsim Ja'far b. Muḥammad informed me on the authority of Muḥammad b. Ya'qūb, on the authority of 'Alī b. Muḥammad, on the authority of Muḥammad b. 'Alī b. Ibrāhīm, who said: Aḥmad b. al-Ḥārith al-Qazwīnī told me:][17]
I (i.e. Aḥmad b. al-Ḥārith al-Qazwīnī) was with my father at Sāmarrā'. My father was employed as a veterinary surgeon in the stable of Abū Muḥammad (al-Hasan al-'Askarī) peace be on him. Al-Musta'īn had a mule whose like in beauty and stoutness has never been seen. Yet it refused (to have anyone on) its back and (to have) reins. The trainers had tried to make it comply but they did not have any trick by which they could ride it. One of his bosom companions said to (al-Musta'īn): "Commander of the faithful, send for al-Ḥasan the descendant of al-Riḍā to come, either he will ride it or it will kill him."

He sent for Abū Muḥammad (al-Ḥasan al-'Askarī), peace be on him. My father went with him. When Abū Muḥammad (al-Ḥasan al-'Askarī) entered the palace, I was with my father. Abu Muḥammad (al-Ḥasan al-'Askarī), peace be on him, looked at the mule standing in the courtyard of the palace. He went straight up to it and put his hand on its buttocks. I looked at the mule and it was sweating so that the sweat was pouring off it. Then he went to al-Musta'īn and greeted

17 *Al-Kāfī*, I, 507, tradition no. 4.

him. The latter welcomed him, brought him close to his seat and said: "Abū Muḥammad (al-Ḥasan al-'Askarī), put reins on this mule."
"Put reins on it, servant," Abū Muḥammad (al-Ḥasan al-'Askarī) told my father.
"You, rein it," al-Musta'īn said to him.

Abū Muḥammad (al-Ḥasan al-'Askarī) put on his cloak. Then he rose and put the reins on it. He went back to his place and sat down
"Abū Muḥammad ," said al-Musta'īn, "saddle it."
"Servant, saddle it," he said to my father.
"You, saddle it," al-Musta'īn said to him.

He rose a second time and saddled it. Then he returned.
"Do you think that you could ride it?" (al- Musta'īn) asked him.
"Yes," answered Abū Muḥammad (al-Ḥasan al-'Askarī).

Then he mounted it without it resisting him. He galloped it through (the courtyard of) the palace. He made it canter at a gentle pace and then it walked beautifully. Then he came back and dismounted.
"How did you find it, Abū Muḥammad ?" al-Musta'īn asked him.
"I have not seen its like in beauty and liveliness," he answered.
"The Commander of the faithful gives it to you," al-Musta'īn told him.
"Servant, take it," Abū Muḥammad (al-Ḥasan al-'Askarī) ordered my father.
My father took it and lead it away.

[Abū Aḥmad b. Rashīd reported on the authority of Abū Hāshim al-Ja'fari, who said:][18]
I (i.e. Abū Hāshim al-Ja'fari) complained to Abū Muḥammad al-Ḥasan b. 'Alī (al-'Askarī), peace be on them, about my needs. He rubbed his whip on the ground. He took out from it an ingot which (was worth) five hundred dīnārs.
"Take it, Abū Hāshim," he said, "and forgive us."

[Abū al-Qāsim (Ja'far b. Muḥammad) informed me on the authority of Muḥammad b. Ya'qūb, on the authority of 'Alī b. Muḥammad, on the authority of Abū 'Abd Allāh b. Ṣāliḥ, on the authority of his father, on the authority of Abū 'Alī al-Muṭahharī:][19]
He (i.e. Abū 'Alī al-Muṭahharī) wrote to him (i.e. al-Ḥasan al-'Askarī) from al-Qādisiyya to inform him of the people's desertion of going on the pilgrimage and that they were afraid of thirst if they went. He (al-Ḥasan al-'Askarī) wrote to him: "Go and have no fear, Allāh willing."

---

18 *Al-Kāfī*, I, 507, tradttion no. 5. Al-Mufīd's *isnād* is shortened.
19 *Al-Kāfī*, I, 507-8, tradition no. 6.

Then those who had held back departed in safety.

[Abū al-Qāsim (Ja'far b. Muḥammad) informed me on the authority of Muḥammad b. Ya'qūb, on the authority of 'Alī b. Muḥammad, on the authority of 'Alī b. al-Ḥasan b. al-Faḍl al-Yamānī, who said:][20]
A great crowd of the supporters of Ja'far (al-Mutawakkil) descended on the area around the river (known as) al-Ja'farī and a man did not have sufficient means to oppose them. He wrote to Abū Muḥammad (al-Hasan al-'Askarī), peace be on him, complaining of that. He wrote back: "You will have enough for them, Allāh willing."

Then that man went against them with a small group while the people were more than twenty thousand souls. He was with less than a thousand but he managed to defeat them.

With the same chain of authorities (*isnād*), on the authority of Muḥammad b. Ismā'īl al-'Alawī, who said:][21]
Abū Muḥammad (al-Ḥasan al-'Askarī), peace be on him, was detained by 'Alī b. Awtāmish. The latter was violent in his hostility to the family of Muḥammad, peace be on them, and severe on the family of Abū Ṭālib. He was told to treat him (badly) and he did so. Yet (al-Ḥasan al-'Askarī) was only with him for a day and he began to treat him with humility. He did not raise his eyes to him out of respect and honour. He would come from him and he had become the most perceptive of men in respect to him and the best of them in his words about him.

[Isḥāq b. Muḥammad al-Nakha'ī reported: Abū Hashim al-Ja'fari told me:][22]
I complained to Abū Muḥammad (al-Ḥasan al-'Askarī) about the oppressiveness of prison and the harshness of the chains. He wrote to me: "You will pray today's noon prayer in your own house."
I was released at noon and prayed the noon prayer in my house as he had said.

I was in a distressed state and I wanted to ask him for help in a letter which I had written to him but I was ashamed to send it. When I went to my house, he sent me a hundred dīnārs and he wrote to me: "When you are in need, do not be ashamed and do not refrain. Ask for it and you will be given what you need, Allāh willing."

[With the same chain of authorities (*isnād*) on the authority of Aḥmad b.

20 *Al-Kāfī*, I, 508, tradition no. 7
21 *Al-Kāfī*, I, 508, tradition no. 8.
22 *Al-Kāfī*, I, 508, tradition no. 10.

Muḥammad al-Aqra', who said: Abū Ḥamza Naṣīr al-Khādim told me:][23]
I (i.e. Abū Ḥamza) heard Abū Muḥammad (al-Ḥasan al-'Askarī) speaking on more than one occasion to his servants in their own languages. Among them were Turks, men from Byzantium and from Ṣaqāliba (in the Caucasus). I was amazed at that and I said: "This man was born in Medina. He did not show himself to anyone until Abū al-Ḥasan (al-Hādī) died, and no one saw him. How is this?"

I was saying this to myself. He came up to me and said: "Allāh has separated His proof (to the world) from the rest of His creatures and has given him knowledge of everything. He knows languages, genealogies and events. If it wasn't for that, there would be no difference between the proof and those who are given the proof."

[With the same chain of authorities (*isnād*): Al-Ḥusayn b. Ẓarīf told me:][24]
Two problems occupied my mind and I (i.e. Al-Ḥusayn b. Ẓarīf) wanted to write to Abū Muḥammad (al-Ḥasan al-'Askarī) peace be on him, about them. I wrote to ask him about how when the one who would undertake (the Imamate for the rest of time) (*al-qā'im*) would undertake his office, he would give his judgements and how his assembly would be in which he gave judgements between the people. I (also) wanted to ask him about something for the quotidian fever. I forgot to mention the fever. The answer came: "You asked about the one who will undertake (the office of the Imamate for the rest of time) (*al-qā'im*). When he undertakes his office, he will give judgements among the people through his knowledge just as David judged without asking for evidence. You wanted to ask about the quotidian fever but you forgot. Write on a paper and hang it over the person with the fever: *O fire, be cold and a place of safety for Abraham* (XXI 69)." I wrote down that and hung it over the person with the fever. He woke up recovered.

[Abū al-Qāsim Ja'far b. Muḥammad informed me on the authority of Muḥammad b. Ya'qūb, on the authority of 'Alī b. Muḥammad, on the authority of Isḥāq b. Muḥammad al-Nakha'ī, who said: Ismā'īl b. Muḥammad b. 'Alī b Ismā'īl b. 'Alī b. 'Abd Allāh b. al-'Abbās told me:][25]
I (Ismā'īl b. Muḥammad) sat waiting for Abū Muḥammad (al-Ḥasan al-'Askarī), peace be on him, at the side of the road. When he passed me, I complained to him of a need (which I had). I swore to him that I did not have a dirham, nor any more than it, nor had I had any breakfast or supper.

23 *Al-Kāfī*, I, 509, tradition no. 11.
24 *Al-Kāfī*, I, 509, tradition no. 13.
25 *Al-Kāfī*, I, 509-10, tradition no. 14.

"You swear by Allāh as a liar," he said. "You have buried two hundred dīnārs. However, I am not saying this as a way of not giving you anything. Servant, give him what you have with you."

His servant gave me a hundred dīnārs. Then he came towards me and said to me: "You will be denied the dīnārs which you buried at a time when your need for them will be much greater than at present."

He, peace be on him, spoke the truth. In fact, I spent what he gave me. Hard necessity forced me to pay for something and the means of gaining provision (from the authorities) were closed to me. I dug for the dīnārs which I had buried and I did not find them. I looked. One of my sons knew where they were. He had taken them and fled. I could not do anything.

[With the same chain of authorities (*isnād*), on the authority of Isḥāq b. Muḥammad al-Nakha'ī, who said: 'Alī b. Zayd b. 'Alī b. al-Ḥusayn told us][26]
I (i.e. 'Alī b. Zayd) had a horse and as a result of it being frequently mentioned in assemblies I was pleased. One day, I visited Abū Muḥammad (al-Ḥasan al-'Askarī), peace be on him. He asked me: "What is your horse doing?"
"It is with me," I answered. "Here it is at your door. I have just dismounted it."
"Exchange it before evening if you can find a purchaser and don't delay," he told me.

A visitor came in and the conversation came to an end. I got up thinking and went to my house. I told my brother and he said to me: "I do not know what to say about this."

However, I was jealous of it and regarded people as unworthy to buy it. Evening came. When I had prayed the night prayer, the groom came to me and said: "My master, your horse has just died."
I was stricken with grief. I knew that (al-Ḥasan al-'Askarī) had meant this by those words. Some days later, I went to visit Abū Muḥammad (al-Ḥasan al-'Askarī), peace be on him. I was saying to myself: "I wish that he would replace it for me with (another) animal."

I sat down and before I could speak, he said to me: "Yes, boy, we will replace it for you. Servant, give him my dark bay horse." Then he said: "This is better and firmer-footed and longer living than your horse was."

[With the same chain of authorities (*isnād*) Muḥammad b. al-Ḥasan b. Shammūn

26 *Al-Kāfī*, I, 510, tradition no. 15.

told us: Aḥmad b. Muḥammad told me:][27]
I (i.e. Aḥmad b. Muḥammad) wrote to Abū Muḥammad (al-Ḥasan al-'Askarī), peace be on him, at the time al-Muhtadī began to kill the slaves (*mawāli*): "My master, praise be to Allāh Who has distracted him from us. I have heard that he is threatening you and saying: 'By Allāh, I will drive them from the face of the earth.'"

Abū Muḥammad (al-Ḥasan al-'Askarī) signed the reply in his own handwriting. (It was as follows:) "There is only a short time for him (i.e. al-Muhtadī) to live. Count from the day you (receive this) five days and he will be killed on the sixth day after humiliation and degradation of his rank."
It happened as he, peace be on him, said.

[Abū al-Qāsim Ja'far b. Muḥammad informed me on the authority of Muḥammad b. Ya'qūb, on the authority of 'Alī b. Muḥammad, on the authority of Muḥammad b. Ismā'īl b. Ibrāhīm b. Mūsā b. Ja'far, who said:][28]
The 'Abbāsids went to Ṣāliḥ b. Waṣīf when Abū Muḥammad (al-Ḥasan al-'Askarī) peace be on him, was imprisoned. They told him:"Be hard On him. Don't give him any ease."
"What can I do with him?" Ṣāliḥ asked them, "I entrusted him to two of the evilest men I could find. They have become (men) of worship, prayer and fasting to an amazing extent"

Then he ordered those two men who had been put in charge of (al-Ḥasan al-'Askarī) to be brought. He said to them: "Shame on you! What is your involvement in the affairs of this man?"

They answered: "What can we say about a man who fasts through the day and stands (in prayer) through the night, who does not speak and occupies himself with nothing except worship? When he looks at us, our limbs shake and within us is (a feeling) which we have never had."
When the 'Abbāsids heard that, they left in despair.

[Abū al-Qāsim Ja'far b. Muḥammad informed me on the authority of Muḥammad b. Ya'qūb, on the authority of 'Alī b. Muḥammad, on the authority of a group of our colleagues, who said:][29]
Abū Muḥammad (al-Ḥasan al-'Askarī), peace be on him, was handed over to Naḥrīr. He was hard on him and did harm to him. A woman said to him: "Fear

27 *Al-Kāfī*, I, 510, tradttion no. 16.
28 *Al-Kāfī*, I, 512, tradttion no. 23.
29 *Al-Kāfī*, I, 513, tradition no. 26.

Allāh, you do not realise who is in your house." She told him about (al-Ḥasan's) righteousness and devotion (to Allāh) and said: "I fear for you as a result of him." "By Allāh, I'll throw him to the wild animals," he declared.

He asked permission to do that and it was granted. He threw him to them. (The authorities) were not disturbed by (wild animals) eating him. They looked at the place in order to find out the situation. They found him, peace be on him. standing in prayer with (the wild animals) around him. (Naḥrīr) ordered him to be taken back to his house.

Reports on these matters are numerous. Those we have given are sufficient for our purpose, Allāh willing.

THE ACCOUNT OF THE DEATH OF ABŪ MUḤAMMAD AL-ḤASAN B. 'ALĪ (AL-'ASKARĪ), PEACE BE ON HIM, THE PLACE OF HIS GRAVE AND THE REPORT ABOUT HIS SON

Abū Muḥammad (al-Ḥasan al- al-'Askarī), fell sick on the 1st on the month of Rabī' al-Awwal in the year 260 A.H. (873). He died on Friday, 8th of that month in the same year. At the time of his death he was twenty-eight years old. He was buried in the house in which his father was buried - the house for both of them was in Sāmarrā'. He left behind his son - the one who is awaited (to bring about) the state of truth. He had concealed his birth and hidden his affair because of the difficulties of the times and the intensity of the search by the authorities of the time for him. This activity by them to enquire into his affair was because of what circulated among the adherents (*madhhab*) of the Shī'a of the Imamites concerning him, and because of what was known about their awaiting him. (Al-Ḥasan al-'Askarī) did not make his son publicly known during his life-time and the ordinary people were not able to recognise him after his death.

Ja'far b. 'Alī, the brother of Abū Muḥammad (al-Ḥasan al-'Askarī), peace be on him, took it upon himself to seize what (al-Ḥasan al- al-'Askarī) had left. He strove to detain the women slaves of Abū Muḥammad (al-Ḥasan al-'Askarī), peace be on him, and to imprison his wives. He made vicious insinuations against (al-Ḥasan's) followers for awaiting his son, for affirming his existence and for maintaining his Imamate. He harassed the people so that he made them afraid and scared them away. Because of that, all this terrible treatment in terms of detention, imprisonment, threats, disparagement, degradation and humiliation occurred for those who were left by Abū Muḥammad (al-Ḥasan al-'Askarī), peace be on him. Yet the authorities did not gain any information. Ja'far took public possession of (the property) which Abū Muḥammad (al-Ḥasan al-'Askarī), peace be on him, had left. He strove to take his place in the eyes of the Shī'a. However, none of them would accept that nor believe him with regard to it. He went to the authorities of the time seeking the position of his brother. He offered them a great deal of money. He offered them everything by which he thought that he could advance himself. Yet he convinced no one of that.

There are numerous reports of Ja'far to this effect, which I feel it appropriate not to mention for reasons whose explanation does not concern this book . They are well-known among the Imamites and those who know the account of the general populace (*'āmma* - non-Shī'a). We seek help from Allāh.

CHAPTER XI

THE TWELFTH IMAM

(This chapter) deals with the one who undertook (the office of the Imamate) (*al-qā'im*) after Abū Muḥammad (al-Ḥasan al-'Askarī), peace be on him, the date of his birth and the evidence for his Imamate. It will mention an extract from the reports about him, his occultation (*ghayba*), his life at the time of his appearance (*qiyam*) and the period of time of his state.

The Imam after Abū Muḥammad (al-Ḥasan al-'Askarī), peace be on him, is his son who is named with the name of the Apostle of Allāh, may Allāh bless Him and His Family, and given his *kunya*. His father did not leave a son who was publicly acknowledged or secretly, except him. He was left behind away from view (*ghā'ib*) and secretly as we have already mentioned. He was born on the night of 15th of Sha'bān in the year 255 A.H. (869). His mother was a slave-wife (*umm walad*) called Narjis. At the time of the death of his father, he was five years old.

Allāh endowed him with wisdom and the distinction of speech. He made him a sign to the worlds. He endowed him with wisdom as He had endowed John the Baptist while still a boy. He made him an Imam while still in the state of apparent childhood just as He made Jesus, son of Mary, a prophet in the cradle. The nomination of him had been given earlier to the community of Islam by the Prophet of guidance, peace be on him, then by the Commander of the Faithful, 'Alī b. Abī Ṭālib, peace be on him, and the Imams, consecutively one after another, down to his own father, al-Ḥasan (al-'Askarī), peace be on him, had nominated him. His father had nominated him in front of the trusted and close members of his Shī'a. Information about his occultation (*ghayba*) was established before his existence. (Information) about his state was widespread before his occultation (*ghayba*). He is the leader with the sword (*ṣāḥib al-sayf*) from the Imams of guidance, peace be on them, the one who will undertake the achievement of truth (*al-qā'im bi-al-ḥaqq*), the one who is awaited (*al-muntaẓar*) to (bring about) the state of faith.

Before his appearance (*qiyām*), he will have two occultations. One of them will be longer than the other as is reported in the traditions. The shortest of them was from the time of his birth to the end of the period of direct representation (*sifāra*) between him and his Shī'a, and the end of the representatives (*sufarā'*) through death. As for the longer (occultation), it will be after the first and at the end of it he will arise with the sword (*yaqūm bi-al-sayf*). Allāh, the Mighty and High, has said: *We want to favour those who were weak on earth. We give them Imams and We give them heirs. We give them power on earth. We show Pharoah and Hāmān and their soldiers but they will not be warned* (XXVIII 5-6). He, exalted be His name, said: *We have written in the Psalms after the message (to Moses): My righteous worshippers will inherit the earth* (XXI 105). The Apostle of Allāh, may Allāh bless Him and His Family, said: "The days and nights will never end until Allāh sends a man from my House, whose name will be the same as mine. He will fill (the earth) with justice and fairness as it was filled with oppression and tyranny." He, may Allāh bless Him and His Family, said: "If only a single day remained for the world, Allāh would lengthen that day so that He could send on it a man from my descendants, whose name is the same as mine. He will fill the world with justice and fairness as it was filled with oppression and tyranny."

Extract from the Evidence for the Imamate of the one who will undertake to (bring about) Truth (*al-Qā'im bi-al-Ḥaqq*) the Son of al-Ḥasan, Peace be on them.

Among the evidence for that is what is required by reason through sound logical deduction (*istidlāl*) with regard to the existence in every age of an Imam, who is infallible, perfect and one who has no need of his subjects with regard to the laws and knowledge, because of the impossibility of those given responsibility (to act) being without an authority by whose existence they may come closer to righteousness and further from corruption. Everyone who is deficient has need of one who will punish criminals, who will correct the disobedient, who will quieten the seducers, who will teach the ignorant, who will remind the careless, who will warn those who have gone astray, who will administer the revealed penal law (*ḥudūd*), who will carry out the laws, who will separate people in dispute, who will appoint the (military) commanders, who will hold the frontiers, who will safeguard property, who will defend the land of Islam, who will join with the people in societies and festivals. The chief proposition in support of the evidence that he is protected from errors is, by agreement, his own lack of need for an Imam. That requires his protection (from sin) without any doubt and by the necessity of the textual definition for every creature who can consider it as a means (of proof) and by virtue of the miracles which he performs in order to distinguish himself from others. The lack of these qualities in everyone except the one whose Imamate was confirmed by the followers of al-Ḥasan b. 'Alī (al-'Askarī), peace be on him - and he is his son the *Mahdī* (the one who is guided and guides) - is based on what we have explained. This is a principle which, nonetheless, requires, with regard to the Imamate, the narration of nominations and the reckoning of the reports which are given concerning them, in order to confirm itself with regard to rational judgement and its validity by the corroboration of logical deduction.

There have been handed down narrations concerning the nomination of the son of al-Ḥasan (al-'Askarī), peace be on him, in ways by which excuses (for not accepting it) are removed. Allāh willing, I will present an extract from them according to the method used earlier of giving a brief outline.

The Reports of the Nomination of the Imamate of the Leader of the (Rest) of Time (*Ṣāḥib al-Zamān*) the Twelfth of the Imams, the Blessings of Allāh on them all, and an Explanation of the Evidence.

[Abū al-Qāsim Ja'far b. Muḥammad informed me on the authority of Muḥammad b. Ya'qūb al-Kulaynī, on the authority of 'Alī b. Ibrāhim, on the authority of Muḥammad b. 'Īsā, on the authority of Muḥammad b. al-Faḍl, on the authority of Abu Ḥamza al-Thumālī, on the authority of Abū Ja'far (al-Bāqir), peace be on him:][1]

He (i.e. al-Bāqir) said: "Allāh, may His name be mighty, sent Muḥammad to *jinn* and mankind. After him He made twelve testamentary trustees of authority (*waṣī*). Of these some have already come before and others remain (to come). A practice has been in operation for each testamentary trustee of authority (*waṣī*). The testamentary trustees of authority (*awṣiyā'*) who came after Muḥammad, may Allāh bless Him and His Family, were accordmg to the practice (established) by Jesus, peace be on him, and they (the *awṣiyā'* of Jesus) were twelve. Thus, the Commander of the Faithful, peace be on him, was (the first *waṣī* after Muḥammad) according to the practice (established) by (Jesus), the Messiah, peace be on him."

[Abū al-Qāsim Ja'far b. Muḥammad informed me on the authority of Muḥammad b. Ya'qūb on the authority of Muḥammad b. Yaḥyā, on the authority of Aḥmad b. Muḥammad b. 'Īsā, Muḥammad b. 'Abd Allāh, Muḥammad b. al-Ḥusayn, all on the authority of Sahl b. Ziyād, on the authority of al-Ḥasan b. al-'Abbās, on the authority of Abū Ja'far the second (i.e. Muḥammad al-Jawād), on the authority of his father back to the authority of the Commander of the Faithful, peace be on them, who said:]

The Apostle of Allāh, may Allāh bless Him and His Family, said to his Companions: "Believe in the Night of Decision (*laylat al-qadr*). On it the command for the religious practice (*sunna*) was revealed and because of that order there exist friends of Allāh (*wulāt*) after me - 'Alī b. Abī Ṭālib and eleven of his descendants."

1 *Al-Kāfī*, I, 532, tradition no. 10.

[With the same chain of authorities (*isnād*):]
The Commander of the faithful, peace be on him, told Ibn 'Abbās, may Allāh have mercy on him: "The Night of Decision is (concerned) with every religious practice (*sunna*). On that night, the command for the religious practice (*sunna*) was revealed and because of that order there are friends of Allāh (*wulāt*) after the Apostle of Allāh, may Allāh bless Him and His Family."

"Who are they?" asked Ibn 'Abbās.
"Myself and eleven (descended) from my loins. Imams who are addressed (by the angels)," he answered.

[Abū al-Qāsim Ja'far b. Muḥammad informed me on the authority of Muḥammad b. Ya'qūb on the authority of Muḥammad b. Yaḥyā, on the authority of Muḥammad b. al-Ḥasan, on the authority of Ibn Maḥbūb, on the authority of Abū al-Jarūd, on the authority of Abū Ja'far Muḥammad b. 'Alī (al-Bāqir), peace be on him, on the authority of Jaīr b. 'Abd Allāh al-Anṣārī, who said:][2]
I (i.e. Jaīr b. 'Abd Allāh) visited Fāṭima, the daughter of the Apostle of Allāh, may Allāh bless Him and His Family. In her hands was a tablet (*lawḥ*) in which was (inscribed) the testamentary trustees of authority (*awṣiyā'*), the Imams from her offspring. I counted twelve names, the last of them was the one who will undertake the office for the rest of time (*al-qā'im*). Of the descendants of Fāṭima, three of the (names) were Muḥammad and three of them were 'Alī.

[Abū al-Qāsim informed me on the authority of Muḥammad b. Ya'qūb, on the authority of Abū 'Alī al-Ash'arī, on the authority of al-Ḥasan b. 'Ubayd Allāh, on the authority of al-Ḥasan b. Mūsā al-Khashshāb, on the authority of 'Alī b. Sumū'a, on the authority of 'Alī b. al-Ḥasan b. Ribāṭ, on the authority of Ibn Udhayna, on the authority of Zurāra, who said:][3]
I (i.e. Zurāra) heard Abū Ja'far (al-Bāqir), peace be on him, say: "The twelve Imams from the family of Muḥammad, all of whom are addressed (by the angels) are 'Alī b. Abī Ṭālib and eleven of his descendants. The Apostle of Allāh and 'Alī b. Abī Ṭālib are the two progenitors (of them), peace be on them both."

[Abū al-Qāsim informed me on the authority of Muḥammad b. Ya'qūb, on the authority of 'Alī b. Ibrāhīm, on the authority of his father (Ibrāhīm b. Hāshim), on the authority of Ibn Abī 'Umayr, on the authority of Sa'īd b. Ghazwān, on the authority of Abū Baṣīr, on the authority of Abū Ja'far (al-Bāqir), peace be on him:][4]

2 *Al-Kāfī*, I, 532, tradition no. 9.
3 *Al-Kāfī*, I, 533, tradition no. 14.
4 *Al-Kāfī*, I, 533, tradition no. 15.

He (al-Bāqir) said: "After al-Ḥusayn, there will be nine Imams, the ninth of them will be the one of them who will undertake the office for the rest of time (*qā'im*)."

[Abū al-Qāsim Ja'far b. Muḥammad informed me on the authority of Muḥammad b. Ya'qūb, on the authority of al-Ḥusayn b. Muḥammad, on the authority of Mu'allā b. Muḥammad, on the authority of al-Washshā, on the authority of Abān, on the authority of Zurāra, who said:][5]
I (i.e. Zurāra) heard Abū Ja'far (al-Bāqir), peace be on him, say: "There will be twelve Imams. Among them are al-Ḥasan and al-Ḥusayn. Then the Imams are from the descendants of al-Ḥusayn, peace be on him."

[Abū al-Qāsim Ja'far b. Muḥammad informed me on the authority of Muḥammad b. Ya'qūb, on the authority of 'Alī b. Muḥammad, on the authority of Muḥammad b. 'Alī b. Bilāl, who said:][6]
There came to me (i.e. Muḥammad b. 'Alī b. Bilāl) (information) from Abu Muḥammad al-Ḥasan b. 'Alī al-'Askarī, peace be on him, informing me of his successor after him two years before his death. Then (again) three days before his death there came to me information (from him) informing me of his successor after him.

[Abū al-Qāsim (Ja'far b. Muḥammad) informed me on the authority of Muḥammad b. Ya'qūb, on the authority of Muḥammad b. Yaḥyā, on the authority of Aḥmad b. Isḥāq, on the authority of Abū Hāshim al-Ja'farī, who said:][7]
I (Abū Hāshim al-Ja'farī) said to Abu Muḥammad al-Ḥasan b. 'Alī (al-'Askarī), peace be on them: "Your exaltedness prevents me from questioning you. Would you permit me to question you?"
"Ask." he said.
"My lord, have you a son?" I asked.
"Yes," he answered.
"If anything happens to you, where will I ask about him?" I said
"In Medina," he replied.

[Abū al-Qāsim Ja'far b. Muḥammad informed me on the authority of Muḥammad b. Ya'qūb, on the authority of 'Alī b. Muḥammad, on the authority of Ja'far b. Muḥammad al-Kūfī, on the authority of Ja'far b. Muḥammad al-Makfūf, on the authority of 'Amr al-Ahwāzī, who said:][8]

5 *Al-Kāfī*, I, 533, tradttion no. 16.
6 *Al-Kāfī*, I, 328, tradition no. 1.
7 *Al-Kāfī*, I, 328, tradition no. 2.
8 *Al-Kāfī*, I, 328, tradition no. 3

Abu Muḥammad (al-Ḥasan al-'Askarī), peace be on him, showed me his son and said: "This is your leader after me."

[Abū al-Qāsim Ja'far b. Muḥammad informed me on the authority of Muḥammad b. Ya'qūb, on the authority of 'Alī b. Muḥammad, on the authority of Ḥamdān al-Qalānisī, on the authority of al-'Umarī, who said:][9]
(al-'Umarī) said: "Abu Muḥammad (al-Ḥasan al-'Askarī), peace be on him, has died and has left his son as his successor."

[Abū al-Qāsim Ja'far b. Muḥammad informed me on the authority of Muḥammad b. Ya'qūb, on the authority of 'Alī b. Muḥammad, on the authority of al-Ḥusayn b. Muḥammad, on the authority of Mu'allā b. Muḥammad, on the authority of Aḥmad b. Muḥammad b. 'Abd Allāh, who said:][10]
(An announcement) came from Abu Muḥammad (al-Ḥasan al-'Askarī), peace be on him, when al-Zubayrī (i.e. al-Muhtadī), may Allāh curse him, was killed: "This is the reward of one who is bold before Allāh, the Exalted, in (his treatment of) His friends (*awliyā'*). He claimed that he would kill me and that I did not have any offspring. How does he consider the power of Allāh now with regard to (that son)?"

[(Aḥmad b.) Muḥammad b. 'Abd Allāh added:]
A son was born to him.

[Abū al-Qāsim Ja'far b. Muḥammad informed me on the authority of Muḥammad b. Ya'qūb, on the authority of 'Alī b. Muḥammad, on the authority of those who report it, on the authority of Muḥammad b. Aḥmad al-'Alawī, on the authority of Dāwud b. al-Qāsim al-Ja'farī (Abū Hāshim), who said:][11]
I (i.e. Dāwud b. al-Qāsim al-Ja'farī) heard Abū al-Ḥasan 'Alī b. Muḥammad (al-Hādī) say: "The successor after me is al-Ḥasan. But how will it be for you with regard to the successor after the successor?"
"May Allāh make me your ransom, why?" I asked.
"You will not see his person," he said, "nor will the mentioning of his name be permitted to you."

"Then how will we refer to him?" I enquired.
"Say - the proof from the family of Muḥammad, peace be on them," he told me.

*****

9 *Al-Kāfī*, I, 329, tradition no. 4.
10 *Al-Kāfī*, I, 329, tradition no. 5. Al-Mufīd omits 256 A.H. as the year of the birth.
11 *Al-Kāfī*, I, 328, tradition no. 13.

This is an extract which comes from the reports handed down concerning the nominations of the twelfth of the Imams, peace be on them. The narrations about that are numerous. The followers of this group have written them and confirmed them in the books which they have compiled. Among those who have presented them with explanation and detail is Muḥammad b. Ibrāhīm, whose *kūnya* is Abu ʻAbd Allāh al-Nuʻmanī, in the book which he compiled on the occultation (*ghayba*). There is no need for us, in view of what we have mentioned, to present them in detail in this place.

AN ACCOUNT OF THOSE WHO SAW THE TWELFTH IMAM, PEACE BE ON HIM, AN EXTRACT FROM THE EVIDENCE AND PROOF FOR HIM.

[Abū al-Qāsim Jaʻfar b. Muḥammad informed me on the authority of Muḥammad b. Yaʻqūb, on the authority of ʻAlī b. Muḥammad, on the authority of Muḥammad b. Ismāʻīl b. Mūsā b. Jaʻfar - he was the oldest leader (*shaykh*) of the family of Muḥammad in Iraq - who said][12]
I (Muḥammad b. Ismāʻīl b. Mūsā) saw the son of al-Ḥasan b. ʻAlī b. Muḥammad (al-ʻAskarī), peace be on them, between the two mosques (i.e between Mecca and Medina). He was a youth.

[Abū al-Qāsim Jaʻfar b. Muḥammad informed me on the authority of Muḥammad b. Yaʻqūb, on the authority of Muḥammad b. Yaḥyā, on the authority of al-Ḥasan b. Rizq Allāh, who said: Mūsā b Muḥammad b. al-Qāsim b. Ḥamza b. Mūsā b. Jaʻfar told me: Ḥakīma, daughter of Muḥammad b. ʻAlī (al-Jawād), peace be on them, and aunt of al-Ḥasan (al-ʻAskarī), peace be on him, told me:][13]
She (Ḥakīma) saw the one who will undertake the office of the Imamate for the rest of time (*al-qā'im*) on the night of his birth and later.

[Abū al-Qāsim Jaʻfar b. Muḥammad informed me on the authority of Muḥammad b. Yaʻqūb, on the authority of ʻAlī b. Muḥammad, on the authority of Ḥamdān al-Qalānisī who said:][14]
I (i.e. Ḥamdān al-Qalānisī) asked Abū ʻAmr al-ʻUmarī, may Allāh have mercy on him: "Has Abū Muḥammad (al-Ḥasan al-ʻAskarī), peace be on him, died?" "He has died," he answered, "but he has left a successor among you, one whose neck is like this." He indicated (his own neck) with his hand (i.e. the successor is already mature).

[Abū al-Qāsim Jaʻfar b. Muḥammad informed me on the authority of Muḥammad

12 *Al-Kāfī*, I, 330, tradition no. 2.
13 *Al-Kāfī*, I, 330-1, tradition no. 3.
14 *Al-Kāfī*, I, 331, trraditlon no. 4.

b. Ya'qūb, on the authority of 'Alī b. Muḥammad, on the authority of Fatḥ, the retainer (*mawlā*) of al-Zurārī, who said:][15]
I (i.e. Fatḥ) heard Abū 'Alī b. Muṭahhar mention that he had seen him and he described his stature.

[Abū al-Qāsim Ja'far b. Muḥammad informed me on the authority of Muḥammad b. Ya'qūb, on the authority of 'Alī b. Muḥammad, on the authority of Muḥammad b. Shādhān b. Nu'aym, on the authority of the maid-servant of Ibrāhīm b. 'Abīda al-Nīsābūrī - she was one of the righteous women - who said:][16]
I (i.e. the maidservant of Ibrāhīm b. 'Abīda) was standing with Ibrāhīm on al-Ṣafā (in Mecca) and the one who possesses authority, peace be on him, came and stood over Ibrāhīm. He took hold of his book of rituals for the pilgrimage and told him about some things.

[Abū al-Qāsim Ja'far b. Muḥammad informed me on the authority of Muḥammad b. Ya'qūb, on the authority of 'Alī b. Muḥammad, on the authority of Muḥammad 'Alī b. Ibrāhīm, on the authority of Abū 'Abd Allāh b. Ṣāliḥ:][17]
He (i.e. Abū 'Abd Allāh b. Ṣāliḥ) saw him opposite the (Black) stone (of the Ka'ba) and the people were struggling with one another to get to it. He said: "They were not ordered to do this."

[Abū al-Qāsim Ja'far b. Muḥammad informed me on the authority of Muḥammad b. Ya'qūb, on the authority of 'Alī b. Muḥammad, on the authority of Aḥmad b. Ibrāhīm b. Idrīs, on the authority of his father (Ibrāhīm b. Idrīs), who said:][18]
I (i.e. Ibrāhīm b. Idrīs) saw him, peace be on him, after the death of Abū Muḥammad (al-Ḥasan al-'Askarī), peace be on him, when he had grown up. I kissed his hand and his head.

[Abū al-Qāsim Ja'far b. Muḥammad informed me on the authority of Muḥammad b. Ya'qūb, on the authority of 'Alī b. Muḥammad, on the authority of Abū 'Abd Allāh b. Ṣāliḥ and Aḥmad b. al-Nadr, on the authority of al-Qanbarī, who said:][19]
A discussion took place about Ja'far b. 'Alī (the brother of al-Ḥasan al-'Askarī). He (an unidentified person) blamed him (i.e. Ja'far) (for claimmg the Imamate).
I (i.e. al-Qanbarī) said: "There is not anyone else except him."
"Yes, there is," he asserted.
"Who." I asked. "And have you see him?"
"I have not seen him," he replied, "but someone else has."

15 *Al-Kāfī*, I, 331, tradition no. 5.
16 *Al-Kāfī*, I, 331, tradition no. 6.
17 *Al-Kāfī*, I, 331, tradition no. 7. Al-Mufīd's *isnād* has been corrected.
18 *Al-Kāfī*, I, 331, tradition no. 8.
19 *Al-Kāfī*, I, 331, tradition no. 9.

"Who is that?" I asked.
"Ja'far has seen him twice," he declared.

[Abū al-Qāsim Ja'far b. Muḥammad informed me on the authority of 'Alī b. Muḥammad, on the authority of Ja'far b. Muḥammad al-Kūfī, on the authority of Ja'far b. Muḥammad al-Makfūf, on the authority of 'Amr al-Ahwāzī, who said:][20]
Abū Muḥammad (al-Ḥasan al-'Askarī), peace be on him, showed me his son and said: "This is your leader (after me)."

[Abū al-Qāsim Ja'far b. Muḥammad informed me on the authority of Muḥammad b. Ya'qūb, on the authority of Muḥammad b. Yaḥyā, on the authority of al-Ḥasan b. 'Alī al-Nīsābūrī, on the authority of Ibrāhīm b. Muḥammad, on the authority of Abū Naṣr Ẓarīf al-Khādim:][21]
He (i.e. Abū Naṣr Ẓarīf al-Khādim) saw him.

*****

Such reports with the meaning which we have mentioned are numerous. The selection which we have given is sufficient for our purpose, since the support of his existence has already been presented by us and what would follow would be merely additional confirmation. If we do not present it, it is not without explanation.

Extract from the Evidence, Proof and Signs for the Leader for the (Rest of) Time

[Abū al-Qāsim Ja'far b. Muḥammad b. Qūlawayh informed me on the authority of Muḥammad b. Ya'qūb, on the authority of 'Alī b. Muḥammad, on the authority of Muḥammad b. Ḥamawayh, on the authority of Muḥammad b. Ibrāhīm b. Mahziyār, who said:][22]
I (i.e. Muḥammad b. Ibrāhīm b. Mahziyā) doubted (if there was a successor) at the death of Abū Muḥammad al-Ḥasan b. 'Alī (al-'Askarī) peace be on them. A great deal of money (for the Imam) had been gathered with my father. He took it and went by boat. I went with him to say farewell to him. He became seriously weakened by a fever. He said: "My son, take me back, it is death."
Then he said: "Fear Allāh with regard to this money," and he entrusted it to my (safe-keeping).

20 *Al-Kāfī*, I, 332, tradition no. 12. This tradition has been repeated by both al-Mufīd and al-Kulaynī.
21 *Al-Kāfī*, I, 332, tradition no. 13.
22 *Al-Kāfī*, I, 518, tradition no. 5.

Three days later he died. I said to myself. "It is not possible for my father to entrust me with something for safe-keeping which is not true. I will take this money to Iraq. I will hire a house on the (river) bank and I won't tell anyone anything. If something becomes clear to me like it was clear at the time of Abū Muḥammad (al-Ḥasan b. 'Alī (al-'Askarī), peace be on him, I will hand it over. If not, I will spend it on enjoying myself and entertainmg myself."

I went to Iraq and hired a house on the river-bank. I remained there for several days. Then suddenly a letter (was brought) by a messenger: "Muḥammad, you have such-and-such . . . ."
(It went on) to describe everything I had, even what I was not aware of, being included in it. I handed it over to the messenger. I remained for some days without a head being raised to me (in greeting) and I was grieved. Then (a message) came to me: "We have put you in the position of your father. So praise Allāh."

[Muḥammad b. Abī 'Abd Allāh reported on the authority of Abū 'Abd Allāh al-Nisā'ī:][23]
I (i.e. Abū 'Abd Allāh) gave some things to al-Marzubānī al-Ḥārithī, among which was a bracelet of gold. They were accepted. However, the bracelet was returned to me and I was told to break it. I broke it. There in the middle of it were weights of iron, copper and brass. I took that away and handed over the gold after that. It was accepted.

['Alī b. Muḥammad reported:][24]
A man from the Sawād (of Iraq) handed over money and it was returned to him. He was told: "Take from it what is due to your nephews. It is four hundred dirhams."

The man had possession of an estate in which his nephews had a share which he had withheld from them. He reflected. When he took out the four hundred dirhams which belonged to his nephews and handed over the rest, it was accepted.

[Al-Qāsim b. al-'Alā' reported:][25]
A number of sons were born to me. I used to write to (the Hidden Imam) and ask for prayers for them. However, he never wrote to me anything about their affair and they all died. When my son al-Ḥusayn was born, I wrote to ask for prayers.

23 *Al-Kāfī*, I, 518, tradition no. 6. Al-Mufīd's *isnād* has been corrected.
24 *Al-Kāfī*, I, 519, tradition no. 8.
25 *Al-Kāfī*, I, 519, tradition no. 9.

I received an answer and he survived. Praise be to Allāh.

['Alī b. Muḥammad (reported) on the authority of Abū 'Abd Allāh b. Ṣāliḥ, who said:][26]
One year I (i.e. Abū 'Abd Allāh b. Ṣāliḥ) went to Baghdād. (At first) I had asked permission to go but it had not been granted to me. So I remained for twenty-two days after the departure of the caravan towards al-Nahrawān. Then I received permission to depart on the Wednesday. I was told to go with it. I set out in despair at catching it up. I reached al-Nahrawān and the caravan was still there. I only had time to feed my camel before the caravan set out and I set out with it. He (the Hidden Imam) had prayed for my safety. Therefore I came to no harm. Praise be to Allāh.

['Alī b. Ibrāhīm (reponed) on the authority of Naḍr b. Ṣabbāḥ al-Bajalī, on the authority of Muḥammad b. Yūsuf al-Shāshī, who said:][27]
Tumours came out on my boltom. I showed them to the doctors and spent a great deal of money to do that. They said that they did not know of any medicine to cure them. I wrote a letter (to the Hidden Imam) to ask him to pray (for me). He sent me a signed letter: "May Allāh clothe you in health. May He make you with us both in this world and the next."

Before Friday came, I was well again and the place where there had been tumours became as smooth as the palm of my hand. I summoned a doctor (who was one) of our colleagues and showed him that. He said: "We do not know of any medicine for that. Health could only have been restored through Allāh directly."

['Alī b. Muḥammad (reported) on the authority of 'Alī b. al-Ḥusayn al-Yamānī, who said:][28]
While I (i.e. 'Alī b. al-Ḥusayn al-Yamānī) was in Baghdād, a caravan of Yamānīs was being prepared for departure. I wanted to go with them. I wrote to ask permission for that and (the message) came: "Do not go with them. No good will come to you through going with them. Stay in Kūfā."
I stayed there and the caravan departed. The Banū Ḥanẓala attacked them and destroyed them.

I wrote to ask permission to make a journey by water and was not given permission. I asked about the boats which were leaving that year by sea but I knew that no boat was safe, for a group of people called *al-Bawāriḥ* used to attack them and stop them.

26 *Al-Kāfī*, I, 519, tradition no. 10.
27 *Al-Kāfī*, I, 519, tradhion no. 11.
28 *Al-Kāfī*, I, 519-20, tradition no. 12.

['Alī b. al-Ḥusayn reported:]
I (i.e. 'Alī b. al-Ḥusayn) went to al-'Askar (Sāmarrā'). I came in by a by-street at dusk. I had spoken to no one and I was not known to anyone. I was praying in the mosque after I had finished my visitation (to the graves of the two Imams al-Hādī and al-'Askarī), when a servant came to me. He said to me. "Arise."
"To where?" I asked.
"To the house," he answered.
"Who am I?" I said. "Perhaps you have been sent to someone else."
"No, I have only been sent to you," he said. "You are 'Alī b. al-Ḥusayn (the messenger of Ja'far b. Ibrāhīm".

He went with me until he installed me in the house of al-Ḥusayn b. Aḥmad).[29] I did not know what he said to him until he brought everything I needed. I remained there for three days. Then I asked permission to make a visitation inside the house (where the two Imams were buried). Permission was granted and I made my visitation at night.

[Al-Ḥasan b. al-Faḍl (b. Zayd al-Yamānī) reported:][30]
My father (i.e. al-Faḍl b. Zayd) wrote a letter in his own handwriting. The reply from the (Hidden Imam) came. (Then I, Al-Ḥasan b. al-Faḍl - wrote in my handwriting, the reply from the Hidden Imam came). Then one of the outstanding scholars among our colleagues wrote in his handwriting and no answer came back. We reflected on that. Indeed the man had changed and become a Qarmaṭī.

[Al-Ḥasan b. al-Faḍl mentioned:]
I (i.e. Al-Ḥasan b. al-Faḍl) went to Iraq (and I went to Tūs). I knew that I would only leave with clear evidence (of an improvement) in my situation and success in my needs even though I might have to stay there untill I had to beg for alms. During that time, my heart became oppressed with my stay and I began to fear that I would miss the pilgrimage. One day I went to Muḥlammad b. Aḥmad - he was the representative of the Hidden Imam (*safīr*) at that time - so that I might get money from him. He said to me: "Go to such-and-such a mosque. There a man will meet you."

I went there. A man came up to me. When he looked at me, he laughed and said: "Don't be worried. You will make the pilgrimage, this year and you will return safely to your family and children."

29 What is between brackets is from *Al-Kāfī*;

30 *Al-Kāfī*, I, 520, tradition no. 13. What is between brackets is from *Al-Kāfī*.

I was relieved and my heart quietened. I said: "This is the real proof of that man."

Then I went to al-'Askar (Sāmarrā'). A bag was sent to me, in which were some dīnārs and some clothes. I was perplexed and said to myself: "Is my reward only that in the eyes of the people (i.e. the Shī'a leaders)?"

I pretended ignorance and sent it back. Then I regretted my action very much. I said to myself: "I have been guilty of unbelief in sending it back to my master."

I wrote a letter apologising for my action, acknowledging my sin and seeking forgiveness for it. Then I sent it. I performed the noon prayer. At that time I was thinking to myself and saying: "If the dīnārs were returned to me, I would not untie the knot (of the purse). I would not do anything with it until I had taken it to my father. He knows better than I."

The messenger, who had brought the purse to me, came to me again. He said to me: "I would throttle you since you do not acknowledge the man (i.e. the Hidden Imam). Sometimes we do that to our followers who have deserted in the first place. Sometimes they ask us to do it to gain relief through it. However, (a message) has come to me that you made a mistake in sending back our beneficence. If you seek the forgiveness of Allāh, then Allāh, the Exalted will forgive you. However, if it is your resolve and your firm intention not to do anything with what we brought to you and not to spend it on your journey, we will deprive you of it. As for the clothes, take them in order to use as the robes for consecration in the pilgrimage (*tuḥrim fihi.*)."

[Al-Ḥasan b. al-Faḍl reported:]
I (i.e. al-Ḥasan b. al-Faḍl) wrote about two problems and wanted to write about a third. However, I stopped myself fearing that that might not be liked. The answer came explaining the two problems and the third which I had kept back. Praise be to Allāh.

[Al-Ḥasan b. al-Faḍl reported:]
I (i.e. al-Ḥasan b. al-Faḍl) agreed with Ja'far b. Ibrāhīm al-Nīsābūrī in Nīsābūr to ride with him to the pilgrimage and give him companionship. When I reached Baghdād, I changed my mind. So I went to look for a partner. Ibn Wajnā' met me. (Earlier) I had gone to him and asked him to hire someone for me. However, he had been unwilling. Now he said: "I have been looking for you, for I was told (i.e. by an instruction from the Hidden Imam) that he (i.e. al-Ḥasan) will be your colleague (within the caravan) so be kind to him and find a partner for him and hire him for him."

['Alī b. Muḥammad (reported) on the authority of al-Ḥasan b. 'Abd al-Ḥamīd, who said:][31]
I (i.e. al-Ḥasan b. 'Abd al-Ḥamīd) doubted about the authority of Ḥājiz. I collected some (dues for the Hidden Imam) and went to al-'Askar. (A message) came to me: "There should be no doubt about us nor about those who act on our behalf with our authority. Return what you have to Ḥājiz b. Yazīd."

['Alī b. Muḥammad (reported) on the authority of Muḥammad b. Ṣāliḥ, who said:][32]
When my father died and his authority came to me (i.e. Muḥammad b. Ṣāliḥ), my father had been holding bills of exchange (which had been given) by people (instead of money) as part of the money owed to the creditor - i.e. the leader of the affair (*ṣāḥib al-amr*), peace be on him.

Al-Shaykh al-Mufīd, may Allāh have mercy on him, explained: This expression (*al-gharīm* - the creditor) is a symbol which the Shī'a had known for a long time among themselves. Their addressing him by it was a form of precautionary dissimulation (*taqiyya*).

I (i.e. Muḥammad b. Ṣāliḥ) wrote to him (the Hidden Imam) to inform me (about what to do). He wrote to me: "Seek them out and get them to pay."

The people paid me except for one man. He owed (the redemption of) a bill of exchange for four hundred dīnārs. I went to him to ask for it. He put off paying me and his son made light of me and ridiculed me. I complained about him to his father. His father said: "What was that?"

I grabbed hold of his beard and took hold of his leg and dragged him to the middle of the house. His son went out to get help from the people of Baghdād. He was shoulmg: "A Qummī, a Rāfiḍite, has killed my father."

A large crowd of them gathered against me. I got on my horse and shouted: "Well done, people of Baghdād, siding with a wrong-doer against a wronged stranger. I am a man from the people of Hamdān from the people of the *sunna* (i.e. non-Shī'a). This man makes claims of me being from the people of Qumm and accuses me of being a Rāfiḍite so that he may take away my rights and my money,"

They began to turn against him and they wanted to go into his shop until I

31 *Al-Kāfī*, I, 521, tradition no. 14.
32 *Al-Kāfī*, I, 521-2, tradition no. 15.

quietened them. The man whose bill of exchange it was came to me and swore by the oath of divorce that he would pay me my money (to redeem the bill) so that I would take them away from him.

['Alī b. Muḥammad (reported) on the authority of a number of our colleagues on the authority of Aḥmad b. al-Ḥasan and al-'Alā' b. Rizq Allāh, on the authority of Badr, the servant of Aḥmad b. al-Ḥasan, on the authority of the latter:][33]
I (i.e. Aḥmad b. al-Ḥasan) came to al-Jabal. I did not yet profess (the doctrine of) the Imamate, nor did I have any love for them (the Shī'a) at all until Yazīd b. 'Abd Allāh died. In his illness, he made (me a trustee of) his will that his horse, his sword and his belt should be given to his Master (i e. the Imam). I was afraid that if I did not give the horse to Udhkūtkīn, he would punish me. I valued the horse, sword and belt in my own view for seven hundred dīnārs and I told no one about it. I gave the horse to Udhkūtkīn. Suddenly there was a letter which came to me from Iraq: "Send seven hundred dīnārs, of the price of the horse, sword and belt which were ours before you."

['Alī b. Muḥammad reported: One of our colleagues told me:][34]
A son was born to me (i.e. one of the Shī'a).

I wrote to ask permission to have him circumcised on the seventh day. (The answer) came: "Do not do that."

The child died on the seventh or eighth day. I wrote about his death. The answer came: "He will be followed by another and another. Name the first Aḥmad and the one after Aḥmad, Ja'far."
It happened just as he said.

[One of our colleagues reported:]
I (i.e. one of the Shī'a) had got ready for the pilgrimage. I said farewell to the people and wrote to depart. (The answer) came "We are averse to that but the decision is yours."

My heart was heavy and I was grieved. I wrote "I remain as one who listens and obeys. However, I am grieved at staying behind from the pilgrimage'"

There came a signed message: "Let your heart not be heavy. You will make the pilgrimage next year. Allāh willing."

---

33 *Al-Kāfī*, I, 522, tradition no. 16.
34 *Al-Kāfī*, I, 522-3, tradition no. 17.

Next year I wrote to ask permssion. Permission came. I wrote (to ask) if I could take Muḥammad b. al-'Abbās as a companion as I trusted in his religious faith and self-restraint. (The answer) came: "The man of the tribe of Asad would be the better companion. If he comes, do not hire (Muḥammad b. al-'Abbās)."

The man of Asad came and l took him as a companion.

[Abu al-Qāsim Ja'far b. Muḥammad reported to me on the authority of Muḥammad b. Ya'qūb, on the authority of 'Alī b. Muḥammad, on the authority of al-Ḥasan b. 'Īsā al-'Uraydī, who said:][35]
When Abū Muḥammad al-Ḥasan b. 'Alī (al-'Askarī), peace be on them, died, a man from the people of Egypt brought money to Mecca for the leader of the affair (*ṣāḥib al-amr*), peace be on him. I (i.e. al-Ḥasan b. 'Īsā al-'Uraydī) used to visit him. He said: "Some of the people (say) that Abū Muḥammad (al-Ḥasan al-'Askarī), peace be on him, died without a successor. Others say that the successor after him is Ja'far. Others say that the successor after him is his son. A man with the *kunya* Abū Ṭālib was sent to al-'Askar (Sāmarrā') to study the matter and (find out) the truth about it. He had a letter with him. The man went to Ja'far and asked him for proof (ofhis Imamate). He answered: 'It is not yet ready for me.' The man went to the door and he sent the letter to our colleagues who are charged with direct representation of the Hidden Imam (*sifāra*). The message came to him: 'May Allāh reward you through your leader.' Then the man died and he entrusted the money which was with him to do with what he was intending (i.e. pay it to the agents of the Hidden Imam). His letter had been answered and the matter was as he had been told."

[With the same chain of authorities (*isnād*) on the authority or 'Alī b. Muḥammad, who said:][36]
A man from the people of Āba brought some things to hand over to him (the Hidden Imam). He forgot his sword which he had also intended to give. When the things arrived, he was informed by letter of their arrrival. In the letter it also said: "What is the news of the sword which you forgot?"

[With the same chain of authorities (*isnād*) on the authority of 'Alī b. Muḥammad, on the authority of Muḥammad b. Shādhān al-Nīsābūrī, who said:][37]
I (i.e. Muḥammad b. Shādhān) had collected five hundred dirhams less twenty. I did not want to send them while they were less (than five hundred). so I paid out twenty dirhams of my own and sent them to al-Asadī. I did not write about what

35 *Al-Kāfī*, I, 523, tradition no. 19.
36 *Al-Kāfī*, I, 523, tradition no. 20.
37 *Al-Kāfī*, I, 523-4, tradition no. 23.

was my own (money) in (the sum). The reply came: " Five hundred dirhams have arrived, of which twenty belongs to you."

[al-Ḥasan b. Muḥammad al-Ash'arī reported:][38]
A letter from Abū Muḥammad (al-Ḥasan al-'Askarī), peace be on him, came about entrusting a salary to al-Junayd, who assassinated Fāris b. Ḥātim b. Māhawayh, to Abū al-Ḥasan and my brother. After Abū Muḥammad (al-Ḥasan al-'Askarī), peace be on him, died, a message came, renewing the salary of Abū al-Ḥasan and his companion. Nothing came with regard to the affairs of al-Junayd. I was troubled at that but then (another message) came later announcmg the death of al-Junayd.

['Alī b. Muḥammad (reported) on the authority of Abū 'Aqīl 'Īsā b. Naṣr, who said:][39]
'Alī b. Ziyād al-Ṣīmarī wrote asking for a shroud. (The reply) was written to him: "You will need it in the year (2)80 A.H."

He died in the year (2)80 A.H. and the shroud was sent to him before his death.

['Alī b. Muḥammad (reported) on the authonty of Muḥammad b. Hārūn b. 'Imrān al-Hamdānī, who said][40]
I (i.e. Muḥammad b. Hārūn) owed five hundred dīnārs to (the Hidden Imam). I did not have enough money to pay it. Then I said to myself: "I have several shops which I had bought for five hundred and thirty dīnārs I could give them (to the Hidden Imam) instead of the five hundred dīnārs."

However, I did not say anythjng about them. (A message) was written to Muḥammad b. Ja'far: "Take the shops from Muḥammad b. Hārūn for the five hundred dīnārs which be owes us."

[Abū al-Qāsim (Ja'far b. Muḥammad) informed me on the authority of Muḥammad b. Ya'qūb, on the authority of 'Alī b. Muḥammad, who said:][41]
An announcement was issued: "It is prohibited to make visitations to the cemetery of Quraysh and Karbalā' (al-Hā'ir)."

Some months later the vizier summoned al-Baqṭānī. He said to him: "Go to (the families of) the Banū Furāt and the people of al-Burs and tell them not to visit the

38 *Al-Kāfī*, I, 524, tradition no. 24.
39 *Al-Kāfī*, I, 524, tradition no. 27.
40 *Al-Kāfī*, I, 524, tradition no. 28.
41 *Al-Kāfī*, I, 525, tradltion no. 31.

cemetery of Quraysh. The caliph has ordered that everyone who visits it should be searched out and arrested."

*****

The Signs of the Reappearance (*Qiyām*) of the (Imam) who undertakes the Office (*al-Qā'im*), Peace be on him, the Period of Time of his Appearance, an Explanation of his Life and an Extract of what is revealed about his State.

Traditions have been reported mentioning the signs for the time of the appearance of the Imam who will arise (*qā'im*), peace be on him, and the events which will take place before his appearance, together with the indications and features of it. Among them are: The Sufyānī will come out in revolt; the Ḥasanid will be killed; the 'Abbāsids will dispute over worldly kingdom; there will be an eclipse of the sun in the middle of the month of Ramaḍān; there will be an eclipse of the moon at the end of that month in contrast to ordinary happenings; the land will be swallowed up at al-Bayḍā'; it will be swallowed in the east - it will be swallowed up in the west; the sun will stay still from the time of its decline to the middle of the time for the afternoon prayer; it will rise from the west; a pure soul (*nafs zakiyya*) will be killed in the outskirts of Kūfā with seventy righteous men; a Hāshimite will be slaughtered between the corner (of the Ka'ba and the station of Abraham); the wall of the mosque of Kūfā will be destroyed; black standards will advance from Khurāsān; al-Yamānī will come out in revolt; al-Maghribī will appear in Egypt and take possession of it from Syria; the Turk will occupy the region of al-Jazīra; the Byzantines will occupy Ramla; the star will appear in the east giving light just like the moon gives light; then (the new moon) will bend until its two tips almost meet; a colour will appear in the sky and spread to its horizons; a fire will appear for a long time in the east remaining in the air for three or seven days; the Arabs will throw off the reins and take possession of their land, throwing out the foreign authority; the people of Egypt will kill their ruler and destroy Syria; and three standards will dispute over it (Syria); the standards of Qays and the Arabs will come among the people of Egypt; the standards of Kinda (will go) to Khurāsān; horses will come from the west until they are stabled in al-Ḥīra; the black standards will advance towards them from the east; the Euphrates will flood so that the water comes into the alleys of Kūfā; sixty liars will come forward, all of them claiming prophethood, and twelve will come forward from the family of Abū Ṭālib, all of them claiming the Imamate; a man of important rank of the supporters of the 'Abbāsids will be burnt between Jalūlā' and Khāniqīn; the bridge next to Karkh in the city of Baghdād will be established; a black wind will raise it at the beginning of the day and then an earthquake will occur so that much of it will be swallowed up; fear will cover the people of Iraq and Baghdād; swift death (will occur) there and there will be a loss of property, lives and harvests; locusts will appear at their usual times and at times not usual so that they attack agricultural land and crops and there will be little harvest for what the people planted; two kinds of foreigners will dispute and much blood will be shed in their quarrel; slaves will rebel against obedience to their masters and kill their masters (*mawālī*); a group of heretics (*ahl al-bida'*) will be transformed until they become monkeys and pigs; slaves will conquer the land of their masters; a cry (will come) from the sky (in such a way) that all the people will hear it in their own languages; a face and a chest will appear in the sky before the people in the centre of the sun; the dead will arise from their graves so that they will return to the world and they will recognize one another and visit one another; that will come to an end with twenty-four continous rainstorms and the land will be revived by them after being dead and it will recognize its blessings; after that every disease will be taken away from those of the Shī'a of the Mahdī, peace be on him, who believe in the truth; at that time they will know of his appearance in Mecca and they will go to him to support him.

(These signs) are as the reports have mentioned. Among the total of these events are some which are bound (to happen) and other which are conditional. Allāh knows best what will take place. We have only mentioned them on the basis of what is recounted in basic sources of tradition (*uṣūl*) because of their inclusion in traditions which have been handed down. From Allāh we seek help and Him do we ask for success.

[Abū al-Ḥasan 'Alī b. Bilāl al-Muhallabī informed me: Muḥammad b. Ja'far al-Mu'addib told me on the authority of Aḥmad b. Idrīs, on the authority of 'Alī b. Muḥammad b. Qutayba, on the authority of al-Faḍl b. Shādhān, on the authority of Ismā'īl b. al-Ṣabbāḥ, who said: I heard an old man among our colleagues mention on the authority of Sayf b. 'Umayra, who said:]
I (i.e. Sayf b. 'Umayra) was with Abu Ja'far al-Manṣūr and he said to me of his own accord: "There will certainly be a voice calling from the sky the name of a man from the descendants of Abū Ṭālib."

"May I be your ransom, Commander of the faithful," I said, "do you relate that?"
"Indeed, by Him in Whose hands is my life," he replied, "because my own ears have heard it."

"Commander of the faithful," I said, "this tradition which you have heard is before my time."
"Sayf, it is the truth," he told me. "When it happens, we will be the first to answer

it. Indeed the call will be for a man from the descendants of our uncle."

"A man from the descendants of Fāṭima, peace be on her?" I asked.
"Yes," he replied. "Sayf, if it was not for the fact that I have heard from Abū Ja'far Muḥammad b. 'Alī (al-Bāqir), who told me about it, even though all the people of the earth have told me about it, I would not accept it from them. However it was Muḥammad b. 'Alī (al-Bāqir), peace be on them, (who told me)."

[Yaḥyā b. Abī Ṭālib reported on the authority of 'Alī b. 'Āṣim, on the authority of 'Aṭā' b. al-Sā'ib, on the authority of his father on the authority of 'Abd Allāh b. 'Umar, who said:]
The Apostle of Allāh, may Allāh bless Him and His Family, said: "The hour (of the end of the world) will not arise until the Mahdī from my descendants comes forth. The Mahdī will not come forth until sixty liars come forward, all of them declaring: 'I am a prophet.'"

[al-Faḍl b. Shādhān reported on the authority of one who reported it on the authority of Abū Ḥamza al-Thumālī, who said:]
I (i.e. Abū Ḥamza al-Thumālī) asked Abū Ja'far (al-Bāqir), peace be on him: "Is the revolt of the Sufyānī one of the things which must happen?"

"Yes," he replied. "The call is one of the things which must happen as is the rising of the sun from the west one of the things which must happen. The dispute of the 'Abbāsids over the state is also one of them and the killing of the pure soul (*al-nafs al-zakiyya*). The appearance of the one who will arise (*al-qā'im*) from the family of Muḥammad, may Allāh bless Him and His Family, is another of the things which must happen."

"How will the call be?" I asked.
"There will be a call from the sky at the beginning of the day - indeed the truth is with 'Alī and his Shī'a,'" he said. "Then at the end of the day, Satan will call from the earth - indeed the truth is with 'Uthmān and his supporters. At that the false one will feel doubt."

[al-Ḥasan b. 'Alī al-Washshā' (reported) on the authority of Aḥmad b. 'Ā'idh, on the authority of Abū Khadīja, on the authority of Abū 'Abd Allāh (Ja'far al-Ṣādiq, peace be on him:]
(Ja'far al-Sadiq) said: "The one who will arise (*al-qā'im*) will not come forth until twelve of the Banū Hāshim come forth before him, all of them summoning men to themselves."

[Muḥammad b. Abī al-Bilād (reported) on the authority of 'Alī b. Muḥammad al-Azdī, on the authority of his father, on the authority of his grandfather, who said:]
The Commander of the Faithful, peace be on him, said: "Before the one who will arise (*al-qā'im*), there will be red death and white death; there will be locusts at their usual time and at their unusual time like the colours of blood. As for red death that is (from) the sword,while white death is (from) plague."

[al-Ḥasan b. Maḥbūb (reported) on the authority of 'Amr b. Abī Miqdām, on the authority of Jābir al-Ju'fī on the authority of Abū Ja'far (al-Bāqir), peace be on him:]
(Al-Bāqir) said: "Stay close to the ground. Don't move an arm or a leg until you see the signs which I will mention to you - I don't think that you will live until that time. The 'Abbāsids will dispute; a voice will call from the sky; one of the villages of Syria called al-Jābiyya will be swallowed up; the Turks will occupy the region of al-Jazīra; the Byzantines will attack al-Ramla; at that time there will be much conflict throughout the land until Syria is destroyed. The cause of its destruction will be the meeting of three standards there: the standard of the Red, the standard of the Spotted and the standard of the Sufyanī."

['Alī b. Abī Ḥamza (reported) on the authority of Abū al-Ḥasan Mūsā, peace be on him:]
Concerning the words of Him, the Mighty and High: *We will show them our signs on the horizons and in themselves so that it will become clear to them that it is the truth* [XLI 53], (Mūsā) said: "(There will be) a disturbance on the horizons and the enemies of truth will be changed in form."

[Wahb b. (Abī) Ḥafṣ (reported) on the authority of Abū Baṣīr, who said:]
I (i.e. Abū Baṣīr) heard Abū Ja'far (al-Bāqir) speak concerning the words of Him, the Exalted: *If We wish, We will send down on them signs from the sky, and their necks will remain bent submissively to them* (XXVI 4). He said: "Allāh will do that to them."

"Who are they?" I asked.
"The Umayyads and their supporters," he answered.

"What is the sign?" I asked.
"Between the decline of the sun (at noon) and the time of the afternoon prayer, the sun will remain still," he said. "The chest and face of man will appear in the centre of the sun, who will be recognized by his standing and genealogy. That will occur in the time of the Sufyani. At that moment his destruction will occur and the destruction of his people."

['Abd Allāh b. Bukayr (reported) on the authority of 'Abd al- Malik b. Ismā'īl, on the authority of his father, on the authority of Sa'īd b. Jubayr:]
(Sa'īd b. Jubayr) said: "In the year in which the Mahdī will rise, twenty rain storms will rain on the earth. You will see their effects and benefits."

[al-Faḍl b. Shādhān (reported) on the authority of Aḥmad b. Muḥammad b. Abī Naṣr , on the authority of Tha'laba al-Azdī, who said:]
Abū Ja'far (al-Bāqir), peace be on him, said: "Two signs will come before the one who will arise (*al-qā'im*), peace be on him: there will be an eclipse of the sun in the middle of the month of Ramaḍān and an eclipse of the moon at the end of it."

"Son of the Apostle of Allāh," I said, "usually the eclipse of the sun occurs at the end of the month and the eclipse of the moon occurs in the middle of it?"

"I know what I have said," replied Abū Ja'far (al-Bāqir), peace be on him. "They are signs which have not occurred since Adam came down."

[Tha'laba b. Maymūn (reported) on the authority of Shu'ayb al-Ḥaddād, on the authority of Ṣāliḥ b. Maytham, who said:]
I (i.e. Ṣāliḥ b. Maytham) heard Abū Ja'far (al-Bāqir), peace be on him, say: "There is no longer than fifteen nights between the appearance of the one who will rise (*al-qā'im*), peace be on him, and the killing of the pure soul (*al-nafs al-zakiyya*)."

['Amr b Shāmir (reported) on the authority of Jabīr (al-Ju'fī) who said:]
I (i.e. Jabīr al-Ju'fī) said to Abū Ja'far (al-Bāqir), peace be on him: "When will this event occur?"

"Jabīr, that will occur at a time when the killing between al-Ḥīra and Kūfā is considerable," he replied.

[Muḥammad b. Sinān (reported) on the authority of al-Ḥusayn b. al-Mukhtār, on the authority of Abū 'Abd Allāh (Ja'far al-Ṣādiq), peace be on him:]
(Ja'far al-Ṣādiq) said: "When the wall of the mosque of Kūfā, which adjoins the house of 'Abd Allāh b. Mas'ūd is destroyed, then at that time the ruler of the people will disappear. At his disappearance, the one who will rise (*al-qā'im*), peace be on him, will come forth."

[Sayf b. 'Umayra (reported) on the authority of Bakr b. Muḥammad, on the authority of Abū 'Abd Allāh (Ja'far al-Ṣādiq), peace be on him:]

(Ja'far al-Ṣādiq) said: "There will be three appearances in one year, one month and one day - the Sufyānī, the Khurasānī and the Yamānī. The standard of guidance will not be among them, except the standard of the Yamānī, because he will summon (people) to the truth."

[al-Faḍl b. Shādhān (reported) on the authority of Aḥmad b. Muḥammad b. Abī Naṣr, on the authority of Abū al-Ḥasan al-Riḍā, peace be on him:]
(Al-Riḍā) said: "What you stretch your necks for will not occur until you are able to discern and to be tested. Only a few of you will remain."

Then he recited: *Alif Lam. Do the people consider that they can abandon saying "We believe" whenever they are tempted?* [XXIX 1-2]. He said: "Among the signs of the relief is an event which will occur between the two mosques (of Mecca and Medina). So-and-so from the descendants of so-and-so will kill fifteen leaders of the Arabs."

[Al-Faḍl b. Shādhān (reported) on the authority of Mu'ammar b. Khallād, on the authority of Abū al-Ḥasan (al-Riḍā), peace be on him:]
(Al-Riḍā) said: "(It is as if I see) standards, dyed green, coming from Egypt until they come to the Syrian (standards). Then they will be guided to the descendant of the one who gave the testamentary bequests of authority (to the Imams)."

[Ḥammād b. 'Īsā (reported) on the authority of Ibrāhīm b. 'Umar al-Yamānī on the authority of Abū Baṣīr, on the authority of Abū 'Abd Allāh (Ja'far al-Ṣādiq), peace be on him:]
(Ja'far al-Ṣādiq) said: "The kingdom of these men will not disappear until they slaughter people in Kūfā on Friday. It is as if I was looking at heads falling between the Gate of al-Fīl and (the place of) the soap-sellers."

['Alī b. Asbāṭ (reported) on the authority of (Abū) al-Ḥasan b. al- Jahm, who said:]
A man asked Abū al-Ḥasan (Mūsā), peace be on him, about the relief. He asked: "Do you want most of it or shall I give you a summary?"

"Would you give me a summary?" he said.

"(It will be) when the standards of Qays are carried in Egypt and the standards of Kinda in Khurāsān," he replied.

[Al-Ḥusayn b. Abī 'Alā' (reported) on the authority of Abū Baṣīr, on the authority of Abū 'Abd Allāh (Ja'far al-Ṣādiq), peace be on him:]

(Ja'far al-Ṣādiq) said: "Because of the sons of so-and-so there will be a battle at your mosque - meaning the mosque of Kūfā. On one Friday four thousand will be killed between the Gate of al-Fīl to (the place of) the soap-sellers. Beware of this street. Avoid it. Those who are in the best situation will take the street of the Anṣār."

['Alī b. Abī Ḥamza (reported) on the authority of Abū Baṣīr, on the authority of Abū 'Abd Allāh (Ja'far al-Ṣādiq), peace be on him:]
(Ja'far al-Ṣādiq) said: "Before (the coming of) the one who will rise (*al-qā'im*), peace be on him, there will be a year of abundant rain in which the fruits and the dates on the palms will be destroyed. But don't complain of that."

[Ibrāhīm b. Muḥammad (reported) on the authority of Ja'far b. Sa'd, on the authority of his father, on the authority of Abū 'Abd Allāh (Ja'far al-Ṣādiq), peace be on him:]
(Ja'far al-Ṣādiq) said: "In the year of the Conquest (by the Mahdī) the Euphrates will flood so that the water goes into the alleys of Kūfā."

[It is reported in the account (*ḥadīth*) of Muḥammad b. Muslim, who said:]
I (i.e. Muḥammad b. Muslim) heard Abū 'Abd Allāh (Ja'far al-Ṣādiq), peace be on him, say: "Before (the coming) of the one who will rise (*al-qā'im*) there will be a trial from Allāh."

"May I be your ransom, what is that?" I asked him.
He recited: *Let Us test you with fear, with hunger, and with lack of money, of lives and of harvests. Good news will come to those who are steadfast* [II 155]. Then he said: "The fear will be from the kings of the Banū so-and-so; the hunger will be as a result of exorbitant prices; the lack of money will be due to the failure of trade and the scarcity of surplus (goods) in it; the lack of lives will be because of swift death; the lack of harvest will be due to the great rains and the little benefit they bring to the crops." Then he continued: "The good news for those who are steadfast is that the one who will rise (*al-qā'im*) will soon come forth."

[Al-Ḥusayn b. Sa'īd (reported) on the authority of Mundhir al-Jawzī, on the authority of Abū 'Abd Allāh (Ja'far al-Ṣādiq), peace be on him:]
(Mundhir al-Jawzī) said: I heard (Ja'far al-Ṣādiq) say: "Before the coming of the one who will rise (*al-qā'im*), peace be on him, the people will be chided for their acts of disobedience by a fire which will appear in the sky and a redness which will cover the sky. It will swallow up Baghdād, it will swallow up Kūfā. There blood will be shed and houses destroyed. Death (*fanā'*) will occur amid their people and a fear will come over the people of Iraq from which they shall have no rest."

THE YEAR IN WHICH THE *QĀ'IM* WILL ARISE.

As for the exact year and day on which the one who will rise (*al-qā'im*), peace be on him and his fathers, rises, there have been handed down reports concerning that on the authority of truthful men.

[Al-Ḥasan b. Maḥbūb reported on the authority of 'Alī b. Abī Ḥama, on the authonty of Abū Baṣīr, on the authority of Abū 'Abd Allāh (Ja'far al-Ṣādiq), peace be on him:]

(Ja'far al-Ṣādiq) said: "The one who will rise (*al-qā'im*) will not come forth in an odd year: one, three, five seven or nine."

[al-Faḍl b. Shādhānn (reported) on the authority of Muḥammad b. 'Alī al-Kūfī, on the authority of Wahb b. Ḥafṣ, on the authority of Abu Baṣīr, who said:]

Abū 'Abd Allāh (Ja'far al-Ṣādiq), peace be on him, said: "(A voice) will summon the one who will rise (*al-qā'im*) on the night of the twenty-third of the month and he will rise on the day of 'Āshūrā', the day on which al-Ḥusayn b. 'Alī, peace be on them, was killed. It is as if I could see him on Saturday, 10th of the month of al-Muḥarram, standing between the corner (of the Ka'ba) and the station (of Abraham) and Gabriel, peace be on him, on his right will call for the pledge of allegiance to Allāh. His Shī'a will come to him from the ends of the earth, rolling up in great numbers to pledge allegiance to him. Then Allāh will fill the earth with justice just as it was filled with injustice".

THE DIRECTION FROM WHICH THE *QĀ'IM* WILL COME.

The report has come that he, peace be on him and his fathers, will go from Mecca until he comes to Kūfā. He will stay on its sand-dunes and scatter the soldiers into the cities.

[Al-Ḥajjāl has reported on the authority of Tha'laba, on the authority of Abū Bakr al-Ḥaḍramī, on the authority of Abu Ja'far (al-Bāqir), peace be on him:]

(al-Bāqir said:) "It is as if (I could see) the one who will rise (*al-qā'im*), peace be on him, on the sand dunes of Kūfā. He came there from Mecca with five thousand angels. Gabriel was on his right and Michael on his left. The believers were (standing) in front of him and he was scattering the soldiers into the land."

[It is reported on the narration (*riwāya*) of 'Amr b. Shamir, on the authority Abu Ja'far (al-Bāqir), peace be on him:]

al-Bāqir mentioned the Mahdī and said: "He will enter Kūfā and there there will be three standards which will have become confused. They will be clear to him. He will go in until he comes to the pulpit. Then he will preach but the people will not know what he says because of the weeping. On the second Friday the people Will ask him to pray the Friday prayer with them. He will order that a place of prostration be marked for him with red dye and he will pray there with them. Then he will order that a river should be dug from the back of the shrine of al-Ḥusayn, peace be on him, which would flow to the Ghariyyayn so that the water would descend into al-Najaf. At its entrance bridges and mills would be working. It is as if I (could see) an old woman, on her head a basket, in which is wheat which is brought to those mills and they grind it without charging."

[In the narration of Ṣāliḥ b. Abī al-Aswad of Abū 'Abd Allāh (Ja'far al-Ṣādiq), peace be on him:]
(Ṣāliḥ b. Abī al-Aswad) said that (Ja'far al-Ṣādiq) mentioned the mosque of al-Sahla. He described it as being of our leader (*ṣāḥib*) when he came with his people.

[In the narration of al-Mufaḍḍal b. 'Umar: the latter said:]
I (i.e. al-Mufaḍḍal b. 'Umar) heard Abū 'Abd Allāh (Ja'far al-Ṣādiq), peace be on him, say "When the one who will rise (*qā'im*) from the family or Muḥammad, peace be on him, rises, he will build a mosque in the outskirts of Kūfā, which will have a thousand doors and the houses of Kūfā will be connected to the river flow of Kalbalā'."

THE DOMINION OF THE *QĀ'IM*.

Reports bave been handed down concerning the period of time of the dominion of the one who will rise (*qā'im*), peace be on him, his times, the circumstances of his Shī'a during them and the position of the world and those on it.

['Abd al-Karīm al-Ju'fī reported:]
I (i.e. 'Abd al-Karīm al-Ju'fī) asked Abū 'Abd Allāh (Ja'far al-Ṣādiq), peace be on him: "How long will the one who will arise (*qā'im*), peace be on him, rule?"

"Seven years," he answered, "but the days will lengthen for him so that one of his years will be the same length as ten of your years. So the years of his dominion will be seventy of your years here. On his coming it will rain on the people during the month of Jumādā al-Ākhira and for ten days during the month of Rajab with rain, the like of which creatures have never seen. By it Allāh will bring forth the flesh and bodies of the believers in the graves. It is as if I could see them advancing from Juhayna shaking off the soil from their hair."

[Al-Mufaḍḍal b. 'Umar reported:]

I (i.e. al-Mufaḍḍal b. ʻUmar) heard Abū ʻAbd Allāh (Jaʻfar al-Ṣādiq), peace be on him, "When the one of us who rises (*qā'im*) rises, the earth will shine with the light of its lord. Men will not need the light of the sun and darkness will vanish. In his dominion a man will live so that he could have a thousand male sons born to him without a female. The earth will show its treasures so that the people will see them on its surface. Men will search for some one among you to receive their money and to take their alms-tax (*zakāt*) but they will find no one to accept that from them. The people will not need it because of what Allāh has provided for them out of His beneficence."

The Description of the *Qā'im* and His Appearance.

Reports have been handed down about the descriptIon of the one who will arise and his kindness, peace be on him.

[ʻAmr b. Shamir reported on the authority of Jābir al-Juʻfī, who said:]
I (i.e. Jābir al-Juʻfī) heard Abū Jaʻfar (al-Bāqir), peace be on him, say: "ʻUmar b. al-Khaṭṭāb questioned the Commander of the Faithful, peace be on him. He said: ʻTell me about the Mahdī, what is his name?'. He answered ʻAs for his name (the Apostle), peace be on him, took a promise from me that I would never mention it until Allāh sent him'. ʻUmar said: ʻGive me his description.' He answered: ʻHe is a young man of medium stature with a handsome face and beautiful hair. His hair flows on to his shoulders. A light rises on his face. The hair of his beard and head is black. By my father, he is the son of the best of mothers.'

The Actions and Manner of the Laws of the Qā'im at his Coming.

The action of him, peace be on him, at his coming and the manner of his laws as well as his signs which Allāh, the Exalted, has explained have been recorded in traditions as we have said before.

[al-Mufaḍḍal b. ʻUmar al-Juʻfī reported:]
I (i.e. al-Mufaḍḍal b. ʻUmar al-Juʻfī) heard Abū ʻAbd Allāh Jaʻfar b. Muḥammad (al-Ṣādiq), peace be on them, say: "When Allāh gives the one who will rise (*qā'im*) permission to come forth, he will go up on the pulpit and summon the people to himself. He will commend them to Allāh and summon them to His truth. He will practise among them the practice (*sunna*) of the Apostle ofAllāh, may Allāh bless Him and His Family. Allāh, may His majesty be extolled, will send Gabriel, peace be on him, to go to him. He will come down on the wall of the Kaʻba saying: ʻWhat are you calling people for?' The *Qā'im*, peace be on him, will inform him. Gabnel will say: ʻI will be the first to pledge allegiance to

you. Stretch out your hand.' He will rub it. Three hundred and some tens of men will come to him and pledge allegiance to him. He will stay in Mecca until his followers number ten thousand (thousand) persons. Then he will go to Medina"

[Muḥammad b. 'Ajlān reported on the authority of Abū 'Abd Allāh (Ja'far al-Ṣādiq), peace be on him.]
(Ja'far al-Ṣādiq) said: "When the *Qā'im*, peace be on him, rises, he will summon the people to Islam anew and guide them to a matter which had become lost and from which people had gone astray. He is only called the Mahdī (the one who guides) because he guides to a matter from which (men) have deviated. He is only called the *Qā'im* (the one who rises) because of his rising."

['Abd Allāh b. al-Mughīra reported on the authority of Abū 'Abd Allāh (Ja'far al-Ṣādiq), peace be on him.]
(Ja'far al-Ṣādiq) said: "When the *Qā'im* from the family of Muḥammad, the blessings of Allāh be on them, rises, five hundred members of Quraysh will come (against him) and he will strike off their heads. Then another five hundred will come (against him) and he will strike off their heads. A further five hundred will come (against him) until he has done that six times."

"Then the number of these men would be this?" I asked.
"Yes," he replied, "of them and of their retainers (*mawāli*)."

[Abū Baṣīr reported:]
Abū 'Abd Allāh (Ja'far al-Ṣādiq) said: "When the *Qā'im*, peace be on him, rises, he will destroy the Sacred Mosque so that it is reduced to its foundations. He will move the station to the place in which it was. He will cut off the hands of the Banū Shayba and hang them on the Ka'ba. On it he will write: 'These are the thieves of the Ka'ba.'

[Abū al-Jārūd reported on the authority of Abū Ja'far (al-Bāqir), peace be on him, in a long account (*ḥadīth*):]:
(al-Bāqir) said: "When the *Qā'im*, peace be on him, rises, he will go to Kūfā and some ten thousand persons called the Batriyya[42] who will be wearing arms will come out (against him). They will say: 'Go back where you came from. We have no need of the sons of Fāṭima.' He will put them to the sword until he comes to the last of them. Then he will enter Kūfā. There he will kill every doubting hypocrite and he will destroy their palaces. He will kill those who fight for them until Allāh, the Mighty and High, is satisfied."

42 Abū al-Jārūd became the founder of a sect of Zaydīs with strong Imāmī influence. Their opponents within the Zaydī movement were the Batriyya.

[Abu Khadīja reported on the authority of Abū 'Abd Allāh (Ja'far al-Ṣādiq), peace be on him:]
(Ja'far al-Ṣādiq) said: "When the *Qā'im*, peace be on him, rises, he will come with a new commandment (from Allāh) just as the Apostle of Allāh, may Allāh bless Him and His Family, summoned (men) to a new commandment (from Allāh) at the beginning of Islam."

['Alī b. 'Uqba reported on the authority of his father, who said:]
(He - an Imam - said:) "When the *Qā'im*, peace be on him, rises, he will rule with justice. In his time, injustice will be removed and the roads will be safe. The earth will produce its benefits and every due will be restored to its proper person. No people of any other religion will remain without being shown Islam and confessing faith in it. Have you not heard Allāh, may He be praised. say: *Those in the heavens and the earth submitted (aslama) to Him willingly and reluctantly To Him you will return* (III 83). He will judge between the people with the judgement of David and the law of Muḥammad, may Allāh bless Him and His Family. At that time the earth will reveal its treasures and show its blessings. At that time men will not find any place to give alms nor be generous because wealth will encompass all the believers." Then he added: "Our state is the last of the states, no House which has a state will remain except that they ruled before us, so that they will not be able to say when they see our actions, if we ruled, we would act in the same way as these. It is the word of Allāh, the Exalted: *The final result is for those who are pious* (VII 128)."

[Abū Baṣīr reported on the authority of Abū Ja'far (al-Bāqir), peace be on him, to a long account:]
(al-Bāqir) said: "When the *Qā'im*, peace be on him, rises, he will go to Kūfā. There he will destroy four mosques. There will not remain a mosque on the face of the earth which has a verandah except he will destroy it and make it flat. He will expand the main street and every (building) which juts out along the road will be destroyed. He will destroy the latrines and waste pipes (which jut out) on to the roads. There will be no innovation left which he does not remove and no religious practice (*sunna*) which he does not establish. He will conquer Constantinople, China and the mountains of al-Daylam. He will remam (doing) that for seven years, each year being ten of your years. Then Allāh will do what He wishes."

"May I be your ransom, how will He lengthen the years?" I asked.
"Allāh, the Exalted, will order the universe to slow down and lessen its movement and the days and the years will be longer because of that," he answered.

"It is said that if the universe changes, it will be destroyed," I said.
"Those are the words of atheists (*zanādiqa*)." he replied. "There is no way for a Muslim to hold that view. Allāh, the Exalted, has split the moon for His Prophet, may Allāh bless Him and His Family, and He has sent the sun back to its earlier position for Joshua. He has informed us of the length of the day of the Resurrection. It will be like a thousand years in your reckoning."

[Jabīr (al-Ju'fi) reported on the authority of Abū Ja'far (al-Bāqir), peace be on him, to a long account:]
(al-Bāqir) said: "When the *Qā'im* from the family of Muḥammad, may Allāh bless Him and His Family, arises, he will set up encampments and he will teach the people the Qur'ān as it was revealed by Allāh, the Mighty and High. The greatest difficulty will be for those who have learnt it as it is today, because it differs from its (original) composition."

[al-Mufaḍḍal b. 'Umar reported on the authority of Abū 'Abd Allāh (Ja'far al-Ṣādiq), peace be on him:]
(Ja'far al-Ṣādiq) said: "There will come with the *Qā'im,* peace be on him, from the outskirts of Kūfā, twenty-seven men. Fifteen of the people of Moses, who shed their blood for the truth and remained true to it, seven people from the cave, Joshua, Salmān, Abū Dujāna al-Anṣarī, al-Miqdād and Mālik al-Ashtar. They will act as helpers (*anṣār*) and judges in his presence."

['Abd Allāh b. 'Ajlān reported on the authority of Abū 'Abd Allāh (Ja'far al-Ṣādiq), peace be on him:]
(Ja'far al-Ṣādiq) said: "When the *Qā'im* of the family of Muḥammad, may Allāh bless Him and His Family, comes he will judge among the people with the judgement of David, peace be on him. Through the inspiration of Allāh, the Exalted, he will not need evidence. He will judge through his knowledge and he will inform each people about what is their innermost secret. He will know his friend from his enemy by a process of immediate recognition (*tawassum*). Allāh, may He be praised and exalted, said: *Indeed in that there are signs for those capable of recognising them and they are a sure means* (XV 75-76)."

*****

It is reported that the period of time of the state of the *Qā'im* will be nineteen years, whose days and months will be lengthened as we have already described. This is a matter which is hidden from us. From it, it has been made known to us that what Allāh, the Exalted, does is through the condition that He, may His name be exalted, knows the best interest. We do not positively assert anyone of the two matters (whether the state will be seven or nineteen years), even though the reports about the seven years are clearer and more numerous. There is no state to anyone after the state of the *Qā'im,* peace be on him, except that there is a narration of one under the control of his sons, if Allāh wishes that. However there is no positive assertion and proof for that. The majority of reports (maintain) that the Mahdī of the community will never depart except forty days before the Resurrection in which there will be ease and the dead arising and the coming of the Hour of Reckoning and Punishment. Allāh knows best what will happen. May Allāh bring success and correctness. Him do we ask for protection from error and we seek His help towards the path of guidance. May Allāh bless our lord, Muḥammad the Prophet, and his pure family.

CONCLUSION

Al-Shaykh al-Sa'id al-Mufīd Muḥammad b. Muḥammad b. Nu'mān, may Allāh be pleased with him and gather him with the steadfast, said:

We have presented in every chapter of this book an extract from the reports (*akhbār*) in accordance with what the circumstances made possible. We have not related everything which has been handed down on each particular subject out of reluctance of being diffuse in our words and out of fear of causing boredom and annoyance by that. From the reports about the *Qā'im*, the Mahdī, peace be on him, we have put forward what is similar in brevity to what went before. It would not be appropriate for anyone to attribute what we have omitted of that to neglect, nor to blame it on lack of knowledge by us, nor oversight, nor carelessness. In what we have laid out as a summary of the proof of the Imamate of the Imams, peace be on them, and an extract from the report about them, there is sufficient for our purpose. May Allāh bring success. He is sufficient for us and the best Agent.

www.ingramcontent.com/pod-product-compliance
Lightning Source LLC
Chambersburg PA
CBHW032020290426
44110CB00012B/616
9780940368118